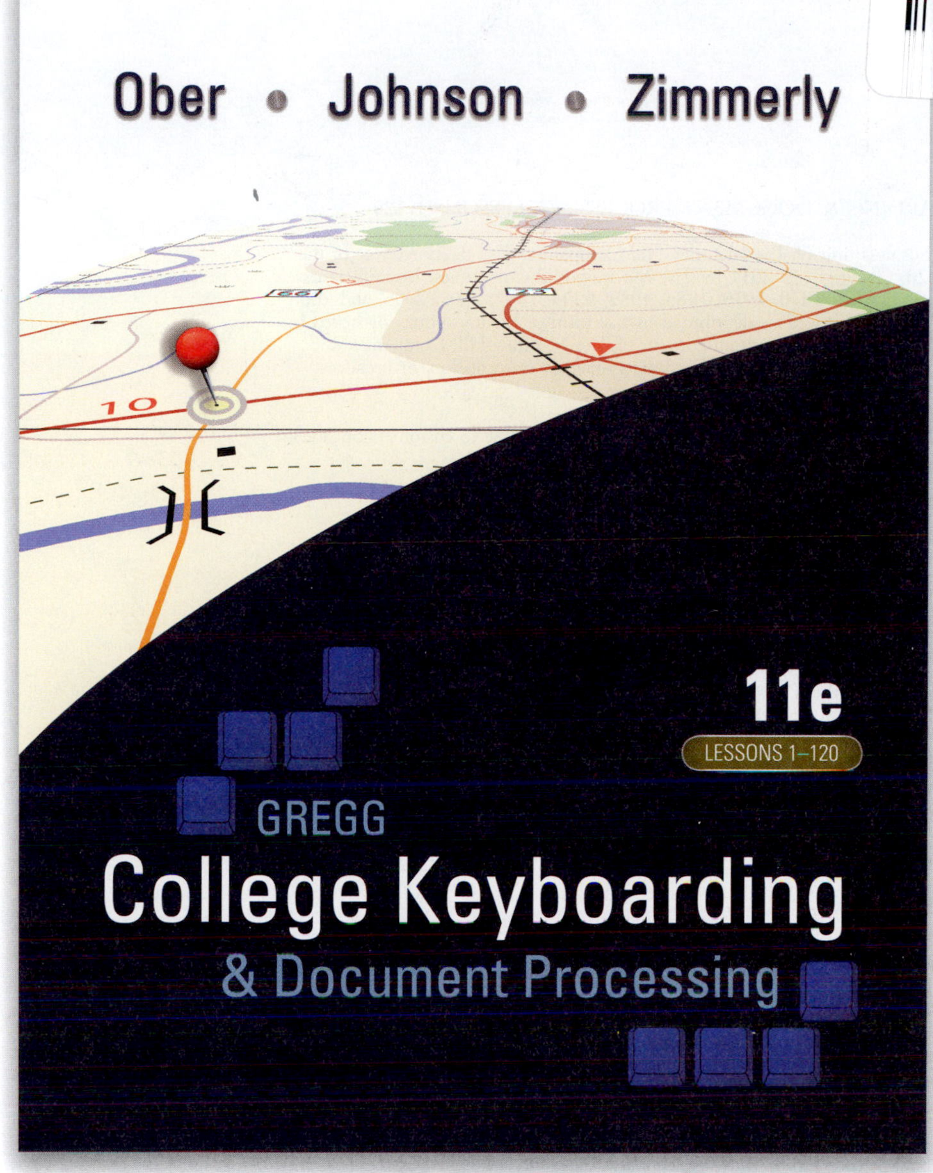

Scot Ober
Ball State University
Jack E. Johnson
University of West Georgia
Arlene Zimmerly
Los Angeles City College

Visit the *College Keyboarding* Web site at **www.mhhe.com/gdp11**

The McGraw-Hill Companies

GREGG COLLEGE KEYBOARDING & DOCUMENT PROCESSING, LESSONS 1–120

Published by McGraw-Hill, a business unit of The McGraw-Hill Companies, Inc., 1221 Avenue of the Americas, New York, NY, 10020.

This book is printed on acid-free paper.

13 14 15 16 17 RMN 20 19 18 17 16

ISBN 978-0-07-337219-8
MHID 0-07-337219-6

Vice President/Editor in Chief: *Elizabeth Haefele*
Vice President/Director of Marketing: *John E. Biernat*
Executive editor: *Scott Davidson*
Director of Development, Business Careers: *Sarah Wood*
Editorial coordinator: *Alan Palmer*
Marketing manager: *Tiffany Wendt*
Lead digital product manager: *Damian Moshak*
Senior digital product manager: *Lynn M. Bluhm*
Digital product specialist: *Randall Bates*
Director, Editing/Design/Production: *Jess Ann Kosic*
Project manager: *Marlena Pechan*
Senior production supervisor: *Janean A. Utley*
Senior designer: *Marianna Kinigakis*
Senior photo research coordinator: *Lori Kramer*
Digital production coordinator: *Brent Dela Cruz*
Digital developmental editor: *Kevin White*
Outside development house: *Debra Matteson*
Cover credit: *© Robert Adrian Hillman/Shutterstock*
Cover design: *Jessica M. Lazar*
Interior design: *Jessica M. Lazar and Laurie J. Entringer, BrainWorx Studio, Inc.*
Typeface: *11/13.5 Adobe Garamond Pro*
Compositor: *Lachina Publishing Services*
Printer: RR Donnelley, Menasha
Credits: The credits section for this book begins on page I-16 and is considered an extension of the copyright page.

Library of Congress Cataloging-in-Publication Data

Ober, Scot, 1946–
Gregg college keyboarding & document processing. Lessons 1–120 / Scot Ober, Jack E. Johnson, Arlene Zimmerly. — 11th ed.
p. cm
Includeds index.
ISBN-13: 978-0-07-337219-8 (Lessons 1–120)
ISBN-10: 0-07-337219-6 (Lessons 1–120)
ISBN-13: 978-0-07-734422-1 (Lessons 1–20)
ISBN-10: 0-07-734422-7 (Lessons 1–20)
ISBN-13: 978-0-07-731936-6 (Lessons 1–60)
ISBN-10: 0-07-731936-2 (Lessons 1–60)
ISBN-13: 978-0-07-731940-3 (Lessons 61–120)
ISBN-10: 0-07-731940-0 (Lessons 61–120)
1. Word processing—Problems, exercises, etc. 2. Keyboarding—Problems, exercises, etc. 3. Commercial correspondence—Problems, exercises, etc. 4. Report writing—Problems, exercises, etc. I. Johnson, Jack E. II. Zimmerly, Arlene. III. Title. IV. Title: Gregg college keyboarding and document processing.

Z52.3.G74 2011
652.3'0076—dc22 2009037843

www.mhhe.com

Welcome to

Gregg College Keyboarding & Document Processing 11th Edition

Your complete learning/teaching *system*

Your guide to success

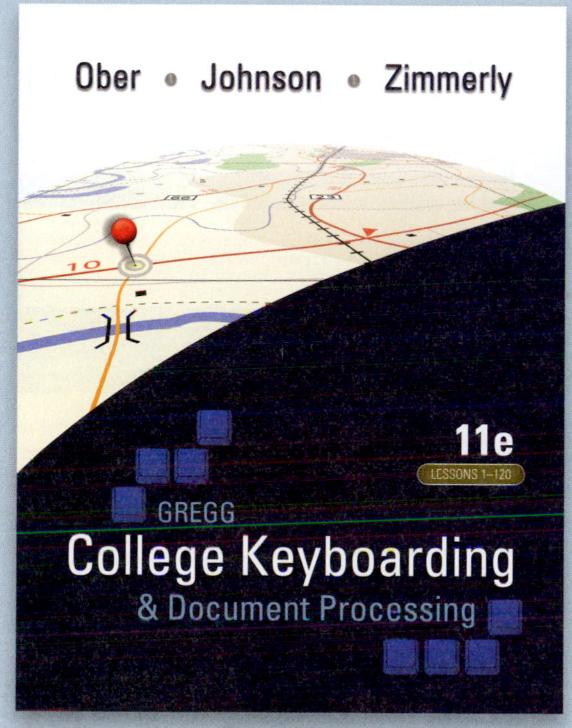

Textbook

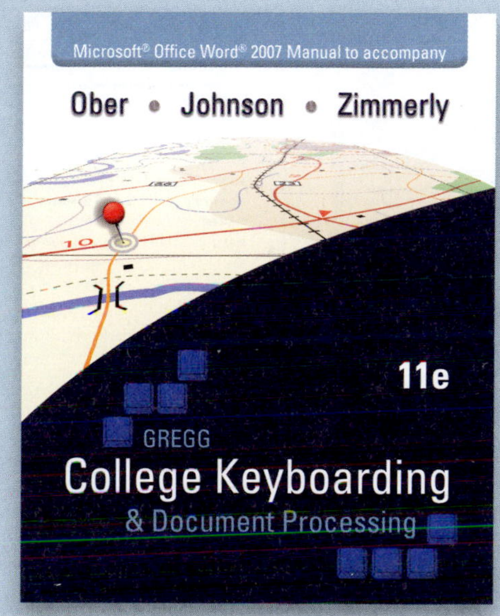

Word Manual

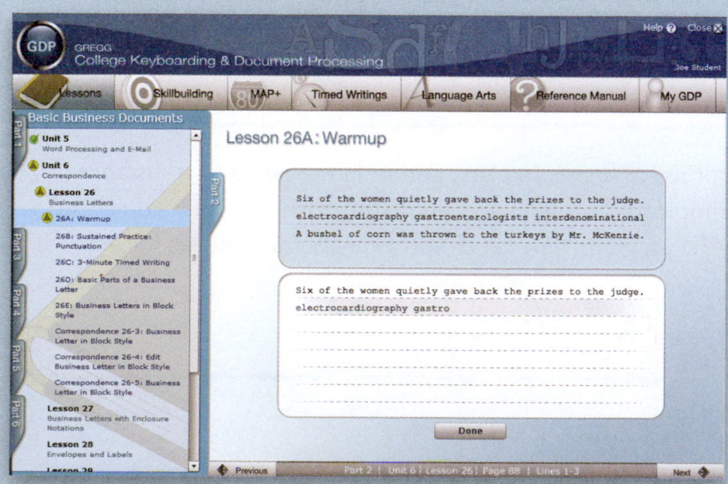

GDP (Gregg Document Processing) Web-Based Software

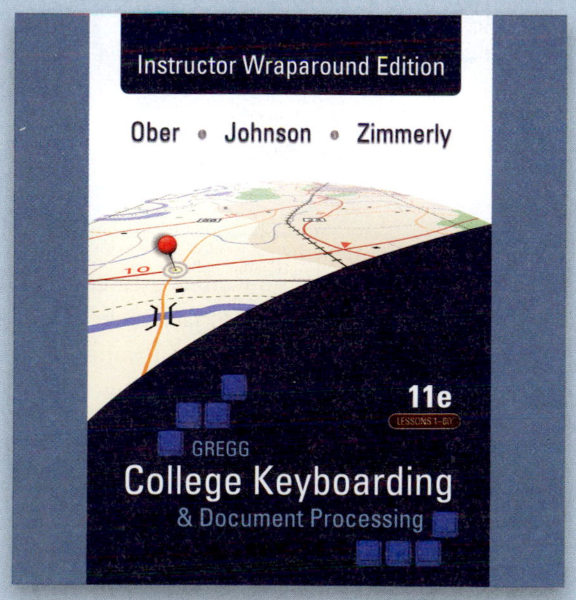

Instructor Wraparound Edition

Online GDP Software

New! Online functionality
Same program; *now* Web-based

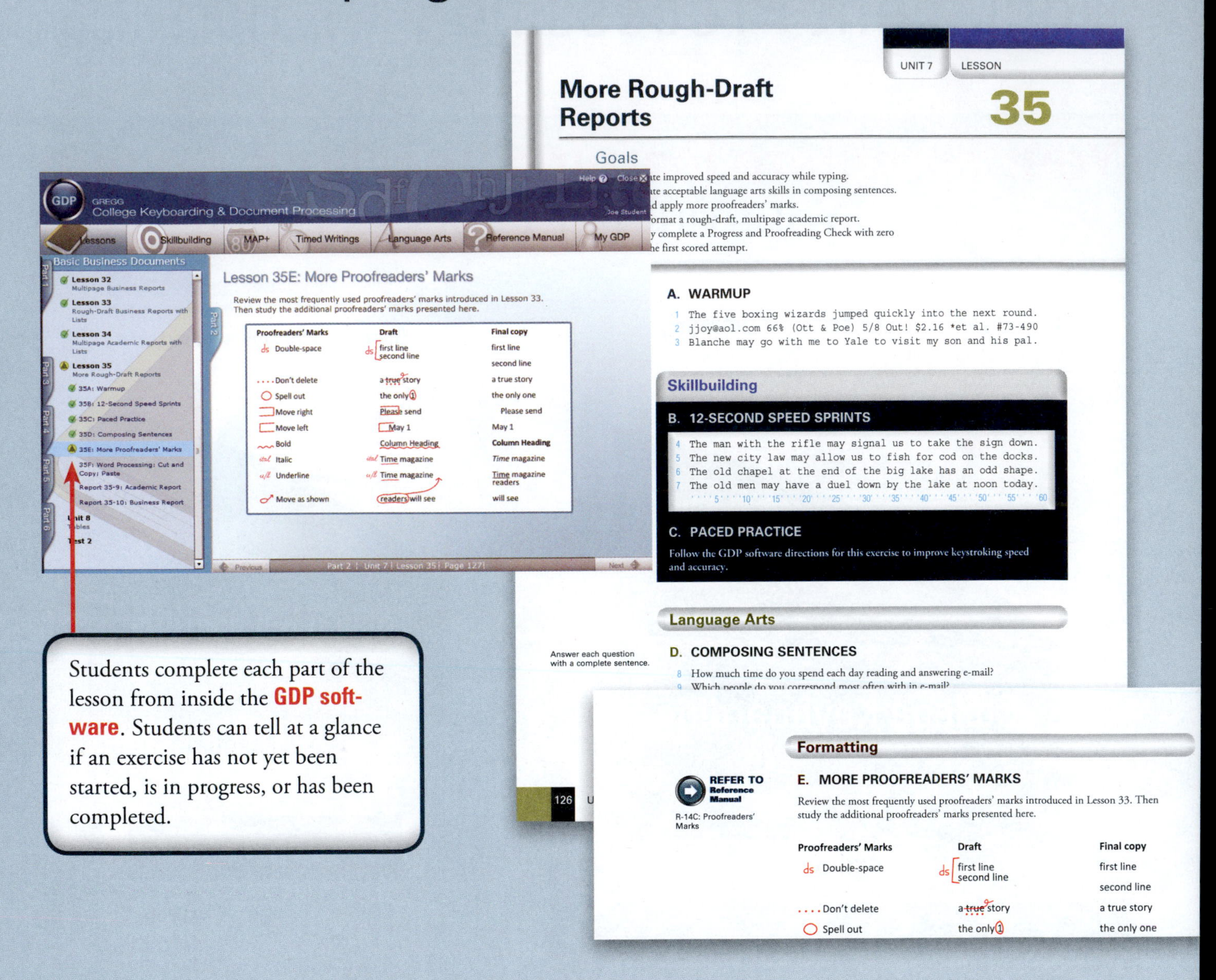

Students complete each part of the lesson from inside the **GDP software**. Students can tell at a glance if an exercise has not yet been started, is in progress, or has been completed.

This online software now offers greater accessibility for use at home, in class, and in labs—perfect for distance learning! Its easy-to-use interface makes this system simple for both you and your students . . . so that you spend more time teaching the skills you want, not learning the program. The GDP software also now allows for automatic keystroking and format scoring.

With GDP's new online functionality, updates are now seamless.

MAP+
The best just got better!

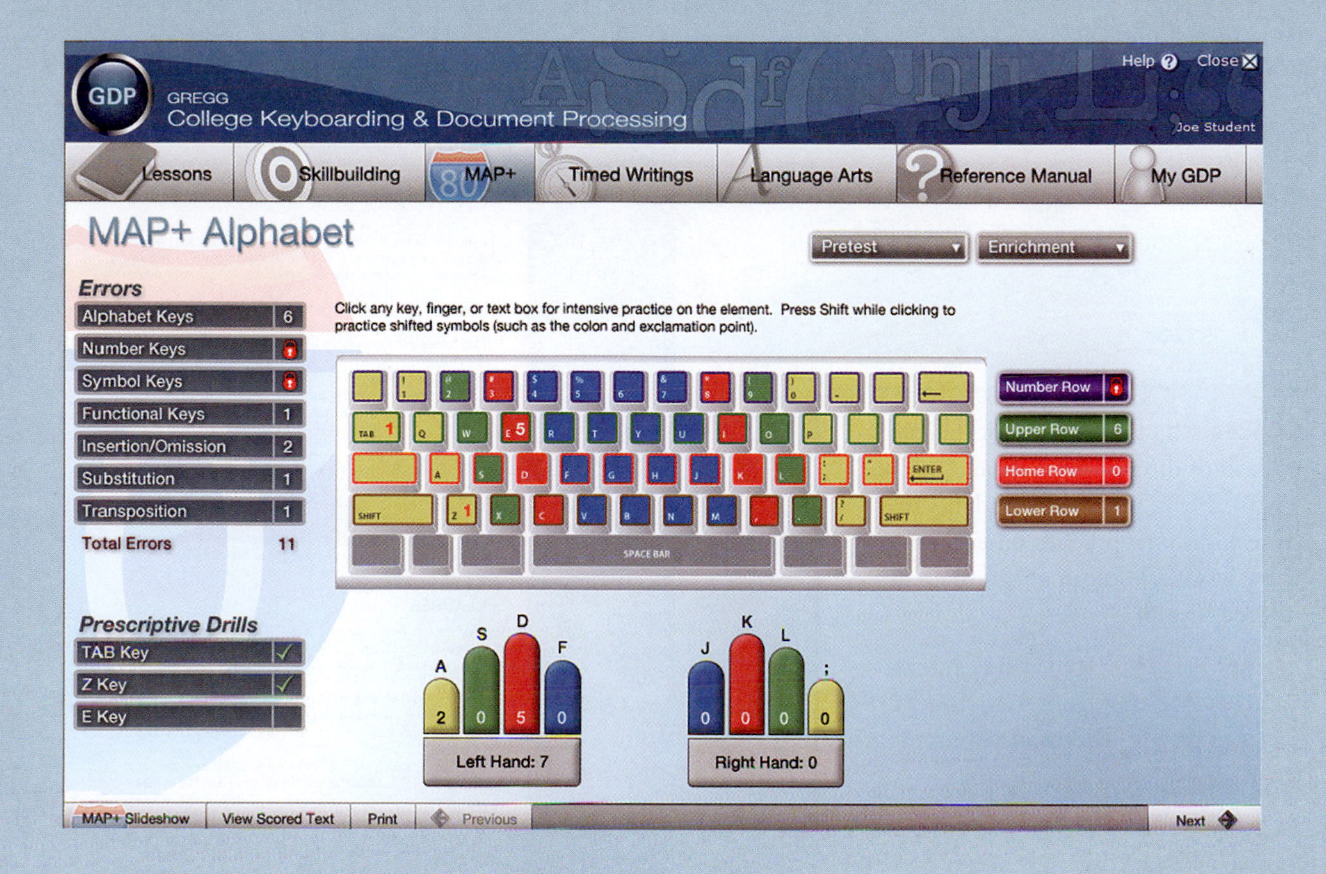

MAP+ (Misstroke Analysis and Prescription) is a *diagnostic tool* within GDP/11 that analyzes each student's pretest misstrokes and prescribes individualized remediation drills based on a powerful new scoring algorithm. MAP+ includes these features:

- **New! Unlimited drill lines**—*Now begin with Lesson 1.*
- **Interactive**—Features a streamlined interactive screen, which allows students to click anywhere for intensive practice on that key or kind of reach.
- **Continuous new drills**—Generate three *new* drill lines every time the student clicks a key or specific reach.
- **New! Deeper content**—Allows students to take a pretest and practice either alphabetic copy, numbers, or numbers and symbols.
- **Integrated**—Is a required part of each unit, although students can access MAP+ at any time from the lesson menu.

New! Enrichment Pages

More drill lines for faster touch-typing skills

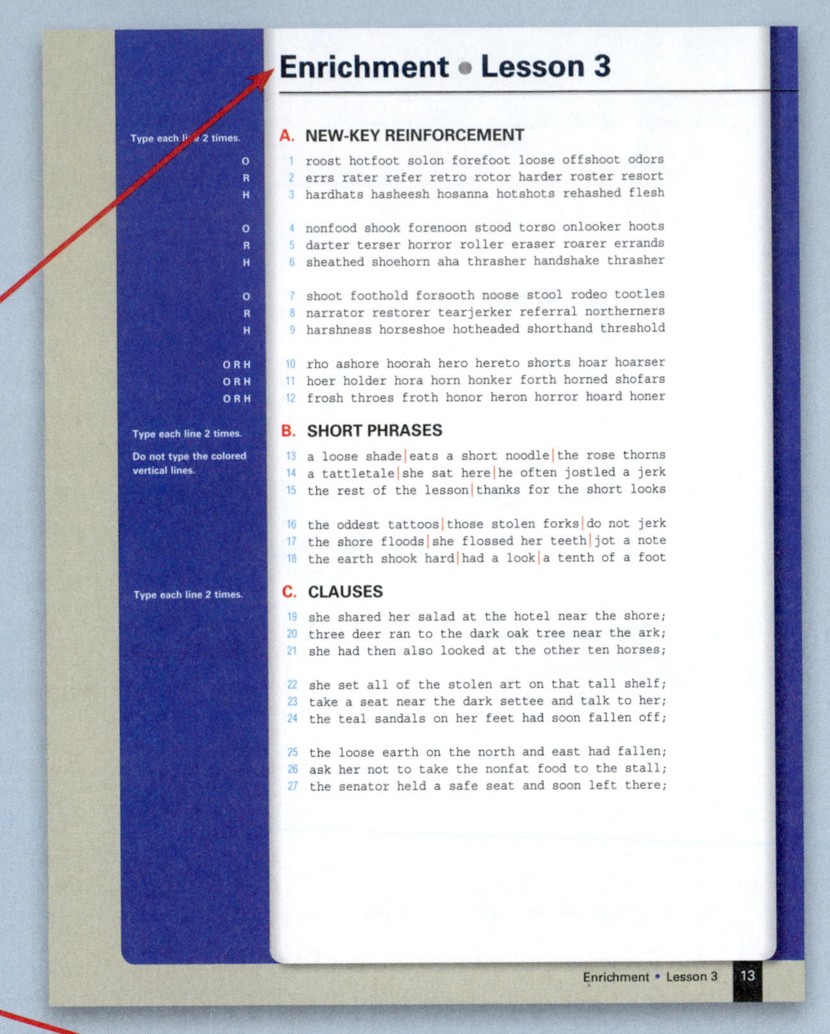

Enrichment • Lesson 3

A. NEW-KEY REINFORCEMENT

Type each line 2 times.

```
O   1 roost hotfoot solon forefoot loose offshoot odors
R   2 errs rater refer retro rotor harder roster resort
H   3 hardhats hasheesh hosanna hotshots rehashed flesh

O   4 nonfood shook forenoon stood torso onlooker hoots
R   5 darter terser horror roller eraser roarer errands
H   6 sheathed shoehorn aha thrasher handshake thrasher

O   7 shoot foothold forsooth noose stool rodeo tootles
R   8 narrator restorer tearjerker referral northerners
H   9 harshness horseshoe hotheaded shorthand threshold

ORH 10 rho ashore hoorah hero hereto shorts hoar hoarser
ORH 11 hoer holder hora horn honker forth horned shofars
ORH 12 frosh throes froth honor heron horror hoard honer
```

B. SHORT PHRASES

Type each line 2 times.

Do not type the colored vertical lines.

```
13 a loose shade|eats a short noodle|the rose thorns
14 a tattletale|she sat here|he often jostled a jerk
15 the rest of the lesson|thanks for the short looks

16 the oddest tattoos|those stolen forks|do not jerk
17 the shore floods|she flossed her teeth|jot a note
18 the earth shook hard|had a look|a tenth of a foot
```

C. CLAUSES

Type each line 2 times.

```
19 she shared her salad at the hotel near the shore;
20 three deer ran to the dark oak tree near the ark;
21 she had then also looked at the other ten horses;

22 she set all of the stolen art on that tall shelf;
23 take a seat near the dark settee and talk to her;
24 the teal sandals on her feet had soon fallen off;

25 the loose earth on the north and east had fallen;
26 ask her not to take the nonfat food to the stall;
27 the senator held a safe seat and soon left there;
```

Enrichment • Lesson 3 13

Enrichment pages appear at the end of each of the new-key lessons (Lessons 1–20). If you want your students to have additional practice on each of these lessons, you can assign them as desired.

Using the GDP system, you can customize GDP to include Enrichment pages as part of the lesson requirements.

With **MAP+**, students also have unlimited new practice drills—*beginning with Lesson 1.* Every time they access MAP+ for a specific lesson, new drill lines appear that contain only those words students can type up to that point.

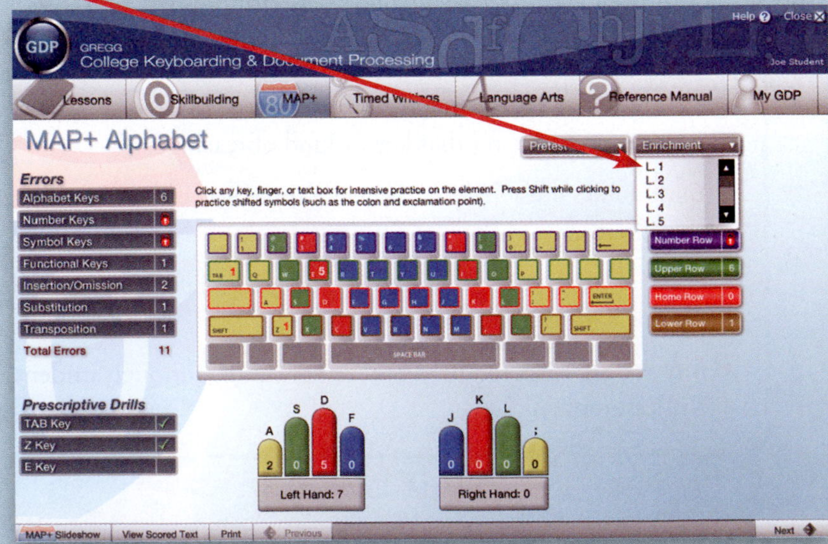

Individualized Skillbuilding
In every lesson

Warmups at the start of each lesson comprise 3 lines. Line 1 is an alphabetic sentence to review all reaches; Line 2 practices a particular type of reach; Line 3 contains easy words to help build speed.

Skillbuilding (building straight-copy speed and accuracy) is built into *every lesson*—15′–20′ of *individualized* skill-building routines.

Each student always practices on the type of drill that is appropriate for him or her and for which the **individualized** goals are challenging—but attainable.

The **timed writings** in every even-numbered lesson are controlled for difficulty, contain all letters of the alphabet, and are the exact length needed to achieve that lesson's speed goal.

UNIT 7 LESSON

Rough-Draft Business Reports With Lists **33**

Goals

- Demonstrate improved speed and accuracy while typing.
- Correctly identify and apply basic proofreaders' marks.
- Correctly use Word's bullet and numbering features.
- Correctly format a rough-draft business report with lists.

A. WARMUP

```
alphabet        1 Jay began removing six dozen black quilts with petty flaws.
practice: s and d  2 sod sad deeds desks dosed dudes dusts sheds sides soda suds
easy            3 The men may be busy but they may go to the social with her.
```

Skillbuilding

B. PROGRESSIVE PRACTICE: NUMBERS

Follow the GDP software directions for this exercise to improve keystroking speed.

C. TECHNIQUE PRACTICE: ENTER KEY

Type each line 2 times. Type each sentence on a separate line by pressing ENTER after each sentence.

```
4 Who? Go. So? Get it? Why not? Well? See to it. Why me? Eat!
5 Read it. Whew! Go slow. Where? Finished? Who, Tom? Type it.
6 Roll over. Wait. Sit. Beg. See him. What gives? Truly! Why?
7 Do it. Be there. Taxi? See me. All? Why him? We did. Don't!
```

D. 3-MINUTE TIMED WRITING

Take two 3-minute timed writings.

Goal: At least 34wpm/3′/5e

```
8      Companies that place major ads on the Internet use a     11
9  process called data mining. They look for patterns in the   22
10 quantities of data they get from those who visit Web sites.  34
11     Data mining tracks buying habits of customers and then   46
12 decides to send ads to them based on their current and past  58
13 buying patterns. Data mining can also be used to explain     69
14 buyer behavior and to look at trends. First, a survey is     80
15 filled out, and then the results are gathered and stored in  92
16 a file to be analyzed in detail at a later time.            102
     1 | 2 | 3 | 4 | 5 | 6 | 7 | 8 | 9 | 10 | 11 | 12
```

Language Arts
A critical document processing skill

Language arts (punctuation rules, usage, proofreading, composing, and spelling) are systematically covered. Short, easy-to-grasp exercises are incorporated throughout Lessons 21–120 with increasing difficulty.

The rules are presented, practiced, and then illustrated in the documents that students type in that lesson—for immediate reinforcement.

Language Arts

Study the rules at the right.

RULE
, independent clause

The underline calls attention to a point in the sentence where a comma might mistakenly be inserted.

D. COMMAS AND SENTENCES

Use a comma between independent clauses joined by a coordinate conjunction (unless both clauses are short).

Ellen left her job with IBM, and she and her sister went to Paris.
But: Ellen left her job with IBM and went to Paris with her sister.
But: John drove and I navigated.

Note: An independent clause is one that can stand alone as a complete sentence. The most common coordinate conjunctions are *and, but, or,* and *nor.*

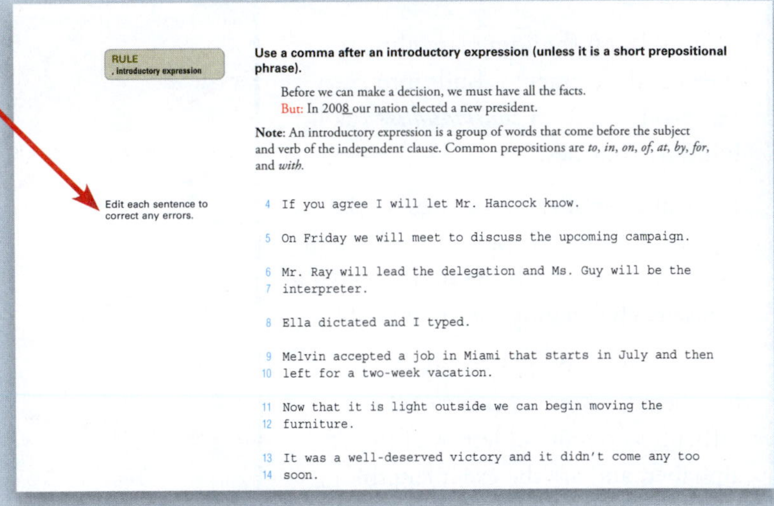

RULE
, introductory expression

Use a comma after an introductory expression (unless it is a short prepositional phrase).

Before we can make a decision, we must have all the facts.
But: In 2008 our nation elected a new president.

Note: An introductory expression is a group of words that come before the subject and verb of the independent clause. Common prepositions are *to, in, on, of, at, by, for,* and *with.*

Edit each sentence to correct any errors.

```
 4 If you agree I will let Mr. Hancock know.
 5 On Friday we will meet to discuss the upcoming campaign.
 6 Mr. Ray will lead the delegation and Ms. Guy will be the
 7 interpreter.
 8 Ella dictated and I typed.
 9 Melvin accepted a job in Miami that starts in July and then
10 left for a two-week vacation.
11 Now that it is light outside we can begin moving the
12 furniture.
13 It was a well-deserved victory and it didn't come any too
14 soon.
```

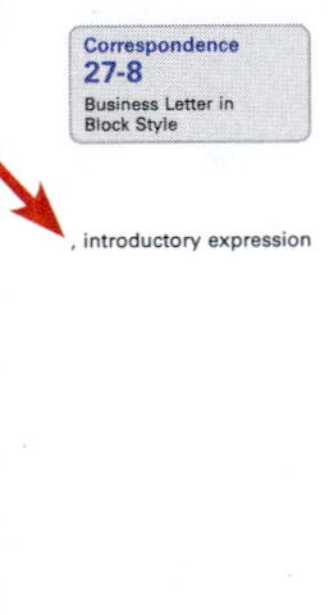

Correspondence
27-8
Business Letter in Block Style

, introductory expression

, independent clause

October 10, 20-- | Mr. Nick Limpett | Marketing Manager | Secure Investments Inc. | 398 East Wacker Drive | Chicago, IL 60601 | Dear Mr. Limpett:

¶ Are you searching for a suitable conference site for your next corporate meeting? If so, the Paradise Valley Resort in Scottsdale, Arizona, offers you every amenity imaginable.

¶ Our luxury resort accommodations and stunning Sonoran Desert views are minutes away from the largest mall in the Southwest and hundreds of shops, galleries, and Scottsdale eateries. We are conveniently located only 12 miles from Phoenix Sky Harbor International Airport. Paradise Valley Resort has 40,000 square feet of flexible meeting space, including stunning outdoor venues. Our in-house audiovisual staff will make sure that your event is flawless.

¶ I've enclosed several brochures for your convenience. Let me know if I can be of service in any way. Your success is our success, and I hope to hear from you soon.

Sincerely yours, | Ms. Julie Mays | Corporate Event Specialist | urs | Enclosures

New! Expanded Ten-Key Practice

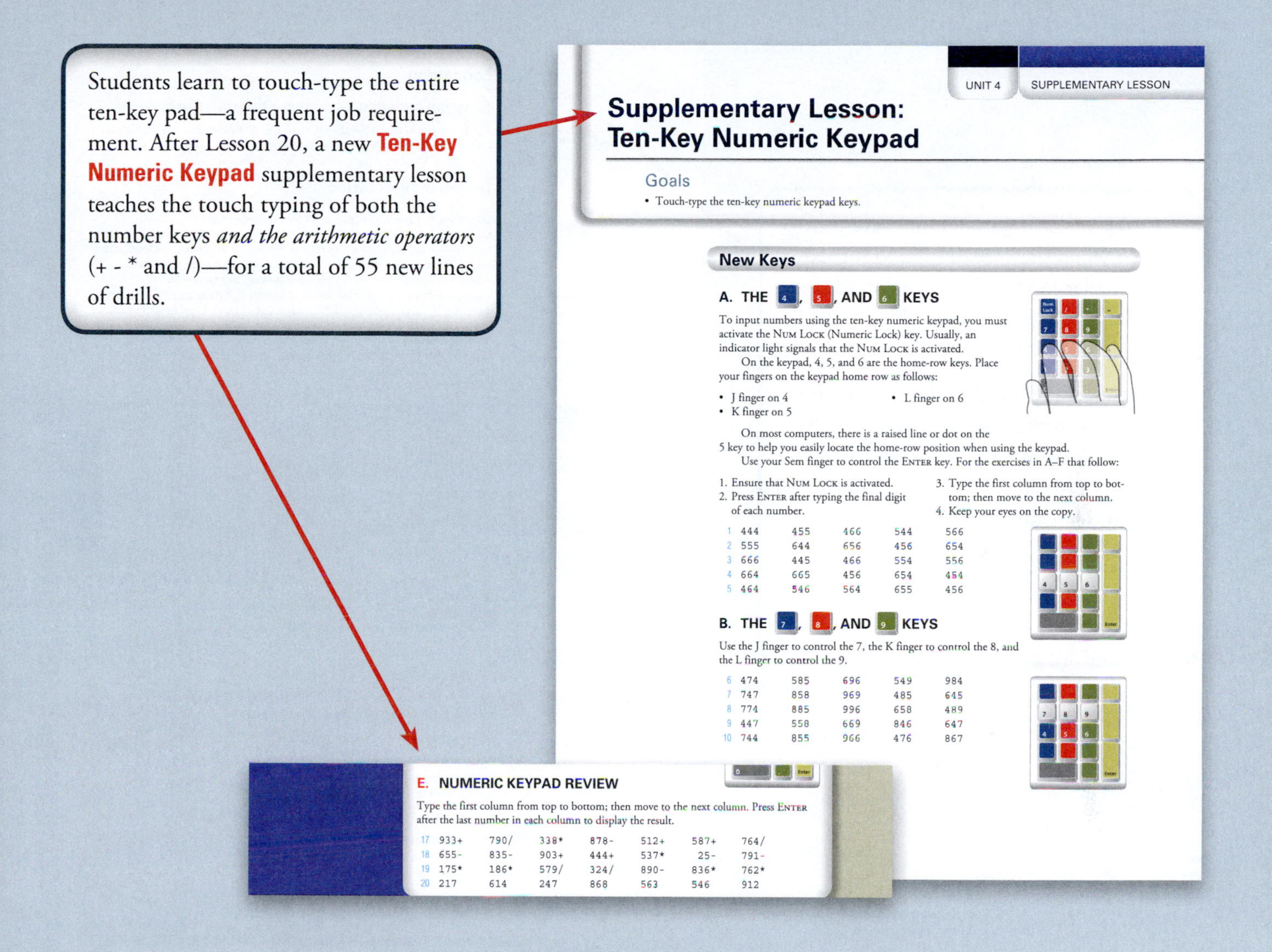

UNIT 4 | SUPPLEMENTARY LESSON

Supplementary Lesson: Ten-Key Numeric Keypad

Goals

- Touch-type the ten-key numeric keypad keys.

New Keys

A. THE 4, 5, AND 6 KEYS

To input numbers using the ten-key numeric keypad, you must activate the NUM LOCK (Numeric Lock) key. Usually, an indicator light signals that the NUM LOCK is activated.

On the keypad, 4, 5, and 6 are the home-row keys. Place your fingers on the keypad home row as follows:

- J finger on 4
- K finger on 5
- L finger on 6

On most computers, there is a raised line or dot on the 5 key to help you easily locate the home-row position when using the keypad.

Use your Sem finger to control the ENTER key. For the exercises in A–F that follow:

1. Ensure that NUM LOCK is activated.
2. Press ENTER after typing the final digit of each number.
3. Type the first column from top to bottom; then move to the next column.
4. Keep your eyes on the copy.

1	444	455	466	544	566
2	555	644	656	456	654
3	666	445	466	554	556
4	664	665	456	654	454
5	464	546	564	655	456

B. THE 7, 8, AND 9 KEYS

Use the J finger to control the 7, the K finger to control the 8, and the L finger to control the 9.

6	474	585	696	549	984
7	747	858	969	485	645
8	774	885	996	658	489
9	447	558	669	846	647
10	744	855	966	476	867

E. NUMERIC KEYPAD REVIEW

Type the first column from top to bottom; then move to the next column. Press ENTER after the last number in each column to display the result.

17	933+	790/	338*	878-	512+	587+	764/
18	655-	835-	903+	444+	537*	25-	791-
19	175*	186*	579/	324/	890-	836*	762*
20	217	614	247	868	563	546	912

Word Processing Commands
Introduced on a *need-to-know* basis

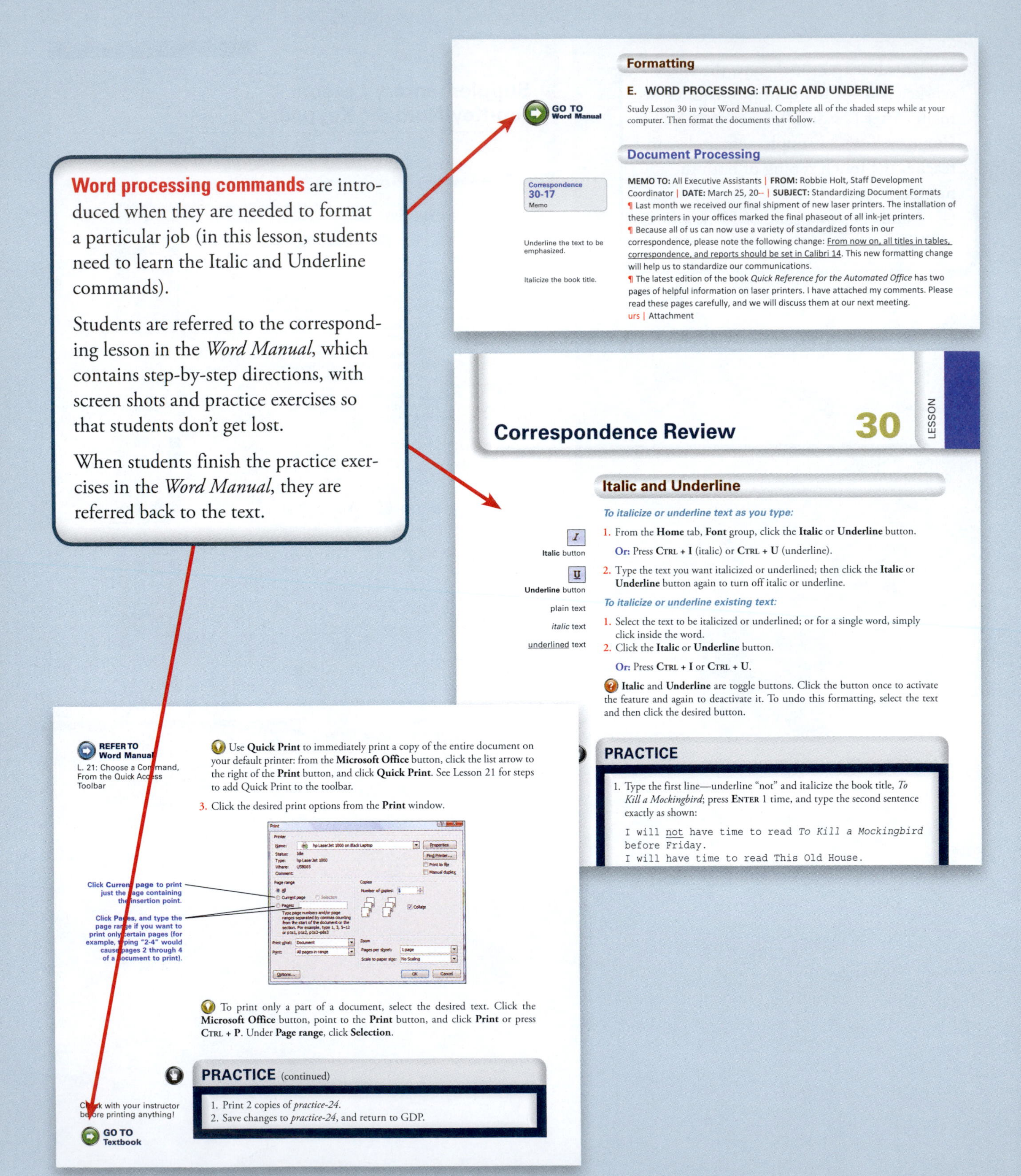

Word processing commands are introduced when they are needed to format a particular job (in this lesson, students need to learn the Italic and Underline commands).

Students are referred to the corresponding lesson in the *Word Manual,* which contains step-by-step directions, with screen shots and practice exercises so that students don't get lost.

When students finish the practice exercises in the *Word Manual,* they are referred back to the text.

Formatting

E. WORD PROCESSING: ITALIC AND UNDERLINE

GO TO Word Manual

Study Lesson 30 in your Word Manual. Complete all of the shaded steps while at your computer. Then format the documents that follow.

Document Processing

Correspondence 30-17 Memo

MEMO TO: All Executive Assistants | **FROM:** Robbie Holt, Staff Development Coordinator | **DATE:** March 25, 20-- | **SUBJECT:** Standardizing Document Formats

¶ Last month we received our final shipment of new laser printers. The installation of these printers in your offices marked the final phaseout of all ink-jet printers.

¶ Because all of us can now use a variety of standardized fonts in our correspondence, please note the following change: From now on, all titles in tables, correspondence, and reports should be set in Calibri 14. This new formatting change will help us to standardize our communications.

Underline the text to be emphasized.

¶ The latest edition of the book *Quick Reference for the Automated Office* has two pages of helpful information on laser printers. I have attached my comments. Please read these pages carefully, and we will discuss them at our next meeting.

Italicize the book title.

urs | Attachment

Correspondence Review — LESSON 30

Italic and Underline

To italicize or underline text as you type:

1. From the **Home** tab, **Font** group, click the **Italic** or **Underline** button.

   Or: Press CTRL + I (italic) or CTRL + U (underline).

2. Type the text you want italicized or underlined; then click the **Italic** or **Underline** button again to turn off italic or underline.

To italicize or underline existing text:

1. Select the text to be italicized or underlined; or for a single word, simply click inside the word.
2. Click the **Italic** or **Underline** button.

   Or: Press CTRL + I or CTRL + U.

Italic and **Underline** are toggle buttons. Click the button once to activate the feature and again to deactivate it. To undo this formatting, select the text and then click the desired button.

Italic button

Underline button

plain text

italic text

underlined text

PRACTICE

1. Type the first line—underline "not" and italicize the book title, *To Kill a Mockingbird*; press ENTER 1 time, and type the second sentence exactly as shown:

```
I will not have time to read To Kill a Mockingbird
before Friday.
I will have time to read This Old House.
```

REFER TO Word Manual

L. 21: Choose a Command, From the Quick Access Toolbar

Use **Quick Print** to immediately print a copy of the entire document on your default printer: from the **Microsoft Office** button, click the list arrow to the right of the **Print** button, and click **Quick Print**. See Lesson 21 for steps to add Quick Print to the toolbar.

3. Click the desired print options from the **Print** window.

Click Current page to print just the page containing the insertion point.

Click Pages, and type the page range if you want to print only certain pages (for example, typing "2-4" would cause pages 2 through 4 of a document to print).

To print only a part of a document, select the desired text. Click the **Microsoft Office** button, point to the **Print** button, and click **Print** or press CTRL + P. Under **Page range**, click **Selection**.

PRACTICE (continued)

1. Print 2 copies of *practice-24.*
2. Save changes to *practice-24,* and return to GDP.

Check with your instructor before printing anything!

GO TO Textbook

GDP Instructor Help

Right where you need it!

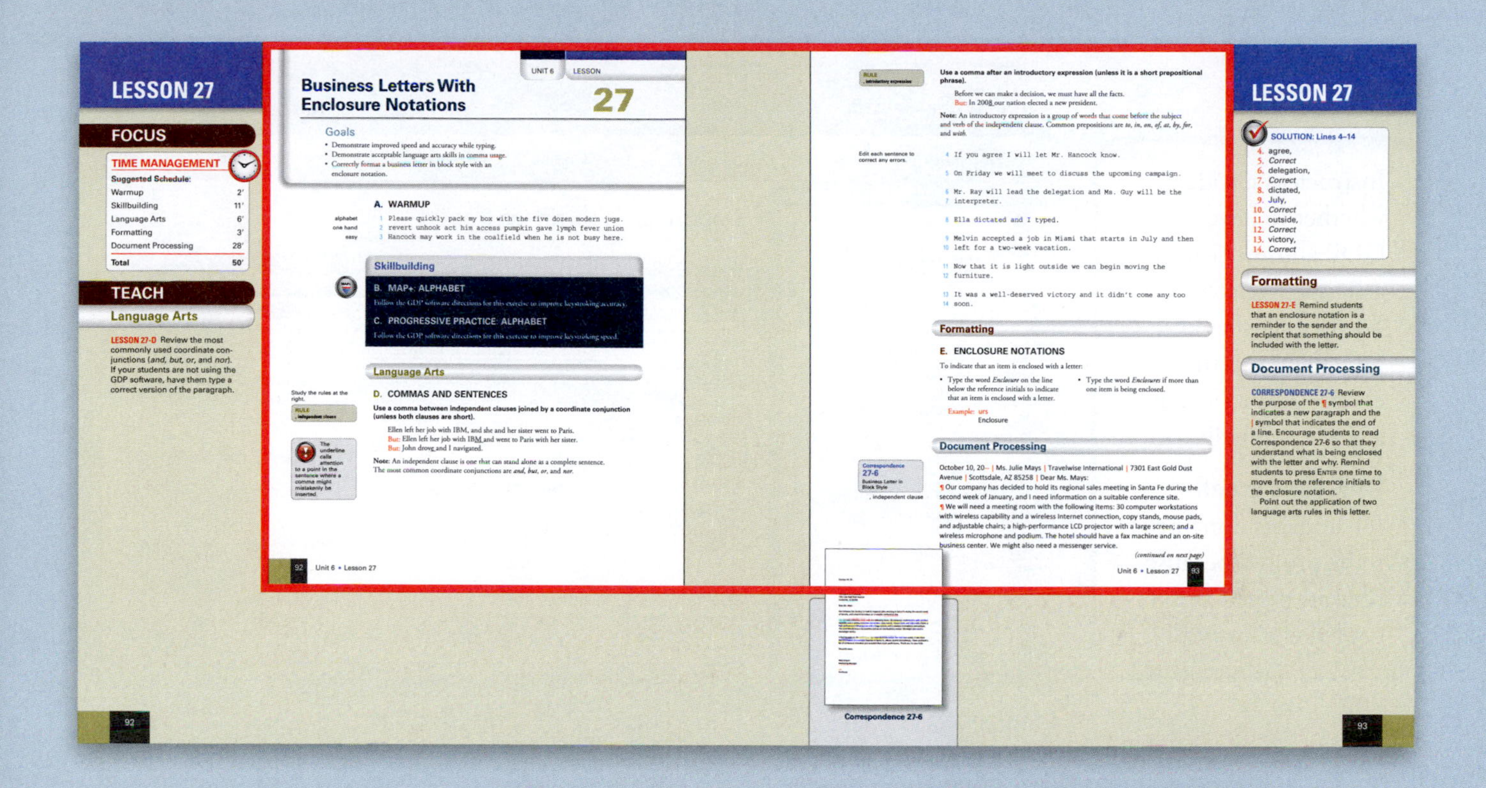

The ***Instructor Wraparound Edition (IWE)*** offers lesson plans and reduced-size student pages (shown in the red border above) to enhance classroom instruction. In addition to a mini-methods section at the front of the *IWE*, the side and bottom panels on each lesson page contain:

- Suggested times for each lesson part
- Miniature copies of the solutions for the documents students type in that lesson
- Solutions to language arts activities
- Marginal teaching notes—right where they are needed

No More Grading Papers!

New! GDP now scores both keystroking and *formatting* errors

Instructors decide whether to have GDP automatically assign a grade to each document—based on parameters they choose—or to assign a grade manually.

GDP goes green. Documents don't need to be printed because they are stored and graded electronically.

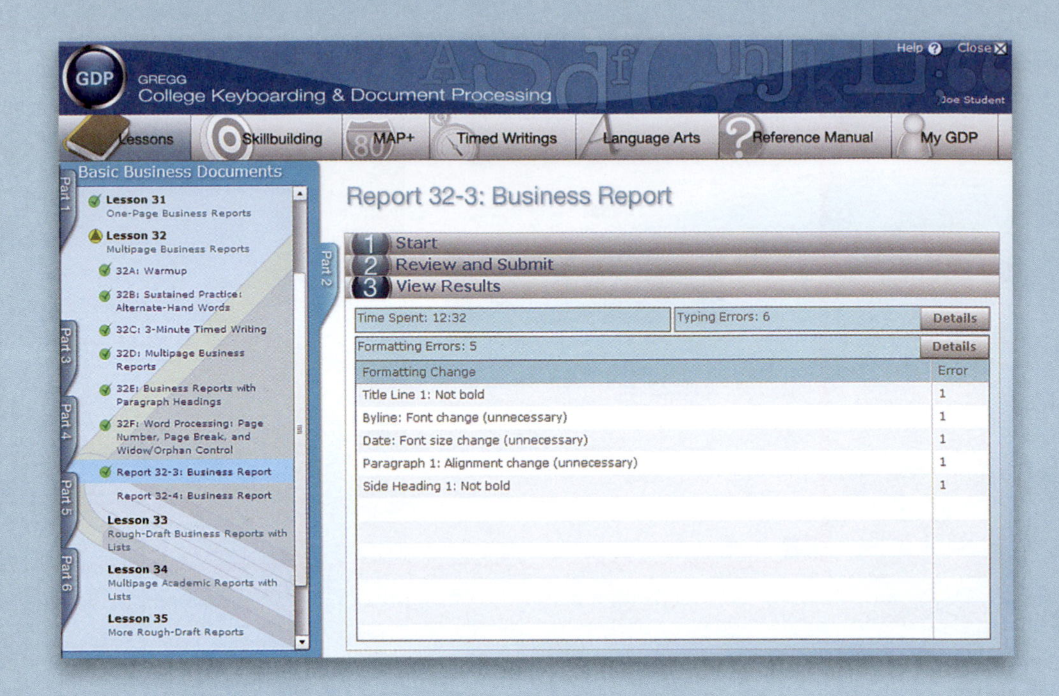

New! The customizable **GPS (Grade Posting System)** gradebook allows complete flexibility in setting up grades—with an easy-to-use, intuitive interface. Students can check their current average at any point in the school term, and instructors can save the gradebook in a comma-delimited format for uploading to Excel or to learning management systems (LMS) such as Blackboard or Angel.

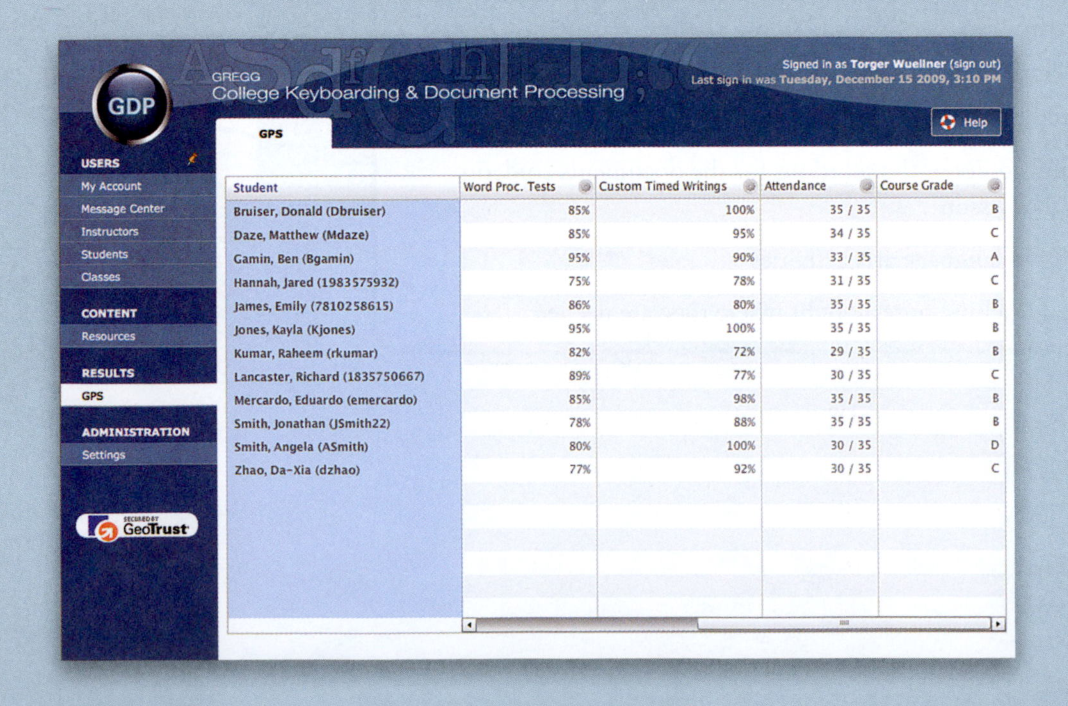

Student	Word Proc. Tests	Custom Timed Writings	Attendance	Course Grade
Bruiser, Donald (Dbruiser)	85%	100%	35 / 35	B
Daze, Matthew (Mdaze)	85%	95%	34 / 35	C
Gamin, Ben (Bgamin)	95%	90%	33 / 35	A
Hannah, Jared (1983575932)	75%	78%	31 / 35	C
James, Emily (7810258615)	86%	80%	35 / 35	B
Jones, Kayla (Kjones)	95%	100%	35 / 35	B
Kumar, Raheem (rkumar)	82%	72%	29 / 35	B
Lancaster, Richard (1835750667)	89%	77%	30 / 35	C
Mercardo, Eduardo (emercardo)	85%	98%	35 / 35	B
Smith, Jonathan (JSmith22)	78%	88%	35 / 35	B
Smith, Angela (ASmith)	80%	100%	30 / 35	D
Zhao, Da-Xia (dzhao)	77%	92%	30 / 35	C

Contents

Preface xxv
Introduction to the Student xxvii
Reference Manual R-1–R-22

PART 1
The Alphabet, Number, and Symbol Keys

UNIT 1 KEYBOARDING: THE ALPHABET 2

1	Home-Row Keys	A S D F J K L ; SPACE BAR ENTER BACKSPACE	3
2	New Keys	E N T	7
3	New Keys	O R H	11
4	New Keys	I LEFT SHIFT .	14
5	New Keys	B U C	18

UNIT 2 KEYBOARDING: THE ALPHABET 21

6	New Keys	RIGHT SHIFT W M	22
7	New Keys	X P TAB	25
8	New Keys	Q , G	28
9	New Keys	V Y Z	31
10	Review		34

UNIT 3 KEYBOARDING: NUMBERS AND SYMBOLS 37

11	New Keys	- 2 9	38
12	New Keys	8 5 '	41
13	New Keys	4 7 :	44
14	New Keys	6 3 /	47
15	Review		50

UNIT 4 KEYBOARDING: NUMBERS AND SYMBOLS 53

16	New Keys	& $ 0	54
17	New Keys	1 ? @	57
18	New Keys	% ( ) #	60

19 New Keys ” ! * 63
20 Review 67
Supplementary Lesson: Ten-Key Numeric Keypad 70

PART 2
Basic Business Documents

UNIT 5 WORD PROCESSING AND E-MAIL 74
21 Orientation to Word Processing—A 75
22 Orientation to Word Processing—B 77
23 Orientation to Word Processing—C 79
24 Orientation to Word Processing—D 81
25 E-Mail Messages 83
Correspondence 25-1: E-Mail Message
Correspondence 25-2: E-Mail Message

UNIT 6 CORRESPONDENCE 87
26 Business Letters 88
Correspondence 26-3: Business Letter in Block Style
Correspondence 26-4: Business Letter in Block Style
Correspondence 26-5: Business Letter in Block Style
27 Business Letters With Enclosure Notations 92
Correspondence 27-6: Business Letter in Block Style
Correspondence 27-7: Business Letter in Block Style
Correspondence 27-8: Business Letter in Block Style
28 Envelopes and Labels 95
Correspondence 28-9: Envelope
Correspondence 28-10: Envelope
Correspondence 28-11: Mailing Labels
Correspondence 28-12: Mailing Labels
Correspondence 28-13: Envelope
29 Memos and E-Mail With Attachments 100
Correspondence 29-14: Memo
Correspondence 29-15: Memo
Correspondence 29-16: E-Mail Message
30 Correspondence Review 106
Correspondence 30-17: Memo
Correspondence 30-18: E-Mail Message
Correspondence 30-19: Business Letter in Block Style

UNIT 7 REPORTS 109
31 One-Page Business Reports 110
Report 31-1: Business Report

Report 31-2: Business Report

32 Multipage Business Reports 114
Report 32-3: Business Report
Report 32-4: Business Report

33 Rough-Draft Business Reports With Lists 118
Report 33-5: Business Report
Report 33-6: Business Report

34 Multipage Academic Reports With Lists 122
Report 34-7: Academic Report
Report 34-8: Academic Report

35 More Rough-Draft Reports 126
Report 35-9: Academic Report
Report 35-10: Business Report

UNIT 8 TABLES 130

36 Boxed Tables 131
Table 36-1: Boxed Table
Table 36-2: Boxed Table
Table 36-3: Boxed Table
Table 36-4: Boxed Table

37 Open Tables 134
Table 37-5: Open Table
Table 37-6: Open Table
Table 37-7: Open Table

38 Open Tables With Column Headings 137
Table 38-8: Open Table
Table 38-9: Open Table
Table 38-10: Open Table
Table 38-11: Open Table

39 Ruled Tables With Number Columns 140
Table 39-12: Ruled Table
Table 39-13: Ruled Table
Table 39-14: Ruled Table

40 Formatting Review 144
Report 40-11: Academic Report
Correspondence 40-20: Business Letter in Block Style
Table 40-15: Ruled Table

TEST 2 Outcomes Assessment on Part 2 147
Correspondence Test 2-21: Business Letter in Block Style
Report Test 2-12: Academic Report
Table Test 2-16: Ruled Table

PART 3
Correspondence, Reports, and Employment Documents

UNIT 9 CORRESPONDENCE 150

41 Personal Titles and Complimentary Closings in Letters 151
Correspondence 41-22: Business Letter in Block Style
Correspondence 41-23: Business Letter in Block Style

42 Personal-Business Letters 154
Correspondence 42-24: Personal-Business Letter in Block Style
Correspondence 42-25: Personal-Business Letter in Block Style
Correspondence 42-26: Personal-Business Letter in Block Style

43 Memos and E-Mail With Lists 158
Correspondence 43-27: Memo
Correspondence 43-28: Memo
Correspondence 43-29: E-Mail Message

44 Letters With Indented Displays and Copy Notations and E-Mail With Copies 161
Correspondence 44-30: Business Letter in Block Style
Correspondence 44-31: E-Mail Message

45 Letters in Modified-Block Style 164
Correspondence 45-32: Business Letter in Modified-Block Style
Correspondence 45-33: Business Letter in Modified-Block Style
Correspondence 45-34: Business Letter in Modified-Block Style

UNIT 10 REPORTS 168

46 Left-Bound Business Reports With Indented Displays and Footnotes 169
Report 46-13: Left-Bound Business Report
Report 46-14: Left-Bound Business Report

47 Reports in APA Style 173
Report 47-15: Report in APA Style
Report 47-16: Report in APA Style

48 Reports in MLA Style 177
Report 48-17: Report in MLA Style
Report 48-18: Report in MLA Style

49 Report Citations 180
Report 49-19: Bibliography
Report 49-20: References in APA Style
Report 49-21: Works Cited in MLA Style

50 Preliminary Report Pages 185
Report 50-22: Title Page
Report 50-23: Table of Contents
Report 50-24: Title Page
Report 50-25: Left-Bound Business Report

UNIT 11 EMPLOYMENT DOCUMENTS 191

51 Resumes 192
Report 51-26: Resume
Report 51-27: Resume

52 Letters of Application 196
Correspondence 52-35: Personal-Business Letter in Modified-Block Style
Correspondence 52-36: Personal-Business Letter in Block Style
Correspondence 52-37: Personal-Business Letter in Modified-Block Style

53 Interview Communications 199
Report 53-28: Academic Report
Table 53-17: Ruled Table

54 Follow-Up Letters 202
Correspondence 54-38: Personal-Business Letter in Block Style
Correspondence 54-39: Personal-Business Letter in Modified-Block Style
Correspondence 54-40: Personal-Business Letter in Modified-Block Style

55 Integrated Employment Project 205
Report 55-29: Resume
Correspondence 55-41: Personal-Business Letter in Block Style
Correspondence 55-42: Personal-Business Letter in Modified-Block Style
Report 55-30: Resume
Correspondence 55-43: Personal-Business Letter in Block Style
Correspondence 55-44: Personal-Business Letter in Modified-Block Style

UNIT 12 SKILLBUILDING AND IN-BASKET REVIEW 209

56 In-Basket Review—Insurance 210
Correspondence 56-45: Business Letter in Block Style
Correspondence 56-46: Memo
Table 56-18: Boxed Table

57 In-Basket Review—Hospitality 214
Table 57-19: Open Table
Correspondence 57-47: Business Letter in Modified-Block Style
Report 57-31: Business Report

58 In-Basket Review—Retail 218
Correspondence 58-48: E-Mail Message
Correspondence 58-49: Memo
Table 58-20: Ruled Table

59 In-Basket Review—Nonprofit 221
Report 59-32: Business Report
Table 59-21: Boxed Table

60 In-Basket Review—Manufacturing 225
Correspondence 60-50: Business Letter in Block Style
Table 60-22: Open Table
Correspondence 60-51: E-Mail Message
Correspondence 60-52: Memo

TEST 3 Outcomes Assessment on Part 3 229
Correspondence Test 3-53: Business Letter in Block Style
Correspondence Test 3-54: E-Mail Message
Report Test 3-33: Business Report

PART 4
Advanced Formatting

UNIT 13 SKILL REFINEMENT 234

61 Skillbuilding and Letter Review 235
Correspondence 61-55: Business Letter in Block Style
Correspondence 61-56: Personal-Business Letter in Block Style
Correspondence 61-57: Business Letter in Modified-Block Style

62 Skillbuilding, Memo, and E-Mail Review 238
Correspondence 62-58: Memo
Correspondence 62-59: E-Mail Message
Correspondence 62-60: Memo
Correspondence 62-61: Memo

63 Skillbuilding and Report Review 241
Report 63-34: Business Report
Report 63-35: Academic Report
Report 63-36: Left-Bound Business Report

64 Skillbuilding and Table Review 245
Table 64-23: Boxed Table
Table 64-24: Open Table
Table 64-25: Ruled Table

65 Skillbuilding and Employment Document Review 248
Report 65-37: Resume
Correspondence 65-62: Application Letter in Block Style
Correspondence 65-63: Follow-Up Letter in Block Style

UNIT 14 CORRESPONDENCE 251

66 Multipage Letters 252
Correspondence 66-64: Business Letter in Modified-Block Style
Correspondence 66-65: Business Letter in Block Style
Correspondence 66-66: Business Letter in Modified-Block Style

67 Special Correspondence Features 256
Correspondence 67-67: Business Letter in Block Style
Correspondence 67-68: Business Letter in Block Style
Correspondence 67-69: Personal-Business Letter in Block Style

68 More Special Correspondence Features 261
Correspondence 68-70: Business Letter in Block Style
Correspondence 68-71: E-Mail Message
Correspondence 68-72: Business Letter in Modified-Block Style

69 Multipage Memos With Tables 267
Correspondence 69-73: Memo
Correspondence 69-74: Memo
Correspondence 69-75: Memo

70 Memo Reports 271
Report 70-38: Memo Report
Report 70-39: Bibliography
Report 70-40: Memo Report

UNIT 15 REPORTS 275

71 Itineraries 276
Report 71-41: Itinerary
Report 71-42: Itinerary
Report 71-43: Itinerary

72 Agendas and Minutes of Meetings 280
Report 72-44: Agenda
Report 72-45: Agenda
Report 72-46: Minutes of a Meeting
Report 72-47: Minutes of a Meeting

73 Procedures Manual 286
Report 73-48: Procedures Manual
Report 73-49: Procedures Manual
Report 73-50: Procedures Manual

74 Reports Formatted in Columns 291
Report 74-51: Magazine Article
Report 74-52: Magazine Article
Report 74-53: Magazine Article

75 Report Review 297
Report 75-54: Agenda
Report 75-55: Minutes of a Meeting
Report 75-56: Magazine Article

UNIT 16 TABLES 300

76 Tables With Footnotes or Source Notes 301
Table 76-26: Boxed Table
Table 76-27: Boxed Table
Table 76-28: Boxed Table

77 Tables With Braced Column Headings 305
Table 77-29: Boxed Table
Table 77-30: Boxed Table
Table 77-31: Boxed Table

78 Tables in Landscape Orientation 308
Table 78-32: Boxed Table
Table 78-33: Boxed Table
Table 78-34: Boxed Table

79 Multipage Tables 312
Table 79-35: Boxed Table
Table 79-36: Ruled Table
Table 79-37: Boxed Table

80 Tables With Predesigned Formats 316
Table 80-38: Predesigned Table
Table 80-39: Predesigned Table
Table 80-40: Predesigned Table

TEST 4 Outcomes Assessment on Part 4 320
Report Test 4-57: Memo Report
Correspondence Test 4-76: Business Letter in Block Style
Table Test 4-41: Boxed Table

PART 5

Specialized Applications

UNIT 17 INTERNATIONAL FORMATTING 324

81 International Formatting—Canada 325
Correspondence 81-77: Business Letter in Modified-Block Style
Table 81-42: Boxed Table
Table 81-43: Boxed Table

82 International Formatting—Mexico 330
Correspondence 82-78: E-Mail Message
Report 82-58: Business Report

83 International Formatting—France 335
Correspondence 83-79: Business Letter in Block Style
Table 83-44: Boxed Table
Correspondence 83-80: E-Mail Message

84 International Formatting—Germany 339
Correspondence 84-81: E-Mail Message
Correspondence 84-82: Business Letter in Block Style
Report 84-59: Business Report

85 International Formatting—China 344
Correspondence 85-83: Business Letter in Block Style
Correspondence 85-84: E-Mail Message
Table 85-45: Boxed Table

UNIT 18 FORMAL REPORT PROJECT 347

86 Formal Report Project—A 348
Report 86-60: Business Report

87 Formal Report Project—B 353
Report 87-61: Business Report (Continued)

88 Formal Report Project—C 357
Report 88-62: Business Report (Continued)

89 Formal Report Project—D 360
Table 89-46: Boxed Table
Report 89-63: Business Report (Continued)

90 Formal Report Project—E 364
Report 90-64: Cover Page
Report 90-65: Table of Contents
Report 90-66: Bibliography

UNIT 19 MEDICAL OFFICE DOCUMENTS 368

91 Medical Office Documents—A 369
Correspondence 91-85: Business Letter in Block Style

Table 91-47: Boxed Table
Correspondence 91-86: Memo

92 Medical Office Documents—B 373
Report 92-67: Business Report
Table 92-48: Predesigned Table

93 Medical Office Documents—C 378
Correspondence 93-87: Business Letter in Modified-Block Style
Report 93-68: Business Report

94 Medical Office Documents—D 382
Table 94-49: Ruled Table
Correspondence 94-88: Business Letter in Block Style
Table 94-50: Predesigned Table

95 Medical Office Documents—E 386
Table 95-51: Open Table
Correspondence 95-89: E-Mail Message
Report 95-69: Business Report

UNIT 20 LEGAL OFFICE DOCUMENTS 389

96 Legal Office Documents—A 390
Report 96-70: Warranty Deed
Table 96-52: Boxed Table
Correspondence 96-90: E-Mail Message

97 Legal Office Documents—B 395
Report 97-71: Last Will and Testament
Correspondence 97-91: Business Letter in Block Style

98 Legal Office Documents—C 399
Report 98-72: Affidavit of Possession
Correspondence 98-92: Business Letter in Block Style

99 Legal Office Documents—D 402
Report 99-73: Summons
Correspondence 99-93: Memo
Table 99-53: Predesigned Table

100 Legal Office Documents—E 406
Report 100-74: Complaint
Report 100-75: Warranty Deed
Report 100-76: Judgment

TEST 5 Outcomes Assessment on Part 5 411
Correspondence Test 5-94: Business Letter in Block Style
Table Test 5-54: Boxed Table
Report Test 5-77: Summons

PART 6

Using and Designing Business Documents

UNIT 21 USING AND DESIGNING OFFICE FORMS 414

101 Using Correspondence Templates 415

Form 101-1: Memo Template
Form 101-2: Memo Template
Form 101-3: Memo Template

102 Using Report Templates 418

Form 102-4: Report Template
Form 102-5: Report Template

103 Designing Letterheads 422

Form 103-6: Letterhead Form
Form 103-7: Letterhead Form
Form 103-8: Letterhead Form

104 Designing Notepads 427

Form 104-9: Notepad Form
Form 104-10: Notepad Form
Form 104-11: Notepad Form

105 Designing Miscellaneous Office Forms 432

Form 105-12: Directory Form
Form 105-13: Sign-In Form
Form 105-14: Memo Template

UNIT 22 DESIGNING OFFICE PUBLICATIONS 436

106 Designing Cover Pages 437

Report 106-78: Cover Page
Report 106-79: Cover Page
Report 106-80: Cover Page

107 Designing Announcements and Flyers 442

Report 107-81: Announcement
Report 107-82: Announcement
Report 107-83: Announcement or Flyer

108 Designing Newsletters—A 447

Report 108-84: Newsletter
Report 108-85: Newsletter

109 Designing Newsletters—B 450

Report 109-86: Newsletter (Continued)
Report 109-87: Newsletter (Continued)

110 Designing Newsletters—C 454

Report 110-88: Newsletter (Continued)
Report 110-89: Flyer

UNIT 23 ONLINE RESUMES AND MERGED DOCUMENTS 459

111 Designing an Online Resume 460

Report 111-90: Online Resume
Report 111-91: Online Resume

112 Mail Merge—A 463
Correspondence 112-95: Business Letter in Block Style

113 Mail Merge—B 467
Correspondence 113-96: Business Letter in Modified-Block Style

114 Mail Merge—C 470
Correspondence 114-97: Business Letter in Block Style

115 Mail Merge—D 473
Correspondence 115-98: Envelopes
Correspondence 115-99: Mailing Labels
Correspondence 115-100: Business Letter in Block Style

UNIT 24 SKILLBUILDING AND IN-BASKET REVIEW 477

116 Skillbuilding and In-Basket Review—Banking 478
Form 116-15: Memo Template
Table 116-55: Boxed Table
Form 116-16: Letterhead Form

117 Skillbuilding and In-Basket Review—Education 482
Report 117-92: Academic Report
Report 117-93: Flyer
Report 117-94: Left-Bound Business Report

118 Skillbuilding and In-Basket Review—Nursing Facility 486
Correspondence 118-101: Business Letter in Block Style
Report 118-95: Itinerary
Report 118-96: Newsletter

119 Skillbuilding and In-Basket Review—Government 490
Correspondence 119-102: Business Letter in Block Style
Table 119-56: Ruled Table
Correspondence 119-103: E-Mail Message

120 Skillbuilding and In-Basket Review—Software Development 493
Report 120-97: Business Report
Correspondence 120-104: Business Letter in Modified-Block Style

TEST 6 Outcomes Assessment on Part 6 498
Form Test 6-17: Memo Template
Report Test 6-98: Online Resume
Report Test 6-99: Flyer

SKILLBUILDING

Progressive Practice: Alphabet SB-2
Progressive Practice: Numbers SB-7
Paced Practice SB-10
Supplementary Timed Writings SB-26

INDEX I-1

Preface

Gregg College Keyboarding & Document Processing is a multicomponent instructional program designed to give the student and the instructor a high degree of flexibility and a high degree of success in meeting their respective goals. The textbook is offered in several volumes: *Lessons 1–20*, *Lessons 1–60*, *Lessons 61–120*, and *Lessons 1–120*. The GDP software is a Web-delivered, PC-compatible program providing complete lesson-by-lesson instruction for each of the 120 text lessons. The document processing *Word Manual*, used in conjunction with the textbook for Lessons 21–120, teaches the document processing skills needed to create efficient business documents using Microsoft Word.

The Kit Format

For student and instructor convenience, the core components of this instructional system—the textbook, the *Word Manual*, and the Gregg College Keyboarding & Document Processing (GDP) software—are available in a variety of kit formats.

Kit 1: Lessons 1–60 This kit, designed for the first keyboarding course, provides the Lessons 1–60 textbook, the *Word Manual*, and an access card to the GDP software. Since this kit is designed for the beginning student, its major objectives are to develop touch control of the keyboard and proper keyboarding techniques, to build basic speed and accuracy, and to provide practice in applying those basic skills to the formatting of e-mails, reports, letters, memos, tables, and other kinds of personal and business communications.

Kit 2: Lessons 61–120 This kit, designed for the second course, provides the Lessons 61–120 textbook, the *Word Manual*, and an access card to the GDP software. This course continues the development of basic keyboarding skills and emphasizes the formatting of various kinds of business correspondence, reports, tables, electronic forms, and desktop publishing projects from arranged, unarranged, handwritten, and rough-draft sources.

Kit 3: Lessons 1–120 This kit, designed for both the first and second course, provides the Lessons 1–120 textbook, the *Word Manual*, and an access card to the GDP software.

Kit 4: Lessons 1–20 This kit, designed for shorter keyboarding courses, provides the Lessons 1–20 text and an access card to the GDP software.

Supporting Materials

Gregg College Keyboarding & Document Processing offers the following instructional materials:

- The special ***Instructor Wraparound Edition (IWE)*** offers lesson plans and reduced-size student pages to enhance classroom instruction. Distance-learning tips, instructional methodology, adult learner strategies, and special needs features also are included in this wraparound edition. New to this edition are miniature solutions for each document the students type; they are shown in the margins of the IWE.
- The ***Tests and Solutions Manual*** provides solution keys for all of the formatting in Lessons 25–120 in addition to objective tests and alternative document processing tests for each part.

What's New in the 11th Edition Text?

New-Key Introduction (Lessons 1–20)

- A new Enrichment page has been added to each of the first 20 lessons—for additional practice and faster development of touch-typing skills.
- MAP+ (Misstroke Analysis and Prescription) can now be used beginning with Lesson 1, thus providing unlimited new practice drills for each of the new-key lessons.
- A new supplementary lesson, Ten-Key Numeric Keypad, follows Lesson 20; it teaches the touch typing of both the number keys and arithmetic operators (+, -, /, and *), with 55 new drill lines.
- Only 3 new keys are introduced in each lesson (instead of 4)—to provide more intensive practice on each new key; all keys are still introduced in Lessons 1–20.
- The order in which new keys are introduced has been refined to balance the workload between each hand and to take into consideration how frequently keys are used. For example, in previous editions, the hyphen key was introduced early (in Lesson 6) because students used it for manual word division. With Word's automatic hyphenation feature, students don't use this key as much anymore, and the hyphen is now introduced in Lesson 11.

Skillbuilding

- MAP+ now provides an analysis and prescription of the number and symbol keys (previously, only alphabetic reaches were included). Because of this, (a) Diagnostic Practice: Symbols and Punctuation and (b) Diagnostic Practice: Numbers have been removed.
- Every Warmup exercise has been revised. Line 1 of each Warmup is now an alphabetic sentence to review all reaches, Line 2 practices a particular type of reach, and Line 3 contains easy words to build speed.

Document Processing

- Formatting correspondence (new Unit 6) is now introduced before formatting reports (new Unit 7).
- The formatting of bulleted/numbered lists in Lesson 33 and table column headings in Lesson 38 has been simplified.
- More e-mail messages are included with added coverage of formatting, such as bulleted lists, tables, and attachments.
- Eleven new Word commands are introduced: Zoom (L. 24), Widow/Orphan Control (L. 32), Table—Align Bottom (L. 38), AutoCorrect—Hyperlink (L. 49), Bookmarks and Hyperlinks (L. 89), Cover Page—Insert (L. 90), Table—Tab (L. 92), Page Color (L. 107), Mail Merge (L. 113–115), Style Set—Word 2007 (Appendix A), and PDF Format (Appendix C).
- The electronic resume in Lesson 52 (which is not being used much anymore) has been replaced by job-interviewing documents.
- The Web project in Unit 23 has been changed from creating a company home page to (a) creating an online resume and (b) introducing Mail Merge.
- Each lesson of the *Instructor's Wraparound Edition* now displays a miniature solution for each document students type in that lesson.

Introduction to the Student

Starting a Lesson

Each lesson begins with the goals for that lesson. Read the goals carefully so that you understand the purpose of your practice. In the example at the right (from Lesson 26), the goals for the lesson are to type at least 30 wpm (words per minute) on a 3-minute timed writing with no more than 5 uncorrected errors and to correctly format a business letter in block style with standard punctuation.

Goals

- Type at least 30wpm/3′/5e by touch.
- Correctly format a business letter in block style with standard punctuation.

Building Straight-Copy Skill

Warmups. Each lesson begins with a Warmup that reinforces learned alphabet, number, and/or symbol keys; practices specific reaches; and builds speed.

Skillbuilding. The Skillbuilding portion of each lesson includes a variety of drills to individualize your keyboarding speed and accuracy development. Instructions for completing the drills are always provided beside each activity.

Additional Skillbuilding drills are included in the back of the textbook and on the GDP correlated software. These drills are intended to help you meet your individual goals.

Measuring Straight-Copy Skill

Straight-copy skill is measured in wpm. All timed writings are the exact length needed to meet the speed goal for the lesson. If you finish a timed writing before time is up, you have automatically reached your speed goal for the lesson.

Counting Errors. Specific criteria are used for counting errors. The GDP software counts an error when

1. Any stroke is incorrect.
2. Any punctuation after a word is incorrect or omitted. The word before the punctuation is counted as incorrect.
3. The spacing after a word or after its punctuation is incorrect. The word is counted as incorrect.
4. A letter or word is omitted or repeated.
5. A direction about spacing, indenting, and so on, is not followed.
6. Words are transposed.

(**Note:** Only one error is counted for each word, no matter how many errors it may contain. The GDP correlated software automatically proofreads your copy and marks any errors for you.)

Determining Speed. To compute your typing speed in wpm, the GDP software counts every 5 strokes, including spaces, as 1 "word." Horizontal word scales below an activity divide lines into 5-stroke words. Vertical word scales to the right of an activity show the number of words in each line cumulatively totaled.

For example, the illustration that follows is for a 2-minute timed writing. If you complete line 30, you have typed 11 words. If you complete line 31, you have typed 22 words. Use the bottom word scale to determine the word count of a partial line. Add that number to the cumulative total for the last complete line. The GDP correlated software automatically computes your wpm speed for you.

Take two 2-minute timed writings.

Goal: At least 19wpm/2′/5e

```
30     Zachary just paid for six seats and quit because he     11
31  could not get the views he required near the middle of the 22
32  field. In August he thinks he may go to the ticket office  34
33  to purchase tickets.                                        38
      1 | 2 | 3 | 4 | 5 | 6 | 7 | 8 | 9 | 10 | 11 | 12
```

Correcting Errors

You will make numerous errors while you are learning the keyboard; do not be overly concerned about them. Errors will decrease as you become familiar with the keyboard. Error-correction settings in the GDP software determine whether you can correct errors in timed writings and drills. Consult your instructor for error-correction guidelines.

To correct an error, press Backspace (shown as ← on some keyboards) to delete the incorrect character(s). Then type the correct character(s).

If you notice an error on a different line, use the up, down, left, or right arrows to move the insertion point immediately to the left or right of the error. Press Backspace to delete a character to the left of the insertion point or Delete to delete a character to the right of the insertion point.

Typing Technique

Correct position at the keyboard enables you to type with greater speed and accuracy and with less fatigue. When typing for a long period, rest your eyes occasionally by looking away from the screen. Change position, walk around, or stretch when your muscles feel tired. Making such movements and adjustments may help prevent your body from becoming too tired. In addition, long-term bodily damage, such as carpal tunnel syndrome, can be prevented.

Follow these ergonomic principles when typing:

Workstation

1. Position your chair so that your upper and lower legs form a greater-than-90-degree angle and your lower back is supported, with your knees slightly lower than your hips.
2. Position your text on either side of the monitor as close to the monitor vertically and horizontally as possible.
3. Position the mouse on a pad next to and at the same height as your keyboard.
4. Tilt the top of the monitor slightly away from you and slightly farther than an arm's length from you.

Position at the Keyboard

5. Center your body in front of the keyboard.
6. Sit slightly reclined, with your lower back touching the back of the chair and your feet flat on the floor.
7. Keep your elbows close to your body in a relaxed position.
8. Curve your fingers naturally over the home-row position, with the back of your hands at the same angle as the keyboard.
9. Move the mouse with your whole arm—not just your wrist.

Keystroking

10. Operate all keys by touch, using the correct fingers.
11. Keep your eyes on the copy most of the time while typing.

12. Keep your forearms at a slight downward slant and raise your hands slightly when typing so that your wrists do not touch the keyboard.
13. Make quick, light strokes, returning your fingers immediately to the home-row position or moving to the next position after each stroke.

Tension-Reducing Exercises

A variety of government and health sources recommend the following exercises for computer users. Perform one exercise from each group, hold each position for three seconds, and repeat each exercise three times.

Neck

1. Look forward and slowly tilt your head as far to the left as possible. Then slowly tilt your head as far to the right as possible.
2. Slowly tilt your head forward until your chin rests on your chest. Then slowly tilt your head as far back as possible.

Shoulders

3. Roll your shoulders forward in a large circle. Then roll your shoulders backward in a large circle.
4. Extend both arms out to your side. Then slowly stretch them toward your back and squeeze your shoulder blades together. Finally, slowly bring your arms forward and touch the tops of your hands together in front of you.

Back

5. Place both hands behind your head, and slowly stretch your upper body backward. Then slowly bend all the way forward, stretching your arms toward the floor.
6. While seated, grab your left knee with both hands and slowly pull your leg in toward your body. Then repeat with your right knee.

Eyes

7. Close your eyes tightly. Then open them as wide as you can, blinking rapidly.
8. Follow the 20/20/20 rule: every 20 minutes, stare at an object 20 feet away for 20 seconds.

Reference Manual

COMPUTER SYSTEM
keyboard, R-2B
parts of, R-2A

CORRESPONDENCE
application letter, R-12B
attachment notation, R-4D, R-7C
blind copy notation, R-5B
block style, R-3A
body, R-3A
company name, R-5B
complimentary closing, R-3A
copy notation, R-3C, R-5B
date line, R-3A
delivery notation, R-3C, R-4A, R-5B
e-mail, R-5C–D
enclosure notation, R-3B, R-5B
envelope formatting, R-6A
executive stationery, R-4A
half-page stationery, R-4B
indented displays, R-3A
inside address, R-3A
international address, R-3D, R-5A
letter folding, R-6B
letterhead, R-3A
lists, R-3B–C, R-5B, R-12C–D
memo, R-4D, R-7C, R-9C
modified-block style, R-3B, R-3D
multiline lists, R-3B, R-5B, R-12C–D
multipage, R-5A–B, R-8A–D, R-13C
on-arrival notation, R-5A
open punctuation, R-4C
page number, R-5A–B, R-8A–D, R-10A–D, R-13C
personal-business, R-3D, R-12B
postscript notation, R-5B
quotation, long, R-3A
reference initials, R-3A, R-4D, R-5B
return address, R-3D, R-12B
salutation, R-3A
simplified style, R-3C
single-line lists, R-3C, R-12C–D
standard punctuation, R-3A
subject line, R-3C, R-4D, R-5A, R-7C
tables in, R-4D, R-5A, R-13C–D
window envelope, folding for, R-6B
window envelope, formatted for, R-4C
writer's identification, R-3A

EMPLOYMENT DOCUMENTS
application letter, R-12B
resume, R-12A

FORMS
R-14A

LANGUAGE ARTS
abbreviations, R-22
adjectives and adverbs, R-20
agreement, R-19
apostrophes, R-17
capitalization, R-21
colons, R-18
commas, R-15 to R-16
grammar, R-19 to R-20
hyphens, R-17
italics (or underline), R-18
mechanics, R-21 to R-22
number expression, R-21 to R-22
periods, R-18
pronouns, R-20
punctuation, R-15 to R-18
quotation marks, R-18
semicolons, R-16
sentences, R-19
underline (or italics), R-18
word usage, R-20

PROOFREADERS' MARKS
R-14C

REPORTS
academic style, R-8C–D
agenda, meeting, R-11A
APA style, R-10A–B
author/page citations, R-10C
author/year citations, R-10A
bibliography, R-9B
business, R-8A–B, R-9A
byline, R-8A, R-10A
citations, R-9D, R-10A–D
date, R-8A
endnotes, R-8C–D, R-9C
footnotes, R-8A–B, R-9A
hanging indent, R-10D
header, R-10A–B, R-10D
headings, R-9D, R-10C
headings, main, R-10A
headings, paragraph, R-8A, R-8C, R-9A
headings, side, R-8A–C, R-9A
indented display, R-8B, R-8D
itinerary, R-11C
left-bound, R-9A
legal document, R-11D
line numbers, R-11D
lists, R-8A, R-8C, R-9A, R-9C, R-11A, R-12A, R-12C–D
margins, R-9D
memo report, R-9C
minutes of a meeting, R-11B
MLA style, R-10C–D
multiline lists, R-8A, R-8C, R-11A, R-12A, R-12C–D
multipage academic, R-8C–D
multipage business, R-8A–B
outline, R-7A
page number, R-8B, R-8D, R-10A–B
paragraph heading, R-8A, R-9C
quotation, long, R-8B, R-8D
references page, APA style, R-10B
resume, R-12A
side heading, R-8A, R-9C
single-line lists, R-9A, R-9C, R-11A, R-12A, R-12C–D
spacing, R-9D
special features, R-9D
subheadings, R-10A
subject line, 2-line, R-9C
subtitle, R-8A
table of contents page, R-7D
tables in, R-8B
title, R-7A–B, R-8A–C, R-10A, R-10C
title, 2-line, R-8C, R-9A, R-10A, R-10C
title page, R-7B
transmittal memo, R-7C
works-cited page, MLA style, R-10D

TABLES
2-line column heading, R-13B
body, R-13A
bottom-aligned, R-13A–B
boxed, R-5A, R-8B, R-13A
braced column headings, R-13A
capitalization, columns, R-13D
column headings, R-4D, R-5A, R-8B, R-13A–D
dollar signs, R-8B, R-13A–B, R-13D
heading block, R-5, R-8B, R-13A–D
in correspondence, R-4D, R-5A, R-13C
in reports, R-8B
note, R-8B, R-13A
number, R-8B, R-13C
numbers in, R-4D, R-8B, R-13A–C
open, R-13B
percent signs, R-13B, R-13D
ruled, R-4D, R-13C
source, R-8B
special features, R-13D
subtitle, R-8B, R-13A–B, R-13D
table number, R-8B, R-13C
tables, R-4D, R-5A, R-8B, R-13A–C
title, R-5A, R-8B, R-13A–D
total line, R-13A, R-13C–D
vertical placement, R-13D

U.S. POSTAL SERVICE STATE ABBREVIATIONS
R-14B

A. MAJOR PARTS OF A COMPUTER SYSTEM

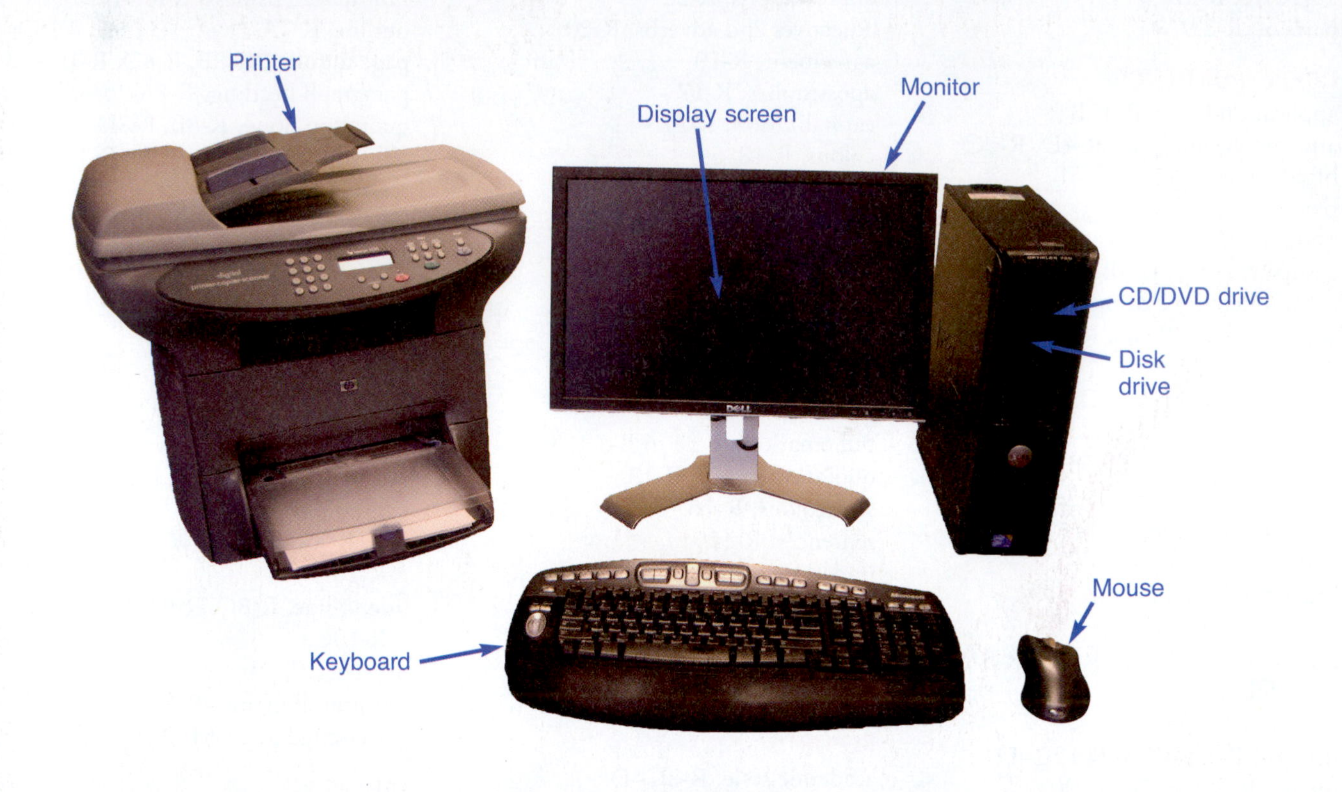

B. THE COMPUTER KEYBOARD

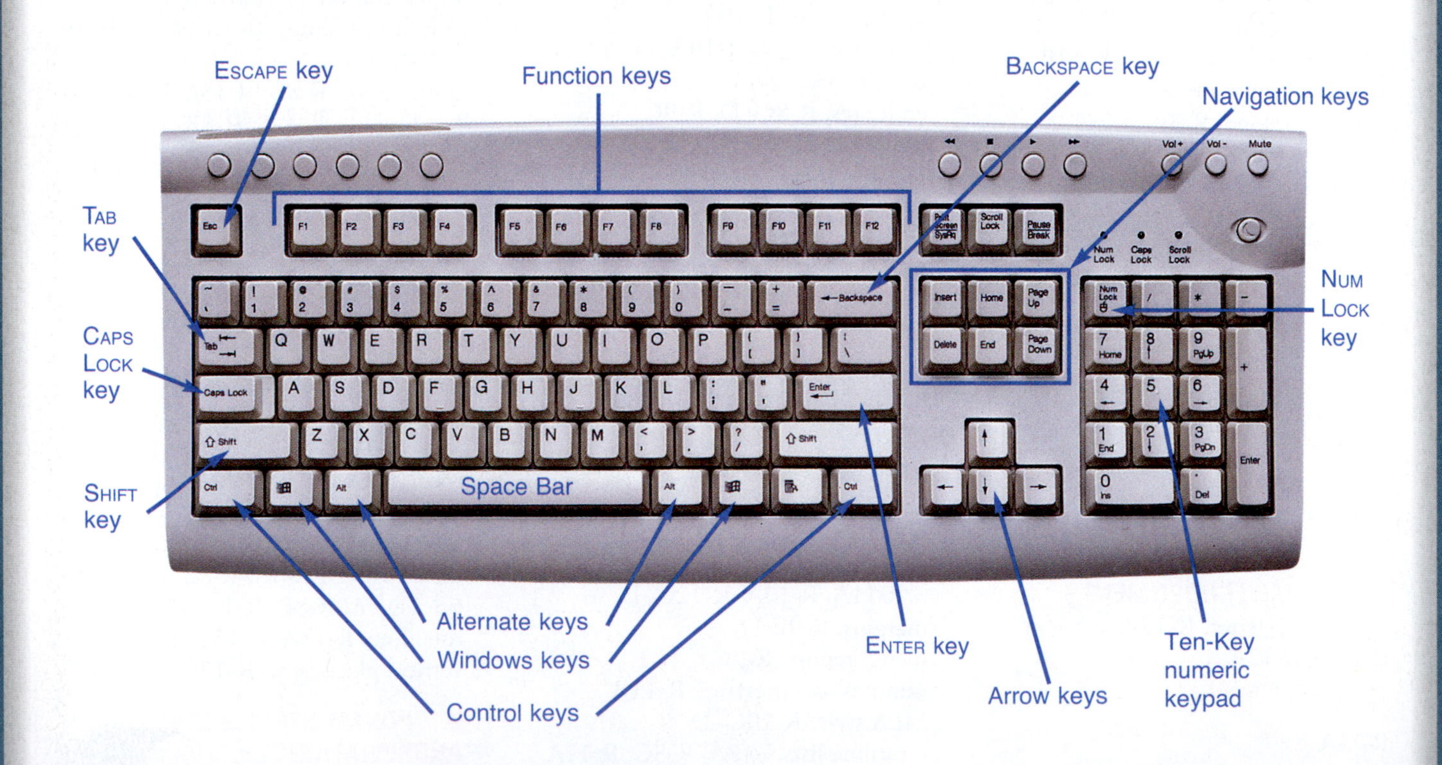

Reference Manual

A. BUSINESS LETTER IN BLOCK STYLE

(with standard punctuation and indented display)

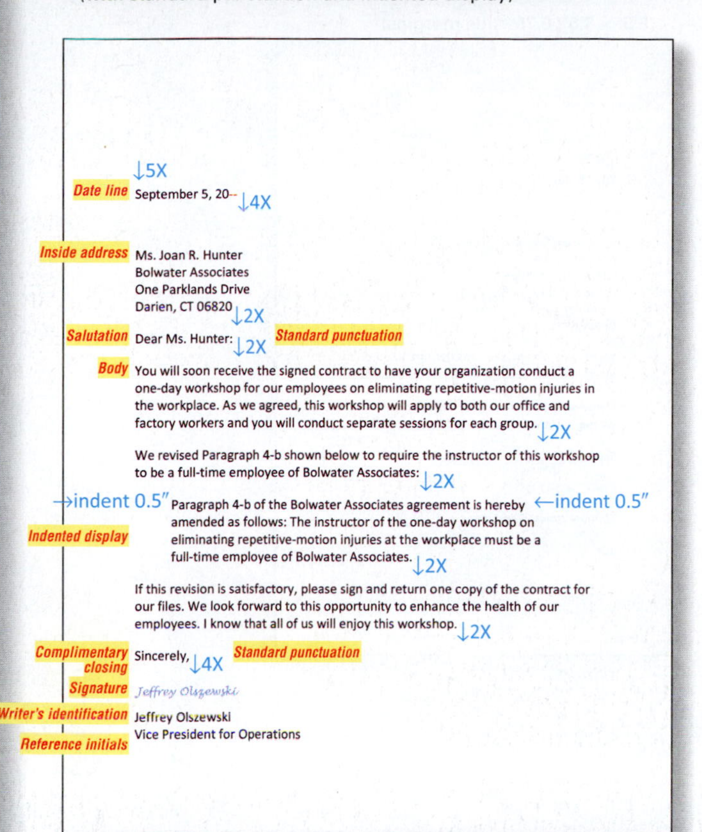

↓5X

Date line — September 5, 20-- ↓4X

Inside address — Ms. Joan R. Hunter
Bolwater Associates
One Parklands Drive
Darien, CT 06820 ↓2X

Salutation — Dear Ms. Hunter: ↓2X — Standard punctuation

Body — You will soon receive the signed contract to have your organization conduct a one-day workshop for our employees on eliminating repetitive-motion injuries in the workplace. As we agreed, this workshop will apply to both our office and factory workers and you will conduct separate sessions for each group. ↓2X

We revised Paragraph 4-b shown below to require the instructor of this workshop to be a full-time employee of Bolwater Associates: ↓2X

→indent 0.5″ Paragraph 4-b of the Bolwater Associates agreement is hereby amended as follows: The instructor of the one-day workshop on eliminating repetitive-motion injuries at the workplace must be a full-time employee of Bolwater Associates. ↓2X ←indent 0.5″ — Indented display

If this revision is satisfactory, please sign and return one copy of the contract for our files. We look forward to this opportunity to enhance the health of our employees. I know that all of us will enjoy this workshop. ↓2X

Complimentary closing — Sincerely, ↓4X — Standard punctuation

Signature — *Jeffrey Olszewski*

Writer's identification — Jeffrey Olszewski
Vice President for Operations

Reference initials

B. BUSINESS LETTER IN MODIFIED-BLOCK STYLE

(with multiline list and enclosure notation)

left tab: 3.25″ (centerpoint)

↓5X

→ tab 3.25″ (centerpoint) May 15, 20-- ↓4X

Mr. Ichiro Xie
Bolwater Associates
One Parklands Drive
Darien, CT 06820 ↓2X

Dear Mr. Xie: ↓2X

I am returning a signed contract to have your organization conduct a one-day workshop for our employees on eliminating repetitive-motion injuries in the workplace. We have made the following changes to the contract: ↓2X

Multiline list

1. We revised Paragraph 4-b to require the instructor of this workshop to be a full-time employee of Bolwater Associates.
2. We made changes to Paragraph 10-c to require our prior approval of the agenda for the workshop. ↓2X

If these revisions are satisfactory, please sign and return one copy of the contract for our files. We look forward to this opportunity to enhance the health of our employees. I know that all of us will enjoy this workshop. ↓2X

→ tab 3.25″ (centerpoint) Sincerely, ↓4X

Jeffrey Olszewski

Jeffrey Olszewski
Vice President for Operations ↓2X

pec

Enclosure notation — Enclosure

C. BUSINESS LETTER IN SIMPLIFIED STYLE

(with subject line, single-line list; enclosure, delivery, and copy notations)

↓5X

October 5, 20-- ↓4X

Mr. Dale P. Griffin
Bolwater Associates
One Parklands Drive
Darien, CT 06820 ↓3X

Subject line — WORKSHOP CONTRACT ↓3X

I am returning the signed contract, Mr. Griffin, to have your organization conduct a one-day workshop for our employees on eliminating repetitive-motion injuries in the workplace. We have amended the following sections of the contract: ↓2X

Single-line list

- Paragraph 4-b
- Table 3
- Attachment 2 ↓2X

If these revisions are satisfactory, please sign and return one copy of the contract for our files. We look forward to this opportunity to enhance the health of our employees. I know that all of us will enjoy this workshop. ↓4X

Rogena Kyles

ROGENA KYLES, DIRECTOR ↓2X

iww

Enclosure notation — Enclosure
Delivery notation — By e-mail
Copy notation — c: Legal Department

D. PERSONAL-BUSINESS LETTER IN MODIFIED-BLOCK STYLE

(with international address and return address)

left tab: 3.25″ (centerpoint)

↓5X

→ tab 3.25″ (centerpoint) July 15, 20-- ↓4X

Mr. Luis Fernandez
Vice President
Arvon Industries, Inc.
21 St. Claire Avenue East
Toronto, ON M4T IL9
CANADA ↓2X — International address

Dear Mr. Fernandez: ↓2X

As a former employee and present stockholder of Arvon Industries, I wish to protest the planned sale of the Consumer Products Division. ↓2X

According to published reports, consumer products accounted for 19 percent of last year's corporate profits, and they are expected to account for even more this year. In addition, Dun & Bradstreet predicts that consumer products nationwide will outpace the general economy for the next five years.

I am concerned about the effect that this planned sale might have on overall corporate profits, on our cash dividends for investors, and on the economy of Melbourne, where the two consumer-products plants are located. Please ask your board of directors to reconsider this matter. ↓2X

→ tab 3.25″ (centerpoint) Sincerely, ↓4X

Jeanine Ford

Return address — Jeanine Ford
901 East Benson, Apt. 3
Fort Lauderdale, FL 33301
U.S.A.

Reference Manual

A. BUSINESS LETTER ON EXECUTIVE STATIONERY

(7.25" × 10.5"; 1" side margins; with delivery notation)

↓5X
July 18, 20-- ↓4X

Mr. Rodney Eastwood
BBL Resources
523 Northern Ridge
Fayetteville, PA 17222 ↓2X

Dear Rodney: ↓2X

I see no reason why we should continue to consider the locality around Geraldton for our new plant. Even though the desirability of this site from an economic view is undeniable, there is not sufficient housing readily available for our workers. ↓2X

In trying to control urban growth, the city has been turning down the building permits for much new housing or placing so many restrictions on foreign investment as to make it too expensive.

Please continue to seek out other areas of exploration where we might form a joint partnership. ↓2X

Sincerely, ↓4X

Jennifer Gwatkin

Jennifer Gwatkin, Director ↓2X

mme
By fax

Delivery notation

B. BUSINESS LETTER ON HALF-PAGE STATIONERY

(5.5" × 8.5"; 0.75" side margins)

↓4 X
July 18, 20-- ↓4X

Mr. Aristeo Olivas
BBL Resources
52A Northern Ridge
Fayetteville, PA 17222 ↓2X

Dear Aristeo: ↓2X

We should discontinue considering Geraldton for our new plant. Housing is not readily available.

Please seek out other areas of exploration where we might someday form a joint partnership. ↓2X

Sincerely, ↓4X

Chimere Jones

Chimere Jones, Director ↓2X

adk

C. BUSINESS LETTER FORMATTED FOR A WINDOW ENVELOPE

(with open punctuation)

↓5X
July 18, 20-- ↓3X

Ms. Reinalda Guerrero
BBL Resources
52A Northern Ridge
Fayetteville, PA 17222 ↓3X

Dear Ms. Guerrero ↓2X **Open punctuation**

I see no reason why we should even continue to consider the locality around Geraldton for our new plant. Even though the desirability of this site from an economic view is undeniable, there is insufficient housing readily available for our workers. ↓2X

In trying to control urban growth, the city has been turning down the building permits for new housing or placing so many restrictions on foreign investment as to make it too expensive.

Please continue to seek out other areas of exploration where we might form a joint partnership. ↓2X

Sincerely ↓4X **Open punctuation**

Augustus Mays

Augustus Mays
Vice President for Operations ↓2X

woc

D. MEMO

(with ruled table, left- and right-aligned columns, and attachment notation)

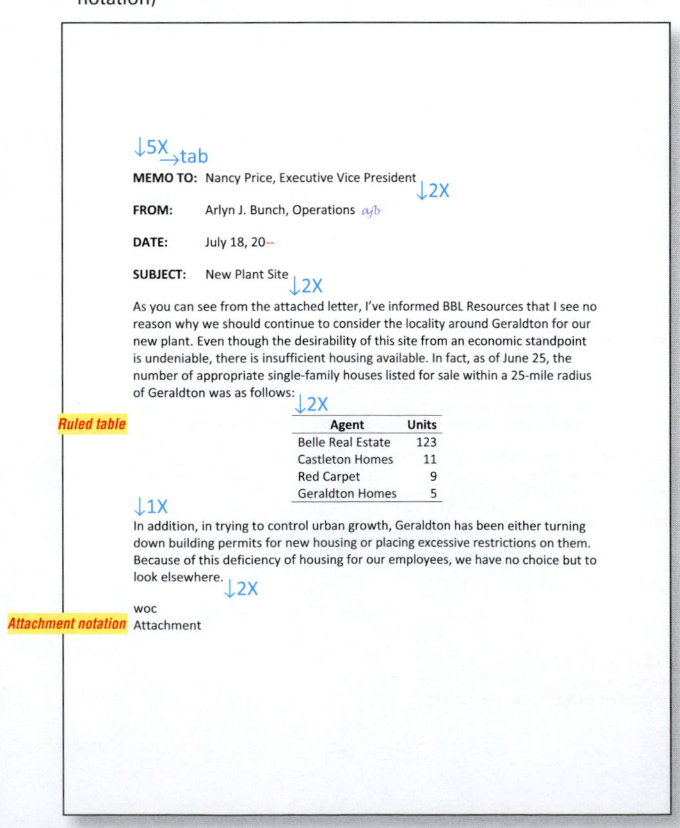

↓5X →tab

MEMO TO: Nancy Price, Executive Vice President ↓2X

FROM: Arlyn J. Bunch, Operations *ajb*

DATE: July 18, 20--

SUBJECT: New Plant Site ↓2X

As you can see from the attached letter, I've informed BBL Resources that I see no reason why we should continue to consider the locality around Geraldton for our new plant. Even though the desirability of this site from an economic standpoint is undeniable, there is insufficient housing available. In fact, as of June 25, the number of appropriate single-family houses listed for sale within a 25-mile radius of Geraldton was as follows: ↓2X

Ruled table

Agent	Units
Belle Real Estate	123
Castleton Homes	11
Red Carpet	9
Geraldton Homes	5

↓1X

In addition, in trying to control urban growth, Geraldton has been either turning down building permits for new housing or placing excessive restrictions on them. Because of this deficiency of housing for our employees, we have no choice but to look elsewhere. ↓2X

woc
Attachment notation Attachment

A. MULTIPAGE BUSINESS LETTER

(page 1; with on-arrival notation, international address, subject line, and boxed table)

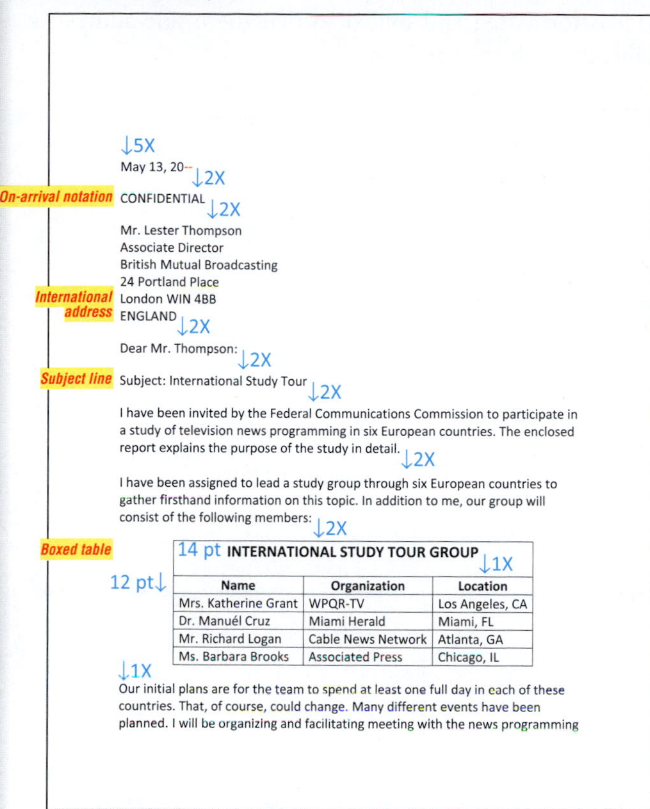

May 13, 20--

CONFIDENTIAL

Mr. Lester Thompson
Associate Director
British Mutual Broadcasting
24 Portland Place
London WIN 4BB
ENGLAND

Dear Mr. Thompson:

Subject: International Study Tour

I have been invited by the Federal Communications Commission to participate in a study of television news programming in six European countries. The enclosed report explains the purpose of the study in detail.

I have been assigned to lead a study group through six European countries to gather firsthand information on this topic. In addition to me, our group will consist of the following members:

INTERNATIONAL STUDY TOUR GROUP		
Name	**Organization**	**Location**
Mrs. Katherine Grant	WPQR-TV	Los Angeles, CA
Dr. Manuél Cruz	Miami Herald	Miami, FL
Mr. Richard Logan	Cable News Network	Atlanta, GA
Ms. Barbara Brooks	Associated Press	Chicago, IL

Our initial plans are for the team to spend at least one full day in each of these countries. That, of course, could change. Many different events have been planned. I will be organizing and facilitating meeting with the news programming

B. MULTIPAGE BUSINESS LETTER

(page 2; with page number; multiline list; company name; and enclosure, delivery, copy, postscript, and blind copy notations)

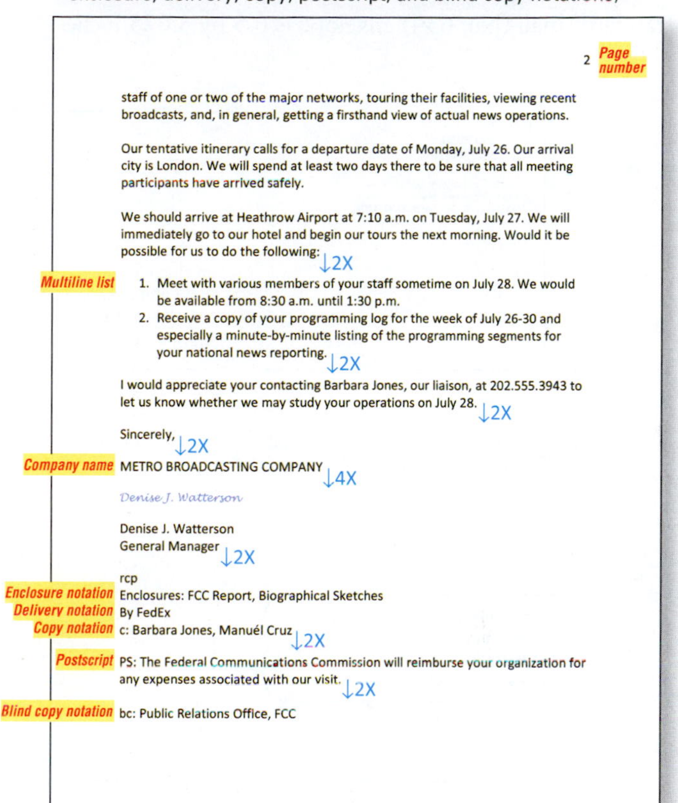

2

staff of one or two of the major networks, touring their facilities, viewing recent broadcasts, and, in general, getting a firsthand view of actual news operations.

Our tentative itinerary calls for a departure date of Monday, July 26. Our arrival city is London. We will spend at least two days there to be sure that all meeting participants have arrived safely.

We should arrive at Heathrow Airport at 7:10 a.m. on Tuesday, July 27. We will immediately go to our hotel and begin our tours the next morning. Would it be possible for us to do the following:

1. Meet with various members of your staff sometime on July 28. We would be available from 8:30 a.m. until 1:30 p.m.
2. Receive a copy of your programming log for the week of July 26-30 and especially a minute-by-minute listing of the programming segments for your national news reporting.

I would appreciate your contacting Barbara Jones, our liaison, at 202.555.3943 to let us know whether we may study your operations on July 28.

Sincerely,

METRO BROADCASTING COMPANY

Denise J. Watterson

Denise J. Watterson
General Manager

rcp
Enclosures: FCC Report, Biographical Sketches
By FedEx
c: Barbara Jones, Manuél Cruz

PS: The Federal Communications Commission will reimburse your organization for any expenses associated with our visit.

bc: Public Relations Office, FCC

C. E-MAIL MESSAGE IN MICROSOFT OUTLOOK

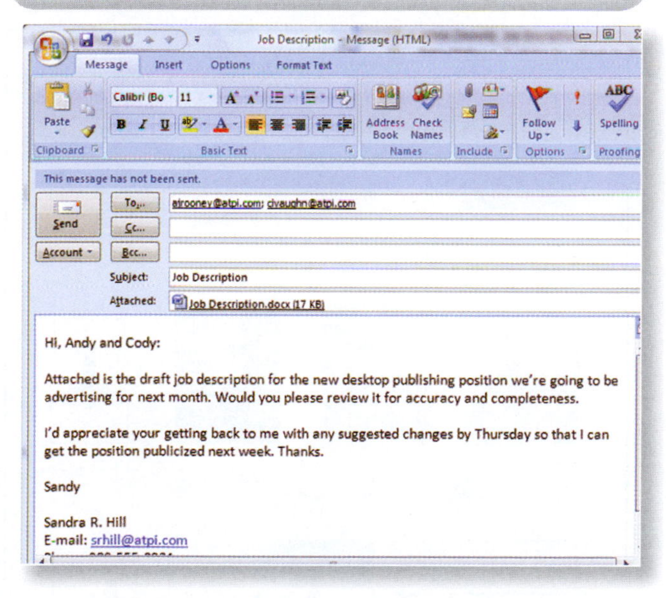

Hi, Andy and Cody:

Attached is the draft job description for the new desktop publishing position we're going to be advertising for next month. Would you please review it for accuracy and completeness.

I'd appreciate your getting back to me with any suggested changes by Thursday so that I can get the position publicized next week. Thanks.

Sandy

Sandra R. Hill
E-mail: srhill@atpi.com

D. E-MAIL MESSAGE IN MSN HOTMAIL

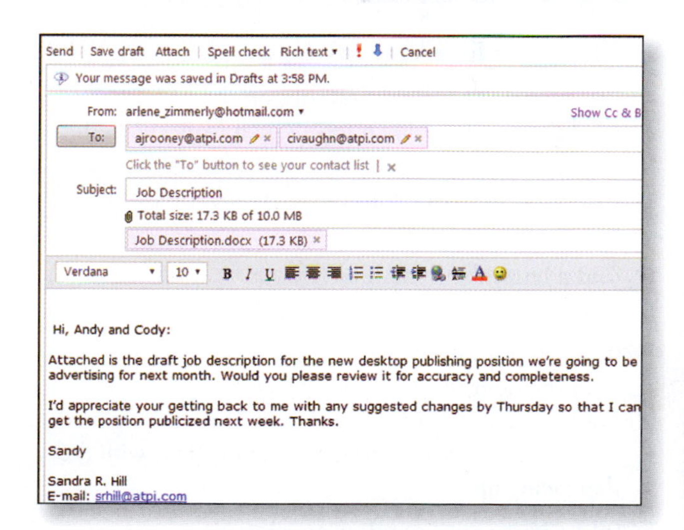

Hi, Andy and Cody:

Attached is the draft job description for the new desktop publishing position we're going to be advertising for next month. Would you please review it for accuracy and completeness.

I'd appreciate your getting back to me with any suggested changes by Thursday so that I can get the position publicized next week. Thanks.

Sandy

Sandra R. Hill
E-mail: srhill@atpi.com

A. FORMATTING ENVELOPES

A standard large (No. 10) envelope is 9.5 by 4.125 inches. A standard small (No. 6¾) envelope is 6.5 by 3.625 inches.

A window envelope requires no formatting, since the letter is formatted and folded so that the inside address is visible through the window.

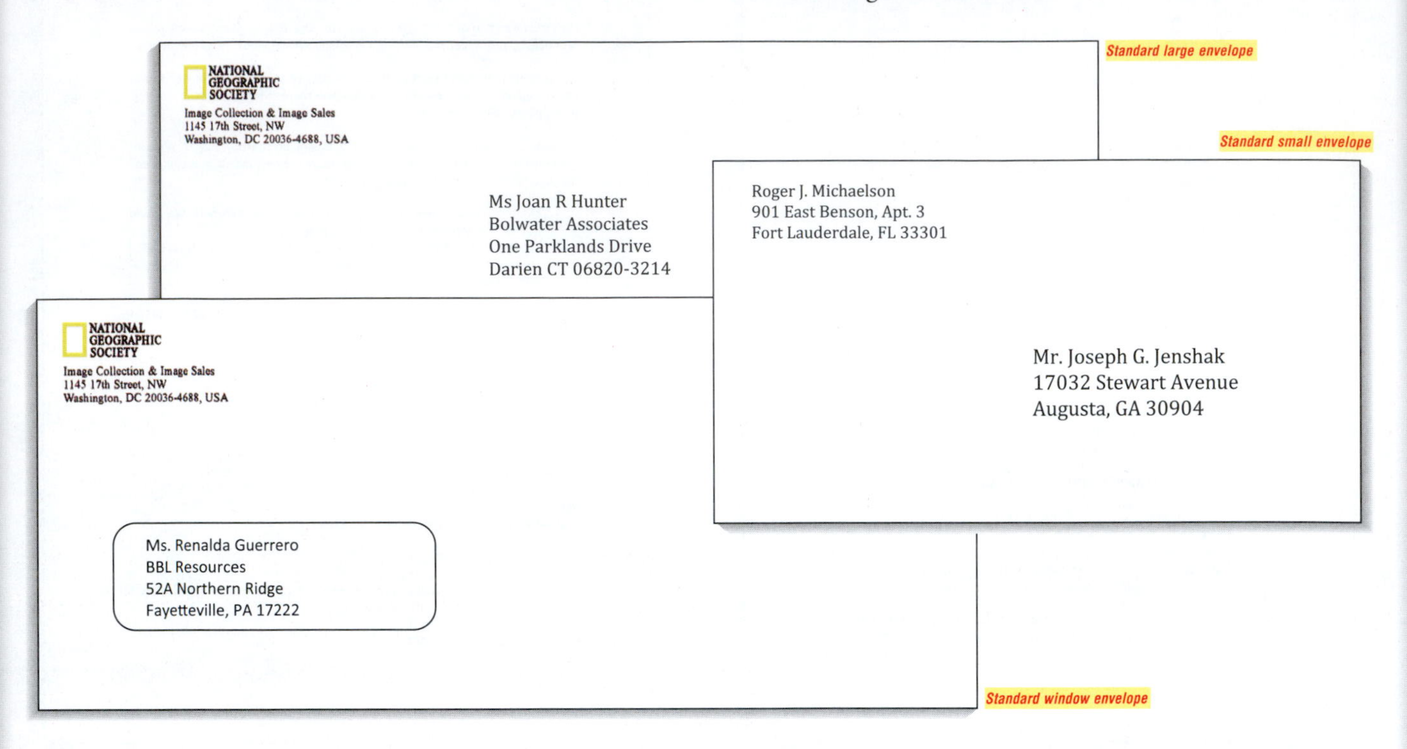

B. FOLDING LETTERS

To fold a letter for a large envelope:

1. Place the letter *face up,* and fold up the bottom third.
2. Fold the top third down to 0.5 inch from the bottom edge.
3. Insert the last crease into the envelope first, with the flap facing up.

To fold a letter for a small envelope:

1. Place the letter *face up,* and fold up the bottom half to 0.5 inch from the top.
2. Fold the right third over to the left.
3. Fold the left third over to 0.5 inch from the right edge.
4. Insert the last crease into the envelope first, with the flap facing up.

To fold a letter for a window envelope:

1. Place the letter *face down* with the letterhead at the top, and fold the bottom third of the letter up.
2. Fold the top third down so that the address shows.
3. Insert the letter into the envelope so that the address shows through the window.

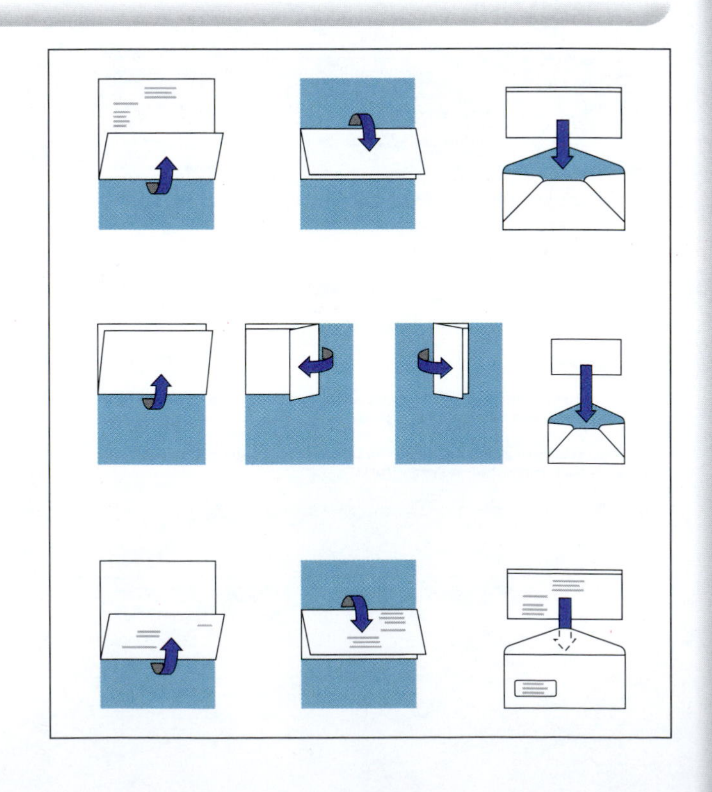

A. OUTLINE

(with 2-line title)

right tab: 0.3"
left tabs: 0.4", 0.7"

↓5X
2-line title 14 pt **AN ANALYSIS OF THE SCOPE AND EFFECTIVENESS OF ONLINE ADVERTISING** ↓2X

12 pt ↓ **The Status of Point-and-Click Selling** ↓2X

Jonathan R. Evans ↓2X

January 19, 20-- ↓2X

→ tab 0.3"
→ tab 0.4"
→ tab 0.7"

I. INTRODUCTION ↓2X

II. SCOPE AND TRENDS IN INTERNET ADVERTISING
- A. Internet Advertising
- B. Major Online Advertisers
- C. Positioning and Pricing
- D. Types of Advertising ↓2X

III. ADVERTISING EFFECTIVENESS
- A. The Banner Debate
- B. Increasing Advertising Effectiveness
- C. Measuring ROI

IV. CONCLUSION

B. TITLE PAGE

(with 2-line title)

center page ↓

2-line title 14 pt **AN ANALYSIS OF THE SCOPE AND EFFECTIVENESS OF ONLINE ADVERTISING** ↓2X

12 pt ↓ **The Status of Point-and-Click Selling** ↓12X

Submitted to ↓2X

Luis Torres
General Manager
ViaWorld, International ↓12X

Prepared by ↓2X

Jonathan R. Evans
Assistant Marketing Manager
ViaWorld, International ↓2X

January 19, 20--

C. TRANSMITTAL MEMO

(with 2-line subject line and attachment notation)

↓5X →tab

MEMO TO: Luis Torres, General Manager ↓2X

FROM: Jonathan R. Evans, Assistant Marketing Manager *jre*

DATE: January 19, 20--

2-line subject line **SUBJECT:** An Analysis of the Scope and Effectiveness of Current Online
→tab Advertising in Today's Marketplace ↓2X

Here is the final report analyzing the scope and effectiveness of Internet advertising that you requested on January 5. ↓2X

The report predicts that the total value of the business-to-business e-commerce market will continue to increase by geometric proportions. New technologies aimed at increasing Internet ad interactivity and the adoption of standards for advertising response measurement and tracking will contribute to this increase. Unfortunately, as discussed in this report, the use of "rich media" and interactivity in Web advertising will create its own set of problems.

I enjoyed working on this assignment, Luis, and learned quite a bit from my analysis of the situation. Please let me know if you have any questions about the report. ↓2X

plw
Attachment notation Attachment

D. TABLE OF CONTENTS

left tab: 0.5"
right dot-leader tab: 6.5"

↓5X
14 pt **CONTENTS** ↓2X

12 pt ↓

INTRODUCTION .... →tab 6.5" 1 ↓2X

SCOPE AND TRENDS IN ONLINE ADVERTISING .... 3 ↓2X

→tab 0.5" Internet Advertising Spending .... →tab 6.5" 4
Major Online Advertisers 5
Positioning and Pricing 7
Types of Advertising .... 8 ↓2X

ADVERTISING EFFECTIVENESS 9

The Banner Debate 9
Increasing Advertising Effectiveness 11
Measuring ROI 12

CONCLUSION 13

APPENDIX

Sample Internet Advertising 15
Proposed WEFA Standards 18

BIBLIOGRAPHY 19

A. MULTIPAGE BUSINESS REPORT

(page 1; with side and paragraph headings, multiline list, footnote references, and footnotes)

↓5X

2-line title — 14 pt **AN ANALYSIS OF THE SCOPE AND EFFECTIVENESS OF ONLINE ADVERTISING** ↓2X

Subtitle — 12 pt ↓ **The Status of Point-and-Click Selling** ↓2X

Byline — **Jonathan R. Evans** ↓2X

Date — **January 19, 20--** ↓2X

Online advertising uses the Internet for the sole purpose of delivering marketing messages to customers. Some examples of online advertising are ads on search engine results pages, banner ads, interactive media ads, and online classified advertising. One major benefit of online advertising is the immediate publishing of content that is not limited by geography or time. Interactive advertising presents fresh challenges for advertisers.[1] ↓2X Footnote reference

Side heading — **GROWTH FACTORS** ↓2X

Online business has grown in tandem with the expanding number of Internet users. That trend will only increase as time goes on. ↓2X

Paragraph heading — **Uncertainty**. The uncertainties surrounding advertising on the Internet remain one of the major impediments to the expansion. ↓2X

Reasons for Not Advertising Online. A recent survey found two main reasons cited for not advertising online:[2] ↓2X

Multiline list

1. The difficulty of determining return on investment, especially in terms of repeat business and first-time shoppers.
2. The lack of reliable tracking and measurement data.

Footnotes

[1] Shannon Newsome, "Effective Online Advertising," *E-Mail Marketing Daily*, August 12, 2010, p. R6.

[2] "eWebStats: Online Trends in the United States," *eWebStats Home page*, August 11, 2010, <http://www.ewebstats.com/trends/ad>, accessed on September 7, 2010.

B. MULTIPAGE BUSINESS REPORT

(last page; with page number, indented display, side heading, boxed table with table number and note, and footnote)

3 

who argue that banners have a strong potential for advertising effectiveness point out that it is not the banner format itself that presents a problem to advertising effectiveness, but rather the quality of the banner and the attention to its placement. According to Steven Mocha, president of Web Ads International: ↓2X

Indented display — →indent 0.5″ ←indent 0.5″

> A banner ad notifies visitors of the product or service and presents reasons why the consumer should choose the product in question. If the reasons are not compelling, then the banner ad has failed to achieve its purpose. If the banner ad is unattractive and obtrusive, it will alienate the consumer. When written and designed well, the banner ad is extremely effective in garnering business.[4] ↓2X

Thus, while some analysts continue to argue that the banner advertisement is passé, there is little evidence of its abandonment. Instead, ad agencies are focusing on increasing the banner's effectiveness. ↓2X

SCOPE AND TRENDS IN ONLINE ADVERTISING ↓2X

Starting from zero in 1994, analysts agree that the volume of Internet advertising spending has risen rapidly. However, as indicated in Table 3, analysts provide a wide range of the exact amount of such advertising. ↓2X

Table number title — 14 pt **Table 3. INTERNET ADVERTISING**

12 pt ↓ **Current Year Estimates** ↓1X

Source	Estimate
Internet Advertising Conference	$3.92 billion
Forecaster	3.30 billion
IPC International	3.20 billion
Brown Media	980 million
Note: This information is subject to change.	

Table note ↓1X

The differences in estimates of total Web advertising spending is generally attributed to the different methodologies used by the research agencies to gather the data. Further research is pending and will be reported next month.

[4] Steven Mocha, "Banner Ads That Really Work," *The Online Advertising Journal*, June 17, 2010, p. D1.

C. MULTIPAGE ACADEMIC REPORT

(page 1; with 2-line title, endnote references, and multiline list)

↓5SS

2-line title — 14 pt **AN ANALYSIS OF THE SCOPE AND EFFECTIVENESS** ↓1DS

OF ONLINE ADVERTISING ↓1DS

12 pt ↓ **The Status of Point-and-Click Selling** ↓1DS

Jonathan R. Evans ↓1DS

January 19, 20-- ↓1DS

One major benefit of online advertising is the immediate publishing of content that is not limited by geography or time. ↓1DS

GROWTH FACTORS ↓1DS

Online business has grown in tandem with the expanding number of Internet users, which is growing exponentially each year.[i] ↓1DS Endnote reference

Reasons for Not Advertising Online. A recent survey conducted by TAIR found two main reasons cited for not advertising online:[ii]

Multiline list

1. The difficulty of determining return on investment, especially in terms of repeat business and first-time shoppers.
2. The lack of reliable tracking and measurement data.

Obviously, there are many other reasons in addition to these two for not advertising online. However, with the growing number of Internet users, these

D. MULTIPAGE ACADEMIC REPORT

(last page; with page number, indented display, and endnotes)

14 Page number

advertising effectiveness, but rather the quality of the banner and the attention to the banner placement. According to Mike Windsor, president of Ogilvy Interactive: ↓1DS

Indented display — →indent 0.5″ ←indent 0.5″

> It's more a case of bad banner ads, just like there are bad TV ads. The space itself has huge potential. As important as using the space within the banner creatively is to aim it effectively. Unlike broadcast media, the Web offers advertisers the opportunity to reach a specific audience based on data gathered about who is surfing at a site and what their interests are.[vii] ↓2SS

From an advertiser's perspective, most effective Internet ads do more than just deliver information to the consumer and grab the consumer's attention—they also gather information about consumers (e.g., through "cookies" and other methodologies). From the consumer's perspective, this type of interactivity may represent an intrusion and an invasion of privacy.

Endnotes

[i] Shannon Newsome, "Effective Online Advertising," *E-Mail Marketing Daily*, July 12, 2010, p. R6.

[ii] "eWebStats: Online Trends in the United States," *eWebStats Home page*, August 11, 2010, <http://www.ewebstats.com/trends/ad>, accessed on September 7, 2010.

[iii] Barbara Fisher, "Net Ratings Index Predicts Rise in Web Ads," *Advertising Today*, July 19, 2010, p. 10.

[iv] Ron Heisman, "Internet Banner Ads Growth Trends," *Internet Associates Conference Home page*, November 13, 2010, <http://www.iac.net/conference>, accessed on December 8, 2010.

[v] Alexis Dirkson, "Point-and-Click Bargains for Internet Ad Surfers," *Internet Age*, March 8, 2010, p. 12.

[vi] Andrew Romero, "Gathering Statistics to Grow Your Internet Business," *The Wall Street Journal*, March 2, 2010, p. C20.

[vii] Lisa Gunderson, "Banner Banter" *The London Financial Times*, June 17, 2010, p. D1.

A. LEFT-BOUND BUSINESS REPORT

(page 1; with 2-line title, single-line list, and footnotes)

left margin: 1.5"
right margin: *default* 1"

↓5X

2-line title 14 pt **AN ANALYSIS OF THE SCOPE AND EFFECTIVENESS OF ONLINE ADVERTISING** ↓2X

12 pt ↓ **The Status of Point-and-Click Selling** ↓2X

Jonathan R. Evans ↓2X

January 19, 20-- ↓2X

Online advertising uses the Internet for the sole purpose of delivering marketing messages to customers. Some examples of online advertising are as follows: ads on search engine results pages, banner ads, interactive media ads, and e-mail marketing. One major benefit of online advertising is the immediate publishing of content that is not limited by geography or time. Interactive advertising presents new challenges for advertisers.[1] ↓2X

GROWTH FACTORS ↓2X

Online business has grown in tandem with the expanding number of Internet users. That trend will only increase as time goes on. ↓2X

Uncertainty. The uncertainties surrounding advertising on the Internet remain one of the major impediments to the expansion. All of the Internet advertising industry is today in a state of flux. ↓2X

Reasons for Not Advertising Online. A recent survey found two main reasons cited for not advertising online:[2] ↓2X

Single-line list
1. The difficulty of determining return on investment.
2. The lack of reliable tracking and measurement data.

Footnotes
[1] Shannon Newsome, "Effective Online Advertising," *E-Mail Marketing Daily*, July 12, 2010, p. R6.
[2] "eWebStats: Online Trends in the United States," *eWebStats Home page*, August 11, 2010, <http://www.ewebstats.com/trends/ad>, accessed on September 7, 2010.

B. BIBLIOGRAPHY

(for business or academic style using either endnotes or footnotes)

hanging indent ↓ ↓5X

14 pt **BIBLIOGRAPHY** ↓2X

12 pt ↓

Book—one author: Adams, Ana B., *Internet Advertising*, Brunswick Press, Boston, 2009. ↓2X

Annual report: AdNet Incorporated, *2010 Annual Report*, BCI, Inc., San Francisco, 2010.

Newspaper article: An, Sang Jin, "Banner Ad Frenzy," *The Wall Street Journal*, July 12, 2010, p. R6.

Book—two authors: Arlens, Rachel, and Seymour Schell, *E-Vertising*, New England Publishing, Cambridge, Mass., 2009. → hanging indent

Book—organization as author: *Directory of Internet Business Services*, International Corporate Libraries Assoc., New York, 2009.

WWW page: "eWebStats: Online Trends in the United States," *eWebStats Home page*, August 11, 2010, <http://www.ewebstats.com/trends/ad>, accessed on September 7, 2010.

Journal article—paged continuously: Ingram, Fred, "Hiring Trends in Online Advertising," *Personnel Quarterly*, Vol. 30, September 2009, pp. 104-116.

Journal article—paged each issue: Johnson, Jennifer, "WebRatings Index Shows 8% Rise in Web Ads," *Advertising Today*, July 19, 2010, p. 18.

Online database: "Motivational Advertising Techniques," *Advertising Encyclopedia*, N.D., <http://www.adtech.com/motivational_advertising_techniques.html>, accessed on January 7, 2010.

Government document: National Institute of Psychology, *Who Clicks? An Analysis of Internet Advertising*, TNIP Publication No. ADM 82-1195, U.S. Government Printing Office, Washington, 2009.

E-mail: Williams, Dennis V., "Reaction to Analysis of Internet Ads," e-mail message, August 18, 2010.

C. MEMO REPORT

(page 1, with 2-line subject line, endnote references, and single-line list)

↓5X →tab

MEMO TO: Luis Torres, General Manager ↓2X

FROM: Jonathan R. Evans, Assistant Marketing Manager *jre*

DATE: January 19, 20--

2-line subject line **SUBJECT:** An Analysis of the Scope and Effectiveness of Current Online →tab Advertising in Today's Marketplace ↓2X

Online advertising uses the Internet and World Wide Web for the sole purpose of delivering marketing messages to customers. Some examples of online advertising are ads on search engine results pages, banner ads, interactive media ads, social network site advertising, online classified advertising, advertising networks, and e-mail marketing, including e-mail spam. ↓2X

One major benefit of online advertising is the immediate publishing of information and content that is not limited by geography or time. To that end, the emerging area of interactive advertising presents fresh challenges for advertisers.[i] Endnote reference Such challenges are opportunities for growth. ↓2X

GROWTH FACTORS ↓2X

Online business has grown in tandem with the expanding number of Internet users. That trend will only increase as time goes on. ↓2X

Uncertainty. The uncertainties surrounding advertising on the Internet remain one of the major impediments to the expansion. All of the Internet advertising industry is today in a state of flux.

Reasons for Not Advertising Online. A recent survey found two main reasons cited for not advertising online:[ii] ↓2X

Single-line list
1. The difficulty of determining return on investment.
2. The lack of reliable tracking and measurement data.

D. FORMATTING REPORTS

Margins, Spacing, and Indents. Begin the first page of each section (for example, the table of contents, first page of the body, and bibliography pages) 2 inches from the top of the page. Begin other pages 1 inch from the top. Use 1-inch default side and bottom margins for all pages. For a left-bound report, add 0.5 inch to the left margin. Single-space business reports. Double-space academic reports and indent paragraphs.

Titles and Headings. Center the title in 14-pt. font. Single-space multiline titles in a single-spaced report, and double-space multiline titles in a double-spaced report. Insert 1 blank line before and after all parts of a heading block (may include the title, subtitle, author, and/or date), and format all lines in bold. Format side headings in bold, at the left margin, with 1 blank line before and after them. Format paragraph headings at the left margin for single-spaced reports and indented for double-spaced reports in bold, followed by a period in bold and one space.

Citations. Format citations using Word's footnote (or endnote) feature.

Margins, Spacing, Headings, and Citations for APA- or MLA-Style Reports. See page R-10.

A. REPORT IN APA STYLE

(page 3; with header, 2-line title, byline, main heading, subheading, and citations)

top, bottom, and side margins: *default* (1")
double-space throughout

Online Advertising 3 **Header**

2-line title An Analysis of the Scope and Effectiveness

of Online Advertising

Byline Jonathan R. Evans

→ tab Online advertising uses the Internet for the sole purpose of delivering marketing messages to customers. Some examples of online advertising are ads on search engine results pages, banner ads, interactive media ads, online classifieds, advertising networks, and e-mail marketing (Gunderson, 2011, p. D1). **Citation**

One major benefit of online advertising is the immediate publishing of content that is not limited by geography or time. To that end, interactive advertising presents fresh challenges for advertisers (Newsome, 2010).

Main heading Growth Factors

Online business has grown in tandem with the expanding number of Internet users. That trend will only increase as time goes on (Arlens & Schell).

Subheading *Uncertainty* ← Italic

The uncertainties surrounding Internet advertising are impeding its expansion. A recent survey found two main reasons cited for not advertising online. The first is the difficulty of determining return on investment, especially in terms of repeat business and first-time shoppers. The second is the lack of reliable tracking and measurement data ("eWebStats," 2010).

B. REFERENCES IN APA STYLE

(page 14; with header)

top, bottom, and side margins: *default* (1")
double-space throughout

Online Advertising 14 **Header**

hanging indent ↓ References

Book—one author Adams, A. B. (2009). *Internet advertising and the upcoming electronic upheaval.*
→ hanging indent Boston: Brunswick Press.

Annual report AdNet Incoporated. (2010). *2010 annual report.* San Francisco: BCI, Inc.

Newspaper article An, S. J. (2010, July 12). Banner ad frenzy. *The Wall Street Journal,* p. R6.

Book—two authors Arlens, R., & Seymour, S. (2010). *E-vertising.* Cambridge, MA: New England Publishing.

Book—organization as author *Directory of business and financial services.* (2009). New York: International Corporate Libraries Association.

WWW page eWebStats: Advertising revenues and trends. (n.d.). New York: eMarketer. Retrieved August 11, 2010, from http://www.emarketer.com/ewebstats/2507manu.ad

Journal article—paged continuously Ingram, F. (2009). Trends in online advertising. *Personnel Quarterly, 20,* 804-816.

Journal article—paged each issue Johnson, J. (2010, July 19). WebRatings Index shows 4% rise in Web ads. *Advertising Today, 39,* 18.

Online database *Motivational advertising techniques.* (2010, January). *Advertising Encyclopedia.* Retrieved January 7, 2010, from http://www.adtech.com/ads.html

Government document National Institute of Psychology (2009). *Who clicks? An analysis of Internet advertising* (TNIP Publication No. ADM 82-1195). Washington, DC.

C. REPORT IN MLA STYLE

(page 1; with header, heading, 2-line title, and citations)

top, bottom, and side margins: *default* (1")
double-space throughout

Evans 1 **Header**

Heading Jonathan R. Evans

Professor Inman

Management 302

19 January 20--

2-line title An Analysis of the Scope and Effectiveness

of Online Advertising

→ tab Online advertising uses the Internet for the sole purpose of delivering marketing messages to customers. Some examples of online advertising are ads on search engine results pages, banner ads, interactive media ads, social network site advertising, online classifieds, and e-mail marketing (Gunderson D1). **Citation**

One major benefit of online advertising is the immediate publishing of information and content that is not limited by geography or time. To that end, interactive advertising presents fresh challenges for advertisers (Newsome 59).

Online business has grown in tandem with the expanding number of Internet users. That trend will only increase as time goes on (Arlens & Schell 376-379). The uncertainties surrounding Internet advertising remain one of the major impediments to the expansion. A recent survey found two main reasons cited for not advertising online. The first is the difficulty of determining return on investment. The second is the lack of reliable tracking and measurement data.

D. WORKS CITED IN MLA STYLE

(page 14; with header and hanging indent)

top, bottom, and side margins: *default* (1")
double-space throughout

Evans 14 **Header**

hanging indent ↓ Works Cited

Book—one author Adams, Ana. B. *Internet Advertising and the Upcoming Electronic Upheaval.*
→ hanging indent Boston: Brunswick Press, 2009.

Annual report AdNet Incoporated. *2010 Annual Report.* San Francisco: BCI, Inc., 2010.

Newspaper article An, Sang Jin. "Banner Ad Frenzy." *The Wall Street Journal,* 12 July 2010: R6.

Book—two authors Arlens, Rachel, and Seymour Schell. *E-vertising.* Cambridge, MA: New England Publishing, 2009.

Book—organization as author Corporate Libraries Association. *Directory of Business and Financial Services.* New York: Corporate Libraries Association, 2009.

WWW page "eWebStats: Advertising Revenues and Trends." 11 Aug. 2009. 7 Jan. 2010 <http://www.emarketer.com/ewebstats/ad>.

Journal article—paged continuously Ingram, Frank. "Trends in Online Advertising." *Personnel Quarterly* 20 (2010): 804-816.

Journal article—paged each issue Johnson, June. "WRI shows 4% rise in Web ads." *WebAds Today* 19 July 2010: 18.

Online database *Motivational Advertising Techniques.* 2010. Advertising Encyclopedia. 7 Jan. 2010 <http://www.adtech.com/ads.html>.

Government document National Institute of Psychology. *Who clicks?* TNIP Publication No. ADM 82-1195. Washington, DC. GPO: 2010.

E-mail Williams, Dan V. "Reaction to Internet Ads." E-mail to the author. 18 Aug. 2010.

A. MEETING AGENDA

↓5X
14 pt **MILES HARDWARE EXECUTIVE COMMITTEE** ↓2X

12 pt ↓ **Meeting Agenda** ↓2X

June 7, 20-- ↓2X

Numbered list: default format

1. Call to order
2. Approval of minutes of May 5 meeting
3. Progress report on building addition and parking lot restrictions (Norman Hodges and Anthony Pascarelli)
4. May 15 draft of Five-Year Plan
5. Review of National Hardware Association annual convention
6. Employee grievance filed by Ellen Burrows (John Landstrom)
7. New expense-report forms (Anne Richards)
8. Announcements
9. Adjournment

B. MINUTES OF A MEETING

↓5X
14 pt **RESOURCE COMMITTEE** ↓2X

12 pt ↓**Minutes of the Meeting** ↓2X

March 13, 20-- ↓1X

ATTENDANCE	The Resource Committee met on March 13, 20--, at the Airport Sheraton in Portland, Oregon, with all members present. Michael Davis, chairperson, called the meeting to order at 2:30 p.m. ↓1X
APPROVAL OF MINUTES	The minutes of the January 27 meeting were read and approved as presented.
OLD BUSINESS	The members of the committee reviewed the sales brochure on electronic copyboards and agreed to purchase one for the conference room. Cynthia Giovanni will secure quotations from at least two suppliers.
NEW BUSINESS	The committee reviewed a request from the Purchasing Department for three new computers. After extensive discussion regarding the appropriate use of the computers and software to be purchased, the committee approved the request.
ADJOURNMENT	The meeting was adjourned at 4:45 p.m. The next meeting is scheduled for April 13 in Suite B. ↓2X Respectfully submitted, ↓4X *D. S. Madsen* D. S. Madsen, Secretary

(Note: Table shown with "View Gridlines" active.)

C. ITINERARY

↓5X
14 pt **PORTLAND SALES MEETING** ↓2X

12 pt ↓ **Itinerary for Dorothy Turner** ↓2X

March 12-15, 20-- ↓1X

THURSDAY, MARCH 12	↓1X
5:10 p.m.-7:06 p.m.	Flight from Detroit to Portland; Northwest 83 (800-555-1212); e-ticket; Seat 8D; nonstop. ↓2X Jack Weatherford (Home: 503-555-8029; Office: 503-555-7631) will meet your flight on Thursday, provide transportation during your visit, and return you to the airport on Saturday morning. Airport Sheraton (503-555-4032) King-sized bed, nonsmoking room; late arrival guaranteed; Reservation No. 30ZM6-02. ↓1X
FRIDAY, MARCH 13	
9 a.m.-5:30 p.m.	Portland Sales Meeting 1931 Executive Way, Suite 10 Portland, OR 97211 (503-555-7631)
SATURDAY, MARCH 14	
7:30 a.m.-2:47 p.m.	Flight from Portland to Detroit; Northwest 360; e-ticket; Seat 9a; nonstop.

(Note: Table shown with "View Gridlines" active.)

D. LEGAL DOCUMENT

(with line numbers)

left tabs: 1", 3.25"
right tab: 6.5"

line numbers (court documents only)

```
1  STATE OF NEVADA                 → tab 6.5"  IN DISTRICT COURT ↓2X
2
3  COUNTY OF CLARK                    NORTHEAST JUDICIAL DISTRICT ↓2X
4
5  JOHN C. SMITH         → tab 3.25") → tab 6.5"  NO. ____ 1 space, 20 underscores
6  209 East Clark Avenue             )
7  Las Vegas, NV 89155-1603          )
8                                    )
9  → tab 1"  Plaintiff,  → tab 3.25")
10                                   )
11           vs.                     )   → tab 6.5"  SUMMONS
12                                   )
13 FAITH GEORGIA                     )
14                                   )
15           Defendant.              ) ↓2X
16
17 THE STATE OF NEVADA TO THE ABOVE-NAMED DEFENDANT: ↓2X
18
19 → tab 1"  You are hereby summoned and required to appear and defend
20 against the Complaint in this action, which is hereby served upon you by serving
21 upon the undersigned an Answer or other proper response within twenty (20)
22 days after the service of the Summons and Complaint upon you, exclusive of the
23 day of service. ↓2X
24
25           If you fail to do so, judgment by default will be taken against you for
26 the relief demanded in the Complaint.
27
28           SIGNED this _____ day of July, 20--. ↓2X
29
30 1 space; 5 underscores; 1 space     underscores to the right margin
31               → tab 3.25"  Jim Roe  → tab 6.5" Attorney at Law
32                            229 South Civic Way
33                            Laughlin, NV 89029-2648
34                            Telephone: 702-555-1205
35                            Attorney for Plaintiff
```

A. RESUME

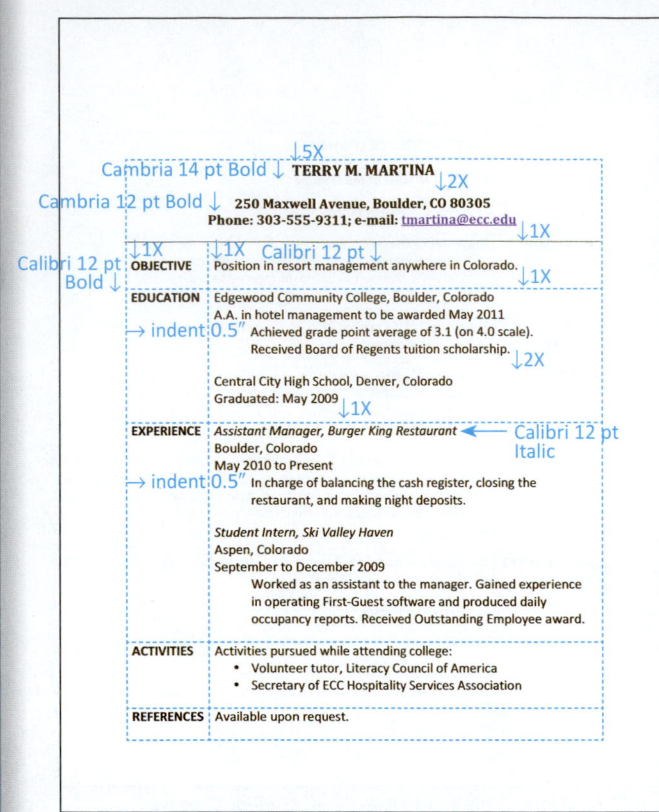

TERRY M. MARTINA

250 Maxwell Avenue, Boulder, CO 80305
Phone: 303-555-9311; e-mail: tmartina@ecc.edu

OBJECTIVE	Position in resort management anywhere in Colorado.
EDUCATION	Edgewood Community College, Boulder, Colorado A.A. in hotel management to be awarded May 2011 Achieved grade point average of 3.1 (on 4.0 scale). Received Board of Regents tuition scholarship. Central City High School, Denver, Colorado Graduated: May 2009
EXPERIENCE	*Assistant Manager, Burger King Restaurant* Boulder, Colorado May 2010 to Present In charge of balancing the cash register, closing the restaurant, and making night deposits. *Student Intern, Ski Valley Haven* Aspen, Colorado September to December 2009 Worked as an assistant to the manager. Gained experience in operating First-Guest software and produced daily occupancy reports. Received Outstanding Employee award.
ACTIVITIES	Activities pursued while attending college: • Volunteer tutor, Literacy Council of America • Secretary of ECC Hospitality Services Association
REFERENCES	Available upon request.

(Note: Table shown with "View Gridlines" active.)

B. APPLICATION LETTER IN BLOCK STYLE

(with return address)

↓5X

March 1, 20-- ↓4X

Mr. Lou Mansfield, Director
Human Resources Department
Rocky Resorts International
P.O. Box 1412
Denver, CO 80214 ↓2X

Dear Mr. Mansfield: ↓2X

Please consider me an applicant for the position of concierge for Suite Retreat, as advertised in last Sunday's *Denver Times*. ↓2X

I will receive my A.A. degree in hotel management from Edgewood Community College in May and will be available for full-time employment immediately. In addition to my extensive coursework in hospitality services and business, I've had experience in working for a ski lodge similar to Suite Retreats in Aspen. As a lifelong resident of Colorado and an avid skier, I would be able to provide your guests with any information they request.

After you've reviewed my enclosed resume, I would appreciate having an opportunity to discuss with you why I believe I have the right qualifications and personality to serve as your concierge. I can be reached at 303-555-9311. ↓2X

Sincerely, ↓4X

Terry M. Martina

Return address Terry M. Martina
250 Maxwell Avenue, Apt. 8
Boulder, CO 80305 ↓2X

Enclosure

C. FORMATTING LISTS

Numbers or bullets are used in documents to call attention to items in a list and to increase readability. If the sequence of the list items is important, use numbers rather than bullets.

- Insert 1 blank line before and after the list.
- Use Word's default format for all lists in either single- or double-spaced documents, including lists in documents such as a meeting agenda. Any carryover lines will be indented automatically.
- Use the same line spacing (single or double) between lines in the list as is used in the rest of the document.

The three bulleted and numbered lists shown at the right are all formatted correctly.

D. EXAMPLES OF DIFFERENT TYPES OF LISTS

According to the Internet Advertising Bureau, the following are the most common types of advertising on the Internet:

- Banner ads that feature some type of appropriate animation to attract the viewer's attention and interest.
- Sponsorship, in which an advertiser sponsors a content-based Web site.
- Interstitials, ads that flash up while a page downloads.

There is now considerable controversy about the effectiveness of banner advertising. As previously noted, a central goal of banner advertisements is to

*****

According to the Internet Advertising Bureau, the following are the most common types of advertising on the Internet, shown in order of popularity:

1. Banner ads
2. Sponsorship
3. Interstitials

There is now considerable controversy about the effectiveness of banner advertising. As previously noted, a central goal of banner advertisements is to

*****

According to the Internet Advertising Bureau, the following are the most common types of advertising on the Internet:

- Banner ads that feature some type of appropriate animation to attract the viewer's attention and interest.
- Sponsorship, in which an advertiser sponsors a Web site.
- Interstitials, ads that flash up while a page downloads.

There is now considerable controversy about the effectiveness of banner advertising. As previously noted, a central goal of banner advertisements is to

A. BOXED TABLE

(with subtitle; bottom-aligned and braced column headings; left- and right-aligned columns; total line and table note)

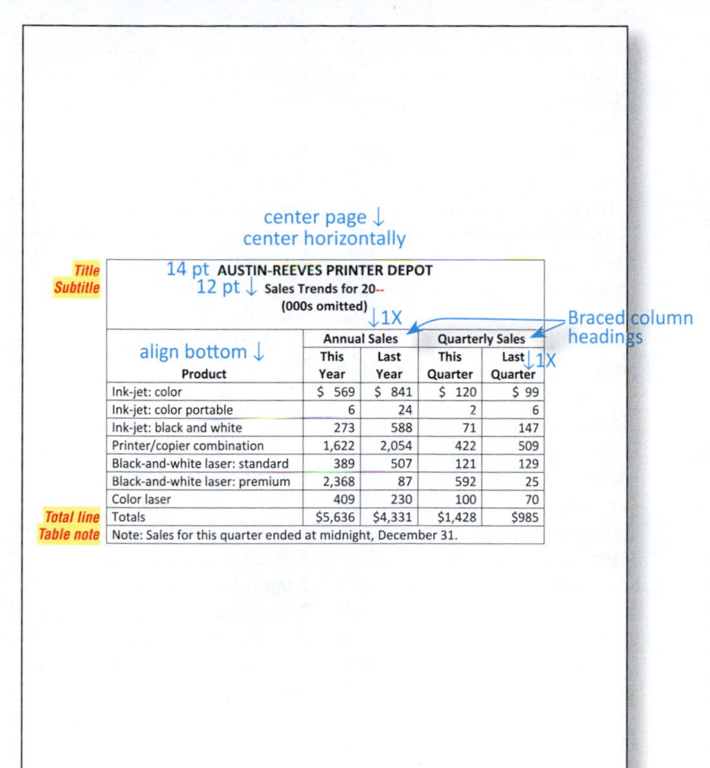

AUSTIN-REEVES PRINTER DEPOT Sales Trends for 20-- (000s omitted)				
	Annual Sales		Quarterly Sales	
Product	This Year	Last Year	This Quarter	Last Quarter
Ink-jet: color	$ 569	$ 841	$ 120	$ 99
Ink-jet: color portable	6	24	2	6
Ink-jet: black and white	273	588	71	147
Printer/copier combination	1,622	2,054	422	509
Black-and-white laser: standard	389	507	121	129
Black-and-white laser: premium	2,368	87	592	25
Color laser	409	230	100	70
Totals	$5,636	$4,331	$1,428	$985
Note: Sales for this quarter ended at midnight, December 31.				

B. OPEN TABLE

(with 2-line title; 2-line centered, bottom-aligned column headings; left- and right-aligned columns; column entries with dollar and percent signs)

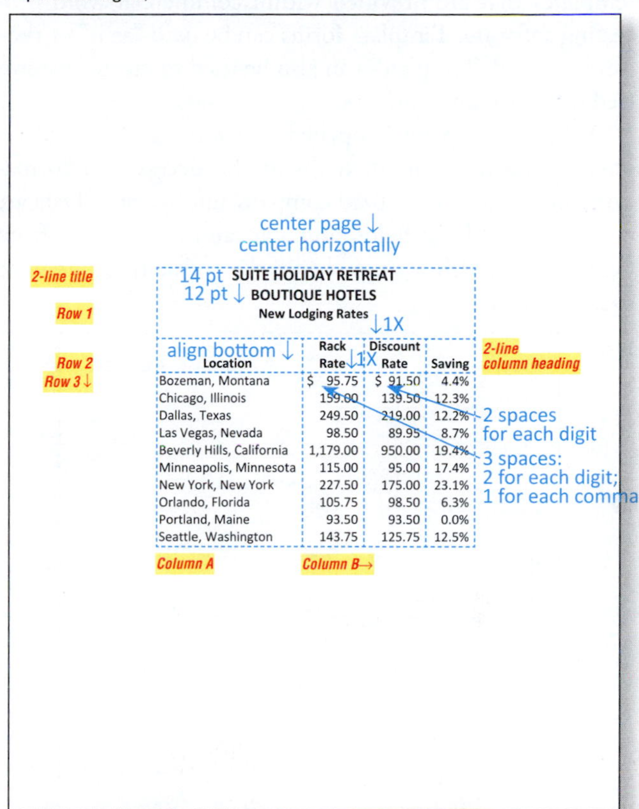

SUITE HOLIDAY RETREAT BOUTIQUE HOTELS New Lodging Rates			
Location	Rack Rate	Discount Rate	Saving
Bozeman, Montana	$ 95.75	$ 91.50	4.4%
Chicago, Illinois	159.00	139.50	12.3%
Dallas, Texas	249.50	219.00	12.2%
Las Vegas, Nevada	98.50	89.95	8.7%
Beverly Hills, California	1,179.00	950.00	19.4%
Minneapolis, Minnesota	115.00	95.00	17.4%
New York, New York	227.50	175.00	23.1%
Orlando, Florida	105.75	98.50	6.3%
Portland, Maine	93.50	93.50	0.0%
Seattle, Washington	143.75	125.75	12.5%

(Note: Table shown with "View Gridlines" active.)

C. RULED TABLE

(with table number, title, centered column headings, and total line)

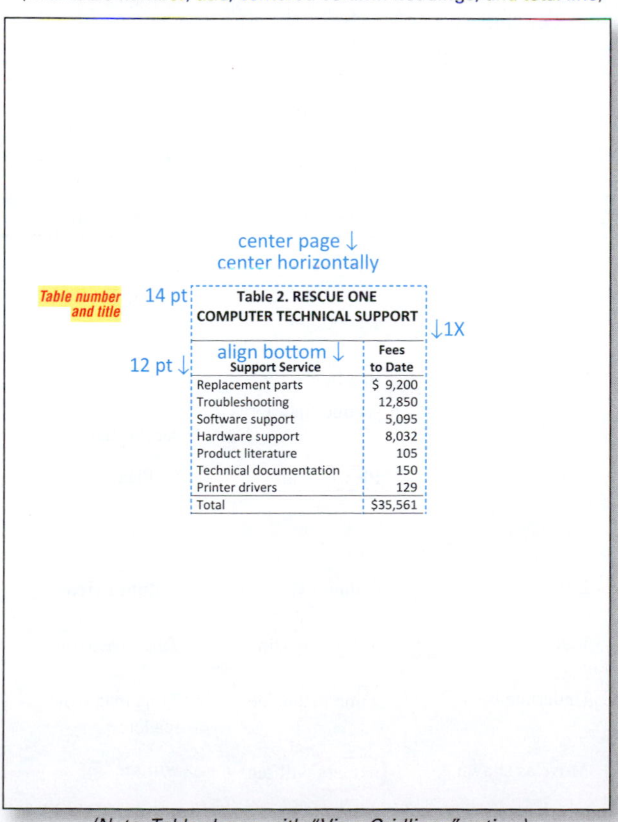

Table 2. RESCUE ONE COMPUTER TECHNICAL SUPPORT	
Support Service	Fees to Date
Replacement parts	$ 9,200
Troubleshooting	12,850
Software support	5,095
Hardware support	8,032
Product literature	105
Technical documentation	150
Printer drivers	129
Total	$35,561

(Note: Table shown with "View Gridlines" active.)

D. FORMATTING TABLES

The three basic styles of tables are boxed, open, and ruled. Tables have vertical columns (Column A), horizontal rows (Row 1), and intersecting cells (Cell A1). Center a table vertically that appears alone on the page. Insert 1 blank line before and after a table that appears within a document. Automatically adjust column widths and horizontally center all tables.

Heading Block. Merge any cells in Row 1, and type the heading block. Center and bold throughout. Type the title in all-caps, 14-pt. font, and the subtitle in upper- and lowercase, 12-pt. font. If a table has a number, type *Table* in upper- and lowercase. Follow the table number with a period and 1 space. Insert 1 blank line below the heading block.

Column Headings. Center column headings. Type in upper- and lowercase and bold. Bottom-align all column headings if a row includes a 2-line column heading. Merge desired cells for braced headings.

Column Entries. Left-align text columns, and right-align number columns. Capitalize only the first word and proper nouns in column entries.

Column Entry Dollar and Percent Signs. Insert the dollar sign only before the amount in the first entry and before a total amount entry. Align the dollar sign with the longest amount in the column, inserting spaces after the dollar sign as needed (allowing for 2 spaces for each digit and 1 space for each comma). Repeat the percent sign for each number in each column entry (unless the column heading identifies the data as percentages).

Table Note and Total Line. For a note line, merge the cells of the last row and use "Note" followed by a colon. For a total line, add a top and bottom border, use "Total" or "Totals" as appropriate, and add a percent or dollar sign if needed.

Reference Manual

A. FORMATTING BUSINESS FORMS

Many business forms can be created and filled in by using templates that are provided within commercial word processing software. Template forms can be used "as is" or they can be edited. Templates can also be used to create customized forms for any business.

When a template is opened, the form is displayed on screen. The user can then fill in the necessary information, including personalized company information. Data are entered into cells or fields, and you can move quickly from field to field with a single keystroke—usually by pressing TAB or ENTER.

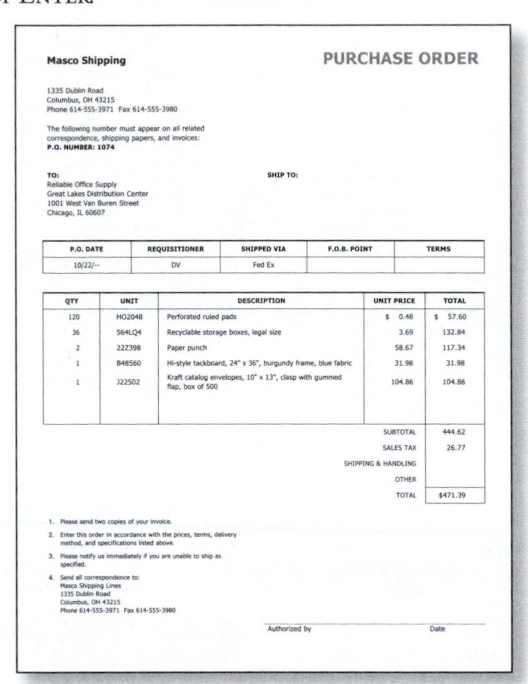

Masco Shipping | **PURCHASE ORDER**

1335 Dublin Road
Columbus, OH 43215
Phone 614-555-3971 Fax 614-555-3980

The following number must appear on all related correspondence, shipping papers, and invoices:
P.O. NUMBER: 1074

TO:
Reliable Office Supply
Great Lakes Distribution Center
1001 West Van Buren Street
Chicago, IL 60607

SHIP TO:

P.O. DATE	REQUISITIONER	SHIPPED VIA	F.O.B. POINT	TERMS
10/22/--	DV	Fed Ex		

QTY	UNIT	DESCRIPTION	UNIT PRICE	TOTAL
120	HO2048	Perforated ruled pads	$ 0.48	$ 57.60
36	564LQ4	Recyclable storage boxes, legal size	3.69	132.84
2	22Z398	Paper punch	58.67	117.34
1	B48560	Hi-style tackboard, 24" x 36", burgundy frame, blue fabric	31.98	31.98
1	J22502	Kraft catalog envelopes, 10" x 13", clasp with gummed flap, box of 500	104.86	104.86
			SUBTOTAL	444.62
			SALES TAX	26.77
			SHIPPING & HANDLING	
			OTHER	
			TOTAL	$471.39

1. Please send two copies of your invoice.
2. Enter this order in accordance with the prices, terms, delivery method, and specifications listed above.
3. Please notify us immediately if you are unable to ship as specified.
4. Send all correspondence to:
   Masco Shipping Lines
   1335 Dublin Road
   Columbus, OH 43215
   Phone 614-555-3971 Fax 614-555-3980

Authorized by | Date

B. U.S. POSTAL SERVICE ABBREVIATIONS

(for States, Territories, and Canadian Provinces)

States and Territories

State/Territory	Abbreviation
Alabama	AL
Alaska	AK
Arizona	AZ
Arkansas	AR
California	CA
Colorado	CO
Connecticut	CT
Delaware	DE
District of Columbia	DC
Florida	FL
Georgia	GA
Guam	GU
Hawaii	HI
Idaho	ID
Illinois	IL
Indiana	IN
Iowa	IA
Kansas	KS
Kentucky	KY
Louisiana	LA
Maine	ME
Maryland	MD
Massachusetts	MA
Michigan	MI
Minnesota	MN
Mississippi	MS
Missouri	MO
Montana	MT
Nebraska	NE
Nevada	NV
New Hampshire	NH
New Jersey	NJ
New Mexico	NM
New York	NY
North Carolina	NC
North Dakota	ND
Ohio	OH
Oklahoma	OK
Oregon	OR
Pennsylvania	PA
Puerto Rico	PR
Rhode Island	RI
South Carolina	SC
South Dakota	SD
Tennessee	TN
Texas	TX
Utah	UT
Vermont	VT
Virgin Islands	VI
Virginia	VA
Washington	WA
West Virginia	WV
Wisconsin	WI
Wyoming	WY

Canadian Provinces

Province	Abbreviation
Alberta	AB
British Columbia	BC
Labrador	LB
Manitoba	MB
New Brunswick	NB
Newfoundland	NF
Northwest Territories	NT
Nova Scotia	NS
Ontario	ON
Prince Edward Island	PE
Quebec	PQ
Saskatchewan	SK
Yukon Territory	YT

C. PROOFREADERS' MARKS

Proofreaders' Marks	Draft	Final Copy
Omit space	data base	database
∨ or ∧ Insert	if hes going (not)	if he's not going,
≡ Capitalize	Maple street	Maple Street
Delete	a final draft	a draft
# Insert space	allready to	all ready to
when / if Change word	and if you	and when you
/ Use lowercase letter	our President	our president
¶ Paragraph	… to use it.¶We can	… to use it. We can
••• Don't delete	a true story	a true story
○ Spell out	the only 1	the only one
Transpose	they all see	they see all

Proofreaders' Marks	Draft	Final Copy
SS Single-space	SS first line second line	first line second line
ds Double-space	ds first line second line	first line second line
Move right	Please send	Please send
Move left	May I	May I
Bold	Column Heading	**Column Heading**
ital Italic	ital Time magazine	*Time* magazine
u/l Underline	u/l Time magazine	Time magazine readers
Move as shown	readers will see	will see

Language Arts For Business

(50 "must-know" rules)

PUNCTUATION

Commas

RULE 1
, direct address
(L. 21)

Use commas before and after a name used in direct address.

Thank you, John, for responding to my e-mail so quickly.
Ladies and gentlemen, the program has been canceled.

RULE 2
, independent clause
(L. 27)

Use a comma between independent clauses joined by a coordinate conjunction (unless both clauses are short).

Ellen left her job with IBM, and she and her sister went to Paris.
But: Ellen left her job with IBM and went to Paris with her sister.
But: John drove and I navigated.

Note: An independent clause is one that can stand alone as a complete sentence. The most common coordinate conjunctions are *and*, *but*, *or*, and *nor*.

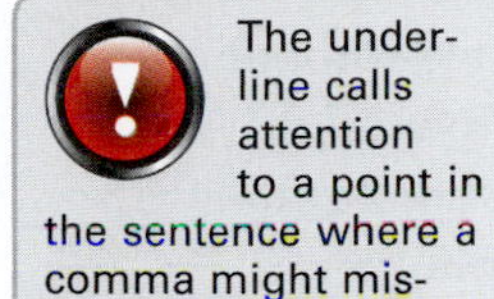

The underline calls attention to a point in the sentence where a comma might mistakenly be inserted.

RULE 3
, introductory expression
(L. 27)

Use a comma after an introductory expression (unless it is a short prepositional phrase).

Before we can make a decision, we must have all the facts.
But: In 2004 our nation elected a new president.

Note: An introductory expression is a group of words that come before the subject and verb of the independent clause. Common prepositions are *to*, *in*, *on*, *of*, *at*, *by*, *for*, and *with*.

RULE 4
, direct quotation
(L. 41)

Use a comma before and after a direct quotation.

James said, "I shall return," and then left.

RULE 5
, date
(L. 51)

Use a comma before and after the year in a complete date.

We will arrive on June 2, 2006, for the conference.
But: We will arrive on June 2 for the conference.

RULE 6
, place
(L. 51)

Use a comma before and after a state or country that follows a city (but not before a ZIP Code).

Joan moved to Vancouver, British Columbia, in May.
Send the package to Douglasville, GA 30135, by Express Mail.
But: Send the package to Georgia by Express Mail.

RULE 7
, series
(L. 61)

Use a comma between each item in a series of three or more.

We need to order paper, toner, and font cartridges for the printer.
They saved their work, exited their program, and turned off their computers when they finished.

Note: Do not use a comma after the last item in a series.

RULE 8
, transitional expression
(L. 61)

Use a comma before and after a transitional expression or independent comment.

It is critical, therefore, that we finish the project on time.
Our present projections, you must admit, are inadequate.
But: You must admit our present projections are inadequate.

Note: Examples of transitional expressions and independent comments are *in addition to, therefore, however, on the other hand, as a matter of fact,* and *unfortunately.*

RULE 9
, nonessential expression
(L. 71)

Use a comma before and after a nonessential expression.

Andre, who was there, can verify the statement.
But: Anyone who was there can verify the statement.
Van's first book, *Crisis of Management*, was not discussed.
Van's book *Crisis of Management* was not discussed.

Note: A nonessential expression is a group of words that may be omitted without changing the basic meaning of the sentence. Always examine the noun or pronoun that comes before the expression to determine whether the noun needs the expression to complete its meaning. If it does, the expression is *essential* and does *not* take a comma.

RULE 10
, adjacent adjectives
(L. 71)

Use a comma between two adjacent adjectives that modify the same noun.

We need an intelligent, enthusiastic individual for this job.
But: Please order a new bulletin board for our main conference room.

Note: Do not use a comma after the second adjective. Also, do not use a comma if the first adjective modifies the combined idea of the second adjective and the noun (for example, *bulletin board* and *conference room* in the second example above).

Semicolons

RULE 11
; no conjunction
(L. 97)

Use a semicolon to separate two closely related independent clauses that are not joined by a conjunction (such as *and, but, or,* or *nor*).

Management favored the vote; stockholders did not.
But: Management favored the vote, but stockholders did not.

RULE 12
; series
(L. 97)

Use a semicolon to separate three or more items in a series if any of the items already contain commas.

Staff meetings were held on Thursday, May 7; Monday, June 7; and Friday, June 12.

Note: Be sure to insert the semicolon *between* (not within) the items in a series.

Hyphens

RULE 13
- number
(L. 57)

Hyphenate compound numbers between twenty-one and ninety-nine and fractions that are expressed as words.

Twenty-nine recommendations were approved by at least three-fourths of the members.

RULE 14
- compound adjective
(L. 67)

Hyphenate compound adjectives that come before a noun (unless the first word is an adverb ending in *-ly*).

We reviewed an up-to-date report on Wednesday.

But: The report was up to date.

But: We reviewed the highly rated report.

Note: A compound adjective is two or more words that function as a unit to describe a noun.

Apostrophes

RULE 15
' singular noun
(L. 37)

Use *'s* to form the possessive of singular nouns.

The hurricane's force caused major damage to North Carolina's coastline.

RULE 16
' plural noun
(L. 37)

Use only an apostrophe to form the possessive of plural nouns that end in *s*.

The investors' goals were outlined in the stockholders' report.

But: The investors outlined their goals in the report to the stockholders.

But: The women's and children's clothing was on sale.

RULE 17
' pronoun
(L. 37)

Use *'s* to form the possessive of indefinite pronouns (such as *someone's* or *anybody's*); do not use an apostrophe with personal pronouns (such as *hers, his, its, ours, theirs,* and *yours*).

She could select anybody's paper for a sample.

It's time to put the file back into its cabinet.

Colons

RULE 18
: explanatory material
(L. 91)

Use a colon to introduce explanatory material that follows an independent clause.

The computer satisfies three criteria: speed, cost, and power.

But: The computer satisfies the three criteria of speed, cost, and power.

Remember this: only one coupon is allowed per customer.

Note: An independent clause can stand alone as a complete sentence. Do not capitalize the word following the colon.

Periods

RULE 19
. polite request
(L. 91)

Use a period to end a sentence that is a polite request.

Will you please call me if I can be of further assistance.

Note: Consider a sentence a polite request if you expect the reader to respond by doing as you ask rather than by giving a yes-or-no answer.

Quotation Marks

RULE 20
" direct quotation
(L. 41)

Use quotation marks around a direct quotation.

Harrison responded by saying, "Their decision does not affect us."

But: Harrison responded by saying that their decision does not affect us.

RULE 21
" title
(L. 41)

Use quotation marks around the title of a newspaper or magazine article, chapter in a book, report, and similar terms.

The most helpful article I found was "Multimedia for All."

Italics (or Underline)

RULE 22
title or title
(L. 41)

Italicize (or underline) the titles of books, magazines, newspapers, and other complete published works.

Grisham's *The Brethren* was reviewed in a recent *USA Today* article.

GRAMMAR

Sentences

RULE 23
fragment
(L. 21)

Avoid sentence fragments.

Not: She had always wanted to be a financial manager. But had not had the needed education.

But: She had always wanted to be a financial manager but had not had the needed education.

Note: A fragment is a part of a sentence that is incorrectly punctuated as a complete sentence. In the first example above, "but had not had the needed education" is not a complete sentence because it does not contain a subject.

RULE 24
run-on
(L. 21)

Avoid run-on sentences.

Not: Mohamed is a competent worker he has even passed the MOS exam.

Not: Mohamed is a competent worker, he has even passed the MOS exam.

But: Mohamed is a competent worker; he has even passed the MOS exam.

Or: Mohamed is a competent worker. He has even passed the MOS exam.

Note: A run-on sentence is two independent clauses that run together without any punctuation between them or with only a comma between them.

Agreement

RULE 25
agreement singular
agreement plural
(L. 67)

Use singular verbs and pronouns with singular subjects; use plural verbs and pronouns with plural subjects.

I was happy with my performance.

Janet and Phoenix were happy with their performance.

Among the items discussed were our raises and benefits.

RULE 26
agreement pronoun
(L. 81)

Some pronouns (*anybody, each, either, everybody, everyone, much, neither, no one, nobody,* and *one*) are always singular and take a singular verb. Other pronouns (*all, any, more, most, none,* and *some*) may be singular or plural, depending on the noun to which they refer.

Each of the employees has finished his or her task.

Much remains to be done.

Most of the pie was eaten, but most of the cookies were left.

RULE 27
agreement intervening words
(L. 81)

Disregard any intervening words that come between the subject and verb when establishing agreement.

That box, containing the books and pencils, has not been found.

Alex, accompanied by Tricia and Roxy, is attending the conference and taking his computer.

RULE 28
agreement nearer noun
(L. 101)

If two subjects are joined by *or, either/or, neither/nor,* or *not only/but also,* make the verb agree with the subject nearer to the verb.

Neither the coach nor the players are at home.

Not only the coach but also the referee is at home.

But: Both the coach and the referee are at home.

Pronouns

RULE 29
nominative pronoun
(L. 107)

Use nominative pronouns (such as *I, he, she, we, they,* and *who*) as subjects of a sentence or clause.

The programmer and he are reviewing the code.
Barb is a person who can do the job.

RULE 30
objective pronoun
(L. 107)

Use objective pronouns (such as *me, him, her, us, them,* and *whom*) as objects of a verb, preposition, or infinitive.

The code was reviewed by the programmer and him.
Barb is the type of person whom we can trust.

Adjectives and Adverbs

RULE 31
adjective/adverb
(L. 101)

Use comparative adjectives and adverbs (*-er, more,* and *less*) when referring to two nouns or pronouns; use superlative adjectives and adverbs (*-est, most,* and *least*) when referring to more than two.

The shorter of the two training sessions is the more helpful one.
The longest of the three training sessions is the least helpful one.

Word Usage

RULE 32
accept/except
(L. 117)

***Accept* means "to agree to"; *except* means "to leave out."**

All employees except the maintenance staff should accept the agreement.

RULE 33
affect/effect
(L. 117)

***Affect* is most often used as a verb meaning "to influence"; *effect* is most often used as a noun meaning "result."**

The ruling will affect our domestic operations but will have no effect on our Asian operations.

RULE 34
farther/further
(L. 117)

***Farther* refers to distance; *further* refers to extent or degree.**

The farther we drove, the further agitated he became.

RULE 35
personal/personnel
(L. 117)

***Personal* means "private"; *personnel* means "employees."**

All personnel agreed not to use e-mail for personal business.

RULE 36
principal/principle
(L. 117)

***Principal* means "primary"; *principle* means "rule."**

The principle of fairness is our principal means of dealing with customers.

MECHANICS

Capitalization

RULE 37
≡ sentence
(L. 31)

Capitalize the first word of a sentence.

Please prepare a summary of your activities.

RULE 38
≡ proper noun
(L. 31)

Capitalize proper nouns and adjectives derived from proper nouns.

Judy Hendrix drove to Albuquerque in her new Pontiac convertible.

Note: A proper noun is the official name of a particular person, place, or thing.

RULE 39
≡ time
(L. 31)

Capitalize the names of the days of the week, months, holidays, and religious days (but do not capitalize the names of the seasons).

On Thursday, November 25, we will celebrate Thanksgiving, the most popular holiday in the fall.

RULE 40
≡ noun #
(L. 77)

Capitalize nouns followed by a number or letter (except for the nouns *line, note, page, paragraph,* and *size*).

Please read Chapter 5, which begins on page 94.

RULE 41
≡ compass point
(L. 77)

Capitalize compass points (such as *north, south,* or *northeast*) only when they designate definite regions.

From Montana we drove south to reach the Southwest.

RULE 42
≡ organization
(L. 111)

Capitalize common organizational terms (such as *advertising department* and *finance committee*) only when they are the actual names of the units in the writer's own organization and when they are preceded by the word *the*.

The report from the Advertising Department is due today.

But: Our advertising department will submit its report today.

RULE 43
≡ course
(L. 111)

Capitalize the names of specific course titles but not the names of subjects or areas of study.

I have enrolled in Accounting 201 and will also take a marketing course.

Number Expression

RULE 44
general
(L. 47)

In general, spell out numbers zero through ten, and use figures for numbers above ten.

We rented two movies for tonight.

The decision was reached after 27 precincts sent in their results.

RULE 45
figure
(L. 47)

Use figures for

- **Dates. (Use *st, d,* or *th* only if the day comes before the month.)**

  The tax report is due on April 15 (not *April 15th*).

  We will drive to the camp on the 23d (or *23rd* or *23rd*) of May.

- **All numbers if two or more *related* numbers both above and below ten are used in the same sentence.**

  Mr. Carter sent in 7 receipts, and Ms. Cantrell sent in 22.

  But: The 13 accountants owned three computers each.

- **Measurements (time, money, distance, weight, and percent).**

  The $500 statue we delivered at 7 a.m. weighed 6 pounds.

- **Mixed numbers.**

  Our sales are up 9½ (or *9.5*) percent over last year.

RULE 46
word
(L. 57)

Spell out

- **A number used as the first word of a sentence.**

  Seventy-five people attended the conference in San Diego.

- **The shorter of two adjacent numbers.**

  We have ordered 3 two-pound cakes and one 5-pound cake for the reception.

- **The words *million* and *billion* in round numbers (do not use decimals with round numbers).**

  Not: A $5.00 ticket can win $28,000,000 in this month's lottery.

  But: A $5 ticket can win $28 million in this month's lottery.

- **Fractions.**

  Almost one-half of the audience responded to the question.

Abbreviations

RULE 47
abbreviate none
(L. 67)

In general business writing, do not abbreviate common words (such as *dept.* or *pkg.*), compass points, units of measure, or the names of months, days of the week, cities, or states (except in addresses).

Almost one-half of the audience indicated they were at least 5 feet 8 inches tall.

Note: Do not insert a comma between the parts of a single measurement.

RULE 48
abbreviate measure
(L. 87)

In technical writing, on forms, and in tables, abbreviate units of measure when they occur frequently. Do not use periods.

14 oz   5 ft 10 in   50 mph   2 yrs 10 mo

RULE 49
abbreviate lowercase
(L. 87)

In most lowercase abbreviations made up of single initials, use a period after each initial but no internal spaces.

a.m.   p.m.   i.e.   e.g.   e.o.m.

Exceptions: mph   mpg   wpm

RULE 50
abbreviate ≡
(L. 87)

In most all-capital abbreviations made up of single initials, do not use periods or internal spaces.

OSHA   PBS   NBEA   WWW   VCR   MBA

Exceptions: U.S.A.   A.A.   B.S.   Ph.D.   P.O.   B.C.   A.D.

The Alphabet, Number, and Symbol Keys

1 PART

Keyboarding in Arts, Audio, Video Technology, and Communication Services

Occupations in this cluster deal with organizing and communicating information to the public in various forms and media.

This cluster includes jobs in radio and television broadcasting, journalism, motion pictures, the recording industry, the performing arts, multimedia publishing, and the entertainment services. Book editors, computer artists, technical writers, radio announcers, news correspondents, camera operators, and home page designers are just a few jobs within this cluster.

Qualifications and Skills

Strong oral and written communication skills and technical skills are necessary for anyone in communications and media. Without a doubt, competent keyboarding skill is extremely advantageous.

Working in the media requires creativity, talent, and accurate use of language. In journalism, being observant, thinking clearly, and seeing the significance of events are all of utmost importance. Announcers must have exceptional voices, excellent speaking skills, and a unique style. The ability to work under pressure is important in all areas of media.

Goals

Keyboarding

- Type by touch the letter, number, and symbol keys.
- Demonstrate proper typing technique.
- Use the correct spacing with punctuation.
- Type at least 28 words per minute on a 2-minute timed writing with no more than 5 errors.

Objective Test

- Answer questions with acceptable accuracy on an objective test.

UNIT 1

Keyboarding: The Alphabet

LESSON 1

Home-Row Keys: A S D F J K L ; SPACE BAR ENTER BACKSPACE

LESSON 2

New Keys: E N T

LESSON 3

New Keys: O R H

LESSON 4

New Keys: I LEFT SHIFT .

LESSON 5

New Keys: B U C

Home-Row Keys 1

Goals

- Touch-type the home-row keys—A S D F J K L ;.
- Touch-type the Space Bar, Enter, and Backspace keys.
- Type at least 10wpm/1′/3e; that is, type at least 10 words per minute (wpm) on a 1-minute timed writing while making no more than 3 uncorrected errors.

New Keys

A. HOME-ROW POSITION

The A S D F J K L and ; keys are called the *home-row keys.*

1. Place the fingers of your left hand lightly over the A, S, D, and F keys and the fingers of your right hand lightly over the J, K, L, and ; keys, as shown in the illustration below.
2. Feel the raised markers on the F and J keys; they will help you keep your fingers on the home-row keys. You are now in home-row position. Each finger is named for the home-row key it controls. Thus, your left little finger is known as the A finger, and your right little finger is known as the Sem finger (short for *semicolon*).

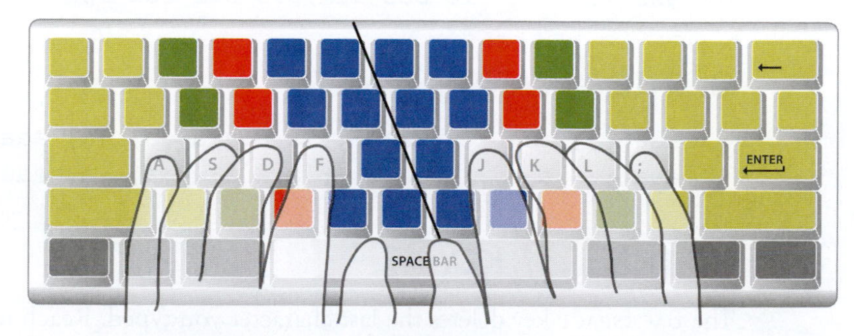

B. THE SPACE BAR AND ENTER KEYS

The Space Bar is located beneath the letter keys and is used to space between words and after punctuation marks. Tap the Space Bar with a downward and inward (toward your body) motion of the right thumb.

The ENTER key moves the insertion point to the beginning of a new line. Reach to the ENTER key with the Sem finger (the little finger of your right hand), keeping your J finger at home. Quickly return the Sem finger to home-row position after tapping ENTER.

C. PRACTICE THE HOME-ROW KEYS

Type each line 1 time, pressing the SPACE BAR where you see a space and pressing the ENTER key at the end of each line (indicated by ↵). Tap ENTER 2 times (indicated by ↵ ↵) to insert a blank line between each set of drill lines.

```
1  asdf jkl; asdf jkl; asdf jkl; ↵
2  asdf jkl; asdf jkl; asdf jkl; ↵↵

3  asdf jkl; asdf jkl; asdf jkl; ↵
4  asdf jkl; asdf jkl; asdf jkl; ↵
```

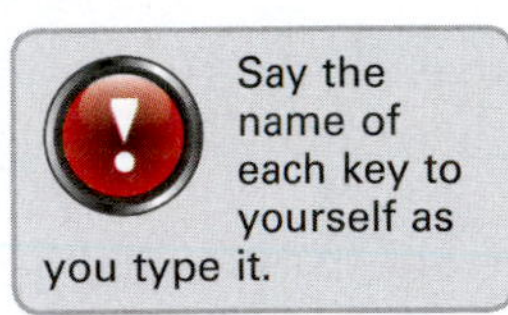

D. THE F AND J KEYS

```
5  fff fff jjj jjj fff jjj fjf fjf jfj jfj fff fj jf
6  fff fff jjj jjj fff jjj fjf fjf jfj jfj fff fj jf
```

E. THE D AND K KEYS

```
7  ddd ddd kkk kkk ddd kkk dkd dkd kdk kdk ddd dk kd
8  ddd ddd kkk kkk ddd kkk dkd dkd kdk kdk ddd dk kd
```

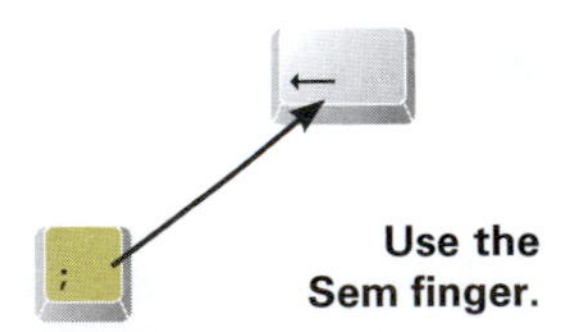

Rest your other fingers *lightly* over the keys while you're typing.

F. THE S AND L KEYS

```
9  sss lll sss lll sss lll sls sls lsl lsl sss sl ls
10 sss lll sss lll sss lll sls sls lsl lsl sss sl ls
```

G. THE A AND ; KEYS

```
11 aaa ;;; aaa ;;; aaa ;;; a;a a;a ;a; ;a; aaa a; ;a
12 aaa ;;; aaa ;;; aaa ;;; a;a a;a ;a; ;a; aaa a; ;a
```

Use the Sem finger.

H. THE ← KEY

The BACKSPACE key deletes the last character you typed. Reach to the BACKSPACE key with the Sem finger (the little finger of your right hand), keeping your J finger at home. Quickly return the Sem finger to home-row position after tapping BACKSPACE.

Looking at your keyboard and keeping your J finger at home, reach for and quickly press the BACKSPACE key and immediately return your little finger to the Sem key. Do this several times—until you can make the reach without looking at your fingers.

In the drill line below, follow these directions:

1. Type the group of letters as shown.
2. When you reach the BACKSPACE sign (←), backspace 1 time to delete the last keystroke typed.
3. Then type the next letter. For example, you will type *as*, press BACKSPACE 1 time, and then type *d*, thus changing *as* to *ad*.

Space 1 time after a semicolon (but not before).

```
13  as←d; dadk←s; sas←d; laf←d; jal←k; sal←d; lasd←s;
```

Skillbuilding

I. WORD BUILDING

```
14  a ad ads; l la las lass; f fa fad; s sa sal sala;
15  d da dad; f fa fal fall; l la lad; j ja jas jass;

16  s sa sad; f fl fla flak; a as ask; s sa sas sass;
17  a ad add; a al alf alfa; j ja jak; a al ala alas;
```

J. 1-MINUTE TIMED WRITING

Goal: At least 10wpm/1′/3e

See "Introduction to the Student" at the front of your text for guidance on how speed and accuracy are measured.

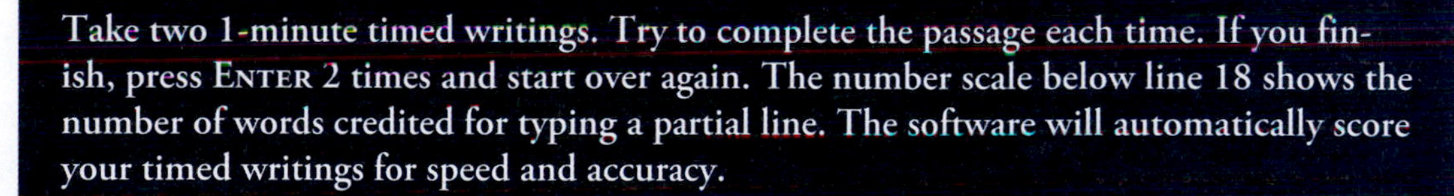

Take two 1-minute timed writings. Try to complete the passage each time. If you finish, press ENTER 2 times and start over again. The number scale below line 18 shows the number of words credited for typing a partial line. The software will automatically score your timed writings for speed and accuracy.

```
18  ask a sad lad; a fall fad; add a jak salad; a lad
       1  |  2  |  3  |  4  |  5  |  6  |  7  |  8  |  9  |  10
```

Enrichment • Lesson 1

Type each line 2 times.

A. NEW-KEY REINFORCEMENT

```
1  a dads jass la daff ad add dak lad lads daks adds
2  ads fad lall lass fads alas alfa fala sad alfalfa

3  sal falda all fall sala as falls salad salsa flak
4  asks flask sass dad flasks skald dada jak ask lad

5  alas ask salads dads dak sala fad falda flask sal
6  alfalfa add fads all salad flak lass flask ads as
```

B. SHORT PHRASES

Type each phrase on a separate line; that is, press Enter 1 time at the end of each line. Type each line 2 times; then press Enter 2 times to insert a blank line between each line. Do not space after a semicolon if it is the last character on the line; instead, immediately after typing the semicolon, press Enter.

```
7  a lad;
8  a lass;
9  a fall;

10 ask dad;
11 add all;
12 as a fad;

13 a fall ad;
14 dad falls;
15 jak salad;

16 add a lad;
17 ask a lass;
18 all flasks;

19 fall salads;
20 a lad asks dad;
21 a sad lass falls;
```

C. PARAGRAPH TYPING

First, type the following paragraph 1 time. Do not press Enter at the end of each line; instead, let Word wrap end your lines for you. After you type the three lines 1 time, press Enter 2 times and then type the three-line paragraph again.

```
22 fall salad; add a jak ad; alfalfa salad; ask a
23 sad lad; a lad asks dad; a lass asks dad; a sad
24 lad falls; a sad lad asks a dad; as a lass falls;
```

New Keys

Goals

- Touch-type the E, N, and T keys.
- Type at least 11wpm/1′/3e.

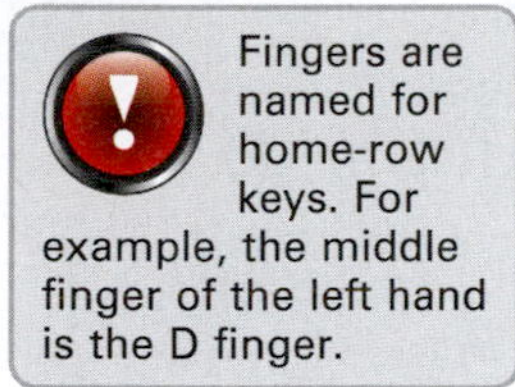

A. WARMUP

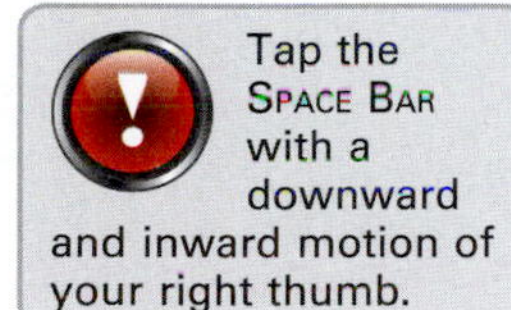


```
1  aa ss dd ff jj kk ll ;; fj dk sl a; asdf jkl; a;s
2  ask dad; a flask; a salsa salad; as sad as a lass
3  add salsa; fall fads; alas a sad lass; a dad; jak
```

New Keys

B. NEW-KEY PROCEDURE

Follow this procedure when learning a new key:

1. Place your fingers on the home-row keys.
2. Look in the left margin of your lesson to see which finger controls the new key.
3. While looking at your keyboard and without actually typing, move the correct finger to the new key and back to home-row position. Do this several times—until you can make the reach without looking at your fingers.
4. Now, with your fingers still on the home-row keys, type the drill lines while keeping your eyes on the copy.
5. If you forget the location of a key, stop typing and repeat step 3.
6. You will make numerous errors while you are learning the keyboard; do not be overly concerned about them. Errors will decrease as you become more familiar with the keyboard.

Keep the A finger at home as you reach for E.

Use the D finger.

C. THE E KEY

```
4  ddd ded ded ede ede eee alae dead eels fed jelled
5  eke lead see fed fee safe eel ease seal deal dead
6  deed feed jell keel lead seal elks fade leek seek
7  a fake deal; feed a flea; lease a desk; sell ale;
```

Keep the Sem finger at home as you reach for N.

Use the J finger.

D. THE N KEY

```
8  jjj jnj jnj njn njn nnn and sadness ends deafness
9  knee kennel sneak an fan dens fen lens sedan lend
10 dean sane lane sank keen lens seen fend lank send
11 lend a needle; send jeans and sandals; needs land
```

Keep the A finger at home as you reach for T.

Use the F finger.

E. THE T KEY

```
12 fff ftf ftf tft tft ttt ate jet aft felt ant east
13 latte tat test at fat jest let ate late east daft
14 deft feet lent state taste tenet sets detest lets
15 a fast jet left at ten; staked a tent; tall tales
```

Skillbuilding

F. MINIMUM-CHANGE PRACTICE

Only one letter changes in each word.

```
16 lent sent send tend tent test nest lest fest jest
17 lake take tale tall tell fell felt feet feat seat
18 seed teed tend send sand land lend fend feed feel

19 lens tens fens fans tans tens dens dent lent sent
20 sank tank talk tale kale dale date late lane lank
21 jets lets less lass last fast fest feet feat seat
```

G. NEW-KEY REVIEW

E 22 easel deafen deed defeat defend delete dense ease
N 23 annals fanned kennel tenant tan and dean den fend
T 24 at attend attest detest estate fatten jest jetted

E 25 deaden dented detest eases eaten eel effete elate
N 26 keen land lend neat sent need net sedan seen send
T 27 tests kettle latent tent latest nettle tee settee

E 28 eke jested else ended estate fee lessee feed fete
N 29 tanned ant sense eaten knee sneak stand tend tent
T 30 settle state talent tan taste tenant tenet tsetse

H. CLAUSES

31 a tense staff deleted data; test a fast delta jet
32 a tenant dented a sedan; a sad tale ended at ten;
33 fasten a tan anklet; a lad ate a steak at a feast
34 a tall dean sat at a sedate settee; take an asset

I. 1-MINUTE TIMED WRITING

Take two 1-minute timed writings. Let word wrap end each line. Press ENTER only at the end of line 36.

Goal: At least 11wpm/1′/3e

35 a tenant leased a fast jet and landed at a sedate 10
36 lake; 11

1 | 2 | 3 | 4 | 5 | 6 | 7 | 8 | 9 | 10

Enrichment • Lesson 2

Type each line 2 times.

A. NEW-KEY REINFORCEMENT

E 1 fleet steel assets deafen lessee deed elate kneel
N 2 annals fanned nene anneal needle fennel leaden an
T 3 tats detest latest jet tsetse stats attest settle

E 4 detest lessen see leek skeet elands estate fallen
N 5 flan keen lean send knee sank land keen lane fend
T 6 aft let eta net alt fat sat ant ate set jet tanks

E 7 sleek leaden leaded needle easel knell sleets eke
N 8 and ant den end fan fen ken nee nets ten tan sane
T 9 settee state kettle tattle taste task kaftan test

ENT 10 nest detent tens sanest knelt neat teens dent net
ENT 11 tensed ante tanned talent sent nest latent fanjet
ENT 12 anklet tenant tend eaten attend assent ten fasten

Type each line 2 times.

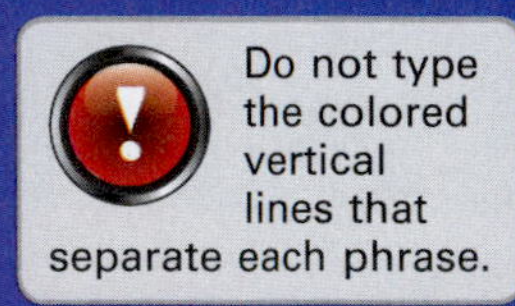

Do not type the colored vertical lines that separate each phrase.

B. SHORT PHRASES

13 jet lease | sent fast | tan sedan | sent less | ten seats
14 dense lad | ten deeds | sent east | ten tasks | least tan
15 jet fleet | let feast | neat deal | neat feat | least sad

16 let stall | net leads | let stand | stale ale | let sneak
17 sent left | net deals | ten dates | sent data | ten lakes
18 ten desks | neat seat | ten deals | ate steak | let taste

Type each line 2 times.

C. CLAUSES

19 a teen ate at least ten dates and sat at a stand;
20 fasten a faded saddle and sandal at a sad estate;
21 a tall tan fanjet landed at a flat delta and sat;

22 all lasses tasted a lean steak and felt less sad;
23 a tenant sent kale salads and ate fat leeks fast;
24 a dad skated at a lake and leaned left at a tent;

25 take a seat at a settee and taste tea and salads;
26 a tall tenant leased a sedate teal sedan and sat;
27 at least a lad tasted steak and ale and ate fast;

New Keys

Goals

- Touch-type the O, R, and H keys.
- Type at least 12wpm/1′/3e.

A. WARMUP

learned keys	1	take a jet and taste a flat steak at a tall tent;
concentration	2	skedaddle attendant senseless flatlands steadfast
easy	3	an ant lent an elf a snake; an elk let an ant eat

New Keys

B. THE O KEY

Keep the J finger at home as you reach for O.

Use the L finger.

4 lll lol lol olo olo ooo do eons foe jot kook lots
5 no too so to not ton eon foe jot lot no dodo dojo
6 took soon solo onto oleo tool look foot fool soon
7 a felon loaded a lot of loose loot on an old lot;

C. THE R KEY

Keep the A finger at home as you reach for R.

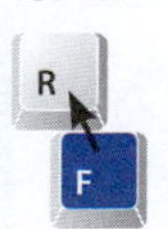

Use the F finger.

8 fff frf frf rfr rfr rrr are drat erased fro okras
9 enroll ore errs tree rear ardor drear raked radar
10 erred rotor retro error rare rater rear errs dare
11 a red deer ran free for an area near a rear door;

D. THE H KEY

Keep the Sem finger at home as you reach for H.

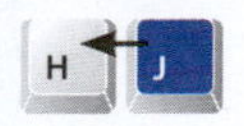

Use the J finger.

12 jjj jhj jhj hjh hjh hhh ah adhere heh offhand shh
13 ankh oh rho she the ha he oh hah haha harsh heath
14 shah hallah the that she three here there her hot
15 she and he had heard that other short heron here;

Skillbuilding

Only one letter changes in each word.

E. MINIMUM-CHANGE PRACTICE

```
16 dash hash sash lash last lost host hoss loss less
17 hall tall tale kale hale hole role dole dolt jolt
18 hero here hare hard hark lark dark dank rank rant

19 jeer seer seek leek leak teak tear teal seal real
20 horn torn tort fort fore fare hare hard hart dart
21 heat seat feat fear hear sear dear dean lean leak
```

F. NEW-KEY REVIEW

```
O  22 food noon soon fool nook root solo tool donor oho
R  23 err rear ardor dares freer rarer roar order erred
H  24 hash hardhat harsher hath shah harsh heath hashed

O  25 foot odor toot oho drool oleo too hoof rook drool
R  26 radar raker rooter rare arrest reader rafter sort
H  27 heathen hashes health hearth hoorah heather trash

O  28 dodo lost toro doors onto flood hooks roof honors
R  29 errata orator darker render rather tartar terrors
H  30 rehash hothead sheath thrash thresh handheld hash
```

G. CLAUSES

```
31 she folded the sheets and he held her hands free;
32 he heard an oath and told her to note the reason;
33 the odd raft had floated onto the north seashore;
34 then she joked that he had stolen the old shades;
      1 | 2 | 3 | 4 | 5 | 6 | 7 | 8 | 9 | 10
```

H. 1-MINUTE TIMED WRITING

Take two 1-minute timed writings. Let word wrap end each line. Press Enter only at the end of line 36.

```
35 the jaded steno learned a hard lesson on the trek   10
36 to a tree;                                          12
      1 | 2 | 3 | 4 | 5 | 6 | 7 | 8 | 9 | 10
```

Goal: At least 12wpm/1′/3e

Enrichment • Lesson 3

Type each line 2 times.

A. NEW-KEY REINFORCEMENT

O 1 roost hotfoot solon forefoot loose offshoot odors
R 2 errs rater refer retro rotor harder roster resort
H 3 hardhats hasheesh hosanna hotshots rehashed flesh

O 4 nonfood shook forenoon stood torso onlooker hoots
R 5 darter terser horror roller eraser roarer errands
H 6 sheathed shoehorn aha thrasher handshake thrasher

O 7 shoot foothold forsooth noose stool rodeo tootles
R 8 narrator restorer tearjerker referral northerners
H 9 harshness horseshoe hotheaded shorthand threshold

ORH 10 rho ashore hoorah hero hereto shorts hoar hoarser
ORH 11 hoer holder hora horn honker forth horned shofars
ORH 12 frosh throes froth honor heron horror hoard honer

Type each line 2 times.

Do not type the colored vertical lines.

B. SHORT PHRASES

13 a loose shade | eats a short noodle | the rose thorns
14 a tattletale | she sat here | he often jostled a jerk
15 the rest of the lesson | thanks for the short looks

16 the oddest tattoos | those stolen forks | do not jerk
17 the shore floods | she flossed her teeth | jot a note
18 the earth shook hard | had a look | a tenth of a foot

Type each line 2 times.

C. CLAUSES

19 she shared her salad at the hotel near the shore;
20 three deer ran to the dark oak tree near the ark;
21 she had then also looked at the other ten horses;

22 she set all of the stolen art on that tall shelf;
23 take a seat near the dark settee and talk to her;
24 the teal sandals on her feet had soon fallen off;

25 the loose earth on the north and east had fallen;
26 ask her not to take the nonfat food to the stall;
27 the senator held a safe seat and soon left there;

New Keys

Goals

- Touch-type the I, LEFT SHIFT, and Period keys.
- Type at least 13wpm/1′/3e.

A. WARMUP

learned keys	1	the soda jerks fell onto a stall and told a joke;
concentration	2	horseshoe northeast shorthand therefore threshold
easy	3	half of an oak had torn and also half of a shelf;

New Keys

B. THE I KEY

Keep the J finger at home as you reach for I.

Use the K finger.

4 kkk kik kik iki iki iii aid die lei fit hit radii
5 jilt kid lit nit oil rid sits tie id if in is ilk
6 aid sin did fie kid jail kid lid nil tie oils ail
7 nine irises in a lei did die in a sink in a deli;

C. THE LEFT  KEY

Use the A finger.

To capitalize letters on the right half of the keyboard:

1. With the F finger at home, press and hold down the LEFT SHIFT key with the A finger.
2. Press the letter key to be capitalized.
3. Immediately release the LEFT SHIFT key and return fingers to the home-row position.

8 aaa Jaa Jaa Kaa Kaa Laa Laa Naa Iaa Oaa Jane Hank
9 Hans Hale Jade Jake Ian Kate Nan Oak Ian Hal Lara
10 Nan Halle Ian Karl Lara Lena Oates Jan Katie Lars
11 Neither Jake Hanks nor Nathan Karl is in Oakland;

Keep the J finger at home as you reach for the period.

Use the L finger.

D. THE . KEY

Follow these rules for spacing with periods:

- Do not space before a period.
- Space 1 time after a period following an abbreviation.
- Do not space after a period within an abbreviation.
- Space 1 time after each initial in a person's name.
- Space 1 time after a period ending a sentence in the middle of a paragraph. Do *not* space after a period at the end of a paragraph.

```
12 lll l.l l.l .l. .l. ... i.e. addl. intl. n.d. Jr.
13 Jan. Ill. a.k.a. N.J. Ind. anon. asst. N.H. Okla.
14 No. et al. i.e. I did. He is not. Ian ate. I sat.
15 J. L. Harris is in Okla. or Ill. for addl. tasks.
```

Skillbuilding

E. MINIMUM-CHANGE PRACTICE

```
16 sink link fink find kind kink link rink rind kind
17 file tile till kill sill silk silt lilt tilt tint
18 fail tail sail said laid lair hair hail nail rail

19 sill kill fill fall tall Hall Hill Jill jilt jolt
20 list fist fish dish dash Nash Nast fast last Lash
21 Jane Lane Kane Kant rant rent Lent lint tint hint
```

F. NEW-KEY REVIEW

```
I            22 idiot initial kiddie raisin finish initiate if in
Left Shift   23 John Hall Lisa Jane Olaf Jill Joan Lois Joel Koto
.            24 H. I. J. K. L. N. O. n.d. Jr. i.e. No. Jan. asst.
I Left Shift . 25 Ida J. Harris; Indira K. Little; Lillian N. Iris;
```

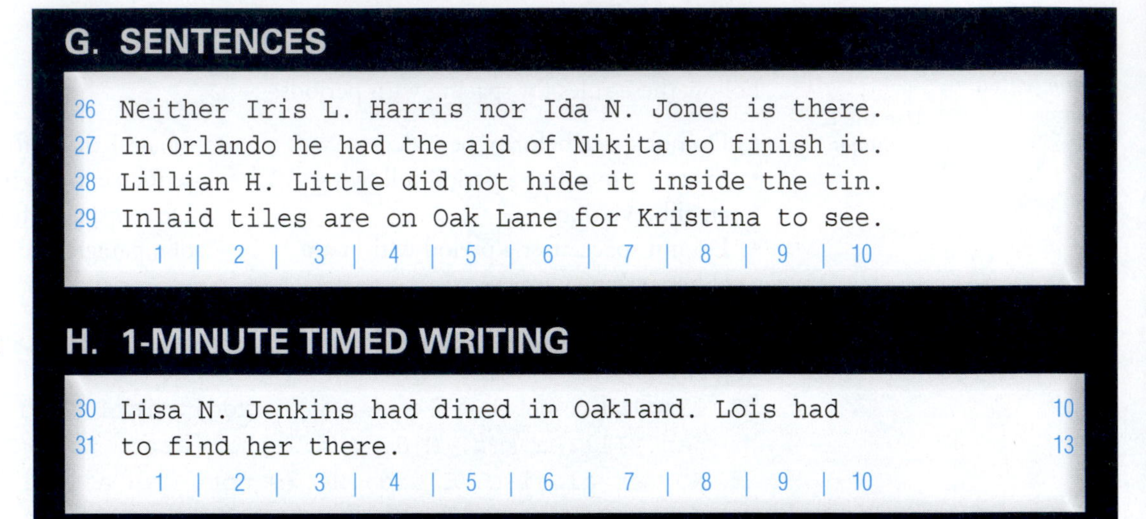

G. SENTENCES

```
26 Neither Iris L. Harris nor Ida N. Jones is there.
27 In Orlando he had the aid of Nikita to finish it.
28 Lillian H. Little did not hide it inside the tin.
29 Inlaid tiles are on Oak Lane for Kristina to see.
      1 | 2 | 3 | 4 | 5 | 6 | 7 | 8 | 9 | 10
```

H. 1-MINUTE TIMED WRITING

Take two 1-minute timed writings.

Goal: At least 13wpm/1′/3e

```
30 Lisa N. Jenkins had dined in Oakland. Lois had      10
31 to find her there.                                  13
      1 | 2 | 3 | 4 | 5 | 6 | 7 | 8 | 9 | 10
```

Enrichment • Lesson 4

A. NEW-KEY REINFORCEMENT

Type each line 2 times.

I / LEFT SHIFT / .

1 aid air din fir fit hit ilk ink inn ire iris this
2 Joe Kid Les Ian Ned Ida Noe Lil Jon Ira Kent John
3 a.k.a. addl. Okla. N.J. N.H. n.d. intl. asst. Jr.

I / LEFT SHIFT / .

4 lid ail did fit tin tie sin oil irk if it is in I
5 Lee Joe Ida Ina Joel Leo John Koto Olaf I. N. Jai
6 anon. et al. i.e. Ill. Ind. Jan. n.d. No. Ltd. H.

I / LEFT SHIFT / .

7 idea iris nail dial edit into file sink soil hint
8 Jill Lisa Nina Lois Hall Jane Joel Hart Olaf Joan
9 I. J. K. L. N. O. Joe. H. Nie; Leo K. Kale; L. J.

I LEFT SHIFT . / I LEFT SHIFT . / I LEFT SHIFT .

10 Keith N. Harris; Irene I. Olson; Katie O. Hinder;
11 Hilario I. Oleans; Kristen N. Jai; Leila N. Jain;
12 Keiko O. Ikeda; Ida H. Jenkins; Lillie N. Little;

B. SHORT PHRASES

Type each line 2 times.

13 that diet soda; an inlaid tile; finish the tasks;
14 tried to aid her; a dirt floor; I. I. Johnson Jr.
15 initial on the fifth line; it is OK; hire Ida Li;

16 a fair deal; a kosher deli; kiss the thin kiddie;
17 other ideas; tidied the dens; inside this raisin;
18 H. and I. and J. and K. and L. and N. and O.; OK;

C. SENTENCES

Type each line 2 times.

19 Olla needs to freshen the tired look of the nook.
20 Keith did not find the softened toast in the tin.
21 I think either N.H. or N.J. is OK for the hotels.

22 Leo Jones insisted on the three lessons in there.
23 Iris Joel had fished here and had liked it a lot.
24 Leila sifted and stirred the soil that needed it.

25 Lois N. Henderson is a dentist there in Lakeland.
26 Ina has to attend the initial session in Oakland.
27 Jill had not finished the task so I assisted her.

New Keys

Goals

- Touch-type the B, U, and C keys.
- Type at least 14wpm/1′/3e.

A. WARMUP

learned keys	1	Jake Nort had not led a fast life; he had rested.
concentration	2	Hadassah Henderson Jonathan Jeanette Leonardo Lee
easy	3	Keith Idle and Henri did tie a fish to the dials.

New Keys

B. THE B KEY

Keep the A finger at home as you reach for B.

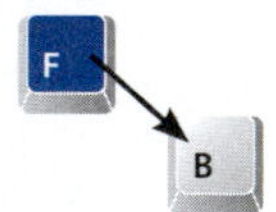

Use the F finger.

4 fff fbf fbf bfb bfb bbb label ebbs tidbits rebels
5 offbeat bib inkblot alb inbred job orb hotbed lab
6 babes barbs bobbin blab babble blob bobbed bobble
7 His best baseball and bat are near a blond table.

C. THE U KEY

Keep the Sem finger at home as you reach for U.

Use the J finger.

8 jjj juj juj uju uju uuu tau but dun euro fun huts
9 radius jut kudos flu nut out run sub tub flu aunt
10 luaus lulu tutus dufus undue usual bureau unusual
11 Kudos to Luke for the debut of his book on burns.

D. THE C KEY

Keep the A finger at home as you reach for C.

Use the D finger.

12 ddd dcd dcd cdc cdc ccc aces bobcat occur redcoat
13 deck ashcan ice bookcase talc inch dock arc discs
14 etch duck etch buck doc arc chic cacti cubic cock
15 Our church choirs can cancel our recitals on cue.

Skillbuilding

E. MINIMUM-CHANGE PRACTICE

16 buck luck lock rock rack race lace late Kate Kane
17 cube tube tune tone tine tint hint hind hand hard
18 curb carb cart dart dark lark Lars bars cars care

19 bout boat coat coal foal foul four tour hour sour
20 cure cute lute lube tube tune tone hone hose nose
21 bare barn bard lard lord cord curd card hard hark

F. NEW-KEY REVIEW

B 22 baker banjo bark basin bribe brake bond boast bit
U 23 unit uke urn use fuel hulk sun tusk house duo sub
C 24 cab chat carol chili check church condo cell aces
B U C 25 cub buck curb scuba scrub biscuit cubicle cutback

G. SENTENCES

26 Joe and Lee think the surf and turf is delicious.
27 Kent said a bunch of bandits robbed a local bank.
28 Unit costs of the industrial knob are reasonable.
29 Nine of the jurors can render the decisions soon.

H. 1-MINUTE TIMED WRITING

Take two 1-minute timed writings.

Goal: At least 14wpm/1′/3e

30 Her old brick condo near Lake Huron has just the 10
31 features Luis needed. 14
1 | 2 | 3 | 4 | 5 | 6 | 7 | 8 | 9 | 10

Enrichment • Lesson 5

A. NEW-KEY REINFORCEMENT

Type each line 2 times.

B	1	bans bar bud rib fib bad bin bat bee job ebb labs
U	2	dub jut run rubs sue but bud ours dud bun fur due
C	3	act can aces cab cat cod cot cad ice con cuts cue
B	4	babe debt bank able book snub blob boat both stab
U	5	euro haul Luke hush loud feud cure sour foul husk
C	6	ache duck cent each Nick cake inch fact lack care
B	7	abode board tribe boast beret burros brake rabbis
U	8	fruits audit crush abuse routes found ruler adult
C	9	catch crude acute clicks cross check chosen black
BUC	10	because buck butcher cube curb scuba subject club
BUC	11	cutback cubic cherub bucket biscuit bounce buckle
BUC	12	cubicle obscure brunch cubs curable scrub bunches

B. SHORT PHRASES

Type each line 2 times.

13 a brisk canter; because of us; a bunch of bananas
14 a rude subject; a tribe of Indians; choke a horse
15 the color of chalk; adults and children; a cherub

16 the noble cause; cost a fortune; a crust of bread
17 a unit of blood, a bleak outlook; hurt just a bit
18 black belt in karate; blue suede shoes; fur coats

C. SENTENCES

Type each line 2 times.

19 Little obscure cutbacks did not affect their job.
20 Her old cubicle is near the corner of the office.
21 Jack had a bacon biscuit and cola for his brunch.

22 Jed beat the odds because the disease is curable.
23 Haul the bucket of nuts and bolts to the shelter.
24 Look for the subject of the broken link to arise.

25 Just fill in the blank line and send it all back.
26 His adobe house near our house has not been sold.
27 One black briefcase is on the bureau in the hall.

UNIT 2

Keyboarding: The Alphabet

LESSON 6
New Keys: Right Shift W M

LESSON 7
New Keys: X P Tab

LESSON 8
New Keys: Q , G

LESSON 9
New Keys: V Y Z

LESSON 10
Review

New Keys

Goals

- Touch-type the RIGHT SHIFT, W, and M keys.
- Type at least 15wpm/1′/3e.

A. WARMUP

learned keys	1	Her brief research could land Kate her first job.
concentration	2	abundance incurable obstructs bucketful clubhouse
speed	3	Keith has both an auto and a bus but is not rich.

New Keys

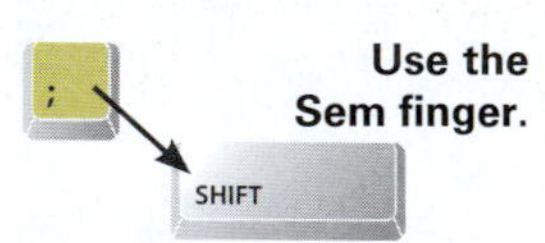

Use the Sem finger.

B. THE RIGHT 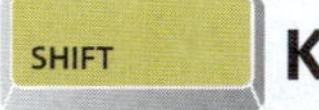 KEY

To capitalize letters on the left half of the keyboard:

1. With the J finger at home, press and hold down the RIGHT SHIFT key with the Sem finger.
2. Press the letter key to be capitalized.
3. Immediately release the RIGHT SHIFT key and return fingers to the home-row position.

```
4  ;;; A;; S;; D;; F;; Ali Sol Don Fido Eli Todd Ron
5  Burr Cora Bo Che Alan Dick Sue Dot Chris Rob Ruth
6  Bob Ana Don Blake Diane Bud Ann Rufus Rod Al Elon
7  Diane S. Dickens likes the East Coast of Florida.
```

Use the S finger.

C. THE W KEY

```
8  sss sws sws wsw wsw www bawls cobwebs dwarf fewer
9  thwart kiwi awkward bulwark unwed owe Darwin swab
10 two Kuwait bowwow owls news laws ewe haw how owns
11 Wanda went to the World Wide Web for the lowdown.
```

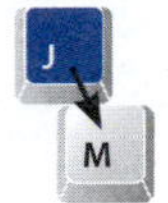

Use the J finger.

D. THE M KEY

12 jjj jmj jmj mjm mjm mmm am submit acme admit hems
13 Hoffman ohm him Hackman calm ammo unmet moms arms
14 ism Batman hums Newman Emma maim memos mime madam
15 Mamie can make a commitment to the mammal museum.

Skillbuilding

E. WORD BUILDING

16 A Al Ala Alan; D Do Don; R Ru Rut Ruth; m mu mum;
17 m mo mow; w wa war warm; M Ma Mac; w wh who whom;
18 m ma mai maim; e el elm; a ar arm; M Ma Mam Mama;

19 a ai aim; o oh ohm; s sw swa swam; T To Tod Todd;
20 M Mo Mom; w wh who whom; w wo wor worm; w wa war;
21 E Em Emm Emma; m ma mar; w wa war warm; M Mi Mia;

F. NEW-KEY REVIEW

Right Shift 22 Adam Walt Carl Emma Rick Taft Ward Tate Rita Eric
W 23 news wire dawn owls wish awes dews town wake wolf
M 24 mill name demo home mast mind dime mini omen dome

Right Shift 25 Will Aida Chad Erie Rome Tara Tess Ross Ewan Weir
W 26 wood twin bows bowl slaw know webs wool flaw claw
M 27 item mate mint room stem miss jamb dorm ammo lamb

Right Shift 28 Alan Alma Webb Fern Ruhr Thad West Theo Fiji Cuba
W 29 fowl stew work stow whom crew wife crow wall wind
M 30 math mist team lima drum arms limo mean term monk

G. 1-MINUTE TIMED WRITING

Take two 1-minute timed writings. Press Enter only at the end of line 32.

Goal: At least 15wpm/1'/3e

31 Then Barbra just left them at the house since the 10
32 men and women were awake. 15
1 | 2 | 3 | 4 | 5 | 6 | 7 | 8 | 9 | 10

Enrichment • Lesson 6

Type each line 2 times.

A. NEW-KEY REINFORCEMENT

Right Shift
1 Anne Arab Dade Finn Sara Thor Tito Saul Fisk Dale
W
2 arrow crown dews word watch awe water towel award
M
3 aim number him album human dam alumni amend dream

Right Shift
4 Asia Wolf Baja Dana Ford Scot Toto Will Seth Demi
W
5 owner we row drawl bow elbow brawl towel who when
M
6 sum mob me arm elm macro aroma female month woman

Right Shift
7 Barb Bess Dodd Adam Shaw Finn Dean Shea Webb Earl
W
8 jewel waist straw law swine crowd war allow drown
M
9 man method Ms. mud crime hum admit am amuse armed

Right Shift W M
10 Awesome Somehow Swims Warmer Winsome Wisdom Warms
Right Shift W M
11 Twosome Swami Warmed Cutworm Dimwit Swarm Walkman
Right Shift W M
12 Wartime Snowman Woman Welcomes Swimmer Whom Women

Type each line 2 times.

B. SHIFT KEY PRACTICE

13 Jack Neal Shea Nell Jane Alan Dodd Jean Nero Jeff
14 Earl Alma Anne Ella Emil Thad Theo Emma Oahu Thor
15 Tito Kane Kate Kent Fiji Bill Finn Ural Bonn Fisk

16 Otto Urdu Ford Owen Uris Utah Fuji Laos Utes Rice
17 Hank Hans Rick Rita Hera Herb Mack Mali Chad Chen
18 Marc Wild Will Mari Cook Cuba Matt Wolf Wood Mead

C. SENTENCES

19 Mr. Taft admitted that his claim was turned down.
20 Ms. Wu used her Web cam and also browsed the Web.
21 Blossoms bloom when it rains twice in four weeks.
22 I wasted much time when I was in town last month.

Type each paragraph 2 times, letting word wrap end each line for you.

D. PARAGRAPH TYPING

23 Ms. Cara Fields listed Milwaukee Tech as her alma 10
24 mater on her resume. I think that she majored in 20
25 business administration and minored in science. 29

26 We rode in a sleek limousine from the hotel to 9
27 Jackson Hole and ate dinner at the Camelback 19
28 Restaurant. We both ordered seafood and wine. 28

29 The newest member of our firm is Ms. Caroline K. 10
30 Smith; she will start work tomorrow as our labor 20
31 relations assistant and will work in New Hall. 29

1 | 2 | 3 | 4 | 5 | 6 | 7 | 8 | 9 | 10

New Keys

Goals

- Touch-type the X, P, and TAB keys.
- Type at least 16wpm/1'/3e.

A. WARMUP

learned keys
1 Ask Al and Jan to be in the room with Ms. Fuchs.

alternate hand
2 rituals socials downtown anthems dorms authentic

speed
3 Chris has to make an enamel dish for the mantel.

New Keys

Use the S finger.

B. THE X KEY

4 sss sxs sxs xsx xsx xxx ax ox fox box tax fix mix
5 axis jinx crux exam taxi exit hoax text coax flex
6 next lax inbox index sexism exhaust exists deluxe
7 The next wax exhibit will excite the anxious fox.

Use the Sem finger.

C. THE P KEY

8 ;;; ;p; ;p; p;p p;p ppp pi ape subplot mudpie pep
9 ashpit pips inkpad helps imps input opt apps warp
10 spa output up cowpea pa Alp top apes cap map cops
11 Pat put up a pinup that he ripped from the paper.

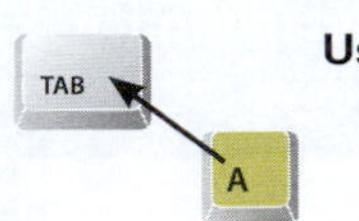

Use the A finger.

D. THE TAB KEY

The TAB key is used to indent paragraphs 0.5 inch. As shown on the next page, you can also align words in columns by pressing the TAB key.

Keep your F finger in home-row position as you quickly press the TAB key, and return your A finger to home-row position immediately after you press the TAB key.

Press TAB when you see the → symbol.

12 aah→ abs→ ace→ act→ add→ ado→ ads→ aft→ aha
13 aid→ ail→ aim→ air→ ale→ all→ alt→ amp→ and
14 ant→ ape→ app→ apt→ arc→ are→ ark→ arm→ art
15 ash→ ask→ asp→ ate→ auk→ awe→ awl→ awn→ axe

Skillbuilding

E. WORD BUILDING

16 p pr pro prop; b bo box; p pa pac pack; s se sex;
17 p pa pad; e ex exa exam; p pe pep; e ex exi exit;
18 f fo fox; p pi pin pint; p pa par part; w wa wax;

19 j ji jin jinx; r ra rap; p pi pin; t te tex text;
20 p po por port; f fi fix; p pl pla plan; m mi mix;
21 o op opt; f fl fle flex; p pu put; c co coa coax;

F. NEW-KEY REVIEW

X 22 box exile apex exec minx fox boxers ox inbox flux
P 23 pack dope pair ripe pest wipe plan sped jeep shop
TAB 24 is→ no→ on→ to→ we→ in→ he→ be→ at

X 25 expo wax next sax axed excess oxen maxi axle taxi
P 26 pain spam park upon pile bump plot apex camp whip
TAB 27 ad→ as→ do→ hi→ if→ it→ of→ or→ up

X 28 excuse tax expense reflex textbook except mailbox
P 29 palm hope part stop pine cope poem kept wrap deep
TAB 30 us→ so→ oh→ me→ id→ ho→ ha→ an→ am

G. 1-MINUTE TIMED WRITING

Take two 1-minute timed writings. Press ENTER only at the end of line 32.

Goal: At least 16wpm/1′/3e

Note: The word counts in this book credit you with 1 stroke for each paragraph indention in a timed writing. The timed writing starts when you press the TAB key.

31   Just ask the six of them to wait in place 9
32 for Brenda to complete that last job. 16
1 | 2 | 3 | 4 | 5 | 6 | 7 | 8 | 9 | 10

Enrichment • Lesson 7

A. NEW-KEY REINFORCEMENT

Type each line 2 times.

X	1	execute fixture exercise excuse mailbox exert tax
P	2	paper piper pauper prop pompom peep pope pulp pop
TAB	3	at→ is→ ho→ on→ to→ up→ in→ he→ be
X	4	lax maximum annex exception inexact examine extra
P	5	people pulpit pupil puppies pepper pump pinup opt
TAB	6	an→ as→ do→ hi→ if→ it→ of→ or→ we
X	7	example exclude experience except experts excuses
P	8	puppet pipe poplar up slipup rapper supper tiptop
TAB	9	us→ no→ so→ oh→ me→ id→ ha→ ad→ am
X, P, TAB	10	max→ mix→ cop→ tax→ pit→ pro→ pox→ hip→ lap
X, P, TAB	11	ape→ pad→ box→ cap→ fix→ pod→ cup→ tip→ rap
X, P, TAB	12	pep→ lax→ pet→ sip→ fox→ pun→ sax→ map→ wax

B. CORRESPONDING-FINGER PRACTICE

Type each line 2 times.

A and Sem	13	abase; fatal; axial; afar; area; ahead; ajar; Al;
S and L	14	else slap lets self list oils also lose last slam
W and O	15	word blow down owes flow show know whom crow work
D and K	16	dark dike eked kind deck kids disk skid desk duck
E and I	17	edit line bite nice bike side ripe cite tire deli
R and U	18	rule true burn sour four rule ours curb sure hour

C. SENTENCES

19 Paul was anxious to drop off the box of old maps.
20 The extra income Pam earned is exempt from taxes.
21 People expect excellent results on their laptops.
22 Please exit the plane and step on the purple box.

D. PARAGRAPH TYPING

Type each paragraph 2 times.

23	Just a few taxis were on the roads on that	9
24	black and cold late afternoon. I needed a map to	19
25	find the street to the second job consultation.	28
26	Blake used his own expertise to prepare the	9
27	report on the success of the annual fall flower	19
28	show. He reported that the show was a major hit.	28
29	We mixed up the names in random order so	8
30	that no one could know when he or she would be	18
31	called on to strum the banjo for the audience.	27

1 | 2 | 3 | 4 | 5 | 6 | 7 | 8 | 9 | 10

New Keys

Goals

- Touch-type the Q, Comma, and G keys.
- Type at least 17wpm/1′/3e.

A. WARMUP

learned keys 1 Ned Black spotted the four women at that jukebox.
one hand 2 best jump card noun debt mink base pump read upon
speed 3 Six of their chaps spent their profit in Orlando.

New Keys

Use the A finger.

B. THE Q KEY

4 aaa aqa aqa qaq qaq qqq aquas acquit equals pique
5 kumquat banquet croquet torque squad bouquet quip
6 quad quid pique quaff equip quiet quit quack quod
7 Quin quoted from his unique request for a quorum.

Use the K finger.

C. THE , KEY

Space 1 time after a comma (but not before). However, do not space after a punctuation mark or word that ends a line; instead, immediately press Enter.

8 kkk k,k k,k ,k, ,k, ,,, ma, cab, arc, ad, be, of,
9 oh, ask, Al, am, pin, too, up, ore, is, eat, emu,
10 ho, box; Al, Bo, Ed, Jo, Di, or I; a, b, c, or d;
11 Li, Ed, and I wrote, proofread, and formatted it.

Use the F finger.

D. THE G KEY

12 fff fgf fgf gfg gfg ggg ages edge begs afghan egg
13 dig ginkgo alga Eng cog popgun urge disgust outgo
14 bug gag gang gouge aging gongs gauge gorged going
15 Greg Rigg is going to see ping pong in Hong Kong.

Skillbuilding

E. BACKSPACE-KEY PRACTICE

Type each word as shown until you reach the backspace sign (←). Then backspace 1 time and replace the previously typed character with the one shown; for example, in line 16, *gale* becomes *gall.*

```
16 gale←l at←n gag←p had←m he←i bad←n if←n ad←h or←n
17 gut←n mask←h big←n me←u her←m dire←k slaw←p age←o
18 us←p die←m as←n box←o of←h kit←n hut←m mad←n it←n
```

F. NEW-KEY REVIEW

```
Q   19 banquet quotas squalor square quote quail bouquet
,   20 ago, rub, can, pop, jag, lax, men, owe, air, fun,
G   21 blog sign gold sing drag edge good wing gain high

Q   22 liquid quid request squid quark queen clique quit
,   23 one, lag, ton, aid, sex, two, ear, jar, use, new,
G   24 logo rage cage glad ring huge guru long urge gate

Q   25 croquet quarrel sequel quilt quarter equator quip
,   26 own, aim, ten, let, cap, its, our, ask, kin, bad,
G   27 goal king glow golf wage drug grow page grew gift
```

G. SENTENCES

```
28 Gus was quick to go to Quebec, Canada, in August.
29 He began to quarrel, argue, and quibble about it.
30 Gosh, Peg sighed at the quietness at the equator.

31 Bring the unique graph, ledger, and plaques here.
32 Grace brought a gold liqueur to the golf banquet.
33 Megan quit using that croquet equipment long ago.
```

H. 1-MINUTE TIMED WRITING

Take two 1-minute timed writings.

Goal: At least 17wpm/1′/3e

```
34      Just ask Phil to quit making that big racket     9
35 and, in addition, to fix the wood pipe.               17
      1 | 2 | 3 | 4 | 5 | 6 | 7 | 8 | 9 | 10
```

Enrichment • Lesson 8

A. NEW-KEY REINFORCEMENT

Type each line 2 times.

Q	1	equals quirk squid quote quest squat unique quick
,	2	ajar, jeeps, jump, joke, joins, jerk, junk, just,
G	3	agents range align cargo right guides judge globe
Q	4	squad quits equip quads liquid quiet square quota
,	5	book, kick, kind, like, risks, pack, neck, keeps,
G	6	grants light fight angles grasp great dough agree
Q	7	quarts quilt squab queen quips squeal quail quite
,	8	apex, oxen, taxi, coax, jinx, axles, text, exams,
G	9	gains begins images grade might doing being greed

B. VERTICAL REACHES

Type each line 2 times.

Up Reaches	10	at atlas match later plate water batch fatal late
	11	dr drums draft drift drawn drain drama dress drab
	12	ju jumps juror junks jumbo julep judge juice just
Down Reaches	13	ca cadet cable cabin camel cameo cards carts cash
	14	nk trunk drink prank rinks brink drank crank sink
	15	ba baked batch badge bagel banjo barge basis bank

C. ROW PRACTICE

Type each line 2 times.

Top Row	16	We were to take our trucks to Pete at the window.
	17	There were two tired people at the hut in Warsaw.
	18	Please write to their home to tell Tom in a week.
Home Row	19	Jake asked his dad for small red flags in Dallas.
	20	She is glad he added a dash of salt to the salad.
	21	Dale said she sold her glasses at that fall sale.
Bottom Row	22	He can come to the annex in Macon to meet Maxine.
	23	Their maximum number from Mexico can come to box.
	24	Mabel Baxter connected with the Nixons in Benson.

New Keys

Goals

- Touch-type the V, Y, and Z keys.
- Type at least 18wpm/1′/3e.

A. WARMUP

learned keys	1	The quick boxing warden jumped and flipped sides.
one hand	2	were lion card hump base join feat hook axes hulk
speed	3	A half bushel of corn was thrown to the big duck.

New Keys

Use the F finger.

B. THE V KEY

4 fff fvf fvf vfv vfv vvv avows obvious advice even
5 five salve Humvee anvil doves curved outvoted luv
6 vie event Van vat vie vexes vim vet vow via vivid
7 Eva and Vi visited the vast civic event in Provo.

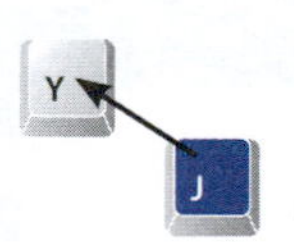

Use the J finger.

C. THE Y KEY

8 jjj jyj jyj yjy yjy yyy aye by icy dyes eyes defy
9 gym shy sky fly my any boys spy cry busy sty guys
10 ivy dewy sexy buy guy joy pay way yes yew you yet
11 Kelly may buy the forty gray kayaks for the navy.

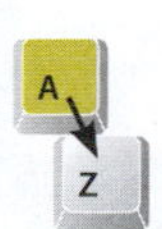

Use the A finger.

D. THE Z KEY

12 aaa aza aza zaz zaz zzz daze subzero czar adz fez
13 zigzagged biz unzip cozy ditz ouzo frowzy analyze
14 buzz pizzazz fuzzy jazz abuzz zit gaze razzmatazz
15 Zeke rented a cozy Mazda from Hertz in the plaza.

Skillbuilding

E. SPACE BAR PRACTICE

Space without pausing.

```
16 a b c d e f g h i j k l m n o p q r s t u v w xyz
17 an as be by go in is it me no of or to we ad Al I
18 ah am at do he hi but id if ma my on so up us for

19 Do not go to Ada or Ida for work every day or so.
20 I am sure he can go with you if he has some time.
21 He is to be at the car by the time you get there.
```

F. NEW-KEY REVIEW

```
V  22 cove gave vane love vein ever verb vast avow oven
Y  23 army ally city many copy navy gray away yell only
Z  24 buzz whiz gaze quiz zinc fez zeal fizzy zany daze

V  25 dove five vain diva over vest have vote vent move
Y  26 clay envy baby type Tony hype pays myth pony easy
Z  27 lazy ooze zips zero size daze Hazel zoo zoom jazz

V  28 five save even view dive veto void live vine avid
Y  29 busy lady play typo body holy defy nosy vary boxy
Z  30 gaze zest hazy cozy zone zaps ziti haze wiz dozen
```

G. SENTENCES

```
31 Hazel gave Zeke some advice on verbs and adverbs.
32 You really need to try out your new frozen pizza.
33 Forty or fifty of you have yet to give any money.

34 I eyed the dazzling piece made of topaz and onyx.
35 You have to visit my newest exhibit in Las Vegas.
36 Zelda vividly gazed at the ritzy piazza in Provo.
```

H. 1-MINUTE TIMED WRITING

Take two 1-minute timed writings.

Goal: At least 18wpm/1′/3e

```
37     David quickly spotted those four old women      9
38 who were just dozing over in the new jury box.     18
     1 | 2 | 3 | 4 | 5 | 6 | 7 | 8 | 9 | 10
```

Enrichment • Lesson 9

A. NEW-KEY REINFORCEMENT

Type each line 2 times.

V	1	cover value level movie never drive advice clever
Y	2	bylaw entry money every angry needy anyway typify
Z	3	craze seize klutz unzip dizzy zesty zealot wizard
V	4	grave valid avoid solve rival voice device avenue
Y	5	lucky annoy maybe decay imply dirty heyday yearly
Z	6	pizza dozen razor blaze ritzy hazel guzzle sizzle
V	7	cover prove never event leave civic behave divide
Y	8	decoy hurry carry glory diary empty byways mayday
Z	9	ozone prize amaze zebra gauze froze puzzle nozzle

B. COMMON LETTER COMBINATIONS

Type each line 2 times.

Word Beginnings	10	comply comedy combat coming common commit compels
	11	forget forbid forced forest formal former formats
	12	permit perils peruse perish period person peruses
	13	subtle submit subdue subtly suburb sublet subways
Word Endings	14	enable liable nimble edible doable usable jumbles
	15	joyful fitful useful armful sinful lawful boxfuls
	16	caring typing losing hiring seeing having rulings
	17	action option notion vision region nation motions

C. PARAGRAPH TYPING

Type each paragraph 2 times.

18	Back in July, we were authorized to acquire	9
19	five boxes of green letterhead stationery. That	19
20	amount should be ample for the entire year.	27
21	Kate took a quick jet to Phoenix, Arizona,	9
22	to enjoy the weather and to have time to begin	19
23	fall duties with the Girl Scouts of America.	27
24	Please just fix the copier quickly so that	9
25	we can minimize our downtime and get productivity	19
26	back in shape. We have to meet our monthly quota.	29
	1 | 2 | 3 | 4 | 5 | 6 | 7 | 8 | 9 | 10	

Review

Goals

- Reinforce key reaches.
- Type at least 19wpm/1'/3e.

A. WARMUP

alphabet 1 Five boxing wizards jumped quickly into the ring.
shift keys 2 Mr. Ho and Ms. Yu let Al, Bo, Ed, Jo, and Ty eat.
speed 3 Dick may air the new anthem on the eighth of May.

Skillbuilding

B. REVIEW: A–D

4 alpaca acacia banana cabana armada azalea pajamas
5 Bob bobbin babble bubble blubber bumblebee bobble
6 Cy cyclic concentric eclectic climactic eccentric
7 do added daddy addled nodded doodad dodged kidded

C. REVIEW: E–H

8 epees eerie emcees geese levee peeve tepee beeper
9 fisticuffs fluffy foodstuff liftoff falloff fluff
10 groggy eggnog giggle baggage gauging digging gigs
11 hitchhike high hashish hashes highlight Chihuahua

D. REVIEW: I–L

12 idiotic bikini if illicit inhibit initial militia
13 jobs jog jam jar jaws jay jet jig jut jog jot joy
14 kick kinky kook knock key kayak khaki kiosk knack
15 lull locally fulfill loyally lullaby ill billfold

E. REVIEW: M–P

16 mommy mammal mummy mammoth medium maximum minimum
17 nanny cannon inning antenna canning pennant ninny
18 outdoor outlook offshoot option onlooker orthodox
19 peppy poppy puppies pepper popped puppets propped

F. REVIEW: Q–T

20 quip aqua equal quay quid equip quip quit Quakers
21 rarer errors horror mirror terror arrears barrier
22 sass sissy Swiss assess says assets assist senses
23 tattoo attest tattle attempt tilt attract statute

G. REVIEW: U–X

24 unusual gurus usurious luau luxurious sunup undue
25 valve viva savvy verve vivid evolve revive velvet
26 widows willow window awkward swallow wows walkway
27 ax ox box fix fox hex lax mix nix sax sex tax tux

H. REVIEW: Y–Z, COMMA, PERIOD

28 yearly byway gypsy pygmy shyly anyway payday your
29 zigzag buzz pizzazz jazz fuzzy pizza buzzer zesty
30 am, we, in, is up, an, to, be, no, do, my, go, it
31 Mr. Ms. Dr. Mrs. Esq. Inc. pp. Nos. Wed. Oct. Pa.

Take two 1-minute timed writings.

Goal: At least 19wpm/1′/3e

I. 1-MINUTE TIMED WRITING

32 Back in June, we delivered oxygen equipment 9
33 of odd sizes to the new hospital near Ogden, 18
34 Utah. 19

1 | 2 | 3 | 4 | 5 | 6 | 7 | 8 | 9 | 10

Enrichment • Lesson 10

Type each line 2 times.

A. REVIEW: A–E

1 Allan asked Alma Adams to fly to Alaska and Asia.
2 Both Barbara and Robb bought a rubber basketball.
3 Carly can accept a classic car at a Cairo clinic.
4 Dade suddenly dined in the dark diner in Detroit.
5 Reeves said Eddie edited the entire eleven texts.

Type each line 2 times.

B. REVIEW: F–J

6 Five friars focused on the four offensive fables.
7 George gave the bag of green grapes to Gina Gaye.
8 Haughty Hugh hoped Hal had helped Seth with this.
9 Iris liked to pickle pickles in the acidic brine.
10 Jo Jones joined a junior jogging team in pajamas.

Type each line 2 times.

C. REVIEW: K–O

11 Ken kept a sleek kayak for the ski trek to Akron.
12 Luella played a well-planned ball game in Lowell.
13 I made more money on many markups of the pompoms.
14 Ned and Ginny knew ten men in a main dining room.
15 Opal Orr opened four boxes of oranges at the zoo.

Type each line 2 times.

D. REVIEW: P–T

16 Pat paid to park the plane at the pump in Pompey.
17 Quincy quickly quit his quarterly quiz in Quebec.
18 Robin carried four rare rulers into that library.
19 Sam signed, sealed, and sent six leases to Jesse.
20 Matt caught the little trout near Twelfth Street.

Type each line 2 times.

E. REVIEW: U–Z

21 Uncle Rubin urged Judy to go see a guru in Utica.
22 Vivian moved to veto five voice votes in Ventura.
23 Walt waited while Wilma went to Watts for a week.
24 Alexi mixed sixty extra extracts exactly as told.
25 Yes, your young son plays cymbals anyway at Yale.
26 Liza saw the zany zebras zigzag in the Ozark zoo.

1 | 2 | 3 | 4 | 5 | 6 | 7 | 8 | 9 | 10

UNIT 3

Keyboarding: Numbers and Symbols

LESSON 11
New Keys: - 2 9

LESSON 12
New Keys: 8 5 '

LESSON 13
New Keys: 4 7 :

LESSON 14
New Keys: 6 3 /

LESSON 15
Review

New Keys 11

Goals

- Touch-type the -, 2, and 9 keys.
- Type at least 19wpm/2′/5e.

A. WARMUP

alphabet
1 Big July earthquakes confounded the zany experimental vows.

concentration
2 uncommunicativeness departmentalization electrocardiography

easy
3 It is the duty of the busy ensigns to dismantle the panels.

New Keys

B. THE - KEY

Keep the J finger in home-row position.

Use the Sem finger.

Do not space before or after a hyphen.

4 ;;; ;p; ;-; ;-; -;- -;- --- no-no to-do mix-up run-in X-ray
5 pop-up sit-in add-on get-go set-to can-do U-turn up-to-date
6 Jo Dye-Lee, a well-to-do jack-of-all-trades, had a boo-boo.
7 Le-Sam is a shut-in who drank a pick-me-up from the get-go.

C. THE 2 KEY

Keep either the A or F finger in home-row position.

Use the S finger.

8 sss sws s2s s2s 2s2 2s2 222 22 sets; 22 seas; 2 sons; 2 men
9 222 suns 22 subs 222 sins 22 saps 222 saws 22 sips 222 sirs
10 He got 22 pens, 22 pads, 22 pencils, and 22 clips on May 2.
11 The 22 seats in Row 22 were sold to 22 coeds from Room 222.

D. THE 9 KEY

Keep the Sem finger in home-row position.

Use the L finger.

12 lll lol l9l l9l 9l9 9l9 999 9 laws; 99 lots; 9 lies; 9 laps
13 99 labs 9 keys 9,992 kits 299 leis 999 legs 99 logs 29 lips
14 She moved from 929 29th Street to 922 92nd Avenue on May 9.
15 On May 9, the 99 men and 29 women baked 9 pies and 9 cakes.

Skillbuilding

E. NEW-KEY REVIEW

```
16 29-22 majority; 99-92 lead at half-time; 929 one-way roads;
17 92 cave-ins; 99 walk-ins; 92 up-to-date items; 22 tune-ups;
18 299 sign-ups; 929 fill-in-the-blank questions; 99 push-ups;
19 929 look-alikes; 922 go-getters; 29 T-shirts; 292 boo-boos;
```

F. PROGRESSIVE PRACTICE: ALPHABET

Follow the GDP software directions for this exercise to improve keystroking accuracy.

G. TECHNIQUE PRACTICE: HYPHEN

Make a dash by typing two hyphens with no space before, between, or after (lines 21 and 24). Note: Microsoft Word (but not the GDP software) automatically converts two hyphens into a formatted dash (—).

```
20      Larry will go to the next tennis tournament. I am
21 positive that he--like Lane--will find the event to be a
22 first-class sports event. If he can go, I will get all of
23 us first-rate seats.
24      Larry--but not Ella--enjoys going to tournaments that
25 are always first-rate, first-class sporting events.
```

H. 12-SECOND SPEED SPRINTS

Take three 12-second timed writings on each line. The scale below the last line shows your wpm speed for a 12-second timed writing.

```
26 Jan owns a pair of old gowns and a new hat she got from me.
27 He may go with us to the giant dock down by the handy lake.
28 His civic goal for the city is for them to endow the chair.
29 I may make us one set of maps to aid us when we visit them.
   ''''5''''10''''15''''20''''25''''30''''35''''40''''45''''50''''55''''60
```

I. 2-MINUTE TIMED WRITING

Take two 2-minute timed writings.

Goal: At least 19wpm/2'/5e

```
30      Zachary just paid for six seats and quit because he     11
31 could not get the views he required near the middle of the  22
32 field. In August he thinks he may go to the ticket office    34
33 to purchase tickets.                                         38
     1 | 2 | 3 | 4 | 5 | 6 | 7 | 8 | 9 | 10 | 11 | 12
```

Enrichment • Lesson 11

Type each line 2 times.

A. NEW-KEY REINFORCEMENT

1 29-92 99-22 92-29 22-99 99-92 22-92 22-29 29-99 22-92 99-29
2 99-29 29-92 92-29 22-99 99-22 99-92 22-92 29-99 22-92 22-29
3 99-22 29-92 99-92 22-92 92-29 22-99 22-92 99-29 22-29 29-99

4 99 also-rans; 29 set-asides; 92 cure-alls; 29 two-by-fours;
5 92 free-for-alls; 29 do-it-yourselfers; 22 merry-go-rounds;
6 292 look-alikes; 929 flip-flops; 292 I-beams; 922 A-frames;

7 She had 92 pens, 29 pads, 99 pencils, 29 clips and 2 notes.
8 To dry-clean the 92 suits, use the 229 high-pressure hoses.
9 Only 22 off-the-record comments were heard from 292 people.

10 The 29 high-ranking men had to attend 22 black-tie affairs.
11 Over 99 part-time jobs were posted at the all-day job fair.
12 Use a 92-29 ratio in the 9-liter container on September 29.

Type each line 2 times.

B. ROW PRACTICE

Top Row

13 uproot Peter treetop typewriter witty purity quieter tiptoe
14 equity Europe prettier teeter quitter troop tutor write wee

Home Row

15 Dallas salads flask gassed ladled leash saddle shall shakes
16 slash ladles flakes flesh safes Allah salsa faked jags fall

Bottom row

17 Amman anemic annexing numb Venice menace examine Mexico ebb
18 Nancy convey become combat machine convene inn Manchu comma

Type each paragraph 2 times.

C. PARAGRAPH TYPING

19 This note is just to confirm my order on the basis of 11
20 the prices you quoted me on the phone. Let me know when you 23
21 ship five dozen boxes of staples for my light-duty machine. 35

22 Yes, I will be quite pleased to have you see the house 11
23 next week on Wednesday, if convenient. I feel sure you will 23
24 think it is just as great a prize as your main residence. 34

25 If we are to have an exciting project of any real size 11
26 this year, we need a more vigorous chair for it, so I will 23
27 request that you serve. I hope that will be okay with you. 35

1 | 2 | 3 | 4 | 5 | 6 | 7 | 8 | 9 | 10 | 11 | 12

New Keys

Goals

- Touch-type the 8, 5, and ' keys.
- Type at least 20wpm/2'/5e.

A. WARMUP

alphabet 1 Dr. Jekyll vowed to finish zapping the quixotic bumblebees.
one hand 2 secret hominy dew hip beasts nonunion edge monk staff nylon
easy 3 Pamela may use a kayak and map to come to the old city dam.

New Keys

Use the K finger.

B. THE 8 KEY

4 kkk kik k8k k8k 8k8 8k8 888 88 kits; 88 kegs; 8 kin; 8 keys
5 828 kites 982 kings 828 kids 988 kilts 828 knees 998 knocks
6 On July 28, I saw 88 cats, 82 dogs, 88 birds, and 28 foxes.
7 Of the 828 people, 28 were at the free-for-all on April 28.

Use the F finger.

C. THE 5 KEY

8 fff frf f5f f5f 5f5 5f5 555 5 fans; 5 fibs; 5 figs; 58 firs
9 5 figs 5 foes 5 tins 5 taps 55 tons 58 bays 85 bids 95 boys
10 Just call me at 585-555-5955 or on my cell at 585-555-5585.
11 The 585 men, 952 women, and 852 children left on August 25.

Use the Sem finger.

D. THE ' KEY

12 ;;; ;'; ;'; ';' ';' ''' he'd; I've; Al's; it's; she's; I'll
13 all's can't cont'd dep't gov't we'll you're I'll lad's we'd
14 It's too bad that he'd eaten Kate's dessert at Abe's Diner.
15 I'm sure he won't mind if Joe's car isn't in Alan's garage.

Skillbuilding

E. NEW-KEY REVIEW

```
16 Li's 85-58 lead; Moe's and Bob's 82 ads; I'll take 59 bids;
17 Bob's sister can't type 85 wpm; 8585 East 85th Lane; 89-58;
18 pages 558-582; call her at 858-555-8958; 558 part-time ads;
19 Invoice 88-595; Apt. 58-B; I'll be in Room 588-D; May 5-28;
```

F. SUSTAINED PRACTICE: CAPITALS

Take a 1-minute timed writing on the boxed paragraph to establish your base speed. Then take a 1-minute timed writing on the following paragraph. As soon as you equal or exceed your base speed on this paragraph, move to the next, more difficult paragraph.

```
20      Even though he was only about thirty years old, Jason  11
21 knew that it was not too soon to begin thinking about his   23
22 retirement. He learned that many things were involved.      33

23      Even without considering the uncertainty of social     10
24 security, Jason knew that he should plan his career moves,  22
25 so he opened a new Individual Retirement Account in May.    34

26      When he became aware that The Longman Company would    11
27 match his contributions, Jason asked the Payroll Department 23
28 to open a retirement account for him with the Coplin Group. 34

29      He also learned that The Longman Company retirement    11
30 plan and his Individual Retirement Plan are all deferred    22
31 savings. Then, Jason purchased New Venture Group mutuals.   33
     1 | 2 | 3 | 4 | 5 | 6 | 7 | 8 | 9 | 10 | 11 | 12
```

G. 2-MINUTE TIMED WRITING

Take two 2-minute timed writings.

Goal: At least 20wpm/2′/5e

```
32      Jack and Alex ordered six pizzas at a price that was   11
33 quite a bit lower than was the one they ordered yesterday.  23
34 They will order from the same place tomorrow for the party  34
35 they are wanting to provide.                                40
     1 | 2 | 3 | 4 | 5 | 6 | 7 | 8 | 9 | 10 | 11 | 12
```

Enrichment • Lesson 12

Type each line 2 times.

A. NEW-KEY REINFORCEMENT

1 Mary's pages 58-85; John's 2,585 sales; 8858 O'Hara Street;
2 Call me at 858-555-8258; I'm in Room 859-B; Al's 58 errors;
3 cont'd on p. 285; 29,858 employees; 825 boys and 589 girls;

4 Pacers' final score of 89-82; May 28, '99; go to Room 2858;
5 Take I-85 to 92-B; Apt. 28-C; I'm 28.5 years old. He's out;
6 A tie score of 58-58; I'm out; the combination is 28-95-85;

Type each line 2 times.

B. ALPHABET PRACTICE

7 A Jack in the Box quickly varied its menu with fudge pizza.
8 Ban all foul toxic smog which can quickly jeopardize lives.
9 Five or six big jet planes zoomed quickly by the old tower.

10 Grumpy wizards made toxic brew for Jack and the evil queen.
11 If fog makes Max shiver, quickly zip down and buy a jacket.
12 Just keep examining every low bid quoted for zinc etchings.

13 Six crazy kings vowed to abolish my quite pitiful projects.
14 The jobs of waxing linoleum frequently peeved chintzy kids.
15 Weekly magazines request help for and by junior executives.

Type each paragraph 2 times.

C. PARAGRAPH TYPING

16 When I was at the gym today, I met Bill Saxon, the 10
17 former Jets quarterback. Bill is leaving football and needs 22
18 a job like the one we have open in hazardous control. 33

19 Folks do not want to live near airports because of 10
20 the extreme racket of the planes. The roar and whine as a 22
21 jet zooms by cannot be equaled by ten giant bulldozers. 33

22 If you accept this job, as we hope, please plan to 10
23 arrive next week so that we may zero in on those fashion 22
24 shows we have in Denver, Boston, Raleigh, and Quebec. 32

25 This is in response to your inquiry about Elizabeth 11
26 Jones. Ms. Jones worked for us for six years. We were sorry 23
27 to lose her to a company that gave her a larger salary. 34

1 | 2 | 3 | 4 | 5 | 6 | 7 | 8 | 9 | 10 | 11 | 12

New Keys

Goals

- Touch-type the 4, 7, and : keys.
- Type at least 21wpm/2'/5e.

A. WARMUP

alphabet
1 Prized waxy jonquils choked the weeds in the big farm vats.

practice: *f* and *g*
2 gruff fig finger flag frogs gift golf gulf goofs fogs flags

easy
3 The new formal audit may be paid for by the downtown firms.

New Keys

Use the F finger.

B. THE 4 KEY

4 fff frf f4f f4f 4f4 4f4 444 4 fans; 4 fibs, 4 figs, 44 firs
5 4 figs 4 foes 4 tins 4 taps 44 tons 49 bays 45 bids 94 boys
6 The 44 men and 54 boys used 494 liters in 42 days on May 4.
7 Please add Items 428, 84, 944, 42, and 488 to Order 44-482.

Use the J finger.

C. THE 7 KEY

8 jjj juj j7j j7j 7j7 7j7 777 77 jugs; 7 jets; 7 jars; 7 jabs
9 74 jays 47 jobs 77 jots 74 hams 74 hats 47 hits 77 hugs 777
10 I bought Item 74 that weighs 47 pounds 7 ounces on June 27.
11 Allen covered pages 472-479, and Sue covered pages 277-789.

Use the Sem finger.

D. THE : KEY

The colon is the shift of the semicolon key. Do not space before or after a colon used with numbers. Space 1 time after a colon following a word except at the end of a line.

12 ;;; ;:; ;:; :;: :;: ::: 7:47 a.m.; 47:74 odds; Dear Mr. Ng:
13 Dr. Poole: Ms. Shu: Mr. Rose: Mrs. Tam: Dear Ed: Dear John:
14 Dear Johnny: Let's meet at 2:45 to discuss the 57:47 ratio.
15 Do not forget the Date:, To:, From:, and Subject: headings.

Skillbuilding

E. NEW-KEY REVIEW

```
16 The 47 managers had 74 tickets for the 4:47 game on May 24.
17 as follows: these people: this motion: here it is: Dear Jo:
18 Ed's 97-42 lead at 4:25 p.m.; pages 477-747; a 747 jet; Hi:
```

PRETEST » PRACTICE » POSTTEST

PRETEST

Take a 1-minute timed writing.

F. PRETEST: Common Letter Combinations

```
19     The condo committee was hoping the motion would not be 11
20 forced upon it, realizing that viable solutions ought to be 23
21 developed. It was forceful in seeking a period of time.     34
     1 | 2 | 3 | 4 | 5 | 6 | 7 | 8 | 9 | 10 | 11 | 12
```

PRACTICE

Speed Emphasis:
If you made 2 or fewer errors on the Pretest, type each *individual* line 2 times.

Accuracy Emphasis:
If you made 3 or more errors, type each *group* of lines (as though it were a paragraph) 2 times.

G. PRACTICE: Word Beginnings

```
22 for forum forge forced forgot formal forest foreign forerun
23 con conks conic consul confer convey convex contact concern
24 per perks peril person period perish permit percale percent
```

H. PRACTICE: Word Endings

```
25 ing tying hiking liking edging bowing hoping having nursing
26 ble fable pebble treble tumble viable dabble fumble fusible
27 ion union legion nation region motion potion option bastion
```

POSTTEST

Repeat the Pretest timed writing and compare performance.

I. POSTTEST: Common Letter Combinations

J. 2-MINUTE TIMED WRITING

Take two 2-minute timed writings.

Goal: At least 21wpm/2'/5e

```
28     Jim told Bev that they must keep the liquid oxygen      10
29 frozen so that it could be used by the new plant managers   22
30 tomorrow. The oxygen will then be moved quickly to its new  34
31 location by transport or rail on Tuesday.                   42
     1 | 2 | 3 | 4 | 5 | 6 | 7 | 8 | 9 | 10 | 11 | 12
```

Enrichment • Lesson 13

Type each line 2 times.

A. NEW-KEY REINFORCEMENT

1 Jill bought 29 tickets for the 8:25 or 7:45 show on July 5.
2 Maxine called from 777-555-4278 or 777-555-4279 for Martin.
3 Jackson sold 85 tires, 94 air filters, and 247 oil filters.

4 Flight 4789B departed at 8:45 a.m. and arrived at 9:25 p.m.
5 I'm moving from 4529 East Rogers to 4725 East Eaton in May.
6 Only 247 men and 74 women attended the orientation at 8:45.

7 Ty: Flight 982 on the 747 jet departs at 2:45 on August 27.
8 On November 24-27, we were open from 7:45 a.m. to 9:45 p.m.
9 The 89 men then drove 774 miles on Route 47-B and Route 77.

Type each line 2 times.

B. SUBSTITUTION ERRORS

10 r-t hurt trot trite Trent treat tutor tort trust rotate try
11 m-n mend mine norm unman many naming morn manual hymn amend
12 o-i void silo olio Ohio into icon coin polio folio boil oil

13 a-s tasks visas sodas seams scans areas bases sales say has
14 s-d suds soda sides sheds dusts dudes dosed desks deeds sad
15 r-e rear refer every erred enter emery elder Erie eerie red

16 v-b visible brave bovine vibe livable above bevy bevel verb
17 w-e endow wade wee ewe wide dew wed elbow we where were wet
18 f-g flags fogs gruff goof gulf golf gift frog flag fang fig

Type each paragraph 2 times.

C. PARAGRAPH TYPING

19 The senator quietly voted to legalize marijuana but 11
20 drew the line at making it easily available to teens. He 22
21 also voted for new price controls on all foreign exports. 33

22 The anxious job applicant inquired about the size of 11
23 the firm's overseas business. He also wanted to know the 22
24 weekly sales of gas and other petroleum products to China. 34

25 I jotted down all the questions I wanted to ask the 11
26 five energy czars the next time I met with them. They were 23
27 in town for the big expo being held at the city arena. 33

28 Three weekly magazines requested help for the junior 11
29 executives in the software industry. By now, they must have 23
30 received many responses from their readers and subscribers. 35

1 | 2 | 3 | 4 | 5 | 6 | 7 | 8 | 9 | 10 | 11 | 12

New Keys

Goals

- Touch-type the 6, 3, and / keys.
- Type at least 22wpm/2′/5e.

A. WARMUP

```
alphabet            1  Max did not become eloquent over a zany gift like jodhpurs.
frequent digraphs   2  te tee ate byte tell tea termite ten Ute tent teed teen Ted
easy                3  The auditor's panel had the right to risk a firm's profits.
```

New Keys

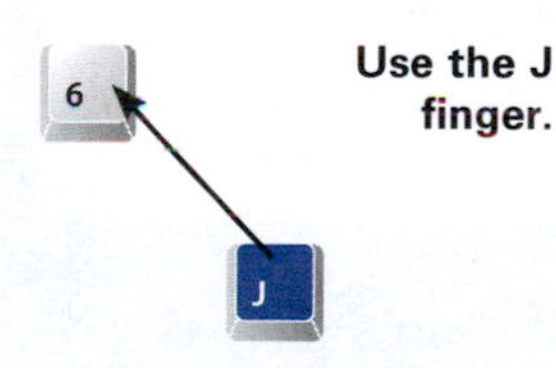

B. THE 6 KEY

```
4  jjj jyj j6j j6j 6j6 6j6 666 66 jugs; 6 jets; 6 jars; 6 jabs
5  64 jays 46 jobs 66 jots 67 hams 76 hats 46 hits 67 hugs 666
6  Tom Quin left at 6:26 p.m. on Train 66 to travel 626 miles.
7  There were 56,646 people in Bath and 26,269 in Hale in May.
```

Use the D finger.

C. THE 3 KEY

```
8  ddd ded d3d d3d 3d3 3d3 333 33 dots; 3 dies; 3 dips; 3 days
9  332 days 36 dogs 63 does 73 duds 37 dies 3:39 p.m.; 323-373
10 The 33 vans moved 36 cases in less than 33 hours on July 3.
11 Please add 55 to 753 and subtract 73 to get a total of 735.
```

Use the Sem finger.

D. THE / KEY

Do not space before or after the slash—unless it is the last character of an expression (line 15).

```
12 ;;; ;/; ;/; /;/ /;/ /// a/an and/or at/about bad/badly I/me
13 both/each disc/disk farther/further fewer/less like/such as
14 On 6/2/99, you asked him/her if he/she selected true/false.
15 Visit http://gdpkeyboarding.com/ for any questions/answers.
```

Skillbuilding

E. NEW-KEY REVIEW: 6, 3, AND SLASH KEY

16 In 6 months, he had walked 36 miles and/or driven 63 miles.
17 I realize that 3/6 of the 66 shipments equals 33 shipments.
18 He was born in New York on 6/3/36 and died there on 6/6/63.
19 Lucille bought 36 his/her towels on 3/3 with terms of n/29.

F. NUMBER-KEY REVIEW: 2, 4, 5, 7, 8, AND 9

20 My staff of 24 worked a total of 87 hours on Project 598-B.
21 Ed's instructor assigned pages 549-782 to be read by May 2.
22 From 2:45 p.m. until 5:45 p.m., I'll be typing in Room 987.
23 Let's visit her at 592 North Elm, Apt. 47, on September 28.

G. TECHNIQUE PRACTICE: SHIFT KEY

Type each line 2 times. After striking the capitalized letter, return the SHIFT key finger immediately to home-row position.

24 Alex Bly and Clara Dye wed. Ella Fochs and Gil Hall talked.
25 Ida Jackson met Kay Lang for a fast lunch at Mamma Nancy's.
26 Otis Pike should call Quint Richards about Sophia Townsend.
27 Ulrich Volte will take Winona Xi to visit Yadkin in Zurich.

H. PROGRESSIVE PRACTICE: ALPHABET

Follow the GDP software directions for this exercise to improve keystroking speed.

I. 2-MINUTE TIMED WRITING

Take two 2-minute timed writings.

Goal: At least 22wpm/2′/5e

28 Jack scheduled a science quiz next week for Gregory, 11
29 but he did not let him know what time the exam was to be 22
30 taken. Gregory must score well on the exam in order to be 34
31 admitted to the class at the private Mount Academy. 44

1 | 2 | 3 | 4 | 5 | 6 | 7 | 8 | 9 | 10 | 11 | 12

Enrichment • Lesson 14

A. NUMBER-KEY REINFORCEMENT

Type each line 2 times.

```
1  The 375 cars traveled 847 miles and used 45 gallons of gas.
2  My staff of 24 worked 48 hours a week from May 6 to May 29.
3  The 6 teams comprised 69 girls and 7 boys and left at 9:45.

4  The 37 men visited the 45 women at 3:25 p.m. on October 26.
5  Larry's 29 basketball players scored 467 points on 6/23/99.
6  The 23 workers packed 87 cartons, which weighed 389 pounds.
```

B. TECHNIQUE PRACTICE: BACKSPACE KEY

Type each line 2 times. Type the 3-letter word, backspace, and type the new letter. Thus, *rat* becomes *ram*.

```
7  rat←m gut←m are←m tip←n rut←n pat←n gut←n did←n bit←n ale←l
8  ash←k woo←k pat←l cot←n fit←n mat←n put←n tap←n wit←n ton←o
9  elk←m ill←k air←l bat←n fur←n owe←n rat←n air←m get←m sin←p
10 inn←k ire←k ilk←l but←n dot←n ink←n pet←n hat←m hit←m air←l
```

C. 12-SECOND SPEED SPRINTS

Take three 12-second timed writings on each line. The scale below the last line shows your wpm speed for a 12-second timed writing.

```
11 The doe and buck by the old lake may dig up the giant oaks.
12 It is a shame she works such an odd bowl into her art work.
13 Jake moved to amend the law to let the worker take the job.
14 He may sign over the title to his autos when he is in town.
   ''''5''''10''''15''''20''''25''''30''''35''''40''''45''''50''''55''''60
```

D. PARAGRAPH TYPING

Type each paragraph 2 times.

```
15      My boss knew that her expert eloquence was just a big   11
16 hazard to effective teamwork, so he asked her to tone down   23
17 her remarks when giving her opinions on our progress.        33

18      Six of the female employees quietly gave back their     11
19 prizes to the judge because they did not agree with his      22
20 decisions regarding the basis for making his decisions.      33

21      Please, just be very quick and careful when you fix     11
22 the size of the tables in your annual report. You should     22
23 get Margaret to help you proofread your final report.        33

24      Our firm should ban all foul toxic smog because it      10
25 can quickly jeopardize the lives of our workers and their    22
26 families. I hope the board will make this decision soon.     33
     1 | 2 | 3 | 4 | 5 | 6 | 7 | 8 | 9 | 10 | 11 | 12
```

Review

Goals

- Type at least 23wpm/2'/5e.

A. WARMUP

alphabet	1	Jack amazed a few girls by dropping the antique onyx vases.
alternate-hand words	2	half height right penalty with visit social lens rigid snap
easy	3	My mangy dog then ran to his bowl in the den to take a sip.

Skillbuilding

B. NUMBER-KEY REVIEW

4 I sent 72 jars, 89 cans, 29 boxes, and 32 bags to 33 homes.
5 The 494 students partied at 576 Dale and then at 5896 Park.
6 We got seats 27, 25, 28, 67, and 79 for the August 98 game.

7 Open Rooms 325, 343, 467, and 456 with Master Key No. 65-7.
8 The equipment shed was 267 by 278 feet, not 289 by 93 feet.
9 Mail the 378 packages to 548 East 65th Lane, not to 46 Elm.

C. PUNCTUATION REVIEW

.	10	Go to Reno. Drive to Yuma. Call Mary. Get Samuel. See Cory.
,	11	We saw Nice, Paris, Bern, Rome, Munich, Bonn, and Shanghai.
;	12	Type the memo; read my report; get pens; get paper; see me.
: -	13	Dear Aldo: Read these pages by 9:45: 2-9, 26-35, and 45-78.
'	14	Ted's car and Ann's truck took the Hills' kids to Shoney's.
/	15	My aunt/best friend was born on 6/22/37 and died on 9/2/95.

D. PROGRESSIVE PRACTICE: ALPHABET

Follow the GDP software directions for this exercise to improve keystroking accuracy.

E. TECHNIQUE PRACTICE: TAB KEY

Press TAB where you see the → symbol.

16 Kim→ apt→ Mac→ art→ Nat→ Meg→ ads→ arm→ all→ ado→ Joy
17 Orr→ awl→ Jan→ Ida→ Moe→ Lin→ zap→ Joe→ zed→ ark→ awe
18 Kai→ Lev→ add→ ask→ Mom→ Uri→ Jeb→ Nan→ aid→ Lot→ amp
19 Jay→ Hal→ Ima→ Ira→ ail→ aim→ Ian→ Max→ Pat→ Liv→ Jim

F. TECHNIQUE PRACTICE: SPACE BAR

20 A toy dog in the pen is apt to be a big hit at the new gym.
21 We may go to the zoo for the day if the sun is not too hot.
22 Eli and Max may use a map to see how to get to the new pub.
23 If it is to be, it is up to you and Ben to do it for a fee.

G. 2-MINUTE TIMED WRITING

Take two 2-minute timed writings.

Goal: At least 23wpm/2'/5e

24 Jeff Melvin was quite busy fixing all of the frozen 11
25 pipes so that his water supply would not be stopped. Last 22
26 winter Jeff kept the pipes from freezing by wrapping them 34
27 with an insulated tape that protected them from snow and 45
28 ice. 46

1 | 2 | 3 | 4 | 5 | 6 | 7 | 8 | 9 | 10 | 11 | 12

Enrichment • Lesson 15

A. NUMBER-KEY REINFORCEMENT

Type each line 2 times.

1 Just call me at 275-555-8346 or on my cell at 748-555-9292.
2 I bought Item 536 that weighs 45 pounds 6 ounces on May 27.
3 She moved from 859 36th Street to 734 82nd Avenue on May 5.

4 On July 26, I saw 67 cats, 92 dogs, 83 birds, and 49 foxes.
5 Please add Items 526, 73, 989, 24, and 453 to Order 56-627.
6 The 587 police met at 2:25 a.m. with 89 agents in Room 324.

B. ALPHABET PRACTICE

Type each line 2 times.

7 A campus TV quiz just asks why gold is buried at Fort Knox.
8 Crazy Fredrick bought Jane many very exquisite opal jewels.
9 All questions asked by five watch experts amazed the judge.

10 Jack quietly gave the dog owners most of his prized boxers.
11 Fred specialized in the job of making very quaint wax toys.
12 Six big devils from Japan then quickly forgot how to waltz.

C. 12-SECOND SPEED SPRINTS

Take three 12-second timed writings on each line. The scale below the last line shows your wpm speed for a 12-second timed writing.

13 He may go with us to the giant dock down by the handy lake.
14 The doe and buck by the old bush may dig up the giant oaks.
15 Ken had a dish of lamb and cut up a mango and a ripe mango.
16 Kay may visit the big island in May when she is down there.
' ' ' ' 5 ' ' ' ' 10 ' ' ' ' 15 ' ' ' ' 20 ' ' ' ' 25 ' ' ' ' 30 ' ' ' ' 35 ' ' ' ' 40 ' ' ' ' 45 ' ' ' ' 50 ' ' ' ' 55 ' ' ' ' 60

D. PARAGRAPH TYPING

Type each paragraph 2 times.

17 Please ship to me by freight sixty dozen quart jars 11
18 and twelve dozen black pans for the opening of our newest 22
19 appliance store in the coming weeks in North Carolina. 33

20 Mr. Dave Jones, the defense attorney, quickly spotted 11
21 four women dozing in the jury box. He moved to have the 22
22 judge quickly declare a mistrial and dismiss the jurors. 33

23 Back in June, our company delivered oxygen equipment 11
24 of odd sizes to the county hospital. It has already been 22
25 installed and is working properly in the emergency room. 33

26 I saw the four brown foxes who were quickly jumping 11
27 over the lazy dogs that were resting out back. The dogs did 23
28 not even open their eyes but continued sleeping heavily. 34
1 | 2 | 3 | 4 | 5 | 6 | 7 | 8 | 9 | 10 | 11 | 12

UNIT 4

Keyboarding: Numbers and Symbols

LESSON 16

New Keys: & $ 0

LESSON 17

New Keys: 1 ? @

LESSON 18

New Keys: % ( ) #

LESSON 19

New Keys: " ! *

LESSON 20

Review

New Keys

Goals

- Touch-type the &, $, and 0 keys.
- Type at least 24wpm/2′/5e.

A. WARMUP

alphabet	1	Jack's man found exactly a quarter in the woven zipper bag.
concentration	2	oversimplifications nonrepresentational professionalization
easy	3	An auditor may sign a form that may name Toby to the panel.

New Keys

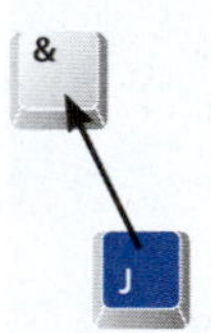

Use the J finger.

B. THE & KEY

The ampersand key (the sign for *and*) is the shift of 7. In normal narrative writing, space 1 time before and after the ampersand.

4 jjj juj j&j j&j &j& &j& &&& Max & Dee & Sue & Tom & Rex & I
5 Brown & Sons shipped to May & Lee and also to Dye & Pearce.
6 John & Loo brought a case against May & Green and Li & Won.
7 Von & Trapp and Den & Sax were joined by Contreras & Duran.

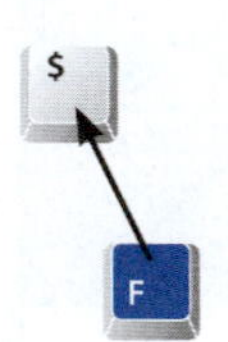

Use the F finger.

C. THE $ KEY

The dollar sign is the shift of 4. Do not space between the dollar sign and the following number.

8 fff frf f$f f$f f f $$$ $44 $434.44 $4,444 $456 $492.85
9 He paid $48, $64, and $94 for the chairs plus $48 shipping.
10 Last season's concert tickets were $35, $45, $75, and $255.
11 If you add $48.62, $49.93, and $324.42, you'll get $422.97.

Keep the J finger in home-row position.

Use the Sem finger.

D. THE 0 KEY

12 ;;; ;p; ;0; ;0; 0;0 0;0 000 00 2:00; 3:00; 4:00; 5:00; 6:30
13 The 80 men met at 3:05 with 20 agents in Room 90 on May 20.
14 I paid $40.05 for 20 pens and $50.50 for 30 pads on May 30.
15 The firm of Mori & Itou at 200 Broad Street owes us $8,000.

Skillbuilding

E. NEW-KEY REVIEW

16 $20.50 & $380.65 & $90.20 & $40.50 & $30.40 & $247.50 & $80
17 We hired Rizzo & Kelly for $20,000 to help Diamond & Green.
18 Arn & Sons owed us $4,000 and paid us only $250.50 in July.
19 Call Penn & Ames at 800-555-2040 and ask about the $48,000.

F. PACED PRACTICE

Follow the GDP software directions for this exercise to improve keystroking speed and accuracy.

G. TECHNIQUE PRACTICE: SHIFT KEY

20 Ann Bonn asked for lunch. Colin Dix and Elaine Fochs moved.
21 Glen Hans filed as Iris James typed. Les Kay talked loudly.
22 Maya Nevins and Orin Parks tried. Quinn Roberts lost a bet.
23 Skye Tynch sat. Uriah Vin and Winn Xung ate. Yosef Zoe hid.

H. PROGRESSIVE PRACTICE: ALPHABET

Follow the GDP software directions for this exercise to improve keystroking speed.

I. 2-MINUTE TIMED WRITING

Take two 2-minute timed writings.

Goal: At least 24wpm/2′/5e

24 Ginny quit her zoo job seven days after she learned 11
25 that she was expected to travel to four zoos in the first 22
26 month of work. After she had quit her job, she found an 34
27 excellent position that did not require her to be away 48
28 from home so much.

1 | 2 | 3 | 4 | 5 | 6 | 7 | 8 | 9 | 10 | 11 | 12

Enrichment • Lesson 16

Type each line 2 times.

A. NEW-KEY REVIEW

&	1	Ali & Wu; Ash & Li; Cho & Ng; Day & Ivy; Gil & Ray; Ho & Yu
$	2	$234.56 and $78.54 and $463.38 and $23,896.25 and $4,993.39
0	3	20 and 30 and 40 and 50 and 60 and 70 and 80 and 90 and 200
& $ 0	4	Ott & Orr owed $5,000 to me; they owed $7,000 to Jay & Poe.

Take a 1-minute timed writing on the boxed paragraph to establish your base speed. Then take a 1-minute timed writing on the following paragraph. As soon as you equal or exceed your base speed on this paragraph, move to the next, more difficult paragraph.

B. SUSTAINED PRACTICE: SYLLABIC INTENSITY

Syllabic intensity refers to the average number of syllables per word in a passage. The higher the syllabic intensity, the more difficult the passage is to type.

```
5       One should always attempt to maintain good health. As     11
6   the first step in keeping good health, one should avoid the   23
7   habit of smoking. Volumes have been written on this topic.    35

8       A second habit that will help maintain your health for    11
9   decades is consuming an appropriate amount of water, day in   23
10  and day out. Most doctors recommend eight glasses a day.      34

11      Making exercise a habit is another important trait for    11
12  staying in good health. Most experts agree that spending a    23
13  few minutes a day in regular, vigorous exercise is helpful.   35

14      A final habit of importance is maintaining appropriate    11
15  body weight. The key to maintaining weight is developing a    23
16  positive eating pattern. Calculating calories is helpful.     34
      1 | 2 | 3 | 4 | 5 | 6 | 7 | 8 | 9 | 10 | 11 | 12
```

Type each paragraph 2 times.

C. PARAGRAPH TYPING

```
17      Jack typed a requisition for white moving boxes of        10
18  various sizes--some long and some short. He will need them    22
19  when we move into our new headquarters sometime next month.   34

20      My grandfather picked up a quartz and onyx necklace       11
21  for my grandmother at the bazaar. He knew that she loved      22
22  jewelry, and he was eager to give it to her on Christmas.     33

23      Jeff had his size, which helped him quickly win over      11
24  Gene in the boxing match. He won based on both his size and   23
25  his abilities as a boxer. My school was quite proud of him.   35
      1 | 2 | 3 | 4 | 5 | 6 | 7 | 8 | 9 | 10 | 11 | 12
```

New Keys

Goals

- Touch-type the 1, ?, and @ keys.
- Type at least 25wpm/2'/5e.

A. WARMUP

alphabet	1	Many big jackdaws quickly zipped over those empty fox pens.
one hand	2	street unholy sad you stated monopoly seat pink treat unpin
easy	3	Duane may try to fix the auditory problems in the city gym.

New Keys

B. THE 1 KEY

Keep the F finger in home-row position.

Use the A finger.

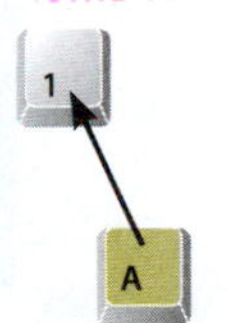

4 aaa aqa ala ala 1a1 1a1 111 11 ants; 11 asps; 1 aim; 11 ads
5 Sam left here at 1:11, Susan at 6:11, and Don at 11:11 a.m.
6 Erich had moved from 1010 Main Street to 1101 Main in 1990.
7 Sarah left at 11:00 a.m. on Train No. 11 to go 1,100 miles.

C. THE ? KEY

Use the Sem finger.

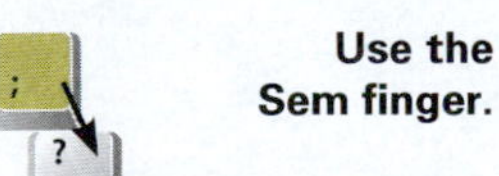

The question mark is the shift of the slash. Space 1 time after a question mark.

8 ;;; ;/; ;?; ;?; ?;? ?;? ??? Who? What? When? Where? Why me?
9 May I? Why not? Who called? Need a job? Which one? Is it I?
10 Who's there? Any questions? Yes? Need some help? Who cares?
11 Is it 11:00? Was it held on 11/11/09? Where is 1101 W. Elm?

Use the S finger.

D. THE @ KEY

The at sign is the shift of 2. Space 1 time before and after the at sign except when it is used in an e-mail address (lines 13 and 15).

```
12 sss sws s@s s@s @s@ @s@ @@@ Buy 15 @ $41.01 and 11 @ $3.15.
13 E-mail me at jfox@tmu.edu or at jfox01@aol.com on April 11.
14 Order 12 pens @ $14, 185 pads @ $16, and 110 clips @ $2.50.
15 Can you e-mail Roger at rlowe@umn.edu to order 250 @ $1.15?
```

Skillbuilding

E. NEW-KEY REVIEW

```
16 Who knows if Randy's e-mail address is rjoyner@hotmail.com?
17 Should she buy 150 shares @ $11.50 and 200 shares @ $11.25?
18 Did she change her e-mail address to dcberkow011@yahoo.com?
19 Did Beverly try cokeefe011@vmu.edu or caroleoke101@msn.com?
```

F. TECHNIQUE PRACTICE: BACKSPACE KEY

Directions: Type the 3-letter word, backspace, and type the new letter.

```
20 bud←m gig←n dew←n rag←m tad←n own←l get←m tie←n toe←n
21 car←p hoe←g yea←n pie←n vat←n hug←m rug←m pod←i per←p
22 job←y yaw←m bus←y pad←l lad←p the←y nag←p fur←n nub←n
23 fad←n max←y jag←m fig←n ice←y oaf←k add←o mow←p log←o
```

G. MAP+: ALPHABET

Follow the GDP software directions for this exercise to improve keystroking accuracy.

H. 2-MINUTE TIMED WRITING

Take two 2-minute timed writings.

Goal: At least 25wpm/2'/5e

```
24      From the tower John saw that those six big planes     11
25 could crash as they zoomed quickly over treetops on their  22
26 way to the demonstration that was scheduled to begin very  33
27 soon. We hope there are no accidents and that the pilots   45
28 reach the airport quickly.                                 50
   1 | 2 | 3 | 4 | 5 | 6 | 7 | 8 | 9 | 10 | 11 | 12
```

Enrichment • Lesson 17

Type each line 2 times.

A. NEW-KEY REINFORCEMENT

```
1  Adam moved from 1101 Oak Lane to 2110 11th Street on May 1.
?  Who knows? Does Karina? Cloris? Gamal? How about Salvatore?
@  Order 328 @ $4.50 and 390 @ $16.75 from renees@comcast.net.
1 ? @  Whose address is luan111@msn.com? Whose is wells101@cc.com?
```

Type each line 2 times.

B. NUMBER PRACTICE

```
5 we 23 ere 343 wry 246 woe 293 ask 128 lay 916 did 383 to 59
6 err 344 I 8 it 85 quit 1785 pup 070 pre 043 rip 480 tie 583
7 yew 632 quip 1780 ow 92 ire 843 per 034 pry 046 is 82 do 39
```

PPP PRETEST » PRACTICE » POSTTEST

PRETEST

Take a 1-minute timed writing.

C. PRETEST: Close Reaches

```
8      Casey hoped that we were not wasting good grub. After  11
9  the sun went down, he swiftly put the oleo and plums in the 23
10 cart. Bart opened a copy of an old book; Grant had a swim.  35
   1 | 2 | 3 | 4 | 5 | 6 | 7 | 8 | 9 | 10 | 11 | 12
```

PRACTICE

Speed Emphasis:
If you made no more than 2 errors on the Pretest, type each *individual* line 2 times.

Accuracy Emphasis:
If you made 3 or more errors, type each *group* of lines (as though it were a paragraph) 2 times.

D. PRACTICE: Adjacent Keys

```
11 op hope flop open mops rope opera droop scope copier trophy
12 we west owed went weld weep weigh weary wedge wealth plowed
13 rt hurt port cart dirt fort court party start hearty parted
```

E. PRACTICE: Consecutive Fingers

```
14 un tune spun unit dune punt under prune sunny hunter uneasy
15 gr grow grim grab grub grew great graze gripe greasy grassy
16 ol role oleo pool sold hole troll folly polka stolen oldest
```

POSTTEST

Repeat the Pretest timed writing and compare performance.

F. POSTTEST: Close Reaches

New Keys

Goals

- Touch-type the % ( ) and # keys.
- Type at least 26wpm/2′/5e.

A. WARMUP

alphabet 1 My woven silk pajamas can be exchanged for the blue quartz.
practice: *s* and *d* 2 ads sad deeds desks dosed dudes dusts sheds sides soda suds
easy 3 Her ruby handiwork is fine, and she is so proficient at it.

New Keys

Use the F finger.

B. THE % KEY

Percent is the shift of 5. Do not space between the number and the percent sign.

4 fff frf f%f f%f %f% %f% %%% 10% 9% 8% 7% 6% 5% 4% 3% 2% 10%
5 Rob quoted rates of 8%, 9%, 10%, 11%, and 12% on the bonds.
6 Sandy scored 82%, Jan 89%, Ken 90%, and me 91% on the exam.
7 Only 55% scored 75% or higher, and 8% scored 90% or higher.

Use the L finger on (. Use the Sem finger on).

C. THE (AND) KEYS

Parentheses are the shifts of 9 and 0. Do not space between the parentheses and the text within them.

8 lll lol l(l l(l (l((l((((;;; ;p; ;); ;););));)))) (a)
9 Please ask (1) Al, (2) Pat, (3) Ted, (4) Dee, and (5) Lise.
10 He'll (a) take two aspirin, (b) go to bed, and (c) rest up.
11 Rosa's (a cafe) had fish (shad) on the menu today (Monday).

Use the D finger.

D. THE # KEY

The # sign stands for *number* if it comes before a figure and *pounds* if it comes after a figure. It is the shift of 3. Do not space between the # sign and the number.

```
12 ddd ded d#d d#d #d# #d# ### #3 #33 #333 33# 83#; 37# of #83
13 Write down 330# of #200 and 380# of #400 using a #2 pencil.
14 We sat in seats #12, #34, #56, #65, and #66 at the concert.
15 Please use 50# lined paper for #373 and 30# paper for #374.
```

Skillbuilding

E. NEW-KEY REVIEW

```
16 Policy 8(b) says to load Truck #48 with 2,000# of 50% sand.
17 We need 85# of #2 grade ore (aluminum) and 45# of #3 grade.
18 Nearly 60% of the males and 50% of the females chose #5738.
19 Just stress (a) speed 50% of the time and (b) accuracy 50%.
```

F. PROGRESSIVE PRACTICE: NUMBERS

Follow the GDP software directions for this exercise to improve keystroking speed.

G. TECHNIQUE PRACTICE: SPACE BAR

```
20 Eli and Max may use a map to see how to get to the new pub.
21 A toy dog in the pen is apt to be a big hit at the new gym.
22 If it is to be, it is up to you and Ben to do it for a fee.
23 We may go to the zoo for the day if the sun is not too hot.
```

H. 2-MINUTE TIMED WRITING

Take two 2-minute timed writings.

Goal: At least 26wpm/2'/5e

```
24      Max had to make one quick adjustment to his television 11
25 set before the football game began. The picture during the  23
26 last game was fuzzy and hard to see. If he cannot fix the   35
27 picture, he may have to purchase a new television set; and  46
28 that may be difficult to do.                                52
    1 | 2 | 3 | 4 | 5 | 6 | 7 | 8 | 9 | 10 | 11 | 12
```

Enrichment • Lesson 18

A. NEW-KEY REINFORCEMENT

Type each line 2 times.

%	1	Of the 85% of the alumni here, 9% gave 28% and 6% gave 25%.
( )	2	Just (a) stop, (b) look, and (c) listen to her (Iphigenia).
#	3	Please record 33# of #200 and 38# of #400 on the #20 paper.
% ( ) #	4	Only 15% of them (the attendees) ordered 30# of item #5011.

B. NUMBER PRACTICE

Type each line 2 times.

5 we 23 ort 945 rep 430 pot 095 toy 596 yip 680 yow 692 it 85
6 tee 533 ore 943 weep 2330 pop 090 poi 098 top 590 quit 1785
7 quip 1780 tip 580 woo 299 try 546 out 975 pro 049 quay 1716

C. SUSTAINED PRACTICE: NUMBERS

Take a 1-minute timed writing on the boxed paragraph to establish your base speed. Then take a 1-minute timed writing on the following paragraph. As soon as you equal or exceed your base speed on this paragraph, move to the next, more difficult paragraph.

8 Michael learned through firsthand experience last week 11
9 that the cost of a week at the beach varies a great deal. 23
10 He says that a rowboat would be about right for his money. 34

11 His Uncle Bo told him that when he was his age, he had 11
12 rented a small cabin for the huge sum of $105 for one week. 23
13 For $23 more, he rented a small boat and outboard motor. 34

14 Then Uncle Bo went on to say that when he rented the 11
15 same cabin last year, the cost had gone up to either $395 22
16 or $410. Boat and motor rentals now cost from $62 to $87. 34

17 Aunt Kate said that she and her husband will be paying 11
18 either $1,946 or $2,073 for a week's sailing on the 53-foot 23
19 yacht. The boat has a 4-person crew and was built in 2006. 35

1 | 2 | 3 | 4 | 5 | 6 | 7 | 8 | 9 | 10 | 11 | 12

D. PACED PRACTICE

Follow the GDP software directions for this exercise to improve keystroking speed and accuracy.

E. PARAGRAPH TYPING

Type each paragraph 2 times.

20 I saw five or six of the big jet planes zoom quickly 11
21 over an old tower by the side of the road. They were flying 23
22 in formation and created a beautiful display for everyone. 34

23 Brown jars of an acidic mixture prevented the solution 11
24 from freezing so quickly. It took about four days for it to 23
25 freeze solid; then we could store it in the lab's freezer. 35

1 | 2 | 3 | 4 | 5 | 6 | 7 | 8 | 9 | 10 | 11 | 12

New Keys

Goals

- Touch-type the " ! and * keys.
- Type at least 27wpm/2'/5e.

A. WARMUP

alphabet 1 The jinxed wizards plucked the ivy stem from the big quilt.
frequent digraphs 2 on bon con none noon don ion one son ton won onto moon font
easy 3 Jan and her son may make a bowl of fish and a cup of cocoa.

New Keys

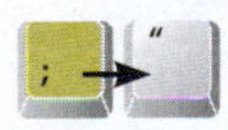

Use the Sem finger.

B. THE " KEY

The quotation key is the shift of the apostrophe. Do not space between quotation marks and the text they enclose.

4 ;;; ;"; ;"; ";" ";" """ "Thanks," he said, "I needed that."
5 I read her article, "Freaking Out," and said, "It is great."
6 "Those were wonderful," Fidel said. "I'll take seven more."
7 Juan wanted to know if the name was "Roberto" or "Roberta."

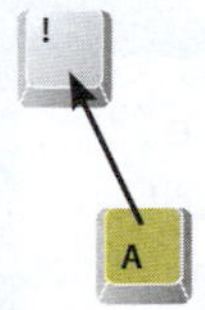

Use the A finger.

C. THE ! KEY

The exclamation mark is the shift of 1. Space 1 time after an exclamation mark.

8 aaa aqa a!a a!a !a! !a! !!! Wow! Now! Go! Stay! Sit! Nurse!
9 Put it down! Do not move! Leave it there! Get out! Move it!
10 Ouch! That hurt! Let's roll! Incredible! Hang in there! No!
11 Congratulations! That was great! Don't shoot! Oh, no! Help!

Use the K finger.

D. THE * KEY

The asterisk is the shift of 8. Do not space before the asterisk but space 1 time after the asterisk.

```
12 kkk kik k*k k*k *k* *k* *** p. 18* as follows:* Note* etc.*
13 An * may be used to indicate a footnote at the page bottom.
14 In the footnote itself, do not leave any space after the *.
15 Did he really call Mr. Baines a *****? Wow! That was awful!
```

Skillbuilding

E. NEW-KEY REVIEW

```
16 The right word* was "parenthesis" instead of "parentheses."
17 "Wow!" Aki said, "That* was an amazing display! Go see it."
18 "Only one* was allowed in," said Jin. "It was Mr. Mystery."
19 The source* was absolutely reliable! "I agree," Yaron said.
```

MAP+

F. MAP+: NUMBERS

Follow the GDP software directions for this exercise to improve keystroking accuracy.

G. PLACEMENT OF QUOTATION MARKS

1. The closing quotation mark is always typed *after* a period or comma (line 20) but *before* a colon or semicolon (line 21).
2. The closing quotation mark is typed *after* a question mark or exclamation point if the quoted material itself is a question or an exclamation (line 22). Otherwise, the quotation mark is typed *before* the question mark or exclamation point (line 23).

```
20 "Hi, there," I said. "My name is Karen, and I am new here."
21 James said, "I'll mail the check tomorrow"; but he did not.
22 Raheem read the article "Will They Succeed on the Economy?"
23 Did Anne say, "We won"? I was shocked when Juan said, "Me"!
```

H. PACED PRACTICE

Follow the GDP software directions for this exercise to improve keystroking speed and accuracy.

I. TECHNIQUE PRACTICE: TAB KEY

Press Tab where you see the →.

24 Orr→ Ike→ zoo→ Jon→ apt→ Pat→ ado→ zap→ Ned→ asp→ zag
25 Jan→ Lev→ Kit→ Ida→ Joy→ ads→ Joe→ ago→ Ima→ are→ ace
26 Mac→ Jim→ ate→ Lou→ Mia→ zed→ add→ Pia→ Moe→ Lot→ Jay
27 zip→ Obi→ Mom→ aft→ Job→ age→ Ham→ Ott→ awl→ art→ Hsu

J. 2-MINUTE TIMED WRITING

Take two 2-minute timed writings.

Goal: At least 27wpm/2'/5e

28 Topaz and onyx rings were for sale at very reasonable 11
29 prices last month. When Jeanette saw the rings with these 23
30 stones, she quickly bought them both for her sons. These 34
31 jewels were difficult to find, and Jeanette was pleased 45
32 she could purchase those rings when she did. 54

1 | 2 | 3 | 4 | 5 | 6 | 7 | 8 | 9 | 10 | 11 | 12

Strategies for Career Success

Being a Good Listener

Silence is golden! Listening is essential for learning, getting along, and forming relationships.

Do you tend to forget people's names after being introduced? Do you look away from the speaker instead of making eye contact? Do you interrupt the speaker before he or she finishes talking? Do you misunderstand people? Answering yes can indicate poor listening skills.

To improve your listening skills, follow these steps. *Hear the speaker clearly.* Do not interrupt; let the speaker develop his or her ideas before you speak. *Focus on the message.* At the end of a conversation, identify major items discussed. Mentally ask questions to help you assess the points the speaker is making. *Keep an open mind.* Do not judge. Developing your listening skills benefits everyone.

Your Turn: Assess your listening behavior. What techniques can you use to improve your listening skills? Practice them the next time you have a conversation with someone.

Enrichment • Lesson 19

Type each line 2 times.

A. NEW-KEY REINFORCEMENT

" 1 "If we go," Arif said, "we will need to find a substitute."
! 2 Goodness! I can't believe that! He must have been in shock!
* 3 The real reason* may never be known about those strangers.*
" ! * 4 "Umberto's exact remarks* were shocking, to say the least!"

PPP PRETEST » PRACTICE » POSTTEST

PRETEST
Take a 1-minute timed writing.

B. PRETEST: Discrimination Practice

5 Few of us were as lucky as Bev was when she joined us 12
6 for golf. She just dreaded the look of the work crew when 24
7 she goofed. But she neatly swung a club and aced the hole. 36
1 | 2 | 3 | 4 | 5 | 6 | 7 | 8 | 9 | 10 | 11 | 12

PRACTICE
Speed Emphasis:
If you made no more than 2 errors on the Pretest, type each *individual* line 2 times.
Accuracy Emphasis:
If you made 3 or more errors, type each *group* of lines (as though it were a paragraph) 2 times.

C. PRACTICE: Left Hand

8 vbv behaves verb bevy vibes bevel brave above verbal bovine
9 wew dewdrop west weep threw wedge weave fewer weight sewing
10 ded precede deed seed bride guide dealt cried secede parted

D. PRACTICE: Right Hand

11 klk kindle kiln lake knoll lanky locks liken kettle knuckle
12 uyu untidy buys your usury unity youth buoys unruly younger
13 oio iodine coin lion oiled foils foist prior oilcan iodized

POSTTEST
Repeat the Pretest timed writing and compare performance.

E. POSTTEST: Discrimination Practice

Type each paragraph 2 times.

F. PARAGRAPH PRACTICE

14 Only a very few phlox grew or even bloomed just in 10
15 back of my old zinc quarry. I think the reason was that the 22
16 zinc had leached into the soil, making plants hard to grow. 34
17 She promptly judged the antique ivory buckles that 10
18 were made for the county fair. They won a prize. Next, we 22
19 moved on to judging the cakes and pies, which we all liked. 34
1 | 2 | 3 | 4 | 5 | 6 | 7 | 8 | 9 | 10 | 11 | 12

Review

Goals

- Type at least 28wpm/2'/5e.

A. WARMUP

alphabet	1	West quickly gave Bert handsome prizes for six juicy plums.
number/symbol	2	gilp@comcast.net (11%) Ng & Ma 4/5 No! $13.86 *Est. #20-972
easy	3	Rodney may risk half of his profits for the old oak mantel.

Skillbuilding

B. NUMBER-KEY REVIEW

4 With 37,548 fans screaming, we won the game 10-9 on May 26.
5 He went to Rome on May 30, 1975, and left on July 24, 1986.
6 Seats 10, 29, 38, 47, and 56 are still unsold for tomorrow.
7 Our store will be open from 7:30 to 9:45 on February 18-26.

8 The 29 teachers and 754 students arrived at 8:30 on May 16.
9 Call 555-3190 and clarify our $826.47 charge for equipment.
10 Order No. 3874 for $165.20 did not arrive until October 19.
11 Al's sales for the last month went from $35,786 to $41,290.

C. PUNCTUATION REVIEW

.	12	Stand here. Sit down. Rest a minute. Relax. Breathe deeply.
?	13	Can it wait? Why not? Can he drive? Where is it? Who knows?
!	14	No! Stop! Don't look! Watch out! Move it over! Jump! Do it!
,	15	Inga, Lev, and I worked, rested, and then worked some more.
;	16	First, read the directions; next, practice; and then build.
:	17	Be on call at these times: 9:30, 12:30, 2:30, and 3:30 p.m.
-	18	It was a once-in-a-lifetime experience for Kay Jones-Lange.
'	19	It's Lynn's job to cover Maria's telephone when she's gone.
/	20	Two/thirds of us and one/fourth of them came on 12/10/2009.
"	21	I watched "Meet the Mets" and "Yankee Power" on the screen.

D. SYMBOL REVIEW

@	22	Order 12 items @ $114, 9 @ $99, and another 18 items @ $87.
#	23	My favorite seats for this year are #92, #83, #74, and #65.
$	24	She received quotes of $48, $52, and $76 for the old radio.
%	25	Ramos scored 93% on the test, Sue had 88%, and Al made 84%.
&	26	Rudd & Sons bought their ten tickets from Cross & Thompson.
*	27	The * sign, the asterisk, is used for reference purposes.**
( )	28	The typist is (a) speedy, (b) accurate, and (c) productive.

E. MAP+: SYMBOLS

Follow the GDP software directions for this exercise to improve keystroking accuracy.

F. 12-SECOND SPEED SPRINTS

Take three 12-second timed writings on each line. The scale below the last line shows your wpm speed for a 12-second timed writing.

29 Kay and she may both visit us in May when they are in town.
30 She may go with me to the city to visit my son and his pal.
31 His body of work may charm the guests who visit the chapel.
32 That new city law may help us to fish for cod on the docks.

5 | 10 | 15 | 20 | 25 | 30 | 35 | 40 | 45 | 50 | 55 | 60

G. 2-MINUTE TIMED WRITING

Take two 2-minute timed writings.

Goal: At least 28wpm/2'/5e

33	Jake or Peggy Zale must quickly fix the fax machine	11
34	so that we can have access to regional reports that we	22
35	think might be sent within the next few days. Without the	33
36	fax, we will not be able to finish all our monthly reports	45
37	by the deadline. Please let Peggy know of any problems.	56

1 | 2 | 3 | 4 | 5 | 6 | 7 | 8 | 9 | 10 | 11 | 12

Enrichment • Lesson 20

A. SUSTAINED PRACTICE: SYMBOLS

Take a 1-minute timed writing on the boxed paragraph to establish your base speed. Then take a 1-minute timed writing on the following paragraph. As soon as you equal or exceed your base speed on this paragraph, move to the next, more difficult paragraph.

```
1      It was quite normal that Patty was somewhat nervous as  11
2  she entered the college building. After four years of work  23
3  as a clerk, she was here to take the college entrance exam. 35

4      Just as you have likely done, Patty took her #2 pencil  11
5  and began to fill in the score sheet. A test administrator  23
6  (Mr. Graham) had said that a grade of 75% would be passing. 35

7      Patty had come to Room #68 (a large lecture hall) from  11
8  the Stone & Carpenter accounting firm. It's a "mighty long  23
9  hike," and almost 100% of the examinees were already there. 35

10     For a $25 fee, everyone in Room #68 (the test site)     11
11 answered the "moderately difficult" true-false or A/B/C/D   23
12 questions; 40% had used the Dun & Bradstreet study guide.   34
     1 | 2 | 3 | 4 | 5 | 6 | 7 | 8 | 9 | 10 | 11 | 12
```

B. TECHNIQUE PRACTICE: ENTER KEY

Type each line 2 times. Type each sentence on a separate line by pressing ENTER after each sentence.

```
13 Ed saw her. Ah. What? We do. Speak. Stop. Go. No. Begin it.
14 Thanks. Stop. Why not? See? Get it? Who, me? Well? She can.
15 See me. Who? Read it. What? Really! Why me? So soon? Do it.
16 Who knew? Enough? What is it? Go now. She did. Why not? So?
```

C. NUMBER PRACTICE

Type each line 2 times.

```
17 we 23 pro 049 too 599 wit 285 toe 593 wet 235 eye 363 IQ 81
18 pit 085 opts 9052 wow 292 quiz 1781 pep 030 pow 092 tow 592
19 you 697 tors 5942 ewe 323 tot 595 ere 343 wry 246 quit 1785
```

D. PARAGRAPH TYPING

Type each paragraph 2 times.

```
20     A campus TV quiz show just asked one contestant why     11
21 gold was buried at Fort Knox. No one knew the answer, so    22
22 they moved on to the business category, which was easier.   33

23     A few of the black taxis drove up the major road on     11
24 the hazy night. Because the hour was so late, they could    22
25 not find passengers needing rides, so they quickly left.    33

26     Jay took a big quiz and exam even though he suffered    11
27 a lower back pain that forced him to be very careful with   22
28 how he moved during the test. Fortunately, he aced it.      33
     1 | 2 | 3 | 4 | 5 | 6 | 7 | 8 | 9 | 10 | 11 | 12
```

Supplementary Lesson: Ten-Key Numeric Keypad

Goals

- Touch-type the ten-key numeric keypad keys.

New Keys

A. THE , , AND  KEYS

To input numbers using the ten-key numeric keypad, you must activate the NUM LOCK (Numeric Lock) key. Usually, an indicator light signals that the NUM LOCK is activated.

On the keypad, 4, 5, and 6 are the home-row keys. Place your fingers on the keypad home row as follows:

- J finger on 4
- K finger on 5
- L finger on 6

On most computers, there is a raised line or dot on the 5 key to help you easily locate the home-row position when using the keypad.

Use your Sem finger to control the ENTER key. For the exercises in A–F that follow:

1. Ensure that NUM LOCK is activated.
2. Press ENTER after typing the final digit of each number.
3. Type the first column from top to bottom; then move to the next column.
4. Keep your eyes on the copy.

1	444	455	466	544	566
2	555	644	656	456	654
3	666	445	466	554	556
4	664	665	456	654	454
5	464	546	564	655	456

B. THE , , AND  KEYS

Use the J finger to control the 7, the K finger to control the 8, and the L finger to control the 9.

6	474	585	696	549	984
7	747	858	969	485	645
8	774	885	996	658	489
9	447	558	669	846	647
10	744	855	966	476	867

C. THE 1, 2, AND 3 KEYS

Use the J finger to control the 1, the K finger to control the 2, and the L finger to control the 3.

11	414	525	636	215	326
12	141	225	336	634	435
13	144	552	663	324	145
14	441	255	636	263	346
15	144	252	363	431	265

D. THE 0 KEY

Use the right thumb to control the 0.

16	404	901	580	407	802
17	505	101	690	508	506
18	606	202	410	609	700
19	707	303	520	140	800
20	808	470	630	250	900

E. THE . KEY

Use the L finger to control the decimal (.) key.

21	6.6	7.6	1.2	6.5	9.8
22	3.2	4.4	7.7	5.5	8.8
23	2.2	6.6	9.3	1.1	1.0
24	3.1	8.4	7.1	9.3	3.4
25	4.5	8.3	9.9	6.5	3.8

Skillbuilding

F. NEW-KEY REVIEW

26	526	081	175	14.7	70.3	868	115
27	451	736	672	80.4	68.0	280	505
28	450	148	761	68.0	69.4	258	739
29	017	856	702	28.0	86.5	42	700
30	023	924	028	63.4	58.2	608	35
31	715	846	315	5.98	7.10	617	290
32	039	760	316	8.40	6.25	74	961
33	401	650	612	5.87	4.20	600	307
34	419	694	427	8.01	9.31	620	3
35	685	948	432	7.50	8.41	929	302

Enrichment • Supplementary Lesson

A. THE  KEY

Use the Sem finger to control the plus (+) key. Press the plus key after each number except the last number in a column. Press ENTER after the last number to display the total.

1	310+	698+	579+	747+	706+
2	845+	252+	999+	833+	126+
3	133+	320+	841+	599+	403+
4	603	484	782	738	180

B. THE / KEY

Use the K finger to control the division (/) key. Press ENTER after the second number in each column to display the result.

5	858/728	912/771	814/238	542/236	956/895
6	595/104	527/970	739/129	771/292	590/485
7	121/494	181/376	984/533	814/820	836/237
8	696/998	293/432	160/189	485/181	922/172

C. THE - KEY

Use the Sem finger to control the minus (-) key. Press ENTER after the second number in each column to display the result.

9	826-477	929-229	332-519	378-112	53.4-31.2
10	569-873	350-847	571-334	878-766	82.6-26.6
11	970-856	528-428	402-986	745-830	55.8-80.2
12	250-152	190-346	439-109	526-923	66.4-41.1

D. THE * KEY

Use the L finger to control the multiplication (*) key. Press ENTER after the second number in each column to display the result.

13	406*363	733*835	923*419	645*618	21.8*18.6
14	214*331	554*843	492*103	135*889	58.8*70.7
15	199*927	572*604	756*375	276*942	84.4*77.1
16	885*286	778*358	601*793	192*672	19.3*99.0

E. NUMERIC KEYPAD REVIEW

Type the first column from top to bottom; then move to the next column. Press ENTER after the last number in each column to display the result.

17	933+	790/	338*	878-	512+	587+	764/
18	655-	835-	903+	444+	537*	25-	791-
19	175*	186*	579/	324/	890-	836*	762*
20	217	614	247	868	563	546	912

Basic Business Documents

PART 2

Opportunities in Business and Administrative Careers

Occupations in the business and administrative services cluster focus on providing management and support services for various companies. The many positions found in this cluster include receptionist, bookkeeper, administrative professional or assistant, claim examiner, accountant, word processor, office manager, and chief executive officer. Managers and administrators are in charge of planning, organizing, and controlling businesses.

Management support workers gather and analyze data to help company executives make decisions. Administrative support workers perform a variety of tasks, such as recordkeeping, operating office equipment, managing their own projects and assignments, and developing high-level integrated software skills as well as Internet research skills. Ideally, everyone in business should be patient, detail-oriented, and cooperative. Excellent written and oral communication skills are definitely an asset as well.

Many companies have been revolutionized by advances in computer technology. As a result, keyboarding skill provides a definite advantage for those who work in business and administrative services. Now, more than ever, success in the business world is dependent upon adaptability and education.

Goals

Keyboarding

- Demonstrate improved speed and accuracy when operating the keyboard by touch.
- Type at least 36 words per minute on a 3-minute timed writing with no more than 4 errors.

Language Arts

- Demonstrate acceptable proofreading skills, including using proofreaders' marks correctly.
- Demonstrate acceptable language arts skills in punctuation and grammar.
- Demonstrate acceptable composing and spelling skills.

Word Processing

- Use appropriate word processing commands necessary to complete document processing activities successfully.

Document Processing

- Correctly format e-mail, correspondence, reports, and tables.

Objective Test

- Answer questions with acceptable accuracy on an objective test.

Word Processing and E-Mail

LESSON 21
Orientation to Word Processing—A

LESSON 22
Orientation to Word Processing—B

LESSON 23
Orientation to Word Processing—C

LESSON 24
Orientation to Word Processing—D

LESSON 25
E-Mail Messages

Orientation to Word Processing—A

Goals

- Demonstrate improved speed and accuracy while typing.
- Demonstrate acceptable language arts skills in comma usage and sentence structure.
- Correctly use the Word Manual and basic Word features.

A. WARMUP

alphabet	1	Jack's eloquence may prove hazardous for the six big shows.
concentration	2	deindustrialization superstitiousnesses comprehensibilities
easy	3	The new dogma may both disorient her and also let her down.

Skillbuilding

B. MAP+: ALPHABET

Follow the GDP software directions for this exercise to improve keystroking accuracy.

C. PROGRESSIVE PRACTICE: ALPHABET

Follow the GDP software directions for this exercise to improve keystroking speed.

Language Arts

Study the rules at the right.

D. COMMAS AND SENTENCES

Note: The callout signals in the left margin indicate which language arts rule from this lesson has been applied.

RULE , direct address

Use commas before and after a name used in direct address.

Thank you, John, for responding to my e-mail so quickly.
Ladies and gentlemen, the program has been canceled.

RULE fragment

Avoid sentence fragments.

Not: She had always wanted to be a financial manager. But had not had the needed education.
But: She had always wanted to be a financial manager but had not had the needed education.

Note: A fragment is a part of a sentence that is incorrectly punctuated as a complete sentence. In the first sentence above, "but had not had the needed education" is not a complete sentence because it does not contain a subject.

RULE
run-on

Avoid run-on sentences.

Not: Mohamed is a competent worker he has even passed the MCSE exam.
Not: Mohamed is a competent worker, he has even passed the MCSE exam.
But: Mohamed is a competent worker; he has even passed the MCSE exam.
Or: Mohamed is a competent worker. He has even passed the MCSE exam.

Note: A run-on sentence is two independent clauses that run together without any punctuation between them or with only a comma between them.

Edit each sentence to correct any errors.

```
4  You must be certain, Sean that every e-mail message is
5  concise. And also complete.

6  In addition, Sean, use a clear subject line the subject line
7  describes briefly the principal content of the e-mail
8  message.

9  You should use a direct style of writing, use short lines
10 and paragraphs.

11 The recipient of your e-mail message will be more likely to
12 read and respond to a short message. Than a long one.

13 Your reader will be grateful for any writing techniques.
14 That save time.

15 Another thing you should do Sean is to include an
16 appropriate closing, your reader should know immediately who
17 wrote the message.
```

Formatting

E. WORD PROCESSING: GETTING STARTED AND ORIENTATION TO WORD PROCESSING—A

Study Getting Started and Lesson 21 in your Word Manual. Complete all of the shaded steps while at your computer.

Orientation to Word Processing—B

Goals

- Type at least 28wpm/3′/5e.
- Correctly use basic Word features.

A. WARMUP

alphabet	1	Jay took a big quiz and exam that forced a vast lower pain.
one hand	2	garage homily sea oil seated Honolulu ever jump eager plunk
easy	3	Nancy may go to the ancient chapel to sign her widow's vow.

Skillbuilding

B. SUSTAINED PRACTICE: CAPITALS

Take a 1-minute timed writing on the boxed paragraph to establish your base speed. Then take a 1-minute timed writing on the following paragraph. As soon as you equal or exceed your base speed on this paragraph, move to the next, more difficult paragraph.

```
 4      The insurance industry will see some changes because   11
 5  of the many natural disasters the United States has seen in 23
 6  the last few years in places like California and Florida.   34

 7      The major earthquakes in San Francisco, Northridge,     11
 8  and Loma Prieta cost thousands of dollars. Faults like      22
 9  the San Andreas are being watched carefully for activity.   33

10      Some tropical storms are spawned in the West Indies     11
11  and move from the Caribbean Sea into the Atlantic Ocean.    22
12  They could affect Georgia, Florida, Alabama, and Texas.     33

13      Some U.S. cities have VHF-FM radio weather stations.    11
14  NASA and NOAA are agencies that launch weather satellites   22
15  to predict the locations, times, and severity of storms.    34
      1 | 2 | 3 | 4 | 5 | 6 | 7 | 8 | 9 | 10 | 11 | 12
```

C. 3-MINUTE TIMED WRITING

Take two 3-minute timed writings.

Goal: At least 28wpm/3′/5e

```
16      Once you learn to use a variety of software programs,   11
17  you will feel confident and comfortable as you are using a  23
18  computer. All you have to do is take that first step and    34
19  decide to strive for excellence.                            41
20      Initially, you might have several questions as you      51
21  gaze up at a screen that is filled with icons. If you try   63
22  to learn to use just one or two commands each day, you may  75
23  soon find that using software is very exciting.             84
      1 | 2 | 3 | 4 | 5 | 6 | 7 | 8 | 9 | 10 | 11 | 12
```

D. WORD PROCESSING: ORIENTATION TO WORD PROCESSING—B

Study Lesson 22 in your Word Manual. Complete all of the shaded steps while at your computer.

Orientation to Word Processing—C

Goals

- Demonstrate improved speed and accuracy while typing.
- Demonstrate acceptable proofreading skills by comparing lines.
- Correctly use basic Word features.

A. WARMUP

alphabet
1 The lazy major was fixing Cupid's broken quiver and arrows.

practice: *o* and *i*
2 oil Rio boil folio polio coin icon into Ohio olio silo void

easy
3 Mr. Richfield is such a busy man he may not go via the bus.

Skillbuilding

B. MAP+: NUMBERS

Follow the GDP software directions for this exercise to improve keystroking accuracy.

PPP PRETEST » PRACTICE » POSTTEST

C. PRETEST: Common Letter Combinations

PRETEST
Take a 1-minute timed writing. Review your speed and errors.

4 He tried to explain the delay in a logical way. The 11
5 man finally agreed to insure the package and demanded to 22
6 know why the postal worker did not record the total amount. 34

1 | 2 | 3 | 4 | 5 | 6 | 7 | 8 | 9 | 10 | 11 | 12

D. PRACTICE: Word Beginnings

PRACTICE
Speed Emphasis:
If you made 2 or fewer errors on the Pretest, type each *individual* line 2 times.
Accuracy Emphasis:
If you made 3 or more errors, type each *group* of lines (as though it were a paragraph) 2 times.

7 re reuse react relay reply return reason record results red
8 in inset inept incur index indeed intend inning insured ink
9 de dents dealt death delay detest devote derive depicts den

E. PRACTICE: Word Endings

10 ly lowly dimly apply daily barely unruly deeply finally sly
11 ed cured tamed tried moved amused tasted billed creamed fed
12 al canal total equal local postal plural rental logical pal

F. POSTTEST: Common Letter Combinations

POSTTEST
Repeat the Pretest timed writing and compare performance.

Language Arts

Study the proofreading techniques at the right.

G. PROOFREADING TECHNIQUES

Proofreading and correcting errors are essential parts of document processing. To become an expert proofreader:

1. Use Word's spelling feature to check for spelling errors; then read the copy aloud to see if it makes sense.
2. Proofread for all kinds of errors, especially repeated, missing, or transposed words; grammar and punctuation; and numbers and names.
3. Check for formatting errors such as line spacing, tabs, margins, and use of bold.

Compare these lines with lines 4–7 on page 83. Edit the lines to correct any errors.

H. PROOFREADING

```
13 A bushal of corn was thrown under the elm trees by the boy.
14 A pair of cosy socks and a cup of soup can fix me right up.
15 Andy will use eight hand singals if he is able to see them.
16 Blanche may go with me to town to visit my son and his pal.
```

Formatting

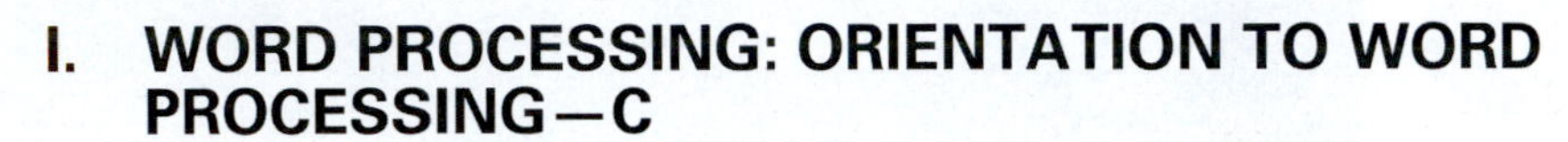

I. WORD PROCESSING: ORIENTATION TO WORD PROCESSING—C

Study Lesson 23 in your Word Manual. Complete all of the shaded steps while at your computer.

Keyboarding Connection

Using Search Engines

How can you most efficiently find information on the Internet? Use a search engine! A search engine guides you to the Internet's resources. It analyzes the information you request, navigates the Internet's many networks, and retrieves a list of relevant Web sites. Google is one of the most popular search engines; others are Yahoo, Ask.com, and Microsoft's Bing.com.

A search engine examines electronic databases, wire services, journals, article summaries, articles, home pages, and user group lists. It can access material found in millions of Web sites. When you search on a specific key word, a search engine scans its large database, searches the content of Web pages, and then displays the information that most closely matches the words you're searching for.

Many large Web sites have a search function built in. This allows you to search only that site for relevant Web pages and information, like job postings on a company Web site or articles about a specific topic on a news Web site.

Your Turn: Try different search engines, and see which ones you like best. Choose three of your favorite search engines. Then conduct a search using the key words "touch typing." (Don't forget the quotation marks, but leave out the period.) Compare the results for each search engine.

Orientation to Word Processing—D

Goals

- Type at least 29wpm/3′/5e.
- Correctly use basic Word features.

A. WARMUP

alphabet 1 Xavier had picked several bright yellow jonquils for Mitzi.
frequent digraphs 2 in ink nine chin pin kind main sin mind tin skinny win inns
easy 3 A bushel of mangos and a box of grapes may be on the canoe.

Skillbuilding

B. PROGRESSIVE PRACTICE: NUMBERS

Follow the GDP software directions for this exercise to improve keystroking speed.

C. TECHNIQUE PRACTICE: SPACE BAR

Type each line 2 times, using your right thumb to strike the SPACE BAR in the center.

4 Ed and Jo can get to the spa if it is on the way to my car.
5 I hid a big car in my new lot, but I may not get it by two.
6 An elk and ape at the zoo do not eat any of the cod or gar.
7 I had a tan dog and a red cat on the big set for Jo to pet.

D. 3-MINUTE TIMED WRITING

Take two 3-minute timed writings.

Goal: At least 29wpm/3′/5e

8 If you ever feel tired as you are typing, you should 11
9 take a rest. Question what you are doing that is causing 22
10 your muscles to be fatigued. You will realize that you 33
11 can change the fundamental source of your anxiety. 43
12 Take a deep breath and enjoy the relaxing feeling as 54
13 you exhale slowly. Check your posture to be sure that you 66
14 are sitting up straight with your back against the chair. 78
15 Stretch your neck and back for full relaxation. 87
1 | 2 | 3 | 4 | 5 | 6 | 7 | 8 | 9 | 10 | 11 | 12

Formatting

E. WORD PROCESSING: ORIENTATION TO WORD PROCESSING—D

Study Lesson 24 in your Word Manual. Complete all of the shaded steps while at your computer.

Strategies for Career Success

Preparing a Job Interview Portfolio

Don't go empty-handed to that job interview! Take a portfolio of items with you. Definitely include copies of your resume and your list of references, with at least three professional references. Your academic transcript is useful, especially if you are asked to complete a company application form. Appropriate work samples and copies of certificates and licenses are also helpful portfolio items.

The interview process provides you the opportunity to interview the organization. Include a list of questions you want to ask during the interview.

A comprehensive portfolio of materials will benefit you by giving you a measure of control during the interview process.

Your Turn: Start today to compile items for your interview portfolio. Include copies of your resume, your reference list, and copies of certificates and licenses. Begin developing a list of interview questions. Think about appropriate work samples to include in your portfolio.

E-Mail Messages

Goals

- Demonstrate improved speed and accuracy while typing.
- Demonstrate acceptable language arts skills in composing sentences.
- Correctly use Word's e-mail feature.
- Correctly format an e-mail message.

A. WARMUP

alphabet 1 Playing jazzy vibe chords quickly excited my wife's senses.
number/symbol 2 (ali41@cs.com) (10%) Guy & Lee 7/8 In! $5.40 *f.o.b. #26-39
easy 3 Did an auditor sign a form that may name Toby to the panel?

Skillbuilding

B. 12-SECOND SPEED SPRINTS

Take three 12-second timed writings on each line.

4 A bushel of corn was thrown under the elm tree by the boys.
5 A pair of cozy socks and a cup of soup may fix me right up.
6 Andy will use eight hand signals if he is able to see them.
7 Blanch may go with me to town to visit my son and his pals.
' ' ' ' 5 ' ' ' ' 10 ' ' ' ' 15 ' ' ' ' 20 ' ' ' ' 25 ' ' ' ' 30 ' ' ' ' 35 ' ' ' ' 40 ' ' ' ' 45 ' ' ' ' 50 ' ' ' ' 55 ' ' ' ' 60

C. PACED PRACTICE

Follow the GDP software directions for this exercise to improve keystroking speed and accuracy.

Language Arts

D. COMPOSING SENTENCES

Answer each question with a complete sentence.

8 What is your favorite class this term, and why?
9 What is your ideal job when you graduate?
10 If you could live in a foreign country, which one would it be, and why?
11 What are your two favorite Internet sites?
12 What qualities do you look for in a friend?

E. BASIC PARTS OF AN E-MAIL MESSAGE

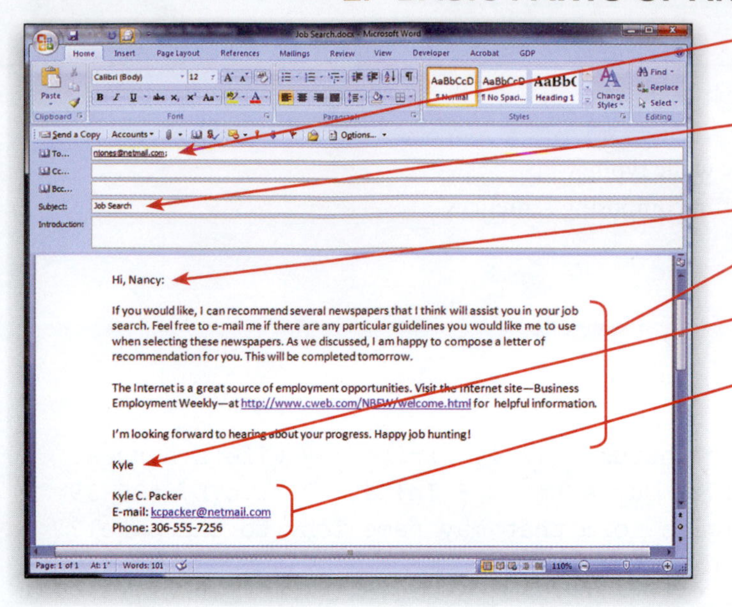

TO BOX. Contains the name or e-mail address of each recipient; each name and/or address is usually separated by a semicolon or comma.

SUBJECT BOX. Contains a descriptive name for the message; typed with upper- and lowercase letters.

GREETING. Friendly opening; followed by a colon.

BODY. Message; type with short lines and paragraphs in plain text.

SENDER'S NAME. Sender's first name or first and last name.

WRITER'S IDENTIFICATION. Writer's identity and contact information; also known as a "signature" in some e-mail software.

F. E-MAIL MESSAGES

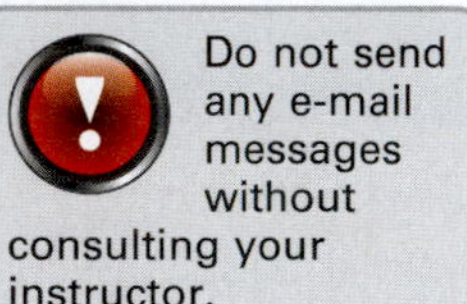
Do not send any e-mail messages without consulting your instructor.

R-5C and R-5D: E-Mail Message in Microsoft Outlook/Internet Explorer and E-Mail Message in MSN Hotmail

To format an e-mail message:

1. Use the address book feature or type the e-mail address of each recipient in the *To*, *Cc*, or *Bcc* box. A semicolon or comma is usually automatically inserted to separate several names.
2. If you use the reply feature, include the original message only if it helps the reader remember the topic more easily.
3. Use a descriptive, concise subject line with upper- and lowercase letters.

   Example: Items for Meeting Agenda

4. Use the attachment feature if you need to attach a file or document.
5. Use a friendly greeting. Follow the greeting with a colon. Use the recipient's first name or a courtesy title and last name for a more businesslike greeting.

   Examples: Hi, Jim: or Jim: or Mr. Andrews:

   Note: A greeting is optional but will be used throughout this book.

6. Keep paragraphs short, and type them with normal capitalization and punctuation. Typing in all-caps is considered shouting.
7. Type paragraphs single-spaced, and do *not* indent paragraphs.
8. Press ENTER 2 times between paragraphs only—do *not* press ENTER when you see a line break in the text.
9. After the last paragraph, press ENTER 2 times.

The remaining steps will vary depending upon your e-mail program. If your e-mail program inserts a signature automatically, you do not have to take any further steps other than proofreading. Refer to your e-mail software Help feature for steps on inserting a signature. If your e-mail software does not include a signature feature (and for the purposes of formatting e-mail messages consistently in this textbook), follow these steps:

1. Type your first name only for a friendlier closing, or type both your first and last name for a more businesslike closing. Press ENTER 2 times.

   Example: Sandy or Sandy Hill

   Note: A closing name is optional but will be used throughout this book.

2. Type your e-mail address, press ENTER, and type your phone number as shown in this example.

   Example:
   Sandra R. Hill
   E-mail: srhill@server.com
   Phone: 661-555-1223

3. Spell-check, proofread, and preview your document for spelling and formatting errors.
4. Type all e-mail messages using standard e-mail format. In this book, you will type only the e-mail greeting, body, and closing for all e-mail messages.
5. Refer to the model document on page 84 for correct formatting.

G. WORD PROCESSING: E-MAIL A DOCUMENT AND GDP REFERENCE MANUAL

Study Lesson 25 in your Word Manual. Complete all of the shaded steps while at your computer. Then format the documents that follow.

Document Processing

Correspondence
25-1
E-Mail Message

Press ENTER 2 times *only between paragraphs* when you see ↓2X. In Word, lines wrap automatically as you approach the right margin. Your line endings in Word will *not* match those in the book.

Hi, Renee: ↓2X

E-mail is easier to read when the message and subject line are short and concise. The paragraphs should be broken up into small ones whenever possible. ↓2X

If you wish to send a social e-mail to a large number of recipients, consider typing their e-mail addresses in the Bcc box, which stands for "blind carbon copy," rather than in the To box. This practice helps reduce spam junk mail, and your friends will appreciate your courtesy.

To add a friendly feeling to your message, greet your recipient by name. Adding your name in the signature also adds a personal touch. Make it easy for your reader to contact you by including a signature line that includes your name, e-mail address, and phone number if desired.

Proofread carefully for errors in typing, spelling, and formatting. Remember, Renee, that once you click the Send button, you can't get it back. Write messages you would be proud to have the world read. It could happen. ↓2X

Edward ↓2X

Edward Garcia
E-mail: egarcia@quickmail.com
Phone: 701-555-4832

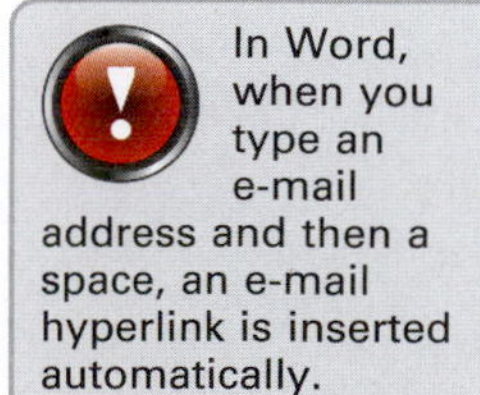

In Word, when you type an e-mail address and then a space, an e-mail hyperlink is inserted automatically.

Correspondence
25-2
E-Mail Message

The ¶ symbol indicates a new, blocked paragraph. The | symbol indicates the end of a line. Press ENTER as many times as needed.

Hi, Kim:
¶ I now have e-mail access using my new phone. You can send me the photos you took at our annual meeting because I will be able to access them immediately.
¶ Thank you, Kim, for bringing your digital camera to the meeting so that we could all enjoy the photos you took.
John | John Sanchez | E-mail: jsanchez@brightway.net | Phone: 404-555-6823

Strategies for Career Success

Goodwill Messages

Would you like to strengthen your relationship with a customer, coworker, or boss? Send an unexpected goodwill message! Your expression of goodwill has a positive effect on business relationships.

Messages of congratulations or appreciation provide special opportunities to express goodwill. These messages can be quite brief. If your handwriting is good, send a handwritten note on a professional note card. Otherwise, send a letter or e-mail.

A note of congratulations might be "I just heard the news about your (award, promotion, etc.). My very best wishes." An appreciation note could be "Thank you for referring me to . . . Your confidence and trust are sincerely appreciated."

Your Turn: Send a goodwill message to someone to express congratulations or appreciation.

UNIT 6

Correspondence

LESSON 26

Business Letters

LESSON 27

Business Letters With Enclosure Notations

LESSON 28

Envelopes and Labels

LESSON 29

Memos and E-Mail With Attachments

LESSON 30

Correspondence Review

UNIT 6 LESSON

Business Letters 26

Goals

- Type at least 30wpm/3'/5e.
- Correctly format a business letter in block style with standard punctuation.

A. WARMUP

alphabet	1	Six of the women quietly gave back the prizes to the judge.
concentration	2	electrocardiography gastroenterologists interdenominational
easy	3	A bushel of corn was thrown to the turkeys by Mr. McKenzie.

Skillbuilding

B. SUSTAINED PRACTICE: PUNCTUATION

Take a 1-minute timed writing on the boxed paragraph to establish your base speed. Then take a 1-minute timed writing on the following paragraph. As soon as you equal or exceed your base speed on this paragraph, move to the next, more difficult paragraph.

4	Anyone who is successful in business realizes that the	11
5	needs of the customer must always come first. A satisfied	23
6	consumer is one who will come back to buy again and again.	34
7	Consumers must learn to lodge a complaint in a manner	11
8	that is fair, effective, and efficient. Don't waste time	22
9	talking to the wrong person. Go to the person in charge.	34
10	State your case clearly; be prepared with facts and	11
11	figures to back up any claim. Warranties, receipts, bills,	22
12	and checks are all very effective. Don't be intimidated.	34
13	If the company agrees to work with you, you're on the	11
14	right track. Be specific: "I'll expect a check Tuesday,"	22
15	or "I'll expect a replacement in the mail by Saturday."	33

1 | 2 | 3 | 4 | 5 | 6 | 7 | 8 | 9 | 10 | 11 | 12

Take two 3-minute timed writings.

Goal: At least 30wpm/3'/5e

C. 3-MINUTE TIMED WRITING

```
16       Holding a good business meeting may require a great      11
17  deal of thought and planning. Your meeting must be well       22
18  organized, and an agenda must be prepared. It may be hard     33
19  to judge how long a meeting will take or how many people      45
20  will discuss important issues.                                51
21       A good leader is required to execute an agenda. He or    62
22  she must know when to move on to the next topic or when to    74
23  continue debate on a topic. After a productive meeting, a     85
24  leader will be pleased.                                       90
      1 | 2 | 3 | 4 | 5 | 6 | 7 | 8 | 9 | 10 | 11 | 12
```

Formatting

D. BASIC PARTS OF A BUSINESS LETTER

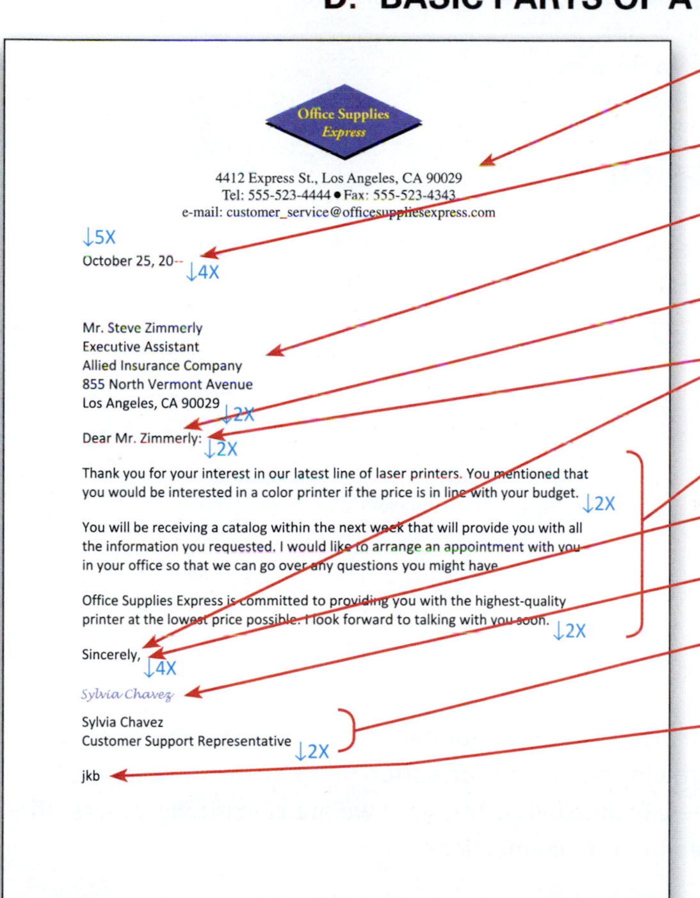

Office Supplies Express

4412 Express St., Los Angeles, CA 90029
Tel: 555-523-4444 • Fax: 555-523-4343
e-mail: customer_service@officesuppliesexpress.com

↓5X

October 25, 20-- ↓4X

Mr. Steve Zimmerly
Executive Assistant
Allied Insurance Company
855 North Vermont Avenue
Los Angeles, CA 90029 ↓2X

Dear Mr. Zimmerly: ↓2X

Thank you for your interest in our latest line of laser printers. You mentioned that you would be interested in a color printer if the price is in line with your budget. ↓2X

You will be receiving a catalog within the next week that will provide you with all the information you requested. I would like to arrange an appointment with you in your office so that we can go over any questions you might have.

Office Supplies Express is committed to providing you with the highest-quality printer at the lowest price possible. I look forward to talking with you soon. ↓2X

Sincerely, ↓4X

Sylvia Chavez

Sylvia Chavez
Customer Support Representative ↓2X

jkb

LETTERHEAD. Printed name, address, and telephone number (and/or fax number and e-mail address) of the company.

DATE LINE. Month, day, and year of the letter; type 2 inches from the top of the page.

INSIDE ADDRESS. Name and address of the party to whom the letter is written; begin 4 lines below the date.

SALUTATION. Opening greeting; type 2 lines below the inside address.

STANDARD PUNCTUATION. A colon after the salutation and a comma after the complimentary closing.

BODY. Text or message of the letter; begin 2 lines below the salutation.

COMPLIMENTARY CLOSING. Closing farewell; type 2 lines below the body.

SIGNATURE. Handwritten signature of the writer.

WRITER'S IDENTIFICATION. Name, or title, or both of the writer; begin 4 lines below the complimentary closing.

REFERENCE INITIALS. Initials of the typist; type 2 lines below the writer's identification.

E. BUSINESS LETTERS IN BLOCK STYLE

To format a business letter in block style:

1. Type all lines beginning at the left margin.
2. Press ENTER 5 times to begin the first line of the letter 2 inches from the top of the page.
3. Type the date, and press ENTER 4 times.
4. Type the inside address. Insert 1 space between the state and ZIP Code.
5. After the inside address, press ENTER 2 times, type the salutation, and type a colon after the salutation for standard punctuation.
6. Press ENTER 2 times after the salutation, and single-space the paragraphs in the body.
7. Press ENTER 2 times between paragraphs only—do *not* press ENTER when you see a line break in the text.
8. Do *not* indent paragraphs in a block-style letter.
9. Press ENTER 2 times after the last paragraph, type the complimentary closing, and type a comma after the complimentary closing for standard punctuation.
10. Press ENTER 4 times after the complimentary closing, and type the writer's identification.
11. Press ENTER 2 times after the writer's identification, and type your reference initials in lowercase letters without periods or spaces.
12. Spell-check, proofread, and preview your document for spelling and formatting errors.

REFER TO Word Manual

Appendix B, Using GDP Features in Document Processing, Reference Initials

Document Processing

Correspondence 26-3
Business Letter in Block Style

Type the current year whenever you see "20--."

↓5X
January 27, 20-- ↓4X

Ms. Laura Green
Account Executive
TurboNet Express
Two Pine Avenue
Long Beach, CA 90802 ↓2X

Dear Ms. Green: ↓2X

Our company is interested in hosting an educational seminar this spring—one that will focus on meeting the growing need for information industry professionals to keep abreast of emerging new technologies. This year we are specifically interested in information on high-speed Internet connections. ↓2X

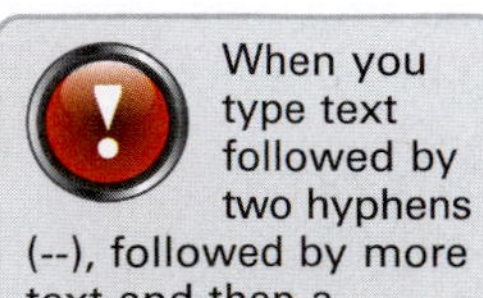

When you type text followed by two hyphens (--), followed by more text and then a space, a formatted em dash (—) will automatically be inserted.

I understand that TurboNet Express specializes in these seminars and that you also help businesses analyze their needs and choose an appropriate solution. I am in the process of contacting several companies similar to yours that might be interested in conducting these seminars. If you will contact me by Thursday or Friday, we can discuss this further.

(continued on next page)

I appreciate the fine service we have always received from you in the past, and I look forward to hearing from you very soon. ↓2X

Sincerely, ↓4X

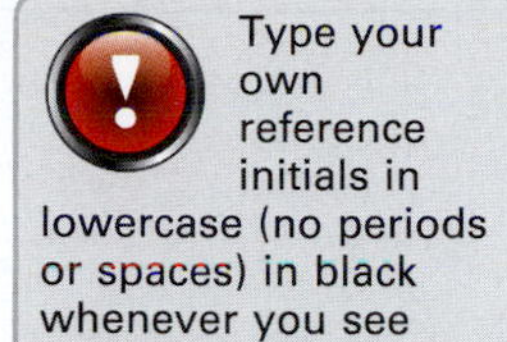

Type your own reference initials in lowercase (no periods or spaces) in black whenever you see urs.

Kathleen Franco
Information Technology Specialist ↓2X

urs

Correspondence 26-4
Business Letter in Block Style

In steps 1 and 3 (and in all similar instances in future jobs) do *not* type the period at the end of text to be revised if that punctuation is not needed.

Open the file for Correspondence 26-3, and make the following changes:

1. Change the date to `February 8`.
2. Delete the last sentence in the first paragraph, and add these sentences:

   `Advances in technology are nothing short of astonishing! This year, we would like to focus on models and procedures to save power in the workplace.`

3. Change the writer's identification to `Joon Soo Han` and the job title to `Technology Engineer`.

Correspondence 26-5
Business Letter in Block Style

May 25, 20-- / Ms. Laura Green / Account Executive / TurboNet Express / Two Pine Avenue / Long Beach, CA 90802 / Dear Ms. Green:

¶ Thank you so much for hosting the educational seminar last Tuesday that focused on the topic of high-speed Internet connections. Our company and our employees are now well prepared to make a decision about the best type of Internet connection for their particular needs.

¶ Because this seminar was so successful, I have been authorized to contract with TurboNet Express for a continuing series of seminars on any topics related to emerging new technologies and trends as they apply to the needs of our company and our employees. I will call you on Monday so that we can arrange for a meeting to finalize some contractual issues.

¶ Once again, thank you for a very successful and productive seminar!

Sincerely, / Kathleen Franco / Information Technology Specialist / urs

Business Letters With Enclosure Notations

27

Goals

- Demonstrate improved speed and accuracy while typing.
- Demonstrate acceptable language arts skills in comma usage.
- Correctly format a business letter in block style with an enclosure notation.

A. WARMUP

alphabet	1	Please quickly pack my box with the five dozen modern jugs.
one hand	2	revert unhook act him access pumpkin gave lymph fever union
easy	3	Hancock may work in the coalfield when he is not busy here.

Skillbuilding

B. MAP+: ALPHABET

Follow the GDP software directions for this exercise to improve keystroking accuracy.

C. PROGRESSIVE PRACTICE: ALPHABET

Follow the GDP software directions for this exercise to improve keystroking speed.

Language Arts

Study the rules at the right.

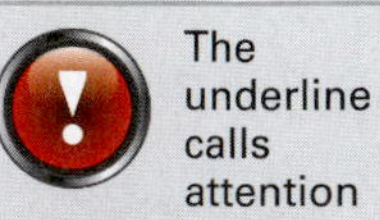

The underline calls attention to a point in the sentence where a comma might mistakenly be inserted.

D. COMMAS AND SENTENCES

Use a comma between independent clauses joined by a coordinate conjunction (unless both clauses are short).

Ellen left her job with IBM, and she and her sister went to Paris.
But: Ellen left her job with IBM_ and went to Paris with her sister.
But: John drove_ and I navigated.

Note: An independent clause is one that can stand alone as a complete sentence. The most common coordinate conjunctions are *and*, *but*, *or*, and *nor*.

RULE
, introductory expression

Use a comma after an introductory expression (unless it is a short prepositional phrase).

Before we can make a decision, we must have all the facts.
But: In 2008_ our nation elected a new president.

Note: An introductory expression is a group of words that come before the subject and verb of the independent clause. Common prepositions are *to, in, on, of, at, by, for,* and *with.*

Edit each sentence to correct any errors.

```
4  If you agree I will let Mr. Hancock know.

5  On Friday we will meet to discuss the upcoming campaign.

6  Mr. Ray will lead the delegation and Ms. Guy will be the
7  interpreter.

8  Ella dictated and I typed.

9  Melvin accepted a job in Miami that starts in July and then
10 left for a two-week vacation.

11 Now that it is light outside we can begin moving the
12 furniture.

13 It was a well-deserved victory and it didn't come any too
14 soon.
```

Formatting

E. ENCLOSURE NOTATIONS

To indicate that an item is enclosed with a letter:

- Type the word *Enclosure* on the line below the reference initials to indicate that an item is enclosed with a letter.
- Type the word *Enclosures* if more than one item is being enclosed.

Example: urs
Enclosure

Document Processing

Correspondence
27-6
Business Letter in Block Style

, independent clause

October 10, 20-- | Ms. Julie Mays | Travelwise International | 7301 East Gold Dust Avenue | Scottsdale, AZ 85258 | Dear Ms. Mays:

¶ Our company has decided to hold its regional sales meeting in Santa Fe during the second week of January, and I need information on a suitable conference site.

¶ We will need a meeting room with the following items: 30 computer workstations with wireless capability and a wireless Internet connection, copy stands, mouse pads, and adjustable chairs; a high-performance LCD projector with a large screen; and a wireless microphone and podium. The hotel should have a fax machine and an on-site business center. We might also need a messenger service.

(continued on next page)

, introductory expression

¶ A final decision on the conference site must be made within the next two weeks. If you have any information on a suitable location in Santa Fe, please send it immediately. I have enclosed a list of conference attendees and included their room preferences. Thank you for your help.
Sincerely yours, | Nick Limpett | Marketing Manager | urs | Enclosure

Correspondence 27-7
Business Letter in Block Style

1. Open the file for Correspondence 27-6.
2. Change the inside address to `5421 North Scottsdale Road` and the ZIP Code to `85250`.
3. Change the first sentence as follows:

   `Our company has decided to hold its annual national sales meeting during the first week of February in Santa Fe, and I need information on a suitable conference site.`

4. Change the writer's name to `William McDougal`.

Correspondence 27-8
Business Letter in Block Style

, introductory expression

, independent clause

October 10, 20-- / Mr. Nick Limpett / Marketing Manager / Secure Investments Inc. / 398 East Wacker Drive / Chicago, IL 60601 / Dear Mr. Limpett:
¶ Are you searching for a suitable conference site for your next corporate meeting? If so, the Paradise Valley Resort in Scottsdale, Arizona, offers you every amenity imaginable.
¶ Our luxury resort accommodations and stunning Sonoran Desert views are minutes away from the largest mall in the Southwest and hundreds of shops, galleries, and Scottsdale eateries. We are conveniently located only 12 miles from Phoenix Sky Harbor International Airport. Paradise Valley Resort has 40,000 square feet of flexible meeting space, including stunning outdoor venues. Our in-house audiovisual staff will make sure that your event is flawless.
¶ I've enclosed several brochures for your convenience. Let me know if I can be of service in any way. Your success is our success, and I hope to hear from you soon.
Sincerely yours, / Ms. Julie Mays / Corporate Event Specialist / urs / Enclosures

Envelopes and Labels

Goals

- Type at least 31wpm/3′/5e.
- Correctly use Word's envelope, view gridlines, and label features.
- Correctly format an envelope and label, and fold a letter.

A. WARMUP

alphabet
practice: *a* and *s*
easy

```
1 Jack amazed a few girls by dropping the antique onyx vases.
2 ask has say sales bases areas scans seams sodas visas tasks
3 My neighbors may bid on the islands if the profit is there.
```

Skillbuilding

B. PACED PRACTICE

Follow the GDP software directions for this exercise to improve keystroking speed and accuracy.

C. 3-MINUTE TIMED WRITING

Take two 3-minute timed writings.

Goal: At least 31wpm/3′/5e

```
4        Credit cards can make shopping very convenient, and     11
5  they frequently help you record and track your spending.      22
6  However, many card companies charge high fees for using       33
7  their credit cards.                                           37
8        You must realize that it may be better to pay in cash   48
9  and not use a credit card. Look at all your options. Some     60
10 card companies do not charge yearly fees. Some may give       71
11 you extended warranties on goods you buy with their credit    83
12 cards. Judge all the details; you may be surprised.           93
     1 | 2 | 3 | 4 | 5 | 6 | 7 | 8 | 9 | 10 | 11 | 12
```

Formatting

D. ENVELOPES

Word's envelope feature simplifies your task of addressing a standard No. 10 envelope measuring 9½ by 4⅛ inches.

To format an envelope:

1. Use Word's envelope feature to create an envelope.
2. The inside address is automatically inserted in Word's delivery address box if you are adding an envelope to an existing letter. Or you can type the recipient's name and address in upper- and lowercase style in Word's delivery address box.
3. If a return address is not printed on the envelope, type the sender's name and address in upper- and lowercase style in Word's return address box.
4. Use Word's default placement and default font for the delivery address and the return address.
5. Print the envelope immediately after creating it, or add the envelope to the document, and print it later.

Trend Electronics
2206 31st Street
Minneapolis, MN 55407-1911

Mr. Charles R. Harrison
Reliable Software Inc.
5613 Brunswick Avenue
Minneapolis, MN 55406

Standard large envelope, No. 10, is $9\frac{1}{2}$ x $4\frac{1}{8}$ inches.

E. FOLDING LETTERS

To fold a letter for a No. 10 envelope:

1. Place the letter face up, and fold up the bottom third of the page.
2. Fold the top third of the page down to about 0.5 inch from the bottom edge of the page.
3. Insert the last crease into the envelope first with the flap facing up.

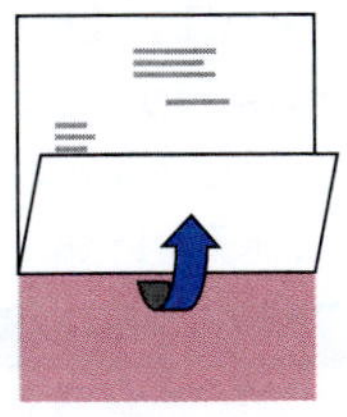

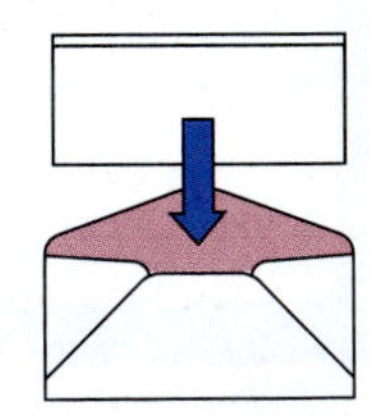

F. LABELS

Word's label feature simplifies the task of preparing various labels. You can use different label settings to print a full sheet of labels or to print a single label. You may want to use a mailing label as an alternative to printing an envelope.

To format a label:

1. Select the desired label, and note the label vendor and form number.
2. Use Word's label feature to create a single label or to create a full page of labels for the desired label form.
3. Use Word's default placement and default font for the labels.
4. After you prepare the labels, test the label position by printing your labels on a blank page before you print them on the actual label form. Make any necessary adjustments.

Ms. Irma Mayberry Garden Concepts Today 75-3982 Alii Drive Kailua-Kona, HI 96740	Ms. Irma Mayberry Garden Concepts Today 75-3982 Alii Drive Kailua-Kona, HI 96740	Ms. Irma Mayberry Garden Concepts Today 75-3982 Alii Drive Kailua-Kona, HI 96740
Ms. Irma Mayberry Garden Concepts Today 75-3982 Alii Drive Kailua-Kona, HI 96740	Ms. Irma Mayberry Garden Concepts Today 75-3982 Alii Drive Kailua-Kona, HI 96740	Ms. Irma Mayberry Garden Concepts Today 75-3982 Alii Drive Kailua-Kona, HI 96740
Ms. Irma Mayberry Garden Concepts Today 75-3982 Alii Drive Kailua-Kona, HI 96740	Ms. Irma Mayberry Garden Concepts Today 75-3982 Alii Drive Kailua-Kona, HI 96740	Ms. Irma Mayberry Garden Concepts Today 75-3982 Alii Drive Kailua-Kona, HI 96740
Ms. Irma Mayberry Garden Concepts Today 75-3982 Alii Drive Kailua-Kona, HI 96740	Ms. Irma Mayberry Garden Concepts Today 75-3982 Alii Drive Kailua-Kona, HI 96740	Ms. Irma Mayberry Garden Concepts Today 75-3982 Alii Drive Kailua-Kona, HI 96740
Ms. Irma Mayberry Garden Concepts Today 75-3982 Alii Drive Kailua-Kona, HI 96740	Ms. Irma Mayberry Garden Concepts Today 75-3982 Alii Drive Kailua-Kona, HI 96740	Ms. Irma Mayberry Garden Concepts Today 75-3982 Alii Drive Kailua-Kona, HI 96740
Ms. Irma Mayberry Garden Concepts Today 75-3982 Alii Drive Kailua-Kona, HI 96740	Ms. Irma Mayberry Garden Concepts Today 75-3982 Alii Drive Kailua-Kona, HI 96740	Ms. Irma Mayberry Garden Concepts Today 75-3982 Alii Drive Kailua-Kona, HI 96740
Ms. Irma Mayberry Garden Concepts Today 75-3982 Alii Drive Kailua-Kona, HI 96740	Ms. Irma Mayberry Garden Concepts Today 75-3982 Alii Drive Kailua-Kona, HI 96740	Ms. Irma Mayberry Garden Concepts Today 75-3982 Alii Drive Kailua-Kona, HI 96740
Ms. Irma Mayberry Garden Concepts Today 75-3982 Alii Drive Kailua-Kona, HI 96740	Ms. Irma Mayberry Garden Concepts Today 75-3982 Alii Drive Kailua-Kona, HI 96740	Ms. Irma Mayberry Garden Concepts Today 75-3982 Alii Drive Kailua-Kona, HI 96740
Ms. Irma Mayberry Garden Concepts Today 75-3982 Alii Drive Kailua-Kona, HI 96740	Ms. Irma Mayberry Garden Concepts Today 75-3982 Alii Drive Kailua-Kona, HI 96740	Ms. Irma Mayberry Garden Concepts Today 75-3982 Alii Drive Kailua-Kona, HI 96740
Ms. Irma Mayberry Garden Concepts Today	Ms. Irma Mayberry Garden Concepts Today	Ms. Irma Mayberry Garden Concepts Toda

Full page of the same label, Avery standard, 5160, Address
(Note: Label form shown with "View Gridlines" active.)

G. WORD PROCESSING: ENVELOPES, VIEW GRIDLINES, AND LABELS

Study Lesson 28 in your Word Manual. Complete all of the shaded steps while at your computer. Then format the documents that follow.

Document Processing

Correspondence 28-9
Envelope

1. Prepare an envelope with the following mailing address:

   Mr. Brad Everett | Business Software Solutions | 1410 Monterey Road | San Jose, CA 95110

2. Insert the following return address:

   Marie Fletcher | ABV Systems Inc. | 7200 Cedar Street | Omaha, NE 68124

3. Add the envelope to a blank document.

Correspondence 28-10
Envelope

1. Open the file for Correspondence 27-8, and prepare an envelope for the letter.
2. Do not insert a return address.
3. Add the envelope to the letter.

Correspondence 28-11
Mailing Labels

1. Select an address label product about 1 inch deep, large enough to fit a 4-line address. Label choices will vary; however, Avery standard, 5160, Address is a good choice for laser and ink-jet printers.
2. Prepare address labels for the names and addresses that follow.
3. Type the addresses in order from left to right as you see them displayed next in the first row of labels.
4. Move to the second row of labels, and type them again from left to right.

Purchasing Department
Abbott Laboratories
351 Abbott Park
Chicago, IL 60064

Frank Zimmerly
Cartridges, Etc.
1220 Charleston Road
Oso Park, CA 90621

John Sanchez
Adobe Systems
1585 Charleston Road
Los Angeles, CA 90029

Mike Rashid
Internet Services
901 Thompson Place
Sunnyvale, CA 94088

Jennifer Reagan
Aetna Life
151 Farmington Avenue
Hartford, CT 06156

Bob Patterson
Affiliated Publishing
135 Morrisey Blvd.
Boston, MA 02107

Correspondence 28-12
Mailing Labels

1. Select an address label product about 1 inch deep, large enough to fit a 4-line address. Label choices will vary; however, Avery standard, 5160, Address is a good choice for laser and ink-jet printers.
2. Prepare a full page of the same label with the following address:

   Shipping and Receiving | E-Office Outlet | 1122 North Highland Street | Arlington, VA 22201

Correspondence 28-13
Envelope

1. Open the file for Correspondence 27-6, and prepare an envelope for the letter.
2. Insert the following return address:

   Nick Limpett | Viatech Communications | 9835 Harvard Road, NE | Albuquerque, NM 87111

3. Add the envelope to the letter.

Keyboarding Connection

Decoding the E-Mail Address

With most e-mail software, a header at the top of each e-mail message contains the sender's address. What is the meaning of the strange configuration of an e-mail address?

An e-mail address contains three parts: anyname@server.com. First is the identity of the e-mail user, whether a person's name or a general name for the recipient, such as helpdesk or customer service (before the @ symbol). Next is the name of the host computer or domain name the person uses (before the period). The third part is the zone, or domain, for the type of organization or institution or even the country indicator to which the host belongs (e.g., *.edu* = education; *.gov* = government; *.com* = company; or a country indicator such as *.de* for Germany, *.uk* for United Kingdom, *.fr* for France).

Be careful to include each part of an e-mail address, and check the spelling and punctuation completely. Even a small error will prevent your message from reaching the recipient. When creating an e-mail address for job searching, try to choose a user name close to your own and as professional as possible.

Your Turn: Have you ever sent an e-mail that did not reach its recipient because of an address error? What type of error did you make?

Memos and E-Mail With Attachments

Goals

- Demonstrate improved speed and accuracy while typing.
- Demonstrate acceptable language arts skills in spelling.
- Correctly use Word's e-mail attachment feature.
- Correctly format a memo and an e-mail message with an attachment notation.

A. WARMUP

alphabet	1	Five jumbo oxen graze quietly with the nearby pack of dogs.
frequent digraphs	2	an and ant any ban can fan man pan ran tan van wan nana Ana
easy	3	Turn the handle to the right to dismantle the usual signal.

Skillbuilding

B. MAP+: SYMBOL

Follow the GDP software directions for this exercise to improve keystroking accuracy.

PPP PRETEST » PRACTICE » POSTTEST

PRETEST

Take a 1-minute timed writing. Review your speed and errors.

C. PRETEST: Close Reaches

4 The growth in the volume of company assets is due to 11
5 the astute group of twenty older employees. Their answers 22
6 were undoubtedly the reason for the increase in net worth. 34
1 | 2 | 3 | 4 | 5 | 6 | 7 | 8 | 9 | 10 | 11 | 12

PRACTICE

Speed Emphasis:
If you made 2 or fewer errors on the Pretest, type each *individual* line 2 times.

Accuracy Emphasis:
If you made 3 or more errors, type each *group* of lines (as though it were a paragraph) 2 times.

D. PRACTICE: Adjacent Keys

7 as ashes cases class asset astute passes chased creased ask
8 we weave tweed towed weigh wealth twenty fewest answers wet
9 rt worth alert party smart artist sorted charts turtles art

E. PRACTICE: Consecutive Fingers

10 un undue bunch stung begun united punish outrun untie funny
11 gr grand agree angry grade growth egress hungry group graph
12 ol older solid tools spool volume evolve uphold olive scold

POSTTEST

Repeat the Pretest timed writing and compare performance.

F. POSTTEST: Close Reaches

Language Arts

Type these frequently misspelled words, paying special attention to any spelling problems in each word.

G. SPELLING

13 personnel information its procedures their committee system
14 receive employees which education services opportunity area
15 financial appropriate interest received production contract
16 important through necessary customer employee further there
17 property account approximately general control division our

Edit the sentences to correct any misspellings.

18 All company personel will receive important information.

19 Are division has some control over there financial account.

20 There comittee has received approximately three contracts.

21 The employe and the customer have an oportunity to attend.

22 We have no farther interest in the property or it's owner.

23 When it is necessary, follow apropriate proceedures.

Strategies for Career Success

Preparing to Conduct a Meeting

Do you want to conduct a successful meeting? Meetings tend to fail because they last too long and attendees do not stay focused. First, determine the meeting's purpose (e.g., to make a decision or obtain/provide information).

Decide who needs to attend the meeting. Include those who can significantly contribute, as well as decision makers. Prepare an agenda, that is, a list of items to be discussed. Distribute it to attendees a few days before the meeting.

Choose where you will conduct the meeting, and schedule a room. Determine if you will be teleconferencing, videoconferencing, or needing audiovisual equipment. If appropriate, arrange for refreshments. Check the room temperature, acoustics, and lighting. Attention to these details will increase your chances for a successful outcome.

Your Turn: Think about a meeting you attended that was a failure. What could the meeting leader have done to better prepare for the meeting?

H. BASIC PARTS OF A MEMO

A memo is usually sent from one person to another in the same organization. E-mail in recent years has replaced memos as an efficient means of interoffice communication in many offices. However, memos are better suited for detailed messages of a more formal nature.

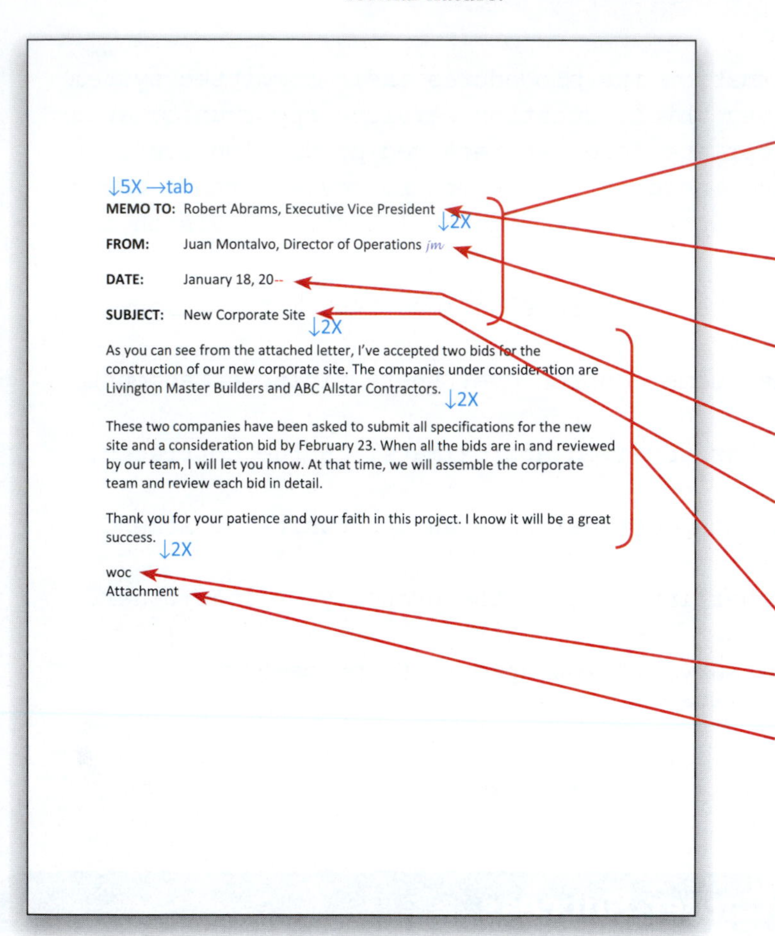

MEMO TO: Robert Abrams, Executive Vice President

FROM: Juan Montalvo, Director of Operations *jm*

DATE: January 18, 20--

SUBJECT: New Corporate Site

As you can see from the attached letter, I've accepted two bids for the construction of our new corporate site. The companies under consideration are Livington Master Builders and ABC Allstar Contractors.

These two companies have been asked to submit all specifications for the new site and a consideration bid by February 23. When all the bids are in and reviewed by our team, I will let you know. At that time, we will assemble the corporate team and review each bid in detail.

Thank you for your patience and your faith in this project. I know it will be a great success.

woc
Attachment

MEMO HEADINGS. Printed guide words typed in bold (including the colon); press TAB after the colon as needed to align the heading entries at the same point; begin 2 inches from the top of the page.

MEMO TO HEADING. Name of recipient; if a title is included, separate the name and title with a comma.

FROM HEADING. Name of writer; if a title is included, separate the name and title with a comma; followed by handwritten initials of sender.

DATE HEADING. Month, day, and year the memo was typed.

SUBJECT HEADING. Subject of the memo; if the subject wraps to a second line, press TAB at the start of the second line as needed to align the second line at the same point as the first line.

BODY. Text or message of the memo; type 2 lines below the subject heading.

REFERENCE INITIALS. Initials of the typist; type 2 lines below the body.

ATTACHMENT NOTATION. Indicates that something is attached; if used, type directly below the reference initials.

I. MEMOS

To format a memo on plain paper or on letterhead stationery:

1. Press ENTER 5 times to begin the first line of the memo 2 inches from the top of the page.
2. Type the headings (including the colons) in all-caps and bold: `MEMO TO:`, `FROM:`, `DATE:`, and `SUBJECT:`.
3. Press TAB as many times as needed to reach the point where each heading entry begins.
4. Press ENTER 2 times between each line of the heading and after the last line in the heading.
5. Type the body of the memo using blocked paragraphs, and press ENTER 2 times between paragraphs.
6. Press ENTER 2 times after the last paragraph in the body, and type your reference initials (not "`urs`") in lowercase letters without periods or spaces.
7. Spell-check, proofread, and preview your document for spelling and formatting errors.

J. MEMOS WITH ATTACHMENT NOTATIONS

To format a memo with an attachment, type the word *Attachment* (rather than *Enclosure*) on the line below the reference initials when material is physically attached (stapled or clipped) to a memo.

Example: urs
Attachment

K. E-MAIL WITH ATTACHMENTS

Use the attachment feature in your e-mail software to attach one or more electronic files to an e-mail message.

To format an e-mail message with an attachment:

- Format the e-mail message as usual.
- No special formatting steps are needed when an attachment is sent. Do *not* type an attachment notation at the bottom of the e-mail message.
- Use the e-mail attachment feature to attach a file of some type to the message. A file attachment is automatically denoted by a special symbol (usually a paper clip).

L. WORD PROCESSING: E-MAIL—ATTACHMENT NOTATIONS

Study Lesson 29 in your Word Manual. Complete all of the shaded steps while at your computer. Then format the documents that follow.

Document Processing

Correspondence 29-14
Memo

Highlighted words are spelling words from the language arts activities; do *not* highlight them when you type.

↓5X →tab
MEMO TO: All Company Personnel ↓2X

FROM: Jerry Mitchell, Employee Relations Division *jm*

DATE: October 15, 20--

SUBJECT: Holiday Committee ↓2X

There has been a great deal of interest regarding the appropriate procedures for planning our upcoming holiday event next month. ↓2X

I have received requests from approximately 80 percent of our customers to organize some type of annual charitable event. This event will include all interested employees and customers and will provide an opportunity for everyone to contribute financially to local families in need.

It will be necessary to gather general information regarding the cost of renting a facility in our area, which will be ready next week. When I am through with that process and a contract has been signed, I will contact all interested personnel. If you are interested in participating in this important event, please return the attached sign-up sheet. ↓2X

urs
Attachment

Correspondence 29-15
Memo

MEMO TO: Amy Vigil, Human Resources | **FROM:** Dan Westphal | **DATE:** November 23, 20-- | **SUBJECT:** MedNet Benefit Plan
¶ Thank you for the brochure I received detailing the various options offered to employees through the MedNet plan. I need clarification on some of the important services included in the plan.
¶ Because both my wife and I are employees of Allied Aerospace Industries, do we have the choice of enrolling separately under different options? In our present plan, I know that this is appropriate.
¶ We have two dependents. Can we enroll each dependent under a different plan option, or is it necessary to choose either one option or the other for both? I know that in the past you have asked for evidence of their dependent status and dates of birth, which I have attached.
¶ If you need any further information, please let me know. Thank you very much for your help.
urs | Attachments

Correspondence
29-16
E-Mail Message

Hi, Doug:

¶ I now have appropriate health insurance for my family. As a fellow employee, you might be very interested in obtaining further details. I have attached a file I received with a list of resources, procedures, services, and general information that I found useful.

¶ Researching these important health insurance contracts is necessary so that you can make an informed choice for your own family. Feel free to contact me with any questions.

Elizabeth | Elizabeth Chavez | E-mail: echavez@freeweb.net | Phone: 661-555-3623

Correspondence Review

Goals

- Type at least 32wpm/3'/5e.
- Correctly use Word's italic and underline features.
- Correctly format a memo and an e-mail message with an attachment notation.
- Successfully complete a Progress and Proofreading Check with zero errors on the first scored attempt.

A. WARMUP

alphabet
1 A dumpy kibitzer jingled coins as the exchequer overflowed.

number/symbol
2 eck@hotmail.com 92% Cho & Orr 9/13 (Shh!) $4.57 *2010 #86-3

easy
3 When they visit downtown, the auditors fight for their bid.

Skillbuilding

B. 12-SECOND SPEED SPRINTS

Take three 12-second timed writings on each line.

4 The giant wiry dog put half of the bones down on the chair.
5 Leo may visit the island by the giant oaks on his tan bike.
6 Do not blame my firm for the low level of fuel in the tank.
7 Jake may try to fix the leaks in the pipes in the city gym.
' ' ' ' 5 ' ' ' ' 10 ' ' ' ' 15 ' ' ' ' 20 ' ' ' ' 25 ' ' ' ' 30 ' ' ' ' 35 ' ' ' ' 40 ' ' ' ' 45 ' ' ' ' 50 ' ' ' ' 55 ' ' ' ' 60

C. TECHNIQUE PRACTICE: TAB KEY

Press Tab 1 time between words where you see the → symbol. Type each line 2 times.

8 ale→ and→ Poe→ aha→ Ian→ ape→ ask→ Jew→ Lin→ Mel→ amp
9 Kai→ Meg→ Mag→ Ira→ adz→ Kim→ Liz→ Hal→ Ivy→ aid→ all
10 ark→ Jeb→ arc→ arm→ Una→ air→ Mel→ Lew→ aim→ Peg→ Nan
11 Uzi→ Leo→ Uri→ awe→ ail→ May→ axe→ Max→ Kim→ Nat→ Liv

Take two 3-minute timed writings.

D. 3-MINUTE TIMED WRITING

```
12      If you want to work in information processing, you      10
13 may realize that there are steps that you must take to      21
14 plan for such an exciting career. First, you must decide    33
15 whether or not you have the right personality traits.       44
16      Then you must be trained in the technical skills you   54
17 need in such an important field. The technology is changing 66
18 each day. You must stay focused on keeping up with these    78
19 changes. Also, you must never quit wanting to learn new     89
20 skills each day you are on the job.                         96
     1 | 2 | 3 | 4 | 5 | 6 | 7 | 8 | 9 | 10 | 11 | 12
```

Formatting

E. WORD PROCESSING: ITALIC AND UNDERLINE

Study Lesson 30 in your Word Manual. Complete all of the shaded steps while at your computer. Then format the documents that follow.

Document Processing

Correspondence
30-17
Memo

MEMO TO: All Executive Assistants | **FROM:** Robbie Holt, Staff Development Coordinator | **DATE:** March 25, 20-- | **SUBJECT:** Standardizing Document Formats
¶ Last month we received our final shipment of new laser printers. The installation of these printers in your offices marked the final phaseout of all ink-jet printers.
¶ Because all of us can now use a variety of standardized fonts in our correspondence, please note the following change: <u>From now on, all titles in tables, correspondence, and reports should be set in Calibri 14</u>. This new formatting change will help us to standardize our communications.
¶ The latest edition of the book *Quick Reference for the Automated Office* has two pages of helpful information on laser printers. I have attached my comments. Please read these pages carefully, and we will discuss them at our next meeting.
urs | Attachment

Underline the text to be emphasized.

Italicize the book title.

Correspondence
30-18
E-Mail Message

Hi, Louise:

¶ The League of Women Voters is looking for volunteers to work at the various polling places during the upcoming elections. If you think you will be able to volunteer your time, please fill out and mail the attached schedule of availability. After I receive your schedule, I will contact you to confirm a location, time, and date.

¶ We are sending you the best-selling book *Great American Presidents* as a small token of our appreciation. Concerned citizens like you make it possible for the public to have a convenient place to vote. Thank you for your interest in this very worthy cause!

Paige | Paige Jones | E-mail: pjones@hotweb.net | Phone: 314-555-6972

Correspondence
30-19
Business Letter in Block Style

Progress and Proofreading Check

Documents designated as Proofreading Checks serve as a check of your proofreading skill. Your goal is to have zero typographical errors when the GDP software first scores the document.

April 3, 20-- / Ms. Robbie Holt / Staff Development Coordinator / Health Care Incorporated / 1129 Market Street / Philadelphia, PA 19107 / Dear Ms. Holt:

¶ I understand that you were in charge of selecting some fabulous new laser printers for Health Care Incorporated in Philadelphia. I know you researched the needs of your branch and considered those needs in your choice. I certainly appreciate your effort.

¶ Several of us at Health Care Incorporated here in Los Angeles would be very interested in seeing the printers demonstrated as we are planning a major printer upgrade with training to follow as well. Would it be possible to schedule a demonstration soon? We are particularly interested in learning about any features that particularly influenced your printer choice.

Italicize the magazine title.

¶ I have enclosed an article on laser printers from the latest issue of Office Technology. Please let me know your reaction to the article. If I can help you in any way to arrange the demonstration, I would be more than happy to do so.

Sincerely, / Jeffrey Keller / Staff Development Coordinator / urs / Enclosure

UNIT 7

Reports

LESSON 31
One-Page Business Reports

LESSON 32
Multipage Business Reports

LESSON 33
Rough-Draft Business Reports With Lists

LESSON 34
Multipage Academic Reports With Lists

LESSON 35
More Rough-Draft Reports

One-Page Business Reports

Goals

- Demonstrate improved speed and accuracy while typing.
- Demonstrate acceptable language arts skills in capitalization.
- Correctly use Word's alignment and font size features.
- Correctly format a business report with side headings.

A. WARMUP

alphabet
1 Jack's man found exactly a quarter in the woven zipper bag.

concentration
2 incomprehensibility counterinsurgencies distinguishableness

easy
3 The towns of Sydney and Burma are both due for a May visit.

Skillbuilding

B. MAP+: ALPHABET

Follow the GDP software directions for this exercise to improve keystroking accuracy.

C. PROGRESSIVE PRACTICE: ALPHABET

Follow the GDP software directions for this exercise to improve keystroking speed.

Language Arts

Study the rules at the right.

D. CAPITALIZATION

RULE ≡ sentence

Capitalize the first word of a sentence.

Please prepare a summary of your activities.

RULE ≡ proper noun

Capitalize proper nouns and adjectives derived from proper nouns.

Judy Hendrix drove to Albuquerque in her new Pontiac convertible.

Note: A proper noun is the official name of a particular person, place, or thing.

RULE ≡ time

Capitalize the names of the days of the week, months, holidays, and religious days (but do not capitalize the names of the seasons).

On Thursday, November 25, we will celebrate Thanksgiving, the most popular holiday in the fall.

Edit each sentence to correct any errors.

4 The american flag can be seen flying over the White House in
5 Washington, DC.

6 Our Country's flag is often seen flying over Government
7 buildings on holidays like July 4, independence day.

8 Memorial Day signals the end of spring and the start of
9 Summer.

10 Most Americans consider Labor day the beginning of the fall
11 season.

12 In december many people observe christmas and Hanukkah.

13 most government holidays are scheduled to fall on either a
14 Monday or a friday.

15 Sometimes the birthdays of Historical figures are also
16 celebrated.

Formatting

E. BASIC PARTS OF A BUSINESS REPORT

The two basic styles of reports are business and academic. An illustration for a business report with side headings, paragraph headings, and a list follows.

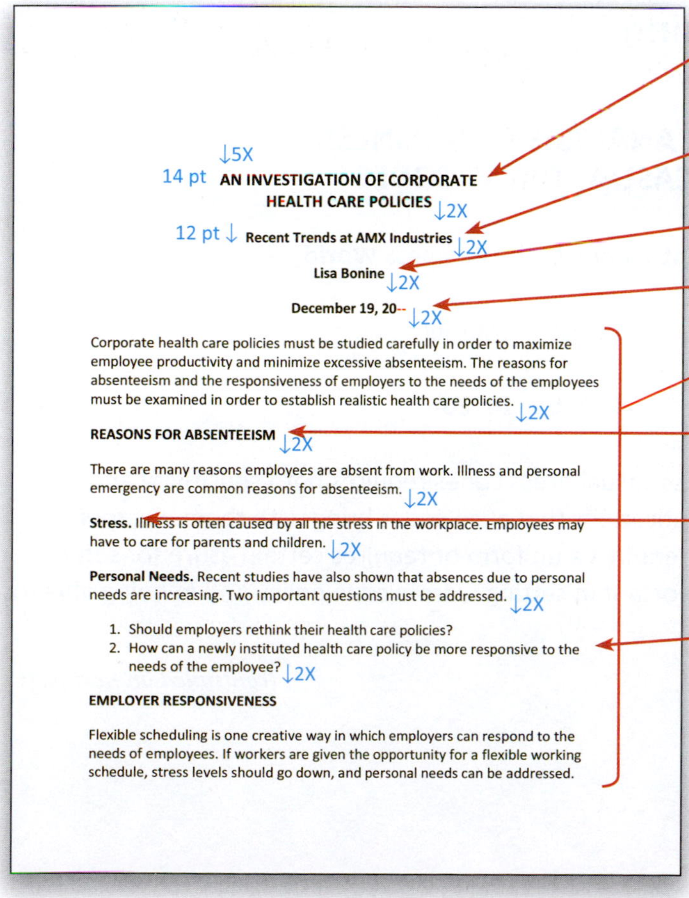

↓5X

14 pt **AN INVESTIGATION OF CORPORATE HEALTH CARE POLICIES** ↓2X

12 pt ↓ **Recent Trends at AMX Industries** ↓2X

Lisa Bonine ↓2X

December 19, 20-- ↓2X

Corporate health care policies must be studied carefully in order to maximize employee productivity and minimize excessive absenteeism. The reasons for absenteeism and the responsiveness of employers to the needs of the employees must be examined in order to establish realistic health care policies. ↓2X

REASONS FOR ABSENTEEISM ↓2X

There are many reasons employees are absent from work. Illness and personal emergency are common reasons for absenteeism. ↓2X

Stress. Illness is often caused by all the stress in the workplace. Employees may have to care for parents and children. ↓2X

Personal Needs. Recent studies have also shown that absences due to personal needs are increasing. Two important questions must be addressed. ↓2X

1. Should employers rethink their health care policies?
2. How can a newly instituted health care policy be more responsive to the needs of the employee? ↓2X

EMPLOYER RESPONSIVENESS

Flexible scheduling is one creative way in which employers can respond to the needs of employees. If workers are given the opportunity for a flexible working schedule, stress levels should go down, and personal needs can be addressed.

TITLE. Subject of the report; type 2 inches from the top of the page with a 14-point font size, in all-caps, in bold; center all title lines, and single-space 2-line titles.

SUBTITLE. Secondary or explanatory title; center, bold, and type 1 blank line below the title, in upper- and lowercase letters.

BYLINE. Name of the writer; center, bold, and type 1 blank line below the previous line.

DATE. Date of the report; center, bold, and type 1 blank line below the previous line.

BODY. Text of the report; type single-spaced, 1 blank line below the previous line at the left margin, with 1 blank line between paragraphs.

SIDE HEADING. Major subdivision of the report; type in all-caps and bold, 1 blank line below the previous line at the left margin.

PARAGRAPH HEADING. Minor subdivision of the report; type in bold (followed by a bold period) in upper- and lowercase letters, 1 blank line below the previous line, at the left margin.

LIST. Numbered or bulleted items; insert 1 blank line above and below the list, using Word's default list format; type single-spaced throughout.

F. BUSINESS REPORTS

To format a business report:

1. Use single spacing.
2. Press ENTER 5 times to begin the first line of the report 2 inches from the top of the page.
3. Change the font size to 14 point; and type the title in all-caps, centered, in bold. Single-space a 2-line title.
4. Press ENTER 2 times and change the font size to 12 point.
5. If the report includes a subtitle, byline, or date, type each item centered and in bold upper- and lowercase letters.
6. Press ENTER 2 times after each part of the heading block.
7. Press ENTER 2 times between all paragraphs.
8. Do not number the first page of a report, but insert a page number on all subsequent pages of a multipage report.
9. Spell-check, proofread, and preview your document for spelling and formatting errors.

G. BUSINESS REPORTS WITH SIDE HEADINGS

To format side headings in a business report:

1. Insert 1 blank line before and after side headings.
2. Type side headings in the default 12-point font at the left margin, in bold, and in all-caps.

H. WORD PROCESSING: ALIGNMENT AND FONT—SIZE

Study Lesson 31 in your Word Manual. Complete all of the shaded steps while at your computer. Then format the documents that follow.

Document Processing

Report 31-1
Business Report

↓5X

14 pt **AN ANALYSIS OF BUSINESS CASUAL DRESS CODES** ↓2X

12 pt ↓ **Recent Trends in the Business World** ↓2X

≡ proper noun

Louise McMabel ↓2X

≡ time

October 18, 20-- ↓2X

≡ sentence

Establishing corporate business casual dress codes requires both sensitivity and awareness of all the legal ramifications that such codes bring with them. Factors such as whether or not a job requires a uniform or requires certain attire for safety reasons can be extremely important in setting a dress code policy and in being able to enforce it. ↓2X

(continued on next page)

ESTABLISHING GUIDELINES ↓2X

≡ sentence

A policy manual should include all specifications regarding dress codes, including the more relaxed dress code known as business casual. If your company's policy manual does not precisely define what is considered "acceptable" business casual dress, you are likely to see a range of interpretations. Once expected dress code standards have been lowered due to vague guidelines, you will have a much more difficult time enforcing any guidelines later.

RESPONSIVENESS OF EMPLOYEES

≡ time

≡ proper noun

If employees are convinced that their image and dress directly affect the company's bottom line, they are more likely to be motivated to adhere to stricter dress code guidelines. If they know that a specified workday, such as a Friday, can be a day to relax their dress, they might consider it a reasonable trade-off to the stricter guidelines enforced during the other workdays. A professional image consultant from Dress for Success Inc. could conduct some workshops to educate employees regarding the importance of professional dress and how to dress professionally even when the standard is business casual.

POTENTIAL RESULTS

≡ time

If you decide to adopt a business casual dress code in the spring, note its effect on employee morale. You might find that teamwork increases and creativity rises. All these factors have the potential to increase productivity. Everyone wins!

Report
31-2
Business Report

Open the file for Report 31-1 and make the following changes:

1. Delete the subtitle, and change the byline to `Renee Kare Oke`.
2. Change the date to `November 24`.
3. Change the second side heading to `EMPLOYEE RESPONSIVENESS`.
4. Delete the last two sentences in the last paragraph at the end of the report.
5. Add the following sentences to the end of the last paragraph:

   `Employees will feel empowered by the energy generated by a more casual work environment. When they arrive at work each Friday in casual attire, they will feel more relaxed and ready to work.`

Multipage Business Reports

Goals

- Type at least 33wpm/3'/5e.
- Correctly use Word's page number, page break, and widow/orphan control features.
- Correctly format a multipage business report with side and paragraph headings.

A. WARMUP

alphabet	1	By Jove, my quick study of lexicography won a bronze prize.
one hand	2	adverb hookup was ply target minimum beat knoll acted kinky
easy	3	The auditor from Dubuque had a problem with the amendments.

Skillbuilding

B. SUSTAINED PRACTICE: ALTERNATE-HAND WORDS

Take a 1-minute timed writing on the boxed paragraph to establish your base speed. Then take a 1-minute timed writing on the following paragraph. As soon as you equal or exceed your base speed on this paragraph, move to the next, more difficult paragraph.

4	When eight of them began a formal discussion on some	11
5	of the major issues, the need for a chair was very evident.	23
6	A chair would be sure to handle the usual work with ease.	34
7	The eight people in that group decided that the work	11
8	would be done only if they selected one person to be chair	23
9	of their group. They began to debate all the major issues.	34
10	One issue that needed to be settled right up front was	11
11	the question of how to handle proxy votes. It seemed for a	23
12	short time that a fight over this very issue would result.	35
13	The group worked diligently in attempting to solve the	11
14	issues that were being discussed. All of the concerns that	23
15	were brought to the group were reviewed in depth by them.	34
	1 | 2 | 3 | 4 | 5 | 6 | 7 | 8 | 9 | 10 | 11 | 12	

Take two 3-minute timed writings.

Goal: At least 33wpm/3'/5e

C. 3-MINUTE TIMED WRITING

```
16      Be zealous in your efforts when you write business      10
17  letters. Your business writing must convey clearly what     22
18  it is you want people to read. All of your letters should   33
19  be formatted neatly in proper business letter format.       44
20      Before sending your letters, read them quickly just to  55
21  make sure that they explain clearly what you want to say.   67
22  Proofread the letters you write for correct grammar and     78
23  spelling. Use all of your writing skills to display the     89
24  best image. Your readers will welcome the effort.           99
      1 | 2 | 3 | 4 | 5 | 6 | 7 | 8 | 9 | 10 | 11 | 12
```

Formatting

D. MULTIPAGE BUSINESS REPORTS

To format a multipage business report:

1. Press Enter 5 times to begin the first line of the report 2 inches from the top of the page.
2. Do not number the first page. Suppress the page number on the first page, and insert a page number in the top right-hand corner of the page header of all continuing pages.
3. Do not end any page with a single line, and do not begin any subsequent page with a single line.
4. Spell-check, proofread, and preview your document for spelling and formatting errors.
5. Refer to the illustration that follows to format the second page of a multipage business report.

2

Job candidates lie for any number of reasons. Many applicants have families to support and are willing to do anything to get the job.

CONCLUSION

It is clear that falsification is at hand more than ever, and it is equally clear that the value of ethics has been lost on some applicants. It is therefore up to the employer to figure out how best to test a potential employee's integrity.

PAGE NUMBER. Inserted on continuing pages only; typed inside the document header at the right margin.

BODY. Continues at the default top margin, 1 inch from the top of the page.

E. BUSINESS REPORTS WITH PARAGRAPH HEADINGS

To format paragraph headings in a business report:

1. Insert 1 blank line above the paragraph that includes a paragraph heading.
2. Type paragraph headings at the left margin, in bold, and in upper- and lowercase letters.
3. Follow the paragraph heading by a bold period and 1 space.

F. WORD PROCESSING: PAGE NUMBER, PAGE BREAK, AND WIDOW/ORPHAN CONTROL

GO TO Word Manual

Study Lesson 32 in your Word Manual. Complete all of the shaded steps while at your computer. Then format the documents that follow.

Document Processing

Report 32-3
Business Report

Remember to insert a page number on the second page and suppress it on the first page.

Your page endings in Word will not match those in the book.

ETHICAL ISSUES FACING EMPLOYERS AND JOB APPLICANTS

Mary Lincoln

February 12, 20--

¶Some job applicants "pad" their application with false information, such as phony salaries and nonexistent jobs. Even some well-known political figures have been guilty of listing a job on their resume during a period of time in which such a job never existed. When applicants are eager or even desperate to find a job, such ethical dilemmas will rise to the forefront.

FALSIFICATION

¶What is falsification? Certainly, adding information that is not true would seem to indicate a clear intent on the part of the applicant to falsify information. But how do you judge whether or not leaving out pertinent information or information that would cast you in a bad light qualifies as intentional falsification? These are gray areas that are not always easy to define.

Italicize the words as shown.

¶**Honors and Grades.** Let's take a look at a more specific example. What if your grade point average at graduation had been just slightly higher to qualify you for a degree designation of *cum laude*, *magna cum laude*, or even *summa cum laude*? Clearly, it would be falsification to claim one of these designations when that designation was not earned. However, there is an ethical way to place yourself in the best light without falsifying information. If you earned an outstanding grade point average in the courses for your given major, it is certainly acceptable to state your correct grade point average and specify that the average reflects grades only for courses related to your declared college major or minor.

¶**School Activities.** Many applicants are willing to exaggerate or totally falsify their participation in school activities. In order to prove leadership ability, an applicant might be willing to say that he or she was president of a nonexistent club or perhaps organized some type of fictional fund-raising activity. Such deception is clearly falsification.

¶**Job Titles.** Another area rampant with deception is the list of previous job titles. In order to make a former job sound more impressive, a job contender might add a word or two to the title or perhaps rename the title altogether.

REASONS FOR LYING

Job candidates lie for any number of reasons. Some of them see getting a job as some sort of game in which the rules really don't matter. Others equate lying with cheating on an exam and rationalize the deception in some way. Many applicants have families to support and are willing to do anything to get the job.

(continued on next page)

CONCLUSION

It is clear that falsification is at hand more than ever, and it is equally clear that the value of ethics has been lost on some applicants. It is therefore up to the employer to figure out how best to test a potential employee's integrity, to investigate an applicant's history, and then to decide whether or not to hire this individual.

Report 32-4
Business Report

Open the file for Report 32-3 and make the following changes:

1. Change the byline to `Ruth Carter`.
2. Change the date to `October 1`.
3. Change the second side heading to `REASONS FOR FALSIFICATION`.
4. Add this paragraph to the end of the report:

The importance of ethical intentions in a future employee should never be underestimated. There is an old saying that honesty is the best policy. Honesty is expected and required in the workplace, and great dividends await those who make an exemplary work ethic a top priority.

Rough-Draft Business Reports With Lists

33

Goals

- Demonstrate improved speed and accuracy while typing.
- Correctly identify and apply basic proofreaders' marks.
- Correctly use Word's bullet and numbering features.
- Correctly format a rough-draft business report with lists.

A. WARMUP

alphabet
1 Jay began removing six dozen black quilts with petty flaws.

practice: *s* and *d*
2 sod sad deeds desks dosed dudes dusts sheds sides soda suds

easy
3 The men may be busy but they may go to the social with her.

Skillbuilding

B. MAP+: NUMBERS

Follow the GDP software directions for this exercise to improve keystroking accuracy.

PPP PRETEST » PRACTICE » POSTTEST

C. PRETEST: Discrimination Practice

PRETEST

Take a 1-minute timed writing.

```
4      Steven saw the younger, unruly boy take flight as he   11
5  threw the coin at the jury. The brave judge stopped the    22
6  fight. He called out to the youth, who recoiled in fear.   33
     1 | 2 | 3 | 4 | 5 | 6 | 7 | 8 | 9 | 10 | 11 | 12
```

D. PRACTICE: Left Hand

PRACTICE

Speed Emphasis:
If you made 2 or fewer errors on the Pretest, type each *individual* line 2 times.

Accuracy Emphasis:
If you made 3 or more errors, type each *group* of lines (as though it were a paragraph) 2 times.

```
7  vbv verb bevy vibes bevel brave above verbal bovine behaves
8  wew west weep threw wedge weave fewer weight sewing dewdrop
9  fgf gulf gift fight fudge fugue flags flight golfer feigned
```

E. PRACTICE: Right Hand

```
10 uyu buys your usury unity youth buoys unruly untidy younger
11 oio coin lion oiled foils foist prior recoil iodine rejoice
12 jhj jury huge enjoy three judge habit adjust slight jasmine
```

POSTTEST

Repeat the Pretest timed writing and compare performance.

F. POSTTEST: Discrimination Practice

Language Arts

Edit these sentences to correct any errors.

G. PROOFREADING

```
13 It doesnt matter how fast you can type or how well you now a
14 software program if you produce documents that are filled
15 with errors.

16 You must learn to watch for errors in spelling punctuation,
17 and formatting.

18 Look carefully between words and sentences.

19 Make sure that after a period at the end of a sentence, you
20 see one space.

21 Sometime it helps to look at the characters in the sentence
22 justabove the one you are proofreading to ensure accuracy.
```

Formatting

H. BULLETED AND NUMBERED LISTS

REFER TO Reference Manual

R-12D: Examples of Different Types of Lists

Numbers and/or bullets are used in documents to call attention to items in a list and to increase readability. If the sequence of the list items is important, use numbers rather than bullets.

To format bulleted and numbered lists in documents:

- Use the bullets or numbers feature to format the list using Word's default format.
- Use the same line spacing (single or double) between lines in the list as is used in the rest of the document.

I. BUSINESS REPORTS WITH LISTS

To format lists in a business report:

1. Press ENTER 2 times to insert 1 blank line above the list.
2. Between lines in the list, use the same spacing (single in a business report or double in academic reports) as is used in the rest of the document.
3. Insert 1 blank line below the list.
4. Spell-check, proofread, and preview your document for spelling and formatting errors.

J. BASIC PROOFREADERS' MARKS

Proofreaders' marks are used to indicate changes or corrections to be made in a rough-draft document that is being revised for final copy. Study the chart to learn what each proofreaders' mark means.

Proofreaders' Marks	Draft	Final copy
Omit space	data base	database
Insert	if hes going, (not)	if he's not going,
Capitalize	Maple street	Maple Street
Delete	a final draft	a draft
Insert space	allready to	all ready to
Change word	and if you (when)	and when you
Use lowercase letter	our President	our president
Transpose	they all see	they see all
SS Single-space	SS first line second line	first line second line
¶ New paragraph	. . . to use it. ¶ We can	. . . to use it. We can

K. WORD PROCESSING: BULLETS AND NUMBERING

Study Lesson 33 in your Word Manual. Complete all of the shaded steps while at your computer. Then format the documents that follow.

Document Processing

Report 33-5
Business Report

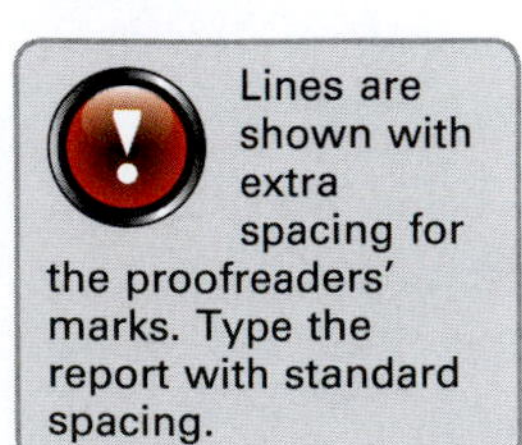

EFFECT IVE WAYS TO
GET ACTIVE AS AFAMILY

By Mike Khouri

February 23, 20--

Thereis no doubt that parenting takes a great deal of time and more energy. Although it would seem that becoming active as a family group would expend even more energy and possibly create more stress the opposite is true. When the whole family participates in hpysical activities, children learn that being active is fun and makes everyone feel better.

(continued on next page)

GETTING STARTED

There are many ways in which you can get all family members up and participating in a newer, healthier lifestyle:

1. Make a list as a Family of activities you would all like to do together and post a schedule.
2. Make sure the list includes things everyone enjoys doing.

SS

3. Plan a monthly activity ~~which~~ that involves walking out doors, such as a trip to the Zoo or camping.

SETTING **Family Rules**

Once you have started this regimen, you will notice probably that the entire family has an increased energy level. However you may still need a few family rules to keep every one on track:

- Set a limit on the number of television hours allowed.
- Set ~~limits~~ a limit on computer games and Internet use.
- Dont use food as a reward for participating in family activities.
- Make these activities a high priority in your daily and weekly routines.

If you practice these methods to create and maintain the energy levels for your ~~entire~~ family, you will find that these routines will become a ~~very~~ natural part of your daily life. Enjoy the change and experiment with new activities each week. You will be likely pleasantly surprised at the changes you see in the family unit

Report
33-6
Business Report

Open the file for Report 33-5 and make the following changes:

1. Change the first side heading to `HOW TO GET STARTED.`
2. Change the second side heading to `HOW TO SET FAMILY RULES.`
3. Change the second numbered item to this: `Make sure the list includes activities that are fun and upbeat.`
4. Change the fourth bulleted item to this: `Don't let things get in the way of family activity time.`

Multipage Academic Reports With Lists

34

Goals

- Type at least 34wpm/3′/5e.
- Correctly use Word's line-spacing feature.
- Correctly format a multipage academic report with a list.

A. WARMUP

alphabet	1	Please pack my boxes with five dozen jugs of liquid veneer.
frequent digraphs	2	on bon con none noon don ion one son ton won onto moon font
easy	3	If she works downtown, Kay may make a visit to the old gym.

Skillbuilding

B. PROGRESSIVE PRACTICE: NUMBERS

Follow the GDP software directions for this exercise to improve keystroking speed.

C. TECHNIQUE PRACTICE: ENTER KEY

Type each line 2 times. Type each sentence on a separate line by pressing ENTER after each sentence.

4 Who? Go. So? Get it? Why not? Well? See to it. Why me? Eat!
5 Read it. Whew! Go slow. Where? Finished? Who, Tom? Type it.
6 Roll over. Wait. Sit. Beg. See him. What gives? Truly! Why?
7 Do it. Be there. Taxi? See me. All? Why him? We did. Don't!

D. 3-MINUTE TIMED WRITING

Take two 3-minute timed writings.

Goal: At least 34wpm/3′/5e

8	Companies that place major ads on the Internet use a	11
9	process called data mining. They look for patterns in the	22
10	quantities of data they get from those who visit Web sites.	34
11	Data mining tracks buying habits of customers and then	46
12	decides to send ads to them based on their current and past	58
13	buying patterns. Data mining can also be used to explain	69
14	buyer behavior and to look at trends. First, a survey is	80
15	filled out, and then the results are gathered and stored in	92
16	a file to be analyzed in detail at a later time.	102

1 | 2 | 3 | 4 | 5 | 6 | 7 | 8 | 9 | 10 | 11 | 12

R-8A–B: Multipage Business Report

E. BASIC PARTS OF AN ACADEMIC REPORT

The two basic styles of reports are business and academic. An illustration for a multipage academic report with side headings, paragraph headings, and a list follows.

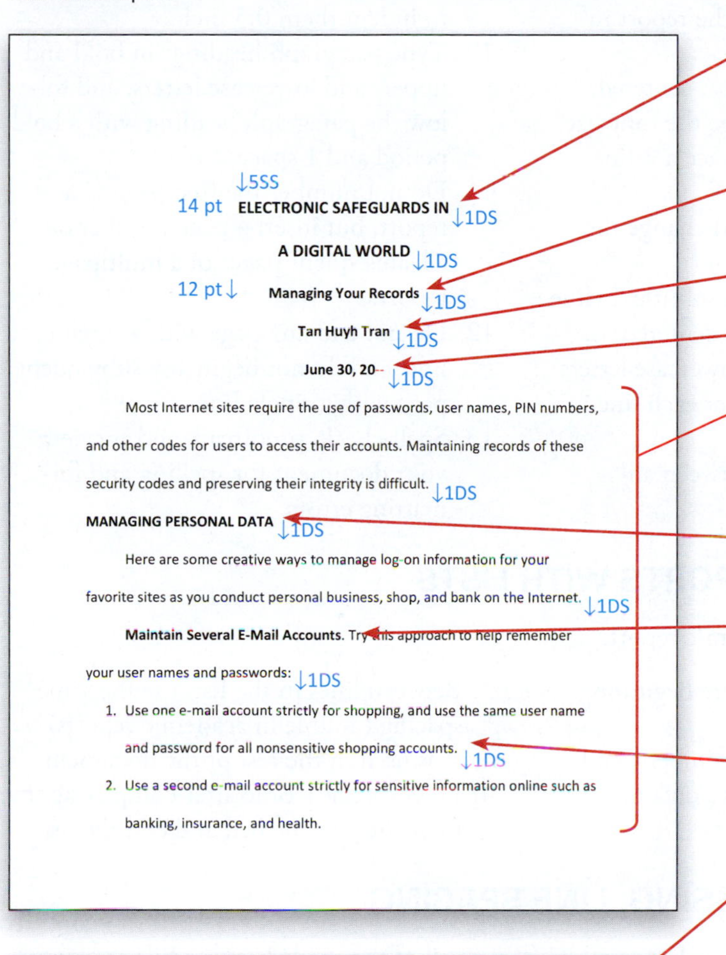

ELECTRONIC SAFEGUARDS IN

A DIGITAL WORLD

Managing Your Records

Tan Huyh Tran

June 30, 20--

Most Internet sites require the use of passwords, user names, PIN numbers, and other codes for users to access their accounts. Maintaining records of these security codes and preserving their integrity is difficult.

MANAGING PERSONAL DATA

Here are some creative ways to manage log-on information for your favorite sites as you conduct personal business, shop, and bank on the Internet.

Maintain Several E-Mail Accounts. Try this approach to help remember your user names and passwords:

1. Use one e-mail account strictly for shopping, and use the same user name and password for all nonsensitive shopping accounts.
2. Use a second e-mail account strictly for sensitive information online such as banking, insurance, and health.

2

Keep User Names and Passwords Secure. Obviously, you should keep these user names written down somewhere or on some removable media. But you must be sure to lock these in a secure location.

TITLE. Subject of the report; centered; typed 2 inches from the top of the page (single-space, press ENTER 5 times, and change to double spacing) in bold and all-caps, with a 14-point font size; 2-line titles are double-spaced.

SUBTITLE. Secondary or explanatory title; centered; typed 1 double space below the title, in bold, with upper- and lowercase letters.

BYLINE. Name of the writer; centered; typed 1 double space below the previous line, in bold.

DATE. Date of the report; centered; typed 1 double space below the previous line, in bold.

BODY. Text of the report, double-spaced; the first line of each paragraph is indented 0.5 inch, with 1 blank line between paragraphs. Subsequent pages continue at the default top margin, 1 inch from the top of the page.

SIDE HEADING. Major subdivision of the report; typed 1 double space below the previous line at the left margin, in bold and all-caps.

PARAGRAPH HEADING. Minor subdivision of the report; typed 1 double space below the previous line indented 0.5 inch from the left margin, in bold, with upper- and lowercase letters; followed by a period (also in bold).

LIST. Numbered or bulleted items in a report; typed using Word's default list indent, double-spaced, with 1 double space above and below the list.

PAGE NUMBER. Inserted on the continuing pages only inside the document header at the right margin.

F. ACADEMIC REPORTS

To format a multipage academic report with side headings and paragraph headings:

1. Press ENTER 5 times to begin the first line of the academic report 2 inches from the top of the page.
2. Change line spacing to double, and type the remainder of the report in double spacing.
3. Type the title in all-caps, centered, and in bold, and change the font size to 14 point. Double-space a 2-line title.
4. Press ENTER 1 time and change the font size to 12 point.
5. If the report includes a subtitle, byline, or date, type each item centered, in bold and upper- and lowercase letters.
6. Press ENTER 1 time after each line in the heading block.
7. Press ENTER 1 time between all paragraphs.
8. Type side headings at the left margin, in bold and all-caps.
9. Press TAB 1 time at the start of each paragraph and each paragraph heading to indent them 0.5 inch.
10. Type paragraph headings in bold and upper- and lowercase letters, and follow the paragraph heading with a bold period and 1 space.
11. Do not number the first page of a report, but insert a page number on all subsequent pages of a multipage report.
12. Do not end any page with a single line, and do not begin any subsequent page with a single line.
13. Spell-check, proofread, and preview your document for spelling and formatting errors.

G. ACADEMIC REPORTS WITH LISTS

R-12D: Examples of Different Types of Lists

To format lists in an academic report:

1. Press ENTER 1 time before beginning the list.
2. Apply either bullets or numbers, and type the list using Word's default format.
3. Between lines in the list, use the same spacing (double in academic reports) as is used in the rest of the document.
4. Press ENTER 1 time after completing the final entry in the list, and end the list.

H. WORD PROCESSING: LINE SPACING

Study Lesson 34 in your Word Manual. Complete all of the shaded steps while at your computer. Then format the documents that follow.

Document Processing

Report 34-7
Academic Report

↓5SS

14 pt **COMMUNICATION DYNAMICS WHEN** ↓1DS

SOCIALIZING AT WORK ↓1DS

12 pt↓ **Informal Social Support Systems** ↓1DS

Linda Padilla ↓1DS

October 30, 20-- ↓1DS

Longer work hours and increasing job demands are leading to social networking on the job. Mixing socially with coworkers requires a different tactic than socializing with friends and family. ↓1DS

(continued on next page)

BE YOURSELF ↓1DS

Conversation does not have to be trivial. You can take many approaches and may find that you are actually enjoying the process. ↓1DS

Talk About Personal Interests. Personal interests are usually great points to launch a conversation that is relaxed and interesting. Try this: ↓1DS

1. Talk about your favorite hobby. This is an easy way to help you relax since our hobbies bring up pleasant memories. ↓1DS
2. Food is always a safe topic that everyone enjoys. Chat about your favorite restaurant or your favorite exotic dish. ↓1DS

Ask Questions About Others. Obviously, you should avoid personal questions. Try not to ask anything you wouldn't want someone to ask you.

JUST LISTEN

Finally, don't be afraid to just listen. You don't have to talk all the time. Your coworkers will appreciate a supportive listener, and you might learn something in the process.

Report 34-8
Academic Report

Open the file for Report 34-7 and make the following changes:

1. Change the byline to `Faith Tolerencia`.
2. Add this paragraph at the end of the report:

```
Maintain good eye contact, avoid distractions, and stay active by asking mental questions. Let the other person know that you're listening by body language and meaningful responses. You might be surprised at the support you receive in return.
```

Keyboarding Connection

Business E-Mail Style Guide

Even though e-mail is relatively informal, you need to be succinct and clear. Greet your reader with a formal "Dear . . . ," or an informal "Hi . . . ," and so on. Put the most important part of your message first. Watch the length of your paragraphs; four to five lines per paragraph won't put off your reader.

Use asterisks, caps, dashes, and so forth, for emphasis. Avoid unfamiliar abbreviations, slang, or jargon. Not everyone who receives your business e-mail may know a particular catchword or phrase. Proofread your e-mail. Be concerned about grammar, punctuation, and word choice. Use your e-mail's spell checker.

End your business e-mail politely. Expressions of appreciation (e.g., "Thanks") or goodwill (e.g., "Best wishes") let your reader know you are finishing your message.

Your Turn: In Lesson 25 you learned how to format and compose e-mail messages. Create an e-mail message to send to a coworker, colleague, or friend. Review the e-mail for adherence to the guidelines listed above.

More Rough-Draft Reports

Goals

- Demonstrate improved speed and accuracy while typing.
- Demonstrate acceptable language arts skills in composing sentences.
- Identify and apply more proofreaders' marks.
- Correctly format a rough-draft, multipage academic report.
- Successfully complete a Progress and Proofreading Check with zero errors on the first scored attempt.

A. WARMUP

alphabet	1	The five boxing wizards jumped quickly into the next round.
number/symbol	2	jjoy@aol.com 66% (Ott & Poe) 5/8 Out! $2.16 *et al. #73-490
easy	3	Blanche may go with me to Yale to visit my son and his pal.

Skillbuilding

B. 12-SECOND SPEED SPRINTS

Take three 12-second timed writings on each line.

4 The man with the rifle may signal us to take the sign down.
5 The new city law may allow us to fish for cod on the docks.
6 The old chapel at the end of the big lake has an odd shape.
7 The old men may have a duel down by the lake at noon today.
' ' ' ' 5 ' ' ' 10 ' ' ' 15 ' ' ' 20 ' ' ' 25 ' ' ' 30 ' ' ' 35 ' ' ' 40 ' ' ' 45 ' ' ' 50 ' ' ' 55 ' ' ' 60

C. PACED PRACTICE

Follow the GDP software directions for this exercise to improve keystroking speed and accuracy.

Language Arts

D. COMPOSING SENTENCES

Answer each question with a complete sentence.

8 How much time do you spend each day reading and answering e-mail?
9 Which people do you correspond most often with in e-mail?
10 What kinds of errors do you find most often in e-mail?
11 Do you proofread your own e-mail messages before sending them?
12 What advice do you have for improving e-mail messages?

Formatting

R-14C: Proofreaders' Marks

E. MORE PROOFREADERS' MARKS

Review the most frequently used proofreaders' marks introduced in Lesson 33. Then study the additional proofreaders' marks presented here.

Proofreaders' Marks	Draft	Final copy
ds Double-space	ds first line second line	first line second line
.... Don't delete	a true story	a true story
◯ Spell out	the only 1	the only one
Move right	Please send	Please send
Move left	May 1	May 1
Bold	Column Heading	**Column Heading**
ital Italic	*ital* Time magazine	*Time* magazine
u/l Underline	u/l Time magazine	Time magazine
Move as shown	readers will see	readers will see

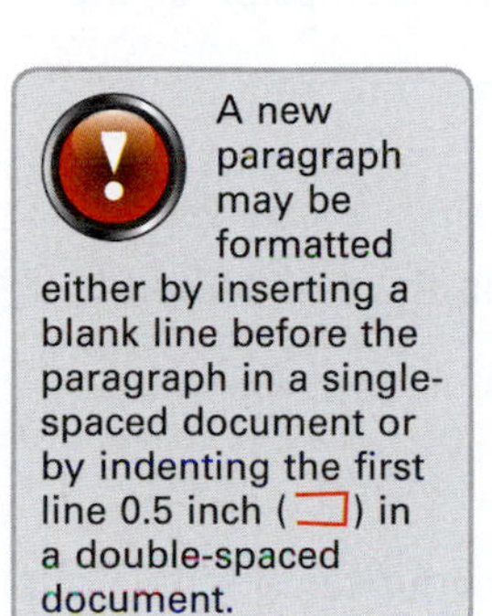

A new paragraph may be formatted either by inserting a blank line before the paragraph in a single-spaced document or by indenting the first line 0.5 inch ( ) in a double-spaced document.

F. WORD PROCESSING: CUT AND COPY; PASTE

GO TO Word Manual

Study Lesson 35 in your Word Manual. Complete all of the shaded steps while at your computer. Then format the documents that follow.

Document Processing

Report 35-9
Academic Report

ENDING PROCRASTINATION

Steven Rice

Every one at one time or another has put of some task, goal or important plan at work for any number of reasons. perhaps you think time is too short or the task isn't really that important. Either way, procrastination can lead to a stalled life and career.

EVALUATE YOUR SITUATION

Joyce Winfrey of Time Management Incorporated has some very good advice that will help you to begin to move forward. She says that you should ask yourself 2 very basic questions about why you are procrastinating:

2. 1. Is there a valid reason for my procrastination?
1. 2. Am I procrastinating because the task at hand is not really what I want?

(continued on next page)

After you have asked yourself these questions, look deep within yourself. If you are looking for excuses, then asking these questions will be a waste of time. However, honest answers will clarify your situation. Several techniques will help you get back on task.

PRACTICE NEW TECHNIQUES

Identifying and understanding the techniques which follow is the first step. Once you know what to do you can begin to practice these steps daily.

Take Baby Steps. Don't make any task bigger than it really is by looking at the whole thing at once. Break it down into babysteps that are manageable.

Dont Strive for Perfectionism. If you are waiting for the perfect solution or the perfect opportunity, you will immobilized. Accept the fact that no one and nothing is perfect. Then accept your mistakes and move on.

Enjoy the Task. Enjoy the task at hand and find something in the task at hand that is positive and rewarding. Confront your fears with a plan of action.

Remind yourself of all these techniques daily. Post them by your telephone, your desk, or your car. You will find that your personal life and career will gain momentum, and success will soon be yours.

Report
35-10
Business Report

Block paragraphs in a business report.

Progress and Proofreading Check

Documents designated as Proofreading Checks serve as a check of your proofreading skill. Your goal is to have zero typographical errors when the GDP software first scores the document.

TIPS FOR HELPING YOU

PREPARE FOR YOUR EXAM

Betty Goldberg

June 8, 20--

in school you have taken some exams. Whether you are an excellent exam taker or a novice at the task, you have experienced a degree of stress related to your performance on an exam. There are some steps you can take to reduce the stress of taking an exam, and these suggestions will likely help you throughout your life.

PREPARING FOR THE EXAM

Of course, it's always easier to take an exam from an Instructor whom you have had in previous classes, because you know what to expect.

(continued on next page)

¶ **Know What to Expect.** If you don't know what to expect, however, you need to prepare for all possibilities. Be sure that you review all pertinent materials for the exam—whether they come from classnotes, the textbook, field trips, or class room presentations.

¶ **Rely on Past Experience.** From past experience, you know whether the Instructor likes to use objective or subjective questions, whether the Instructor focuses on the textbook or on class notes, and the difficulty of the questions the Instructor asks.

SURVIVING THE DAY BEFORE THE EXAM

¶ Be sure you know where and at what time the exam will be administered. Organize the materials you need to bring with you to the exam. You need a computer pencils, pens, a calculators, CDs, or paper. Try to get a good nights sleep the night before the exam.

Taking the Exam

¶ Now that the day of the exam has arrived, try this to ensure that you perform well:

1. Arrive at the test sight early so that you are ready to take the exam when the instructor announces the beginning time. That means that you have to be sure to get up early enough to have a light breakfast before leaving for the exam.
2. Read the instructions provided very carefully on the exam to be sure you answer the questions correctly.
3. Keep track of time so that you don't get stuck and spend too much of your time on any one part of the exam.

a. Try to keep a positive attitude.

¶ Relax as best you can. A relaxed performance is much more productive than a

stressed performance.

UNIT 8

Tables

LESSON 36
Boxed Tables

LESSON 37
Open Tables

LESSON 38
Open Tables With Column Headings

LESSON 39
Ruled Tables With Number Columns

LESSON 40
Formatting Review

Boxed Tables

Goals

- Type at least 35wpm/3'/4e.
- Correctly use Word's table features to insert and resize a table.
- Correctly format a boxed table.

A. WARMUP

alphabet	1	Jack typed a requisition for long-sized white moving boxes.
concentration	2	interchangeableness paleoanthropologist extraterritoriality
easy	3	Bob owns a pair of ancient bicycles and a giant ivory bowl.

Skillbuilding

B. SUSTAINED PRACTICE: ROUGH DRAFT

Take a 1-minute timed writing on the boxed paragraph to establish your base speed. Then take a 1-minute timed writing on the following paragraph. As soon as you equal or exceed your base speed on this paragraph, move to the next, more difficult paragraph.

4 The pattern of employment in our country is undergoing 11
5 some major changes. Companies are slowly paring down their 23
6 permanent staffs to just a core group of critical managers. 35

7 This trend promotes what is called an acordion affect 11
8 in the workforce: The ability to expand and contract as the 23
9 time and balance sheets dictate. This provides flexibility. 35

10 All of these changes would make it tought for all unions 11
11 to stay a float. They donot possess satisfactory proceedures 23
12 for organizing employes. Unions are trying to adapt faster. 35

13 Such services as elder or child care, counseling, debt 11
14 managment, and even health care maybe of great asistance 23
15 to employees, but employers may *find it difficult to offer them.* 35

1 | 2 | 3 | 4 | 5 | 6 | 7 | 8 | 9 | 10 | 11 | 12

Take two 3-minute timed writings.

Goal: At least 35wpm/3′/4e

C. 3-MINUTE TIMED WRITING

16 Technology that tracks eye movements is used by Web 11
17 designers to judge how people interact with Web pages. It 22
18 must find out which zone of the page is viewed first, which 34
19 feature is viewed most often, and how quickly a page comes 46
20 to the screen. 49
21 Eye movements are tracked by use of hardware and data 60
22 analysis software. A camera is employed to find out the eye 72
23 movements of people who watch a screen. Pupil dilations and 84
24 scanning patterns of the eyes are measured to document the 96
25 amount of mental strain that has been exerted. 105

1 | 2 | 3 | 4 | 5 | 6 | 7 | 8 | 9 | 10 | 11 | 12

Formatting

D. BASIC PARTS OF A TABLE

Tables have vertical columns (identified by a letter, such as Column A) and horizontal rows (identified by a number, such as Row 1). A table cell (identified by the column letter and row number, such as Cell A1) is created where a column and a row intersect. An illustration for a boxed table follows.

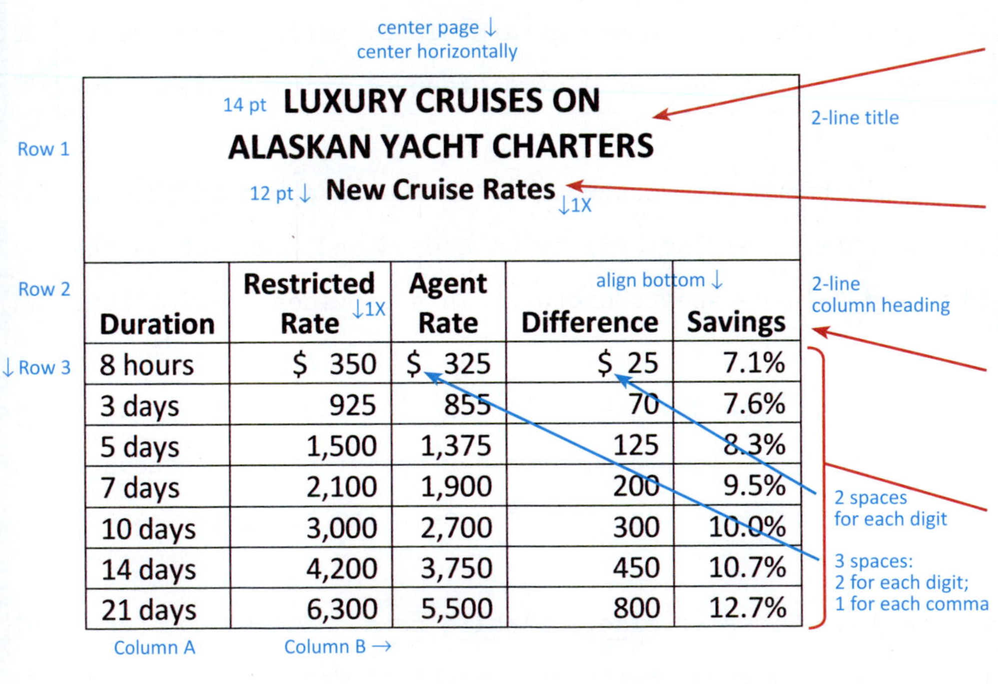

LUXURY CRUISES ON ALASKAN YACHT CHARTERS				
New Cruise Rates				
Duration	**Restricted Rate**	**Agent Rate**	**Difference**	**Savings**
8 hours	$ 350	$ 325	$ 25	7.1%
3 days	925	855	70	7.6%
5 days	1,500	1,375	125	8.3%
7 days	2,100	1,900	200	9.5%
10 days	3,000	2,700	300	10.0%
14 days	4,200	3,750	450	10.7%
21 days	6,300	5,500	800	12.7%

TITLE. Merge cells in Row 1; center and type the title with a 14-point font, in all-caps and bold; if a subtitle is not used, insert 1 blank line after the title; single-space a 2-line title.

SUBTITLE. Center and type the subtitle on the line below the title, in upper- and lowercase bold letters; press ENTER 1 time to insert a blank line below the subtitle.

COLUMN HEADINGS. Center all column headings; press ENTER 1 time to split a 2-line column heading; bottom-align all column headings.

COLUMN ENTRIES. Left-align text column entries and right-align number column entries; capitalize only the first word and proper nouns; add spaces after a dollar sign to align with the widest column entry below (add 2 spaces for each digit and 1 space for each comma).

E. TABLES

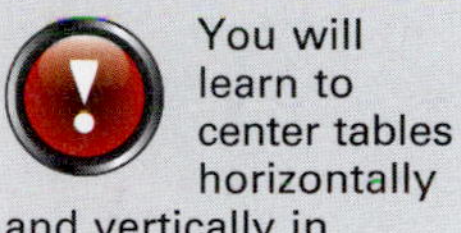

You will learn to center tables horizontally and vertically in Lesson 38.

To format a table:

1. Use single spacing.
2. Insert a table with the desired number of columns and rows.
3. Format other parts of a table as indicated in the model document in Section D.
4. Capitalize only the first word and proper nouns in column entries.
5. Type all tables using standard table format.
6. Automatically adjust the column widths.
7. Spell-check, proofread, and preview your document for spelling and formatting errors.

F. WORD PROCESSING: TABLE—INSERT AND TABLE—AUTOFIT TO CONTENTS

GO TO Word Manual

Study Lesson 36 in your Word Manual. Complete all of the shaded steps while at your computer. Then format the documents that follow.

Document Processing

Table 36-1
Boxed Table

Brenda Riggs	President	Clausen Hall
Cameron Smith	Dean	Roosevelt Hall
Jamie Summers	Chairperson	Strathern Hall

Table 36-2
Boxed Table

Bonnie Frank, Executive Editor	Trenton, New Jersey
Robert Gales, Associate Editor	Lincoln, Nebraska
Omar Quinlan, Contributing Writer	Jefferson City, Missouri
Elena Plummer, Art Director	Santa Fe, New Mexico

Table 36-3
Boxed Table

1. Open the file for Table 36-2.
2. Change the name and title in Cell A1 to `Corinne Easton, Film Editor`.
3. Change the city and state in Cell B2 to `Albany, New York`.
4. Change the name in Cell A3 to `Blanca Puscani`.
5. Change the title in Cell A4 to `Special Effects Animator`.

Table 36-4
Boxed Table

Angel Barcos	Storyboard Artist	Academy of Fine Arts
Maggie Lester	Art Director	Art Institute of California
Chang Jin Lee	Special Effects Animator	Digital Media Technologies
Anita Bergman	Visual Effects Artist	Video Game Design School

Open Tables

Goals

- Demonstrate improved speed and accuracy while typing.
- Demonstrate acceptable language arts skills in using apostrophes.
- Correctly use Word's table features to merge cells and remove borders.
- Correctly format an open table with a table heading block.

A. WARMUP

alphabet	1	Def may just bring very exciting news to the plaza quickly.
one hand	2	street unholy sad you stated monopoly seat pink treat unpin
easy	3	Hal bought an authentic bible of the gospels in the chapel.

Skillbuilding

B. MAP+: ALPHABET

Follow the GDP software directions for this exercise to improve keystroking accuracy.

C. PROGRESSIVE PRACTICE: ALPHABET

Follow the GDP software directions for this exercise to improve keystroking speed.

Language Arts

D. APOSTROPHES

Study the rules at the right.

RULE ' singular noun

Use *'s* to form the possessive of singular nouns.

The hurricane's force caused major damage to North Carolina's coastline.

RULE ' plural noun

Use only an apostrophe to form the possessive of plural nouns that end in *s*.

The investors' goals were outlined in the stockholders' report.

But: The investors outlined their goals in the report to the stockholders.

But: The women's and children's clothing was on sale.

RULE ' pronoun

Use *'s* to form the possessive of indefinite pronouns (such as *someone's* or *anybody's*); do not use an apostrophe with personal pronouns (such as *hers, his, its, ours, theirs,* and *yours*).

She could select anybody's paper for a sample.

It's time to put the file back into its cabinet.

Edit each sentence to correct any errors.

```
4  The womans purse was stolen as she held her childs hand.

5  If the book is yours, please return it to the library now.

6  The girls decided to send both parents donations to the school.

7  The childs toy was forgotten by his mothers good friend.

8  The universities presidents submitted the joint statement.

9  The four secretaries salaries were raised just like yours.

10 One boys presents were forgotten when he left the party.

11 If these blue notebooks are not ours, they must be theirs.

12 The plant was designed to recycle its own waste products.
```

Formatting

E. TABLE HEADING BLOCK

The table heading block is typed in Row 1 and includes the title and subtitle (if any). To format a table heading block:

1. Merge the cells in Row 1.
2. Inside Row 1, center and type the title in all-caps and bold, with a 14-point font.
3. Single-space a 2-line title.
4. If a subtitle is *not* used, insert 1 blank line after the title.
5. Center and type the subtitle (if any) 1 line below the title in upper- and lowercase bold letters.
6. Insert 1 blank line after any subtitle.

F. WORD PROCESSING: TABLE—MERGE CELLS AND TABLE—BORDER

GO TO Word Manual

Study Lesson 37 in your Word Manual. Complete all of the shaded steps while at your computer. Then format the documents that follow.

Document Processing

Table 37-5
Open Table

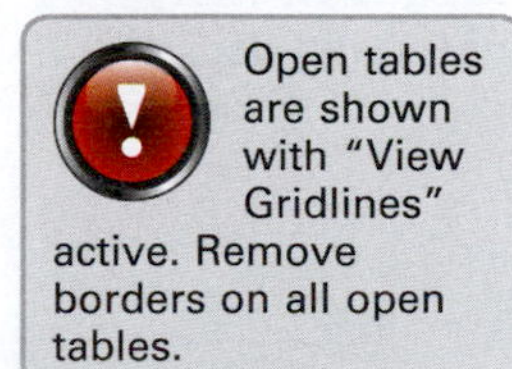
Open tables are shown with "View Gridlines" active. Remove borders on all open tables.

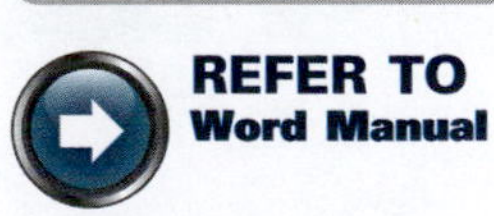

L. 28: View Gridlines

14 pt

CONTEMPORARY DESIGN'S NEWEST LOCATIONS ↓1X	
The Glen Town Center	Tallahassee, Florida
Highland Park Square	Evergreen Park, Illinois
Myrtle Beach Mall	Myrtle Beach, South Carolina
Greenway Mall	Atlanta, Georgia

12 pt ↓

Table 37-6
Open Table

' singular noun

' plural noun

LOS ANGELES COUNTY'S ↓1X PREREGISTRATION SCHEDULE Regional Supervisors' Calendar ↓1X		
Artesia	Monday, February 14	11 a.m.
Stevenson Ranch	Monday, February 21	10 a.m.
San Gabriel	Monday, February 28	11 a.m.
Huntington Park	Monday, March 7	10 a.m.

Table 37-7
Open Table

' singular noun

' plural noun

MAR VISTA REALTY'S MILLION-DOLLAR AGENTS' LIST First-Quarter Data	
James Kealing	Santa Clarita
Carol Pajaro	Malibu
Patricia Morelli	Woodland Hills
Jan McKay	Northbridge
Daniel Aboud	San Luis Obispo

Strategies for Career Success

Turning Negative Messages Positive

Accentuate the positive. When communicating bad news (e.g., layoffs, product recalls, price increases, or personnel problems), find the positive.

People respond better to positive rather than negative language, and they are more likely to cooperate if treated fairly and with respect. Avoid insults, accusations, criticism, or words with negative connotations (e.g., *failed, delinquent,* or *bad*). You also should avoid humor, as it is often misinterpreted as callousness or disdain. Focus on what the reader can do rather than on what you won't or can't let the reader do. Instead of "You will not qualify unless . . . ," state, "You will qualify if you are . . ." An example of finding the positive is "Due to budget cuts, we will not be having a holiday party. Instead, we are planning to give everyone an afternoon off around the end of the year."

Manage your audience's response by providing an explanation to support your decision and examples of how they might benefit. Analyze your audience, and decide whether to give the negative news at the beginning, middle, or end of your message. Regardless of your approach, always maintain goodwill.

Your Turn: Review some of your written documents, and observe if they have a positive tone.

Open Tables With Column Headings

Goals

- Type at least 35wpm/3′/4e.
- Correctly use Word's features to align table information and center a table horizontally and vertically.
- Correctly format an open table with column headings.

A. WARMUP

alphabet
1 Just be very quick when fixing the zip codes for your mail.

practice: *r* and *e*
2 red Rex eerie Erie elder emery enter erred every refer rear

easy
3 Kay may visit the big island in May when she is down there.

Skillbuilding

B. PACED PRACTICE

Follow the GDP software directions for this exercise to improve keystroking speed and accuracy.

C. 3-MINUTE TIMED WRITING

Take two 3-minute timed writings.

Goal: At least 35wpm/3′/4e

```
 4      Telecommuting is a word you may have heard before but    11
 5  do not quite understand. Very simply, it means working at    23
 6  home instead of driving in to work. Many people like the     34
 7  convenience of working at home. They realize they can save   46
 8  money on expenses like gas, food, or child care.             56
 9      Most home office workers use a computer in their job.    67
10  When their work is done, they can just fax or e-mail it to   78
11  the office. If they must communicate with other workers,     90
12  they can use the phone, fax, or computer and never have to  102
13  leave their home.                                           105
      1 | 2 | 3 | 4 | 5 | 6 | 7 | 8 | 9 | 10 | 11 | 12
```

Formatting

D. COLUMN HEADINGS

Column headings describe the information contained in the column entries below them. To format column headings:

- Center all column headings.
- Type the column headings in upper- and lowercase letters and bold.
- If any column heading requires 2 lines, press ENTER 1 time to create the 2-line column heading; then bottom-align all column headings in that row.

Do not insert a blank line before a single-line column heading.

center page ↓
center horizontally

TOP FIVE MANAGEMENT COMPANIES
Capital Growth Funds ↓1X

Metro Area ↓1X Market	align bottom ↓ **Business**
Atlanta, Georgia	Cedar Properties, Inc.
Charlotte, North Carolina	Kenco Realty Corporation
Norfolk, Virginia	The Westfall Group
New Orleans, Louisiana	Eden Pyramid Companies

(Note: Table shown with "View Gridlines" active.)

E. WORD PROCESSING: TABLE—ALIGN BOTTOM, TABLE—CENTER HORIZONTALLY, AND TABLE—CENTER PAGE

GO TO Word Manual

Study Lesson 38 in your Word Manual. Complete all of the shaded steps while at your computer. Then format the documents that follow.

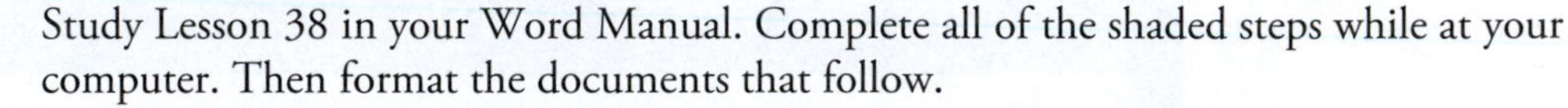

Document Processing

Table 38-8
Open Table

center page ↓

14 pt **OFFICE SUPPLIES VENDOR LIST**
12 pt ↓ **Pacific Print Works** ↓1X

Product ↓1X Category	align bottom ↓ **Vendor**
Binders	Executive Offices Unlimited
Calendars	Savings to You Inc.
File folders	Office Products Today
Business forms	Atlantic-Pacific Systems

Center all tables horizontally and vertically from now on.

Table 38-9
Open Table

COMMITTEE ASSIGNMENTS	
Academic Committee Assignments	**Professor**
Institutional Integrity	Anne McCarthy
Educational Programs	Bill Zimmerman
Student Services	John Yeh
Financial Resources	Steve Williams

Table 38-10
Open Table

1. Open the file for Table 38-8.
2. Change the subtitle to `Office Supplies Max`.
3. Change the four product categories in Column A to these:

```
Envelopes
Shredders
Hole punches
Sticky notes
```

Table 38-11
Open Table

AVAILABILITY OF CABLESERVICES	
Type Of Service	**Available Currently**
Life line	Scottsdale
Basic	Phoenix
Expanded	Glendale
Expanded (per channel)	Camelback city

Ruled Tables With Number Columns

Goals

- Demonstrate improved speed and accuracy while typing.
- Demonstrate acceptable language arts skills in spelling.
- Correctly use Word's table features to align text and apply borders.
- Correctly format a ruled table with number columns.

A. WARMUP

alphabet
1 Six of the gunboats would be jeopardized by my quick moves.

frequent digraphs
2 en end den deny gene hen men lend menu pen ten oven yen Ben

easy
3 The city panel may work on an amendment to audit the firms.

Skillbuilding

B. MAP+: SYMBOL

Follow the GDP software directions for this exercise to improve keystroking accuracy.

PPP PRETEST » PRACTICE » POSTTEST

PRETEST
Take a 1-minute timed writing.

C. PRETEST: Horizontal Reaches

4 The chief thinks the alarm was a decoy for the armed 11
5 agent who coyly dashed away. She was dazed as she dodged 22
6 a blue sedan. He lured her to the edge of the high bluff. 34
1 | 2 | 3 | 4 | 5 | 6 | 7 | 8 | 9 | 10 | 11 | 12

PRACTICE
Speed Emphasis:
If you made 2 or fewer errors on the Pretest, type each *individual* line 2 times.
Accuracy Emphasis:
If you made 3 or more errors, type each *group* of lines (as though it were a paragraph) 2 times.

D. PRACTICE: In Reaches

7 oy foyer loyal buoys enjoy decoy coyly royal cloy ploy toys
8 ar argue armed cared alarm cedar sugar radar area earn hear
9 lu lucid lunch lured bluff value blunt fluid luck lush blue

E. PRACTICE: Out Reaches

10 ge geese genes germs agent edges dodge hinge gear ages page
11 da daily dazed dance adapt sedan adage panda dash date soda
12 hi hints hiked hired chief think ethic aphid high ship chip

POSTTEST

Repeat the Pretest timed writing and compare performance.

F. POSTTEST: Horizontal Reaches

Language Arts

G. SPELLING

Type these frequently misspelled words, paying special attention to any spelling problems in each word.

13 prior activities additional than faculty whether first with
14 subject material equipment receiving completed during basis
15 available please required decision established policy audit
16 section schedule installation insurance possible appreciate
17 benefits requirements business scheduled office immediately

Edit the sentences to correct any misspellings.

18 We requierd the office to schedule all prior activities.

19 The business scheduled the instalation of the equipment.

20 The decision established the basis of the insurance policy.

21 Please audit any additionl material available to faculty.

22 If possible, they would appreciate recieving them soon.

23 Section requirements to receive benefits were completed.

Formatting

H. RULED TABLES WITH NUMBER COLUMNS

R-13B: Open Table
R-13C: Ruled Table

To format a ruled table with number columns:

1. Remove all table borders.
2. Apply borders to the top and bottom of Row 2 and to the bottom of the last row.
3. Center column headings, left-align text columns (or a mix of text and numbers), and right-align column entries with numbers that could be used in mathematical calculations.
4. Insert the dollar sign only before the amount in the first entry and before a total amount entry.

CLASS A SHARES

American World Growth and Income Fund

Investment	Offering Price	Dealer Commission
$ 205,000	2.5%	$ 4,100
500,000	2.0%	8,000
750,000	1.5%	9,000
1,000,000	0.5%	10,000

(Note: Table shown with "View Gridlines" active.)

borders: Row 2 last row—bottom

3 spaces: 2 for each digit; 1 for each comma

2 spaces for each digit

5. Align the dollar sign with the longest amount in the column, inserting spaces after the dollar sign as follows: allow 2 spaces for each digit and 1 space for each comma. In the first example, allow 2 spaces after the dollar sign. In the second, allow 3 spaces.

Examples:

$ 5
75
15

$ 375
2,150
49

6. If a table includes a total line, add a border above and below the total line. Use the word *Total* or *Totals* as appropriate, and add a percent or dollar sign if needed.

I. WORD PROCESSING: TABLE—ALIGN TEXT RIGHT AND TABLE—BORDERS, RULED

Study Lesson 39 in your Word Manual. Complete all of the shaded steps while at your computer. Then format the documents that follow.

Document Processing

Table 39-12
Ruled Table

Highlighted words are spelling words from the language arts activities; do *not* highlight them when you type. This first ruled table is shown with "View Gridlines" active.

center page ↓
center horizontally

ACCOUNT SUMMARY
Vanguard Faculty Insurance Policy ↓1X

align bottom ↓ **Account Balance**	**Current Period**	**Year-to-Date Totals**
Fees	$ 4.25	$ 145.76
Highest available balance	98.16	5,326.48
Employer contributions	9.95	499.95
Completed transactions	25.43	39.76
Totals	$137.79	$6,011.95

Table 39-13
Ruled Table

HOLIDAY RESORT SUITES
Additional Rate Charges

Hotel	**Rack Rate**	**Club Rate**	**3-Night Savings**
Porter Ranch Inn	$ 92.00	$36.00	$168.00
Jamaican Inn	119.00	59.50	178.50
Casitas Suites	120.00	60.00	180.00
The Desert Inn Resort	135.00	75.50	178.50
First Street Courtyard	150.00	75.00	225.00

Table
39-14
Ruled Table

ESTABLISHED FUNDING RESOURCES		
Fund	Current Year	Previous Year
Duncan Insurance	16.3%	2.0%
Strident Nova	9.3%	3.5%
First Value	10.7%	12.1%
Safeguard Policy	11.1%	9.7%
Vanguard Life	8.5%	10.1%

Keyboarding Connection

Searching the Web

Online search engines seek out Web pages based upon text the user types into the search box. The best results occur when users keep their search simple and specific. To search for a phrase, sentence, name, or title, put quotation marks around it; this instructs the search engine that you want results that have all those words together. For example, a search for **red bicycle** without quotation marks results in pages that may have *red* and *bicycle*, but maybe not both together. Using "red Schwinn bicycle" will produce pages that use that exact phrase.

Your Turn: From your Web browser, open a Web search engine site. Type various searches in the entry box of the search engine, and start the search. Compare the results you get from different search engines.

Formatting Review

Goals

- Type at least 36wpm/3′/4e.
- Correctly format an academic report, a business letter in block style, and a ruled table with a variety of features.
- Successfully complete a Progress and Proofreading Check with zero errors on the first scored attempt.

A. WARMUP

alphabet
1 Two joyful vixens squirted some milk upon the caged zebras.

number/symbol
2 edow@msn.com 38% Ely & May (6/9) Wow! $4.12 *ibid. #573-012

easy
3 The ten hens and turkeys in the cornfields may lay low now.

Skillbuilding

B. 12-SECOND SPEED SPRINTS

Take three 12-second timed writings on each line.

4 Bob owns a pair of old bikes and a new car he got from her.
5 Keith must work with a tutor when he has need of more help.
6 Nan may sign over the title to her car when she is in town.
7 The firm did not sign a form that may name me to the panel.
' ' ' ' 5 ' ' ' ' 10 ' ' ' ' 15 ' ' ' ' 20 ' ' ' ' 25 ' ' ' ' 30 ' ' ' ' 35 ' ' ' ' 40 ' ' ' ' 45 ' ' ' ' 50 ' ' ' ' 55 ' ' ' ' 60

C. TECHNIQUE PRACTICE: SHIFT KEY

Type each line 2 times. After striking the capitalized letter, return the SHIFT KEY finger immediately to home-row position.

8 Andrew Bishop hid me from Cindy Dunn. Emma Ford owed money.
9 Gordon Harris and Irene Jenkins spied on Kelsey Lambertson.
10 Marie Nakamura asked Orlando Pena what Quentin Rice wanted.
11 Sid Tuy and Uri Vincent ate. Will Xiang and Yasir Zito won.

Take two 3-minute timed writings.

Goal: At least 36wpm/3'/4e

D. 3-MINUTE TIMED WRITING

```
12      Complaints by workers are often viewed as a negative     11
13 force in a workplace. In fact, the complaints should be        22
14 viewed as a chance to communicate with the employee and to     34
15 improve morale. To ignore the complaint does not make it go    46
16 away. If you just listen to complaints, you may help to        57
17 solve small problems before they turn into bigger ones.        68
18      Often workers expect a chance to be heard by a person     79
19 who is willing to listen to them quite openly. That person     91
20 must recognize that the employee has concerns that need       102
21 to be addressed at this time.                                 108
    1 | 2 | 3 | 4 | 5 | 6 | 7 | 8 | 9 | 10 | 11 | 12
```

Document Processing

Report 40-11
Academic Report

RELATIONSHIPS AT WORK

Shannon Pacencia

Do you believe that as long as you get your work done at the end of the day, you have had a successful day on the job? If so, you are badly mistaken. Doing the work is only half the job. The other half is relating to and working with the people around you.

TAKE A TEAM APPROACH

Everything you do and every action you take affects those around you in a close working relationship. Operating as a team means thinking about others and taking actions that will help them reach their goals and achieve the goals of the company.

MAINTAIN A SPIRIT OF COOPERATION

When you work in a spirit of cooperation, those around you will reflect that spirit. Your job will be easier because you will minimize resistance.

VALIDATE THE OPINIONS OF OTHERS

You will find that this simple act of validation will go a long way in helping the spirit of your coworkers. Here are two simple ways to validate the opinions of others:

1. Take time to listen to the issues and accomplishments of those around you.
2. Reflect their opinions in your own words in a spirit of genuine interest.

There is a saying that states, "Your success is my success." Adopt this as your motto, and you will find a great deal of satisfaction at the end of each day.

Correspondence
40-20
Business Letter in Block Style

1. Prepare an envelope for this letter; do not insert an inside address.
2. Add the envelope to the letter.

December 1, 20-- | Mrs. Janet Broers | 1291 ~~Bahama~~ Obama Court | Richmond, KY 40475 |

Dear mrs. Broers:

¶ Thank you for choosing Alliance Insurance Of America. Open enrollment for your ~~medical~~ insurance plan is scheduled to begin the first day of January. I hope it was possible for you to review the materials you received last week. ¶ Selecting the right benefit plan for you and your family can be an over whelming task. To make ~~this~~ your decision a little easier, I have enclosed a brochure ~~with this letter~~ that summarizing the key features of each policy.

¶ Please call me if I can help in any way. You might want to browse through our website at www.iaa.com for further details.

Sincerely, | Denise Montoya | Customer Support | urs | enclosures

Table
40-15
Ruled Table

Progress and Proofreading Check

Documents designated as Proofreading Checks serve as a check of your proofreading skill. Your goal is to have zero typographical errors when the GDP software first scores the document.

PERSONAL ASSET ACCOUNTS
Albert Trevino

Account	Amount	Interest Rate
Interest Checking	$ 972.55	3.10%
Money Market	4,500.35	4.90%
Smart Saver	3,250.76	5.07%
Certificate of Deposit	550.00	7.41%

Outcomes Assessment on Part 2

Test 2

3-Minute Timed Writing

```
 1      From the first day of class, you have continuously     10
 2  worked to improve your typing skill. You have worked hard  22
 3  to increase your typing speed and accuracy. You have also  34
 4  learned to format letters, memos, reports, and tables. All 45
 5  of this work is quite an amazing accomplishment.           55
 6      In your lessons, you have worked on learning a wide    66
 7  range of word processing skills. You can expect to make    77
 8  even more progress if you will just practice your skills   88
 9  often. Learn as much as you can each day. Ask questions,  100
10  and then move toward a new goal each day.                 108
    1 | 2 | 3 | 4 | 5 | 6 | 7 | 8 | 9 | 10 | 11 | 12
```

Correspondence Test 2-21

Business Letter in Block Style

1. Add an envelope to the document.
2. Omit the return address.

January 10, 20-- | Ms. Christine Beltran | World wide Temp Professionals | 1200 Interstate Park Drive | Montgomery, AL 36109 | Dear Ms. Beltran:

¶ Each year many of the students in the computer applications department work on our campus and gain valuable experience on-the-job. This semester I have 3 students who have developed very exceptional skills. I have enclosed a list of their names in case you are interested in arranging any interviews. ¶ These students have all taken a variety of classes within our department and have worked in other disciplines with different supervisors. This exposure has given them valuable experience and insite sight into the demands of the working world. I know that you will be impressed with their backgrounds and experience.

¶ I will be calling you in the next few days so that we can discuss these students adn their qualifications in more detail.

sincerely, | Michelle Betts | Chair person | urs | Enclosure

Report Test
2-12
Academic Report

PROPER TECHNIQUE AT THE KEYBOARD

Alex Harrington

April 13, 20--

Appropriate technique at the keyboard is essential for productivity as well as for health reasons. Two essential elements of keyboarding technique are proper placement of the computer monitor and the keyboard.

MONITOR

The computer monitor should be positioned in line with the keyboard, centered on the user. Ideally, the monitor should be slightly below eye level for the most comfortable viewing and should be tilted slightly away from you, forcing you to look down slightly.

In general, position the monitor as far away as possible while still being able to read the text clearly. To position the monitor appropriately, sit back in the chair and extend your arm horizontally; your middle finger should touch the middle of the screen. This way, you won't need to make excessive head movements to see the viewing area of the screen.

Monitors and Document Holders. To minimize head movement, place the document holder at the same height and distance as the monitor and at the same angle as the monitor, tilted slightly upward. Place the document holder next to the monitor opposite the mouse.

Monitors and Laptop Computers. Despite their convenience of use, laptop computers are not ergonomic because you cannot adjust the screen and keyboard independently for the most comfort. If you do a lot of typing on a laptop, consider purchasing an external monitor or an external keyboard to avoid straining yourself.

KEYBOARD

The keyboard should be in a straight line between your body and the monitor. There is no research showing that ergonomic (split) keyboards are superior to traditional keyboards; therefore, using an ergonomic keyboard design is an individual preference.

Table Test
2-16
Ruled Table

UNIVERSITY PHONE SERVICES

Current Rates

Category	One-Time Charge	Proposed Increase
Caller ID	$ 5	$ 1
Caller ID block	5	1
Analog line	35	5
Extension	26	10

Correspondence, Reports, and Employment Documents

3 PART

Keyboarding in Education Careers

The education field has many career opportunities, including positions such as instructor, counselor, instructor assistant, administrator, media specialist, and curriculum specialist. Although two of three workers in educational services have professional and related occupations, the education field employs many administrative support, managerial, and service workers.

Instructor assistants provide support for classroom instructors in many ways, allowing instructors more time for lesson planning and actual teaching. Instructor assistants also grade assignments and tests, check homework, keep attendance records, and perform typing, data entry, and filing. Office administration staff perform similar functions for the heads of departments in colleges and universities and for the principals and education boards of elementary and secondary schools.

The use of computer technology in the educational setting is constantly growing. Proficiency with a computer, including keyboarding and formatting skills, is essential for success in the field. The use of the Internet in classrooms has expanded significantly, by helping instructors and students to communicate with each other, as well as to perform research for class assignments. Online learning is growing as well. Increasing numbers of higher education institutions use Internet-based technology to post lessons and coursework electronically, as well as to communicate with students. The *Gregg College Keyboarding & Document Processing* textbook and software are good examples of this development.

Goals

Keyboarding

- Type at least 40 words per minute on a 5-minute timed writing with no more than 5 errors.

Language Arts

- Demonstrate acceptable proofreading skills, including using proofreaders' marks.
- Demonstrate acceptable language arts skills in punctuation and grammar.
- Demonstrate acceptable language arts skills in composing and spelling.

Word Processing

- Use appropriate word processing commands to complete document processing activities successfully.

Document Processing

- Correctly format business and academic reports, business letters and personal-business letters, memos, e-mail, and resumes.

Objective Test

- Answer questions with acceptable accuracy on an objective test.

Correspondence

LESSON 41

Personal Titles and Complimentary Closings in Letters

LESSON 42

Personal-Business Letters

LESSON 43

Memos and E-Mail With Lists

LESSON 44

Letters With Indented Displays and Copy Notations and E-Mail With Copies

LESSON 45

Letters in Modified-Block Style

Personal Titles and Complimentary Closings in Letters

UNIT 9 LESSON **41**

Goals

- Demonstrate improved speed and accuracy while typing by touch.
- Demonstrate acceptable language arts skills in using quotation marks and italics (or underline).
- Correctly format a personal title in correspondence.
- Correctly format a complimentary closing in correspondence.

A. WARMUP

alphabet	1	We have quickly spotted four women dozing in that jury box.
concentration	2	oversimplifications nonrepresentational professionalization
easy	3	The town may pay my neighbor for the work she did for them.

Skillbuilding

B. MAP+: ALPHABET

Follow the GDP software directions for this exercise to improve keystroking accuracy.

C. PROGRESSIVE PRACTICE: ALPHABET

Follow the GDP software directions for this exercise to improve keystroking speed.

Language Arts

Study the rules at the right.

D. QUOTATION MARKS AND ITALICS (OR UNDERLINE)

RULE
" direct quotation

Use quotation marks around a direct quotation.

Harrison responded by saying, "Their decision does not affect us."

But: Harrison responded by saying that their decision does not affect us.

RULE
" title

Use quotation marks around the title of a newspaper or magazine article, chapter in a book, report, and similar terms.

The most helpful article I found was "Multimedia for All."

RULE
title or <u>title</u>

Italicize (or underline) the titles of books, magazines, newspapers, and other complete published works.

Grisham's *The Brethren* was reviewed in a recent *USA Today* article.

RULE
, direct quotation

Use a comma before and after a direct quotation.

James said, "I shall return," and then left.

Edit each sentence to correct any errors.

```
4  The newspaper ad in the March 1 "Tribune" was very
5  effective.

6  The Power of e-Commerce is an excellent chapter.

7  Maria answered the question by saying, "I agree."

8  Her title for the report was "The Internet in Action."

9  The magazine cover for "Newsweek" last month was excellent.

10 Karen interrupted by saying, That's exactly right!

11 The realtor replied "The first thing to consider is
12 location."

13 "The margin of error is very small" said Andy.
```

Formatting

E. PERSONAL TITLES IN LETTERS

Standard punctuation refers to the use of a colon after the salutation and a comma after the complimentary closing.

Inside Addresses

Always use a courtesy title before a person's name in the inside address of a letter; for example, *Mr.*, *Mrs.*, or *Dr.*

Type a person's title on the same line with the name (separated by a comma), if the title is short, or on the line below. The title and business name may be typed on the same line (separated by a comma) if they are both short.

Personal Titles in Inside Addresses

Mr. James R. Yamamoto, Manager
National Security Systems

Mrs. Marilyn Broquette
Executive Director
Perimeter Hospital

Dr. Raymond Bishop
Manager, Velletti Oil Co.

Salutations

When possible, use a person's name in the salutation. The correct form for the salutation is the courtesy title and the last name. If you do not know the name of the other person, use a job title or *Ladies and Gentlemen*. A colon is used after the salutation in standard punctuation.

Dear Ms. Winston:

Dear Dr. Hamner:

Dear Mr. Sparanta:

Dear Sales Manager:

Ladies and Gentlemen:

F. COMPLIMENTARY CLOSINGS IN LETTERS

Every letter should end with a complimentary closing. Some frequently used complimentary closings are *Sincerely*, *Sincerely yours*, *Yours truly*, *Cordially*, and *Respectfully yours*.

In the closing lines, do not use a courtesy title before a man's name. If a woman wants to use her personal title, she may include it in parentheses in her handwritten signature or without parentheses in her typed signature (but not in both). A comma is used after the complimentary closing in standard punctuation.

Closing Lines

Sincerely yours,
Linda Humphries
Linda Humphries
Account Manager

Yours truly,
Juliet McCoy
Ms. Juliet McCoy
Marketing Director

Cordially,
Chris S. VanVliet
Chris S. VanVliet
Regional Supervisor

Document Processing

Correspondence 41-22
Business Letter in Block Style

January 10, 20-- | Mrs. Gwen Hanover | 4034 Kennedy Lane | Mount Vernon, WA 98274-2340 | Dear Mrs. Hanover:

¶ You are one of several prospective buyers of a SunCity townhouse, and we thank you for the interest you have shown in our development project. The SunCity model received three national awards last month, and these awards were announced in the *SunCity Register* last week. *(title)*

¶ I am enclosing a brochure that illustrates all six of our model townhouses. The specific square footage for each townhouse is included in this brochure, with details on room size, electrical outlets, and cable access points. Our builder said, "I will give a bonus for the first ten customers who purchase a townhouse," and he plans to follow through with his offer. The bonus is a free cable subscription for your first year of residency. *(" direct quotation)*

¶ Thank you, Mrs. Hanover, for the opportunity to work with you these past few days. If you have any questions, please let us know.

Sincerely, | Mrs. Kathryn Bennett | Sales Director | urs | Enclosure

Correspondence 41-23
Business Letter in Block Style

May 20, 20-- | Mr. Winston A. Kahn | 1800 East Hollywood Avenue | Salt Lake City, UT 84108 | Dear Mr. Kahn:

¶ This past week we heard from many of our readers who enjoyed your rebuttal to our editorial in the *Utah Times* about the proposed airport site in Provo, Utah. Actually, you are 1 of over 30 listeners who indicated your desire for us to air your rebuttal. *(title)*

¶ Of the more than 100 request letters for equal time, we selected yours because you touched on most of the relevant points of this topic. We especially liked your comment in which you said, "The airport site would be better situated in the heavily populated north side." *(" direct quotation)*

¶ We will contact you further about taping your rebuttal on June 4. Please read the enclosed disclaimer that we would like you to sign before airing the rebuttal.

Yours truly, | Sandra L. Green | General Manager | urs | Enclosure

Personal-Business Letters

Goals

- Type at least 36wpm/3'/3e.
- Correctly format a personal-business letter.

A. WARMUP

alphabet	1	Six crazy kings vowed to abolish my quite pitiful projects.
one hand	2	secret hominy dew hip beasts nonunion edge monk staff nylon
easy	3	The chairman may risk an amendment for the downtown island.

Skillbuilding

B. SUSTAINED PRACTICE: SYLLABIC INTENSITY

Take a 1-minute timed writing on the boxed paragraph to establish your base speed. Then take a 1-minute timed writing on the following paragraph. As soon as you equal or exceed your base speed on this paragraph, move to the next, more difficult paragraph.

```
4      Taking care of aging parents is not a new trend. This   11
5  issue has arisen more and more, since we are now living     22
6  longer. Companies are now trying to help out in many ways.  34

7      Help may come in many ways, ranging from financial aid  11
8  to sponsoring hospice or in-home respite care. Workers may  23
9  find it difficult to work and care for aging parents.       34

10     Why are employers so interested in elder care? Rising   11
11 interest is the result of a combination of several things.  23
12 The most notable is a marked increase in life expectancy.   34

13     Another trend is the increased participation of women,  11
14 the primary caregivers, in the workforce. Businesses are    23
15 recognizing that work and family life are intertwined.      33
     1 | 2 | 3 | 4 | 5 | 6 | 7 | 8 | 9 | 10 | 11 | 12
```

Take two 3-minute timed writings.

Goal: At least 36wpm/3'/3e

C. 3-MINUTE TIMED WRITING

```
16      The size of their first paycheck after they finish      10
17 college seems quite high to a few young men and women. They  22
18 rent a place to live that is just too much to pay, or they   34
19 may buy a car with a huge monthly payment. For some, it      45
20 takes a while to learn that there are other items in the     57
21 monthly budget.                                              60
22      Some other budget items are food, student loans, car    71
23 insurance, rental insurance, credit card debts, health       82
24 insurance, utilities, and miscellaneous expenses. A good     93
25 goal is to put a regular amount from each paycheck into a   105
26 savings account.                                            108
     1 | 2 | 3 | 4 | 5 | 6 | 7 | 8 | 9 | 10 | 11 | 12
```

Formatting

D. PERSONAL-BUSINESS LETTERS

Personal-business letters are prepared by individuals to conduct their personal business. To format a personal-business letter:

1. Type the letter on plain paper or personal stationery, not letterhead.
2. Include the writer's return address in the letter directly below the writer's name in the closing lines.
3. Since the writer of the letter usually types the letter, do not use reference initials.
4. Spell-check, proofread, and preview your document for spelling and formatting errors.

Document Processing

Correspondence 42-24
Personal-Business Letter in Block Style

↓5X
October 1, 20-- ↓4X

Ms. Ruth Lee, Director
City Parks and Recreation Department
7034 Renwick Avenue
Syracuse, NY 13210-0475 ↓2X

Dear Ms. Lee: ↓2X

(continued on next page)

Thank you for the excellent manner in which your department accommodated our family last summer. About 120 Killians attended the reunion at Rosedale Park on August 21. Jeffrey Sparks said that Building 5 was an excellent facility for us to use for the reunion. ↓2X

As many of the Killian family pointed out to me, "We are not likely to find a facility as nice as Rosedale Park for holding our reunion." I would like to again request that Building 5 be reserved for our next year's family reunion on August 20. A confirmation of the date from your office will be appreciated. ↓2X

Sincerely, ↓4X

Jerry Killian
2410 Farnham Road
Syracuse, NY 13219

Correspondence
42-25
Personal-Business Letter in Block Style

July 13, 20-- / Mr. Alan R. Diaz, Administrator / Glencrest Nursing Home / 2807 Crossgate Circle / Lawrence, KS 66047 / Dear Mr. Diaz:
¶ Thanks to you and dozens of other people, the fall crafts sale at Glencrest was highly successful. I am very appreciative of the ways in which you helped. The highlights of the sale are going to be displayed in next Monday's issue of Glencrest Crafts.
¶ I particularly wish to thank you for transporting the display tables and chairs to Glencrest and back to the community center. Many people from the community center attended the sale and commented about how nice it was of you and your staff to support such an activity.
¶ Please accept my special thanks to you and your staff for supporting the many activities that benefit all Glencrest residents.
Sincerely, / Charles C. Brewster / 482 22d Street East / Lawrence, KS 66049

Italicize (but do not underline) the title of the magazine.

Correspondence
42-26
Personal-Business Letter in Block Style

June 4, 20-- | Mr. Randall Mitchell | 5270 Rosecrans Avenue | Topeka, KS 67284 |

Dear Mr. Mitchell:

¶ Your presentation at the Sand Hills Country Club, "Steps for Succesful Employment," was one of the most enjoyable our members have observed. I especially enjoyed the question-and-answer session at the conclusion of your wonderful presentation, and I received favorable comments from other attendees as well.

¶ Our professor has suggested that we take the information you gave us and prepare a website that focuses on the points 6 you mentioned in your speech. That way, many of our class mates can take advantage of your excellent advice when preparing for 1st search job. We have also found several other sources to use on the world wide web that we plan to include in our Web site that will be posted by the 10th of next month.

¶ This has been a very interesting assignment, thanks to the excelent information you provided. The project has given students an incentive to construct their own Web sites pertaining to job searches and interviewing techniques.

¶ Again, thank you for all your ideas.

Sincerely, | James Fetter | 3421 Carlisle Avenue | Topeka, KS 67209

Strategies for Career Success

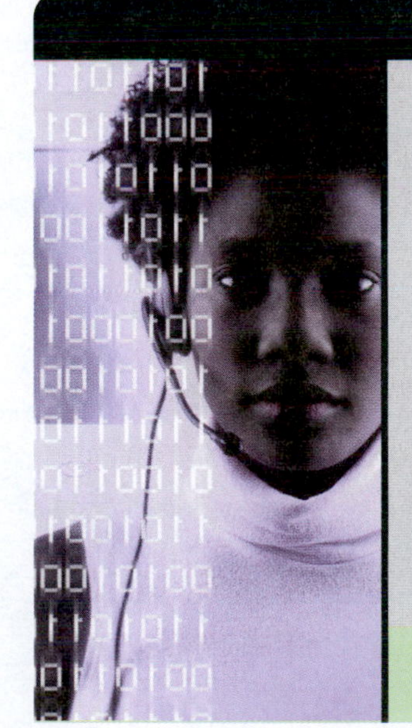

Nonverbal Communication

"It's not what he said, but how he said it." More than 90 percent of your spoken message contains nonverbal communication that expresses your feelings and desires. People respond to this nonverbal language.

Posture can convey your mood. For example, leaning toward a speaker indicates interest. Leaning backward suggests dislike or indifference. Your handshake, an important nonverbal communicator, should be firm but not overpowering.

Your head position provides many nonverbal signals. A lowered head usually expresses shyness or withdrawal. An upright head conveys confidence and interest. A tilted head signifies curiosity or suspicion. Nodding your head shows positive feeling, while left-right head shakes signify negative feeling. Your face strongly expresses your emotions. Narrow, squinting eyes signify caution, reflection, or uncertainty. Wide-open eyes convey interest and attention.

Your Turn: Turn off the sound on a television program. How much of the plot can you understand just from the nonverbal communication signals?

Memos and E-Mail With Lists

Goals

- Demonstrate improved speed and accuracy while typing by touch.
- Demonstrate acceptable proofreading skills by comparing lines of copy.
- Correctly format a list in correspondence.

A. WARMUP

alphabet	1	Joann packed my boxes with those five dozen jugs of liquor.
practice: *v* and *b*	2	verb Bev bevel bevy above livable vibe bovine brave visible
easy	3	She or I may pay for the Bible if we go to the busy chapel.

Skillbuilding

B. MAP+: NUMBERS

Follow the GDP software directions for this exercise to improve keystroking accuracy.

PPP PRETEST » PRACTICE » POSTTEST

C. PRETEST: Vertical Reaches

PRETEST
Take a 1-minute timed writing.

```
4      Kim knew that her skills at the keyboard made her a      11
5  top rival for that job. About six persons had seen her race 23
6  home to see if the mail showed the company was aware of it. 34
     1 | 2 | 3 | 4 | 5 | 6 | 7 | 8 | 9 | 10 | 11 | 12
```

D. PRACTICE: Up Reaches

PRACTICE
Speed Emphasis:
If you made 2 or fewer errors on the Pretest, type each *individual* line 2 times.
Accuracy Emphasis:
If you made 3 or more errors, type each *group* of lines (as though it were a paragraph) 2 times.

```
7  se seven reset seams sedan loses eases serve used seed dose
8  ki skids kings kinks skill kitty kites kilts kind kids kick
9  rd board horde wards sword award beard third cord hard lard
```

E. PRACTICE: Down Reaches

```
10 ac races pacer backs ached acute laced facts each acre lace
11 kn knave knack knife knows knoll knots knelt knew knee knit
12 ab about abide label above abode sable abbey drab able cabs
```

POSTTEST

Repeat the Pretest timed writing and compare performance.

F. POSTTEST: Vertical Reaches

Language Arts

Compare these lines with lines 4–7 on page 164. Edit the lines to correct any errors.

G. PROOFREADING

```
13 The eighty old books are to be thrown into the field today.
14 Alan may not take a part both of the toys out on the lanai.
15 Due to the big quake, our city may start to move all autos.
16 Glenn can take apart the old robot when he comes into town.
```

Formatting

H. CORRESPONDENCE WITH LISTS

Numbers or bullets may be used in correspondence to call attention to items in a list and to increase readability. If the sequence of the items is important, use numbers rather than bullets.

To format lists in correspondence:

1. Press ENTER 2 times to insert 1 blank line before the list.
2. Type the list using Word's default format.
3. Use single spacing between lines in the list.
4. Insert 1 blank line below the list.
5. Spell-check, proofread, and preview your document for spelling and formatting errors.

Document Processing

Correspondence
43-27
Memo

↓5X →tab

MEMO TO: Members of the Convention Committee ↓2X

FROM: Alfred A. Long, Convention Director

DATE: September 8, 20--

SUBJECT: Convention Locations ↓2X

As you know, this year's convention will meet in Kansas City, Missouri. It is the Executive Board's decision to rotate the convention site to each of the districts in our region. Our next three conventions will be held in the following locations: ↓2X

- Oklahoma City, Oklahoma
- Omaha, Nebraska
- Minneapolis, Minnesota ↓2X

(continued on next page)

In May the Board will travel to Oklahoma City to visit the location of our next convention site. When we return, we will draft our convention site proposal for you. ↓2X

urs

Correspondence 43-28
Memo

MEMO TO: Marian Dalton | **FROM:** Phyllis Schulte | **DATE:** April 9, 20-- | **SUBJECT:** Program Descriptions

¶ As you requested, I have contacted the speakers for our afternoon session discussions. All three speakers have sent me a brief description of their sessions, and they are listed in the order of presentation as follows:

1. Salon A. This session will discuss the economic growth of Pacific Rim nations.
2. Salon B. This session will present the impact of the World Wide Web on marketing strategies.
3. Salon C. This session will discuss the dynamics of econometrics.

¶ By next Monday I will send you an introduction for each speaker.
urs

Correspondence 43-29
E-Mail Message

Marian,
¶ As I indicated to you last week, I am sending you information on our three speakers' presentation titles for the Economic Seminar we have scheduled for October 20. Their presentation titles are as follows:

- Ms. Marcia Cantrell is vice president of economic forecasting for Business Trends Inc. She will be addressing the group in Salon A on the topic of "The Economic Growth of Pacific Rim Nations."
- Mr. Leonard Sanchez is marketing director for Superior Industries. He will be presenting in Salon B on the topic of "The Impact of the World Wide Web on Marketing Strategies."
- Dr. Adrian Guzman is CEO of Global Economic Research. His presentation will be held in Salon C. The title of his speech is "Dynamic Econometrics."

¶ I will send you each speaker's resume next week so that you can prepare suitable introductions for their sessions.
Phyllis Schulte | E-mail: pschulte@quickmail.com | Phone: 701-555-4832

Letters With Indented Displays and Copy Notations and E-Mail With Copies

UNIT 9 LESSON 44

Goals

- Type at least 37wpm/3′/3e.
- Correctly format a letter with a copy notation and e-mail with copies.
- Correctly format correspondence with an indented display.

A. WARMUP

alphabet 1 Five bright vixens jumped while dozing fowl quacked loudly.
frequent digraphs 2 at ate bat cat eat tat fat hat mat oat pat rat sat vat beat
easy 3 It is a shame she works such chaotic anthems into her urns.

Skillbuilding

B. PROGRESSIVE PRACTICE: NUMBERS

Follow the GDP software directions for this exercise to improve keystroking speed.

C. TECHNIQUE PRACTICE: BACKSPACE KEY

Type each line 2 times, using your Sem finger to strike the Backspace key.

The ← symbol means to backspace. For example, type *saw*, backspace, and type *y*, thus changing *saw* to *say*.

4 saw←y are←k mud←m aid←l her←n air←m hot←p box←y sot←y
5 keg←y spa←y ill←k mob←m tag←m tow←y ski←y age←o par←n
6 dad←m pat←y and←y rut←n rat←p zag←p cue←p dab←y big←n
7 via←m who←y flu←y gee←l cab←n bar←n was←y sue←m bog←o

D. 3-MINUTE TIMED WRITING

Take two 3-minute timed writings.

Goal: At least 37wpm/3′/3e

8 Each business should have its code of ethics. A code 11
9 contains rules of conduct and moral guidelines that serve 22
10 the company and its employees. Some general ethics that may 34
11 be recognized in the code are equal and fair treatment, 46
12 truth, and zeal on the job. 51
13 Companies may include a few rules in the code that 62
14 relate to their type of work. For example, if some laws 73
15 govern how they conduct business, an owner just might ask 85
16 employees to conduct all activities in a just and lawful 96
17 process. The code of business ethics should be equal for 107
18 all these workers. 111
1 | 2 | 3 | 4 | 5 | 6 | 7 | 8 | 9 | 10 | 11 | 12

Formatting

E. LETTERS WITH COPY NOTATIONS

At times you may need to send a copy of your correspondence to people other than the addressee of the original document. A copy notation is included to indicate that someone else besides the addressee is receiving a copy.

To format a letter or memo with a copy notation:

1. Type the copy notation on the line below the reference initials or below the attachment or enclosure notation.
2. At the left margin, type a lowercase *c* followed by a colon.
3. Press the Space Bar 1 time, and type the name of the person receiving the copy.
4. If more than one person is receiving a copy, type the names on one line separated by a comma and space between each name.
5. Spell-check, proofread, and preview your document for spelling and formatting errors.

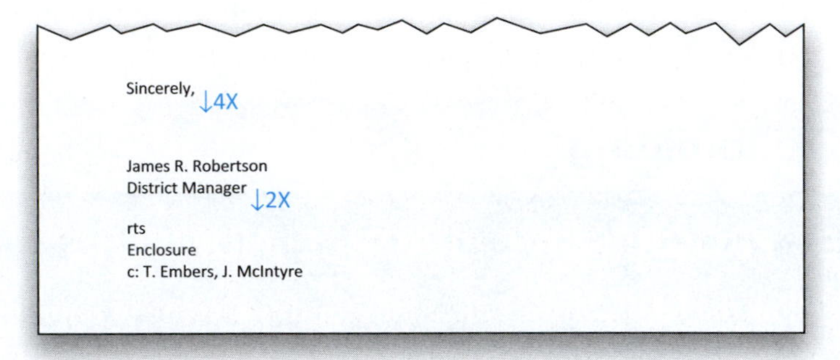

F. E-MAIL WITH COPIES

Use the copy feature in your e-mail software when you wish to send the e-mail message to additional addressees.

To format an e-mail message with a copy:

- Format the e-mail message as usual.
- No special formatting steps are needed when a copy is sent. Therefore, do not type a copy notation at the bottom of the e-mail message.
- Type e-mail addresses for recipients as desired in the Cc box.

G. INDENTED DISPLAYS

To set off a quoted paragraph that has 4 or more lines of text or to emphasize a paragraph, format it as an indented display. To format a paragraph as an indented display:

- Insert 1 blank line before and after the indented display.
- Type the paragraph single-spaced and indented 0.5 inch from both the left and right margins (instead of enclosing it in quotation marks).
- Use the indent command in Word to format a displayed paragraph.
- Spell-check, proofread, and preview your document for spelling and formatting errors.

Some students work part-time and take classes over an extended period of years. Others obtain skills by attending career-specific schools. ↓2X

→indent 0.5" No matter what path is taken, all who seek advanced training face ←indent 0.5"
Indented display
the problem of paying the ever-increasing costs of higher education. Financial aid can be the answer. There are scholarships, loans, and grants that do not have to be repaid. ↓2X

It is important that you start your research early so that you have enough time to locate and meet application deadlines for a variety of awards. ↓2X

Sincerely, ↓4X

Charles R. Stone
Branch Manager ↓2X

mtr
Enclosure
Copy notation c: Mrs. Coretta D. Rice, Dr. Thomas Moore

H. WORD PROCESSING: INDENTATION AND E-MAIL—COPIES

Study Lesson 44 in your Word Manual. Complete all of the shaded steps while at your computer. Then format the documents that follow.

Document Processing

Correspondence 44-30
Business Letter in Block Style

May 11, 20-- | Mr. James Becker | 783 Wellcourt Lane | Mount Vernon, WA 98273-4156 | Dear Mr. Becker:

¶ Marvin Sirinek has informed me that you have a question pertaining to the maintenance proposal that was submitted by the directors and approved by management at the April board meeting. Specifically, your concern focused on the following segment from that proposal:

Format this paragraph as an indented display.

> All maintenance proposals are subject to review within a reasonable timeframe, as initially defined in the RFP. Therefore, it is strongly recommended that no company representative sign a contract with the designated provider until the deadline to receive objections expires and all protests have been settled.

¶ To clarify any future misunderstandings with the interpretation of this paragraph, it should be recognized that all parties may object to any portion of the RFP for a period not to exceed 30 days from the date the RFP was officially signed by all parties.

Sincerely, | Susan Booth | Director of Maintenance | urs | c: Marvin Sirinek

Correspondence 44-31
E-Mail Message

Sarah,

¶ Thank you for your article on "The Essentials for Computer Security." As you asked, I have reviewed the article and have the following suggestions for adding some additional points to those you mentioned:

1. Never leave your computer unattended.
2. Don't lock your computer in your car where it can be seen.
3. Consider investing in a cable lock system to secure your computer to your workstation.

¶ You have some excellent suggestions in your article. I am copying my assistant editor, Alan Kramer, so that he can provide any additional suggestions.

Kevin | Kevin R. Stone | E-mail: kstone@quickmail.com | Phone: 701-555-8039

UNIT 9 LESSON

Letters in Modified-Block Style

45

Goals

- Demonstrate improved speed and accuracy when typing by touch.
- Demonstrate acceptable language arts skills in composing.
- Correctly format a letter in modified-block style.
- Successfully complete a Progress and Proofreading Check with zero errors on the first scored attempt.

A. WARMUP

alphabet 1 A Jack in the Box quickly varied its menu with fudge pizza.
number/symbol 2 coy20@cox.net 70% Hsu & Van 5/7 Win! ($4.93) *op. cit #16-8
easy 3 Andy will use eight hand signals if he is able to see them.

Skillbuilding

B. 12-SECOND SPEED SPRINTS

Take three 12-second timed writings on each line.

4 The eight old books are to be thrown into the fields today.
5 Alan may then take apart both of the toys out on the lanai.
6 Due to the big quake, the city may start to move all autos.
7 Glen may take apart the old robots when he comes into town.
' ' ' ' 5 ' ' ' ' 10 ' ' ' ' 15 ' ' ' ' 20 ' ' ' ' 25 ' ' ' ' 30 ' ' ' ' 35 ' ' ' ' 40 ' ' ' ' 45 ' ' ' ' 50 ' ' ' ' 55 ' ' ' ' 60

C. PACED PRACTICE

Follow the GDP software directions for this exercise to improve keystroking speed and accuracy.

Language Arts

D. COMPOSING SENTENCES

Answer each question with a complete sentence.

8 What are your best traits that you will bring to your job when you graduate?
9 Would you rather work for a large or a small company?
10 How much money do you expect to earn on your first job?
11 Would you like your first job to be in a small town or a large city?
12 What do you see yourself doing in ten years?

E. MODIFIED-BLOCK STYLE LETTERS

Modified-block style is a commonly used format for business letters. The date, the complimentary closing, and the writer's identification line(s) begin at the horizontal centerpoint for each of these lines. **Note:** These lines are *not* centered horizontally.

1. Set a left tab at the centerpoint (at 3.25 inches).
2. Press ENTER 5 times to begin the letter 2 inches from the top of the page.
3. Press TAB 1 time to move to the centerpoint; then type the date of the letter.
4. Press ENTER 4 times; then type the inside address at the left margin.
5. Press ENTER 2 times; then type the salutation at the left margin, and press ENTER 2 times again.
6. Type the paragraphs blocked at the left margin; press ENTER 2 times after all paragraphs.
7. After typing the final paragraph, press ENTER 2 times; then press TAB 1 time to move to the centerpoint.
8. Type the complimentary closing; then press ENTER 4 times.
9. Press TAB 1 time to move to the centerpoint; then type the writer's identification. If the writer's identification is to be typed on 2 lines, press ENTER and TAB 1 time again for any additional line.
10. Press ENTER 2 times; then type the reference initials and remaining letter parts at the left margin.
11. Spell-check, proofread, and preview your document for spelling and formatting errors.

Insurance Alliance of America
3457 Plainfield Avenue
Highland Park, NJ 08904
http://www.iaa.org

↓5X

→tab 3.25" (centerpoint) December 1, 20-- ↓4X

Mrs. Yvonne Spillotro
105 Northfield Avenue
Edison, NJ 08837 ↓2X

Dear Mrs. Spillotro: ↓2X

Thank you for choosing Insurance Alliance of America. Open enrollment for your medical insurance plan is scheduled to begin the first day of January. I hope it was possible for you to review the materials you received last week. ↓2X

Selecting the right benefit plan for you and your family can be an overwhelming task. To make your decision a little easier, I have enclosed a brochure that summarizes the key features of each policy.

You might want to browse through our Web site at www.iaa.com for further details. Please call me if I can help in any way. ↓2X

→tab 3.25" (centerpoint) Sincerely, ↓4X

Denise Broers

Denise Broers
Customer Support ↓2X

nl
Enclosure
c: Human Resources Department

F. WORD PROCESSING: TAB SET—RULER TABS

GO TO Word Manual

Study Lesson 45 in your Word Manual. Complete all of the shaded steps while at your computer. Then format the documents that follow.

Document Processing

Correspondence 45-32
Business Letter in Modified-Block Style

October 28, 20-- | Mr. and Mrs. Jacob Fang | 2308 Hannegan Road | Bellingham, WA 98226 | Dear Mr. and Mrs. Fang:
¶ We are pleased that you are interested in a Jennings home. Ollie Lucas, the agent who showed you the lot on Garfield Street, has referred your unanswered questions to me.
¶ Typically, 20 percent of the selling price is required as a down payment, but some of the lending agencies with which we work require a smaller down payment depending on your financial liquidity. Jennings Homes is not itself involved in home financing, but we work with several financial institutions in the Bellingham area. I encourage you to call on any of those included in the enclosed list to arrange for your financing needs.
¶ Yes, the Garfield lot can accommodate a full basement. If you prefer to add a basement to your new home, please let Mr. Lucas know of your intentions. We hope to hear from you soon so that we can start landscaping the lot to your satisfaction.
Sincerely, | Gayle R. Sloan | Sales Director | urs | Enclosure | c: Loan Processing Dept.

Correspondence 45-33
Business Letter in Modified-Block Style

December 8, 20-- / Mr. Darryl Ward, Sales Manager / Bachmann's Nursery and Landscaping / 6823 Oneta Avenue / Youngstown, OH 44500-2175 / Dear Mr. Ward:
¶ As you requested on the telephone, I am providing the following list of events relating to the trees I purchased from your nursery:

1. *On May 4, I purchased at your nursery in Salem four silver maples for the atrium outside our Salem office. We also purchased four Yoshino cherry trees at your branch in Canton the next day.*
2. *After about six months, one of the silver maples and one cherry tree had died. I phoned both the Salem and Canton branches the week of November 15, but no one returned my calls.*
3. *On November 20, I phoned your nursery in Salem in an attempt to have these trees replaced. Again, no one responded to my call.*

(continued on next page)

¶ As these trees are under warranty for one year from the date of purchase, I expect that you will replace them at no charge. I look forward to hearing from you as to when the trees will be replaced.
Sincerely, | Roger Blalock | Grounds Manager | urs

Correspondence
45-34
Business Letter in Modified-Block Style

Progress and Proofreading Check

Documents designated as Proofreading Checks serve as a check of your proofreading skill. Your goal is to have zero typographical errors when the GDP software first scores the document.

December 21, 20-- | Mr. Roger Blalock | 4782 Saranac Avenue | Youngstown, OH 44505-6207 | Dear Mr. Blalock:
¶ As you requested in your December 8 letter, we will replace your trees without cost to you. The replacement trees will match the others you purchased in both size and color. I am enclosing a warranty for these new trees so that you can feel confident that we stand behind our product.
¶ We cannot predict the survival rate for any tree; however, for those that do not survive for a reasonable lifespan, we stand behind our warranty and replace those that expire during the first year they are planted.
¶ The communication breakdown that you experienced with our branch offices should not have occurred. We will take steps to ensure that this will not happen again. You can be confident that the appearance of your atrium will be restored. Thank you for shopping at Bachmann's.
Sincerely, | Mrs. Alice G. Schmidt | Co-owner | urs | Enclosure | c: Mr. Darryl Ward

Keyboarding Connection

Inedible Cookies

Is that cookie good for you? A cookie is a short text entry stored on your computer that identifies your preferences to the server of the Web site you are viewing.

Certain Web sites use cookies to customize pages for return visitors. Only the information you provide or the selections you make while visiting a Web site are stored in a cookie. You can control how your browser uses cookies.

Use the Help feature in your browser to find out how to control cookies. Try using the keywords "cookie" or "security" when you search the Help index. You will probably find some great tips on how to increase security when working on the Internet.

Your Turn: Access your browser's cookie policy defaults. Decide if you want to change them.

UNIT

10

Reports

LESSON 46
Left-Bound Business Reports With Indented Displays and Footnotes

LESSON 47
Reports in APA Style

LESSON 48
Reports in MLA Style

LESSON 49
Report Citations

LESSON 50
Preliminary Report Pages

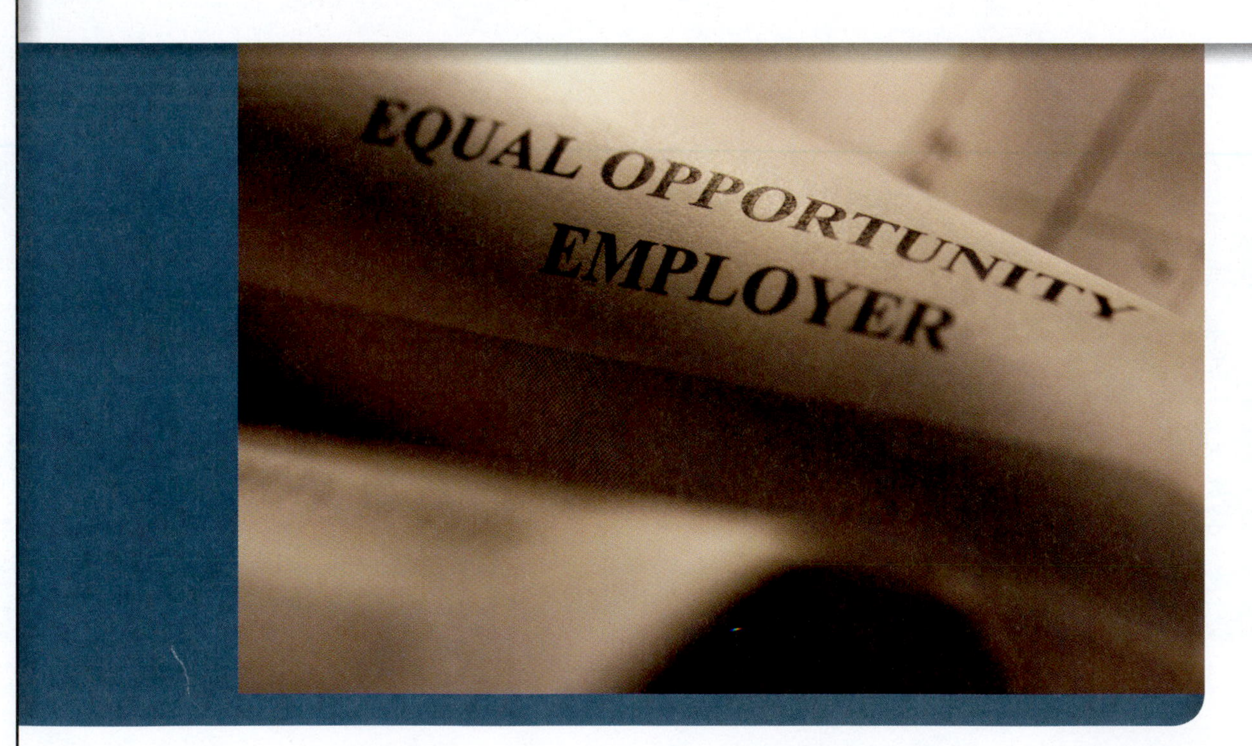

Left-Bound Business Reports With Indented Displays and Footnotes

UNIT 10 LESSON 46

Goals

- Type at least 37wpm/3′/3e.
- Correctly use Word's margin and footnote features.
- Correctly format a left-bound business report with a long quotation and footnotes.

A. WARMUP

alphabet	1	At the zoo a roving ox was quickly fed a tasty jumping bug.
concentration	2	straightforwardness uncommunicativeness departmentalization
easy	3	A pair of cozy socks or a cup of cocoa may fix me right up.

Skillbuilding

B. SUSTAINED PRACTICE: NUMBERS AND SYMBOLS

Take a 1-minute timed writing on the boxed paragraph to establish your base speed. Then take a 1-minute timed writing on the following paragraph. As soon as you equal or exceed your base speed on this paragraph, move to the next, more difficult paragraph.

4	The proposed road improvement program was approved by	10
5	the county commissioners at their last meeting. There were	23
6	about ten citizens who spoke on behalf of the project.	34
7	The plan calls for blacktopping a 14-mile stretch on	11
8	County Road 42356. This is the road that is commonly called	23
9	the "roller coaster" because of all the curves and hills.	34
10	There will be 116 miles blacktopped by J & J. Bros.	10
11	(commonly referred to as the Jeremy Brothers*). J & J's	22
12	office is at 1798 30th Avenue past the 22d Street bridge.	33
13	Minor road repair costs range from $10,784 to a high	11
14	of $163,450 (39% of the total program costs). The "county	22
15	inspector" is to hold the project costs to 105% of budget!	34

1 | 2 | 3 | 4 | 5 | 6 | 7 | 8 | 9 | 10 | 11 | 12

Take two 3-minute timed writings.

Goal: At least 37wpm/3'/3e

C. 3-MINUTE TIMED WRITING

```
16      Now is a great time for you to look for a job. Most        11
17 employers look for people who have mastered a few office        22
18 skills. For example, if you have acquired good computer         33
19 skills and are capable of working with people around you        45
20 and are steadfast, you can find a good job. There are some      56
21 who will pay top dollar to find and keep good workers.          67
22      Your first impression on a prospective employer will       78
23 be a lasting one. Your resume should list your job skills,      90
24 your experience, and your personal information. Your zeal      102
25 when you interview for a job must come through.                111
     1 | 2 | 3 | 4 | 5 | 6 | 7 | 8 | 9 | 10 | 11 | 12
```

Formatting

D. LEFT-BOUND REPORTS WITH FOOTNOTES

A left-bound report requires a wider left margin to allow for binding so that text is not hidden after the report is bound. To format a left-bound report, increase the left margin to 1.5 inches.

Footnote references indicate the sources of facts or ideas used in a report. Although footnotes may be formatted in various ways, they have many characteristics in common:

1. Footnote references are indicated in the text by superior figures.
2. Footnotes are numbered consecutively throughout a report.
3. Footnotes appear at the bottom of the page on which the references appear and are preceded by a divider line, which is automatically inserted when the footnote is created.
4. A footnote should include the name of the author, the title of the book (italicized) or article (in quotation marks), the publisher, the place of publication, the year of publication, and the page number(s).
5. If a footnote lists an online reference, it should also include the URL address and the date the source was accessed.
6. Spell-check, proofread, and preview your document for spelling and formatting errors.

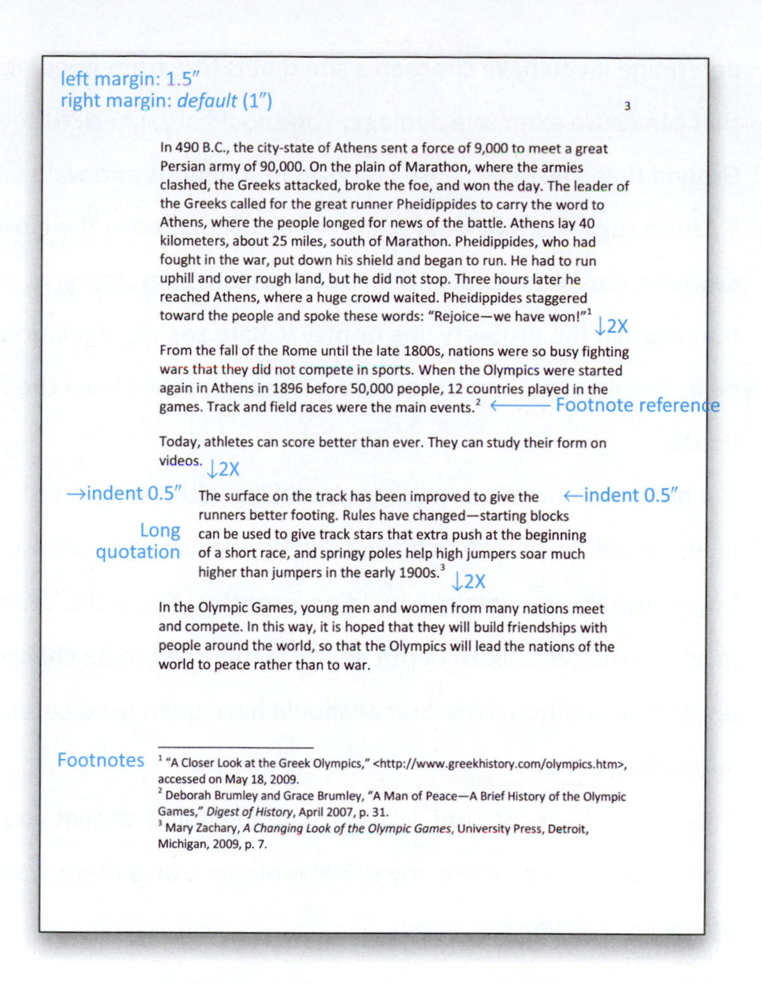
left margin: 1.5″
right margin: *default* (1″)

3

In 490 B.C., the city-state of Athens sent a force of 9,000 to meet a great Persian army of 90,000. On the plain of Marathon, where the armies clashed, the Greeks attacked, broke the foe, and won the day. The leader of the Greeks called for the great runner Pheidippides to carry the word to Athens, where the people longed for news of the battle. Athens lay 40 kilometers, about 25 miles, south of Marathon. Pheidippides, who had fought in the war, put down his shield and began to run. He had to run uphill and over rough land, but he did not stop. Three hours later he reached Athens, where a huge crowd waited. Pheidippides staggered toward the people and spoke these words: "Rejoice—we have won!"[1] ↓2X

From the fall of the Rome until the late 1800s, nations were so busy fighting wars that they did not compete in sports. When the Olympics were started again in Athens in 1896 before 50,000 people, 12 countries played in the games. Track and field races were the main events.[2] ←—— Footnote reference

Today, athletes can score better than ever. They can study their form on videos. ↓2X

→indent 0.5″ ←indent 0.5″

Long quotation

> The surface on the track has been improved to give the runners better footing. Rules have changed—starting blocks can be used to give track stars that extra push at the beginning of a short race, and springy poles help high jumpers soar much higher than jumpers in the early 1900s.[3] ↓2X

In the Olympic Games, young men and women from many nations meet and compete. In this way, it is hoped that they will build friendships with people around the world, so that the Olympics will lead the nations of the world to peace rather than to war.

Footnotes

[1] "A Closer Look at the Greek Olympics," <http://www.greekhistory.com/olympics.htm>, accessed on May 18, 2009.
[2] Deborah Brumley and Grace Brumley, "A Man of Peace—A Brief History of the Olympic Games," *Digest of History*, April 2007, p. 31.
[3] Mary Zachary, *A Changing Look of the Olympic Games*, University Press, Detroit, Michigan, 2009, p. 7.

E. WORD PROCESSING: MARGINS AND FOOTNOTES

Study Lesson 46 in your Word Manual. Complete all of the shaded steps while at your computer. Then format the documents that follow.

Document Processing

Report 46-13
Left-Bound Business Report

SHOPPING FOR A HOME

Antonio Valdez

¶ Buying a home is a proces s that many of us will go through in our life time. If we are like many other prospective buyers, we will experience this decision three or four major times in our working years. A home is often the largest purchase we will make, and it deserves therefore our careful attention. ~~We must be certain to look carefully at all the information available to us.~~

¶ "Many people think that the most important criteria on in shopping for a home is its site,"[1] ~~says James Carson.~~ The site should be on land that is well drained and free ~~from~~ from flooding ~~that can cause extensive damage.~~ Check the ~~area~~ local city zoning plan to

(continued on next page)

determine if you have choosen a site that is free from flooding and highwater levels that can cause extensive damage. You should also check to see if the ground is stable. Ground that shifts can cause cracks in foundations and walls.

¶ Cruise suggests that a home survey be conducted in the early stages of your search:

Key problems are encroachments such as buildings, trees, or additions to the house that overlap the property line or may violate zoning regulations. The solution can be as simple as moving or removing trees or bushes from the front or back of your house.[2]

¶ A home purchase is a major under taking with a long list of items that must be investigated. To ensure that the building is structurally sound, many prospective buyers use the services of a building inspector. The walls, ceiling, and floors need proper insulation. "Both depth and 'r' factor need to be checked for appropriate levels."[3] In addition, crossbraces should have been used between the beams supporting a floor.

¶ Carefully check the roof. Walk around the house so that you can view the roof lines from all angles. Are there any shingles missing, or is there water damage? Make note of any inconsistencies.

---

[1] David Sanders, "A New Home for the Millennium," *home planning magazine,* April 12, 2009, pp. 8-14.

[2] Karen Cruise, "Settlement Issues when Buying a New Home," *Home Finances,* 2010 July, p. 73.

[3] Raymond Stiles, "Home Construction Ideas," *The Do-It-Yourself Builder,* October 17, 2009, p. 22.

Report
46-14
Left-Bound Business Report

Open the file for Report 46-13 and make the following changes:

1. Delete the final paragraph in the report.
2. Add the following as the final paragraph in the report; insert the footnote as indicated.

The roof should be checked to see if any shingles are missing. Finally, a thorough check should be made of the heating, cooling, and electrical systems in the home. "These features are as critical as any others to be examined."[4]

---

[4] Jennifer Corsi, Home Facilities Planning, University Press, Chicago, 2009, p. 184.

In the footnote, format the book title in italics.

Reports in APA Style

47

Goals

- Demonstrate improved speed and accuracy while typing by touch.
- Demonstrate acceptable language arts skills in expressing numbers.
- Correctly use Word's header feature.
- Correctly format a report in APA style with author/year citations.

A. WARMUP

alphabet 1 His graceful bisque vases whizzed past in my taxi--no joke!
one hand 2 exceed kimono ads mop geared opinion cast onion weave plump
easy 3 Guthrie may clench his hand when they chant the old anthem.

Skillbuilding

B. MAP+: ALPHABET

Follow the GDP software directions for this exercise to improve keystroking accuracy.

C. PROGRESSIVE PRACTICE: ALPHABET

Follow the GDP software directions for this exercise to improve keystroking speed.

Language Arts

Study the rules at the right.

D. NUMBER EXPRESSION

RULE # general

In general, spell out numbers zero through ten, and use figures for numbers above ten.

We rented two movies for tonight.
The decision was reached after 27 precincts sent in their results.

RULE # figure

Use figures for

- **Dates. (Use *st, d,* or *th* only if the day comes *before* the month.)**
  The tax report is due on April 15 (not *April 15th*).
  We will drive to the camp on the 23d (or *23rd* or *23rd*) of May.
- **All numbers if two or more related numbers both above and below ten are used in the same sentence.**
  Mr. Carter sent in 7 receipts, and Ms. Cantrell sent in 22.
  But: The 13 accountants owned three computers each.

- **Measurements (time, money, distance, weight, and percent).**
  The $500 statue we delivered at 7 a.m. weighed 6 pounds.
- **Mixed numbers.**
  Our sales are up 9½ (or *9 1/2* or *9.5)* percent over last year.

Edit each sentence to correct any errors.

```
4  On the 3d of June, when she turns 60, 2 of her annuities will
5  have earned an average of 10 3/4 percent.

6  All seven investors were interested in buying 14 condos if
7  they were located within fifteen miles of one another.

8  The credit fee is fifteen dollars, and the interest is set
9  at 8 percent; escrow will close on March 23rd before five
10 p.m.

11 The parcel weighed two pounds.

12 She also mailed three large packages and twelve small
13 packages on June 4.

14 They paid 2.5 points on the loan amount.
```

Formatting

E. REPORTS IN APA STYLE

In addition to the traditional academic style, academic reports may also be formatted in APA (American Psychological Association) style. In the APA style, format the report as follows:

1. Use the default 1-inch margins, and 12-pt. Calibri throughout the report.
2. Double-space the entire report.
3. Insert a header for all pages; type a shortened title and insert an automatic page number that continues the page-numbering sequence from the previous page right-aligned inside the header. **Note:** APA style requires that page 1 be a title page and page 2 be an abstract. Thus, the first page of your APA report should be page number 3.
4. Type the title 1 inch from the top of the page centered using upper- and lowercase letters. Press ENTER 1 time and type the byline centered using upper- and lowercase letters. (Do not bold either the title or the byline.)
5. Indent all paragraphs 0.5 inch.
6. Type main headings centered, using upper- and lowercase letters. Press ENTER 1 time before and after the main heading.
7. Type subheadings at the left margin in italics using upper- and lowercase letters. Press ENTER 1 time before and after the subheading.
8. Spell-check, proofread, and preview your document for spelling and formatting errors.

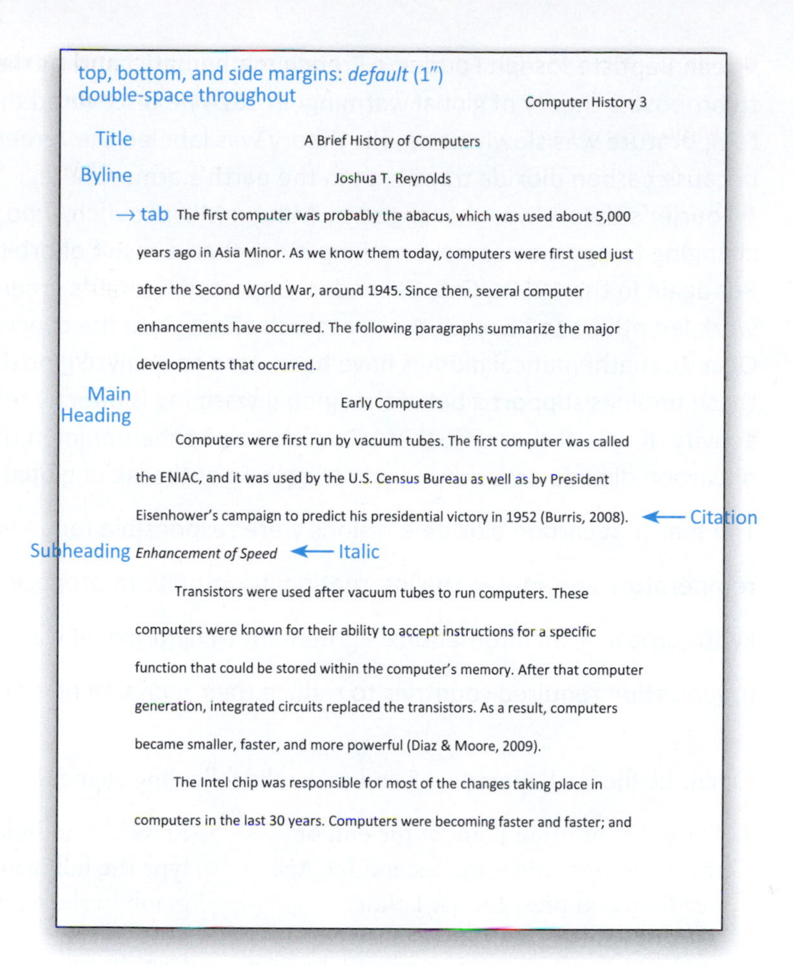
Computer History 3

A Brief History of Computers

Joshua T. Reynolds

The first computer was probably the abacus, which was used about 5,000 years ago in Asia Minor. As we know them today, computers were first used just after the Second World War, around 1945. Since then, several computer enhancements have occurred. The following paragraphs summarize the major developments that occurred.

Early Computers

Computers were first run by vacuum tubes. The first computer was called the ENIAC, and it was used by the U.S. Census Bureau as well as by President Eisenhower's campaign to predict his presidential victory in 1952 (Burris, 2008).

Enhancement of Speed

Transistors were used after vacuum tubes to run computers. These computers were known for their ability to accept instructions for a specific function that could be stored within the computer's memory. After that computer generation, integrated circuits replaced the transistors. As a result, computers became smaller, faster, and more powerful (Diaz & Moore, 2009).

The Intel chip was responsible for most of the changes taking place in computers in the last 30 years. Computers were becoming faster and faster; and

F. AUTHOR/YEAR CITATIONS

Any information based on other sources and used in a report must be documented or cited. The author/year method of citation includes the source information in parentheses at the appropriate point within the text. For more detailed information on APA citations, refer to the illustration in this book or consult the current APA style guide.

G. WORD PROCESSING: HEADERS

GO TO Word Manual

Study Lesson 47 in your Word Manual. Complete all of the shaded steps while at your computer. Then format the documents that follow.

Document Processing

Report 47-15
Report in APA Style

Global Warming 3

A Brief History of Global Warming | April R. Baumgartner

¶ Earth's climate constantly changes, and many scientists believe that the temperature rises we see in this decade are a natural phenomenon that occurs every so many years. Around 25,000 years ago, it is believed that earth was covered by large areas of ice. And then, about 7,000 years ago, temperatures began to rise and the "Ice Age" came to an end.

general

general

Second Ice Age

¶ In the 14th century earth experienced the start of another Ice Age where much of the land mass was covered by glaciers, mostly in three areas: Alaska, Iceland, and the Scandinavian countries. By 1850, however, earth's temperatures had warmed to the point where the glaciers receded, uncovering millions of acres of fertile soil.

general

(continued on next page)

¶ Jean Baptiste Joseph Fourier, a French mathematician, was the first scientist to propose a theory of global warming. In 1824 he discovered that the earth's temperature was slowly rising. His theory was labeled the "greenhouse effect" because carbon dioxide traps heat in the earth's atmosphere.

¶ Fourier's theory was challenged by Milutin Milankovitch, who proposed that earth's changing temperatures were nothing more than a result of orbital changes of earth. But again in the 1950s, G. S. Callendar supported Fourier's greenhouse effect, and his work led others to increase their research efforts into the concept of global warming. Over 20 mathematical models have been used to analyze global temperatures, and these findings support a belief that global warming is directly related to human activity. It was at that time that scientists voiced their opinion that an increased level of carbon dioxide emissions would trigger an outbreak of global warming.

general

¶ The fear that carbon dioxide emisions were responsible for an increase in temperatures prompted the international comunity to propose the creation of the kyoto protocol, an international agreement to fight global warming. Members of the organization required countries to reduce their emission of green house gases.

(Proofreaders' marks: insert "s" in "emisions"; insert "global" after "in"; insert "m" in "comunity"; capitalize "kyoto protocol"; replace "the" with "this"; close up "green house".)

Report 47-16
Report in APA Style

Open the file for Report 47-15 and make the following changes:

1. Place the insertion point at the end of the paragraph under the Second Ice Age heading, and press ENTER 1 time.
2. Type the subheading `Global Warming Theories` in italics at the left margin; then press ENTER 1 time.
3. Move the insertion point to the end of the document.
4. Press ENTER 1 time; then type `Global Warming Today` as a subheading; press ENTER 1 time.
5. Press TAB to indent the paragraph; then type the following text as the final paragraph in the report:

```
Scientists today disagree as
to cause of global warming.
Most support two theories:
that the increased level
of carbon dioxide emissions
is responsible for global
warming or that global
warming is a natural
phenomenon. All do agree,
however, that global warming
is an imminent problem that
needs to be addressed in the
future.
```

Reports in MLA Style

Goals

- Type at least 38wpm/3′/3e.
- Correctly format a report in MLA style.

A. WARMUP

alphabet	1	Meghan deftly picked valuable jewels, like onyx and quartz.
practice: *w* and *e*	2	web wet were where we elbow wed dew wide ewe wee wade endow
easy	3	Maud may signal her skepticism by her amendment to the bid.

Skillbuilding

B. PACED PRACTICE

Follow the GDP software directions for this exercise to improve keystroking speed and accuracy.

C. 3-MINUTE TIMED WRITING

Take two 3-minute timed writings.

Goal: At least 38wpm/3′/3e

```
 4      Some of us like to use the Internet for shopping. With  11
 5  just a simple click of the mouse, you can shop for almost   23
 6  any type of product. You can purchase books, cars, food,    34
 7  games, toys, zippers, boxes, and even golf clubs by using   46
 8  the computer to shop online.                                52
 9      The advantages of using the Web to shop with such ease  63
10  are many. First, you can shop from any place that has some  75
11  access to the Internet. Second, you can compare all prices  86
12  with other places before you make any purchase. Third, you  98
13  can have your purchases shipped directly to you. All the   110
14  savings mount quickly.                                     114
     1 | 2 | 3 | 4 | 5 | 6 | 7 | 8 | 9 | 10 | 11 | 12
```

D. REPORTS IN MLA STYLE

In addition to the traditional academic style and APA style, academic reports may also be formatted in MLA (Modern Language Association) style. If citations are used, usually the author's last name and page number are cited inside parentheses. For more detailed information on MLA style, refer to the illustrations in this book or consult the current MLA style guide.

In the MLA style, format the report as follows:

1. Use the default 1-inch margins, and 12-pt. Calibri throughout the report.
2. Double-space the entire report.
3. Insert a header for all pages; type the author's last name and the page number right-aligned inside the header.
4. Type each element of the heading information (your name, your instructor's name, the class name, and the date) on a separate line at the left margin.
5. Type the date using the day-month-year style (15 April 20--).
6. Center and type the title using upper- and lowercase letters. (Do not bold the title.)
7. Indent all paragraphs 0.5 inch.
8. Spell-check, proofread, and preview your document for spelling and formatting errors.

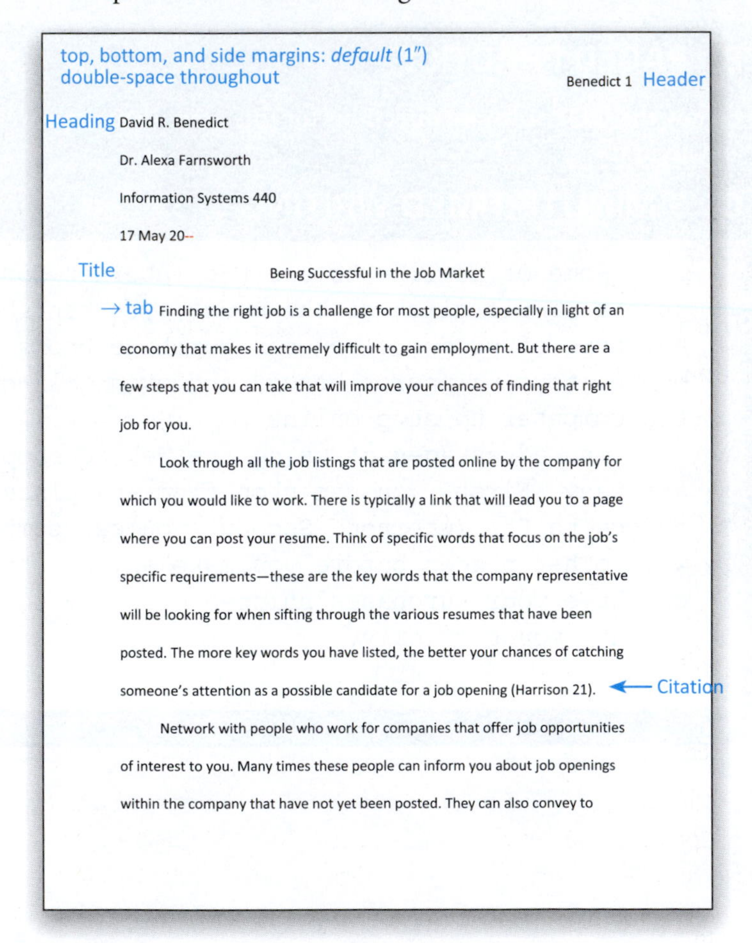
top, bottom, and side margins: *default* (1")
double-space throughout

Benedict 1 ← Header

Heading → David R. Benedict

Dr. Alexa Farnsworth

Information Systems 440

17 May 20--

Title → Being Successful in the Job Market

→ tab Finding the right job is a challenge for most people, especially in light of an economy that makes it extremely difficult to gain employment. But there are a few steps that you can take that will improve your chances of finding that right job for you.

Look through all the job listings that are posted online by the company for which you would like to work. There is typically a link that will lead you to a page where you can post your resume. Think of specific words that focus on the job's specific requirements—these are the key words that the company representative will be looking for when sifting through the various resumes that have been posted. The more key words you have listed, the better your chances of catching someone's attention as a possible candidate for a job opening (Harrison 21). ← Citation

Network with people who work for companies that offer job opportunities of interest to you. Many times these people can inform you about job openings within the company that have not yet been posted. They can also convey to

Document Processing

Report
48-17
Report in MLA Style

Remember to type the author's last name and page number right-aligned in the header.

Remember to double-space the entire report.

Chu 1

Michael Chu
Dr. Katherine Sanchez
Telecommunications 414
14 October 20--

Evaluating a Computer System

¶ Judging the effectiveness of a computer system has taken on a new dimension in the past few years, if for no other reason than the wide range of computer systems from which the user can select. It is, therefore, important that we investigate the criteria that should be considered in making this important decision.

¶ Probably the most obvious criterion to be considered when one purchases a computer system is speed. The value of a computer is directly related to its speed, and a computer's speed is typically measured in gigahertz (GHz). A gigahertz is one billion cycles per second, and the more gigahertz you have to work with, the faster your computer will run. However, computer manufacturers are starting to drop the gigahertz rating from computers because there are so many other factors that determine a computer's speed (Phillips 243).

¶ Another important consideration is memory. Software programs continue to expand and need more memory to run on today's computers. If a computer does not have sufficient memory, your computer will process slowly or not at all. When purchasing your new computer, do not settle for anything less than 8 to 12 GBytes of Dual or Tri-Channel memory.

¶ *Flexibility is also important because of the rapid turnover of hardware and software in the computer industry. The flexibility of a computer system is important for two reasons: to accommodate a variety of programs and to permit expandability. Hundreds and possibly thousands of software packages are available today to meet the needs of computer users. The computer you purchase must be able to accommodate this variety of software and be flexible enough to change with the increasing sophistication of software packages.*

Report
48-18
Report in MLA Style

Open the file for Report 48-17 and make the following changes:

1. Change the title of the report to `Computer System Evaluation`.
2. Delete the last sentence in the first paragraph of the report.
3. Place the insertion point at the end of the fourth paragraph; then add a new paragraph with the text that follows:

```
Because of the substantial investment you make in a computer, you do not want to commit your resources to a computer that cannot be expanded to handle (1) newer, more powerful operating systems; (2) "memory-hungry" software packages; (3) network interfaces; and (4) additional users (Goebels and Hallock 129).
```

UNIT 10 LESSON 49

Report Citations

Goals

- Demonstrate improved speed and accuracy while typing by touch.
- Demonstrate acceptable language arts skills in spelling.
- Correctly use Word's hanging indent and AutoCorrect features.
- Correctly format a bibliography, a reference page in APA style, and a works-cited page in MLA style.

A. WARMUP

alphabet	1	The jinxed wizards plucked the ivy stem from the big quilt.
frequent digraphs	2	es ekes yes espy eves less desires ewes exes eyes fees mess
easy	3	Pamela may use a kayak and map to come to the old city dam.

Skillbuilding

B. MAP+: SYMBOL

Follow the GDP software directions for this exercise to improve keystroking accuracy.

PPP PRETEST » PRACTICE » POSTTEST

PRETEST

Take a 1-minute timed writing.

C. PRETEST: Alternate- and One-Hand Words

```
4      The chair of the trade committee served notice that     11
5  the endowment grant exceeded the budget. A million dollars  22
6  was the exact amount. The greater part might be deferred.   34
     1 | 2 | 3 | 4 | 5 | 6 | 7 | 8 | 9 | 10 | 11 | 12
```

PRACTICE

Speed Emphasis:
If you made 2 or fewer errors on the Pretest, type each *individual* line 2 times.

Accuracy Emphasis:
If you made 3 or more errors, type each *group* of lines (as though it were a paragraph) 2 times.

D. PRACTICE: Alternate-Hand Keys

```
7  amendment turndown visible suspend visual height signs maps
8  authentic clemency dormant figment island emblem usual snap
9  shamrocks blandish problem penalty profit thrown chair form
```

E. PRACTICE: One-Hand Words

```
10 pumpkin eastward plumply barrage poplin greater holly trade
11 manikin cassette opinion seaweed kimono created union exact
12 minimum attracts million reserve unhook scatter plump defer
```

POSTTEST

Repeat the Pretest timed writing and compare performance.

F. POSTTEST: Alternate- and One-Hand Words

Language Arts

Type these frequently misspelled words, paying special attention to any spelling problems in each word.

G. SPELLING

```
13 per other receipt present provided commission international
14 service position questions following industrial maintenance
15 well absence support proposal mortgage corporate management
16 upon balance approval experience facilities recommendations
17 paid because premium procedure addition directors currently
```

Edit the sentences to correct any misspellings.

```
18 The international comission provided a list of proceedures.
19 That industrial maintainance proposal is curently in place.
20 The directers and management supported the recomendations.
21 Those present raised a question about a corporate morgage.
22 Six of the folowing persons have now given their aproval.
23 In edition, Kris has other experience at the facilitys.
```

Formatting

R-9B: Bibliography

H. BIBLIOGRAPHIES

A bibliography is an alphabetic listing of all sources of facts or ideas used or cited in a report. The bibliography is typed on a separate page at the end of a report. In general, titles of major works like books or magazine titles are italicized, and titles of minor works like articles from magazines are typed in quotation marks. For more detailed information on entries in a bibliography, refer to the illustrations in this book or consult a current style guide.

To format a bibliography:

1. Press ENTER 5 times to begin the first line 2 inches from the top of the page.
2. Center and type BIBLIOGRAPHY in all-caps, 14-pt. font, and bold; then press ENTER 2 times.
3. Apply a hanging indent and type the first line. Each entry will begin at the left margin, and the carryover lines will automatically be indented 0.5 inch by the hanging indent.
4. Single-space each entry in the bibliography, and press ENTER 2 times between each entry.

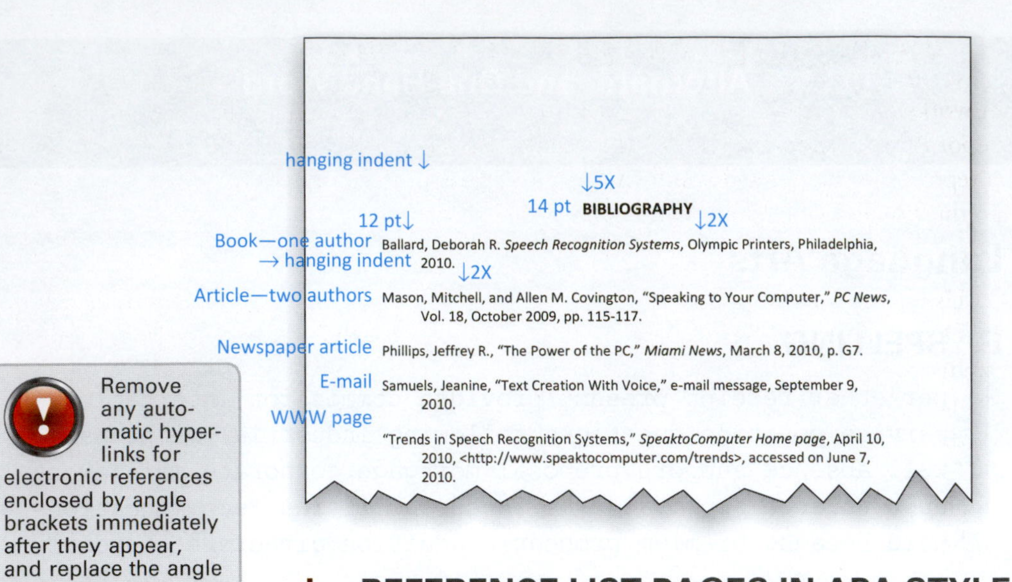

hanging indent ↓

↓5X

14 pt **BIBLIOGRAPHY** ↓2X

12 pt↓

Book—one author → hanging indent: Ballard, Deborah R. *Speech Recognition Systems*, Olympic Printers, Philadelphia, 2010. ↓2X

Article—two authors: Mason, Mitchell, and Allen M. Covington, "Speaking to Your Computer," *PC News*, Vol. 18, October 2009, pp. 115-117.

Newspaper article: Phillips, Jeffrey R., "The Power of the PC," *Miami News*, March 8, 2010, p. G7.

E-mail: Samuels, Jeanine, "Text Creation With Voice," e-mail message, September 9, 2010.

WWW page: "Trends in Speech Recognition Systems," *SpeaktoComputer Home page*, April 10, 2010, <http://www.speaktocomputer.com/trends>, accessed on June 7, 2010.

Remove any automatic hyperlinks for electronic references enclosed by angle brackets immediately after they appear, and replace the angle brackets as needed.

I. REFERENCE LIST PAGES IN APA STYLE

REFER TO Reference Manual

R-10B: References in APA Style

A reference list is an alphabetic listing of all sources of facts or ideas used or cited in a report formatted in APA style. The reference list is typed on a separate page at the end of a report. For more detailed information on reference list entries, refer to the illustrations in this book or consult a current APA style guide.

To format an APA reference list page:

1. Use the default margins.
2. Double-space the entire page.
3. Insert a header, type a shortened title, and insert an automatic page number that continues the page-numbering sequence from the previous page right-aligned inside the header.
4. Center and type `References` at the top of the page in upper- and lowercase letters; then press ENTER 1 time.
5. Apply a hanging indent and type the first line. Each reference will begin at the left margin, and the carryover lines will automatically be indented 0.5 inch by the hanging indent.

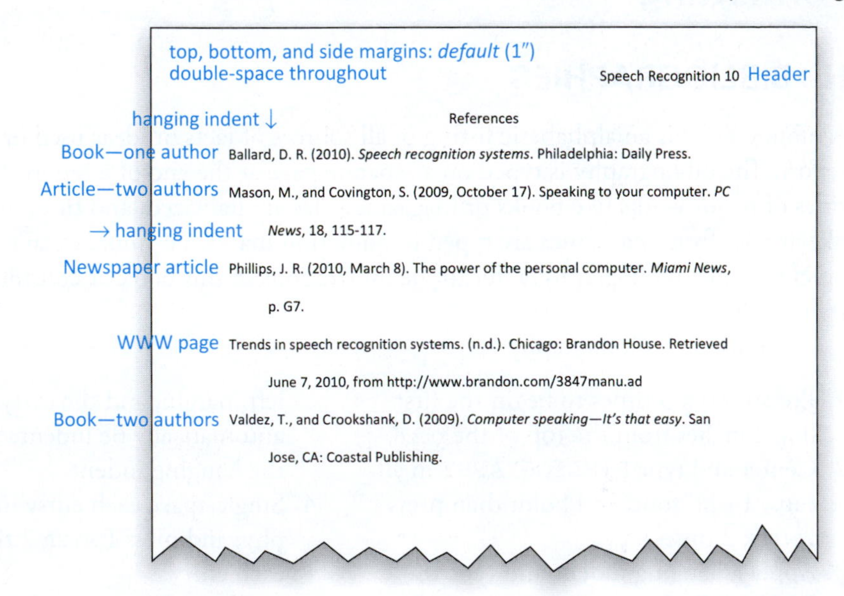

top, bottom, and side margins: *default* (1")
double-space throughout

Speech Recognition 10 Header

hanging indent ↓

References

Book—one author: Ballard, D. R. (2010). *Speech recognition systems*. Philadelphia: Daily Press.

Article—two authors → hanging indent: Mason, M., and Covington, S. (2009, October 17). Speaking to your computer. *PC News*, 18, 115-117.

Newspaper article: Phillips, J. R. (2010, March 8). The power of the personal computer. *Miami News*, p. G7.

WWW page: Trends in speech recognition systems. (n.d.). Chicago: Brandon House. Retrieved June 7, 2010, from http://www.brandon.com/3847manu.ad

Book—two authors: Valdez, T., and Crookshank, D. (2009). *Computer speaking—It's that easy*. San Jose, CA: Coastal Publishing.

J. WORKS-CITED PAGES IN MLA STYLE

R-10D: Works Cited in MLA Style

A works-cited page is an alphabetic listing of all sources of facts or ideas used or cited in a report formatted in MLA style. This reference list is typed on a separate page at the end of a report. For more detailed information on reference list entries, refer to the illustrations in this book or consult a current MLA style guide.

To format a works-cited page:

1. Use the default margins.
2. Double-space the entire page.
3. Insert a header, type the author's last name, insert an automatic page number that continues the page-numbering sequence from the previous page right-aligned inside the header, and close the header.
4. Type `Works Cited` centered at the top of the page; then press ENTER 1 time.
5. Apply a hanging indent, and type the first line at the left margin; the carry-over lines will automatically be indented 0.5 inch by the hanging indent.

Kramer 10

Works Cited

Ballard, Deborah R. *Speech Recognition Systems*. Philadelphia: Olympic Printers, 2010.

Mason, Mitchell, and Allen M. Covington. "Speaking to Your Computer." *PC News* 18 Oct. 2009: 115-117.

Phillips, Jeffrey R. "The Power of the PC." *Miami News* 8 March 2010: G7.

Samuels, Jeanine. "Text Creation with Voice." E-mail to the author. 18 Sept. 2010.

"Trends in Speech Recognition Systems." 10 Apr. 2010. 7 Sept. 2010 <http://www.speaktocomputer.com/trends/ad>.

K. WORD PROCESSING: INDENTATION—HANGING AND AUTOCORRECT—HYPERLINK

Study Lesson 49 in your Word Manual. Complete all the shaded steps while at your computer. Then format the documents that follow.

Document Processing

Report 49-19
Bibliography

Italicize (but do not underline) the publication titles.

Highlighted words are spelling words from the language arts activities; do *not* highlight them when you type.

BIBLIOGRAPHY

Becker, Arnie, "Management Policies in Industrial Nations," Modern Management, Vol. 24, January 2010, pp. 22-24.

Champagne, Lester R., CEO Questions and Recommendations, Tennessee Valley Press, Nashville, 2009.

Driscoll, Andy, and Cynthia Rogge, "Procedures for Boards of Directors," Daily Press, San Francisco, 2009.

(continued on next page)

Hartwing Institute, Premium Mortgages, Lohr Press, Phoenix, 2008.

"Overdue Debts of our Nation," Corpamerica, June 18, 2010, <http://www.corporatedebt.com>, accessed on July 8, 2010.

Pearson, Jack E., "International Investment Guide Proposal," e-mail message, February 17, 2010.

Report 49-20
References in APA Style

An Economic Overview 12

References

Currin, C.D., & Terwilliger, Ernest, S. E. (2010). *A director's position on mortgage loans*. Burr Ridge, IL: Mcgraw-Hill/Irwin.

Dodsworth, W. R. (2009). Current guide to insurance premiums, *The Review Insurance, XIX*, 24-34.

Freeberg, S. A., Kingsford, M. A., & Soderbloom, Z. E. (2009). *The absence of experience in job interviews.* Minneapolis: The University Press.

Mueller, D. T., & Isaacson, R. D. (2010). *Questions about the present economic condition.* Retreived June 11, 2010, from the world wide web: http://www.economicforecasts.com/june digest/forecasts.htm

Tindall, M. G. (2008). Adjusting the balance of additional indicators. *The Midwest Economic Forecaster,* 23.

Waldon, J. R. (2010). *american capitalism following the economic down turn.* Seattle: Puget Sound Press.

Report 49-21
Works Cited in MLA Style

Worthington 18

Works Cited

Anderson, Cody M. "Corporate Management Policies." E-mail to the author. 9 Nov. 2010.

Bartoletti, Lynda, et al. "E-commerce Support on the Internet." *Online Today*. Vol. 10. Aug. 2009: 123-124.

Conner, Shelby. *Recommendations for the New Online Resources*. Cheyenne: Mountain Press, 2010.

"Industrial Maintenance Facilities." *National Entrepreneur.* 18 Oct. 2009. 22 July 2010 <http://www.entrepreneurnews.com/facilities.htm>.

Lewis, Michael, and Walter R. Arnold. *Proposal for Approval of Online Purchases.* Miami: Keys Publishing House, 2010.

Tucker, James, and Arlene Hoffman. "International Commission on Internet Services." *Indianapolis Gazette*, 12 June 2009: B3.

Preliminary Report Pages

Goals

- Type at least 38/3′/3e.
- Correctly format a title page and a table of contents.
- Correctly use Word's tab set and dot leaders features.
- Successfully complete a Progress and Proofreading Check with zero errors on the first scored attempt.

A. WARMUP

alphabet
1 The judges quickly gave back six prizes to the famed women.

number/symbol
2 pnoe@att.net 270% Ivy & Day 3/8 Go! $17.59 *sic (#6423-145)

easy
3 The haughty widow with the auditory problem may ask for it.

Skillbuilding

B. 12-SECOND SPEED SPRINTS

Take three 12-second timed writings on each line.

4 Chris may clap his hands when they chant the songs at camp.
5 Hale saw a Bible of the gospel in the chapel near the lake.
6 Half of the maps may be for the land and half for the lake.
7 Ray may work in the field of coal when he is not busy here.
' ' ' ' 5 ' ' ' ' 10 ' ' ' ' 15 ' ' ' ' 20 ' ' ' ' 25 ' ' ' ' 30 ' ' ' ' 35 ' ' ' ' 40 ' ' ' ' 45 ' ' ' ' 50 ' ' ' ' 55 ' ' ' ' 60

C. TECHNIQUE PRACTICE: SPACE BAR

Type each line 2 times, using your right thumb to strike the Space Bar in the center.

8 My dad may ask me to dig up an old oak if it is in the way.
9 Ty can be at the bus by six if he can hop a cab on the way.
10 We may ask a tax pro to pay our tax for us if we owe a lot.
11 My new ad on the air may get a lot of men to buy a new car.

Take two 3-minute timed writings.

Goal: At least 38wpm/3'/3e

D. 3-MINUTE TIMED WRITING

```
12      The Web is a vast source of facts and data on many      10
13  topics. You can view many newspapers, zip through weather   22
14  reports, find a tax form and learn how to complete it, and  34
15  search for a job. You can find answers to health questions  46
16  and learn about world events almost as soon as they occur.  57
17      E-mail is another part of the Internet that people are  69
18  using more often. They use e-mail to keep in touch with     80
19  friends and family in a quick and efficient way that costs  92
20  very little. They can write down their thoughts and send   103
21  messages just as if they were writing a letter or memo.    114
      1 | 2 | 3 | 4 | 5 | 6 | 7 | 8 | 9 | 10 | 11 | 12
```

Formatting

E. TITLE PAGE

Reports may have a title page, which includes information such as the report title, to whom the report is submitted, the writer's name and identification, and the date. To format a title page, follow these steps:

1. Center the page vertically and center all lines horizontally.
2. Center the title in all-caps and bold, using a 14-pt. font.
3. Press ENTER 2 times; then center the subtitle in upper- and lowercase and bold, using a 12-pt. font.
4. Press ENTER 12 times; then center the words `Submitted to`.
5. Press ENTER 2 times; then center the recipient's name and identification on separate lines, single-spaced.
6. Press ENTER 12 times; then center the words `Prepared by`.
7. Press ENTER 2 times; then center the writer's name and identification on separate lines, single-spaced.
8. Press ENTER 2 times; then center the date.

Strategies for Career Success

Cover Letters

A cover letter, also known as a letter of transmittal or an executive summary, introduces a report or proposal. Such letters provide an overview of the report in an informal, conversational writing style.

Let the recipient know what you are sending; for example, "Enclosed is the proposal you requested." If you're submitting an unsolicited report, explain why you've written the report. Include the report topic, and identify the person or persons who authorized the report. Recap the main points. Cite any specific information that would help your audience comprehend the material, such as whether it's a draft. Keep your cover letter short and concise.

Conclude with a note of appreciation, a willingness to discuss the report, and intended follow-up action. Will you do something? Do you want feedback? If you want the reader to act, explain what you need and provide a deadline; for example, "Please provide your comments by July 15."

Your Turn: List some ways that a cover letter can promote goodwill between the sender and recipient.

center page ↓

14 pt **USING TECHNOLOGY TO REACH STUDENTS**
AT A DISTANCE ↓2X

12X ↓ **Distance Learning Classrooms** ↓12X

Submitted to ↓2X

Alicia T. Gonzalez
Technology Coordinator
Media Systems, Inc. ↓12X

Prepared by ↓2X

Tracy Weller
Computer Specialist
Media Systems, Inc. ↓2X

October 21, 20--

F. TABLE OF CONTENTS

A table of contents is usually included in a long report. The table of contents identifies the major and minor sections of a report and includes page numbers preceded by dot leaders. Dot leaders are a series of periods that guide the reader's eye across the page to the page number typed at the right margin. To format a table of contents:

1. Press ENTER 5 times to begin the first line 2 inches from the top of the page.
2. Center and type CONTENTS in all-caps, 14-pt. font, and bold; then press ENTER 2 times.
3. Set a left tab at 0.5 inch; then set a right tab at 6.5 inches with dot leaders.
4. Change to 12-pt. font, and type the first main heading in all-caps.
5. Press TAB to insert dot leaders and to move to the right margin; then type the page number, and press ENTER 2 times.
6. Type the next main heading in a similar fashion. If the next item is a subheading, press TAB 1 time to indent the subheading 0.5 inch.
7. Type the subheading, and then press TAB to insert dot leaders and to move to the right margin; then type the page number.
8. Press ENTER 1 time to type the next subheading or 2 times to type a new main heading.
9. Continue in like fashion until the table of contents is complete.

left tab: 0.5"
right dot-leader tab: 6.5"

↓5X

14 pt **CONTENTS** ↓2X

12 pt ↓ OUR COMPUTER SOCIETY .... → tab 6.5" 2 ↓2X

HOW COMPUTERS WORK .... 5 ↓2X

→ tab 0.5" Input 5
Processing 7
Storage 8
Output .... 12 ↓2X

USING COMPUTER SOFTWARE 14

Word Processing 16
Spreadsheet 17
Database 19
Graphics 20

COMPUTERS AND YOUR CAREER 21

Management Information Systems 25
Careers in the Computer Industry 28
Careers in Business and Industry 32
Careers in Government 36

COMPUTERS AND YOUR FUTURE 38

BIBLIOGRAPHY 41

G. WORD PROCESSING: TAB SET—DOT LEADERS

GO TO Word Manual

Study Lesson 50 in your Word Manual. Complete all of the shaded steps while at your computer. Then format the documents that follow.

Document Processing

Report 50-22
Title Page

GLOBAL WARMING AND ITS IMPACT ON EARTH'S CLIMATE

Including a Discussion on Future Trends

Submitted to

Brandon T. Alexander
Technology Coordinator
Anthropogenic Division

Prepared by

Richelle R. Simmons
Science Coordinator
Anthropogenic Division

February 9, 20--

Report
50-23
Table of Contents

CONTENTS

INTRODUCTION 2
HISTORICAL EVIDENCE 5
Ancient History 6
Last 1,000 Years 8
Last 100 Years 9
THE EFFECTS OF GLOBAL WARMING 10
Impact on Icebergs 12
Impact on Oceans 15
Temperature Extremes 16
Disease 18
PREDICTING FUTURE TEMPERATURES 20
Computer Modeling 22
Trends in Forecasting 24
Scientific Proof 25
Climate Sensitivity 27
CLIMATE CHANGE POLICIES 30
SUMMARY 35

Report
50-24
Title Page

THE POWER OF COMPUTERS

Some Predictions for the Internet and Artificial Intelligence

Submitted to

Jerry Santiago
Division Chief
Computer Dynamics Inc.

Prepared by

Marilyn R. Hasamara
Computer Consultant
Computer Dynamics Inc.

May 24, 20--

Report
50-25
Left-Bound Business Report

Progress and Proofreading Check

Documents designated as Proofreading Checks serve as a check of your proofreading skill. Your goal is to have zero typographical errors when the GDP software first scores the document.

THE POWER OF COMPUTERS

Some Predictions for the Internet and Artificial Intelligence

Marilyn R. Hasamara

¶ Much has been written about the impact of computers and how they will alter almost every activity in our lives for years to come. There is strong evidence that this prediction will soon become a reality. The purpose of this report is to summarize changes that we will likely see in the areas of Internet activity and artificial intelligence.

THE INTERNET REVOLUTION

¶ There is little doubt that connectivity to the Internet will continue to grow in this decade. The speed at which we access the Internet will also continue to grow. The transmission of information on the Internet today will be considered but a "snail's pace" when compared to what we can expect in just a few short years. Most

(continued on next page)

information will be transmitted at gigabit speeds and higher.[1] Computer security will also be enhanced exponentially, and the safety of transmitting sensitive data over the Internet will encourage many users to increase their use of online communications to conduct everyday business activities without fear of outside interference.

ARTIFICIAL INTELLIGENCE

¶ Artificial intelligence—generally known as AI—can be described as a computer's ability to assume an intelligence similar to that of the human brain. It enables a computer to reason and make decisions based on a preassigned set of facts or data.[2] But many experts predict that the computer's power will not stop there. They predict that computers will soon become much smarter than humans by a process in which "intelligent" computers create even more intelligent computers.

¶ It is also predicted that robots will displace humans from farms and factories; we will travel in cars, planes, and trains that are operated solely by computers; and traveling on the interstate highways will be as safe as watching television at home.

---

[1] Delores R. Polaski, "Tomorrow's Brainpower," *Internet for Tomorrow*, Vol. 8, February 2010, pp. 75-77.

[2] Timothy T. Reynolds, "Artificial Intelligence," *Journal of Computer Trends*, September 2009, pp. 23-24, 36.

Keyboarding Connection

Evaluating Internet Sources

Are you sure your Internet source has valid information? Because of the broad availability of the Internet and the lack of careful review stages like the ones built into print publishing, you must be cautious about the dependability of information you find on the Internet. Evaluate information on the Internet by the same standards you use to evaluate other sources of information.

The best way to ensure that information is valid is to get it from a reputable source. The Internet versions of established, reputable journals in medicine (for example, *Journal of the American Medical Association*), business (for example, *Harvard Business Review*), engineering, computer science, and so forth, warrant the same level of trust as the printed versions.

When you do not use established, reputable Web sites, use caution. Keep in mind that anyone can publish on the Internet. For many sources, there are no editorial review safeguards in place.

Your Turn: Search the Web for more assessment methods.

UNIT 11

Employment Documents

LESSON 51
Resumes

LESSON 52
Letters of Application

LESSON 53
Interview Communications

LESSON 54
Follow-Up Letters

LESSON 55
Integrated Employment Project

Resumes 51

Goals

- Demonstrate improved speed and accuracy while typing by touch.
- Demonstrate acceptable language arts skills in comma usage.
- Correctly format a resume.
- Correctly use Word's font and table column width features.

A. WARMUP

alphabet	1	`Viewing those quizzical abstracts mixed up the hefty jocks.`
concentration	2	`interchangeableness incontrovertibility nonadministratively`
easy	3	`The men paid for their neighbor to make a robot for profit.`

Skillbuilding

B. MAP+: ALPHABET

Follow the GDP software directions for this exercise to improve keystroking accuracy.

C. PROGRESSIVE PRACTICE: ALPHABET

Follow the GDP software directions for this exercise to improve keystroking speed.

Language Arts

D. COMMAS

Study the rules at the right.

RULE
, date

Use a comma before and after the year in a complete date.

We will arrive on June 2, 2009, for the conference.

But: We will arrive on June 2 for the conference.

But: Work should be submitted between November 2009 and December 2009.

RULE
, place

Use a comma before and after a state or country that follows a city (but not before a ZIP Code).

Joan moved to Vancouver, British Columbia, in May.

Send the package to Douglasville, GA 30135, by Express Mail.

But: Send the package to Georgia by Express Mail.

Edit each sentence to correct any errors.

```
4  The warehouse building will be ready in September, 2008.

5  The attorney told a clerk to use June 30, 2009 as the date.

6  The books were sent to Los Angeles, CA, 90029 on July 13,
7  2009 and will arrive soon.

8  The move to Toledo, Ohio, was scheduled for November, 2008.

9  The meeting began on May 3 in Chicago at 9 a.m.

10 We shopped for souvenirs in Nogales, Sonora on Friday.

11 January 1, 2012 will be a special date for our company.
```

Formatting

E. BASIC PARTS OF A RESUME

When you apply for a job, you may be asked to submit a resume. The purpose of a resume is to convey your qualifications for the position you are seeking. A resume should include the following:

- Personal information (name, address, telephone number, and e-mail address).
- Your career objective (optional).
- A summary of your educational background and special training.
- Previous work experience.
- Any activities or personal achievements that relate to the position for which you are applying.
- References (optional). If an employer requests references, you should have at least three people who can tell a prospective employer what kind of worker you are.

Often, your resume creates the first impression you make on a prospective employer; be sure it is free of errors.

A resume can be formatted in various styles. Choose a style (or design one) that is attractive and that enables you to get all the needed information on one or two pages.

F. RESUME

To format a resume:

1. Press Enter 5 times.
2. Insert an open table with 2 columns and 1 row for each section of the resume. **Note:** In the illustration on page 194, you would use 6 rows.
3. Merge the cells in Row 1.
4. Change to center alignment.
5. Type your name in all-caps in Cambria 14-pt. Bold in Row 1.
6. Change font size to 12 pt. and press Enter 2 times.
7. Type your street address followed by a comma and 1 space; type your city followed by a comma and 1 space; then type your state followed by 1 space and your ZIP Code. Press Enter 1 time.
8. Type `Phone:` followed by 1 space; then type your area code and phone number followed by a semicolon and 1 space.

9. Type `e-mail:` followed by 1 space and your e-mail address.
10. Press ENTER 1 time.
11. Apply a bottom border to Row 1.
12. Move to Row 2, Column A; then press ENTER 1 time.
13. Change font to Calibri Bold. Type the entry in Column A in all-caps; then press TAB to move to Column B.
14. Press ENTER 1 time, and type the information related to the Column A heading in Column B.
15. Press ENTER as needed in each section to insert 1 blank line between sections.
16. Type job titles and business names in italics.
17. Continue typing all entries until you are finished.
18. For any job descriptions, increase the left indent to 0.5 inch to reposition the information.
19. Decrease the width of Column A to accommodate the longest entry.

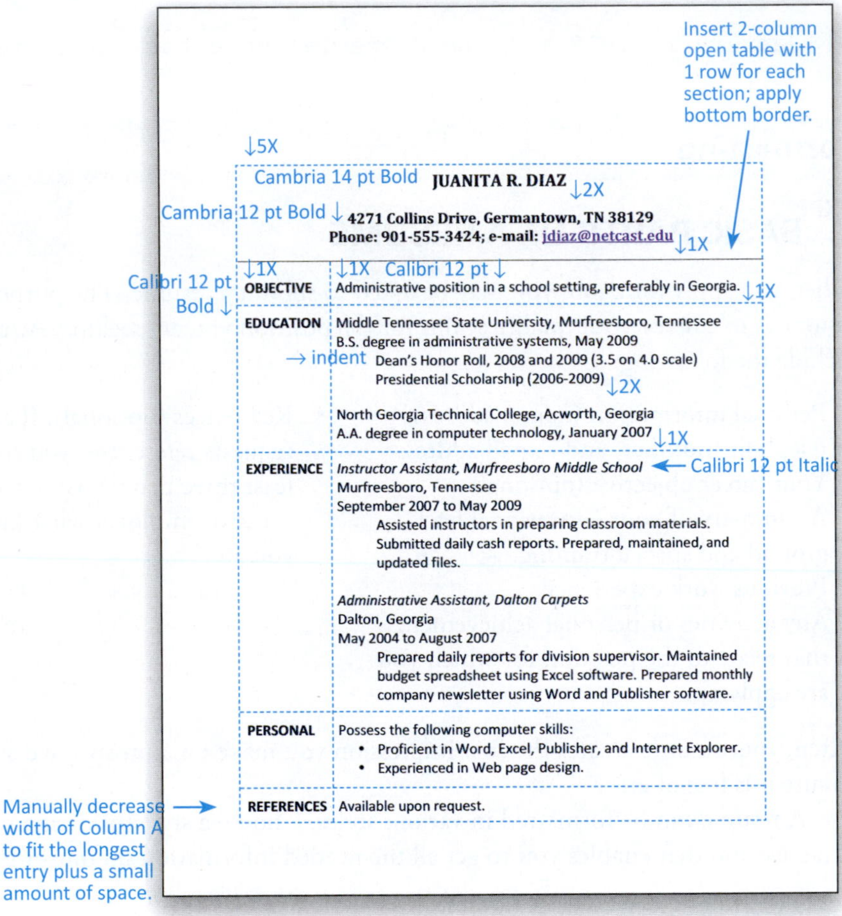

(Note: Table shown with "View Gridlines" active.)

G. WORD PROCESSING: FONT AND TABLE—CHANGE COLUMN WIDTH

Study Lesson 51 in your Word Manual. Complete all of the shaded steps while at your computer. Then format the documents that follow.

Report 51-26
Resume

Document Processing

<table>
<tr><td></td><td colspan="2">MARTINA R. VALDEZ</td></tr>
<tr><td>, place</td><td colspan="2">4826 Foxworth Apartments, #201, Clio, MI 48420</td></tr>
<tr><td></td><td colspan="2">Phone: 810-555-3424; e-mail: mvaldez@quickmail.net</td></tr>
<tr><td></td><td>OBJECTIVE</td><td>To pursue a career in graphic design.</td></tr>
<tr><td>, place</td><td>EDUCATION</td><td>Central Michigan Business College, Mt. Pleasant, Michigan</td></tr>
<tr><td></td><td></td><td>A.A. degree in graphic design</td></tr>
<tr><td>, date</td><td></td><td>Graduated: December 2009</td></tr>
<tr><td>, place</td><td></td><td>Clio High School, Clio, Michigan</td></tr>
<tr><td>, date</td><td></td><td>Graduated: June 2007</td></tr>
<tr><td></td><td>EXPERIENCE</td><td>Office Assistant, Chambers Moving and Storage</td></tr>
<tr><td>, place</td><td></td><td>Mt. Pleasant, Michigan</td></tr>
<tr><td>, date</td><td></td><td>June 2008 to December 2009</td></tr>
<tr><td></td><td></td><td>Composed and typed routine correspondence; filed customer records; placed and answered telephone calls; prepared invoices; updated online customer records.</td></tr>
<tr><td></td><td></td><td>Copy Editor, Clio Daily News</td></tr>
<tr><td>, place</td><td></td><td>Clio, Michigan</td></tr>
<tr><td>, date</td><td></td><td>June 2007 to June 2008</td></tr>
<tr><td></td><td></td><td>Assisted the news editor with designing and preparing copy for the Clio Daily News; solicited subscriptions from local businesses; edited copy for the New Business forum.</td></tr>
<tr><td></td><td>ACTIVITIES</td><td>Activities pursued while attending college:
• Newsletter Editor, 2009
• Member, Spanish Club, 2009
• President, Graphic Design Club, 2008-2009
• Member, Phi Beta Lambda, 2008-2009
• Vice President, Graphic Design Club, 2007</td></tr>
<tr><td></td><td>REFERENCES</td><td>Available upon request.</td></tr>
</table>

Report 51-27
Resume

Open the file for Report 51-26, and make the following changes:

1. Change the name to `Connie R. Cameron`.
2. Change the address to `725 Dearborn Street, Lapeer, MI 48446`.
3. Change the phone number to `810-555-8956`.
4. Change the e-mail address to `ccameron@quickmail.net`.
5. Change the high school attended to `Lapeer Central High School, Lapeer, Michigan`.
6. Delete the third activity and replace it with the following: `Member, Intramural Tennis Team, 2009`.

Letters of Application

Goals

- Type at least 39wpm/5'/5e.
- Correctly format a letter of application.

A. WARMUP

alphabet	1	Sympathizing with those Quakers would fix their objectives.
one hand	2	stages phylum wet pop affect jumpily tact junky beard pinky
easy	3	The ancient emblem is the handiwork of the haughty prodigy.

Skillbuilding

B. SUSTAINED PRACTICE: CAPITALS

Take a 1-minute timed writing on the boxed paragraph to establish your base speed. Then take a 1-minute timed writing on the following paragraph. As soon as you equal or exceed your base speed on this paragraph, move to the next, more difficult paragraph.

4	There are several different approaches that one can	11
5	take when considering a major purchase. Some people make	22
6	the mistake of simply going to a store and making a choice.	34
7	When one couple decided to buy a chest-type freezer,	11
8	they looked at a consumer magazine in the library. The	22
9	Sears, Amana, and General Electric were shown as best buys.	34
10	That same issue of their magazine compared electric	11
11	ranges. Jonathan and Mary Anne found that the Maytag, Magic	23
12	Chef, Amana, and Gibson were determined to be best buys.	34
13	Best buys for full-size microwave ovens were the Sharp	11
14	Carousel, Panasonic, and GoldStar Multiwave. Good midsize	23
15	models were the Frigidaire, Panasonic, and Sears Kenmore.	34

1 | 2 | 3 | 4 | 5 | 6 | 7 | 8 | 9 | 10 | 11 | 12

Take two 5-minute timed writings.

Goal: At least 39wpm/5'/5e

C. 5-MINUTE TIMED WRITING

```
16      Have you completed your education when you graduate     11
17  from high school or finish your college work? Most people   22
18  look forward to reaching milestones, such as graduation or  34
19  completing a course. Have they learned everything they will 46
20  need to know to be successful in the real world? The answer 58
21  is not so simple.                                           62
22      Learning continues to occur long after you leave the    72
23  classroom. No matter what job or career you pursue, you     84
24  will learn something new every day. When you investigate    95
25  new ideas, ask questions, or find a different way to do a  107
26  job, you are continuing to learn. In the process, you gain 118
27  additional experience, develop new skills, and become a    130
28  better worker.                                             133
29      Getting along with your peers, for example, is not     143
30  something that you learn from studying books. You learn to 155
31  be a team player when you listen to your coworkers and     166
32  share your ideas with them. Do not hesitate to acquire new 178
33  skills or to initiate new ideas. Be zealous in your efforts 190
34  to continue your education.                                195
      1 | 2 | 3 | 4 | 5 | 6 | 7 | 8 | 9 | 10 | 11 | 12
```

Formatting

D. LETTERS OF APPLICATION

REFER TO Reference Manual

R-12B: Application Letter

A letter of application is a personal-business letter sent along with a resume to a prospective employer. Together, the letter and the resume serve to introduce a person to the organization.

The letter of application should be no longer than one page and should include (1) the job you are applying for and how you learned of the job, (2) the highlights of your enclosed resume, and (3) a request for an interview.

Document Processing

Correspondence 52-35
Personal-Business Letter in Modified-Block Style

March 8, 20-- | Ms. Violet Logan | Human Resource s Director | proctor computer systems | 2489 Highland Ave. | Park City, UT 84060 | Dear Ms. Logan:

¶ Please consider me an applicant for the position of Data System s Operator that was advertised in the February 25th edition of the Park City Press. ital

¶ In May I will graduate with an A.A. degree in office systems from Northern Utah Business College. My enclosed resume shows that I have completed courses in excel, Publisher, and Word. I also have considerable experience in working with web page

(continued on next page)

design. The skills I gained in using these software packages will be helpful extremely to your Branch Office in Provo.

¶ The position with your company is very apealing to me. I would like an opportunity to interview with Proctor Computer Systems and can be reached at either 801-555-8332 (cell) or 801-555-3872 (home).

¶ I look forward to hearing from you soon.

Sincerely, | Marlene Hooper | 387 Amber Ave. | Lehi, UT 84043 | Enclosure

Correspondence 52-36
Personal-Business Letter in Block Style

May 17, 20-- | Mr. Daniel R. Gantz | Human Resources Director | Carrington Communications | 3024 Maple Lane | Commerce, TX 75428-2314 | Dear Mr. Gantz: ¶ Please consider me as an applicant for a position with Carrington Communications. As you can see on the enclosed resume, my strength is in communication arts. I have completed a number of courses in speech, English, and communication technology. My part-time employment with your company for the past three years convinced me that Carrington Communications is the place where I would like to work. ¶ I would like to arrange an interview with you for any possible openings this summer or fall. I can be reached at 903-555-7823. Feel free to leave a message on my answering machine if I am not home when you call. I look forward to the possibility of working for Carrington Communications.
Sincerely, | Carmen S. Diamond | 489 Crescent Avenue | Greenville, TX 75401 | Enclosure

Correspondence 52-37
Personal-Business Letter in Modified-Block Style

Open the file for Correspondence 52-36, and make the following changes:

1. Use a modified-block style.
2. Change Mr. Gantz's title to `Director, Personnel Services.`
3. Delete the first sentence in the letter, and insert the following replacement: `I would like to apply for the Communications Specialist position advertised in the` *`Commerce Journal`* `on May 15.`
4. Add the following words at the end of the third sentence in the first paragraph: `that uniquely qualify me for an entry-level position.`
5. Change the telephone number to `903-555-3398.`

Interview Communications

Goals

- Demonstrate improved speed and accuracy while typing by touch.
- Demonstrate acceptable proofreading skills by editing lines of copy.
- Correctly format an academic report and a ruled table.

A. WARMUP

alphabet	1	If fog makes Max shiver, quickly zip down and buy a jacket.
substitution: *f* and *g*	2	fig fang flag frog fang gift golf gulf goof gruff fogs flag
easy	3	His civic goal for the city is for them to endow the chair.

Skillbuilding

B. MAP+: NUMBERS

Follow the GDP software directions for this exercise to improve keystroking accuracy.

PPP PRETEST » PRACTICE » POSTTEST

PRETEST

Take a 1-minute timed writing.

C. PRETEST: Common Letter Combinations

4	They formed an action committee to force a motion for	11
5	a ruling on your contract case. This enabled them to comply	23
6	within the lawful time period and convey a common message.	35
	1 | 2 | 3 | 4 | 5 | 6 | 7 | 8 | 9 | 10 | 11 | 12	

PRACTICE

Speed Emphasis:
If you made 2 or fewer errors on the Pretest, type each *individual* line 2 times.

Accuracy Emphasis:
If you made 3 or more errors, type each *group* of lines (as though it were a paragraph) 2 times.

D. PRACTICE: Word Beginnings

7	for forget formal format forces forums forked forest formed
8	per perils period perish permit person peruse perked pertly
9	com combat comedy coming commit common compel comply comets

E. PRACTICE: Word Endings

10	ing acting aiding boring buying ruling saving hiding dating
11	ble bubble dabble double enable feeble fumble tumble usable
12	ion action vision lesion nation bunion lotion motion legion

POSTTEST

Repeat the Pretest timed writing and compare performance.

F. POSTTEST: Common Letter Combinations

Language Arts

G. PROOFREADING

Edit these sentences to correct any errors.

```
13 The Smith were please to learn from their insurance
14 agent that the covrage ona $50,000 life insurance policy
15 policy would be increased by $ 20,000 at no extra cost.

16 The continued to pay the same premum, not knowing that the
17 cash value of there original policy was being tappped each
18 month to pay an addition premium for hte new coverage.
```

Document Processing

Report 53-28
Academic Report

SUCCESSFUL INTERVIEWING TECHNIQUES

Raymond T. Argue

March 28, 20--

One of the chal^l^lenges that faces all prospective employees is thier performance during an interview. To be successful during an interview, there are ^certain^ steps you should take to ensure that you get the job.

DRESSING PROFESSIONALLY

You need to dress professionally for ~~your~~ ^an^ interview. How you dress says a lot about you, especially during a job interview. If you don't take care and dress professiona^l^ly, you may be telling the interview^er^ that this is the kind of attitude (you'll) display while on the job.[1]

DURING THE INTERVIEW

It's always a good idea to arrive a few minutes early for the interview. If you are late for an interview, you may be conveying to ~~the~~ ^an^ interviewer that you will bring this ^same^ behavior with you to the job. When you are greeted by the interviewer, give a ^firm^ handshake. When you enter the /Interview /Room, (don't) sit down until the interviewer suggests that you do so. Be cons^c^ious of your posture when you sit. The manner in which you maintain good posture can relay an appearance of confidence and attentiveness. Use grammar correct and speak in complete sentences. Project your voice so that the interviewer can hear your responses. Answer ^clearly^ the questions you are asked. Be brief and concise, and be careful not to ramble.

(continued on next page)

ENDING THE INTERVIEW

Near the end of the interview, the interviewer will likely ask you if you have any questions. Be prepared to ask questions, because your questions may tell the interviewer that you are interested in working for this company. Do your research before hand so that you are prepared to ask questions particular to the job for which you are aplying and about the company itself.

End the interview on a positive note. Reaffirm your interest in working for the company and briefly restate how your visit to the company has enhanced your desire to be hired for the position for which you have applied. And lastly, don't forget to express a thanks to all the people who interviewed you.[2]

Though some of the above suggestions are critical to successful interviewing research shows that some interviewes continue to exhibit inappropriate behavior during the interview. See Table 1 below.

Table 1. INTERVIEW BEHAVIORS
As observed by 100 interviewers

Observed Behavior	Percentage
Poorly dressed for the interview	25
Incorrect grammer	12
Responses inaudible	9
Not prepared with question	7

---

[1] James Sabin, "Effective Interviewing Techniques," *Interviewing Today,* August 7, 2010, p. 18.

[2] Roshena Karis, "Online Interviewing Techniques," *Your Interview,* February 22, 2010, <http://www.yourinterview.net/april>, accessed on May 8, 2010.

Table 53-17 Ruled Table

INTERVIEW SCHEDULE
Todd Giordelli
August 18, 20--

Scheduled Time	Location	Interviewer
7:30 a.m. to 9:00 a.m.	Cafeteria	Mr. Alan Spitzer, Communications Director
9:00 a.m. to 10:00 a.m.	Room B-212	Ms. Karen Eisner, Human Resources Director
10:00 a.m. to 11:30 a.m.	Room D-134	Ms. Maureen Schiller, Chief Marketing Officer
11:30 a.m. to 1:00 p.m.	Dining Room	Members of the Search Committee
1:00 p.m. to 1:30 p.m.	Building R	Tour of Building, David Carpenter
1:30 p.m. to 2:00 p.m.	Room C-220	Mr. Vince Moore, Executive Vice President
2:00 p.m. to 2:30 p.m.	Room C-226	Ms. Gayle Hartman, Senior Vice President
2:30 p.m. to 3:00 p.m.	Room C-230	Mr. Richard DeClark, CEO

Follow-Up Letters

Goals

- Type at least 39wpm/5'/5e.
- Correctly format a follow-up letter.

A. WARMUP

alphabet	1	Dave quickly spotted the four women dozing in the jury box.
frequent digraphs	2	ed edge wed Eddy bed eyed cede lied fed edited led axed red
easy	3	Disney World is a land of enchantment to the civic visitor.

Skillbuilding

B. PROGRESSIVE PRACTICE: NUMBERS

Follow the GDP software directions for this exercise to improve keystroking speed.

C. TECHNIQUE PRACTICE: TAB KEY

Press TAB 1 time between words. Type each line 2 times.

```
4 Kit→ Ida→ Joy→ ads→ Joe→ Jan→ Lev→ ago→ Ima→ are→ ace
5 Mom→ aft→ Job→ age→ Ham→ zip→ Obi→ Ott→ awl→ art→ Hsu
6 zoo→ Jon→ apt→ Pat→ ado→ zap→ Orr→ Ike→ Ned→ asp→ zag
7 ate→ Lou→ Mia→ Mac→ Jim→ zed→ add→ Pia→ Moe→ Lot→ Jay
```

Strategies for Career Success

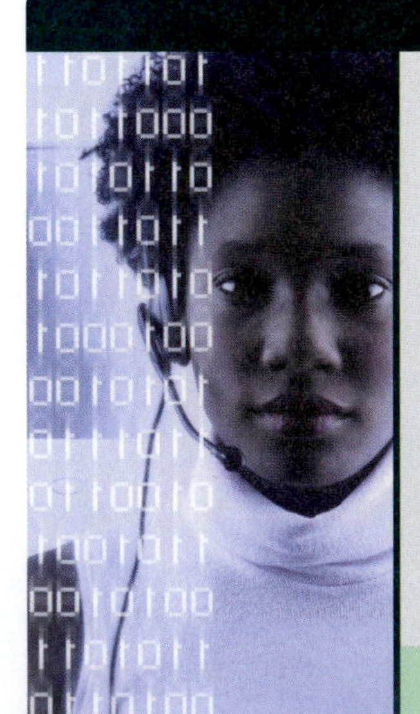

Reducing Bias in Business Communication

Everything we do in business communication attempts to build goodwill. Bias-free language and visuals help maintain the goodwill we work so hard to create.

Bias-free language does not discriminate against people on the basis of gender, physical condition, race, age, or any other characteristic. Do not emphasize gender-specific words in your business vocabulary. Instead, incorporate gender-neutral words (for example, use *chair* instead of *chairman*) into your business communication.

Organizations that treat people fairly also should use language that treats people fairly. The law is increasingly intolerant of biased documents and hostile work environments. Practice nondiscriminatory behavior by focusing on individual merits, accomplishments, skills, and what you might share in common rather than illustrating differences. Treating every group with respect and understanding is essential to gaining loyalty and future business while cultivating harmonious relationships.

Your Turn: Review a document that you have recently written. Is the document bias-free?

Take two 5-minute timed writings.

Goal: At least 39wpm/5'/5e

D. 5-MINUTE TIMED WRITING

```
8       In the past, typing was a skill that was used only by     11
9  those who were secretaries, students, and office workers.      23
10 High school students who were in school and who had plans      34
11 for going on took a typing class so that they could type       46
12 their work with ease and skill. Often, students who wanted     57
13 to be hired to work in an office would make plans to take      69
14 advanced courses in typing.                                     75
15      As prices drop and as we have more and more advances      85
16 in technology of all types, people are recognizing that        97
17 they need typing skills. From the top executive to the        108
18 customer service agents, everyone needs to be able to use a   120
19 computer keyboard. Workers in almost any kind of business     131
20 use their keyboarding skills to perform their daily tasks.    143
21      Employers are looking for skilled workers who type       154
22 with consistent speed and accuracy. People who are able to    166
23 type documents accurately and enter data quickly are needed   178
24 for many types of careers. Keyboarding skills are important   190
25 for every manner of job.                                      195
     1 | 2 | 3 | 4 | 5 | 6 | 7 | 8 | 9 | 10 | 11 | 12
```

Formatting

E. FOLLOW-UP LETTERS

As soon as possible after your interview (preferably the next day), you should send a follow-up letter to the person who conducted your interview. In the letter you should:

- Use a positive tone.
- Thank the person who conducted the interview.
- Mention some specific information you learned during the interview.
- Highlight your particular strengths.
- Restate your interest in working for that organization, and mention that you look forward to a favorable decision.

Document Processing

Correspondence
54-38
Personal-Business Letter in Block Style

May 25, 20-- / Mr. Daniel R. Gantz / Human Resources Director / Carrington Communications / 3024 Maple Lane / Commerce, TX 75428-2314 / Dear Mr. Gantz:
¶ It was a pleasure meeting with you yesterday and learning of the wonderful career opportunities at Carrington Communications. I enjoyed meeting everyone

(continued on next page)

in the Technology Division. Thank you for taking the time to share with me a brief history of the company and its move to the Commerce area.

¶ I believe my experience and job skills match very well with those you are seeking for a technology consultant, and this position is exactly what I had in mind when applying to Carrington Communications.

¶ I would appreciate hearing from you when you have made your hiring decision for this position. I am very much interested in joining the professional ranks at Carrington.

Sincerely yours, | Carmen S. Diamond | 489 Crescent Avenue | Greenville, TX 75401

Correspondence
54-39
Personal-Business Letter in Modified-Block Style

May 8, 20-- | Ms. Violet Logan | Human Resources director | Proctor Computer Systems | 2498 Highland Avenue | Park City, UT 84060 | Dear Ms. Logan:

¶ Thank you for the opportunity of interviewing yesterday with Proctor Computer Systems. Please extend my apreciation to those in your Division who participated in the interview process.

¶ The interview gave me a good feeling about your company. The positive information you shared with me about proctor convinced me that your Company is indeed where I'd like to work. I was very impressed with the pro gress you have made in the area of system enhancements and the positive outlook for future expansion in to the Park City market area.

¶ You may recall that I have had experience with the equipment you use at proctor. My strengths in computer software applications would blend well with your company profile.

¶ I look forward to hear from you soon regarding your immediate hiring decision.

Sincerely, | Marlene D. Hoper | 387 Amber Avenue | Logon, UT 84043

Correspondence
54-40
Personal-Business Letter in Modified-Block Style

Open the file for Correspondence 54-39 and make the following changes:

- Change the date of the letter to `June 25, 20--`
- Send the letter to `Mr. Donald F. Hallada | Vice President of Human Resources | Technology Solutions, Inc. | Sulphur Springs, TX 75483`
- Replace the first sentence with the following: `Thank you for the opportunity to interview with Technology Solutions on June 24.`
- Replace "Proctor" with `Technology Solutions` in the first, second, and third paragraphs.

Integrated Employment Project

Goals

- Demonstrate improved speed and accuracy while typing by touch.
- Demonstrate acceptable language arts skills in composing paragraphs.
- Correctly format an application letter, a resume, and a follow-up letter.
- Successfully complete a Progress and Proofreading Check with zero errors on the first scored attempt.

A. WARMUP

```
alphabet       1 A campus TV quiz just asks why gold is buried at Fort Knox.
number/symbol  2 gilp@comcast.net (11%) Ng & Ma 4/5 No! $13.86 *Est. #20-972
easy           3 Blair's penchant for a duck dish may make him go to a lake.
```

Skillbuilding

B. 12-SECOND SPEED SPRINTS

Take three 12-second timed writings on each line.

```
4 I am at my best when I am on a boat on an icy lake at home.
5 I will lend a hand to anyone if he or she signals for help.
6 We may take a number of maps to aid me when we visit there.
7 If they work in town, they may make a visit to the old gym.
  ''''5''''10''''15''''20''''25''''30''''35''''40''''45''''50''''55''''60
```

C. PACED PRACTICE

Follow the GDP software directions for this exercise to improve keystroking speed and accuracy.

Language Arts

D. COMPOSING PARAGRAPHS

Choose one of the phrases at the right; then compose a paragraph of three to four sentences on that topic.

8 My computer was working fine until it . . .
9 The Internet has helped me complete my class assignments by . . . .
10 The one thing I like best about e-mail is . . . .
11 I have several skills, but my best skill is . . . .

Document Processing

In the previous unit you learned how to prepare a resume, an application letter, and a follow-up letter—all of which are frequently used by job applicants. You will now use these skills in preparing the documents necessary to apply for the job described in the newspaper ad illustrated below.

DESKTOP PUBLISHER

InfoJobs' mission is to shape the future of desktop publishing. We have an immediate opening to work in a team environment with desktop publishers and technical editors.

This is an entry-level position within the Marketing Department in our Denver office. Applicant must have experience in using Word, Photoshop, and PageMaker. Good verbal and written communication skills are required. Should possess the ability to acquire new knowledge through formal and self-training. Associates degree or equivalent experience required.

InfoJobs offers an excellent medical and dental program for all employees.

If interested, send a letter of application and resume to:

Mr. Harrison Campbell
HRM Department
InfoJobs, Inc.
4590 Emerson Avenue
Denver, CO 80014

InfoJobs is an Equal Opportunity Employer.

Report 55-29
Resume

Prepare a resume for yourself as though you are applying for the job described in the ad above. Use actual data in the resume. Assume that you have just graduated from a postsecondary program. Include school-related activities, courses you have completed, and any part-time or full-time work experience you may have acquired. Make the resume as realistic as possible, and provide as much information as you can about your background.

Correspondence 55-41
Personal-Business Letter in Block Style

Prepare an application letter to apply for the position described in the ad. Date your letter April 15. Emphasize the skills you have acquired during your years in school and while working in any part-time or full-time positions. Use Correspondence 52-35 or 52-36 as guides for your letter.

Correspondence 55-42
Personal-Business Letter in Modified-Block Style

Assume that your interview was held on April 30 and that you would very much like to work for InfoJobs. It is now the day after your interview. Prepare a follow-up letter expressing your positive thoughts about working for InfoJobs. Use Correspondence 54-38 or 54-39 as guides for your letter.

Report
55-30
Resume

JEFF METCALF

10454 Melody Drive, Denver, Co 80234
Phone: 303-555-2241; e-mail: jeffmet@allmail.net

OBJECTIVE To obtain a position as a publisher in the Denver area.

EDUCATION Rocky Mountain Technical College, Colorado Springs, CO
A.A. Degree in Computer Systems
Graduated: December 2009

South City High School, Denver, Colorado
Graduated: May 2007

EXPERIENCE *Desk Clerk, Alpine Blue Resort*
Vail, Colorado
May 2006 to April 2007

Checked guests in and out, provided all information about rates and the kinds of services in the resort, assigning guests to rooms, and made guest reservations within computer reservation system.

Data records technician, Denver health center
Denver, Colorado
April 2007 to December 2009

Responsible for maintaining and updating a computerized system record for all hospital reports on patients. Updated medical histories and charts, and cross-indexed information for access in computer files.

ACTIVITIES Activities pursued:

- Colorado Data Technicians Association President, 2007 to 2008
- National Health care Employees Association, 2009 to present
- Dean's honor list, 2007 to 2009
- National Society, 2005 to 2007
- Class president, South High School, 2006 to 2007

REFERENCES Available upon request.

Correspondence
55-43
Personal-Business Letter in Block Style

Italicize (but do not underline) the name of the newspaper.

June 19, 20-- | Mr. Wayne Durham | McDaniel Computer Communications | 348 Ellsworth Avenue | Denver, CO 80280 | Dear Mr. Durham:

¶ I am responding to your ad in the Denver Post for the position of desktop publisher.

¶ My degree in computer systems and my experience as a data records technician provide me with the computer background you are seeking. As you indicated in your ad, I would welcome the opportunity to complete the two-week formal training course you provide for this position.

¶ I gained valuable personal relations skills as an employee for Blue Alpine Resort, and my technical skills are well documented from 2007 to 2009 in my responsibilities as a data records technician for the Denver Health Center.

¶ I am very interested in working for Computer Enterprises and look forward to hearing from you regarding this position. If you would like to speak to me personally, you can reach me at 303-555-2214 or e-mail me at jeffmet@allmail.net.

Sincerely, | Jeffrey Metcalf | 10454 Melody Drive | Denver, CO 80234

Correspondence
55-44
Personal-Business Letter in Modified-Block Style

Progress and Proofreading Check

Documents designated as Proofreading Checks serve as a check of your proofreading skill. Your goal is to have zero typographical errors when the GDP software first scores the document.

June
~~May~~ 30, 20-- | Mr. Wayne Durham | Mcdaniel Computer Communications | 348 Ellsworth Avenue | Denver, CO 80280 | Dear Mr. Durham ~~Wayne~~:

¶ Thank you for taking ~~the~~ time to interview me about the desk top publishing position with McDaniel Computer communications. The information you shared with me has enhanced my interest in working for McDaniel.

¶ I was very impressed with the responsibilityies you high lighted regarding this position, and your 2-week formal training course focuses precisely on the responsibilities I was seeking in a desktop publishing position.

¶ I hope to hear from you by the end of next week for a positive decision on my employment with McDaniel.

Sincerely, | Jeffrey Metcalf | 10454 Melody Dr. | Denver, CO 80243

UNIT 12

Skillbuilding and In-Basket Review

LESSON 56
In-Basket Review—Insurance

LESSON 57
In-Basket Review—Hospitality

LESSON 58
In-Basket Review—Retail

LESSON 59
In-Basket Review—Nonprofit

LESSON 60
In-Basket Review—Manufacturing

UNIT 12 LESSON

In-Basket Review—Insurance

56

Goals

- Type at least 40wpm/5'/5e.
- Correctly format a business letter, a memo, and a boxed table.

A. WARMUP

alphabet	1	All questions asked by five watch experts amazed the judge.
concentration	2	antirevolutionaries disenfranchisements unconstitutionality
easy	3	All eight authentic antique autos may be lent to the firms.

Skillbuilding

B. SUSTAINED PRACTICE: PUNCTUATION

Take a 1-minute timed writing on the boxed paragraph to establish your base speed. Then take a 1-minute timed writing on the following paragraph. As soon as you equal or exceed your base speed on this paragraph, move to the next, more difficult paragraph.

```
 4      The men in the warehouse were having a very difficult  11
 5  time keeping track of that inventory. Things began to go   23
 6  much more smoothly for them when they got the new computer. 34

 7      Whenever something was shipped out, a computer entry   11
 8  was made to show the changes. They always knew exactly what 22
 9  merchandise was in stock; they also knew what to order.    34

10      Management was pleased with that improvement. "We      11
11  should have made the change years ago," said the supervisor 22
12  to the plant manager, who was in full agreement with him.  34

13      This is just one example (among many) of how the work  11
14  areas can be improved.* Workers' suggestions are listened  23
15  to by alert, expert managers. Their jobs are better, too!  33
      1 | 2 | 3 | 4 | 5 | 6 | 7 | 8 | 9 | 10 | 11 | 12
```

Take two 5-minute timed writings.

Goal: At least 40wpm/5'/5e

C. 5-MINUTE TIMED WRITING

```
16      When you begin to think about a career, you should       10
17 assess your personal abilities and interests. Do you have     22
18 natural aptitudes in a certain area? Do you have special      33
19 interests or hobbies that you would like to develop into a    45
20 career? Do you enjoy working with other people, or do you     56
21 like to work on your own? Would you like to work in a large   68
22 office, or do you prefer to work outdoors? These questions    80
23 are important to consider when you think about your career.   92
24      Your quest to find the perfect career will be more      103
25 successful if you try to maximize the opportunities that     114
26 are available. For example, you might consider working with  126
27 an organization that offers you career counseling. A career  138
28 counselor is trained to help you determine your aptitudes    150
29 and interests.                                               153
30      You may contact some people who work in a career which  164
31 interests you and ask to shadow them on their jobs and ask   176
32 them questions. You might find a service online to help you  188
33 find an interesting career that can meet all of your goals.  200
     1 | 2 | 3 | 4 | 5 | 6 | 7 | 8 | 9 | 10 | 11 | 12
```

Document Processing

Situation: Today is November 17. You are employed in the office of Advantage Insurance of Cedar Rapids, Iowa. Advantage handles auto, home, and life insurance coverage in Iowa and Minnesota. You work for Samuel R. Haney, vice president. Prepare the following letter for Mr. Haney.

Correspondence 56-45
Business Letter in Block Style

November 17, 20-- / Ms. Maribel Valez / District Manager / 568 Curtiss Avenue / Ames, IA 50010-3568 / Dear Ms. Valez:

¶ Several of our service representatives have indicated on our Web site chat room that new clients are becoming increasingly interested in the criteria to consider when evaluating their insurance carriers. Advantage has prided itself in years past on its reputable service record with its policyholders, and the service representatives have undoubtedly shared this record with prospective customers. However, we want to be certain that other characteristics about Advantage are also shared with these potential policyholders.

(continued on next page)

¶ Please be sure that your representatives share the following service characteristics with potential customers:

- Our claims are handled quickly and with a minimum of "red tape."
- Our ratio of number of policies to number of complaints is the highest in the industry.
- No disciplinary actions have been taken against Advantage in the past 50 years.

¶ Please share this information with your service representatives, and inform them that updated information on our services is provided on our home page for their use or for their policyholders' use.

Sincerely, / Samuel R. Haney / Vice President / urs

Correspondence
56-46
Memo

Mr. Haney has dictated the following memo for you to transcribe. As you can see, there are several rough-draft changes that you will have to make to the memo.

MEMO TO: Deanna Crews, training director

FROM: Samuel R. Haney, Vice President

DATE: November 18, 20--

SUBJECT: Training Seminar

¶ Our new agent training seminar will be held on Jan. 10, and we again plan to conduct 2 sessions each for auto and life insurance policies. You will be in charge of the auto life insurance seminars, and Thomas Meeks will conduct the life insurance seminars.

¶ I expect that this year's auto insurance seminars will present our 6 basic coverage areas using the latest software presentation for the following topics:

alphabetize this list

- Collision
- Comprehensive
- Uninsured motorist
- Medical payments or personal injury protection
- Property damage liability
- Bodily injury liability

¶ We are the market leaders in bodily injury liability and property damage liability coverages. Therefore, you should plan to spend at least one-half of your presentation discussing our strengths in these coverages. In your presentation you might like to should include the fact that our coverages in these areas have more than surpassed those of our competitors for the past 5 years.

(continued on next page)

¶ Table 1 is attached to help you explain the ^variety of^ discounts offered for Iowa and Minnesota policyholders. | urs | Attachment

Table
56-18
Boxed Table

R-13B: 2-line column heading
R-13C: Table number title

Prepare Table 56-18 as an attachment for the memo to Deanna Crews.

Table 1. DISCOUNT PROGRAMS **(For Iowa and Minnesota)**	
Discounts Available	**Discount Amount (%)**
Air bag	Up to 6.5
Antitheft device	Up to 10
Driver training course	Up to 2.5
Good driver	Up to 2
Good student	Up to 15
Multipolicy	Up to 5
Multivehicle	Up to 15
Professional driver's program	Up to 14

Keyboarding Connection

Avoiding E-Mail Flame Wars

Don't fan the flames! A flame is an offensive e-mail that expresses anger, criticism, or insults. If flames are transmitted to an e-mail list, they can produce a long list of flames and counterflames known as flame wars. Some e-mail lists have rules against this and will ban people who participate in or cause flame wars.

You may be tempted to join in, but this is a waste of everyone's time. Often the initial offense was merely a poorly worded e-mail that a reader interpreted as an insult. There are those who intentionally send inflammatory e-mail called flame bait. Resist the urge to send a cutting response, and consider whether the writer's intent was to provoke you.

If your reader misjudges something you wrote and becomes offended, just apologize. A timely apology can thwart a potential fire. Avoid miscommunication by watching how you word your e-mail.

Your Turn: Have you ever been insulted by an e-mail? What was your response?

In-Basket Review—Hospitality

Goals

- Demonstrate improved speed and accuracy while typing by touch.
- Demonstrate acceptable language arts skills in number expression and hyphenation.
- Correctly format an open table, a business letter, and a business report.

A. WARMUP

```
alphabet  1 Fred specialized in the job of making very quaint wax toys.
one hand  2 assets linkup bat kin tested phonily wave imply refer puppy
easy      3 He has on a tux and she has on a tan gown for their social.
```

Skillbuilding

B. MAP+: ALPHABET

Follow the GDP software directions for this exercise to improve keystroking accuracy.

C. PROGRESSIVE PRACTICE: ALPHABET

Follow the GDP software directions for this exercise to improve keystroking speed.

Language Arts

Study the rules at the right.

D. NUMBER EXPRESSION AND HYPHENATION

RULE
word

Spell out

- **A number used as the first word of a sentence.**
  Seventy-five people attended the conference in San Diego.
- **The shorter of two adjacent numbers.**
  We have ordered 3 two-pound cakes and one 5-pound cake for the reception.
- **The words million and billion in round numbers (do not use decimals with round numbers).**
  Not: A $5.00 ticket can win $28,000,000 in this month's lottery.
  But: A $5 ticket can win $28 million in this month's lottery.
- **Fractions.**
  Almost one-half of the audience responded to the question.

RULE
- number

Hyphenate compound numbers between twenty-one and ninety-nine and fractions that are expressed as words.

Twenty-nine recommendations were approved by at least three-fourths of the members.

Edit each sentence to correct any errors.

```
4  Seven investors were interested in buying 2 15-unit condos.

5  The purchase price for the buildings will be $3,000,000.00
6  each, which is 1/2 the total.

7  The computers were mailed in 5 40-pound boxes for 2/3 of the
8  price paid yesterday.

9  Our food chain sold hamburgers for $3.00 each last year.

10 I can sell nearly one-half of all the tickets at the gate on
11 November 13.

12 59 parking spaces are located within 1/2 mile of the city
13 center.

14 We must place our mailing pieces in 8 twenty-pound bags for
15 the mail clerk.

16 I don't believe more than 1/5 of the drivers have insurance.
```

Document Processing

Situation: Today is March 25, and you are employed in the office of Pacific Resorts in Oceanside, California. Your employer, the general manager, is Ms. Glenda Flowers. Ms. Flowers is attending a meeting in San Diego and has left the following documents for you to complete.

Table 57-19
Open Table

- number

PACIFIC RESORTS PROPERTIES Beach Rental Units			
Property	**Rooms**	**Rental Rate In Season**	**Rental Rate Off Season**
Buena Vista Landings	5	$4,750	$3,325
Cradle by the Sea	6	5,750	4,025
El Camino Lodge	4	3,500	2,450
Mission Bay Hideaway	5	4,500	3,150
Pacific House	6	5,800	4,050
Poinsettia Palace	4	3,375	2,350
Twenty-Two Pines Estates	5	4,250	2,975

Correspondence
57-47
Business Letter in Modified-Block Style

March 25, 20-- / Mr. Shane O'Keefe / 723 Harrington Avenue / Madison, TN 37115 / Dear Mr. O'Keefe:
¶ We were pleased to hear of your interest in renting one of our prime beach units in Oceanside, California. I have enclosed a listing of all our current properties in the
# word Oceanside area. We have 12 two-bedroom rentals, 16 three-
# word bedroom rentals, and 9 four-bedroom rentals. Five of our
# word three-bedroom units have already been rented for this season;
# word one-half of the other 32 units are still available.
¶ Our Cradle by the Sea and Mission Bay Hideaway units have ocean views and garage facilities. The El Camino Lodge
- number and Twenty-Two Pines Estates have a gorgeous mountain view and tennis courts. The Buena Vista Landings, Pacific House, and Poinsettia Palace have a private golf course. Our most popular units are El Camino Lodge and Poinsettia Palace, and they both rent for under $3,000.
word ¶ If you plan to rent one of our units, please be sure to notify us by e-mail or by calling our toll-free number at 1-800-555-3390.
Sincerely, / Glenda Flowers / General Manager / urs / Enclosure / c: Kimberly England, David Pollard

Report
57-31
Business Report

Ms. Flowers has recently purchased a fishing resort on Lake Henshaw, California, and plans to open it on April 15. Type the following report and send it to the *Oceanside Press* so that it will appear in this Sunday's special *Travel and Tourism* section. Use a standard business format to prepare the report.

KAMP HENSHAW RESORT SCHEDULED TO OPEN | Pacific Resorts Properties | Oceanside, California
¶ Pacific Resorts is celebrating the grand opening of its newest resort property, Kamp Henshaw, located on the shores of Lake Henshaw in Santa Ysabel, California.
GENERAL INFORMATION
¶ The following information will give you an overview of our policies and accommodations:
¶ **Reservations.** The reservation desk will open on April 15 to reserve your cabin at our beautiful resort. You can reach reservations via the Internet by logging on to our Web site at http://www.henshawresort.com.
¶ **Accommodations.** Whether you're looking for deluxe accommodations or rustic surroundings, Kamp Henshaw has it all. You have a choice of rustic cabins nestled in the woods or large chalets overlooking Lake Henshaw. If you enjoy an evening of relaxation, each cabin includes a gazebo, out near the water's edge, that is screened in for a perfect evening of comfort.

(continued on next page)

¶ **Amenities.** Your lodging choice includes full kitchens for those who want to do
# word their own cooking, or you can order a full meal through our catering service. Ten of our larger units have a game room with a large-screen television, DVD player, and computer workstation with Internet connection. We also have a library of DVD movies that you can rent. Outside the sliding glass door is a covered deck, equipped with a barbecue grill and hot tub.

LAKE HENSHAW

¶ Lake Henshaw is located on the southern slope of Palomar Mountain, 60 miles northeast of San Diego, California. Palomar Observatory is close by, and many tourists to the area take in a day to visit that location. Lake Henshaw encompasses approximately 1,100 acres of water and five miles of shoreline. It is widely known for its great crappie fishing and also has populations of catfish, bass, bluegill, and trout. The month of March is the wettest at Lake Henshaw, and June is the driest. Hiking
# word is popular in the area, especially along the Gomez Trail. Twenty-five miles of hiking trails are open to the general public. Summertime temperatures are typically in the 80s, and nighttime temperatures drop down into the 60s. In the winter, temperatures typically run in the mid-50s during the day and in the 30s overnight.

PRICING INFORMATION

word ¶ We are offering a special introductory rate of $275 through December 1. This rate includes the following:

word • Two-night stay for a family of four.
word • Four admission tickets to the Palomar Observatory.
word • Free rental of hiking gear for one 24-hour period.

¶ A full refund will be made on all hiking gear rented if there is inclement weather
# word during the scheduled hike. If only a partial day of hiking is completed, one-half of the charges will be refunded.

In-Basket Review—Retail

Goals

- Type at least 40wpm/5'/5e.
- Correctly format an e-mail message, a memo, and a ruled table.

A. WARMUP

alphabet	1	Maizie quickly paid Joan for the five new taxis she bought.
substitution: *k* and *l*	2	kill Karl luck kilo lake kale lick kilt leak kelp link like
easy	3	The town may suspend its right to make an audit of the bid.

Skillbuilding

B. PACED PRACTICE

Follow the GDP software directions for this exercise to improve keystroking speed and accuracy.

C. 5-MINUTE TIMED WRITING

Take two 5-minute timed writings. Review your speed and errors.

Goal: At least 40wpm/5'/5e

4	Most workers will learn about their success on the job	11
5	at least once a year. The person in charge will be the one	23
6	to conduct these reviews. Even though the job review is	34
7	quite important, either party might not look forward to	45
8	such a meeting.	49
9	Frequently, an employee and a boss can view these	59
10	meetings as a time to discuss everything that the person	70
11	has done wrong in the last year. Such a negative approach	82
12	can add a lot of stress and tension between the employee	93
13	and management. In the long run, work performance suffers.	105
14	A good manager must learn a new way to conduct more	116
15	positive job reviews. Such a meeting might start by sizing	127
16	up what the employee has done to help improve things in the	139
17	past year. Positive comments may include coming to work on	151
18	time, working well with others, and being willing to pitch	163
19	in whenever needed.	167
20	Next, the areas for improvement are discussed. Then,	178
21	the employee should be given the chance to ask questions,	190
22	write a response to the appraisal, and get feedback.	200

1 | 2 | 3 | 4 | 5 | 6 | 7 | 8 | 9 | 10 | 11 | 12

Document Processing

Situation: Today is February 7. You are employed as an administrative assistant for Best Sports, a retailer for sports equipment and clothing in Albuquerque, New Mexico. Your employer is Mr. Raymond E. Abernathy, marketing director for Best Sports. Today, you are to prepare an e-mail message, a memo, and a table.

Correspondence
58-48
E-Mail Message

Hi, Brian:
¶ I talked to Lauren Emory earlier this morning, and she has agreed to host the district meeting in El Paso on April 9 and 10.
¶ In preparation for that meeting, would you please pull together the sales figures for last year and send them to Lauren so that she can include them in the sales presentation. For comparison purposes, here are figures for the year before last:

Quarter	District 1	District 2	District 3
First	$48,924	$72,230	$110,239
Second	45,220	76,137	115,330
Third	43,234	65,200	108,114
Fourth	47,899	73,249	113,233

Ray | Raymond E. Abernathy | E-mail: reabernathy@bestsports.net | Phone: 505-555-5690

Correspondence
58-49
Memo

MEMO TO: Lauren Emory | **FROM:** Raymond E. Abernathy, Marketing Director | **DATE:** February 7, 20-- | **SUBJECT:** District Meetings
¶ As you know, each year we rotate the location of our district meetings to one of our regional offices. This year our meeting will be held in El Paso. Would you please contact hotels in El Paso and select a suitable site for this year's meeting, which will be held on April 9 and 10.
¶ We decided at our last regional managers' meeting that this year's meeting would highlight our Internet sales campaign. Specifically, we want to focus on the following issues:

1. How can we improve our Web page design to attract a higher percentage of the market?
2. How can we improve our e-commerce procedures so that our order-processing routine is easier and faster for the average Web visitor?
3. What links can we add to our home page to encourage visitors to view a greater percentage of our product line?

¶ Please let me know when you have made arrangements for our meeting site. I look forward to meeting with all of you in April.
urs

Table
58-20
Ruled Table

MONTHLY BICYCLE SPECIALS

Febuary 7, 20--

Model	Price	Special Features
Lemans	$590	17.5-inch frame; 27-speed drive train; adjustable seat
Serpentine	575	16-inch frame; light weight; 18-speed drivetrain
Triple Asd	450	17.5-inch frame; Carbon fork; linear-pull brakes
ATB Ultra	400	17-inch frame; Aluminum frame; 18-speed drive train

Strategies for Career Success

Formatting Your Resume

The format of your resume communicates important skills—neatness and the ability to organize. Make a good first impression by following these guidelines.

Watch the spacing on your resume. A crowded resume implies that you cannot summarize. Leave adequate white space between the section headings of your resume. Use different font sizes, boldface, and italics to separate and emphasize information, but avoid using too many different fonts or formatting your text too many different ways, as this can make your resume look busy or unprofessional. Font sizes should be between 10 and 14.

Print your resume on good-quality 8½″ × 11″ white or off-white bond paper (for example, 20-pound stock). Colored paper doesn't provide enough contrast when your resume is copied or faxed.

Proofread your resume for spelling errors and consistency of format. Ask a few friends to review it and provide feedback.

Your Turn: Print one copy of your resume on dark-colored paper and one copy on white paper. Photocopy each resume. Which provides the better contrast for readability?

In-Basket Review—Nonprofit

Goals

- Demonstrate improved speed and accuracy while typing by touch.
- Demonstrate acceptable language arts skills in spelling.
- Correctly format a business report and a boxed table.

A. WARMUP

alphabet	1	The four brawny guards just flocked up to quiz and vex him.
frequent digraphs	2	te tee ate byte tell tea termite ten Ute tent teed teen Ted
easy	3	The penalty for such an amendment may be too gory for them.

Skillbuilding

B. MAP+: SYMBOL

Follow the GDP software directions for this exercise to improve keystroking accuracy.

PPP PRETEST » PRACTICE » POSTTEST

C. PRETEST: Close Reaches

PRETEST
Take a 1-minute timed writing.

```
4      Sally took the coins from the pocket of her blouse    10
5  and traded them for seventy different coins. Anyone could 22
6  see that Myrtle looked funny when extra coins were traded. 34
     1 | 2 | 3 | 4 | 5 | 6 | 7 | 8 | 9 | 10 | 11 | 12
```

D. PRACTICE: Adjacent Keys

PRACTICE
Speed Emphasis:
If you made 2 or fewer errors on the Pretest, type each *individual* line 2 times.
Accuracy Emphasis:
If you made 3 or more errors, type each *group* of lines (as though it were a paragraph) 2 times.

```
7  as asked asset based basis class least visas ease fast mass
8  we weary wedge weigh towel jewel fewer dwell wear weed week
9  rt birth dirty earth heart north alert worth dart port tort
```

E. PRACTICE: Consecutive Fingers

```
10 sw swamp swift swoop sweet swear swank swirl swap sway swim
11 gr grade grace angry agree group gross gripe grow gram grab
12 ol older olive solid extol spool fools stole bolt cold cool
```

F. POSTTEST: Close Reaches

POSTTEST
Repeat the Pretest timed writing and compare performance.

Language Arts

G. SPELLING

Type these frequently misspelled words, paying special attention to any spelling problems in each word.

```
13 development determine enclosed complete members recent site
14 permanent personal facility medical library however purpose
15 representative implementation electrical discussed eligible
16 organization performance minimum discuss expense areas next
17 professional arrangements separate changes reason field pay
```

Edit the sentences to correct any misspellings.

```
18 Members of the medicle and profesional group discussed it.
19 The development of the seperate cite will be completed.
20 A recent representive said the libary facility may be next.
21 A perpose of the electricle organization is to get changes.
22 However, the implimentation of changes will be permenant.
23 Arrangments for the enclosed eligable expenses are listed.
```

Document Processing

Situation: Today is November 15. You work for Quick Ride, a ride-share company located in Newton, Massachusetts. Your job responsibilities include preparing reports that summarize weekly commuter news, typing correspondence to advertise and promote Quick Ride's services, and communicating with area commuters who subscribe to Quick Ride's services. Today, you must (1) prepare a report that summarizes services offered by Quick Ride and (2) create a table that lists drivers scheduled for December.

Report 59-32
Business Report

QUICK RIDE

Newton's Premier Ride-Share

If you're tired of driving that one- to two hour comute into Bostons' busy metropolitan area, then let us take that burden off your shoulders. Quick Ride, the metro's premier ride-share company, is a very convenient, economical way to get to & from work. All you have to do is get on board!

Service AREAS

Quick Ride serves the cities of Newton, Needham, Welesley, Dedham, Dover, and Natick. Next month we will open routes to Boston, Wayland, Waltham, and Sudbury. In all, we have over 100 regular routes state wide, and service is expanding monthly. Easy access is guaranteed with all our routes. To view our entire service area, go to our Web Site, http://www.qr.com, and click the link to the Quick Ride regional service area map. The map gives all our routes, highlights specific pick up points, and

(continued on next page)

identifies our regional facilities service. The site also allows you to link directly with are reservations office to make or change a reservation or confirm your ride-share. Visit our site today and become a ride-share enthusiast.

COSTS OF COMMUTING

A recent article showed that commuting just fifteen miles each way can cost a minimum of 1,200 per year; sharing the ride with someone else can cut your commuting expenses in half.[1] In addition to the cost of gas, you must figure also in other costs of transportation such as maintenance on your vehicle, premiums, depreciation, and finance charges.[2] You should also consider how you are helping the traffic congestion and air pollution problems by ride-sharing. And don't forget about the possibility of being involved in an accident. Finally, you can reduce stress by ride-sharing because you can choose to leave the driving to some one else.

RESERVATIONS AND BENEFITS

If you want to make arrangements to reserve a seat on a Quick ride route, just call one of our professional service representatives at 1-800-555-Trip. Our representatives in the field have information on routes, schedules, ride availability, and other benefits. For example, we have an e-Ride available for you if there is an emergency that requires you to immediately get home. Here are some special benefits with Quick Ride:

- A free commute for every 500 couting miles.
- Separate insurance and medical coverage.
- Flexible payment policy.
- 4 free taxi rides home per year in the event of illness or personal emergency.

---

[1] Angela Snyder, "Environment Clean Up With Ride-Share," *Environmental Planning,* December 21, 2010, p. 18.

[2] Mel Ragsdale, *Cleaning Up America,* Bay Area publishing, Boston, 2010, p. 142.

Table
59-21
Boxed Table

QUICK RIDE DRIVERS
For December

From	To	Name	Telephone
Newton	Boston	M. Rainwater	617-555-8924
Newton	Cambridge	A. Castillo	508-555-8832
Dedham	Boston	M. Lopez	508-555-1223
Dedham	Medford	R. Chandler	774-555-3350
Dover	Boston	T. Blankenship	508-555-9012
Natick	Cambridge	R. Gaston	857-555-7702
Wellesley	Somerville	W. Moore	617-555-8855
Wellesley	Boston	A. Owens	508-555-7812
Needham	Lexington	R. Fairchild	508-555-1240
Needham	Boston	G. Saylor	774-555-3892

In-Basket Review—Manufacturing

Goals

- Type at least 40wpm/5′/5e.
- Correctly format a business letter, an open table, an e-mail message, and a memo.
- Successfully complete a Progress and Proofreading Check with zero errors on the first scored attempt.

A. WARMUP

```
alphabet       1 Two radio jocks helped fax my big quiz for driving lessons.
number/symbol  2 (mloy@usa.net) 45% Eng & Ray 4/7 Grr! $3.67 *p. 259 #28-013
easy           3 They may blame me for my penchant to laugh a lot in Peoria.
```

Skillbuilding

B. 12-SECOND SPEED SPRINTS

Take three 12-second timed writings on each line. The scale below the last line shows your wpm speed for a 12-second timed writing.

```
4 He may go with us to the giant dock down by the handy lake.
5 She is so good at her work and likes what she does as well.
6 His civic goal for the city is for them to endow the chair.
7 His body of work may charm the guests who visit the chapel.
  ''''5''''10''''15''''20''''25''''30''''35''''40''''45''''50''''55''''60
```

C. TECHNIQUE PRACTICE: ENTER KEY

Type each line 2 times. Type each sentence on a separate line by pressing ENTER after each sentence.

```
8 Step on it. Stop now. We are. Get up. Enough? Be here. Why?
9 See me. Who is he? So soon? Do it now. Who knew? We are up.
10 Busy? Find it? Go! Catch. Give. Begin. Who can go? Who did?
11 Why me? We can. Today. Really. Do not. See? When? Says who?
```

Take two 5-minute timed writings. Review your speed and errors.

Goal: At least 40wpm/5'/5e

D. 5-MINUTE TIMED WRITING

```
12      Information technology is among the fastest-growing     11
13  job fields today and is also one of the fields to change    22
14  the quickest. The goal of many schools is to try to prepare 34
15  students to be specialists in a workplace that continues to 46
16  be challenging and will need to change quickly as advances  58
17  are made in technology.                                     63
18      Those who wish to work in a field that will not stand   74
19  still need to know all about the systems with which they    85
20  labor. Network administrators, for example, will often take 97
21  courses to certify that they have a sound knowledge of any 109
22  of the new hardware. They must also learn about specific   120
23  equipment and have an understanding of how new software    131
24  will function with hardware.                               137
25      Those who wish to pass certification exams must have   148
26  the zeal, determination, and drive to complete all of the  160
27  requirements. They know that it will not be long before the 172
28  current systems will be upgraded or new software will be   183
29  released. They need to learn the latest systems and review 195
30  their certification again.                                 200
      1 | 2 | 3 | 4 | 5 | 6 | 7 | 8 | 9 | 10 | 11 | 12
```

Document Processing

Situation: Today is August 31. You are an administrative assistant, and you work for Disk House Inc. in Boulder, Colorado. Your supervisor is Ms. Rhonda Mendoza, sales and marketing director. Ms. Mendoza has asked you to prepare the following documents for her while she is in a staff meeting this morning. The letter is to be prepared for her signature, the table will be enclosed with the letter, the e-mail is to be sent out ASAP, and she will initial the memo before sending it out this afternoon.

Correspondence 60-50
Business Letter in Block Style

August 31, 20-- | Ms. Sharon Chiro | 8731 Paseo de Peralta | Santa Fe, NM 87502-3214 | Dear Ms. Chiro:

¶ We were pleased to see that you have used our Web site at www.diskhouse.com to inquire about our online catalog. We specialize in computer drives of all types: CD-ROM, DVD, and hard drives. I have enclosed a listing of our most popular DVD writers that will appear online next week in our catalog. As a new customer, you are invited to visit our catalog and place your order at these special prices.

¶ Our online customers receive the same privileges as our hard-copy catalog shoppers. These online privileges include:

- No shipping charges.
- Toll-free customer support line.
- Discounts on purchases of ten or more items.
- Ninety-day warranties (parts and labor) on all purchases.

(continued on next page)

¶ We look forward to many years of doing business with you. Please e-mail me at rmendoza@diskhouse.com if you have any questions or would like additional information.

Sincerely, | Rhonda Mendoza | Sales and Marketing Director | urs | Enclosure | c: R. Hsu, S. Horton

Table
60-22
Open Table

DVD/BLU-RAY BURNERS (Effective Dates September 3 to September 9)			
Model No.	**Part No.**	**Price**	**Specifications**
5500 Blu-ray	64702-BR	$154.99	25 to 50 GB capacity
275 DVD	32102-DVD	75.50	8X Lightscribe
303 DVD	33420-DVD	82.50	16X notebook drive
6500 Blu-ray	74781-BR	178.00	6X Blu-ray ReWriter
7000 Blu-ray	81440-BR	185.75	100 GB capacity

Correspondence
60-51
E-Mail Message

Hi, Marlene:

¶ Your order for Internet service has been processed, and you can enjoy surfing the Web immediately. As a customer of Mountain Communications, a subsidiary of Disk House Inc., you will enjoy several benefits:

1. You will receive 24/7 customer service when using our service hotline at 1-800-555-3222.
2. You will be protected by M-Protect, Mountain's virus protection software.
3. You will receive 20 Mbytes of Web page space.
4. You will receive automated credit card billing.

¶ Thank you for joining Mountain Communications. Please e-mail us at support@mc.net if you have any questions, or call us on our service hotline.

Rhonda | Rhonda Mendoza | E-mail: rmendoza@diskhouse.com | Phone: 303-555-1345

Correspondence
60-52
Memo

Progress and Proofreading Check 

Documents designated as Proofreading Checks serve as a check of your proofreading skill. Your goal is to have zero typographical errors when the GDP software first scores the document.

MEMO TO: Martha R. Durham, Publications Department | **FROM:** Rhonda Mendoza, Sales and Marketing Director | **DATE:** August 31, 20-- | **SUBJECT:** Ad in the *Rocky Mountain Daily*

¶ Martha, please include the following criteria in our ad that will run in the *Rocky Mountain Daily* this Sunday:

1. Quarter-page ad.
2. Run-time: 10 days.
3. Location: Business Section and Classified Section.
4. Contact: Include telephone and fax numbers as well as e-mail address and home page URL.

¶ This is our first ad piece in the *Rocky Mountain Daily* since we ran that special promotion last March. Let's add some graphics to make this one an "eye-catcher."
urs

Strategies for Career Success

Writing a Job Application Letter

What's the goal of the letter that accompanies your resume? The goal is to get the interview. No two letters of application are alike.

In the opening paragraph, state your purpose (for example, the position applied for, or how you became aware of it).

In the middle section, sell yourself. Convince the reader that you are the best match for the job. If you respond to a job posting, match your qualifications to the job description. If you send an unsolicited letter, specify how the employer would benefit from your qualifications. Also, refer to your resume.

In the closing paragraph, show confidence in your abilities (for example, "I'm certain I can meet your needs for a . . ."). Then state a specific time you will call to schedule an interview.

Your Turn: Obtain a job description for which you are qualified. List the job requirements, and then list your qualifications that match.

Outcomes Assessment on Part 3

Test 3

5-Minute Timed Writing

```
 1      People are often the most prized assets in a business.  11
 2  Excellent firms know that having well-qualified workers is   23
 3  an important step to ensure the success of the company. The  35
 4  people in charge can play a huge part in how much success a  47
 5  firm will have when they provide a workplace that is meant   58
 6  to support teams of people who can work together to achieve  70
 7  a common goal.                                               74
 8      When people know they are being encouraged to work       84
 9  toward achieving their own goals as well as the goals of     95
10  the company, they will respond by working to their highest  107
11  potential with ardor and zeal.                              113
12      Managers need to show that they value the hard work     124
13  and long hours that employees put in to ensure the success  136
14  of the business. People thrive on compliments that show     147
15  their work is appreciated. They like to be rewarded in some 159
16  way when they have done an exceptional job. When those in   171
17  charge are successful in motivating the employees to work   182
18  to their full potential, their company will prosper. The    194
19  result is that each person wins.                            200
      1 | 2 | 3 | 4 | 5 | 6 | 7 | 8 | 9 | 10 | 11 | 12
```

Correspondence Test 3-53
Business Letter in Block Style

August 10, 20-- / Mr. Randy Strickland / Cambridge Properties / 832 Oldham Avenue / Knoxville, TN 37912-3841 / Dear Mr. Strickland:

¶ Let me introduce myself. I am committee chair of a group that monitors development projects in Knoxville, Tennessee. It was brought to my attention that your proposal to construct 100 three- and four-bedroom homes was approved by the city council last night. As a resident in a neighboring community, I wish to share with you the stipulations we would like you to incorporate in your development project:

- *The new homes should have no fewer than 2,700 square feet of living space.*
- *All structures should have brick frontage.*
- *No external, unattached buildings should be constructed.*

(continued on next page)

¶ *Following these stipulations will ensure that your homes adhere to our community building codes.*
Sincerely, / Dominique Walters / Committee Chair / urs /
c: D. McMillan, N. Snyder

Correspondence Test
3-54
E-Mail Message

Sarah,
¶ Our DTP certificate seminar will be held in Kansas City on March 14. Upon request of last year's participants, we want to be sure to include the topics scheduled in Table 1 below.

Table 1. SEMINAR SESSIONS

Session Topic	Scheduled Room	Scheduled Time
Web Page Design	Dakota	8:00 a.m. to 9:30 a.m.
Computer Graphics	Missouri	10:00 a.m. to 11:30 a.m.
Blu-Ray Technology	Gateway A	1:30 p.m. to 3:00 p.m.
Online Marketing Techniques	Gateway B	3:30 p.m. to 5:00 p.m.

¶ These were the four most popular topics at the regional meeting. Let's use a brochure design similar to the one we used at that meeting. I will send you a copy of the brochure tomorrow.
Chris | Chris Meadows | E-mail: cmeadows@commtech.com | Phone: 816-555-0782

Report Test
3-33
Business Report

AIR POLLUTION

¶ When we hear about pollution, we think of smog, traffic congestion, acid rain, and other pollutant-related terms. However, we also need to consider contaminants in the air we breathe and chemical pollutants around us. We need to be concerned about indoor air because it can affect the health, comfort, and productivity of workers.[1]

POLLUTANTS AND CONTAMINANTS

¶ Chemical pollutants include tobacco smoke and chemical spills. Particles include pollutants such as dust and dirt from drywall, carpets, and copying machines.[2] Biological contaminants can include bacteria, viruses, molds, pollen, and water spills. These contaminants cause allergic reactions that trigger asthma attacks for an estimated 17 million Americans.[3]

IMPROVING AIR QUALITY

¶ The three basic approaches to improving air quality include the use of filters to clean the air, the use of ventilation systems to remove the pollutants, and the use of air pressure to keep the pollutants "at bay." The method we use to improve air quality depends on how difficult it is to separate the impurities.

(continued on next page)

ADMINISTRATIVE RESPONSIBILITIES

¶ Office managers can help by reviewing records pertaining to air conditioning and ventilation systems. They can also help by providing training sessions for employees to learn about maintaining clean air. Finally, they can keep a record of reported health complaints related to polluted air and aid in resolving these complaints.

A TEAM EFFORT

¶ All workers can have a positive impact on improving the quality of the air they breathe. For example, simply making sure that air vents and grills are clean will help improve the quality of air. People who smoke should do so only in areas designated for smoking.

---

[1] Juan Montero, *Pollutants in America*, Southwest Press, El Paso, Texas, 2010.

[2] Julie Bergstrom, "Pollution in the Office," *Boston Globe*, June 17, 2009, p. B4.

[3] "Breathing Clean Air," April 8, 2010, <http://www.airamerica.com/dirty.htm>, accessed on May 13, 2010.

Strategies for Career Success

Interview Thank-You Letter

Expressing your appreciation is a very important follow-up step in your job search. Send a thank-you letter or e-mail within 24 hours after your interview.

In the opening paragraph, thank the interviewer for taking time to meet with you. Make a positive statement about the company or interview feature (for example, meeting potential coworkers).

In the middle paragraph, close the sale. Address any qualifications you neglected to mention. Turn around an interview weakness (for example, reconsider your statement that you wouldn't travel). Strengthen your relationship with the interviewer (for example, refer the interviewer to a good article on a topic in which he or she expressed interest).

In the closing paragraph, ask to be notified when the decision is made. A thank-you letter ensures that your last impression is a positive one.

Your Turn: After your next interview, send a thank-you letter to effectively close the sale.

Advanced Formatting

4 PART

Keyboarding in Health Services

Within the health services job cluster, there is an enormous range of opportunities in the medical and health care job market. Hundreds of different occupations exist in health care practice, including business-oriented positions. In fact, career opportunities within this cluster are among the fastest growing in the national marketplace.

The current job outlook is quite positive because the growth in managed care has significantly increased opportunities for doctors and other health professionals, particularly in the area of preventive care. In addition, the aging population requires more highly skilled medical workers.

Consider health care jobs, medical careers, health care management, and medical management. Various job possibilities exist in positions such as a medical assistant, clinical technician, nurse, medical analyst, surgical technician or surgeon, physical therapist, orderly, pharmacist, or medical researcher. Keyboarding skill is important for all of these positions.

Goals

Keyboarding

- Demonstrate improved speed and accuracy when operating the keyboard by touch.
- Type at least 43 words per minute on a 5-minute timed writing with no more than 5 errors.

Language Arts

- Demonstrate acceptable proofreading skills, including using proofreaders' marks correctly.
- Demonstrate acceptable language arts skills in punctuation, grammar, and mechanics.
- Demonstrate acceptable language arts skills in composing and spelling.

Word Processing

- Use appropriate word processing commands necessary to complete document processing activities successfully.

Document Processing

- Correctly format e-mail, multipage correspondence, multipage reports, and tables.

Objective Test

- Answer questions with acceptable accuracy on an objective test.

UNIT

13

Skill Refinement

LESSON 61
Skillbuilding and Letter Review

LESSON 62
Skillbuilding, Memo, and E-Mail Review

LESSON 63
Skillbuilding and Report Review

LESSON 64
Skillbuilding and Table Review

LESSON 65
Skillbuilding and Employment Document Review

Skillbuilding and Letter Review

Goals

- Demonstrate improved speed and accuracy while typing by touch.
- Demonstrate acceptable language arts skills in comma usage.
- Correctly format a rough-draft document and apply proofreaders' marks.
- Correctly format a business letter and personal-business letter in block style and in modified-block style.

A. WARMUP

alphabet	1	`Six women quietly got the prizes back from the five judges.`
concentration	2	`electromagnetically pseudointellectuals overdiversification`
easy	3	`Di may work as a tutor for the six girls who asked for one.`

Skillbuilding

B. MAP+: ALPHABET

Follow the GDP software directions for this exercise to improve keystroking accuracy.

C. PROGRESSIVE PRACTICE: ALPHABET

Follow the GDP software directions for this exercise to improve keystroking speed.

Language Arts

D. COMMAS

Study the rules at the right.

Note: The callout signals in the left margin indicate which language arts rule from this lesson has been applied.

RULE
, series

Use a comma between each item in a series of three or more.

We need to order paper, toner, and font cartridges for the printer.
They saved their work, exited their program, and turned off their computers when they finished.

Note: Do not use a comma after the last item in a series.

RULE
, transitional expression

Use a comma before and after a transitional expression or independent comment.

It is critical, therefore, that we finish the project on time.
Our present projections, you must admit, are inadequate.
But: You must admit our present projections are inadequate.

Note: Examples of transitional expressions and independent comments are *in addition to, therefore, however, on the other hand, as a matter of fact,* and *unfortunately.*

Edit each sentence to correct any errors.

```
4  The lawyer the bank and the courthouse received copies.
5  The closing was delayed therefore for more than an hour.
6  The contract power of attorney and deed were in order.
7  Ms. Sperry's flight was delayed however for two hours.
8  Happily the drinks snacks and napkins arrived on time.
9  This offer I think will be unacceptable to the board.
10 Please read their report make whatever comments you feel
11 are appropriate and then route it to the others.
```

Formatting

E. ADVANCED FORMATTING

The document processing jobs in this unit review basic formatting for correspondence, reports, tables, and employment documents. Before beginning these jobs, review the introductory lessons in the Word Manual and the pages in the Reference Manual listed next. The fundamental information in these pages will prepare you to format and type the jobs in this unit and those that follow.

In the Word Manual, review Getting Started, Lessons 21–25, and Lesson 28. In the Reference Manual, review R-5C–D, R-14C, R-9D, R-13D, and R-12C–D.

As you format document processing jobs, note the following:

- Whenever you see "20--," type the current year in black.
- The | symbol indicates the end of a line. Press Enter whenever you see it.
- The ¶ symbol indicates a new, blocked paragraph.
- In Word, lines wrap automatically as you approach the right margin. Your line endings in Word may not match those in the book.
- Type your own reference initials in lowercase (no periods or spaces) in black whenever you see urs in letters or memos.
- Lines are shown with extra spacing for proofreaders' marks. Use standard spacing in all jobs.
- Center tables that appear alone on a page horizontally and vertically, and automatically adjust the column widths.
- Tables with borders removed are shown with "View Gridlines" active.

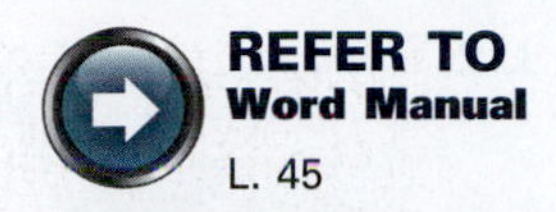

REFER TO
Word Manual
L. 45

Document Processing

Correspondence 61-55
Business Letter in Block Style

REFER TO
Reference Manual
R-3A: Business Letter in Block Style

June 3, 20-- | Mr. Andres Macias | Director of Product Development | Hampton Associates Inc. | 830 Market Street | San Francisco, CA 94102-1925 | Dear Mr. Macias:

¶ Have you had customer groups assist you or provide you with advice related to pending business decisions regarding computer design? Such design standards would include industrywide interfaces and computer hardware and software.

¶ I recently read an article discussing the influence consumer opinion can have on the design of various computer components. This very interesting article concluded that if customers demand standardization in computer hardware, participate in focus groups, and band together with other customers, they will see results reflected in the marketplace.

, series

¶ I am considering organizing several focus groups and, therefore, would appreciate any advice you might have. I know your expertise will prove to be invaluable, and I thank you in advance for your time and consideration.

, transitional expression

Sincerely yours, | Alice Karns | Product Development Manager | urs

Correspondence 61-56
Personal-Business Letter in Block Style

REFER TO
Reference Manual
R-3D: Personal-Business Letter in Modified-Block Style
R-14C: Proofreaders' Marks

september 1, 20--

Dr. David L. Grant | 3329 Market Street | Salem, OR 97301 | Dear Dr. Grant:

¶ Thank you for your letter of August 27 inquiring about my trip to New York city. Your letter brought back a lot of memories of those days when I was your student at Portland State University. We spent many weekends discussing all matters of importance and I'm sure we must have solved the worlds problems many times over. I will leave on Oct. 15th for a 2-week business trip where I will be conducting a workshop at Columbia University on the utilization of voice-activated hardware. When I complete my work on October 22, I would love to have you and your wife join me in New York City. I plan to attend plays, visit the Metropolitan Museum of Art and take one of the sightseeing tours. I would be happy to make hotel reservations and purchase theatre tickets.

, series

¶ I hope you'll consider joining me in the "Big Apple"! It would be great to see you and your wife again. However, I do need to know soon so that I can proceed with our plans. I look forward to hearing from you.

, transitional expression

Sincerely, | Rodney Dorey | 1329 BroadwayStreet | Eureka, California 95501

Correspondence 61-57
Business Letter in Modified-Block Style

REFER TO
Reference Manual
R-3B: Business Letter in Modified-Block Style

Open the file for Correspondence 61-55 and make the following changes:

1. Change the letter format to modified-block style.
2. Change the addressee name to this:
   `Mr. Peng Lim`
3. Change the salutation to this:
   `Dear Mr. Lim:`
4. Delete the last paragraph and replace it with this:

```
I would certainly appreciate
meeting you and discussing
this in person. Your advice
is very valuable, and your
reputation in this industry
is stellar. I will contact
you soon.
```

UNIT 13 LESSON 62

Skillbuilding, Memo, and E-Mail Review

Goals

- Type at least 40wpm/5'/5e.
- Correctly format a memo and an e-mail message.
- Correctly format a rough-draft document and apply proofreaders' marks.

A. WARMUP

alphabet	1	Very few phlox grew or bloomed just back of my zinc quarry.
one hand	2	tracer uplink tax lip regard plumply date phony waste polio
easy	3	The goal of their amendment is to make the city proficient.

Skillbuilding

B. SUSTAINED PRACTICE: ALTERNATE-HAND WORDS

Take a 1-minute timed writing on the boxed paragraph to establish your base speed. Then take a 1-minute timed writing on the following paragraph. As soon as you equal or exceed your base speed on this paragraph, move to the next, more difficult paragraph.

4	The town council decided to shape its destiny when a	11
5	rich landowner lent a hand by proposing to chair the audit	23
6	committee. He will be a good chairman, and eight civic	34
7	club members will work to amend some troublesome policies.	46
8	One problem relates to the change in profit for many	11
9	of the firms in the city. As giant property taxes do not	22
10	relate to income, they wish to make those taxes go down.	33
11	The result means increases in their sales or income taxes.	45
12	All eight members of the town council now agree that	11
13	it is time to join with other cities throughout the state	12
14	in lobbying with the state legislature to bring about the	35
15	needed change. The right balance in taxes is the goal.	46
16	The mayor pointed out that it is not only business	10
17	property owners who would be affected. Homeowners should	22
18	see a decrease in property taxes, and renters might see	33
19	lower rents, as taxes on rental property would be lowered.	45

1 | 2 | 3 | 4 | 5 | 6 | 7 | 8 | 9 | 10 | 11 | 12

Take two 5-minute timed writings. Review your speed and errors.

Goal: At least 40wpm/5'/5e

C. 5-MINUTE TIMED WRITING

```
20      Digital photography has revolutionized the way we take  11
21 pictures. A digital camera puts our photos in a format that  23
22 makes them easy to print and share with others. Using a      34
23 digital camera also has the advantage that we can quickly    46
24 print out our photos and see the result of our efforts.      57
25      We can also insert our photos into word processing      68
26 documents, send them by e-mail to our friends, or post them  80
27 on the Web where they can be viewed by all. We can even      91
28 connect our camera to a television set and have our images 103
29 displayed in a slide show presentation.                     111
30      Another advantage of digital photography is that the   121
31 expense of developing your own photos is much less because 133
32 you do not have to purchase rolls of film, nor do you have 145
33 to have your photos developed by others. Also, your photos 157
34 can be edited if you do not like what you see. You can crop 169
35 the photo, adjust its color or contrast, take out red-eye  180
36 imperfections, and even add or delete elements from the    192
37 photo or from other photos you have taken.                 200
      1 | 2 | 3 | 4 | 5 | 6 | 7 | 8 | 9 | 10 | 11 | 12
```

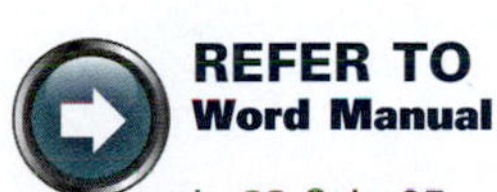

REFER TO Word Manual

L. 23 & L. 25

Document Processing

Correspondence 62-58
Memo

REFER TO Reference Manual

R-4D: Memo

MEMO TO: Min-Hong Dai, Theater Manager | **FROM:** Barbara Cornell, Executive Director | **DATE:** March 1, 20-- | **SUBJECT:** Season Ticket Price Schedule for Orchestra Hall

¶ We have tentatively scheduled 114 concerts for Orchestra Hall for the calendar year beginning September 1. The attached list shows the new season ticket prices for the main floor, mezzanine, balcony, and gallery.

¶ These prices are grouped in 11 different concert categories, which reflect the varied classical tastes of our patrons. These groupings also consider preferences for day of the week, time of day, and season of the year.

¶ Please see me in my office at 3 p.m. on March 10 so that we can review our ticket sales campaign. Last year's season ticket holders have had ample time to renew their subscriptions; we must now concentrate on attracting new season subscribers. I shall look forward to reviewing your plans.

urs | Attachment

Correspondence 62-59
E-Mail Message

Mr. Phillips:

¶ We are interested in implementing a new security program for the personal computers in our main office and would like to study the specifications and features your system provides.

(continued on next page)

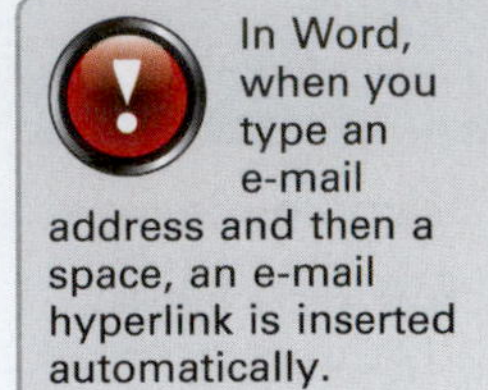

In Word, when you type an e-mail address and then a space, an e-mail hyperlink is inserted automatically.

¶ Please send information and prices on your state-of-the-art security software. The ready availability of the Internet to the general public and others has made the prevention of identity theft, phishing, and other types of related scams a top security priority in our firm.
¶ Thank you for your assistance.
Charles | Charles Cox | E-mail: chcox@mailserver.net | Phone: 770-555-2843

Correspondence
62-60
Memo

MEMO TO: Eduardo Bocelli Cabaret pops Conductor

FROM: Marcia Greene, Executive Director

Date: March 2, 20--

SUBJECT: Erving Berlin Concert

Our Patron Advisory Program Committeee has included several recommendations in it's attached letter. They would like the Irving Berlin concert to begin with some pre-World War I hits, followed by music from the 1920s and 1930s. The first part of the program will focus on favorite hit songs from the 1920s and 1930s. After the intermission, the program will focus on hit songs from the 1940s and 1950s. A planning meeting has been scheduled for you, Dolly Carpenter (the Rehearsals Coordinator), and me on Mar. 9 at 10 A.M. at Orchestra Hall. I look forward to seeing you then.

urs

Attachments

c:Dolly Carpenter

Correspondence
62-61
Memo

MEMO TO: Dolly Carpenter, Rehearsals Coordinator
FROM: Sam Steele, Executive Director
DATE: March 3, 20--
SUBJECT: Summer Cabaret Pops Concerts
¶ We are pleased that you will be our rehearsals coordinator for this summer's Cabaret Pops concerts. The five biweekly concerts will run from June 13 through August 8.
¶ As the concert schedule is much lighter during the summer months, I am quite confident that you will be able to use the Orchestra Hall stage for all rehearsals. This is the preference of Eduardo Bocelli, who will be the conductor for this summer's Cabaret Pops concerts.
¶ I look forward to seeing you on June 1.
¶ urs

Skillbuilding and Report Review

Goals

- Demonstrate improved speed and accuracy while typing.
- Demonstrate acceptable proofreading skills by comparing lines.
- Correctly format a business report and an academic report.

A. WARMUP

alphabet	1	Just keep examining every low bid quoted for zinc etchings.
practice: *u* and *y*	2	yum buy duly yuck fury your guy July busy yuk quay you jury
easy	3	Pam blames all her problems on the rituals of the sorority.

Skillbuilding

B. MAP+: NUMBERS

Follow the GDP software directions for this exercise to improve keystroking accuracy.

PPP PRETEST » PRACTICE » POSTTEST

PRETEST
Take a 1-minute timed writing. Review your speed and errors.

C. PRETEST: Discrimination Practice

```
4      Lois said the rear of the long train was right next    11
5  to the column of poplar trees. A robber had entered a red  22
6  car and stolen a case of grapefruit juice and ten cases of 34
7  soda pop. The officer quickly arrested him on the street.  45
    1 | 2 | 3 | 4 | 5 | 6 | 7 | 8 | 9 | 10 | 11 | 12
```

PRACTICE
Speed Emphasis:
If you made no more than 1 error on the Pretest, type each *individual* line 2 times.
Accuracy Emphasis:
If you made 2 or more errors, type each *group* of lines (as though it were a paragraph) 2 times.

D. PRACTICE: Left Hand

```
8  rtr trip trot sport train alert courts assert tragic truest
9  asa mass salt usage cased cease astute dashed masked castle
10 sds sad used suds said pods based drips curds stride guards
11 rer rear rest overt rerun older before entire surest better
```

E. PRACTICE: Right Hand

```
12 mnm menu numb hymns unmet manly mental namely manner number
13 pop post coop opera pools opens polite proper police oppose
14 olo tool yolk loon spoil lodge color stroll lottery rolling
15 iui unit quit fruit suits built medium guided helium podium
```

POSTTEST

Repeat the Pretest timed writing and compare performance.

F. POSTTEST: Discrimination Practice

Language Arts

Compare this paragraph with the last paragraph of the timed writing on page 239. Edit the paragraph to correct any errors.

G. PROOFREADING

```
16      Another advantage of digital photography is that the
17 the expense of developing your own photos is less because you
18 do not have to buy any rolls of film, nor do you have
19 to have your photos developed by others. Also, your photos
20 can be edited if you do not like what you see. You can crop
21 the photo, adjust it's color or contrast, take out red-eye
22 imperfections and even add or delete elements from the photo
23 or from other photographs you have taken.
```

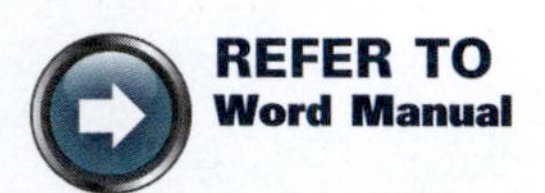

L. 31, L. 32, L. 34 & L. 46

Document Processing

Report
63-34
Business Report

VIDEO-BASED TRAINING PROGRAMS

Rodolfo Madison, Training Consultant

¶ Video-based training programs are being implemented at an ever-increasing rate across the country. While this type of training should certainly not be the only method that is used to train your employees, it is very effective and can offer significant advantages over other training methods.

ADVANTAGES

¶ There are many advantages to video-based training. However, only the most significant ones are discussed here.

Save Development Time. You can shorten your training cycle because you will have the ability to deliver "just-in-time" training where and when you need it. Facilitation materials with activities and discussion points can be used in whole or in part to create training events that run anywhere from one to four hours.

Add Variety to the Delivery Mix. Workshops and lectures can become routine and boring. Video provides a change of pace and can add an entertainment factor that is not possible in a live presentation. Videos can also be used to supplement a face-to-face workshop to stimulate discussion, demonstrate concepts that could not otherwise be presented, and provide meaningful examples of the topic at hand. The more the senses are engaged in the content, the more the participants will learn.

Build a Resource Library. Building a video and/or DVD library allows you to offer a broader range of training. You will no longer be limited to custom in-house development or scheduled classroom events. Trainees can check out a DVD or access video training online.

(continued on next page)

RECOMMENDATION

¶ Video-based training materials save your organization time and money, and they make your business look progressive. Because they help build learning retention, they can also improve the return on your training investment. The next step should be a formal review of your training needs and an evaluation report to be completed by a professional video-based training firm with a proven track record.

Report
63-35
Academic Report

R-8C–D: Multipage Academic Report

BECOMING A FITNESS WORKER

Cal Jordan

According to the U.S. Department of Labor's Bureau of Labor Statistics, "Jobs for fitness workers are expected to increase much faster than the average for all occupations."[1] Fitness workers should have good job prospects due to rapid job growth in health clubs, fitness facilities, and other settings where fitness workers are concentrated.

NATURE OF THE WORK

Fitness workers primarily instruct and motivate individuals or groups in a variety of exercise activities. A rising trend is providing fitness trainers in the workplace as an employee benefit. There are several categories of fitness workers.

Personal Trainers. Personal trainers work one-on-one with individuals to help them assess their level of physical fitness and set and reach fitness goals. Trainers can also demonstrate exercises to help clients improve their exercise techniques. They may keep records of exercise sessions for monitoring progress and offer advice regarding lifestyles outside of the gym to improve fitness. They often work in a variety of places—health clubs, hospitals, fitness studios, resorts, and private homes are typical.

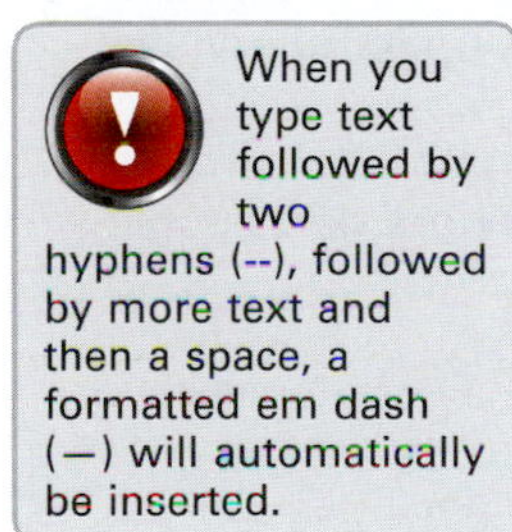

Group Exercise Instructors. Group exercise instructors conduct group exercise sessions, including aerobic exercise, stretching, and muscle conditioning. Classes are often set to music, and Pilates and yoga are often incorporated. Exercise classes should be motivating, safe, and challenging. Louise Byron says that classes that incorporate Pilates and yoga can be more effective than weight training for overall strength and toning.[2]

Fitness Directors. Fitness directors oversee health club or fitness center activities. They might create programs for member orientations, fitness assessments, and workout incentive programs. They also select fitness equipment; coordinate training programs; hire, train, and supervise fitness staff; and carry out other administrative duties.

RELATED OCCUPATIONS

Other workers that focus on physical fitness include athletes, coaches, and physical therapists. For example, a physical therapist is often required to create exercise plans to improve their patients' flexibility, strength, and endurance. Dietitians and nutritionists also have related careers because they offer advice on improving and maintaining good health.

[1] U.S. Department of Labor, *Occupational Outlook Handbook*, <http://www.bls.gov/oco/ocos296.htm>, accessed on April 22, 2010.

[2] Louise Byron, *Pilates and Yoga for Strength and Fitness*, 2nd ed., Midwest Publishing, Chicago, 2010, p. 20.

Report
63-36
Left-Bound Business Report

REFER TO Reference Manual

R-9A: Left-Bound Business Report

Open the file for Report 63-34 and make the following changes:

1. Change the report from a business report to a left-bound business report.
2. Add this new paragraph heading and paragraph as the last paragraph in the ADVANTAGES section of the report:

   Supplement Existing Training Resources. Videos can often be used to support more than one of your training initiatives. For example, you can use a video like *Leadership for the New Millennium* to enhance workshops on decision making, leadership, teamwork, or communication.

3. Add a page number to display on the second page only.

Strategies for Career Success

Looking for a Job

Don't waste time! Start your job search early. Scan the Help Wanted sections in major Sunday newspapers or their Web sites for job descriptions and salaries. The Internet provides access to worldwide job listings at sites like Monster.com, Dice.com, Craigslist.com, and on company and government Web sites, such as the federal government's jobs site (http://www.usajobs.gov/).

Consult references such as the U.S. Department of Labor's *Occupational Outlook Handbook* (http://www.bls.gov/oco/) to research types of jobs in various fields and the requirements for those jobs. Visit your college placement office. Sign up for interviews with companies that visit your campus.

Talk with people in your field to get advice. Look for an internship or join a professional organization in your field. Attend local chapter meetings to network with people in your chosen profession.

Taking the initiative in your job search will pay off!

Your Turn: Visit the Internet site for the *National Business Employment Weekly* at http://www.employmentguide.com, which provides more than 45,000 national and international job listings online.

Skillbuilding and Table Review

64

Goals

- Type at least 40wpm/5′/5e.
- Correctly format a boxed table, an open table, and a ruled table.

A. WARMUP

alphabet	1	George W. Bush quickly fixed prize jam cakes on television.
frequent digraphs	2	ti tie anti tic site tilt tin tithe stir tide tick tip tint
easy	3	I may make a quantity of maps to aid me when I visit Japan.

Skillbuilding

B. PROGRESSIVE PRACTICE: NUMBERS

Follow the GDP software directions for this exercise to improve keystroking speed.

C. TECHNIQUE PRACTICE: SHIFT KEY

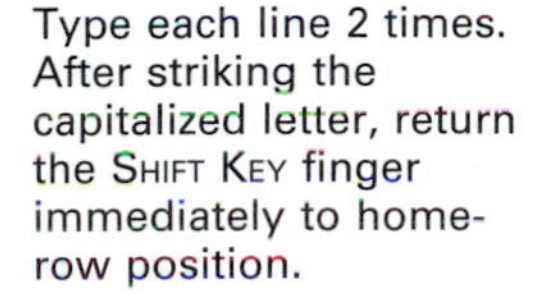
Type each line 2 times. After striking the capitalized letter, return the Shift Key finger immediately to home-row position.

4 Aldo Bonilla skied. Clara Duarte typed. Ellen Fuller filed.
5 Guy Hayes ate dinner. Isabella Jayne hid. Kevin Lee sobbed.
6 Megan Newsome sat. Otis Petrov tried. Quincy Rogers hummed.
7 Syd Tia wed Ursula Vivian. Willie Xin and Yvonne Zola lied.

Take two 5-minute timed writings. Review your speed and errors.

Goal: At least 40wpm/5'/5e

D. 5-MINUTE TIMED WRITING

```
 8       The computer has changed the way you do things in the   11
 9   office today. Jobs that used to take many hours to complete 23
10   now can be done in less time. A quick review of ways in     34
11   which the computer can help you streamline your work may    46
12   be in order.                                                48
13       Most software programs include helpful wizards that     59
14   can guide you through any project. You can use a stored     70
15   template, or you can create your own style. You do not need 82
16   to write your thoughts in longhand on paper before you type 94
17   them. Composing and revising documents as you type them    105
18   will save you lots of time.                                111
19       Your computer is valuable for more than just writing   122
20   letters. Using different software applications, you can    133
21   create dazzling presentations for all to see. You can also 145
22   build databases for sorting and storing all types of data, 156
23   format spreadsheets, create your own calendar and colorful 169
24   charts, and perform calculations. You can even publish your 180
25   own newsletter and make business cards. It is exciting to  192
26   consider the ways you can use a computer.                  200
       1 | 2 | 3 | 4 | 5 | 6 | 7 | 8 | 9 | 10 | 11 | 12
```

REFER TO Word Manual

L. 28 & L. 36–39

Document Processing

Table 64-23

Boxed Table

REFER TO Reference Manual

R-13A: Boxed Table

$700 COMPOUNDED ANNUALLY FOR 7 YEARS AT 7 PERCENT		
Beginning of Year	**Interest**	**Value**
First	$00.00	$ 700.00
Second	49.00	749.00
Third	52.43	801.43
Fourth	56.10	857.53
Fifth	60.03	917.56
Sixth	64.23	981.79
Seventh	68.72	1,050.51
Eighth	78.68	1,129.19

Table
64-24
Open Table

R-13B: Open Table

SALES CONFERENCES All Sessions at Regional Offices		
Date	**City**	**Leader**
October 7	Boston	D. G. Gorham
October 17	Baltimore	James B. Brunner
October 24	Miami	Becky Taylor
November 3	Dallas	Rodney R. Nordstein
November 10	Minneapolis	Joanne Miles-Tyrell
November 17	Denver	Becky Taylor
November 26	Los Angeles	Rodney R. Nordstein

Table
64-25
Ruled Table

R-13C: Ruled Table

COMPARISON OF SALES QUOTAS
AND ACTUAL SALES
July to December

Month	Sales Quotas	Actual Sales
July	$ 935,400	$ 950,620
August	970,750	896,230
September	974,510	725,110
October	990,270	990,110
November	975,890	968,290
December	1,960,470	1,978,690
Totals	$6,807,290	$6,509,050

Keyboarding Connection

Finding Business Information on the Internet

Finding information about businesses on the Internet is easy. If you want to research a company, you can go to its Web site, or you can use a search engine to find out what resources and information are available. Sites like Bloomberg.com and Yahoo! have articles about business trends and companies. Professional organizations like the American Management Association and the Chamber of Commerce also have Web sites where you can learn about their member businesses.

Start by using a search engine like Google, and you'll find plenty of business information available on the Internet. Company Web sites often have an About Us link, where you can learn more about specific companies.

Your Turn: Access the *Selected Business Resources on the Web* site at http://www.bls.gov and explore its offerings.

Skillbuilding and Employment Document Review

UNIT 13 LESSON

65

Goals

- Demonstrate improved speed and accuracy while typing.
- Demonstrate acceptable language arts skills in composing.
- Correctly format a resume, an application letter, and a follow-up letter.
- Successfully complete a Progress and Proofreading Check with zero errors on the first scored attempt.

A. WARMUP

```
alphabet        1  Crazy Fredrick bought Jane many very exquisite opal jewels.
number/symbol   2  wroe@gmail.com 82% Dye & Cox (5/7) Oh! ($6.90) *8:45 #12-63
easy            3  Did a firm fix the problem of the worn element with a disk?
```

Skillbuilding

B. 12-SECOND SPEED SPRINTS

Take three 12-second timed writings on each line. The scale below the last line shows your wpm speed for a 12-second timed writing.

```
4  Jan owns a pair of old gowns and a new hat she got from me.
5  He may go with us to the giant dock down by the handy lake.
6  His civic goal for the city is for them to endow the chair.
7  If she works at home, she may make a visit to the old farm.
   ''''5''''10''''15''''20''''25''''30''''35''''40''''45''''50''''55''''60
```

C. PACED PRACTICE

Follow the GDP software directions for this exercise to improve keystroking speed and accuracy.

Language Arts

D. COMPOSING PARAGRAPHS

What advice can you give students who tend to get nervous when they take timed writings? Compose a paragraph of at least three to four sentences answering this question.

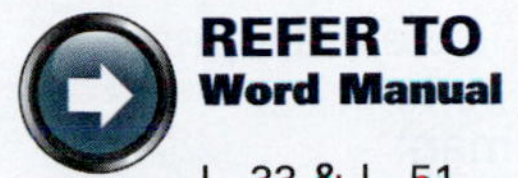

L. 33 & L. 51

Document Processing

Report
65-37
Resume

R-12A: Resume
R-12D: Examples of Different Kinds of Lists

STEPHEN K. HAMILTON

6183 Nicollet Avenue South, Minneapolis, MN 55404
Phone: 612-555-9009; e-mail: shamilton@fastmail.com

OBJECTIVE	To obtain a position as a technology support specialist in a corporate environment or government agency.
EDUCATION	Minneapolis Community College, Minneapolis, Minnesota A.A. degree in information technology Graduated: December 2009 Specialize in analysis, design, and security of modern computer networks. Concentration courses emphasize local area networks, wireless local area networks, wide area networks, and network security South Minneapolis High School, Minneapolis, Minnesota Graduated: May 2008
EXPERIENCE	*Computer Systems Technician, Selkirk & Associates* Minneapolis, Minnesota September 2009 to Present Duties include installing and updating computer software programs throughout the firm. *Administrative Assistant, Kittredge Insurance Agency* Circle Pines, Minnesota August 2008 to August 2009 (part-time) Duties included coordinating office communications and setting up international videoconferences.
ACTIVITIES	Activities pursued: • College Choir, 2008 to 2009 • Business Students Club, 2006 to 2008 • Varsity Basketball, 2007 to 2008
REFERENCES	Available upon request.

Table shown with "View Gridlines" active.

Correspondence
65-62
Application Letter in Block Style

REFER TO Reference Manual

R-12B: Application Letter in Block Style

Mar. 10, 20-- | Denise Klenzman | Director of Human Resources | Cole Enterprises | 3714 Crestmont Ave. | Minneapolis, Mn 55405 | Dear Mrs. Klenzman:

¶ Please consider me an applicant for the position of technology systems specialist with your firm. I becameaware of the position through a friend who is an employee at Cole Enterprises.

¶ I am currently employed at Selkirk & Associates as a computer systems technician and have earned an A.A. degree at Minneapolis Community College in information technology. The resume and transcript enclosed will provide you with details on courses completed. I am confident that my educationl background and my Computer Systems experience make me qualified for this position. I would very much appreciate an opportunity for an interview. Plaese contact me at your convenience at 612-555-9039, or send me an e-mail message at shamilton@fastmail.com.

Sincerely yours | Stephen K. Hamilton | 6183 Nicollet Avenue South | Minneapolis, MN 55404 | Enclosure

Correspondence
65-63
Follow-Up Letter in Block Style

Progress and Proofreading Check

Documents designated as Proofreading Checks serve as a check of your proofreading skill. Your goal is to have zero typographical errors when the GDP software first scores the document.

March 19, 20-- | Mrs. Denise A. Klenzman | Director of Human Resources | Cole Enterprises | 3714 Crestmont Avenue | Minneapolis, MN 55405 | Dear Mrs. Klenzman:

¶ Thank you for the opportunity to meet with you yesterday and to learn of the exciting career opportunities at Cole Enterprises. It was inspiring for me to learn about future plans for your forward-looking company.

¶ I am confident that my education and my experience qualify me in a special way for your position of technology support specialist. I am familiar with all of your present equipment and software.

¶ I would very much like to join the professional staff at Cole Enterprises. Please let me know when you have made your decision.

Sincerely yours, | Stephen K. Hamilton | 6183 Nicollet Avenue South | Minneapolis, MN 55404

UNIT 14

Correspondence

LESSON 66
Multipage Letters

LESSON 67
Special Correspondence Features

LESSON 68
More Special Correspondence Features

LESSON 69
Multipage Memos With Tables

LESSON 70
Memo Reports

Multipage Letters 66

Goals

- Type at least 41wpm/5'/5e.
- Correctly format a multipage letter.

A. WARMUP

alphabet	1	A puzzled woman bequeathed idiotic jerks very exotic gifts.
concentration	2	nonrepresentational counterinsurgencies individualistically
easy	3	A new toxic problem may ensue if we burn the old cornfield.

Skillbuilding

B. SUSTAINED PRACTICE: ROUGH DRAFT

Take a 1-minute timed writing on the boxed paragraph to establish your base speed. Then take a 1-minute timed writing on the following paragraph. As soon as you equal or exceed your base speed on this paragraph, move to the next, more difficult paragraph.

4 The possibility of aging and not being able to live as 11
5 independently as we want to is a prospect that no one wants 23
6 to recognize. One resource designed to counter some of the 35
7 negative realities of aging is called the Handyman Project. 47

8 This type of ~~project~~ *program* helps support elders and disabled 12
9 residents in their efforts to maintain the^*ir* homes. As the 24
10 name implies, "handy" volunte^*e*rs per for^*m* minor home repairs 36
11 such as tight^*e*ning leaky faucets and fixing broken windows. 48

12 ¶Other type^*s* of work include: painting, plumbing, yard 11
13 work, and carpentery. The volunteers are all as divers^*i*fied 23
14 as the word itself. You may find a retire^*e* working next to 35
15 an executive or a student ~~helping~~ *assisting* a lisensed electrician. 47

16 Their back gr^*o*unds may vary, but that they share is the 11
17 ~~hope~~ *desire* to put their capabilities to good use. Volunteers ~~take~~ *find* 23
18 a high level of personal satisfaction after ~~doing~~ *finishing* a job 35
19 ~~but~~ *and* spending time with^ *an elder who really needs the help.* 47

1 | 2 | 3 | 4 | 5 | 6 | 7 | 8 | 9 | 10 | 11 | 12

Take two 5-minute timed writings.

Goal: At least 41wpm/5'/5e

C. 5-MINUTE TIMED WRITING

20	Making a successful presentation to an audience is a	11
21	skill that is absolutely essential in your career. The art	23
22	of speaking before a group requires planning and hard work.	35
23	Although different speakers prepare in many different ways,	47
24	a speaker should try to adhere to certain rules.	56
25	As the speaker, you are quite visible to people in the	68
26	audience. Therefore, you should always try to make a good	79
27	first impression. When you walk to the podium to speak, you	91
28	give the audience a chance to notice your neat appearance,	103
29	good posture, and confident manner. You will improve the	114
30	quality of your voice if you stand up straight and hold	126
31	your shoulders back and stomach in.	133
32	As you talk, use your eyes, face, and hands to help	143
33	you connect with your listeners. Maintain eye contact by	155
34	just moving your eyes over the group without focusing on	166
35	any one person. Use hand movements and facial expressions	178
36	to convey meanings to your audience. By utilizing these	189
37	techniques, you will improve your speaking skills, and your	201
38	effort may be noted.	205
	1 | 2 | 3 | 4 | 5 | 6 | 7 | 8 | 9 | 10 | 11 | 12	

Formatting

D. MULTIPAGE LETTERS

To format a multipage letter:

1. Type the first page on letterhead stationery, and type continuation pages on plain paper that matches the letterhead.
2. Insert a page number in the top right-hand corner of the page header of all continuing pages, and remove the page number from the first page.

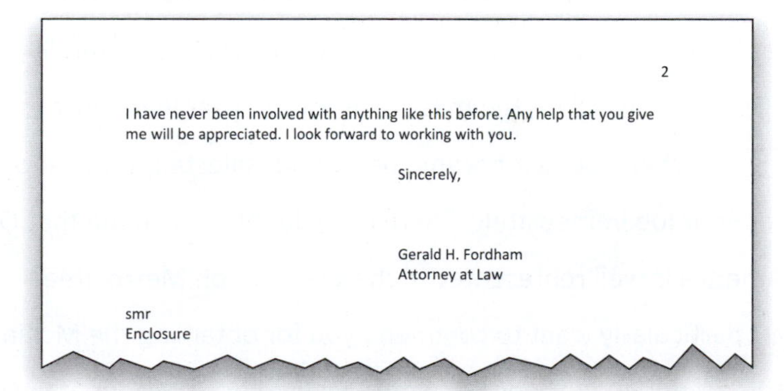

2

I have never been involved with anything like this before. Any help that you give me will be appreciated. I look forward to working with you.

Sincerely,

Gerald H. Fordham
Attorney at Law

smr
Enclosure

Document Processing

Correspondence 66-64
Business Letter in Modified-Block Style

R-5A–B: Multipage Business Letter

July 13, 20-- | Miss Florence B. Glashan | Attorney at Law | 2932 Point Street | Providence, RI 02903 | Dear Miss Glashan:

¶ It was a pleasure to meet you at the convention for trial attorneys in New York last week. In addition to the interesting program highlights of the regular sessions, the informal discussions with people like you are an added plus at these meetings. Your contribution to the program was very beneficial and highly informative.

¶ You may recall that I had just been appointed by the court to defend a woman here in Providence who has been charged with embezzling large sums of money from her previous employer. The defendant had been employed at a large department store for more than 25 years. Because of her valuable years of experience in accounting with the store, she was in charge of accounts receivable at the store. Her previous employer, the plaintiff in the case, claims that she embezzled $18,634 three years ago, $39,072 two years ago, and $27,045 last year.

¶ You mentioned that you had represented defendants in similar cases in previous years. Your assistance would be invaluable as I prepare for this defense. If you are willing to lend your professional expertise in this case, here is what is needed:

1. Within the next week, send the appropriate citations for all similar trials in which you participated.
2. Provide any other case citations that you think might be helpful in this case.
3. Meet with me in approximately two weeks for a case consultation. At that time we can discuss compensation for your work on this matter.

¶ A copy of the formal complaint is enclosed for your review. I will call you in about a week to arrange a time and place for our meeting. Please let me know if there is additional information that would be helpful in preparing for this case.

¶ This type of case will present unique challenges, but I know your guidance and years of experience will be invaluable. I look forward to working with you.

Sincerely, | Gerald H. Fordham | Attorney at Law | urs | Enclosure

Correspondence 66-65
Business Letter in Block Style

April 3, 20--

Mr. ~~Tom~~ *Thomas* Crawford | District Product Manager | Office Supplies of America | 2101 Pennsylvania Avenue, ~~N.W.~~ *NW* | Washington, dc 20006 | Dear Tom:

¶ The Sales Conference in Atlanta last week was out standing. Your winning the "Gold Key" award for the most sales for the year was well deserved indeed.

¶ When you first became part of our sales team, you showed great *ul* enthusiasm for your job immediately. There is no doubt in my mind that Office Supplies of America is well represented in the Washington Metro area.

¶ I particularly want to commend you for obtaining the McKinley account. Acquiring this account ~~have~~ *has* been a major objective for a number of years. None of our other sales representatives ~~has~~ *have* been able to accomplish this feat. What approach did you take, Tom? Did you:

(continued on next page)

1. Spend consider able time with the president, Mr. Arch Davis or one of his associates? If so, who were the individuals involved?
2. Conduct a series of presentations for key personel?

   SS

3. Develop a special marketing campaign for McKinley itself?
4. Use regular campaign model and customize it for McKinley?
5. Combine various strategies in your efforts to obtain this important account?

¶ Please let me know what approaches you used to make this sale. Successes of this nature do not happen without a lot of hard work. You to are be commended for putting forth your best efforts to sign the account.

¶ If we can arrange a time at our annual sales meeting we would like to have you make a presentation to our Sales Representatives. They would benefit greatly from having you share your success story. Our annual meeting will be held in late September in Richmond, VA.

¶ Again, congratulations on receiving this very prestigious award. All of us here in the home office are very pleased with the performance of our entire sales team. Indications that are this will be a year when our sales records will be broken and we will again be in the media spotlight.

Sincerely, | Leonard d. Manchester | President | urs | bc: Maria Olson, Director of Sales

Correspondence
66-66
Business Letter in Modified-Block Style

Open the file for Correspondence 66-64 and make the following changes:

1. Change the inside address to this:

   ```
   2632 East Main Road
   Portsmouth, RI 02871
   ```

2. Replace the last sentence in the first paragraph with these:

   ```
   Networking with colleagues
   like you is always
   enlightening and beneficial.
   I value your input greatly.
   ```

3. Add this sentence after the last sentence in the letter:

   ```
   I will call you in a few
   days to discuss this matter
   further.
   ```

Special Correspondence Features

Goals

- Demonstrate improved speed and accuracy while typing.
- Demonstrate acceptable language arts skills in using hyphens, in subject and verb agreement, and in using abbreviations.
- Correctly use Word's sort feature.
- Correctly format correspondence with multiple addresses, on-arrival notations, and subject lines.

A. WARMUP

alphabet	1	How quickly the daft jumping zebras were vexed by the boys.
one hand	2	career uphill gas pin awards homonym read yummy grade lumpy
easy	3	He has on a tux and she has on a tan gown for their social.

Skillbuilding

B. MAP+: ALPHABET

Follow the GDP software directions for this exercise to improve keystroking accuracy.

C. PROGRESSIVE PRACTICE: ALPHABET

Follow the GDP software directions for this exercise to improve keystroking speed.

Language Arts

Study the rules at the right.

RULE
- compound adjective

D. HYPHENS

Hyphenate compound adjectives that come before a noun (unless the first word is an adverb ending in *-ly*).

We reviewed an up-to-date report on Wednesday.
But: The report was up_to_date.
But: We reviewed the highly_rated report.

Note: A compound adjective is two or more words that function as a unit to describe a noun.

E. AGREEMENT

RULE
agreement singular
agreement plural

Use singular verbs and pronouns with singular subjects; use plural verbs and pronouns with plural subjects.

I was happy with my performance.
Janet and Phoenix were happy with their performance.
Among the items discussed were our raises and benefits.

F. ABBREVIATIONS

RULE
abbreviate none

In general business writing, do not abbreviate common words (such as *dept.* or *pkg.*), compass points, units of measure, or the names of months, days of the week, cities, or states (except in addresses).

Almost one-half of the audience indicated they were at least 5 feet 8 inches tall.

Note: Do not insert a comma between the parts of a single measurement.

Edit each sentence to correct any errors.

```
4  The Sabins visited Hickory to look at four bedroom homes.
5  Cindy Wallace has a part time job after school.
6  The accountants was extremely busy from March through April.
7  Lydia and Margaret were invited to present their report.
8  The portfolio include several technology stocks.
9  The planning committee will meet on Tue., Sept. 26.
10 Please credit the acct. for the amt. of $55.48.
11 The mgr. said the org. will move its headquarters to NC.
12 Appearing last on the agenda was the reports about the
13 urgently needed parts.
```

Formatting

G. MULTIPLE ADDRESSES

Often a letter may be sent to two or more people at the same address or to different addresses:

1. If a letter is addressed to two people at the same address, type each name on a separate line above the same inside address.
2. If a letter is addressed to two people at different addresses, type each name and address, one under the other. Press ENTER 2 times between the addresses.
3. If a letter is addressed to three or more people, type the names and addresses side by side, with one at the left margin and another beginning at the centerpoint. Press ENTER 2 times before typing the third name and address at the left margin.

↓5X
November 19, 20--
↓4X

Dr. Albert Russell, Professor
Department of English
Appalachian State University
Boone, NC 28608
↓2X
Dr. Kay Smith, Professor
Director of Business
Grove City College
Grove City, PA 16127
↓2X
Dear Dr. Russell and Dr. Smith:
↓2X
It is with great pleasure that I announce the scholarship winners for this year's awards banquet to be held in the next month. The awardees' names are listed below.
↓2X

H. ON-ARRIVAL NOTATIONS

On-arrival notations (such as *CONFIDENTIAL*) should be typed on the second line below the date, at the left margin. Type the notation in all-caps. Press ENTER 2 times to begin the inside address.

↓5X
November 19, 20--
↓2X
CONFIDENTIAL
↓2X
Mr. and Mrs. Earl Walters
3408 Washington Boulevard
New Tripoli, PA 18066
↓2X
Dear Mr. and Mrs. Walters:
↓2X
We are very pleased to tell you that your daughter will be the recipient of a prestigious scholarship this semester. She will be recognized at a banquet to be held next month.
↓2X

I. SUBJECT LINES

A *subject line* indicates what a letter is about. Type the subject line below the salutation at the left margin, preceded and followed by 1 blank line. (The term *Re* or *In re* may be used in place of *Subject*.)

↓5X
November 19, 20--
↓4X

Mr. and Mrs. Earl Walters
3408 Washington Boulevard
New Tripoli, PA 18066
↓2X
Dear Mr. and Mrs. Walters:
↓2X
Subject: Scholarship Awarded
↓2X
We are very pleased to tell you that your daughter will be the recipient of a very prestigious scholarship this semester. She will be recognized at a banquet to be held next month.
↓2X

J. WORD PROCESSING: SORT

GO TO Word Manual

Study Lesson 67 in your Word Manual. Complete all of the shaded steps while at your computer. Then format the documents that follow.

Document Processing

Correspondence 67-67
Business Letter in Block Style

November 8, 20-- / CONFIDENTIAL / Mrs. Katie Hollister / 11426 Prairie View Road / Kearney, NE 68847 / Dear Mrs. Hollister: / Subject: Site for New Elementary School

¶ As you are aware, your farm, located in the northeast quarter of Section 26 in Tyro township, is a part of Independent School District 17. Each of our three elementary schools occupies 11 acres and is adjoined by an 18-acre park. We are now in the early planning stages for a fourth elementary school. Because your farm is centrally located, the District 17 Board has directed me to initiate discussions with you on the following topics regarding 11 acres of your land:

- compound adjective

Sort the bulleted list in ascending alphabetical order.

- Purchasing options
- Time frames for purchasing
- Alternative sites

¶ Please call me to arrange a meeting with you and your attorneys, Jonathan Beck and Myra Colter, no later than November 13. They informed me that they will coordinate their schedules around yours. I look forward to our discussions.

abbreviate none

Yours truly, / Irvin J. Hagg / Superintendent / urs / c: District 17 Board

Correspondence
67-68
Business Letter in Block Style

October 4, 20-- | Ms. Deborah Campbell Wallace | 7835 Virginia Avenue, NW | Washington, DC 20037 | Mr. Thomas E. Campbell | 3725 Stevens Road, SE | Washington, DC 20020 | Dear Ms. Wallace and Mr. Campbell:

agreement plural

¶ We received your letter requesting instructions for transferring stock. The most common stock transfer situations are provided below. Determine which type of transfer you require, and select the instructions that apply to your stock transfer.

Sort each bulleted list in ascending alphabetical order.

- Transferring shares to another individual
- Transferring shares to a minor
- Transferring shares from a deceased shareholder (multiple owners)
- Transferring shares from a deceased shareholder (individual ownership)
- Transfers involving a trust
- Transfers involving a power of attorney
- Changing a name

agreement singular

¶ Every transfer requires a letter of instruction specifying how you want your shares transferred. The following items are required for all types of transfers:

- Name and address of new owner
- Social security number or taxpayer identification number
- Dated and signed form
- Preferred form of ownership (that is, joint tenants or tenants in common)
- Total number of shares being transferred

abbreviate none

¶ Please be sure to submit all required documentation no later than November 1, and note that all documents submitted become part of the permanent record of transfer and will not be returned. All transfers must have your signature guaranteed by a financial institution participating in the Medallion Signature Guarantee Program.

- compound adjective

¶ If you need additional information, you may visit our Web site for step-by-step instructions, or you may call one of our customer service representatives at our toll-free number.

Sincerely, | William J. Shawley | Shareholder Services | urs

Correspondence
67-69
Personal-Business Letter in Block Style

Nov. 17, 20--

Doctor Francesca Tuscany | 953 Foster Street | Durham, NC 27701 | Dear Dr.Tuscany: |

SUBJECT: January Meeting Book Selection

¶ Your new book, The Iron Hand, has gotten excellent reviews across the nation. The citizens of durham are pleased that a respected member of one of their local colleges is receiving national attention. Our book discussion group in Morehead, composed of members of the AAUW (American Association of University Women), is going to select 1 of your books below for discussion at our January meeting. All the topics we agreed to discuss were related to your books. We would like you very much to recommend one of these books:

agreement plural

agreement plural

Sort the bulleted list in ascending alphabetical order.

Format book titles in italic.

- *The Iron Hand*
- *Peace in Troubled Times*
- *A House Divided*

I will call you next week. Your presence at our meeting would be a real highlight.

Sincerely | TheresaMayfield | 2901 Garfield Court | Durham, NC 27701

More Special Correspondence Features

Goals

- Type at least 41wpm/5'/5e.
- Correctly use Word's table shading and e-mail blind copy features.
- Correctly format a table within a document.
- Correctly format correspondence with a company name, delivery notation, blind copy notation and postscript.

A. WARMUP

alphabet	1	My folks proved his expert eloquence was just a big hazard.
practice: *f* and *d*	2	fad fold fodder fed doff defy find fled deaf fund deft fade
easy	3	Sign the forms to pay for the ivory bowl she got in Durham.

Skillbuilding

B. PACED PRACTICE

Follow the GDP software directions for this exercise to improve keystroking speed and accuracy.

C. 5-MINUTE TIMED WRITING

Take two 5-minute timed writings.

Goal: At least 41wpm/5'/5e

4	Taking photos with a digital camera is a process that	11
5	is somewhat unique and different from taking photos with	22
6	film. Most digital cameras store images on a device such as	34
7	a memory card or a memory stick. The number of photos you	46
8	can store on a card or stick depends on how many megabytes	58
9	it can hold. Once you reach the limit of the memory device,	70
10	you can store no new images until you either transfer or	81
11	delete the old ones to make room for new ones.	91
12	The advantages of using a memory device are many. For	102
13	example, the card or stick can be used over and over; or,	113
14	when the device is full, just simply remove it and put in a	125
15	new device. You can also move the images to the computer,	137
16	where they can reside on the hard drive for as long as you	149
17	want. If the memory card or stick you have does not have	160
18	enough memory, you can upgrade the size.	168
19	Finally, you will see instantly any images you have	179
20	taken with the camera. If you decide not to keep an image	190
21	in the camera, you can delete it to make space for other	202
22	exciting images.	205

1 | 2 | 3 | 4 | 5 | 6 | 7 | 8 | 9 | 10 | 11 | 12

Formatting

D. TABLES WITHIN DOCUMENTS

To format a table that is part of a letter, e-mail message, memo, or report:

1. In a single-spaced document, press ENTER 2 times before and 1 time after the table. Be sure you are outside the table structure before pressing ENTER 1 time.
2. In a double-spaced document, press ENTER 1 time before and after the table.
3. Single-space the body of the table.
4. Adjust the column widths, and center the table within the margins of the document.
5. Never split a table between two pages if it will fit on one page. If a table will not fit at the bottom of the page on which it is first mentioned, place it at the top of the next page.

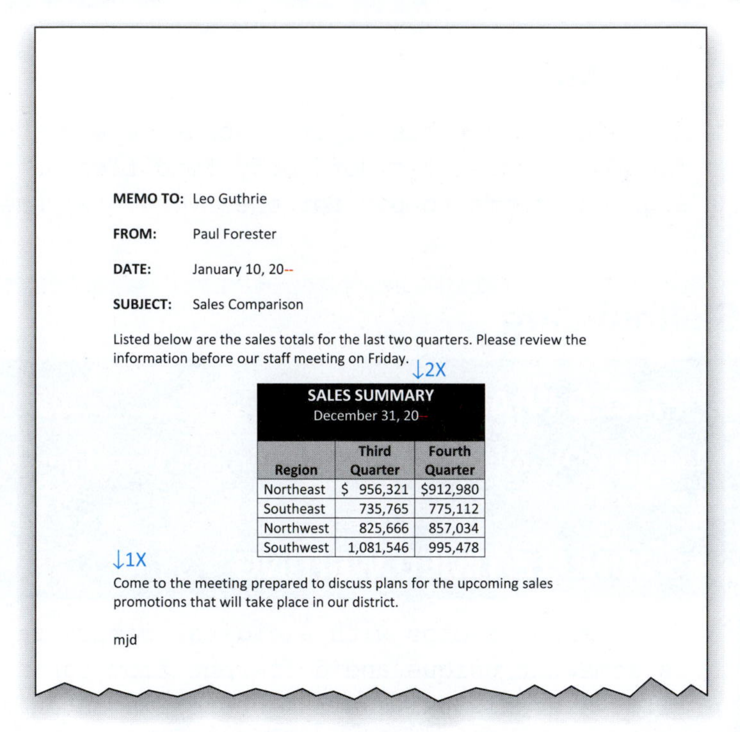

MEMO TO: Leo Guthrie

FROM: Paul Forester

DATE: January 10, 20--

SUBJECT: Sales Comparison

Listed below are the sales totals for the last two quarters. Please review the information before our staff meeting on Friday. ↓2X

SALES SUMMARY December 31, 20--		
Region	**Third Quarter**	**Fourth Quarter**
Northeast	$ 956,321	$912,980
Southeast	735,765	775,112
Northwest	825,666	857,034
Southwest	1,081,546	995,478

↓1X

Come to the meeting prepared to discuss plans for the upcoming sales promotions that will take place in our district.

mjd

E. COMPANY NAMES IN CLOSING LINES

Some business firms show the company name in the closing lines of a letter. Type the company name in all-caps on the second line below the complimentary closing. Then press ENTER 4 times and type the writer's name.

Thank you for inviting me to participate in the discussion concerning this issue. It has been very informative and helpful. ↓2X

Sincerely, ↓2X

HENDERSON AND SONS, INC. ↓4X

Mark Henderson, President ↓2X

mjd

F. DELIVERY NOTATIONS

Type a delivery notation (such as *By fax*, *By e-mail*, *By FedEx*, or *By messenger*) on the line below the enclosure notation (if used) or on the line below the reference initials. A delivery notation comes before a copy notation.

Thank you for inviting me to participate in the discussion concerning this issue. It has been very informative and helpful. ↓2X

Sincerely, ↓4X

Mark Henderson
President ↓2X

imz
Enclosure
By e-mail
c: Mary Stevenson

G. BLIND COPY NOTATIONS

Use the blind copy (*bc:*) notation when the addressee is *not* intended to know that someone else is receiving a copy of the letter. Type the *bc* notation on the file copy at the left margin on the second line after the last item in the letter.

When preparing a letter with a blind copy, print one copy of the letter; then add the blind copy notation and print another.

Thank you for inviting me to participate in the discussion concerning this issue. It has been very informative and helpful. ↓2X

Sincerely, ↓4X

Mark Henderson
President ↓2X

imz ↓2X

bc: Mary Stevenson

H. POSTSCRIPTS

If a postscript (*PS:*) is added to a letter, it is typed as the last item in the letter, preceded by 1 blank line. If a blind copy notation and postscript are used, the blind copy notation follows the postscript.

Thank you for inviting me to participate in the discussion concerning this issue. It has been very informative and helpful. ↓2X

Sincerely, ↓4X

Mark Henderson
President ↓2X

imz
Enclosure ↓2X

PS: You will be reimbursed for all expenses. Complete an expense report and submit it to your supervisor. ↓2X

bc: Mary Stevenson

I. E-MAIL WITH BLIND COPIES

Use the blind copy (*bcc:*) feature when the addressee in the To box is *not* intended to know that someone else is receiving a copy of the e-mail.

To format an e-mail message with a blind copy:

- Format the e-mail message as usual.
- No special formatting steps are needed when a blind copy is sent. Therefore, do *not* type a blind copy notation at the bottom of the e-mail message.
- Type e-mail addresses for recipients as desired in the Bcc box.

J. WORD PROCESSING: TABLE—SHADING AND E-MAIL—BLIND COPIES

Study Lesson 68 in your Word Manual. Complete all of the shaded steps while at your computer. Then format the documents that follow.

Document Processing

Correspondence 68-70
Business Letter in Block Style

March 1, 20-- | Ms. Ramona Gutierrez | Austin Communications | 5 Gulf Street | Concord, NH 03301 | Dear Ms. Gutierrez:

¶ We are indeed interested in designing a new corporate logo and the corresponding stationery for your fine company. As I indicated in our recent telephone conversation, we have a design staff that has won many national awards for letterhead form design.

¶ Within a couple of weeks, we will submit several basic designs to you and your committee for consideration. Here is a modified price list for the printed stationery:

Use 25 percent shading for Row 1.

Stationery	Cost
Letterhead (500 sheets)	$ 80.00
Business cards (1,000 cards)	39.50
Coated brochures (1,000 sheets)	219.30
Envelopes (1,500)	92.00

¶ In the meantime, please call me if we can be of further service.

Sincerely yours, | Samantha A. Steele | General Manager | urs | By fax | bc: Design Department

Correspondence
68-71
E-Mail Message

Hi, Renee:

¶ Samantha Steele of Imperial Graphic Design sent me a modified price list for our printed stationery. I added our own budget to the last column in the table below.

Use 100 percent shading for Row 1.

Stationery	Cost	Budget
Letterhead (500 sheets)	$ 80.00	$120.00
Business cards (1,000 cards)	39.50	25.00
Coated brochures (1,000 sheets)	219.30	300.00
Envelopes (1,500)	92.00	85.50

¶ Let me know your reaction to her proposed price list after reviewing our budget.

Ramona | Ramona Gutierrez | E-mail: gutierrez@acmail.com | Phone: 603-555-3363

Correspondence
68-72
Business Letter in Modified-Block Style

November 5, 20-- | Burlington Fitness Center | 31 Battery Street | Burlington, VT 05401 | Ladies and Gentlemen:

¶ We have 494 apartments at Fountain Ridge. As the recreation coordinator, I have concerns not only about the leisure-time activities of our residents but also about the health and physical fitness of the more than 1,100 people who call Fountain Ridge home.

¶ Our recreation facilities are excellent. In addition to our two outdoor tennis courts, putting green, and swimming pool, we have the following indoor facilities: two racquetball courts, swimming pool, whirlpool bath, sauna, steam room, and two billiard tables. However, we have no workout equipment.

¶ During the next few months we will be equipping a new gymnasium. The dimensions of the gym and schematics are enclosed. We would like to provide our residents with classes that will incorporate the equipment below:

Use 100 percent shading for Row 1 and 25 percent shading for Row 2.

CLASS SCHEDULE Fountain Ridge Sports Complex	
Equipment	**Proposed Classes**
Exercise bicycles	Spinning
Treadmills	Aerobics
Rowing machines	Toning and conditioning

(continued on next page)

¶ The needs and interests of our residents are varied. Some residents will take full advantage of the gymnasium equipment. However, many of our residents have expressed interest in an indoor track for walking; others would like to add a track for running. We hope to accommodate as many of the suggestions as we feel are feasible.

¶ The population of the residents in the Fountain Ridge complex consists of a mixture of young and middle-age adult couples as well as single residents. Some of the couples have children who would be old enough to enjoy the facilities. Therefore, safety and durability of the equipment are very important considerations. In addition, we would like to continue to develop our complex in a way that would invite family participation in our recreational activities.

¶Do you have a sales representative serving this area who could meet with me to discuss this proposal? In the meantime, please send any related information and prices.

Sincerely yours, | FOUNTAIN RIDGE | Rosa Bailey-Judd | Recreation Coordinator | urs | Enclosure | By fax | PS: Please contact me no later than November 10. | bc: Ramona Garcia

Keyboarding Connection

Creating an E-Mail Signature File

Creating a signature file saves you time and adds a personal touch to your e-mail messages. A signature file is a tag of information that is automatically included at the end of your e-mail messages. It may include your signature, a small graphic, your address, your phone number, or a quotation. Use the following guidelines to create a signature file.

Open your e-mail software. Open the menu item that allows you to create a signature file. Type the information you want to include in your signature, and then save and close the file.

Some companies don't allow graphics or quotations in e-mail signature files. E-mailing graphics uses extra bandwidth, which can slow down the network. For this reason, some e-mail software doesn't display graphics at all, instead displaying e-mail in plain text. Quotations may not align with the corporate culture or mission. Check to find out whether your company has corporate guidelines on e-mail signatures before you create your own signature file. When sending e-mail to potential employers, it's useful to add a professional signature to your e-mail that contains your contact information.

Your Turn: Create a signature file, then address an e-mail to yourself. Type "Test" in the Subject box. In the body, type "This is a test of the signature file." Send the e-mail; then open it to see how your signature file looks.

Multipage Memos With Tables

Goals

- Demonstrate improved speed and accuracy while typing.
- Demonstrate acceptable language arts skills in spelling.
- Correctly use Word's find and replace feature.
- Correctly format a multipage memo with a table.

A. WARMUP

alphabet	1	The lazy judge was very quick to pay tax money for the bar.
frequent digraphs	2	or orb for door fort more boor nor odor port orator ore ort
easy	3	The neighbor will do the fieldwork when she is in the glen.

Skillbuilding

B. MAP+: SYMBOL

Follow the GDP software directions for this exercise to improve keystroking accuracy.

PPP PRETEST » PRACTICE » POSTTEST

PRETEST
Take a 1-minute timed writing.

C. PRETEST: Horizontal Reaches

```
4      The legal facts gave our lawyers a sense that we could 11
5 be ready to wrap up this case quickly. Until a written copy 23
6 of our testimony is given to us, we shall all be extremely  35
7 anxious. We added every ounce of our energy to your case.   46
   1 | 2 | 3 | 4 | 5 | 6 | 7 | 8 | 9 | 10 | 11 | 12
```

PRACTICE
Speed Emphasis:
If you made no more than 1 error on the Pretest, type each *individual* line 2 times.
Accuracy Emphasis:
If you made 2 or more errors, type each *group* of lines (as though it were a paragraph) 2 times.

D. PRACTICE: In Reaches

```
8  wr wrap wren wreak wrist wrote writer unwrap writhe wreaths
9  ou pout ours ounce cough fouls output detour ousted coupons
10 ad adds dead adult ready blade advice fading admits adheres
11 py pyre copy pygmy pylon happy pyrene choppy pyrite pyramid
```

E. PRACTICE: Out Reaches

```
12 yo yoga your youth yodel yowls yogurt joyous yonder younger
13 fa fact farm faith sofas fakes faulty unfair famous defames
14 up upon soup upset group upper upturn supply uplift upsurge
15 ga gate gave cigar gains legal gazing legacy gawked garbage
```

POSTTEST

Repeat the Pretest timed writing and compare performance.

F. POSTTEST: Horizontal Reaches

Language Arts

Type these frequently misspelled words, paying special attention to any spelling problems in each word.

G. SPELLING

16 personnel information its procedures their committee system
17 receive employees which education services opportunity area
18 financial appropriate interest received production contract
19 important through necessary customer employee further there
20 property account approximately general control division our

Edit the sentences to correct any misspellings.

21 The revised systom was adopted by the finantial division.

22 Four employes want to serve on the new property commitee.

23 Approximatly ten proceedures were included in the contract.

24 Further informasion will be recieved from the customers.

25 Their was much interest shown by the production personal.

26 The services in that aria are necesary for needed control.

Formatting

H. WORD PROCESSING: FIND AND REPLACE

Study Lesson 69 in your Word Manual. Complete all of the shaded steps while at your computer. Then format the documents that follow.

Document Processing

Correspondence
69-73
Memo

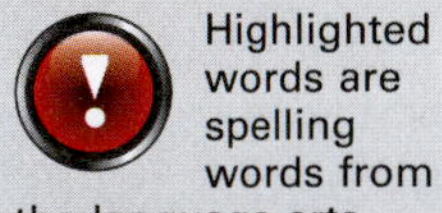

Highlighted words are spelling words from the language arts activities; do *not* highlight them when you type.

MEMO TO: L. B. Chinn, Station Manager | **FROM:** Mitzi Grenell, News Director | **DATE:** May 5, 20-- | **SUBJECT:** FCC European Trip

¶ This memo and others to follow will keep you informed about my upcoming trip to Europe. I have been invited by the Federal Communications Commission to lead a committee that will study television news in European countries. This opportunity came about because Jill Andrews received advance notice about the study and made the necessary arrangements so that I would be invited to participate. I am delighted to take part in this important project, which should be of great interest to all of our employees.

(continued on next page)

¶ A major focus of this study will be to compare the types of technologies used in different European countries to report and broadcast the news. Our study group will visit six European countries to gather further information. We will be visiting England, France, Denmark, Germany, Spain, and Portugal from August 24 through September 23. Four other members will offer their services to this committee:

Sandra Holton	News Director, WSVN	Miami, Florida
Manuel Cruz	News Director, National Public Radio	Boise, Idaho
Jason Chan	Station Manager, WLBZ	Bangor, Maine
Richard Logan	Operations Manager, Cable News System	Provo, Utah

Our initial plans are to spend approximately five full days in each country, meet with the news personnel of one or two of the major networks, tour their facilities, view recent broadcasts, and observe their general operations and various divisions. It should be quite an education.

¶ If you need to contact me during my absence, Barbara Brooks, our liaison at the Federal Communications Commission, is the appropriate contact. She, or any employee on her staff, will be able to provide a location and phone number.

¶ An amendment has been made to my contract that will allow production to continue as usual here at Channel 5 while I am gone. Dave Gelson will assume financial control of the department and will also supervise its day-to-day activities. Further procedures are being finalized so that Dave can make a smooth transition during my absence.

¶ As you can imagine, this is an exciting time for me. Thank you for supporting the project and for taking into account the long-term implications of this important study.

urs | PS: Thank you also for suggesting that I visit John Jacobs, one of our most valued customers. I understand that he owns property in England and France and will be at his estate in France at a time that coincides with my schedule. I will be sure to give him your best wishes.

Correspondence
69-74
Memo

Open the file for Correspondence 69-73 and make the following changes:

1. Address the memo to "All Employees."
2. Change each occurrence of the words "News Director" to "News Analyst." A total of three replacements should be made.
3. Change each occurrence of the word "France" to "Switzerland." A total of three replacements should be made.
4. Delete the fourth paragraph.
5. Add this as the second-to-the-last paragraph:

   When I return from this trip, my committee will compile a comprehensive report and analysis that will be distributed to all personnel. I will then organize some internal focus groups so that we can discuss the implications of the study on our day-to-day operations.

6. Delete the postscript at the end of the memo.

Correspondence
69-75
Memo

MEMO TO: Terri Hackworth Property Manager

FROM: Rosa Bailey-Judd, recreation coordinator

DATE: Apr. 14, 20--

Subject: Fitness Center

¶ The new fitness center will be ready for our residents to use in approximately one month, and interest continues to grow. Your leadership in constructing a fitness center on this property is sincerely appreciated. ¶ As soon as appropriate research is completed I will be requesting further financial support to purchase the following equipment in the quantity specified:

Single-space the table.

No.	Equipment
15 ~~20~~	Exercise Bicycles
10	Treadmills
8	rowing machines

¶ Three types of other equipment were seriously considered, but those ~~the ones~~ listed above are the most important in terms of what is necesary to schedule our proposed fitness classes. I am not quite ready to sign a contract with a specific supplier. We expect that there will be very heavy usage ofthe specified equipment and are requesting inforamtion from vendors regarding durability, warranties, and the support of service personnel. I will receive that information within the week and will read through it carefully before signing a final contract.

SS ¶ Thank you again for your full support and cooperation with this project. The general

contractor you hired has received rave reviews The new fitness center ~~gym~~ is a golden opportunity for all our residents to ~~vastly~~ improve their quality of life.

urs

Memo Reports

Goals

- Type at least 41wpm/5'/5e.
- Correctly format a memo report with report headings and a bibliography.
- Successfully complete a Progress and Proofreading Check with zero errors on the first scored attempt.

A. WARMUP

alphabet	1	Those five lazy movers quit packing the hard jewelry boxes.
number/symbol	2	(fay237@yahoo.com) 33% Coe & Tan 6/8 Hi! $2.41 *Oct. #95-01
easy	3	One half of the endowments may be paid by the town members.

Skillbuilding

B. 12-SECOND SPEED SPRINTS

Take three 12-second timed writings on each line. The scale below the last line shows your wpm speed for a 12-second timed writing.

4 That new city law may help us to fish for cod on the docks.
5 He may sign over the title to his autos when he is in town.
6 She may go with me to the city to visit my son and his pal.
7 The doe and buck by the old bush may dig up the giant oaks.
' ' ' ' 5 ' ' ' ' 10 ' ' ' ' 15 ' ' ' ' 20 ' ' ' ' 25 ' ' ' ' 30 ' ' ' ' 35 ' ' ' ' 40 ' ' ' ' 45 ' ' ' ' 50 ' ' ' ' 55 ' ' ' ' 60

C. TECHNIQUE PRACTICE: BACKSPACE KEY

Type each line 2 times, using your Sem finger to strike the BACKSPACE key when you see the ← symbol. For example, type *bud*, backspace, and type *m*, thus changing *bud* to *bum*.

8 bud←m gig←n dew←n rag←m tad←n own←l get←m tie←n toe←n
9 car←p hoe←g yea←n pie←n vat←n hug←m rug←m pod←i per←p
10 job←y yaw←m bus←y pad←l lad←p the←y nag←p fur←n nub←n
11 fad←n max←y jag←m fig←n ice←y oaf←k add←o mow←p log←o

Take two 5-minute timed writings.

Goal: At least 41wpm/5'/5e

D. 5-MINUTE TIMED WRITING

```
12      In most offices, many products that are used each day    11
13  are made of materials that can now be recycled. Amazingly,   23
14  items made of glass, steel, aluminum, plastics, and paper    34
15  can be recycled to make many products that we need. Also,    46
16  the recycling process can help the environment.              56
17      Some unique examples of the process of recycling the     66
18  items we often throw away are listed here. Those old coffee  78
19  filters can be used to make soles for new shoes. Pieces of   90
20  paper that are thrown away each day can be used to make     101
21  tissue paper or paper towels. Most plastics that are used   113
22  in soda bottles can be recycled for insulation for jackets  125
23  and auto interiors. Used lightbulbs and some glass products 137
24  can also be used to replace the surface on our streets.     148
25      Look around the room in which you are working. If you   159
26  are not already taking part in a recycling program, you may 171
27  want to recycle some items that you no longer need. Items   183
28  such as used paper, file folders, and aluminum cans can be  194
29  collected very quickly. What other items can you add?       205
      1 | 2 | 3 | 4 | 5 | 6 | 7 | 8 | 9 | 10 | 11 | 12
```

Formatting

E. REPORT HEADINGS IN MEMOS

REFER TO Reference Manual

R-9C: Memo Report

There are times when a memo report is used rather than a cover memo to accompany a report. The memo and the report are combined into one, and headings are formatted as they are in a report. If a table is included in the body of the report, it should be formatted as it would be in a report. Use reference initials at the end of a memo report.

Document Processing

Report 70-38 Memo Report

MEMO TO: All Employees | **FROM:** Frank Reynolds, Director | **DATE:** February 24, 20-- | **SUBJECT:** New Security System

¶ Beginning April 1, we will be using a new security access system. Various security system options were researched thoroughly before a final decision was made to implement a fingerprint access system. Complete installation should occur by the end of March, but the system will not be activated until April 1. The system includes digital surveillance cameras and a fingerprint access system at all entrances. This will provide a more secure working environment, especially in the evenings and on weekends. Please carefully read the specifications below and follow the detailed instructions for using the new system:

(continued on next page)

FINGERPRINT ACCESS SYSTEM	
Description	**Specifications**
Fingerprint memory capacity	78 people
Password capacity	78 people
False identification rate	Less than 0.0001%
Password length	8 bytes
Unlock methods	Fingerprint or keypad code

FINGERPRINT AND KEYPAD CODES

¶ Once the new system is installed, you simply touch the fingerprint keypad lock with your index finger for access during nonworking hours. You will also receive a keypad code for alternate access. Although mechanical keys can be used, they will <u>not</u> be created or distributed. Human Resources will begin programming fingerprint codes during the week of March 20. Further instructions will be issued at that time.

ENTRANCE AND EXIT PROCEDURES

¶ Entrances will unlock automatically each day at 8 a.m. and lock automatically at 5 p.m. To enter, touch the fingerprint keypad lock with your index finger. When the green light comes on, open the door. Do <u>not</u> hold the door open longer than 30 seconds when you enter or exit, or the alarm will sound. When you exit the building, do <u>not</u> use the special latch handle to open the door, or the alarm will sound. Instead, use the push bar. Sign in and sign out at the front desk each time you enter and exit.

¶ If you have questions about our new security access system and procedures, send an e-mail message to me at freynolds@infotech.com.

urs

Report 70-39
Bibliography

R-9B: Bibliography

BIBLIOGRAPHY

"Biometric Fingerprint Keypad Locks," *OfficeSecuritySystems,* January 11, 2010, <http://www.officesecuritysystems.com/fingerprint>, accessed on January 15, 2010.

"Business Alarm Monitoring," *SecurityZone,* December 11, 2009, <http://www.securityzone.com/securitymonitoring>, accessed on January 16, 2010.

De La Cruz, Stacey, "Digital Surveillance Systems," *Security Systems Today,* November 19, 2009, p. 18.

Paisley, Robert, "What's New in Business Security Systems," *The Daily Sentinel,* January 12, 2010, p. D6.

Report 70-40
Memo Report

Progress and Proofreading Check

Documents designated as Proofreading Checks serve as a check of your proofreading skill. Your goal is to have zero typographical errors when the GDP software first scores the document.

MEMO TO: All Employees
FROM: Won Chul Lee, President
DATE: March 2, 20--
SUBJECT: New Administrative Center

¶ You will all be very pleased to know that after extensive consultation with several architectural firms, I have finalized plans for a new administrative center to be constructed at 3900 Rockefeller Plaza. This memo will

(continued on next page)

provide you with general information about the exciting plans for the center's exterior and interior development.

ARCHITECTURE AND LANDSCAPING

¶ Exterior plans will maintain the historical integrity and beauty of the surrounding area and reflect the architecture of other buildings in the office park. Landscaping plans include a park area, a picnic area, and a small pond. Paseos (winding walkways) will connect the various businesses within the complex and include both bike paths and foot paths.

DEPARTMENTAL LOCATIONS

¶ Staff will be located within the new facility as follows:

1. Accounting will be located on the first floor in the west wing.
2. Sales and marketing will be located on the first floor in the east wing. All staff will be grouped according to product line.
3. Technical support will be located in the basement level of the east wing. All staff will be grouped according to product support.
4. All other staff will be located on the second floor. Exact locations will be determined at a later date.

SPECIAL FACILITIES

¶ Conference rooms will be located in the center of the building on the first floor to provide easy access for everyone. All rooms will be equipped with state-of-the-art technology. Our new center will also include a full-service cafeteria, a copy center, a library, an athletic center, and an on-site day-care center.

¶ Construction of the new center will begin when the necessary permits have been obtained. I hope you are looking forward to our new location as much as I am. More information will be forthcoming as plans are finalized.

urs

UNIT 15

Reports

LESSON 71
Itineraries

LESSON 72
Agendas and Minutes of Meetings

LESSON 73
Procedures Manual

LESSON 74
Reports Formatted in Columns

LESSON 75
Report Review

Itineraries 71

Goals

- Demonstrate improved speed and accuracy while typing.
- Demonstrate acceptable language arts skills in using commas.
- Correctly format an itinerary.

A. WARMUP

alphabet
1 My faxed jokes won me a pager from the cable TV quiz shows.

concentration
2 electromagnetically antirevolutionaries overdiversification

easy
3 The big dog down by the lake may bury the eighty fishbowls.

Skillbuilding

MAP+

B. MAP+: ALPHABET

Follow the GDP software directions for this exercise to improve keystroking accuracy.

C. PROGRESSIVE PRACTICE: ALPHABET

Follow the GDP software directions for this exercise to improve keystroking speed.

Language Arts

Study the rules at the right.

RULE
, nonessential expression

D. COMMAS

Use a comma before and after a nonessential expression.

Andre, who was there, can verify the statement.
But: Anyone_ who was there_ can verify the statement.
Van's first book, *Crisis of Management,* was not discussed.
Van's book_ *Crisis of Management*_ was not discussed.

Note: A nonessential expression is a group of words that may be omitted without changing the basic meaning of the sentence. Always examine the noun or pronoun that comes before the expression to determine whether the noun needs the expression to complete its meaning. If it does, the expression is *essential* and does *not* take a comma.

RULE
, adjacent adjectives

Use a comma between two adjacent adjectives that modify the same noun.

We need an intelligent, enthusiastic_ individual for this job.
But: Please order a new_ bulletin board for our main_ conference room.

Note: Do not use a comma after the second adjective. Also, do not use a comma if the first adjective modifies the combined idea of the second adjective and the noun (for example, *bulletin board* and *conference room* in the second example).

Edit each sentence to correct any errors.

```
4  The school president Mr. Roberts will address the students.

5  The fall planning meeting which is held in Charlotte has been
6  canceled.

7  Students planning to take the certification test must
8  register for the orientation class.

9  The sleek luxury car is scheduled for delivery next week.

10 Margaret brought her fast reliable laptop to the meeting.

11 A stamped addressed envelope should be included with the
12 survey.
```

Formatting

E. ITINERARIES

R-11C: Itinerary

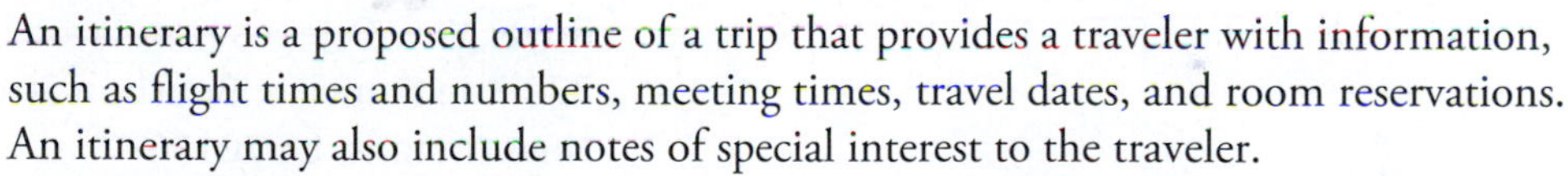

An itinerary is a proposed outline of a trip that provides a traveler with information, such as flight times and numbers, meeting times, travel dates, and room reservations. An itinerary may also include notes of special interest to the traveler.

To format an itinerary:

1. Press ENTER 5 times to begin the first line of the itinerary 2 inches from the top of the page.
2. Insert an open table with 2 columns and enough rows to accommodate the completed itinerary.
3. Insert 1 blank line between each part of the heading block in Row 1.
4. Type the date in Row 2, Column A, in all-caps and bold; press ENTER 1 time.
5. Type the time in Column A and the corresponding information in Column B; press ENTER 1 time as shown after each group of lines in Column B.
6. Repeat these steps until the itinerary is finished, and adjust the column widths as needed.

Document Processing

Report 71-41
Itinerary

↓5X

14 pt **RESOURCE CONSULTANTS SALES MEETING** ↓2X

12 pt↓ **Itinerary for Linda Padilla** ↓2X

March 12-14, 20-- ↓2X

THURSDAY, MARCH 12 ↓1X	
9:39 a.m.-10:07 a.m.	Flight from Atlanta to New Orleans; Delta 1585 (800-555-1222); e-ticket; Seat 8D; nonstop. ↓2X Sharon Lee (Cell: 504-555-8029; Office: 504-555-7631) will meet your flight on Thursday, provide transportation during your visit, and return you to the airport on Saturday morning. Airport Embassy Suites (504-555-4032) King-sized bed, nonsmoking room; late arrival guaranteed; Reservation No. 0312010-AZ. ↓1X
FRIDAY, MARCH 13	
9 a.m.	Resource Consultants Sales Meeting Royal New Orleans Hotel 730 Rue Bienville, Bourbon Street Suite New Orleans, LA 70130 (503-555-7631)
7 p.m.	Dinner at the Royal New Orleans Hotel—The French Quarter Bistro.
SATURDAY, MARCH 14	
6:30 a.m.	Meet Sharon Lee, who will accompany you on the return flight, in the lobby of the Airport Embassy Suites for transportation to the airport.
8:30 a.m.-10:50 a.m.	Flight from New Orleans to Atlanta; Delta 5995; e-ticket; Seat 10D; nonstop.

, nonessential expression

(Note: Table shown with "View Gridlines" active.)

Report 71-42
Itinerary

, nonessential expression

, adjacent adjectives

RSA TECHNOLOGY CONFERENCE | **Itinerary for Mrs. Norma McKinley** | **September 25-29, 20--** | **WEDNESDAY, SEPTEMBER 25** | 1:50 p.m.-4:10 p.m. | Flight from Columbus to Boston; US Airways 2053; Seat 13F; nonstop. | Boston Inn (617-555-3982) | King-sized bed, nonsmoking room; late arrival guaranteed. | Judith Greenburg, who will be at the same conference, will meet you in the lobby at 6 p.m. for dinner. | **THURSDAY, SEPTEMBER 26** | 8:30 a.m.-5 p.m. | RSA Technology Conference, Suite 201 | A compact, full-featured presentations projector will be ready in the suite no later than 8 a.m. | **FRIDAY, SEPTEMBER 27** | 9 a.m.-10:17 a.m. | Flight from Boston to New York City; US Airways 454; Seat 10D; nonstop. | **SUNDAY, SEPTEMBER 29** | 2:07 p.m.-4:18 p.m. | Flight from New York City to Columbus; US Airways 324; Seat 9A; nonstop.

Report 71-43
Itinerary

, adjacent adjectives

, nonessential expression

HEALTH EFFECTS INSTITUTE CONFERENCE | **Itinerary for Dr. Ron Jacobs** | **July 8-10, 20--** | **MONDAY, JULY 8** | 2:45 p.m.-4:05 p.m. | Flight from Houston to Los Angeles; United 834; Seat 10C; nonstop. | Marriott (310-555-1014) | King-sized bed; nonsmoking room; late arrival guaranteed; Reservation No. 45STX78. | **TUESDAY, JULY 9** | 6 a.m.-7:15 a.m. | Flight from Los Angeles to Sacramento; American 206; Seat 4A; nonstop. | Sacramento Garden Inn (916-555-7373) | King-sized bed; nonsmoking room; late arrival guaranteed; Reservation No. QRR6H. | A spacious, well-equipped welcome booth, including computers with Internet access, will be available in the Executive Center, Room 12B. | 10 a.m.-4:30 p.m. | Health Effects Institute Conference, Executive Center, Room 12A. | **WEDNESDAY, JULY 10** | 7 a.m.-11:15 a.m. | Flight from Sacramento to Houston; United 307; Seat 7B; nonstop.

Strategies for Career Success

Successful Interviewing Techniques

The interview is a useful tool for gathering more information about a company. Here are some steps to effective interviewing.

Conduct preliminary research so you can ask intelligent questions and make efficient use of the interview time. Prepare a list of questions to use in the interview. Make sure questions are open-ended, unbiased, and geared toward gathering insights you can't gain through reading about the company. Be prepared to take notes, listen actively, and ask follow-up questions, as needed.

Remember that an interview, whether for a job or for information gathering, is also your opportunity to find out if a company or career would be a good fit for you. It is in everyone's best interest to find out during a job interview if you will be happy at the company, so ask questions about things that are important to you. These might be things like potential for advancement, various career paths within a specialty, and corporate culture (e.g., does the company promote a work-life balance, or is it a place where overtime is routine and can lead to better opportunities?).

Greet the interviewer by name, and thank him or her for taking time to talk to you. If it's not a job interview, explain why you are interested in interviewing him or her. Stay within the scheduled time. In closing the interview, thank the person again, and ask if you can get in touch if other questions come to mind.

Your Turn: Prepare a list of questions you might use in interviewing someone concerning what his or her company does.

Agendas and Minutes of Meetings

Goals

- Type at least 42wpm/5'/5e.
- Correctly format an agenda and the minutes of a meeting.

A. WARMUP

alphabet	1	Quick brown foxes jumped over the lazy dog who was resting.
one hand	2	adverb hookup was ply target minimum beat knoll acted kinky
easy	3	The quantity of profits for the coalfield is a big problem.

Skillbuilding

B. SUSTAINED PRACTICE: SYLLABIC INTENSITY

Take a 1-minute timed writing on the boxed paragraph to establish your base speed. Then take a 1-minute timed writing on the following paragraph. As soon as you equal or exceed your base speed on this paragraph, move to the next, more difficult paragraph.

4	Each of us has several bills to be paid on a monthly	11
5	basis. For most of us, a checkbook is the tool that we use	23
6	to take care of this chore. However, in this electronic	34
7	age, other ways of doing this have received rave reviews.	45
8	You will likely be surprised to learn that the most	11
9	basic way and the cheapest way to pay bills electronically	22
10	involves the use of a Touch-Tone phone. The time required	34
11	is approximately a third of that used when writing checks.	46
12	Several banking institutions offer or plan to offer	11
13	screen phones as a method for paying bills. It is possible	22
14	to buy securities, make transfers, and determine account	34
15	balances. You will save time by using a Touch-Tone phone.	45
16	A third type of electronic bill processing involves	11
17	using a microcomputer and a modem. Software programs have	22
18	on-screen checkbooks linked to bill-paying applications.	34
19	Other microcomputers use online services through a modem.	45

1 | 2 | 3 | 4 | 5 | 6 | 7 | 8 | 9 | 10 | 11 | 12

Take two 5-minute timed writings.

C. 5-MINUTE TIMED WRITING

```
20      Whether you are searching for your first job or are     11
21 looking to change jobs, your networking skills may play a    22
22 crucial role in how successful you are in that endeavor.     34
23 Networking can be defined in some respects as a group of     45
24 people who are linked closely together for the purpose of    57
25 achieving some sort of end result. In this case, the end     68
26 result will be to establish new contacts who might be able   80
27 to assist you in your job search.                            87
28      Your network is made up of dozens of people you have    97
29 met. You can never be sure who has the potential of helping 109
30 you the most in your job search. Therefore, it is important 121
31 that you consider all acquaintances. You should certainly   133
32 network with business associates, and especially those you  145
33 have met at various meetings or conferences. And don't      158
34 forget former teachers in whose classes you were enrolled.  168
35      Former classmates provide an excellent base on which   178
36 to build your network, and friends and family should also   190
37 be included. Also, use the Internet to nurture any online   202
38 contacts you may have made over the years.                  210
      1 | 2 | 3 | 4 | 5 | 6 | 7 | 8 | 9 | 10 | 11 | 12
```

Formatting

D. AGENDAS

R-11A: Meeting Agenda

An agenda is a list of topics to be discussed at a meeting. It may also include a formal program of a meeting and consist of times, rooms, speakers, and other related information.

To format an agenda:

1. Press ENTER 5 times to begin the first line of the agenda 2 inches from the top of the page.
2. Center and type the name of the company or committee in all-caps, bold, and 14-point font.
3. Press ENTER 2 times; then center and type `Meeting Agenda` in upper- and lowercase, bold, and 12-point font.
4. Press ENTER 2 times; then center and type the date in upper- and lowercase, bold, and 12-point font.
5. Press ENTER 2 times and turn off bold.
6. Type all agenda items as a numbered list using Word's default format.

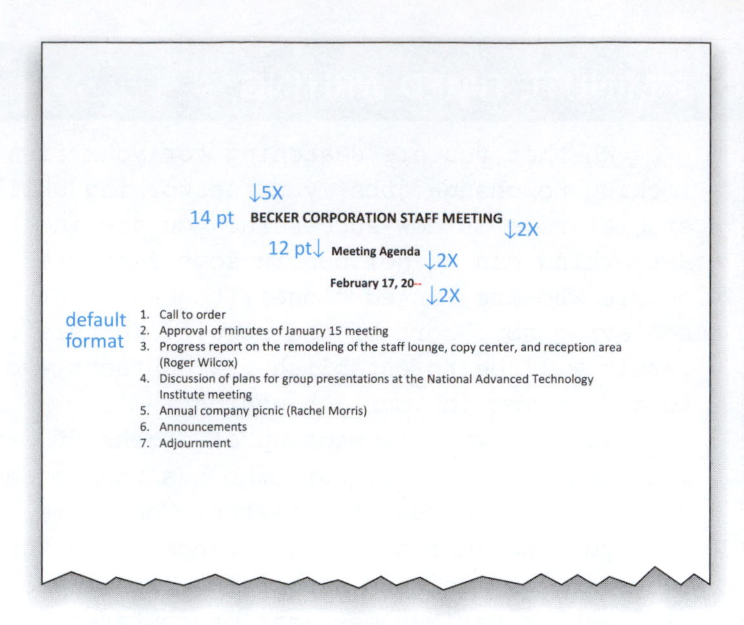

BECKER CORPORATION STAFF MEETING

Meeting Agenda

February 17, 20--

1. Call to order
2. Approval of minutes of January 15 meeting
3. Progress report on the remodeling of the staff lounge, copy center, and reception area (Roger Wilcox)
4. Discussion of plans for group presentations at the National Advanced Technology Institute meeting
5. Annual company picnic (Rachel Morris)
6. Announcements
7. Adjournment

E. MINUTES OF MEETINGS

R-11B: Minutes of a Meeting

Items discussed during a meeting are officially recorded as the minutes of a meeting.

To format the minutes of a meeting:

1. Press ENTER 5 times to begin the first line of the minutes 2 inches from the top of the page.
2. Insert an open table with 2 columns and enough rows to accommodate the completed meeting minutes.
3. Insert 1 blank line between each part of the heading block in Row 1.
4. Type the first section heading in Row 2, Column A, in all-caps and bold.
5. Type the corresponding information in Column B; press ENTER 1 time after the final line in Column B.
6. Move to the next row and repeat steps 4 and 5 until all remaining sections have been completed.
7. Type the closing and signature lines in Column B of the final row; press ENTER 4 times to allow room for the signature.
8. Adjust the width of Column A to accommodate the longest heading as shown in the illustration that follows.

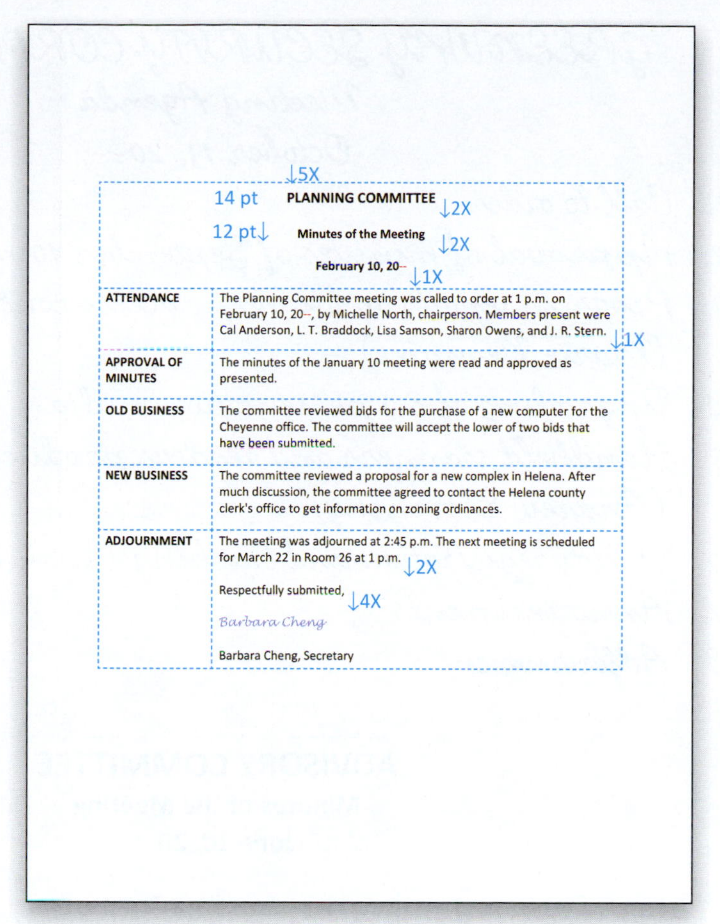

(Note: Table shown with "View Gridlines" active.)

Document Processing

Report
72-44
Agenda

Use Word's default numbering format.

FOX ASSOCIATES STAFF MEETING
Meeting Agenda
April 15, 20--

1. Call to order
2. Approval of minutes of March 15 meeting
3. Progress reports for the construction of new media center
4. Discussion of the upcoming time management seminar (F. Pryor and J. Harrington)
5. Discussion of Internet security and antivirus software (T. Rashid)
6. Annual charity event (J. Simpatico)
7. Announcements
8. Adjournment

Report
72-45
Agenda

GREENWAY SECURITY CORPORATION

Meeting Agenda

October 13, 20--

1. Call to order
2. Approval of minutes of September 10 meeting
3. Progress reports on biometric access control technology (Marie Newsome)
4. Upgrading of 8.0 presentation media
5. Handheld scanners and readers product development (Andrew Slovinsky)
6. Visitor registration and tracking (Juan Mendoza)
7. Announcements
8. Adjournment

Report
72-46
Minutes of a Meeting

ADVISORY COMMITTEE

Minutes of the Meeting

June 10, 20--

ATTENDANCE	The Advisory Committee meeting was called to order at 1 p.m. on June 10, 20--, by Suzanne Higgins-North, chairperson. Members present were Georgia Holton, James Duncan, Mary Benavidez, Pete Bergstrom, Quan Ying Zhao, and Sharon Rose.
APPROVAL OF MINUTES	The minutes of the May 10 meeting were read and approved as presented.
OLD BUSINESS	The committee reviewed recommendations for new hardware and software and new ergonomically sound workstations, lighting, and seating.
NEW BUSINESS	The committee reviewed a proposal for a new classroom complex in Helena. After much discussion, the committee agreed to contact the Helena county clerk's office to get information on zoning ordinances.
ADJOURNMENT	The meeting was adjourned at 2:45 p.m. The next meeting is scheduled for July 10 in Room 16. Respectfully submitted, Nancy Jacobs, Secretary

(Note: Table shown with "View Gridlines" active.)

Report
72-47
Minutes of a Meeting

HUMAN RESOURCES DEPT.

Minutes of The Meeting

May 20, 20--

ATTENDING	On May 14, 20--, A meeting of the Human Resources Department was held in the office of Mr. Choi. Members were present except Donald Clark, who was representedby Monica Cruz. The meeting was called to order at 10 A.M.
APPROVAL OF MINUTES	The minutes of the Apr. 14 meeting were read and approved as presented.
OLD BUSINESS	Andrea Fields was in charge of a staff-development survey. Ninetyseven questionnaires were returned, and a copy of the staff-development survey was discussed. The committee will consider the findings and be prepared to make recomendations for up dated job descriptions at the next monthly meeting.
NEW BUSINESS	Mr. Choi discussed plans to disseminate information about vaacncies that occur within the company to prospective job applicants. Monica Cruz will draft a flyer to be sent to the Lakeview Sentinel. Programs for the N P A convention to be held in Los Angeles were distributed to all members. Each committee member was asked to distribute copies to employees all in his or her department.
ADJOURNMENT	The meetingwas ended at 11:45 a.m. The meeting has been scheduled for July 10 in the Conference Center.

Respectfully submitted,

Brandon Scher Secretary

Procedures Manual

Goals

- Demonstrate improved speed and accuracy while typing.
- Demonstrate acceptable proofreading skills by editing a paragraph.
- Correctly use Word's footer feature.
- Correctly format a procedures manual.

A. WARMUP

alphabet
1 The jobs of waxing linoleum frequently peeved chintzy kids.

practice *u* and *y*
2 yum buy duly yuck fury your guy July busy yuk quay you your

easy
3 Laurie may dismantle her tan bicycle and put it in the van.

Skillbuilding

B. MAP+: NUMBERS

Follow the GDP software directions for this exercise to improve keystroking accuracy.

PPP PRETEST » PRACTICE » POSTTEST

PRETEST

Take a 1-minute timed writing.

C. PRETEST: Vertical Reaches

4 Janice and her escort were late for a dance at the 10
5 resort. The drummers in the band had just started to play 22
6 as they came in. It seems Janice injured the back of her 33
7 knee on the bank of the river during a cruise that morning. 45
1 | 2 | 3 | 4 | 5 | 6 | 7 | 8 | 9 | 10 | 11 | 12

PRACTICE

Speed Emphasis:
If you made no more than 1 error on the Pretest, type each *individual* line 2 times.

Accuracy Emphasis:
If you made 2 or more errors, type each *group* of lines (as though it were a paragraph) 2 times.

D. PRACTICE: Up Reaches

8 at late flatly rebate atomic rather repeat attest atom what
9 dr draft drank dryer drew drain drama dread dream drag drug
10 ju judge juice jumpy junks juror judo julep jumbo jump just
11 es essay nests tests less dress acres makes uses best rests

E. PRACTICE: Down Reaches

12 ca cable caddy cargo scare decay yucca pecan cage calm case
13 nk ankle blank crank blink junk think trunk brink bank sink
14 ba tuba ballot cabana bakery abates global basket balk band
15 sc scar scale scalp scene scent scold scoop scope scan disc

POSTTEST

Repeat the Pretest timed writing and compare performance.

F. POSTTEST: Vertical Reaches

Language Arts

Edit the paragraph to correct any errors.

G. PROOFREADING

```
16       Many home computer user like the challenge of haveing
17 the latest in both hardware and software technology. Their
18 are those however, who's needs likely can be satisfied at
19 a very low costs. A used Pentium personnel computer with
20 color monitor and keyboard might be your's for under $ 300.
21 Check out th Yellow Page, or visit a used-computer store.
```

Formatting

H. PROCEDURES MANUAL

Organizations often prepare procedures manuals to assist employees in identifying the steps or methods they must follow to accomplish particular tasks. The illustration depicts a continuation page in a procedures manual for American Bistro. The title of the manual is "Employee Manual" and the report section name is "Training Program."

To format a procedures manual:

1. Type the manual using standard formatting for the body of a business report.
2. Insert a header (suppressed on the first page) with the company name followed by a comma and the manual title at the left margin.
3. Move to the right margin, and type the name of the report section in italics.
4. Insert a footer with the word "Page" followed by a page number field centered in the footer.

Strategies for Career Success

Corrective Feedback

Sometime in your career, you will give someone corrective feedback. You can use positive communication to do this and not appear to criticize the person.

Here are some things you should not do. Do not correct the person in front of others. Avoid giving feedback when you are angry. Stay away from derogatory or dismissive comments (for example, "That's a useless idea!"). Do not dismiss a person's enthusiasm with comments like "We've never done that before" or "It won't work."

Here are some things you should do. Listen to the other person's side of the situation. Ask for ideas on how to fix the situation. Express yourself in a positive way, such as saying, "You're getting much closer" or "That's an interesting idea." Be specific about what the person can do to correct the situation. Follow up within a short time and identify all progress.

Your Turn: Think about the last time you received corrective feedback. Did the person giving you feedback use techniques to create a positive outcome?

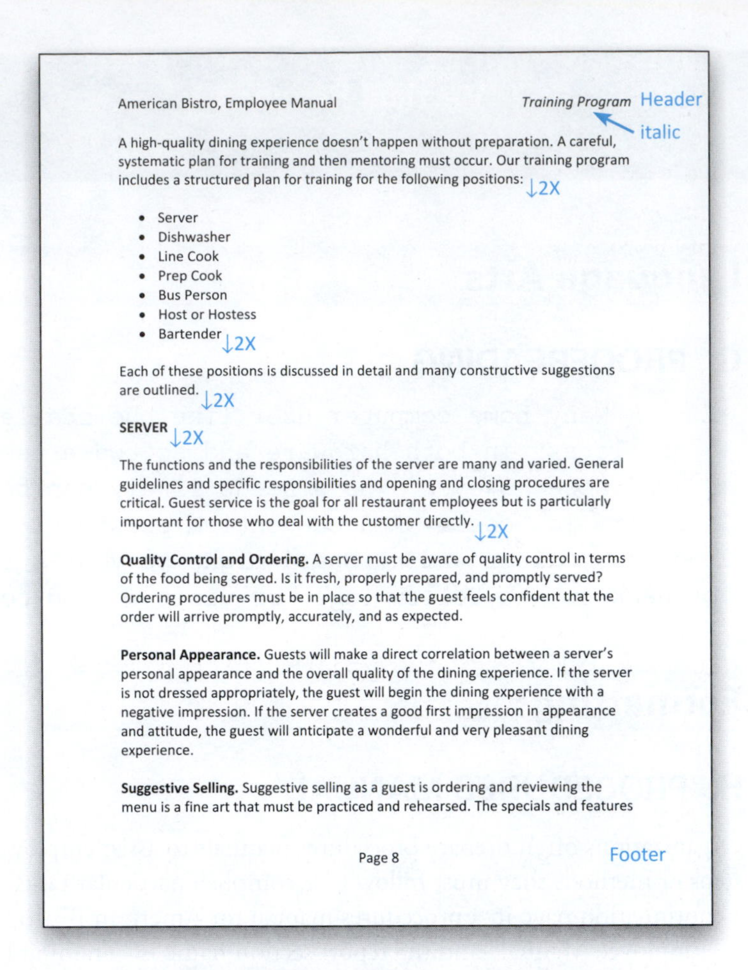
American Bistro, Employee Manual *Training Program* Header

italic

A high-quality dining experience doesn't happen without preparation. A careful, systematic plan for training and then mentoring must occur. Our training program includes a structured plan for training for the following positions: ↓2X

- Server
- Dishwasher
- Line Cook
- Prep Cook
- Bus Person
- Host or Hostess
- Bartender ↓2X

Each of these positions is discussed in detail and many constructive suggestions are outlined. ↓2X

SERVER ↓2X

The functions and the responsibilities of the server are many and varied. General guidelines and specific responsibilities and opening and closing procedures are critical. Guest service is the goal for all restaurant employees but is particularly important for those who deal with the customer directly. ↓2X

Quality Control and Ordering. A server must be aware of quality control in terms of the food being served. Is it fresh, properly prepared, and promptly served? Ordering procedures must be in place so that the guest feels confident that the order will arrive promptly, accurately, and as expected.

Personal Appearance. Guests will make a direct correlation between a server's personal appearance and the overall quality of the dining experience. If the server is not dressed appropriately, the guest will begin the dining experience with a negative impression. If the server creates a good first impression in appearance and attitude, the guest will anticipate a wonderful and very pleasant dining experience.

Suggestive Selling. Suggestive selling as a guest is ordering and reviewing the menu is a fine art that must be practiced and rehearsed. The specials and features

Page 8 Footer

I. WORD PROCESSING: FOOTERS

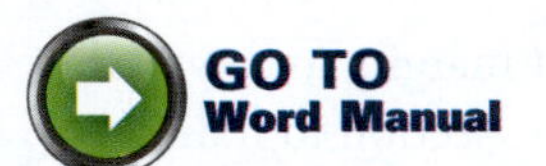

Study Lesson 73 in your Word Manual. Complete all of the shaded steps while at your computer. Then format the documents that follow.

Document Processing

Report
73-48
Procedures Manual

Abbott Industries, Employee Training Manual *Introduction*

¶ Managers are responsible for developing training programs for new employees who have been hired in any of the seven regional branches of Abbott Industries. The basic content of this employee training program is outlined next.

EMPLOYEE TRAINING MANUAL OUTLINE

¶ Abbott Industries will distribute this manual to all new managers to help familiarize them with the day-to-day procedures of the company. Also, answers are provided to the following questions with specific details included in each section:

- Where does the training manual fit within the training program?
- For whom is the manual designed, and what does it contain?
- How should the manual be used?
- Can the manual be used in a classroom setting?
- Can the manual be used as self-paced instructional material?
- Can study guides accompany the manual?

(continued on next page)

EMPLOYEE TRAINING PROGRAM PHILOSOPHY AND GOALS

¶ Well-trained employees are the key to the continued success of Abbott Industries. Studies have shown that the most successful, productive employees are those who have received extensive training. One of the positive results of a training program is that employees often feel they have a strong stake in the company's future. That internalized sense of ownership is highly motivational. The next section in this training manual explains the program guidelines.

Page 2

Report 73-49
Procedures Manual

Studio One Photography, Presentation Software Guide *Presentation Overview*

PRESENTATION ACTION PLAN

¶ An effective presentation does not happen by accident. It must be designed and formatted in a way that is appropriate to the audience and the topic. It must focus carefully on the subject at hand and include the right amount of text and graphics on each slide without appearing busy. Artwork, tables, and charts should be used purposefully to convey information clearly.

¶ Sound and video must be used with discretion as they can become a distraction rather than an enhancement. The same holds true for animation. It can quickly become annoying unless it is used sparingly. A good presentation should include a closing that provides the audience with an opportunity for questions, answers, and discussion.

PRESENTATION SOFTWARE

¶ There are several different computer-assisted presentation methods. However, Studio One Photography is using PowerPresentation software exclusively at this time. Any presentation can be delivered directly from a computer by connecting to a large external monitor or to a projection system.

¶ The software also allows presentations to be saved in a format for publishing on the Internet. Self-running presentations can be created specifically for the Internet; however, some of the special effects and animation may be lost in the process. Presentations can also be saved to a CD that will start automatically when the CD is inserted into a computer. Because the CD contains both the presentation and special viewer software, distributing the presentation is seamless.

Page 7

Report 73-50
Procedures Manual

1. Open Report 73-49.
2. Edit the header, and type `Clip Art Overview` as the section name.
3. Edit the footer so the page number starts at page 8.
4. Delete the entire content of the report body, and replace it with this:

ADDING **Clip Art**

Clip art can enhance the appearance of aslide, and it can be easily added to selected slides or to every slide in your presentation. Several clip art images are included in this presentation package and any 1 of them can be used in slides that you prepare. If you choose, therefore, you can insert clip art images from other packages. To insert a clip art image from your Presentation software package, follow these steps:

1. Click the icon for adding a clip art image.
2. Select the image from the software clip art library and size and move it to its new location.
3. Size and move the image to its correct location on the presentation slide.
4. Copy the image to the slide master if it is to appear on all slides.

You can also change the appearance of a clip art image by changing the colors used or by changing the contrast or brightness. A mirror image is created by flipping the image so that its horizontal or vertical position are reversed. To eliminate un wanted sections of an image, crop the unwanted sections. This process is similar to what happens you when take a printed picture and use scissors to cut off portions of picture except that it happens electronically.

Keyboarding Connection

Observing Netiquette

Netiquette is proper conduct for e-mail users. It shows courtesy and professionalism and conveys a good impression of you and your company. Since e-mail is close to speech, it is the most informal of business documents.

Check your e-mail daily. Try to answer it the same day it arrives. Don't let it accumulate in your mailbox; you risk offending the sender. Use regular capitalization. All-caps indicate SHOUTING; all-lowercase text conveys immaturity. Most readers tolerate an infrequent typo, but if your message is filled with errors, you appear unprofessional. Use your spell checker, and don't overwhelm people with unnecessary e-mail. Use discretion. Don't automatically reply all; make sure the information is relevant to each e-mail recipient.

Be considerate. Be professional. Don't forward jokes or nonwork-related e-mail at work. Anything you write can wind up in your personnel file. E-mail that criticizes another person can be forwarded to him or her without your knowledge.

Your Turn: Review your next e-mail message for the use of netiquette.

UNIT 15 LESSON

Reports Formatted in Columns

74

Goals

- Type at least 42wpm/5′/5e.
- Correctly use Word's column and hyphenation features.
- Correctly format a magazine article.

A. WARMUP

alphabet	1	Amusing quips galvanized a few of the mock jury in the box.
frequent digraphs	2	th that bath them both math then moth the myth theft thirty
easy	3	The doe and buck by the old bush may dig up the giant oaks.

Skillbuilding

B. PROGRESSIVE PRACTICE: NUMBERS

Follow the GDP software directions for this exercise to improve keystroking speed.

C. TECHNIQUE PRACTICE: SPACE BAR

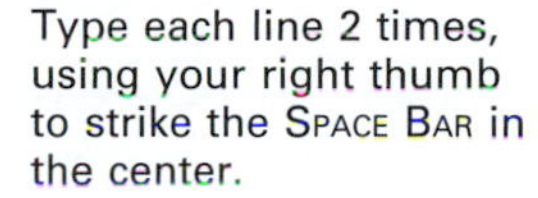

Type each line 2 times, using your right thumb to strike the SPACE BAR in the center.

```
4 Mr. Li may ask an arm and a leg for the new car on the lot.
5 The hot sun in the sky led Ann to ask him for a cup of tea.
6 Bo may use an old key to the gym for the new job if he can.
7 One ton of wet tar on the dam may be a bit too hot for him.
```

Take two 5-minute timed writings.

Goal: At least 42wpm/5'/5e

D. 5-MINUTE TIMED WRITING

```
8       Have you ever given any thought to starting your own      11
9   business? Obviously, there is some risk in starting out in    23
10  a venture such as this. However, if you realize there are     34
11  some issues to starting up a business, it may not seem to     46
12  be such a daunting undertaking. Let's quickly look at just    58
13  some of the issues that are involved in this task.            68
14      First of all, you need to think about whether you want    79
15  to do so badly enough to work long hours without knowing if   91
16  you will make any money at the end of the month. It would    103
17  be advantageous if you had worked previously for another     114
18  company as a manager or have managerial experience.          124
19      You have to have some sense for just how much money      135
20  you will need to start your business. It will take some      146
21  working capital to get you started. If you have put money    158
22  aside to invest in the company, there is a good possibility  170
23  you will succeed. If you don't have enough put aside, can    181
24  you get credit from a lending institution to assist you      193
25  through the first few months? And, of course, you'll need    204
26  to get credit from suppliers.                                 210
      1 | 2 | 3 | 4 | 5 | 6 | 7 | 8 | 9 | 10 | 11 | 12
```

Formatting

E. MAGAZINE ARTICLES

Magazine articles can be formatted as a newspaper-style column in which text flows from the bottom of one column to the top of the next column. Magazine articles are generally formatted as 2-column reports.

To format a magazine article with two columns:

1. Turn hyphenation on.
2. Press ENTER 5 times to begin the first line of the magazine article 2 inches from the top of the page.
3. Center and type the title in all-caps, bold, and 14-point.
4. Press ENTER 2 times; then center and type the byline in upper- and lowercase, bold, and 12-point.
5. Press ENTER 2 times and change to left alignment.
6. Type the article single-spaced; insert 1 blank line before and after all side headings.
7. Select the body of the report, and change to justified alignment.
8. For a multipage article, insert a header (suppressed on the first page) with the author's last name, a space, and the page number aligned at the right.
9. Carefully select text beginning just before the first character in the first paragraph through the last typed character of the document excluding the paragraph formatting following the last character.
10. Format the body into 2 columns.
11. If any heading appears as a one-liner at the bottom of the first page, keep it with the text on the next page.
12. Balance the columns if necessary.
13. Fix any large gaps that might appear between the words of the last line of the body.

↓5X

14 pt **TIME AND PERCEPTION** ↓2X

12 pt ↓ **Shannon Jones** ↓2X

Time is a method human beings use to measure and sequence events, to compare the durations of events, and to measure the intervals between events. Time is a hot topic in terms of religion, philosophy, and science. However, defining time in an objective, accepted way has been nearly impossible among scholarly types. How, in fact, do you compare one moment to the next?

As human beings, our perception of time has grown out of a natural series of rhythms that are linked to daily, monthly, and yearly cycles. No matter how much we live by our wristwatches, our bodies and our lives will always be somewhat influenced by an internal clock. What is of even greater interest, though, are the many uses and perceptions of time based on individuals and their cultures.

RHYTHM AND TEMPO

Rhythm and tempo are ways we relate to time and are discerning features of a culture. In some cultures, people move very slowly; in others, moving quickly is the norm. Mixing the two types may create feelings of discomfort. People may have trouble relating to each other because they are not synchronized. To be synchronized is to subtly move in union with another person; it is vital to a strong partnership.

In general, Americans move at a fast tempo, although there are regional departures. In meetings, Americans tend to be impatient and want to "get down to business" right away. They have been taught that it is best to come to the point quickly and avoid vagueness. Because American business operates in a short time frame, prompt results are often of more interest than the building of long-term relationships.

PERCEPTION AND MEMORY

Picture yourself in a room watching someone enter, walk across the room, and sit down. By the time the person sits down, your brain must remember the actions that happened previous to the act of sitting down. All these memories and perceptions are filed as bits of data in the brain. The perception of the passing of time from the first event of entering the room to the last event of sitting down occurs only if the observer is aware and comparing the events.

What would happen if the observer could not remember one or more of the events from the time the person entered the room to the time that person was seated? The brain might interpret the scene and assign a time frame, but unless the observer remembers, the perception of time passing would not exist.

Jones 2

LIVING IN THE MOMENT

If a human being perceives himself to be of a certain age, this is because he has accumulated data, remembers that data, and has a basis for a comparison. If a person cannot remember his past, such as a person with dementia, then he would not be aware of the existence of such a past. He would only be experiencing the single "moment" he was living in.

F. WORD PROCESSING: COLUMNS AND HYPHENATION

GO TO Word Manual

Study Lesson 74 in your Word Manual. Complete all of the shaded steps while at your computer. Then format the documents that follow.

Document Processing

Report 74-51
Magazine Article

INTERVIEW TECHNIQUES
Sandra Dolan

¶ The interview process enables a company to gather information about you that was not provided on your resume or application form. This information may include such items as your career goals, appearance, personality, poise, and ability to express yourself verbally.

¶ Regardless of where you went to school or how much experience you have, if you aren't able to interview successfully, you won't get the job. Take note of the information in this article to help you interview successfully and get the job you want.

APPEARANCE

¶ Plan your wardrobe carefully because first impressions are lasting ones when you walk into the interviewer's office. If you are not quite certain about what you should wear, dress conservatively.

¶ Whatever you choose, be sure that your clothing is clean, neat, and comfortable. You should also pay attention to details such as personal hygiene, clean hair, shined shoes, well-groomed nails, and appropriate jewelry and other accessories.

MEETING THE INTERVIEWER

¶ Be sure to arrive at the interview site a few minutes early. Stand when you meet the interviewer for the first time. If the interviewer offers to shake hands, shake hands in a confident, firm manner. A great deal of nonverbal communication occurs even in a simple handshake.

THE INTERVIEW PROCESS

¶ Maintain direct eye contact with the interviewer when you respond to his or her questions. Listen intently to everything that is said. Be aware of any movements you make with your eyes, your hands, and other parts of your body during the interview. Too much movement may be a signal to the interviewer that you are nervous, that you lack confidence, or that you are not certain of your answers.

¶ During the interview, the interviewer will judge not only what you say but also how you say it. As you answer questions, you will be judged on grammar, articulation, vocabulary, and tone of voice. The nonverbal skills that the interviewer may judge are your attitude, enthusiasm, listening ability, and promptness in responding to questions.

ENDING THE INTERVIEW

¶ Let the interviewer determine when it is time to close the interview. When this time arrives, ask the interviewer when he or she expects to make a decision on hiring for this position and when you may expect to hear about the job. Thank the interviewer for taking the time to meet with you, and make a graceful, prompt exit.

¶ After the interview, send a follow-up letter to remind the interviewer of your name and your continued interest in the company. This follow-up letter will set you apart from the competition and provide another example of your communication skills. Let the interviewer know how to contact you by providing a telephone number where you can be reached. A cell phone number is preferable to a home phone number. Make it easy for the interviewer to contact you.

Report
74-52
Magazine Article

PACIFIC INSURANCE DISCOUNTS

Sharon Brooks

¶ Policyholders of Pacific Insurance (and their dependents) are eligible for a wide range of discount services. These services provide you with a variety of items you can purchase, from automobiles to computers to jewelry. Here are some examples of the merchandise and services that are available to all Pacific Insurance members.

AUTO PRICING

¶ You can order the most sophisticated auto information guide on the market. The guide will give you information on retail prices, vehicle specifications, safety equipment, and factory-option packages.

¶ When you are ready to place your order for an automobile, a team of company experts will work with you and with the prospective dealer to ensure that you are getting the best possible price through a network of nationwide dealers. You are guaranteed to get the best price for the automobile you have chosen.

¶ Once you have purchased your automobile, Pacific Insurance will provide all your insurance needs. Discounts on policy rates are provided for completion of a driver-training program, for installed antitheft devices, and for installed passive restraint systems, such as air bags.

¶ Finally, Pacific Insurance can make your purchase decision an easy one by always providing a low-rate finance plan for you. You can be certain that you are getting the most competitive interest rate for the purchase of your automobile when you finance with Pacific Insurance.

CAR RENTAL DISCOUNTS

¶ When you need to rent an automobile while traveling, take advantage of special rates available to you from five of the largest car rental agencies. Send us an e-mail message at pacificinsurance@mail.com to receive all details regarding car rental rates and participating agencies.

(continued on next page)

ROAD AND TRAVEL SERVICES

¶ You can enjoy the security of specialized coverage for both towing and roadside emergency through the Pacific Insurance Road and Travel Plan. If you're locked out of your car or need a jump start, a tire changed, or a tow, Pacific Insurance is there.

¶ As a Pacific Insurance traveler, you can take advantage of our exclusive discounts and bonuses on cruises and tours. Our travel plan provides daily and weekend trips to over 100 destinations.

MERCHANDISE BUYING

¶ Each quarter a buying services catalog will be mailed to you. This catalog includes a variety of items that can be purchased through Pacific Insurance, and you'll never find better prices! Through the catalog you can purchase jewelry, furniture, sports equipment, electronics, appliances, computers, and much more. To place an order, simply call Pacific Insurance free at 1-800-555-3838 or visit our Web site.

Report
74-53
Magazine Article

Open the file for Report 74-51 and make the following changes:

1. Change the author's name to "Debra Winger."
2. Add the following section just before the section entitled "ENDING THE INTERVIEW."

   INTERVIEW QUESTIONS
   ¶ Be prepared for common interview questions, and be prepared to ask some of your own. You might ask about the company's mission statement, about the typical career path for this position, or about a typical workday at that organization. Ask some questions that show you are interested in learning more about the company and want to make a commitment to its success as a future employee.

Report Review

Goals

- Demonstrate improved speed and accuracy while typing.
- Demonstrate acceptable language arts skills in composing paragraphs.
- Correctly format an agenda, the minutes of a meeting, and a magazine article.
- Successfully complete a Progress and Proofreading Check with zero errors on the first scored attempt.

A. WARMUP

alphabet 1 I quickly explained that many big jobs involve few hazards.
number/symbol 2 rlow@juno.com 294% (Dix & Wu) 8/9 Yes! $1.34 *Fri. #1257-60
easy 3 Jane did not blame the busy auditor for her usual problems.

Skillbuilding

B. 12-SECOND SPEED SPRINTS

Take three 12-second timed writings on each line.

4 I may make us one set of maps to aid us when we visit them.
5 I hid a big car in my new lot, but I may not get to it by two.
6 It is a shame she works such odd anthems into her busy art.
7 It is the duty of the busy worker to take apart the panels.
' ' ' ' 5 ' ' ' ' 10 ' ' ' ' 15 ' ' ' ' 20 ' ' ' ' 25 ' ' ' ' 30 ' ' ' ' 35 ' ' ' ' 40 ' ' ' ' 45 ' ' ' ' 50 ' ' ' ' 55 ' ' ' ' 60

C. PACED PRACTICE

Follow the GDP software directions for this exercise to improve keystroking speed and accuracy.

Language Arts

D. COMPOSING PARAGRAPHS

Do you think it is safe to make and pay for purchases online? Compose a paragraph of at least three to four sentences answering this question.

Document Processing

Report
75-54
Agenda

UNITED BANK OF THE WEST
Meeting Agenda
May 15, 20--

1. Call to order
2. Approval of minutes of April 15 meeting
3. Installment loans (Gerald Hagen)
4. Mortgage loans (William McKay)
5. Series EE bonds (Francis Montoya)
6. Club memberships (Louise Abbey)
7. Certificates of deposit (Robert Hunt)
8. Closing remarks
9. Adjournment

Report
75-55
Minutes of a Meeting

ART SOCIETY OF MENDO CINO

Minutes of the Meeting

Nov. 19, 20--

ATTENDANCE Linda Scher called the meeting to order at 8 p.m. in the Mendocino Fine arts Center.

APPROVAL OF MINUTES The minutes of the October May 10th meeting were read and approved with 1 correction—the spring arts fair will be held in April rather than in May of next year.

OLDBUSINESS Susan Firtz furnished each member with a list of artists and the names of the watercolor paintings by each artist.

NEW BUSINESS Martha Steward informed members taht a new supply of canvas and oil paint arrived. Members can check out any items they need to begin their winter projects. She reminded everyone that The Winter Arts Fair will be held December 14 at the Centennial Convention Center.

ADJOURNMENT The Meeting was adjourned at 9:45 p.m. The December November meeting will be canceled skipped, and the next meeting will be held January December 12.

Respectfully submitted,

Carole Little

Report
75-56
Magazine Article

Progress and Proofreading Check

Documents designated as Proofreading Checks serve as a check of your proofreading skill. Your goal is to have zero typographical errors when the GDP software first scores the document.

PUBLIC SPEAKING TIPS

Donna Barnes

¶ We have all been giving performances since our very early years. The most terrifying part of each performance was probably the fear that we would "freeze" when it came our turn to perform. Whenever we find ourselves in this predicament, we should accept that fear and learn to let it work for us, not against us. We need to recognize that nervousness or fear may set in during our performance. Then, when it does happen (if it does), we will be ready to cope with it and overcome it.

¶ If you forget some lines in a recitation, try to remember other lines and recite them. Doing so may help those forgotten lines to "pop back" into your memory so that you put them in at a later time.

¶ You always want to leave your audience with the idea that you have given them something worthwhile that they can use or apply to their own lives. For maximum impact on your audience and to make sure that they remember what you say, use audiovisual aids to reinforce your message. Remember, however, that audiovisual aids are nothing more than aids. The real message should come in the words you choose when giving your presentation.

¶ Study your speech well; even rehearse it, if necessary. However, do not practice it to the extent that it appears that you are merely reading what is written down on the paper in front of you. Much of your personality should be exhibited while you are giving your speech. If you are an enthusiastic, friendly person who converses well with people face-to-face, then those same qualities should be evident during your speech. A good piece of advice is to just go out there and be yourself—you will be much more comfortable by doing so, and your audience will relate to you better than if you try to exhibit a different personality when at the podium.

¶ No matter how rapidly you speak, slow down when you are in front of a group. The fact that you are nervous can cause your speech rate to increase. The best way to slow down your speaking is to breathe deeply. Doing so also causes your nervous system to relax, allowing you to proceed with your speech calmly.

¶ Finally, the best advice for giving a successful speech is to be prepared. You will be more confident if you are thoroughly prepared. Do your research, rehearse your speech, and make notes about any points you want to emphasize.

Strategies for Career Success

Audience Analysis

Knowing your audience is fundamental to the success of any message. Ask the following questions to help identify your audience.

What is your relationship with your audience? Are they familiar—people with whom you work—or people unknown to you? The latter will prompt you to conduct some research to better communicate your purpose. What is the attitude of your audience? Are they hostile or receptive to your message? How will your message benefit them? What is your anticipated response? Asking these questions first can help prevent message mishaps later.

When writing to a diverse audience, direct your message to the primary audience. These key decision makers will make a decision or act on the basis of your message. Determine the level of detail, organization, formality, and use of technical terms and theory.

Your Turn: Compose a thank-you e-mail to a friend. How would it differ from an interview thank-you letter?

UNIT 16

Tables

LESSON 76

Tables With Footnotes or Source Notes

LESSON 77

Tables With Braced Column Headings

LESSON 78

Tables in Landscape Orientation

LESSON 79

Multipage Tables

LESSON 80

Tables With Predesigned Formats

Tables With Footnotes or Source Notes

Goals

- Type at least 43wpm/5'/5e.
- Correctly use Word's table features to change text direction and insert or delete rows or columns.
- Correctly format a table with source notes or footnotes.

A. WARMUP

alphabet 1 My wife wove six dozen plaid jackets before the girls quit.
concentration 2 disenfranchisements unconstitutionality contemporaneousness
easy 3 The girl may make a formal gown of fur to go with her hair.

Skillbuilding

B. SUSTAINED PRACTICE: NUMBERS AND SYMBOLS

Take a 1-minute timed writing on the boxed paragraph to establish your base speed. Then take a 1-minute timed writing on the following paragraph. As soon as you equal or exceed your base speed on this paragraph, move to the next, more difficult paragraph.

4 There is a need at this time to communicate our new 11
5 pricing guidelines to our franchise outlets. In addition, 22
6 they must be made aware of inventory implications. They 33
7 will then be in a position to have a successful operation. 45

8 Franchise operators could be requested to use either 11
9 a 20% or a 30% markup. A $50 item would be marked to sell 22
10 for either $60 or $65. Depending on future prospects for 34
11 sales, half of the articles would be priced at each level. 45

12 Ms. Aagard's suggestion is to assign items in Groups 11
13 #1470, #2830, and #4560 to the 20% category. The Series 77 23
14 items* would be in the 30% markup category except for the 34
15 items with a base rate under $100. What is your reaction? 48

16 Mr. Chavez's recommendation is to assign a 30% markup 11
17 to Groups #3890, #5290, #6480, and #7180. About 1/4 of the 23
18 remainder (except for soft goods) would also be in the 30% 35
19 category. Groups #8340 and #9560 would have a 20% markup. 46

1 | 2 | 3 | 4 | 5 | 6 | 7 | 8 | 9 | 10 | 11 | 12

Take two 5-minute timed writings.

Goal: At least 43wpm/5'/5e

C. 5-MINUTE TIMED WRITING

```
20      Starting up your own business may mean that you are      11
21 thinking about acquiring an existing business. If so, is      22
22 that business doing well in the community? If you are going   34
23 to buy out an established business, you need to know the     45
24 reason the current owner wishes to sell the company. If       57
25 there are other businesses in the area, you should first      68
26 find out what reputation that business has built up in the    80
27 community. Do other businesses think highly of the company?   92
28      You must also consider what type of advertising you     102
29 plan to use to get your business off to a good start. You    114
30 might use ads in newspapers, on television, in magazines,    128
31 or on the Internet. When you start your ad campaigns, you    137
32 should consider hiring an ad agency to put out the right     149
33 message for your company and its products. You should also   160
34 consider the types of ads being used by your competitors to  172
35 determine what has worked well for them.                     181
36      Yes, there are major issues that need to be addressed   192
37 when starting up your own business; and all of the issues    203
38 should be dealt with before you decide to take such a step.  215
     1 | 2 | 3 | 4 | 5 | 6 | 7 | 8 | 9 | 10 | 11 | 12
```

Formatting

D. TABLES WITH SOURCE NOTES OR FOOTNOTES

REFER TO Reference Manual

R-8B: Multipage Business Report
R-13A: Boxed Table

To format tables with source notes or footnotes:

1. When you insert a table, include an additional row at the bottom of the table for the source note or footnote.
2. Merge the cells in the bottom row.
3. For a source note, type `Note:` or `Source:` as applicable in the bottom row; then type the corresponding information for the source note.
4. For a footnote, type an asterisk (or another symbol) at the relevant point within the table; then in the bottom row, type an asterisk and the corresponding information for the footnote.

E. WORD PROCESSING: TABLE—TEXT DIRECTION AND TABLE—INSERT, DELETE, AND MOVE ROWS OR COLUMNS

GO TO Word Manual

Study Lesson 76 in your Word Manual. Complete all of the shaded steps while at your computer. Then format the documents that follow.

Document Processing

Table 76-26
Boxed Table

1. In Row 1, set the text direction to display vertically from bottom to top, and change the alignment to bottom center.
2. Adjust the row height so that none of the column heading lines wrap to a second line.
3. In the merged cells in the bottom row, type the table note as shown.

Portfolio Counselor	Years of Experience	Fund Title Code	MSC World Index	Maxim Global Funds Index	Class A Management Fees	Class B Management Fees	Class C Management Fees
Steven Burgess	16	529-A	40.33%	38.78%	.37%	.37%	.37%
Jean Carol	5	529-B	38.78%	5.65%	.23%	1.00%	.25%
Mark Denning	12	361-A	21.42%	1.23%	.15%	.15%	.14%
Rex Humber	3	361-B	38.29%	3.99%	.75%	1.52%	.76%
Note: This information is subject to change.							

Table 76-27
Boxed Table

Open the file for Table 76-26 and make the following changes:

1. Delete the table note row.
2. Delete Column H.
3. Insert a row above Row 3. Type this:

   `Marie Alexander | 20 | 436-C | 26.17% | 24.39% | .52% | 1.25%`

4. Insert a column to the left of Column F. Type this:

   `United Fund Index | 31.29% | 19.07% | 9.73% | 2.75% | 5.41%`

5. Adjust the alignment of the new column heading to bottom center.
6. Move Column D to the right one column so it will become Column E.
7. Move Row 3 up one row so it becomes Row 2.
8. Insert a row at the bottom of the table, merge the cells, and type this left-aligned note: `Note: This information will be updated next quarter.`
9. Apply a 25 percent shading to Row 1.

Table
76-28
Boxed Table

1. In Row 1, set the text direction to display vertically from bottom to top, and change the alignment to bottom center.
2. Adjust the row height so that none of the column heading lines wrap to a second line.
3. In the merged cells in the bottom row, type the table footnote as shown.

Office Supply Account*	LED Laser Printer	Internal Fax Modem	Cash Management System	Plain-Paper Laser Fax
OE-9	$405	$181	$199	$249
DD-7	395	150	205	234
US-2	410	125	183	252
OB-1	420	167	179	245
*Codes are subject to change.				

Keyboarding Connection

Virus and Spam Prevention

Use caution when opening e-mail attachments or downloading files from the Internet. Download files only from reliable Web sites. Do not open files attached to an e-mail from an unknown source. Also question files attached to e-mail from a known source. Some viruses replicate themselves and are sent through e-mail without users' knowledge.

Delete any e-mail with an odd subject, a chain e-mail, or electronic junk mail, commonly known as spam. If you're given the opportunity to unsubscribe from a spammer's list, think twice. Your reply will stop the messages from a reputable mailing list, but replying to e-mail spam lets the spammers know your e-mail address is legitimate and can actually increase the amount of spam you receive.

To protect against lost data, back up your files on a regular basis. Then you will be prepared if a virus infects your computer. New viruses are discovered daily, so update your antivirus software regularly.

Your Turn: How do you handle junk mail via snail mail? Do you notice similarities when dealing with spam?

Tables With Braced Column Headings

Goals

- Demonstrate improved speed and accuracy while typing.
- Demonstrate acceptable language arts skills in capitalization.
- Correctly format a table with braced column headings.

A. WARMUP

alphabet 1 Grumpy wizards made toxic brew for Jack and the evil queen.
one hand 2 assets linkup bat kin tested phonily wave imply refer puppy
easy 3 Kent may fish with me for cod at the docks on their island.

Skillbuilding

B. MAP+: ALPHABET

Follow the GDP software directions for this exercise to improve keystroking accuracy.

C. PROGRESSIVE PRACTICE: ALPHABET

Follow the GDP software directions for this exercise to improve keystroking speed.

Language Arts

Study the rules at the right.

D. CAPITALIZATION

RULE
= noun #

Capitalize nouns followed by a number or letter (except for the nouns *line, note, page, paragraph,* and *size*).

Please read Chapter 5, which begins on page 94.

RULE
= compass point

Capitalize compass points (such as *north, south,* or *northeast*) only when they designate definite regions.

From Montana we drove south to reach the Southwest.

Edit each sentence to correct any errors.

4 The marketing manager had a reservation on flight 505 to
5 Atlanta.

6 Please order two model 6M printers.

7 The desktop publishing seminar will be held in Room 101.

8 Study pages 120-230 for the unit test.

9 Please contact all representatives in the northern states.

10 Didn't line 9 of the directions say to drive south?

11 The population of the south continues to increase.

Formatting

E. TABLES WITH BRACED COLUMN HEADINGS

A braced column heading is a heading that applies to more than one column (for example, *Explore Chicago Pass* and *Chicago City Pass* in the table shown below). To create a braced column heading:

1. Position the insertion point where you want the braced heading to appear.
2. Merge the cells that will hold the braced heading.
3. Center the braced column heading over the appropriate columns.

Document Processing

Table 77-29
Boxed Table

CHICAGO ATTRACTION DISCOUNT CARDS Spring Rates*					
Explore Chicago Pass			Chicago City Pass		
Month	Adult	Child	Month	Adult	Child
March	$60	$45	March	$55	$40
April	70	55	April	65	50
May	90	75	May	85	70
*Read page 2 of "Big City on a Budget" for details.					

≡ noun #

Table 77-30
Boxed Table

CHICAGO TRAVEL BOOKS Sales Trends			
Midwest Publishing		Total Sales	
Region	Sales Representative	Last Year	This Year
Illinois	Jeff Meyer	$1,956,250	$2,135,433
Wisconsin*	Marjorie Matheson	859,435	1,231,332
Indiana	Valerie Harper	737,498	831,352
*Includes only eastern Wisconsin.			

≡ compass point

Table
77-31
Boxed Table

Single-space the table.

AMERICA DISCOVERY TOURS			
Illinois Tour Highlights		San Francisco tour Highlights	
Attraction	**Location**	**Attraction**	**Location**
Land Of Lincoln	Springfield	Golden Gate Park	Central Richmond
Adler Planet arium	South Shore of Chicago	Exploratorium	Presidio
Lincoln Park	North Side ofChicago	Yerba Buena Gardens	South Beach
The Navy Pier	Downtown Chicago	Coit Tower	The Embarcadero
Aquarium Shedd	South Shore of Chicago	Fishermans Wharf	North Beach
Wrigley Building	North Side of Chicago	Palace of Fine Arts	Persidio

Tables in Landscape Orientation

Goals

- Type at least 43wpm/5'/5e.
- Correctly use Word's page orientation feature.
- Correctly format a table in landscape orientation.

A. WARMUP

alphabet 1 Those heavy boxers performed quick waltzes and lively jigs.
practice *r* and *t* 2 rat try rotate trust tort tutor treat Trent trite trot hurt
easy 3 His body of work may disorient the visitors in the chapels.

Skillbuilding

B. PACED PRACTICE

Follow the GDP software directions for this exercise to improve keystroking speed and accuracy.

C. 5-MINUTE TIMED WRITING

Take two 5-minute timed writings.

Goal: At least 43wpm/5'/5e

4 This is the third in a series of timed writings on 10
5 starting up a new business. In this presentation, you will 22
6 consider some expense and merchandise issues as well as 33
7 some thoughts on the building you will move into or build. 45
8 There are several expenses that you will have to look 56
9 at for your new business. For example, do you realize how 68
10 much construction costs will be, or, if you are going to 79
11 rent a building, how much that expense will amount to? You 91
12 must also project expenses for insurance on the building 102
13 and its contents, utilities costs for running the business, 114
14 interest expense on any loans you secure to purchase or 128
15 renovate the building, and any new advertising expenses. 137
16 You must also consider the amount of merchandise you 148
17 will have on hand when you first open your store. If you 159
18 have several lines of merchandise, you need to determine 171
19 how many products and how much of each product you will 182
20 keep on the shelves and how much you will keep in inventory 194
21 in your warehouse. To acquire this merchandise, you must 205
22 locate suppliers who will sell you what you need. 215

1 | 2 | 3 | 4 | 5 | 6 | 7 | 8 | 9 | 10 | 11 | 12

D. TABLES IN LANDSCAPE ORIENTATION

The default page orientation for 8.5- by 11-inch paper is vertical (also known as *portrait*). Sometimes, however, the content of a document would fit better or appear more attractive in horizontal orientation (called *landscape*). Format all tables in this lesson in landscape orientation.

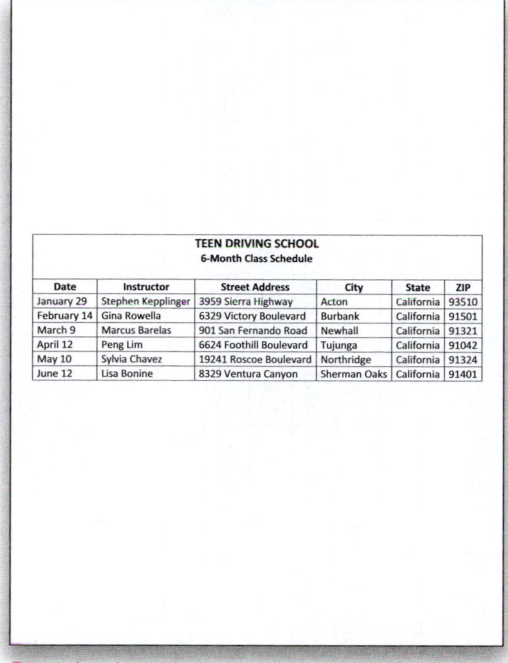

TEEN DRIVING SCHOOL 6-Month Class Schedule					
Date	**Instructor**	**Street Address**	**City**	**State**	**ZIP**
January 29	Stephen Kepplinger	3959 Sierra Highway	Acton	California	93510
February 14	Gina Rowella	6329 Victory Boulevard	Burbank	California	91501
March 9	Marcus Barelas	901 San Fernando Road	Newhall	California	91321
April 12	Peng Lim	6624 Foothill Boulevard	Tujunga	California	91042
May 10	Sylvia Chavez	19241 Roscoe Boulevard	Northridge	California	91324
June 12	Lisa Bonine	8329 Ventura Canyon	Sherman Oaks	California	91401

Portrait orientation.

TEEN DRIVING SCHOOL 6-Month Class Schedule					
Date	**Instructor**	**Street Address**	**City**	**State**	**ZIP**
January 29	Stephen Kepplinger	3959 Sierra Highway	Acton	California	93510
February 14	Gina Rowella	6329 Victory Boulevard	Burbank	California	91501
March 9	Marcus Barelas	901 San Fernando Road	Newhall	California	91321
April 12	Peng Lim	6624 Foothill Boulevard	Tujunga	California	91042
May 10	Sylvia Chavez	19241 Roscoe Boulevard	Northridge	California	91324
June 12	Lisa Bonine	8329 Ventura Canyon	Sherman Oaks	California	91401

Landscape orientation.

E. WORD PROCESSING: PAGE ORIENTATION

Study Lesson 78 in your Word Manual. Complete all of the shaded steps while at your computer. Then format the documents that follow.

Strategies for Career Success

Developing Confidence as a Presenter

Public speaking anxiety is quite common. As many as 77 percent of experienced speakers admit to having some anxiety on each speaking occasion. Normally, stage fright decreases with experience.

Even if there are no physical expressions of anxiety, speakers often assume others can see through their smiles to their fears. However, listeners are actually poor judges of the amount of anxiety that speakers experience.

A little anxiety can actually stimulate a better presentation. The best way to control your anxiety is to be well prepared for the presentation. Carefully analyze your audience, research your topic, organize the speech, practice your delivery, and believe in the ideas. Being well prepared puts you in an excellent position to control your anxiety.

Your Turn: "I'm glad I'm here. I'm glad you're here. I know that I know." What are the benefits of repeating this to yourself before each presentation?

Table
78-32
Boxed Table

THE TRAVEL SHOP
Travel Agent Contact Information*

Name	Street Address	City	State	ZIP	Telephone	E-Mail
Ronald Dahl	8787 Orion Place	Columbus	OH	43240	614-555-4951	rdahl@tts.com
Ming Dai	1415 Elbridge Payne Road	Chesterfield	MO	63017	636-555-9940	mdai@tts.com
Amber Palmer	3100 Breckinridge Boulevard	Duluth	GA	30096	770-555-7007	apalmer@tts.com
Anita Mills	21600 Oxnard Street	Woodland Hills	CA	91367	818-555-2675	amills@tts.com

*Contact information was last updated on July 1.

Table
78-33
Boxed Table

Open the file for Table 78-32 and make the following changes:

1. Change Ronald Dahl's address to this:

   `376 West Lane Avenue`

2. Add this information for another travel agent in a new row just above the table note:

   `Mike Cassidy | 2739 Idaho Avenue | Kenner | LA | 70062 | 504-555-0089 | mcassidy@tts.com`

3. Change the table note to read as follows:

   `*For a complete listing of all travel agents, visit http://www.thetravelshop.com and click "Contact Us."`

Table
78-34
Boxed Table

Ohio CUSTOMER SURVEY RESULTS

Office Products Un limited

July 1 20--

Customer | **Address** | **City** | **Zip** | **Telephone No** | **Most Recent Purchase**

Becker, Steve | 121 North Summit Avenue Street | Toledo | 44426 | 419-555-2384 | Label maker

Cross Mario | 20604 Lucile Rd. South | Columbus | 43230 | 614-555-2074 | Book case and Shelving

Dusenberry, Rich | 322 West Lyons Road | Cleve land | 44902 | 261-555-2002 | Portable hard drive

Ferrer, Marie | 5914 Bay Oaks Place | Chillicothe | 45601 | 614-555-1399 | Portable DVD player

Goodrich, Mike | 10386 Drive Power | Stuebenville | 43952 | 614-555-7821 | Digital camera

Juarez, Ismael | 231 East Front Street | Youngstown | 54401 44502 | 216-555-3885 | Postal scale

Lancaster, Robert | 6823 Creekwood Dr. | Columbus | 43085 | 614-555-2934 | Wireless router

Pastor, Sandra | 26044 Manzano Court | Columbus Youngstown | 44505 | 216-555-1777 | Cordless keyboard

Wee, Ju Jong | 936 East Wind Drive | Cleveland | 44121 | 216-555-8239 | Industrialshredder

Multipage Tables

Goals

- Demonstrate improved speed and accuracy while typing.
- Demonstrate acceptable language arts skills in spelling.
- Correctly use Word's table feature to repeat a heading row.
- Correctly format a multipage table with a heading row.

A. WARMUP

alphabet	1	A large fawn jumped quickly over seven white boxes of zinc.
frequent digraphs	2	or orb for door fort more boor nor odor port orator ore ort
easy	3	Did the naughty lapdog put my pajama top down on the chair?

Skillbuilding

B. MAP+: SYMBOL

Follow the GDP software directions for this exercise to improve keystroking accuracy.

PPP PRETEST » PRACTICE » POSTTEST

PRETEST
Take a 1-minute timed writing.

C. PRETEST: Alternate- and One-Hand Words

4	The usual visitors to the rocky island are from either	11
5	the city of Lakeland or Honolulu. They like to visit hilly	23
6	areas and taste the giant fruit. The eight signs that girl	35
7	made gave us an extra boost and some added revenue as well.	47
	1 | 2 | 3 | 4 | 5 | 6 | 7 | 8 | 9 | 10 | 11 | 12	

PRACTICE
Speed Emphasis:
If you made no more than 1 error on the Pretest, type each *individual* line 2 times.
Accuracy Emphasis:
If you made 2 or more errors, type each *group* of lines (as though it were a paragraph) 2 times.

D. PRACTICE: Alternate-Hand Words

8	also angle field bushel ancient emblem panel sight fish big
9	both blame fight formal element handle proxy signs girl and
10	city chair giant island visitor profit right their laid cut
11	down eight laugh theory chaotic visual shape usual work she

E. PRACTICE: One-Hand Words

12	acts hilly award uphill average poplin refer jolly adds him
13	area jumpy based homily baggage you'll serve union beat ink
14	case onion extra limply greater unholy wages imply draw you
15	gave pupil extra unhook wastage lumpy swears pylon star you

POSTTEST

Repeat the Pretest timed writing and compare performance.

F. POSTTEST: Alternate- and One-Hand Words

Language Arts

G. SPELLING

Type these frequently misspelled words, paying special attention to any spelling problems in each word.

16 assistance compliance initial limited corporation technical
17 operating sufficient operation incorporated writing current
18 advice together prepared recommend appreciated cannot based
19 benefit completing analysis probably projects before annual
20 issue attention location association participation proposed

Edit the sentences to correct any misspellings.

21 The complience by the corporation was sufficient to pass.

22 I cannot reccomend the project based on the expert advise.

23 The location of the proposed annual meeting was an issue.

24 Your assistance in completeing the project is appreciated.

25 Together we prepared an analysis of their current operation.

26 The writing was incorporated in the initial asociation bid.

Formatting

H. MULTIPAGE TABLES

Tables should generally be formatted to fit on one page. However, if a table extends to another page, follow these formatting rules:

1. Repeat the column headings at the top of each new page.
2. Insert a page number in the top right-hand corner of the page header of all continuing pages, and remove the page number from the first page.
3. Do not center a multipage table vertically.

50 LONGEST RIVERS OF THE WORLD
(Miles rounded to nearest 10)

River	Outflow	Miles
Nile	Mediterranean	4,160
Amazon	Atlantic Ocean	4,000
Chang	East China Sea	3,960
Huang	Yellow Sea	3,400
Ob-Irtysh	Gulf of Ob	3,360
Amur	Tatar Strait	2,740
Lena	Laptev Sea	2,730
Congo	Atlantic Ocean	2,720
Mekong	South China Sea	2,600
Niger	Gulf of Guinea	2,590
Yenisey	Kara Sea	2,540
Parana	Rio de la Plata	2,490
Mississippi	Gulf of Mexico	2,340
Missouri	Mississippi River	2,320
Murray-Darling	Indian Ocean	2,310
Volga	Caspian Sea	2,290
Purus	Amazon River	2,100
Medeira	Amazon River	2,010
Sao Francisco	Atlantic Ocean	1,990
Yukon	Bering Sea	1,980
Rio Grande	Gulf of Mexico	1,900
Brahmaputra	Bay of Bengal	1,800
Indus	Arabian Sea	1,800
Danube	Black Sea	1,780
Japura	Amazon River	1,750
Euphrates	Shatt al Arab	1,700
Zambezi	Indian Ocean	1,700
Tocantins	Para River	1,680
Orinoco	Atlantic Ocean	1,600
Amu	Aral Sea	1,580
Paraguay	Parana River	1,580
Ural	Caspian Sea	1,580

2

50 LONGEST RIVERS OF THE WORLD
(Miles rounded to nearest 10)

River	Outflow	Miles
Ganges	Bay of Bengal	1,560
Salween	Andaman Sea	1,500
Arkansas	Mississippi River	1,460
Colorado	Gulf of California	1,450
Dnieper	Black Sea	1,420
Negro	Amazon	1,400
Syr	Aral Sea	1,370
Irrawaddy	Bay of Bengal	1,340
Orange	Atlantic Ocean	1,300
Red	Atchafalaya River	1,290
Columbia	Pacific Ocean	1,240
Don	Sea of Azov	1,220
Peace	Slave River	1,210
Xi	South China Sea	1,200
Tigris	Shatt al Arab	1,180
Angara	Yenisey River	1,150
Songhua	Amur River	1,150
Snake	Columbia River	1,040

I. WORD PROCESSING: TABLE—REPEATING TABLE HEADING ROWS

Study Lesson 79 in your Word Manual. Complete all of the shaded steps while at your computer. Then format the documents that follow.

Document Processing

Table
79-35
Boxed Table

Follow these steps to create a boxed table:

1. Apply a 100 percent shading to Row 1.
2. Apply a 25 percent shading to Row 2. Your completed table may look different from the table shown.

FIFTY FREQUENTLY MISSPELLED WORDS	
Word	Common Business Meaning
Accommodate	House or contain
Advice	Guidance
Apparently	Evidently
Analysis	Examination
Annual	Yearly
Apparent	Obvious or clear
Appreciated	Valued
Argument	Quarrel or squabble
Assistance	Help
Association	Friendship or relationship
Attention	Notice or interest
Believe	Think or accept as true
Based	Found or established
Before	Previous to
Benefit	Advantage; help
Calendar	Datebook or schedule
Category	Group or class
Changeable	Variable or unpredictable
Committed	Dedicated or steadfast
Completing	Finishing
Consensus	Agreement
Compliance	Conformity
Corporation	Company
Current	Present
Definite	Exact or distinct
Exceed	Go beyond
Guarantee	Assurance or promise
Incorporated	Included
Independent	Self-governing or free

FIFTY FREQUENTLY MISSPELLED WORDS	
Word	Common Business Meaning
Initial	First
Issue	Subject or concern
Judgment	Ruling or decision
Limited	Incomplete or restricted
Location	Site or place
Occasionally	Infrequently
Occurrence	Event or incident
Operating	In service or working
Operation	Process or procedure
Participation	Contribution or involvement
Personnel	Employees
Precede	Come first or go before
Prepared	Ready or arranged
Probably	Most likely
Projects	Assignments or tasks
Proposed	Planned or anticipated
Recommend	Advise or suggest
Sufficient	Enough or adequate
Technical	Scientific or procedural
Together	Jointly or collectively
Writing	Script

Table 79-36 Ruled Table

Open the file for Table 79-35 and make the following changes:

1. Change the shading in Row 1 to clear.
2. Change the table format to a ruled table.
3. Insert these new rows of information in alphabetical order within the table:

Noticeable	Visible
Principal	Main or most important
Principle	Belief or theory
Schedule	Timetable or plan

Table 79-37 Boxed Table

Follow these steps to create a boxed table:

1. Format the table in landscape orientation.
2. Apply a 100 percent shading to the title row.
3. Apply a 25 percent shading to the column heading row.

INVESTMENT SUMMARY				
Limited Partnership	**Date of Issue**	**Initial Cost**	**Dividend***	**Owner**
HS Properties	January 2010	$ 50,000	$ 6,066	Alpha Association
Northern Lumber	May 2009	50,000	4,750	CXT Corporation
United Western Real Estate	February 2010	50,000	7,500	Smith & Sons Incorporated
United Inland Real Estate	December 2010	100,000	12,250	Q and S Company
*Annual dividends based on current market analysis.				

Tables With Predesigned Formats

Goals

- Type at least 43wpm/5'/5e.
- Correctly use Word's table styles feature.
- Correctly format a predesigned table.

A. WARMUP

alphabet	1	Judge Hank Powell quickly gave six embezzlers a stiff fine.
number/symbol	2	(ali41@cs.com) (10%) Guy & Lee 7/8 In! $5.40 *f.o.b. #26-39
easy	3	Claudia may sign the title to her auto when she is in town.

Skillbuilding

B. 12-SECOND SPEED SPRINTS

Take three 12-second timed writings on each line.

4 Jake moved to amend the law to let the worker take the job.
5 Jan and her son may make a bowl of fish and a cup of cocoa.
6 Jane can buy fuel for the old blue auto at the nearby lots.
7 Kay and she may both visit us in May when they are in town.
' ' ' ' 5 ' ' ' '10' ' ' '15' ' ' '20' ' ' '25' ' ' '30' ' ' '35' ' ' '40' ' ' '45' ' ' '50' ' ' '55' ' ' '60

C. TECHNIQUE PRACTICE: TAB KEY

Press Tab 1 time between words. Type each line 2 times.

Press Tab where you see the → symbol.

8 are→ Mag→ Uzi→ Lew→ Mel→ adz→ ace→ ale→ Jew→ air→ Poe
9 axe→ Job→ Leo→ Mia→ Jon→ Peg→ arc→ ago→ ate→ Pia→ Una
10 aha→ Ott→ Ivy→ zag→ ape→ Obi→ Ike→ Hsu→ and→ asp→ zip
11 May→ Liz→ Lou→ Kit→ Ned→ Kim→ Ham→ age→ aft→ zoo→ Mel

Take two 5-minute timed writings.

Goal: At least 43wpm/5'/5e

D. 5-MINUTE TIMED WRITING

```
12      Finding a job is a challenge in today's job market,       11
13 but there are some steps you can take to remain competitive    23
14 in the job market. First of all, be sure you know something    35
15 about the company. Does it have offices in a location to       48
16 which you would move, and is the position in that company      58
17 one in which you would like to spend the next five to ten      69
18 years of your working life?                                    75
19      To be successful during the interview, you need to        85
20 know yourself. What are your strengths, and what are your      97
21 weaknesses, if any? Be sure to emphasize your unique skills   109
22 both in your resume and during the interview. Let others      120
23 know what makes you the best candidate for the job. Some      132
24 excellent traits to emphasize would be enthusiasm, a high     143
25 motivation level, and an excellent work ethic.                153
26      When you go for your interview, take into account how   164
27 you dress. Choose your wardrobe as you would for your first   178
28 day on the job. If you are uncertain as to the particular     187
29 dress code, always err on the side of conservatism. Also,     199
30 be mindful of your personal grooming. Make certain your       210
31 hair is trimmed and neat.                                      215
     1 | 2 | 3 | 4 | 5 | 6 | 7 | 8 | 9 | 10 | 11 | 12
```

Formatting

E. PREDESIGNED TABLES

Predesigned table styles are used to quickly refine the look and layout of a table and to format major table elements, such as title blocks and total lines, in unique ways. Bolding and varying font sizes have been used up to this point to distinguish the title, subtitle, and column headings in a table. A table style will distinguish these table elements in a more refined way through colorful, customized designs. As with any style, repeating a table style also ensures design consistency.

Table styles help comprehension by giving readers visual style cues for different content. For example, if the bottom table row includes a total line, a table style option could be used to format that row in a distinct way. Likewise, a unique treatment could be applied to the first column if the content calls for it.

F. WORD PROCESSING: TABLE—STYLES

GO TO Word Manual

Study Lesson 80 in your Word Manual. Complete all of the shaded steps while at your computer. Then format the documents that follow.

Document Processing

Table
80-38
Predesigned Table

Your completed tables may look different from the tables shown.

1. Apply a table style of your choice.
2. In Rows 1 and 2, verify that all text is bolded.
3. In Row 2, align the column headings at the bottom center.

HIGH-YIELD CD RATES 1-Year Deposits			
Institution	Rate	APY	Minimum Deposit
ADSCapital.com	2.45%	2.70%	$10,000
Amber Direct	2.50%	2.50%	10,000
Arizona First National Bank	2.18%	2.20%	5,000
Chorus Bank	2.71%	2.74%	10,000
GCBank.com	2.57%	2.60%	1,000
GMBC Bank	2.71%	2.75%	500
HTSM Direct	2.27%	2.30%	10
New Mercantile	2.35%	2.38%	10,000
Nexus Bank	2.53%	2.56%	1,000
Regal Capital Bank	2.45%	2.45%	2,000
State Bank	2.51%	2.54%	500
State Bank of Indiana	2.30%	2.32%	5,000
UTCDirect.com	2.52%	2.55%	8,000
Average	**2.47%**	**2.51%**	**$ 4,847**

Table
80-39
Predesigned Table

1. Apply a table style of your choice.
2. In Rows 1 and 2, verify that all text is bolded.
3. In Row 2, align the column headings at the bottom center.

BUILDING DIRECTORY National Convention Center			
No.	Room Name	Seating	Square Feet
102	Alabama	35	400
104	Colorado	150	1,600
106	Delaware	25	350
108	Georgia	50	600
202	Montana	35	400
204	Nevada	50	600
206	New Jersey	300	3,200
208	Pennsylvania	350	3,600

Table
80-40
Predesigned Table

1. Apply a table style of your choice.
2. In Rows 1 and 2, verify that all text is bolded.
3. In Row 2, align the column headings at the bottom center.

ABC MEMBER VACATIONS Promotional Sailing Prices*						
	7-Day Cruises			12-Day Cruises		
Location	Interior	Ocean-View	Balcony	Interior	Ocean-View	Balcony
Alaska	$ 599	$ 699	$1,299	$1,199	$1,299	$1,899
Canada	965	1,290	1,445	1,565	1,890	2,045
Caribbean	739	839	1,239	1,139	1,239	1,839
Hawaii	699	799	1,999	1,299	1,399	2,699
Mexico	599	749	849	999	1,149	1,249
Panama Canal	1,299	1,749	2,099	1,699	2,049	2,449
*All prices are subject to change.						

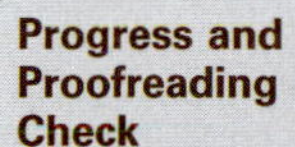

Progress and Proofreading Check

Documents designated as Proofreading Checks serve as a check of your proofreading skill. Your goal is to have zero typographical errors when the GDP software first scores the document.

Strategies for Career Success

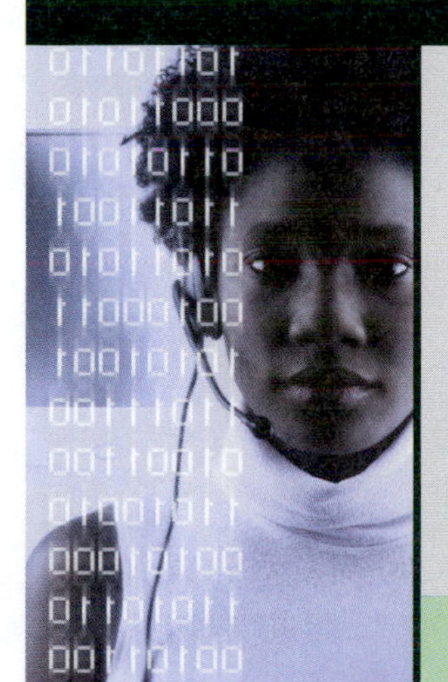

Cell Phone Manners Matter

Mind your cell phone manners! Although the cell phone allows you to keep in touch with your boss, coworkers, and clients, it also requires you to consider your communication etiquette. One of the worst violations of etiquette and safety is driving and talking at the same time. Several states now have laws restricting or forbidding cell phone use while driving. It is much safer to pull off the road to make or answer a call.

Consider others when you use a cell phone in a public place (for example, a restaurant). Don't use your cell phone at the movies or in a public restroom. If you use the phone in public, talk quietly and watch what you say. Cell phones in meetings can distract others or interrupt the meeting completely; some companies prohibit them in business meetings.

Your Turn: Observe cell phone users in a public place. Are they mindful of others when they use their phones?

Outcomes Assessment on Part 4

Test 4

5-Minute Timed Writing

```
 1      Many business firms create their own special documents  11
 2  today by using software packages that are designed to do    23
 3  the job. These packages help people with limited design     34
 4  skills create pages with very little effort. The challenge, 48
 5  though, is for the person to design the pages effectively   57
 6  so that the readers will read them. After all, the reason   69
 7  for putting in all that time and money is to get people to  81
 8  read the articles.                                          85
 9      Designing pages that are easy to read is not quite as   98
10  easy as it seems. For example, a reader may be confused if 107
11  a page has too many headlines. Instead, a reader may want  119
12  to read fewer headlines that are printed in large type.    130
13      Desktop publishers require just a few good tools to    141
14  interest the reader. A good plan to use is to be sure to   152
15  put the most important articles at the top of the first    164
16  page and the less important articles on the inside pages.  175
17  The use of bullets or side headings is also a helpful guide 187
18  to help a reader zip through pages. A final suggestion is  199
19  to use pictures and graphics that can make the text much   210
20  more interesting to read.                                  215
      1 | 2 | 3 | 4 | 5 | 6 | 7 | 8 | 9 | 10 | 11 | 12
```

Report Test
4-57
Memo Report

MEMO TO: All Employees Members

FROM: Judy Greenburg

DATE: July June 23, 20--

SUBJECT: Understanding Your Dental Plan

The Fulton # Community College district sent out a quarterly news letter early in June July explaining the dental plan benefits offered to all of our employees. The highlights of each plan were reviewed and many of you requested further information.

Vanguard Dental PPO

If you are a Dental Vanguard Plan member, ask the dentist specifically if he or she is a Vanguard Dental provider and if he or she is in the ppo or Premiere network. Your benefits will vary greatly depending upon the dentists affiliation. The table below includes examples of the costs you might pay with each of the three types of Vanguard Dental providers.

Bottom-align column headings. Single-space the table.

VANGUARD DENTAL PPO Charges For a Crown*			
Category	PPO Dentist	SS Out-of-Network Premiere Dentist	Out-of-Network Noncontracted Non-Contracted Dentis t
Dentists charge	$1,000	$1,000	$1,000
Vanguard's approved fee	640	800	800
Plan payment	512	640	640
Member payment	128	160	360
*Dentist's charges and approved fees are hypothetical.			

HEALTHGUARD DENTAL HMO

If yuo are a Healthguard Dental Plan member, remember that you may change your dentist any at time and as often as you wish as long as your dentist is a participating

SS

provider. Other covered family members do *not* have to choose the same dentist.

Visit www.vanguard.net and www.healthguard.net for further details and a Directory of Dentists.

urs

Correspondence Test
4-76
Business Letter in Block Style

January 10, 20-- | Mr. James F. Duncan | 229 Foster Street | Durham, NC 27701 | Dear Mr. Duncan:
¶ I am sorry that I had to end our phone call so abruptly yesterday. I would like to respond to both of your questions more specifically and give you a few more details regarding the tax consequences of hiring your daughter as an employee in your business.

1. You will need to issue her a W-2 form if you are paying her as an employee this year.
2. You cannot deduct her wages as a business expense on Schedule C because she is over the age of 19 and because you have paid her more than $600 this year.

¶ Please check with your tax attorney, and read IRS Publication 15 for further details. Sincerely yours, | Arlene R. Weiser | Attorney at Law | urs | PS: You may want to discuss this matter with your daughter before calling your tax attorney for an appointment. | bc: Peggy Jennings

Table Test
4-41
Boxed Table

Apply a 100 percent shading to Row 1 and a 25 percent shading to Row 3 and Row 11.

VALENCIA MEADOWS POOL Lesson Schedule*			
Session A		Session B	
Time	Code	Time	Code
7:10-8:10 a.m.	3508.310	7:05-8:05 a.m.	4001.910
8:20-9:20 a.m.	3509.311	8:25-9:25 a.m.	4002.911
9:30-10:30 a.m.	3510.312	9:40-10:30 a.m.	4003.912
10:45-11:15 a.m.	3511.313	10:35-11:35 a.m.	4004.913
12:05-1:05 p.m.	3512.314	12:15-1:15 p.m.	4005.914
5:40-6:40 p.m.	3513.315	5:10-6:10 p.m.	4006.915
7:15-8:15 p.m.	3514.316	7:15-8:15 p.m.	4007.931
*Session A begins June 15; Session B begins August 1.			

Specialized Applications

5 PART

Keyboarding in Information Technology (IT) Services

Work in the IT services cluster involves designing, developing, managing, and operating communication and IT systems, networks, and related hardware and software for telecommunications and computing services.

Opportunities in IT Services

People working in telecommunications design and maintain telephone, satellite, and laser communication systems. Among the numerous IT jobs are programmer, software engineer, technical support representative, information systems operator/analyst, and network administrator. Satellites above the earth receive and send signals, thus speeding up communications. Skilled engineers design systems that enhance the ways by which people communicate.

We are all globally connected by technology, and IT services support those necessary connections. Technology is spreading at an ever-increasing rate and affecting every aspect of our daily lives. This industry is full of opportunity for individuals with superior technical and mathematical skills. The ability to communicate complex ideas clearly, handle many details, and solve problems is an asset. Of course, keyboarding proficiency is critical.

Goals

Keyboarding

- Demonstrate improved speed and accuracy when operating the keyboard by touch.
- Type at least 47 words per minute on a 5-minute timed writing with no more than 5 errors.

Language Arts

- Demonstrate acceptable proofreading skills, including using proofreaders' marks correctly.
- Demonstrate acceptable language arts skills in punctuation, grammar, and mechanics.
- Demonstrate acceptable language arts skills in composing and spelling.

Word Processing

- Use appropriate word processing commands necessary to complete document processing activities successfully.

Document Processing

- Correctly format international business documents, formal report projects, medical office documents, and legal office documents.

Objective Test

- Answer questions with acceptable accuracy on an objective test.

UNIT 17

International Formatting

LESSON 81
International Formatting—Canada

LESSON 82
International Formatting—Mexico

LESSON 83
International Formatting—France

LESSON 84
International Formatting—Germany

LESSON 85
International Formatting—China

International Formatting—Canada

Goals

- Demonstrate improved speed and accuracy while typing.
- Demonstrate acceptable language arts skills in agreement between pronouns and verbs.
- Correctly use Word's paper size feature.
- Correctly format a letter and a table on metric paper.
- Correctly format a letter with an international address and a date line using the day/month/year format.

A. WARMUP

alphabet	1	Amazingly, a few of the discotheques now provide jukeboxes.
concentration	2	intellectualization disadvantageousness deindustrialization
easy	3	A naughty chap may ambush the fiendish cowhand if he ducks.

Skillbuilding

B. MAP+: ALPHABET

Follow the GDP software directions for this exercise to improve keystroking accuracy.

C. PROGRESSIVE PRACTICE: ALPHABET

Follow the GDP software directions for this exercise to improve keystroking speed.

Language Arts

Study the rules at the right.

D. AGREEMENT

RULE agreement pronoun

Some pronouns (*anybody, each, either, everybody, everyone, much, neither, no one, nobody,* and *one*) are always singular and take a singular verb. Other pronouns (*all, any, more, most, none,* and *some*) may be singular or plural, depending on the noun to which they refer.

Each of the employees has finished his or her task.
Much remains to be done.
Most of the pie was eaten, but most of the cookies were left.

RULE agreement intervening words

Disregard any intervening words that come between the subject and verb when establishing agreement.

That box, containing the books and pencils, has not been found.
Alex, accompanied by Tricia and Roxie, is attending the conference and taking his computer.

Edit each sentence to correct any errors.

4 Everybody who signed up for the trips are to be at Building
5 16.

6 All the tourists are sending cards to us from their hotels.

7 Everyone on the trip, including spouses, have been having
8 fun.

9 Some of the postcards from their vacations are not arriving.

10 Two of the sales reps from Region 4 were given cash bonuses.

11 The fastest runner from all five teams are receiving a
12 trophy.

Formatting

E. METRIC PAPER SIZE

Paper size for correspondence in the United States is typically 8.5 by 11 inches. However, correspondence in most foreign countries is often formatted on metric-sized paper. The most popular of these is called A4 paper, and it measures 210 by 297 millimeters—approximately 8.25 by 11.75 inches.

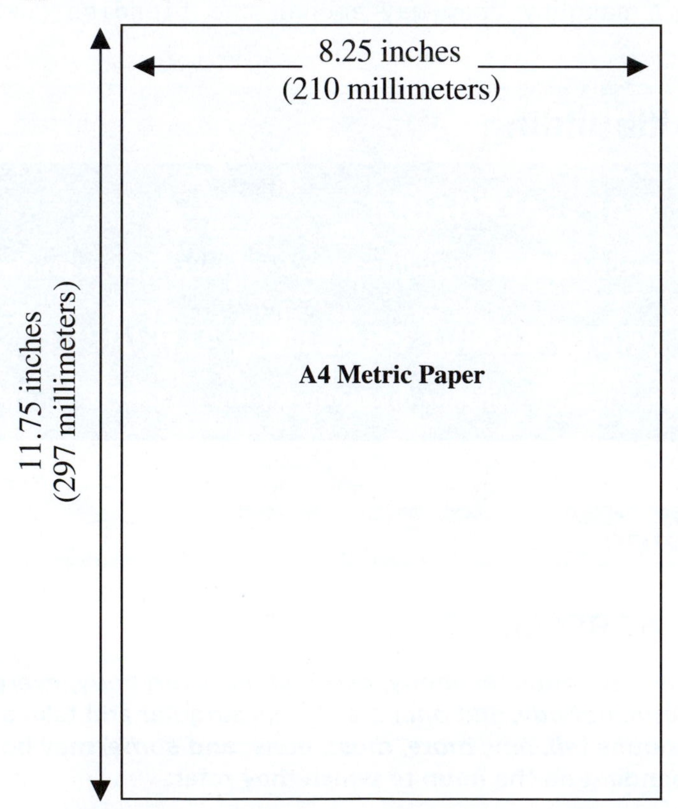

F. METRIC ENVELOPE SIZE

A standard large envelope (No. 10) measures 9.5 by 4.125 inches. A large envelope for metric size paper is called DL, and it measures 110 by 220 millimeters—approximately 4.33 by 8.67 inches. The No. 10 envelope is not as deep as the metric envelope, but it is slightly wider.

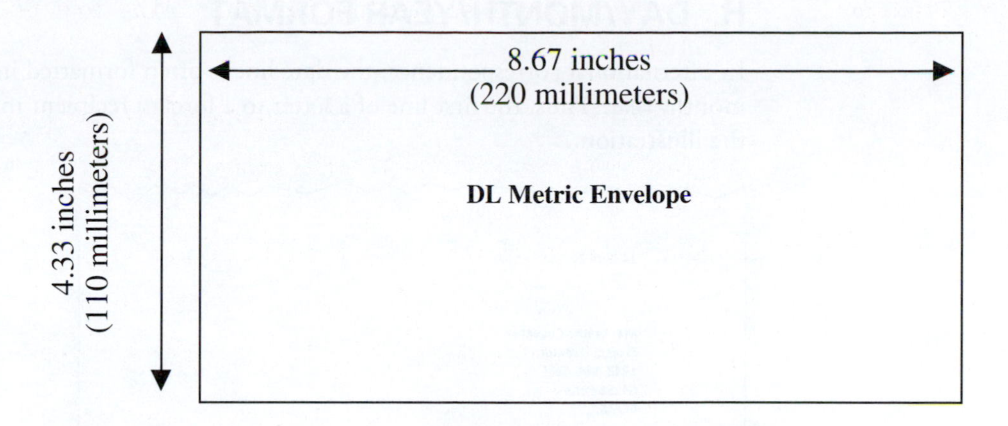

G. INTERNATIONAL ADDRESSES IN LETTERS

International addressing is becoming more common with the increased popularity of the Internet and frequently requires changes to the address lines, such as the addition of special codes, abbreviations, and capitalization. Individual organizational preferences for international address formatting will vary. Therefore, the most technologically efficient formats for international addresses will be used, including the use of all-caps and the name of the country spelled out as the last entry of the address, as shown in the examples below.

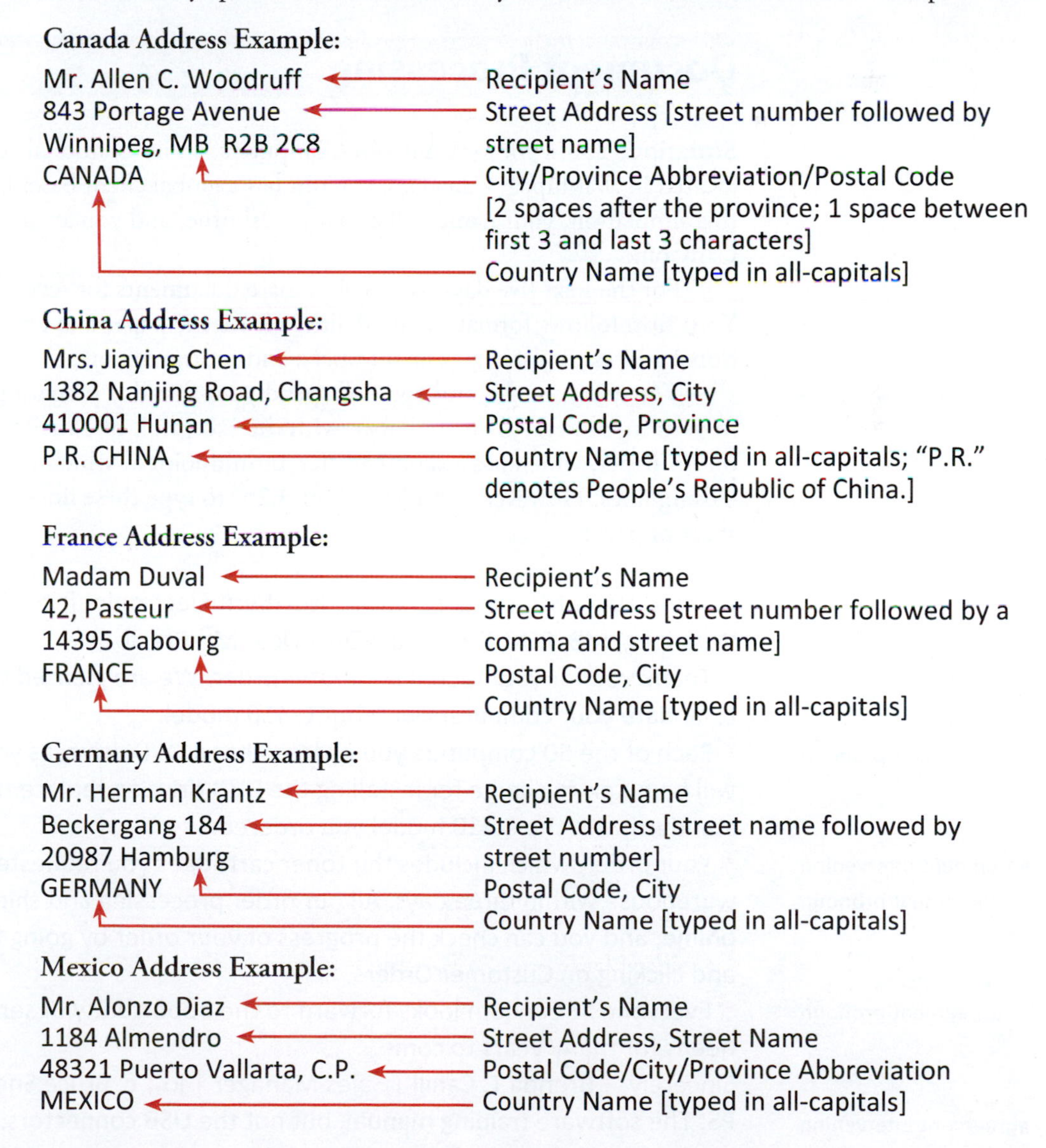

H. DAY/MONTH/YEAR FORMAT

In international correspondence, the date line is often formatted in this sequence: day, month, year. Thus, the first line of a letter to a foreign recipient may appear as shown in the illustration.

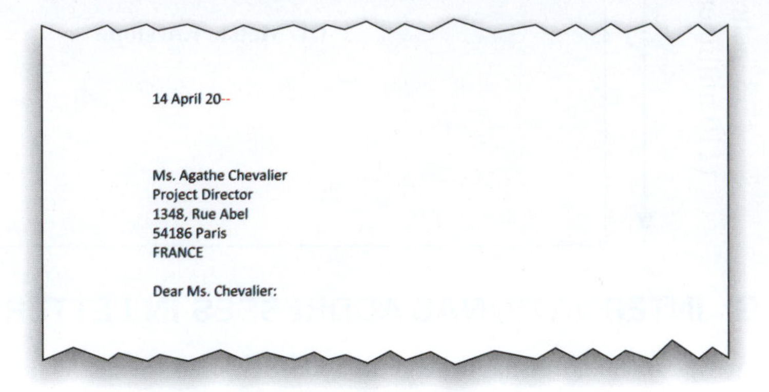

14 April 20--

Ms. Agathe Chevalier
Project Director
1348, Rue Abel
54186 Paris
FRANCE

Dear Ms. Chevalier:

I. WORD PROCESSING: PAPER SIZE

Study Lesson 81 in your Word Manual. Complete all of the shaded steps while at your computer. Then format the documents that follow.

Document Processing

Situation: You work for CanCom Computers, an international computer manufacturer located in Winnipeg, Canada. CanCom has a global client base. For the purposes of this simulation, your name will be Janet Osborne, and you are an executive assistant for CanCom.

For the next five days, you will prepare documents for several CanCom executives. Your firm follows formatting guidelines for metric paper and envelope size and international addresses, dates, phone numbers, and measurements.

Today is June 22, and you will spend your first day preparing documents that appear in your in-basket. All documents—with the exception of e-mail messages—will be typed on A4 paper, which has a slightly different midpoint at which to start typing the date and closing lines. However, use a left tab of 3.25″ to type these lines, as you do on a standard sheet of paper.

Correspondence 81-77
Business Letter in Modified-Block Style

22 June 20-- | Mr. David L. Brazil | Northern Electronics Inc. | 389 Boyd Avenue | Winnipeg, MB ROC 3Z8 | CANADA | Dear Mr. Brazil:

¶ Thank you for your recent computer order. We are pleased that you have decided to update your computers with our C-410 model.

agreement pronoun

¶ Each of the 50 computers you ordered has a DVD drive, as you requested. There will be no extra charge for installing the DVD drive to replace the CD drive that comes standard with the C-410 model you ordered.

agreement intervening
agreement pronoun

¶ Your order, which includes the toner cartridges you requested, is leaving our warehouse within three days. All our order processing and shipping departments are online, and you can check the progress of your order by going to www.cancom.com and clicking on Customer Orders.

agreement pronoun

¶ Everyone at CanCom looks forward to the opportunity of serving your computer needs for many years to come.

Sincerely, | Brenda T. Cahill | Sales Manager | jo | c: Bruce Snell, Lloyd Wilkes |

agreement intervening

PS: The software training manual, but not the USB connectors, is on back order. We anticipate it to be shipped on June 30.

Table 81-42
Boxed Table

Prepare Table 81-42 in landscape orientation. Apply shading of 25 percent to Row 2.

CUSTOMER SHIPPING INFORMATION				
Name	**Address**	**City/Province**	**Postal Code**	**Kilometers**
Abrams, Andrew	2218 College Avenue	Regina, SK	S0G 4C0	571
Brewer, Royce	345 Barr Road, NW	Calgary, AB	T1Y 1A8	1,208
Lazano, Gary	1084 Rue Coderre	Montreal, QC	H1A 1J2	1,821
Osborn, Connie	8701 Pine Street	Sudbury, ON	P3A 1B1	1,254
Purdy, Vickie	383 Jubilee Road	Halifax, NS	B3H 1B4	2,573
Rollins, Helene	811 Pears Avenue	Toronto, ON	M4C 1A3	2,222
Swenson, Hillary	284 Maple Avenue	Brandon, MB	R7A 0C8	199
Tetrault, Brandon	844 Ross Street	Red Deer, AB	T4N 0B6	1,192
Williams, Allen	1840 Oxford Street	Victoria, BC	V8N 1B5	2,295

Table 81-43
Boxed Table

Open the file for Table 81-42 and make the following changes:

1. Add the following entry after Royce Brewer's information:

   `Collins, Steve | 816 55th Street, NW | Edmonton, AB | T5A 0C5 | 1,305`

2. Sort Column E so that the kilometers are displayed in a descending order.

Keyboarding Connection

Finding People on the Internet

Remember that long-lost friend from high school? Well, he or she may not be lost for long if you use the Internet's assistance. It is easy to search for a person on the Internet.

Social networking sites such as LinkedIn, MySpace, and Facebook allow you to search for lost friends, family, and coworkers. You also can use a search engine to search for a person's name. Many schools and organizations have Web sites where you can look for old friends. When searching for someone in a search engine, it can be helpful to type the location or other identifying information along with the person's name.

Your Turn: Access a search engine, and conduct a search on your own name. Then try a search for a high school friend.

International Formatting—Mexico

Goals

- Type at least 44wpm/5'/5e.
- Correctly format international URLs.
- Correctly use Word's insert symbol feature.
- Correctly format an e-mail message, a business report, and a table.

A. WARMUP

alphabet	1	Jack Farmer realized that big yellow quilts were expensive.
one hand	2	barber poplin car joy feared million area hilly craft milky
easy	3	If the town signs an entitlement, the profit may go to her.

Skillbuilding

B. SUSTAINED PRACTICE: CAPITALS

Take a 1-minute timed writing on the boxed paragraph to establish your base speed. Then take a 1-minute timed writing on the following paragraph. As soon as you equal or exceed your base speed on this paragraph, move to the next, more difficult paragraph.

4	A visit to Europe is a vacation that many people dream	11
5	of doing. There are many countries to visit and hundreds of	23
6	sites to see if you can spend at least four weeks on the	34
7	continent. A trip to Europe is one you will never forget.	46
8	If you decide to visit Europe, the months of June and	11
9	July would probably be the prettiest, but they would also	23
10	be the busiest. England, France, and Germany are popular	34
11	countries to visit; Spain is popular for Americans as well.	46
12	In England you will want to visit St. Paul's Cathedral	11
13	and Big Ben. And, of course, when you are in England, you	23
14	do not want to pass up the opportunity to see Buckingham	34
15	Palace. Plan on staying a few days to see all the sites.	45
16	France certainly is a highlight of any European visit.	11
17	Paris offers many sites such as the Arc de Triomphe, the	23
18	Louvre, the Eiffel Tower, and the Gothic Cathedral of Notre	35
19	Dame. Other cities to visit are Nice, Lyon, and Versailles.	46

1 | 2 | 3 | 4 | 5 | 6 | 7 | 8 | 9 | 10 | 11 | 12

Take two 5-minute timed writings.

Goal: At least 44wpm/5'/5e

C. 5-MINUTE TIMED WRITING

```
20      Critical thinking is a skill that can be learned and      11
21  applied to more than a few situations. There are many ways    23
22  to describe critical thinking skill. The common theme that    34
23  runs through each of these descriptions is related to the     46
24  use of cognitive skill.                                       51
25      With this skill, the person thinks with a purpose in      62
26  mind and likely directs some of the focus toward goals. The   74
27  person looks at a situation and decides rationally what to    86
28  believe or not to believe. In critical thinking, the goal     97
29  is to achieve understanding, judge more than one viewpoint,  109
30  and then solve problems.                                     114
31      After a person thinks through all the elements of the    125
32  problem, a decision is made based on all of the facts and    137
33  exact findings. Bias, prejudice, and feelings should not     148
34  sway the final outcome.                                      153
35      Critical thinking is useful in reading, listening,       163
36  speaking, and writing. A critical thinker will ask great     175
37  questions. He or she listens carefully to others and gives   187
38  feedback. A critical thinker seeks the truth with zeal and   198
39  then willingly accepts change when new facts are presented.  210
40  Critical thinking is needed for problem solving.             220
      1 | 2 | 3 | 4 | 5 | 6 | 7 | 8 | 9 | 10 | 11 | 12
```

Formatting

D. INTERNATIONAL URLs

Uniform resource locators (URLs) identify a site on the World Wide Web where specific information can be found. In international URLs, an abbreviation for a country is often included in the URL, as shown in red below.

Country	Uniform Resource Locator (URL)
Canada	http://www.samuels.animate.chap2.ca
Mexico	http://www.reloj.baja.mx
France	http://www.education.grad.up.fr
Germany	http://www.mercedes.de
China	http://www.peking.transportation.costs.cn

E. WORD PROCESSING: SYMBOL—INSERT

Accents and other marks are used in many languages to indicate how words should be pronounced. Some examples of commonly used symbols are shown below.

Symbol	Application
á	Yucatán
é	Quertéro
í	García
ñ	Señor
ó	Torreón
ú	Cancún
ü	Nürnberg

Study Lesson 82 in your Word Manual. Complete all of the shaded steps while at your computer. Then format the documents that follow.

Document Processing

Situation: Today is June 23, your second day, and you will prepare an e-mail message and a business report with a table. Begin with the e-mail. Type the e-mail greeting `Hi, Mr. Sanchez:` and the body shown below in correct format. Type your name (`Janet`) as the sender, with the following writer's identification: `Janet Osborne | E-mail: josborne@cancom.com | Phone: +1.204.555.8823`

Correspondence
82-78
E-Mail Message

R-5C–D: E-Mail Message

¶ As you know, sales in our international divisions have been accelerating since the advent of our new Genesis laptop. As a result, several new manufacturing plants will open in the next eight years. All of the plants are to open in France and Germany.

¶ To market our new manufacturing plants and promote the Genesis, the Marketing Division is planning to open new Web sites on the Genesis home page. The following links will be added to advertise our plant expansion:

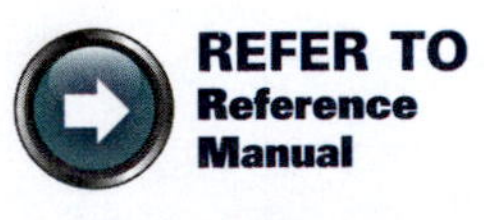

R-12C–D: Formatting Lists

- Lyon, France: http://www.lyon.fr.genesis.new.html
- Reims, France: http://www.reims.fr.genesis.new.html
- Bremen, Germany: http://www.bremen.de.genesis.new.html
- Leipzig, Germany: http://www.leipzig.de.genesis.new.html
- Nürnberg, Germany: http://www.nurnberg.de.genesis.new.html

Use an umlaut in Nürnberg

(continued on next page)

agreement pronoun

agreement intervening

¶ Each of our sites, including the plants in France and Germany, is scheduled to go online in late August. Until then, plan to work with the Marketing Division personnel to implement the marketing plan we discussed at our meeting last month (the International Proposal). When the sites go online in August, we hope to maximize our exposure on the WWW. If they are as successful as we believe they will be, our promotional campaign may also be implemented at our plants in Torreón, Querétaro, and León.

Use accent marks in Torreón, Querétaro, and León.

Report 82-58
Business Report

Use A4 paper.

MEXICO TRAVEL DESTINATIONS
Popular Sites Visited
June 23, 20--

¶ Since the mid-1990s, national parks in Mexico have become popular tourist sites for visitors from the Americas, Asia, and Europe. Because of this popularity, an increasing number of requests have been made for maps and travel brochures from our Visitors' Bureau. Therefore, in the coming weeks, we will be publishing several new maps and brochures to accommodate these requests.

BROCHURES

¶ The brochures will include a detailed description of the site, providing information on beginning and ending visitation schedules, highlights of the site, and popular photography locations. Brochures will be prepared on the sites and locations shown below. The fourth column indicates how many years each site has been ranked among the top ten most popular sites in Mexico.

Use accent marks as shown in the city and state names in this table.

Site	City	State	Top 10
Bosque de la Primavera	Guadalajara	Jalisco	4 yrs.
Cancún	Quintana Roo	Cancún	10 yrs.
Chichén Itzá	Merida	Yucatán	8 yrs.
Dzibilchaltún	Merida	Yucatán	7 yrs.
El Tepozteco	Tepoztlán	Morelos	5 yrs.
Fuerte de San Miguel	Campeche	Campeche	5 yrs.
Parque Papagayo	Acapulco	Guerrero	4 yrs.
Temple Pyramid	Cholula	Puebla	3 yrs.
Uxmal	Merida	Yucatán	6 yrs.

(continued on next page)

MAPS

¶ Maps will be supplied for these sites, with detailed insets to guide visitors from the nearest cities to the tourist attractions. Walking trails and resting stations will be highlighted, and approximate walking times will be noted on the maps. Individual maps will be prepared for each site, and an area map will also be available for each city. Everyone is encouraged to send his or her advertising pieces to Señor Garcia, Public Relations Director.

International Formatting—France

Goals

- Demonstrate improved speed and accuracy while typing.
- Demonstrate acceptable proofreading skills by comparing lines of copy.
- Correctly format a letter, a table, and an e-mail message with dot-style telephone numbers and international telephone access codes.

A. WARMUP

alphabet
1 She was watching Alex Trebek's fun TV quiz game "Jeopardy!"

substitution: *m* and *n*
2 man men amen hymn unman norm name many unmet norm mine mend

easy
3 Six girls may buy a new gown for the big social in the gym.

Skillbuilding

B. MAP+: NUMBERS

Follow the GDP software directions for this exercise to improve keystroking accuracy.

PPP PRETEST » PRACTICE » POSTTEST

C. PRETEST: Common Letter Combinations

PRETEST
Take a 1-minute timed writing.

4 Della Daly will return to Detroit because she believes 11
5 her income will increase. She will share an apartment with 23
6 Joann to save on rent. Their rental was lowered, however, 35
7 because of the intent complaints of the outraged dwellers. 46

1 | 2 | 3 | 4 | 5 | 6 | 7 | 8 | 9 | 10 | 11 | 12

D. PRACTICE: Word Beginnings

PRACTICE
Speed Emphasis:
If you made no more than 1 error on the Pretest, type each *individual* line 2 times.
Accuracy Emphasis:
If you made 2 or more errors, type each *group* of lines (as though it were a paragraph) 2 times.

8 re- repel renew remit relax refer ready react really reveal
9 in- inept insert inert inset input infer index incur inches
10 be- beauty bears beams beach below being began befit beside
11 de- deny decide defend design detain devise depress deforms

E. PRACTICE: Word Endings

12 -ly truly weekly madly lowly early daily apply hilly simply
13 -ed sized hired dated opened cited based acted added showed
14 -nt plant meant giant front event count agent amount fluent
15 -al Val mental cereal bridal fungal normal literal informal

POSTTEST

Repeat the Pretest timed writing and compare performance.

F. POSTTEST: Common Letter Combinations

Language Arts

Compare these lines with lines 35–40 on page 331. Edit the lines to correct any errors.

G. PROOFREADING

```
16      Criticle thinking is useful in reading, listenning,
17 speaking, or writing. A critical thinker may ask great
18 questions. He or she listens carefully to others and gives
19 feedback. A critical tinker seeks truth with zeal and
20 then willingly accepts changes when new facts are presented.
21 Critical thinking is important for problem solving.
```

Formatting

H. DOT-STYLE TELEPHONE NUMBERS

In the United States, hyphens are used in telephone numbers. A hyphen is used after the 3-digit area code and after the first 3 digits of the telephone number; for example, 701-555-1234. Another format, used in many countries, is to replace the hyphens with periods without spaces before or after; for example, 701.555.4832 or 818.555.3424.

I. INTERNATIONAL TELEPHONE ACCESS CODES

Special access codes are needed to make a phone call from one country to another. To make an international call, dial the IDD (International Direct Dialing) code first. Then dial the country code for the country you are calling, next the area code (if any), and finally the telephone number. The IDD code in many countries changes periodically.

The United States and Canada have the same IDD (011) and country code (1). When you provide a United States (or Canadian) telephone number in a document being sent to an international address, use a plus sign (+) in front of the area code, instead of the IDD code, followed by 1 (the country code for the United States). For example, if you are writing a letter to an international address and you are giving your own telephone number in Los Angeles, you would express your number as +1.323.555.8923. Some of the more common access codes are listed on the next page.

Country	From U.S. to Foreign Country		From Foreign Country to U.S.	
	IDD Code	Country Code	IDD Code	Country Code
Canada	011	1	011	1
China	011	86	00	1
France	011	33	00	1
Germany	011	49	00	1
Italy	011	39	00	1
Japan	011	81	001	1
Mexico	011	52	98	1
Taiwan	011	886	002	1
United Kingdom	011	44	00	1
Note: The United States and Canada have the same IDD (011) and country code (1).				

Document Processing

Situation: Today is June 24, your third day, and you will prepare a letter, a table, and an e-mail message. Begin with the letter.

Correspondence
83-79
Business Letter in Block Style

Use A4 paper.

23 June 20-- | Mr. Claude R. Moreau | Human Resources Director | Walther Techtronics | 38, Rue du Caire | 75106 Paris | FRANCE | Dear Mr. Moreau:
¶ I am pleased that we will be involved in an employee exchange this coming year. As we discussed earlier, the exchange of our 36 production employees will benefit both companies.
¶ We plan to rotate all 36 employees through the various units of our production process, starting from the raw materials division and continuing right on through our shipping operations. I have enclosed a projected rotation plan for you to review. Included in the plan are all the employee rotations we discussed at our last meeting. Please review the plan and e-mail me if you have any changes. You can e-mail me at tlambeer@cancom.com; or, if you wish to speak to me directly, you can call +00.1.204.555.9090.
¶ I look forward to working with you this coming year. As soon as we have agreed on the rotation plan, we can make copies for all affected employees. I know that everyone from our end is eagerly anticipating this collaborative effort.
Sincerely, | Tom R. Lambeer | Human Resources Manager | jo | Enclosure | c: Sheila Southern, Geraldine Gouet

Table
83-44
Boxed Table

Add 25 percent shading to Row 2.

Type the body of the table single-spaced.

PROJECTED ROTATION PLAN CanCom Group and Walther Tech tronics		
Department	**Rotation Start Date**	**Rotation End Date**
Raw Materials	3 May 20--	11 June 20--
Board Assembly	14 12 June 20--	22 July June 20--
Drive Assembly	25 July 20--	3 Sept. 20--
Power Unit	6 Sept. 20--	15 October 20--
Testing & Evaluation	October 15 20--	2 November 20--

Type the e-mail greeting, `Hi, Mr. Moreau:`, and the body shown below in correct format. Type `Janet` as the sender's name, and use the following as the writer's identification: `Janet Osborne | E-mail: josborne@cancom.com | Phone: +1.204.555.8823`

Correspondence
83-80
E-Mail Message

¶ I am sending you this e-mail to alert you to a change we must make in the rotation plan I sent you last week. We will have to refit several of our board assembly production unit relay systems during the week of 14 June through 18 June. To avoid significantly altering the remaining rotation plan, I would like to suggest that we use one-half of the drive assembly rotation period to complete the board assembly rotation.

¶ Please respond to my e-mail as soon as possible so that we can make whatever changes are necessary.

International Formatting—Germany

Goals

- Type at least 44wpm/5'/5e.
- Correctly format an e-mail message, a business letter, and a business report that include metric units of measure content.

A. WARMUP

alphabet	1	The foxy General Schwarzkopf jumbled his words on Iraqi TV.
frequent digraphs	2	he heed ache hem heel herb her chef she here shed head hear
easy	3	The proficient sleuth may own both the giant bowl and dish.

Skillbuilding

B. PROGRESSIVE PRACTICE: NUMBERS

Follow the GDP software directions for this exercise to improve keystroking speed.

C. TECHNIQUE PRACTICE: ENTER KEY

Type each line 2 times. Type each sentence on a separate line by pressing ENTER after each sentence.

4	Ah. What? We do. Speak. Stop. Ed saw her. Go. Ah. Begin it.
5	Stop. Why not? See? Get it? Why me? Who, me? Well? She can.
6	Who? See me. Read it. What? Really! Who is? So soon? Do it.
7	Who knew? Enough? What is it? Go slow. She did. How so? So?

Strategies for Career Success

Letter of Complaint

Is a poor product or bad service getting you down? By writing a concise, rational letter of complaint, you have the possibility of the reader honoring your request.

In the first paragraph, give a precise description of the product or service (for example, model and serial number). Include a general statement of the problem (for example, "It does not work properly."). In the middle section, provide the details of what went wrong (for example, when it happened or what failed). Refer to copies of invoices, checks, and so on. Describe how you were inconvenienced, with details about time and money lost. State what you want (for example, a refund, a repair, or a replacement). In the closing paragraph, ask for a timely response to the complaint (for example, "Please resolve this problem within the next two weeks.").

Your Turn: Think about the last time you experienced a poor product or service. Did you write a letter of complaint? If so, what was the response?

Take two 5-minute timed writings.

Goal: At least 44wpm/5'/5e

D. 5-MINUTE TIMED WRITING

```
 8      Proofreading skill is developed with practice. You may  11
 9  want to master several techniques that will help develop    23
10  and improve your proofreading skills.                       30
11      In order to be a successful proofreader, you will want  41
12  to schedule time to read through the completed job several  53
13  times. At the first reading, check your work to see if the  65
14  margins are correct and the page numbers are in the right   76
15  places. Determine if the spacing and the font styles are    88
16  correct. With each reading, zoom in on a specific type of   99
17  error. If possible, read your work out loud and read only  111
18  one word at a time.                                        115
19      You may find that placing a ruler under each line as   126
20  you read it will give your eyes a manageable amount of text 138
21  to read.                                                   140
22      At the next reading, be sure that the content of the   150
23  document follows a logical order. If any cited works are   162
24  included, be sure the citations are in the proper format   173
25  with complete and accurate data. Check to be sure that all 185
26  the basic rules of grammar, spelling, and punctuation have 197
27  been followed. Proofread your document when you are fresh  208
28  and alert. Remember, proofreading takes time and patience. 220
      1 | 2 | 3 | 4 | 5 | 6 | 7 | 8 | 9 | 10 | 11 | 12
```

Formatting

E. METRIC UNITS OF MEASUREMENT

The metric system of measurement was devised in 1670. It is based on units of 10 and is used by almost every nation in the world. The five common measurements in the metric system are length, area, volume, capacity, and weight and mass. The table below gives the basic units of measure used in the metric and U.S. systems.

Quantity	Metric Units of Measure	U.S. Units of Measure
Length	millimeter, centimeter, meter, kilometer	inch, foot, yard, mile
Area	square centimeter, square meter, hectare	square inch, square foot, square yard
Volume	cubic centimeter, cubic decimeter, cubic meter, liter, hectoliter	cubic inch, cubic foot, fluid ounce, pint, gallon
Weight	milligram, gram, kilogram, tonne	ounce, pound, ton

Document Processing

Situation: Today is June 25, your fourth day, and you will prepare an e-mail message, a business letter, and a multipage business report with tables. Begin with the e-mail. Type the e-mail greeting, `Hi, Mr. Kaufmann:`, and the body shown below in correct format. Type `Janet` as the sender's name, and use the following as the writer's identification: `Janet Osborne | E-mail: josborne@cancom.net | Phone: +1.204.555.8823`

Correspondence
84-81
E-Mail Message

Use an umlaut in Düsseldorf.

¶ The total conversion of our manufacturing plants to the metric system, which was discussed previously, is six months away. Ms. Eisenberg has asked for your continuing support and cooperation as you prepare employees who are presently transferring to the Düsseldorf plant in accordance with the provisions of our policies. Please send me the summary report used when you were monitoring the conversion last year.
¶ The metric system will be quite foreign to many employees, especially the younger ones, who were not involved in the planning stages. The summary report will give them a head start on metrication, as indicated in the assessment.
¶ Call Ms. Eisenberg Thursday morning (+1.204.555.8823) to discuss the Frankfurt plant closing. Plant operations will be transferred to Düsseldorf in May. She has asked that you use your judgment to monitor the quality of the operation closely until the transfer has been fully implemented.

Use an umlaut in Düsseldorf.

Correspondence
84-82
Business Letter in Block Style

Use A4 paper.

28 June 20-- | Ms. Faye Fruehauf | Marketing Department | Melitta Bentz Inc. | Hohe Weide 5 | 22753 Hamburg | GERMANY | Dear Ms. Fruehauf:
¶ Frank Sparks has asked that I send a copy of the summary report on metrics that we completed in the last quarter. As you recall, I sent you that report previously to share with the new employees at our Bremen plant.
¶ As many of the employees in the Production Division were transferred to your plant last April, it is likely that they are not yet aware of the actual impact of our metric conversion that we completed late last year. Feel free to share the summary report with all those employees.
¶ If you wish for copies of the report to be mailed directly from our office, e-mail me a list of all employees to whom the report should be sent.
Sincerely, | Sigfried Krause | Human Resources Manager | jo | Enclosure

Report
84-59
Business Report

SUMMARY REPORT ON METRICS

April 7, 20--

¶ The metric system was devised by Gabriel Mouton, a French man, in 1607. It is a system based on units of 10 and is considered by many some to be more accurate and easier to use than the Imperial system of measure used in the U.S.

¶ When it was first defined, a meter was considered to be 1/10,000,000 of the distance from the pole to the equator. This is the basis for all metric measurements; it is a system that is used by an overwhelming majority of nations around the globe.

(continued on next page)

Use an umlaut in Düsseldorf.

¶ The most common metric measurements are for length, area, volume, capacity, and weight and mass. For our Düsseldorf plant, the most crucial measurements for new employees from the U.S. will be volume. Table 1 shows metric and U.S. comparisons for weight. volume

Table 1. METRIC/U.S. COMPARISONS For Volume		
Metric Unit	**Metric Example**	**U.S. Equivalent**
Cubic centimeter	1 cubic centimeter	0.061 cubic inch
Cubic meter decimeter	1,000 cubic centimeters	0.035 cubic feet
Cubic meter	100 1,000 cubic decimeters	1.31 cubic yards
liter	1 cubic decimeter	2.21 1 pints
Hectoliter	100 liters	26.42 gallons

Use an umlaut in Düsseldorf.

The Düsseldorf plant will also be impacted by wieght measurements, though not as prominently as the volume measurements as noted in table 1. The metric and United States U.S. comparisons for weight are displayed in Table 2 below.

Table 2. METRIC/U.S. COMPARISONS For Weight		
Metric Unit	**Metric Example**	**U.S. Equivalent**
Miligram	1 milligram	0.015 grain
Gram	1,000 miligrams	0.035 ounce
Kilogram	1,000 grams	2.205 pounds
tonne	1,000 kilograms	1.01 tons

(continued on next page)

¶ We are convinced that our employees will adapt quickly to the Metric System when they use it on a daily basis. Although we encourage all employees to make calculations in the metric system, it may be helpful for the first few days if they are aware of the conversion factors involved in comparing the measurement systems. The following conversions may therefore be helpful to them:

- Multiply inches by 2.45 to get centimeters
- Multiply feet by 0.305 to get meters
- Multiply miles by 1.6 to get kilometers
- Divide lbs. by 2.2 to get kilograms
- Multiply ounces by 28 to get grams
- Multiply fluid ounces by 30 to get mililiters
- Multiply gallons by 3.8 to get litters

¶ More detailed conversions and metric information can be obtained by visiting the web site for the U.S. Metric Association at http://lamar.colostate.edu/metric.html.

International Formatting—China

Goals

- Demonstrate improved speed and accuracy while typing.
- Demonstrate acceptable language arts skills in composing an e-mail message.
- Correctly format a business letter, an e-mail message, and a table containing international content.
- Successfully complete a Progress and Proofreading Check with zero errors on the first scored attempt.

A. WARMUP

alphabet	1	Four quick brown foxes jumped lazily over the resting dogs.
number/symbol	2	eck@hotmail.com 92% Cho & Orr 9/13 (Shh!) $4.57 *2010 #86-3
easy	3	Jake's amendment may also entitle the prodigy to a new job.

Skillbuilding

B. 12-SECOND SPEED SPRINTS

Take three 12-second timed writings on each line.

```
4 I will lend a hand to anyone if he or she signals for help.
5 A bushel of corn was thrown under the elm tree by the boys.
6 The giant wiry dog put half of the bones down on the chair.
7 A pair of cozy socks and a cup of soup may fix me right up.
  ''''5'''10'''15'''20'''25'''30'''35'''40'''45'''50'''55'''60
```

C. PACED PRACTICE

Follow the GDP software directions for this exercise to improve keystroking speed and accuracy.

Language Arts

D. COMPOSING AN E-MAIL MESSAGE

Compose an e-mail message to your keyboarding instructor. Use an appropriate greeting. Your instructor has a strict policy that cell phones must be turned off during class. In the first paragraph, explain that your sister is expecting her first child any day and that you would like to keep your cell phone on in case your family calls with any news. Explain that you will keep your phone on vibrate and that you will go out into the hallway to accept the call. End the e-mail with an appropriate note of appreciation.

Document Processing

Situation: Today is June 26, your fifth day, and you will prepare a letter, an e-mail message, and a table. Begin with the letter.

Correspondence 85-83
Business Letter in Block Style

Use A4 paper.

26 June 20-- | Mr. Chao Chang | Chief Technology Officer | Tian Hao Technology | 47 Renmin Road, Zhengzhou | 450347 Henan | P.R. CHINA | Dear Mr. Chang:
¶ You are one of six technology executives from various countries with whom we will be working to develop the technology alliance strategic venture. Your company has long been known for its excellence in developing green technology in a global community, and CanCom Computers is pleased to play a collaborative part with you in this venture.
¶ Our development teams have been working with their counterparts from all six participating venture companies over the past several weeks, and we look forward to this continued, cooperative spirit.
¶ Because the strategic venture includes participants from various countries, we believe it would be helpful if you could share with us any particular ideas you have for our upcoming meeting in Hefei that are unique to your country's promotion of green technology. If you could send those ideas to me, we will gladly include them in our agenda.
Sincerely, | Donna T. Parsons | Project Coordinator | jo | c: Chan Huang, Jia Wang, Charlotte Chrisler

Correspondence 85-84
E-Mail Message

Type the e-mail greeting, `Hi, Ms. Parsons:`, and the body shown below in correct format. Type `Janet` as the sender's name, and use the following as the writer's identification: `Janet Osborne` | `E-mail: josborne@cancom.com` | `Phone: +1.204.555.8823`.

¶ It is my pleasure to inform you that Jia Wang will be forwarding to your office a summary of Tian Hao Technology's ideas for the promotion of green technology. Ms. Wang's report presents a very aggressive approach to this technology, and I know many of the venture members will benefit appreciably from her ideas. She has asked that you call her at +00.1.204.555.7788 when her report arrives at CanCom.
¶ After you receive Ms. Wang's report, please forward it immediately to the other committee members. By this time next week, we should have received all six reports and will be able to set our next agenda for the Hefei meeting.

Table
85-45
Boxed Table

Use 25 percent shading for Row 2.

Progress and Proofreading Check

Documents designated as Proofreading Checks serve as a check of your proofreading skill. Your goal is to have zero typographical errors when the GDP software first scores the document.

TECHNOLOGY ALLIANCE STRATEGIC VENTURE Committee Members		
Name	**City/Country**	**Affiliation**
Bachmann, Alexis	Frankfurt, Germany	Volkert Technology
Chang, Chao	Zhengzhou, China	Tian Hao Technology
Chernov, Vasily	Saratov, Russia	Kinetic Technologies
Kapoor, Deepak	Mumbai, India	Kolkata Pradish
Parsons, Donna	Winnipeg, Canada	CanCom Computers
Uda, Yoshifumi	Osaka, Japan	Tadashi Corporation

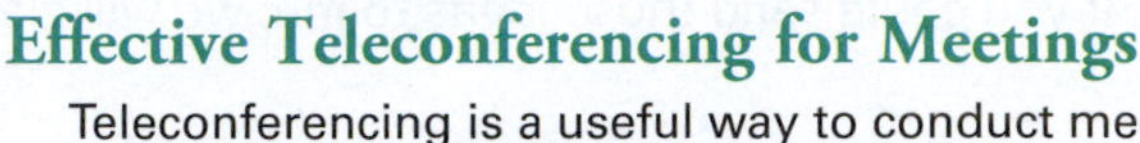

Keyboarding Connection

Effective Teleconferencing for Meetings

Teleconferencing is a useful way to conduct meetings with businesspeople across the globe. To make the best use of teleconferences, follow these guidelines.

Decide whether you will have a teleconference (audio only) or a videoconference (video and audio). Since sound quality varies greatly, use the best equipment available. Your company may already have the necessary equipment, or you might need to rent it from an audiovisual company. If you have a teleconference, there is software such as NetMeeting or WebEx to allow a presentation to be viewed in all locations via the Internet or company intranet. Make sure you test the equipment in advance and that each location has someone who has tested and knows how to use the equipment there.

Allow individual participants enough time to participate in the meeting. Distribute agendas to everyone in advance. Be sensitive to time zone differences. Since it is possible the meetings will be at an inconvenient time for some attendees, especially for international meetings, consider rotating the times of the meetings. Assign someone to prepare and e-mail to the participants a brief summary covering the main discussion topics, decisions, and action items of the meeting.

Your Turn: List what you think are the advantages and disadvantages of conducting meetings via teleconference or videoconference.

UNIT 18

Formal Report Project

LESSON 86
Formal Report Project—A

LESSON 87
Formal Report Project—B

LESSON 88
Formal Report Project—C

LESSON 89
Formal Report Project—D

LESSON 90
Formal Report Project—E

Formal Report Project—A

Goals

- Type at least 45wpm/5'/5e.
- Correctly use Word's styles feature.
- Correctly format a multipage business report.

A. WARMUP

alphabet	1	A zoo quickly bought a jinxed mauve dog with pink fur ears.
concentration	2	superstitiousnesses comprehensibilities incomprehensibility
easy	3	Dudley may then dismantle the tan bicycle out on the lanai.

Skillbuilding

B. SUSTAINED PRACTICE: PUNCTUATION

Take a 1-minute timed writing on the boxed paragraph to establish your base speed. Then take a 1-minute timed writing on the following paragraph. As soon as you equal or exceed your base speed on this paragraph, move to the next, more difficult paragraph.

```
 4      One of the strengths you must have if you are going to  11
 5  be a success in business is good writing skills. You must   23
 6  practice your writing skills every day if you want them to  35
 7  improve. Perfection of writing skills takes much practice.  46

 8      You must always strive to write clearly, concisely,     11
 9  and accurately. Remember always that your writing can be    22
10  examined by more people than just the one to whom you have  34
11  written. It's often looked at by other readers as well.     45

12      You want to be sure that your letters always convey a   11
13  positive, helpful attitude. Don't forget, you represent     22
14  more than yourself when you write--you also represent your  34
15  company! This is an important, useful rule to remember.     45

16      Try to stay away from negative words like "can't" or    11
17  "won't." Readers also do not like phrases such as "because  23
18  of company policies" or "due to unforeseen circumstances."  34
19  Using these words and phrases never helps resolve problems. 46
       1 | 2 | 3 | 4 | 5 | 6 | 7 | 8 | 9 | 10 | 11 | 12
```

Take two 5-minute timed writings.

Goal: At least 45wpm/5'/5e

C. 5-MINUTE TIMED WRITING

```
20      During upbeat economic times, businesses have trouble   11
21  finding and keeping their skilled workers. As a result,     22
22  some places may offer great benefits to the workers. These  34
23  could include such things as sick leave, life insurance,    45
24  profit sharing, paid time off each year, and flextime.      56
25      The concept of flextime was brought to the workforce    67
26  quite a few years ago. Companies implemented this concept   78
27  for a lot of reasons. Among the top reasons for flexible    90
28  work schedules at that time were to reduce the number of   101
29  cars on the road, to help workers to meet their families'  113
30  needs and demands, and also to attract more women back to  124
31  the workforce.                                             127
32      Businesses can manage such a schedule in a few ways.   138
33  Employees may have a chance to choose when to arrive and   150
34  leave for the day. This policy allows people who like to   161
35  work early in the day to start early and end early and vice 173
36  versa. Other companies may allow their employees to work   184
37  extended hours for four days and then enjoy three days off. 196
38      This type of benefit has assisted both workers and     206
39  companies. Companies recognize that their workers are more 218
40  productive and absences are lower.                         225
      1 | 2 | 3 | 4 | 5 | 6 | 7 | 8 | 9 | 10 | 11 | 12
```

Formatting

D. WORD PROCESSING—STYLES

GO TO Word Manual

Study Lesson 86 in your Word Manual. Complete all of the shaded steps while at your computer. Then format the document that follows.

Document Processing

You will begin typing Report 86-60, a formal business report project, in this lesson and will continue adding pages and features to the report in Lessons 87, 88, and 89.

- In Report 86-60, you will apply a Title style and Subtitle style to the title block and a Heading 2 style to the side headings. You will also insert a header and lists.
- In Report 87-61, you will apply styles, insert a list and two tables, format a displayed paragraph, and insert footnotes.
- In Report 88-62, you will apply styles, format a displayed paragraph, and insert clip art and footnotes.
- In Report 89-63, you will apply styles, insert a table, format a displayed paragraph, insert clip art and a footnote, and create bookmarks and hyperlinks.

Follow these steps to create the first two pages of the business report. Do not apply any styles until directed to do so:

1. Press ENTER 5 times, type the title in all-caps, and press ENTER 1 time.
2. Type the byline information in upper- and lowercase letters, and press ENTER 1 time after each line; then type the date, and press ENTER 2 times.
3. Type the first paragraph; then press ENTER 1 time.
4. Type the side heading in all-caps, and press ENTER 1 time. (Additional spacing will be added above the side heading later when the Heading 2 style is applied.)
5. Continue in like manner until all paragraph and side headings have been typed.
6. Insert a header that will display on all pages except the first page; type `Human Resources Department` at the left margin, and type `Page` followed by a space and an automatic page number at the right margin.
7. Select all header text and format it using Cambria 10 pt. Italic.
8. Add a bottom border; then close the header.

After you finish typing the part of the report shown in Lesson 86, do this:

1. Apply the Title style to the report title. (The title style automatically bolds the text.)
2. Apply the Subtitle style to the byline information and date line; then bold these lines.
3. Apply the Heading 2 style to the side headings. (The Heading 2 style automatically applies italic and bold and inserts blank space above the heading.)

Report
86-60
Business Report

↓5X

Title style **INTERCULTURAL SEMINARS** ↓1X

Subtitle style **Heath R. Watkins, Director** ↓1X

Human resources department ↓1X

March 10, 20-- ↓2X

¶ The Marketing department has been conducting surveys of our world wide offices, foreign customers, and prospective foreign customers over the last several months. Information received through the use of our mailed questionnaires has made us aware of an urgent need to improve our communication skills at the international level. Therefore, weare going to conduct a series of Seminars to focus on intercultural awareness issues. This The report addresses the process involved in developing the seminars, the instructional approach to be used, the seminar content that will be provided, and the schedule for conducting the seminars. ↓1X

Calibri 12 pt

Heading 2 style **PROBLEM**

¶ Some incidents have been reported to us in which we have failed to negotiate contracts with foreign customers and foreign prospective customers because of serious breakdowns in communication. Some of these setbacks have been the result of conscious negative acts on the part of our employees. However, the main culprit seems to be lack of awareness of cultural differences and lack of appreciation for the nuances that reflect these cultural differences. Indeed, there are unlimited possibilities almost for misunderstandings, insults, miscues, and avenues for people of good intent to miscommunicate. These issues must be addressed immediately to preclude any future breakdowns in communications.

Heading 2 style **INTERCULTURAL SEMINARS**

¶ Three-day seminars designed to improve intercultural communication skills will be held at regional sites in the United States and in selected forieign cities where we have offices: ↓2X

- Beijing
- Hamburg
- Madrid
- Melbourne
- Oslo
- Rio de Janeiro
- Tokyo
- Warsaw ↓2X

¶ It will be our intent that all employees who have direct contact with people from other countries will participate in these seminars over a four-month period. Depending on

(continued on next page)

the success of these seminars, the programs will be made available in the company to others who express an interest in acuiring or enhancing there cultural awareness. Any future seminars will always be scheduled on an as-needed basis during the up coming calendar year.

¶ It would be unreasonable to assume that a small team of people from our company would have the breadth of knowledge needed to conduct these seminars in 7 foreign cities. However, Celeste Fuhrmann, Robert Driscoll, and Han Lee have agreed to work together as the co-ordinating team for this effort. Ms. Fuhrman, Mr. Driscoll, and Mr. lee will be soliciting volunteers to work with them in areas of expertise. They hope to gain representative views and opinions for the purpose of molding an impressive array of seminar topics. Please contact these individuals if you believe you have the necessary background and/or experience and would like to volunteer.

¶ Each of these individuals has worked over the past 2 months with the managers of our international offices as well as with natives in specific countries to formulate a preliminary plan for these in-service programs. There plan will use the expertise of our employees in each country who have had negotiating experience and who have knowledge of local customs as demonstrated by natives. We are confident that through this team approach, every one will gain an understanding of problems only not from the position of our company but also from the perspective of those with whom they conduct business.

Heading 2 style

BENEFITS OF ATTENDING THE SEMINARS

¶ Besides the benefits that seminars such as these provide, invited speakers will lead discussions on a variety of topics to provide answers to questions such as the following:

- How can I develop a good working relationship with other coleagues?
- How can I avoid offending people?
- Do I need to adopt to another peoples' culture when I travel abroad?
- Is cultural stereo typing harmful or helpful?
- How do people from different cultures approach the decision-making process?
- How can we improve international cooperation?

¶ It is our hope that the Seminars will help all participants gain a much greater awareness and understanding of the environment in which they work. We believe the Seminars will assist all participants in avoiding cultural mistakes that might be costly to the company. Finally, for those employees who frequently work in one of our foreign branches, the Seminars will enable these people to adapt much more quickly to the cultures of the country in which they work.

Save this unfinished report. You will resume work on it in Lesson 87.

Formal Report Project—B 87

Goals

- Demonstrate improved speed and accuracy while typing.
- Demonstrate acceptable language arts skills in using abbreviations.
- Correctly format a multipage business report.

A. WARMUP

alphabet	1	Freight to me sixty dozen quart jars and twelve black pans.
one hand	2	career uphill gas pin awards homonym read yummy grade lumpy
easy	3	The Auburn sorority may dock in England for a formal visit.

Skillbuilding

B. MAP+: ALPHABET

Follow the GDP software directions for this exercise to improve keystroking accuracy.

C. PROGRESSIVE PRACTICE: ALPHABET

Follow the GDP software directions for this exercise to improve keystroking speed.

Language Arts

Study the rules at the right.

D. ABBREVIATIONS

RULE
abbreviate measures

In technical writing, on forms, and in tables, abbreviate units of measure when they occur frequently. Do not use periods.

14 oz 5 ft 10 in 50 mph 2 yrs 10 mo

RULE
abbreviate lowercase

In most lowercase abbreviations made up of single initials, use a period after each initial but no internal spaces.

a.m. p.m. i.e. e.g. e.o.m.
Exceptions: mph mpg wpm

RULE
abbreviate =

In most all-capital abbreviations made up of single initials, do not use periods or internal spaces.

OSHA PBS NBEA WWW VCR MBA
Exceptions: U.S.A. A.A. B.S. Ph.D. P.O. B.C. A.D.

Edit each sentence to correct any errors.

```
4  A mixture of 25 lb of cement and 100 lb of gravel was used.

5  The desk height must be reduced from 2 ft. 6 in. to 2 ft 4
6  in.

7  The 11 a. m. meeting was changed to 1 p. m. because of a
8  conflict.

9  The eom statement was published over the Internet on the
10 W.W.W.

11 She enlisted in the U.S.M.C. after she received her MBA
12 degree.

13 His Ph. D. dissertation deals with the early history of NATO.
```

Document Processing

When you type the remaining report pages in Lessons 87, 88, and 89, do this:

1. Type all lists, tables, displayed paragraphs, and footnotes in standard format.
2. Apply styles as the last step in each lesson.

Report 87-61
Business Report (Continued)

INSTRUCTIONAL APPROACH

¶ Fruehauf and Chang suggest a framework of instruction that has been was recognized by several international groups, and has been used by seminar groups around the globe. This approach includes the following 3 components:

1. The Cognitive component
2. The Affective component
3. The Experiential component

¶ The cognitive component includes information about comm unicating with people of other cultures. The a effective component is the area in which attention is given to attitudes, emotions, and resulting behaviors as they are affected by human interaction in a multicultural environment. The experiential component is the "hands-on" element that suggests several different possibilities. Others who have used this instructional approach have found that the use of simulations is a natural for this type of experience. Writing letters, memos, e-mails, and reports to persons in other cultures also provides beneficial learning experiences. In addition, the use of tutors can be very helpful to workers unfamiliar with a particular culture.[1]

---

[1] Faye Fruehauf and Chao Chang, "Communication Across Cultures," *International Business World*, Monthly April 2010, pp. 33-47.

(continued on next page)

SEMINAR CONTENT

¶ The cognitive, affective, and experiential components would be applied as appropriate for each of the topics included. The coordinating team members have used the resources available to them at our three local universities.

abbreviate ≡

¶ The co ordinating team has found that most colleges and universities now provide instruction in international communication. Many offer separate degrees in international Communication, and the number of majors and minors in this disipline have been growing rapidly for the past several years. While the content of international communication is integrated into several Business Administration and Psychology courses, there has been a trend in recent years to provide a course specifically designed for business interaction in an intercultural setting. The very nature of this type of study makes it very difficult to segment the broad topical areas, as all elements are so closely intertwined.

¶ The seminars must reflect the broad involvement of our international operations. There is a need for many workers in our domestic offices to develop an appreciation of the inter cultural challenge. This is true not only for those in the marketing and sales areas. Those in our finance department and our legal department are increasingly involved only not with foreign companies but also with huge multinational corporations that, at times, are as large as or larger than the biggest companies in the U.S. Table 1, page 4, provides a summary of the largest multinational corporations with whom we have worked on numerous projects since the early 1980s.

R-8B: Tables in Reports

Table 1. Largest International Companies
(Doing Business With CanCom, Inc.)

Company Name	Location	Global Rank
HSBC Holdings	United Kingdom	1
Royal Shell Dutch	Netherlands	6
Toyota Motor	Japan	7
BNP Paribas	France	13
Allianz	Germany	14
Gaz Prom	russia	19
Banco Santander	Spain	24
ENI	Italy	28
China Petro	China	30
Nokia	Finland	69

(continued on next page)

¶ Several seminar topics have been suggested to the coordinating team members, and the literature reviewed by the team suggests that there might be possibly more than a dozen from which to choose. Because of time constraints, however, we have decided to include 8 topics that are recommended by Chernov, Uda, and Kapoor. The topics and presentation times are displayed in Table 2 below.[2]

abbreviate measures

Table 3. SEMINAR TOPICS

Instructional Topic	Time
Body positions and movements	2 hrs
Concept of Culture	3 hrs
Conflict Resolution	2 hrs
Intimacy in Relationships	3 hrs
Language	2 hrs
Male and Female roles	2 hrs
Space & Time	2 hrs
Religion, Values, and Ethics	4 hrs

¶ **Body Positions and Movements.** Body language—that is, facial expressions, gestures, and body movements—convey messages about attitude and may be interpreted by people in different cultures. For example, firm handshakes are the normal in the U.S.; loose handshakes are the custom in some other countries. The way we stand, sit, and hold our arms may convey different messages in different cultural settings.

¶ **concept of culture.** This session will be an over view of the various cultures in which we conduct business, including ecommerce. Clooney identifies the needs for varied marketing strategies within the different economic, political, and cultural environments:

Indent the long quotation ½ inch from each margin.

> International web use and access are growing exponentially, and many businesses are wanting to capitalize on this trend and grab their share of this global market. English-speaking audiences are not expected to continue to dominate this market. Certainly, more than a literal translation will be required to reach this culturally diverse audience.[3]

¶ Case studies will be reviewed that are considered classics in the field of international communication. In addition, summaries of some of our own sucesses and failures will be reported.

---

[2] Vasily Chernov, Yoshifumi Uda, and Deepak Kapoor, *The Dynamics of Intercultural Seminars*, Gateway Publishing, St. Louis, 2009.

Save this unfinished report. You will resume work on it in Lesson 88.

[3] Sandra Boucher, "Cultural Comparisons in E-Commerce," January 17, 2010, <http://www.ecommerce.com/news.htm>, accessed on February 23, 2010.

Formal Report Project—C

Goals

- Type at least 45wpm/5′/5e.
- Correctly use Word's clip art feature.
- Correctly format a multipage business report.

A. WARMUP

alphabet	1	Jeff had his size to help him quickly win over Gene Baxter.
practice: *a* and *s*	2	ask has say sales bases areas scans seams sodas visas tasks
easy	3	Duane may try to fix the auditory problems in the city gym.

Skillbuilding

B. PACED PRACTICE

Follow the GDP software directions for this exercise to improve keystroking speed and accuracy.

C. 5-MINUTE TIMED WRITING

Take two 5-minute timed writings.

Goal: At least 45wpm/5′/5e

```
4       Technology surrounds us. It is everywhere you look.     11
5   People use cellular phones to speak to one another just     22
6   about anywhere. They carry their pagers so that they can be 34
7   reached at any time. Everyone, from the busy executive to   45
8   the college student, is now quite used to being available   57
9   at all hours of the day or night.                           64
10      In recent years, busy travelers have become used to     74
11  using their laptops everywhere. They use computer ports in  86
12  airports, hotel rooms and lobbies, and even taxis. This     97
13  technology allows the busy traveler to have access to the  109
14  Internet while on the go. Using the laptop, the user can   120
15  access the latest weather report, sports scores, and news, 132
16  almost as soon as they happen.                             138
17      Using the latest technology, you can keep up with your 150
18  work and maintain contact with your office. You can even   161
19  access your bank accounts and pay bills while waiting in   172
20  traffic. Also, if you are in a new place, you can find a   184
21  restaurant or call for directions as needed. The technology 196
22  options that have become available to almost everyone are  207
23  quite amazing. We are living in a small world that seems to 219
24  be getting smaller each day.                               225
      1 | 2 | 3 | 4 | 5 | 6 | 7 | 8 | 9 | 10 | 11 | 12
```

Formatting

D. WORD PROCESSING: CLIP ART—INSERT

Study Lesson 88 in your Word Manual. Complete all of the shaded steps while at your computer. Then format the document that follows.

Document Processing

Report
88-62
Business Report
(Continued)

¶ **Conflict Resolution.** Whether people are involved in negotiating a contract, working together to remedy product quality issues, or resolving contract interpretations, the need for tact and skill is particularly important in the foreign setting. Many of the seminar topics have implications in the area of conflict resolution. While every effort should be made to prevent conflict, there is a need for guidance in resolving disagreements in foreign cultures.

¶ **Intimacy in Relationships.** The degree of physical contact that is acceptable varies considerably. Hugs and kisses are the standard, even in the business office, in some countries. By contrast, the act of touching a person is considered an extreme invasion of privacy in other places. The use of first names may or may not be acceptable. To ask a personal question is extremely offensive in some cultures. While socializing with business clients is to be expected in some countries, it would be highly inappropriate in others. These are only a few of the relationship concerns that will be explored.

Insert clip art related to communication, similar to the above example.
Set the clip art width to 1 inch, set the wrap style to square, and align the clip art at the right margin, even with the first line of the Language paragraph.

¶ **Language.** It is obvious that language differences play a major part in business miscommunication. Whenever there is an interpreter or a written translation involved, the chances for error are increased. There are over 3,000 languages used worldwide. Just as with English, there are not only grammar rules but also varied meanings as words are both spoken and written. Even with the English language, there are differences in usage between the English used in the United States and that used in England.

¶ Although English is the language usually used in international communication, the topics identified in Table 2 illustrate the complexity of communicating accurately; and the problem continues to grow. For example, literal translations of American advertising and labeling have sometimes resulted in negative feelings toward products. As world trade increases, so does the need for American businesses to understand the complexities of cultural differences. Matthews offers this example:

> A businessperson must change his or her expectations and assumptions away from what is customary and acceptable in the United States in terms of personal and social conduct to what is customary and acceptable within the culture of the country where he or she is conducting business. Any other assumption can have serious consequences and undesirable results. In the other person's mind, you are the foreigner, and therefore you will be the one who might look out of place or act in a way that is considered socially unacceptable.[4]

---

[4] Craig Matthews, *Comparing Cultural Differences*, Grant Publishing Company, Los Angeles, 2010, p. 37.

(continued on next page)

Insert clip art related to shaking hands, similar to the above example.
Set the clip art width to 1 inch, set the wrap style to square, and align the clip art at the right margin, even with the first line in the Male and Female Roles paragraph.

¶ A good sense of humor is an asset not only in our personal lives but also in the business environment. However, it probably should be avoided in multicultural settings because the possibilities for misinterpretation are compounded. Do not use humor that makes fun of a particular individual, group, or culture. Remember that what may appear to be humorous to you may have a negative connotation in another culture.

¶ **Male and Female Roles.** There are major contrasts in the ways male and female roles are perceived in different cultures. The right to vote is still withheld from women in countries all over the world. Opportunities for female employment in the business environment vary considerably. Pay differentials for men and women continue to exist. Opportunities for advancement for men and women often are not the same.

¶ **Space and Time.** The distance one stands from someone when engaged in conversation is very important. If a person stands farther away than usual, this may signal a feeling of indifference or even a negative feeling. Standing too close is a sign of inappropriate familiarity. However, it should be recognized that different cultures require a variety of space for business exchanges to take place. In the United States, that space is typically from three to five feet, but in the Middle East and in Latin American countries, this distance is considered too far.

abbreviate lowercase

abbreviate lowercase

¶ There is also the element of time—a meeting that is scheduled for 9 a.m. likely will start on time in the United States, but in other cultures the meeting may not start until 9:30 a.m. or even 10 a.m. Punctuality and time concepts vary with the customs and practices of each country. Patience really can be a virtue.

Save this unfinished report. You will work on it again in Lesson 89.

Keyboarding Connection

Protecting Your Files With Antivirus Programs

A virus is a computer program intentionally written to contaminate your computer system. Viruses can enter your system from files downloaded from the Internet or can be acquired from infected files sent to you via e-mail, instant message or chat, or other storage media.

You can protect your computer by purchasing an antivirus program. These programs periodically scan your computer system for viruses. They also scan files that you bring into the system. Some antivirus manufacturers allow you to download a trial copy of their software from their Web site. You can try the software for a few days before you decide if you want to buy it.

Your Turn: If you want to visit antivirus sites to find out what they have to offer, search for *antivirus software* in your search engine.

Formal Report Project—D

Goals

- Demonstrate improved speed and accuracy while typing.
- Demonstrate acceptable language arts skills in spelling.
- Correctly use Word's features to insert a file, add bookmarks, and add hyperlinks.
- Correctly format a boxed table and a multipage business report.

A. WARMUP

alphabet
1 Quick goblins jumped over a lazy dwarf with the onyx rings.

frequent digraphs
2 in ink nine chin pin kind main sin mind tin skinny win inns

easy
3 The right bicycle may fix the problems of the ban on autos.

Skillbuilding

B. MAP+: SYMBOL

Follow the GDP software directions for this exercise to improve keystroking accuracy.

PPP PRETEST » PRACTICE » POSTTEST

C. PRETEST: Close

PRETEST
Take a 1-minute timed writing.

4 Old Uncle Bert lived northeast of the swamp, opposite 11
5 a dirty old shop. Last week we asked him to agree to allow 23
6 Aunt Gretel to purchase a jeweled sword for her birthday. 34
7 He fooled all of us by getting her a new topaz necklace. 46
1 | 2 | 3 | 4 | 5 | 6 | 7 | 8 | 9 | 10 | 11 | 12

D. PRACTICE: Adjacent Keys

PRACTICE
Speed Emphasis:
If you made no more than 1 error on the Pretest, type each *individual* line 2 times.
Accuracy Emphasis:
If you made 2 or more errors, type each *group* of lines (as though it were a paragraph) 2 times.

8 as asked asset based basis class least visas ease fast mass
9 op opera roped topaz adopt scope troop shops open hope drop
10 we weary wedge weigh towed jewel fewer dwell wear weed week
11 rt birth dirty earth heart north alert worth dart port tort

E. PRACTICE: Consecutive Fingers

12 sw swamp swift swoop sweet swear swank swirl swap sway swim
13 un uncle under undue unfit bunch begun funny unit aunt junk
14 gr grade grace angry agree group gross gripe grow gram grab
15 ol older olive solid extol spool fools stole bolt cold cool

POSTTEST

Repeat the Pretest timed writing and compare performance.

F. POSTTEST: Close Reaches

Language Arts

G. SPELLING

Type these frequently misspelled words, paying special attention to any spelling problems in each word.

16 means valve entry patient officer similar expenses industry
17 quality judgment academic provisions previously cooperation
18 foreign closing indicated secretary especially construction
19 monitoring assessment continuing registration manufacturing
20 products policies capacity presently accordance implemented

Edit the sentences to correct any misspellings.

21 Every company offiser will have simaler expenses next week.

22 In my judgement, we must insist on co-operation from all.

23 My secertary said that she traveled to a foriegn country.

24 We must continue monitering the progress for assesment.

25 The new policeis must be implimented for all products.

26 We must implement continuing registeration during the
27 closeing weeks.

Formatting

H. WORD PROCESSING: FILE—INSERT AND BOOKMARKS AND HYPERLINKS

Study Lesson 89 in your Word Manual. Complete all of the shaded steps while at your computer. Then format the documents that follow.

Document Processing

Table
89-46
Boxed Table

This table will later be inserted into Report 89-63.

Table 3. FOREIGN-CITY SEMINARS		
City	First Seminar	Second Seminar
Melbourne	May 2-4	July 5-7
Rio de Janeiro	May 9-11	July 11-13
Beijing	May 16-18	July 18-20
Hamburg	May 23-25	July 25-27
Tokyo	June 6-8	August 1-3
Warsaw	June 13-15	August 8-10
Oslo	June 20-22	August 15-17
Madrid	June 27-29	August 22-24

Report
89-63
Business Report (Continued)

¶ **Religion, Values, and Ethics.** While we can recognize the difficult challenge presented by language differences, this category (religion, values, and ethics) is in some ways the area that can bring about the most serious breakdowns in relations with those from other cultures.

¶ The very nature of religious beliefs suggests that this is a delicate area, especially for those involved in business transactions in foreign countries. Also, religious beliefs affect the consumption of certain products throughout the world. Examples are tobacco, liquor, pork, and coffee.

¶ Values are a reflection of religious beliefs for most people. We have previously heard of references to right and wrong as applied to the ideals and customs of a society. Values relate to a range of similar topics, and they may pertain to areas such as cleanliness, education, health care, and criminal justice. Such values are often very personal and as such can have a variety of interpretations. The more interpretations there are, the more likely it is that miscommunication will occur.

¶ Ethics can be considered as standards of conduct that reflect moral beliefs as applied to both one's personal life and one's business life.

¶ Delaney suggests that now more than ever, a code of ethics is essential within the business environment. When this code of ethics is missing or if it is not enforced, chaos and financial ruin for everyone associated are often the result.

(continued on next page)

Insert clip art related to world travel, similar to the above example.
Set the clip art width to 1 inch, set the wrap style to square, and align the clip art at the right margin, even with the first line of the first paragraph in the TENTATIVE SEMINAR SCHEDULE section.

A quality code of ethics is presently being recognized as an intrinsic and critical component in any business environment. Newspapers are filled with reports of scandalous, unconscionable, unethical behavior that has led to the downfall of otherwise successful businesses.[5]

TENTATIVE SEMINAR SCHEDULE

¶ As indicated earlier, all employees who have direct contact with people in other cultures will participate in these continuing seminars. That means that we need to have two identical three-day seminars scheduled at each site. These seminars will be conducted in the cities shown in Table 3.

(Insert Table 89-46 here)

¶ The Marketing Department is to be commended for calling our attention to the seriousness of our international communication problem. Celeste Fuhrmann, Robert Driscoll, and Han Lee also deserve our sincere thanks for their planning efforts for implementing the intercultural communication seminars. Through their efforts, we have experienced a high level of cooperation from all departments.

¶ As can be seen, special attention is being given to the seminar topics for these in-service programs. Efforts are also being made to identify instructors and resource persons who will develop instructional strategies that will be effective, interesting, and well received by the participants. These seminars will help significantly in increasing our market share in the international market.

---

[5] Denise C. Delaney, *Business Ethics and Workplace Compliance,* Empire Publishing Company, San Francisco, 2009, p. 35.

After completing Report 89-63, add three bookmarks and three hyperlinks by following these directions:

1. Add the first bookmark to Table 1 in the table title on page 4 of the report. Add a text hyperlink to the words "Table 1" found on page 3, last paragraph, to link to this bookmark.
2. Add the second bookmark to Table 2 in the table title on page 4 of the report. Add a text hyperlink to the word "topics" found on page 8, last paragraph, to link to this bookmark.
3. Add the third bookmark to Table 3 in the table title on page 7 of the report. Add a text hyperlink to "seminars," found on page 2, second paragraph, to link to this bookmark.

Formal Report Project—E

Goals

- Type at least 45wpm/5'/5e.
- Correctly use Word's feature to insert a cover page.
- Correctly format a cover page, a table of contents, and a bibliography.
- Successfully complete a Progress and Proofreading Check with zero errors on the first scored attempt.

A. WARMUP

alphabet
1 The wizard's main job was to vex the chimps quickly in fog.

number/symbol
2 jjoy@aol.com 66% (Ott & Poe) 5/8 Out! $2.16 *et al. #73-490

easy
3 Did the fiendish old men fight a duel down by the lakeside?

Skillbuilding

B. 12-SECOND SPEED SPRINTS

Take three 12-second timed writings on each line.

4 We may take a number of maps to aid us when we visit there.
5 Alan may then take apart both of the toys out on the lanai.
6 The eight old books are to be thrown into the fields today.
7 Andy will use eight hand signals if he is able to see them.
' ' ' ' 5 ' ' ' ' 10 ' ' ' ' 15 ' ' ' ' 20 ' ' ' ' 25 ' ' ' ' 30 ' ' ' ' 35 ' ' ' ' 40 ' ' ' ' 45 ' ' ' ' 50 ' ' ' ' 55 ' ' ' ' 60

C. TECHNIQUE PRACTICE: SHIFT KEY

Type each line 2 times. After striking the capitalized letter, return the SHIFT KEY finger immediately to home-row position.

8 Ann Bonn asked for lunch. Colin Dix and Elaine Fochs moved.
9 Glen Hans filed as Iris James typed. Kay Lee talked loudly.
10 Maya Nevins and Orin Parks tried. Quinn Roberts lost a bet.
11 Skye Tynch sat. Uriah Vin and Winn Xung ate. Yates Zyd hid.

Take two 5-minute timed writings.

D. 5-MINUTE TIMED WRITING

```
12      Anyone with a supervisory position will occasionally   11
13 have to deal with a problem employee. If you learn to deal  23
14 with this type of worker in a good way, it will benefit      34
15 everyone within the organization.                             41
16      As a manager, you should address the problem as soon    51
17 as you are made aware of it. However, if you are extremely   63
18 upset, it may be best to wait until you calm down and have   75
19 time to plan what you will say. Avoid using an approach      86
20 based on reaction, which can often be ineffective and too    98
21 emotional. Speaking up too quickly might bring you some     109
22 unwanted results.                                            113
23      When you talk to an employee, be sure you get to the   123
24 real issue. Present the facts and tell the employee exactly 135
25 what he or she is doing wrong on the job. Do not express    147
26 your own personal opinion. You need to present a positive   158
27 and mutually fair solution to the employee in question to   170
28 solve a problem.                                            173
29      At the end of the meeting, ask the person to explain   184
30 his or her problems to you and the changes that are needed. 196
31 By following this procedure, you know everyone understands  208
32 what is happening. Set up a time to meet in a few days to   220
33 follow up with this person.                                 225
     1 | 2 | 3 | 4 | 5 | 6 | 7 | 8 | 9 | 10 | 11 | 12
```

Formatting

E. WORD PROCESSING: COVER PAGE—INSERT

Study Lesson 90 in your Word Manual. Complete all of the shaded steps while at your computer. Then format the documents that follow.

Document Processing

Report 90-64
Cover Page

Create a cover page for Report 89-63 using the Insert Cover Page feature in Word. Use the following information to complete the cover page:

- Select a suitable cover page from the Word gallery that includes (1) company name, (2) report title, (3) author, and (4) name. Delete any extra elements on the page.
- Type `CanCom Inc.` as the company name.
- Type `INTERCULTURAL SEMINARS` as the document title.
- Delete the document subtitle.
- Type `Heath R. Watkins` as the author name.
- Use the current year.
- Delete the company address.

Report
90-65
Table of Contents

Create a table of contents for Report 89-63 as a separate document. Use the illustration that follows as an example. The table of contents shown is incomplete. You must refer to Report 89-63 to compose and complete all of the entries for the table of contents. Make these changes:

1. Type the title in Calibri 14 pt. Bold. A title style will be applied later to conform with the title in your report.
2. Refer to Report 89-63 to compose and type the table of contents. The entries should include all side headings and paragraph headings from the report, as well as the appropriate page numbers for each heading.
3. Type the side headings in all-caps at the left margin.
4. Type the paragraph headings in upper- and lowercase, indented 0.5 inch from the left margin.
5. When you are finished typing the table of contents, apply the Title style to "CONTENTS."

Use a Title style for CONTENTS.

PROBLEM. 1

SEMINAR CONTENT 2

    Body Positions and Movements 4
    Concept of Culture 5
    Space and Time. 6

TENTATIVE SEMINAR SCHEDULE. 7

BIBLIOGRAPHY 9

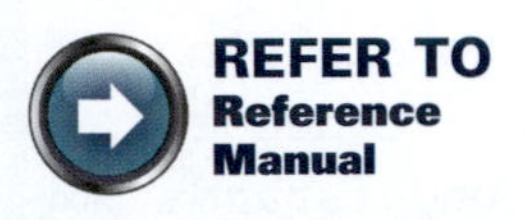

R-7D: Table of Contents

Report
90-66
Bibliography

Type the bibliography for Report 89-63, shown on page 367, as a separate document using standard format. Follow these steps:

1. Type the title in Calibri 14-pt. Bold. A title style will be applied later to conform with the title in your report.
2. Type the bibliography in standard format.
3. When you are finished typing the bibliography, apply the Title style to "BIBLIOGRAPHY."

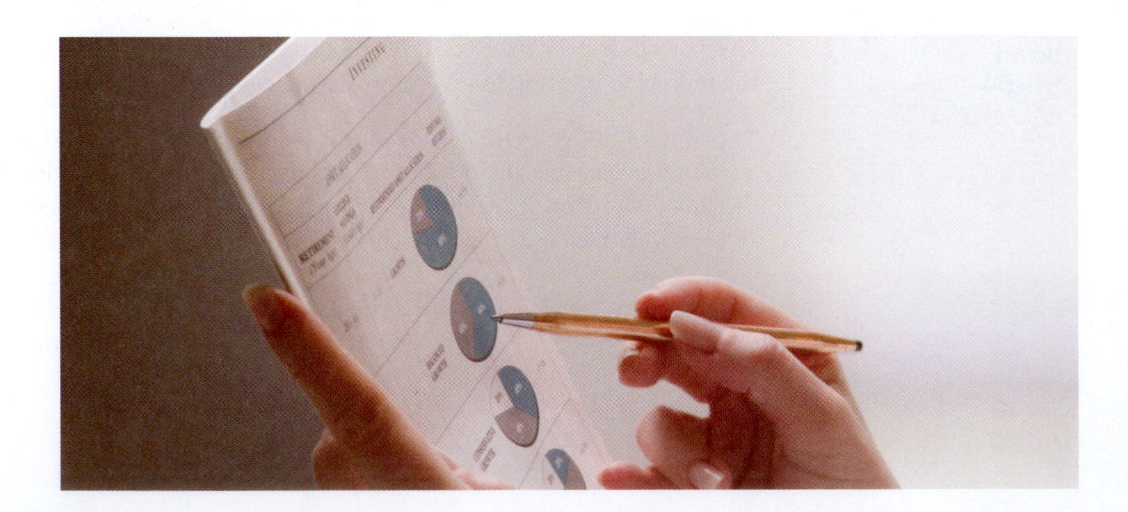

Use a Title style for BIBLIOGRAPHY.

R-9B: Bibliography

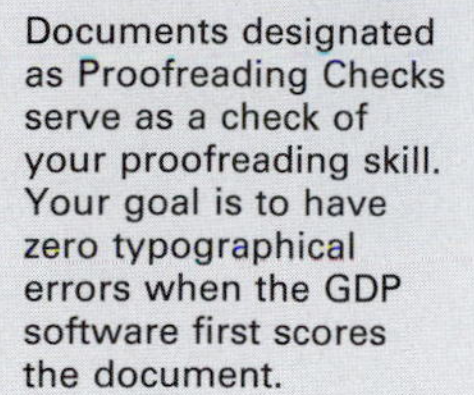

Documents designated as Proofreading Checks serve as a check of your proofreading skill. Your goal is to have zero typographical errors when the GDP software first scores the document.

BIBLIOGRAPHY

Boucher, Sandra, "Cultural Comparisons in E-Commerce," January 17, 2010, <http://www.ecommerce.com/news.htm>, accessed on February 23, 2010.

Chernov, Vasily, Yoshifumi Uda, and Deepak Kapoor, *The Dynamics of Intercultural Seminars,* Gateway Publishing, St. Louis, 2009.

Delaney, Denise C., *Business Ethics and Workplace Compliance*, Empire Publishing Company, New York, 2009, p. 35.

Fruehauf, Faye, and Chao Chang, "Communication Across Cultures," *International Business World,* April 2010, pp. 33-47.

Matthews, Craig, *Comparing Cultural Differences*, Grant Publishing Company, Los Angeles, 2010, p. 37.

Finalize the report project:

- Proofread all the pages for format and typing errors.
- Assemble the pages in this order: cover page, table of contents, body, bibliography, and a blank page for a back cover sheet.
- Staple the report pages in the upper-left corner.

Strategies for Career Success

Business Communication

There are five components to the communication process, whether written or oral.

The sender is the person who initiates the communication process. The message is the information that needs to be communicated (for example, "There will be a meeting at . . ."). The channel is the method for transmitting the message (for example, e-mail, letter, memo, or orally). The audience is the person(s) who receives the message. Feedback is the response given to the sender by the audience that enables the sender to determine if the message was received as intended.

The most effective communication within companies must flow not only downward but also upward.

Your Turn: Suppose you send an e-mail to 20 people in your department announcing a meeting to discuss your company's new policy on flextime. Who is the sender? What is the message? What is the channel you use to transmit the message? Who is the audience? What is the ultimate feedback?

UNIT

19

Medical Office Documents

LESSON 91
Medical Office Documents—A

LESSON 92
Medical Office Documents—B

LESSON 93
Medical Office Documents—C

LESSON 94
Medical Office Documents—D

LESSON 95
Medical Office Documents—E

UNIT 19 LESSON

Medical Office Documents—A

91

Goals

- Demonstrate improved speed and accuracy while typing.
- Demonstrate acceptable language arts skills in colon and period usage.
- Correctly format a business letter, a boxed table, and a memo.

A. WARMUP

alphabet	1	Back in June we delivered oxygen equipment of the odd size.
concentration	2	counterinsurgencies distinguishableness nonrepresentational
easy	3	A problem with the old chapel at the lake is its odd shape.

Skillbuilding

B. MAP+: ALPHABET

Follow the GDP software directions for this exercise to improve keystroking accuracy.

C. PROGRESSIVE PRACTICE: ALPHABET

Follow the GDP software directions for this exercise to improve keystroking speed.

Language Arts

Study the rules at the right.

D. PUNCTUATION

RULE
: explanatory material

Use a colon to introduce explanatory material that follows an independent clause.

The computer satisfies three criteria: speed, cost, and power.
But: The computer satisfies the three criteria of speed, cost, and power.
Remember this: only one coupon is allowed per customer.

Note: An independent clause can stand alone as a complete sentence. Do not capitalize the word following the colon.

RULE
. polite request

Use a period to end a sentence that is a polite request.

Will you please call me if I can be of further assistance.

Note: Consider a sentence a polite request if you expect the reader to respond by doing as you ask rather than by giving a yes-or-no answer.

Edit each sentence to correct any errors.

4 We need the following items, pens, pencils, and paper.

5 May I suggest that you send the report by Tuesday?

6 These are some of your colleagues: Bill, Mary, and Ann.

7 Would you please pay my bills when I am on vacation?

8 Our flag is these three colors; red, white, and blue.

9 Would you please start my car to warm it up for me.

10 One thing is certain: We will be busy that day.

Document Processing

Situation: Today is September 1. You work for Bayfield Hospital in Eugene, Oregon. For the purposes of this simulation, your name will be Carrie N. Garrison. Your e-mail address is cgarrison@bayfield.org, and you use *cg* as your reference initials in correspondence.

For the next five days, you will prepare documents for several units within the hospital—Admissions, Billing, Dermatology, Oncology, and Surgery. You will also format various documents, such as correspondence and medical reports, for these units.

You will spend your first day working for Brenda T. Atwood in the Admissions Office, preparing documents that appear in your in-basket. Proofread your work carefully, and check for spelling, punctuation, grammar, and formatting errors so that your documents are mailable.

Correspondence 91-85
Business Letter in Block Style

September 1, 20-- | Ms. Diane R. Williamson | 3727 Rambling Drive | Springfield, OR 97477 | Dear Ms. Williamson:

¶ Thank you for contacting us and considering us as your primary care provider. We are confident that you will be pleased with our services and our patient care, and we look forward to many years of serving your health needs.

¶ Now that you have made your final selection, we would like you to complete the enclosed Patient Information form. As you can see, the form asks mostly for personal information so that we can contact you or your employer if necessary. In addition, the form requests the following information: the name, address, and telephone number of your insurance company and your insurance policy number. Could you please return the form by Wednesday of next week.

: explanatory material

. polite request

¶ Again, welcome to Bayfield Hospital! If there is any additional information we can provide about our services, do not hesitate to call us at 541-555-4400 or e-mail me at batwood@bayfield.org.

Sincerely, | Brenda T. Atwood | Admissions Manager | cg | Enclosure

Table
91-47
Boxed Table

Create a patient information form using the illustration below and these steps:

1. Insert a table with 1 column and 15 rows.
2. Split cells as shown to provide room for individual entries.
3. Type the information as shown.
4. Type the headings in Cambria 14 pt., and the remaining text in Calibri 12 pt.
5. Bold the information in Rows 1, 7, 11, and 15.
6. Apply 25 percent shading to Rows 1, 7, 11, and 15.
7. Manually adjust the width of the cells so that they appear similar to those shown in the illustration.

↓1X

Cambria 14 pt

↓1X

↓1X

Calibri 12 pt

<table>
<tr><td colspan="3">PATIENT INFORMATION</td></tr>
<tr><td colspan="3">Date:</td></tr>
<tr><td colspan="2">Name (last, first):</td><td>Birth Date:</td></tr>
<tr><td colspan="2">Street Address:</td><td>Phone:</td></tr>
<tr><td>City:</td><td>State:</td><td>ZIP:</td></tr>
<tr><td colspan="3">E-Mail:</td></tr>
<tr><td colspan="3">EMPLOYER INFORMATION</td></tr>
<tr><td colspan="3">Employer:</td></tr>
<tr><td colspan="2">Street Address:</td><td>Phone:</td></tr>
<tr><td>City:</td><td>State:</td><td>ZIP:</td></tr>
<tr><td colspan="3">INSURANCE INFORMATION</td></tr>
<tr><td colspan="3">Name of Company:</td></tr>
<tr><td colspan="3">Address:</td></tr>
<tr><td>Phone:</td><td colspan="2">Policy Number:</td></tr>
<tr><td>Signature:</td><td colspan="2">Date:</td></tr>
</table>

Correspondence
91-86
Memo

MEMO TO: All Employees / FROM: Lucille R. Medford / DATE: September 1, 20-- / SUBJECT: Flu Shot

¶ Next week Bayfield Hospital will make flu shots available for all employees. If you would like to schedule a flu shot, call one of these nurses: R.N. Tim Bradford at Extension 224 or R.N. Karen Fishburn at Extension 228.

: explanatory material

¶ The clinic will be open from 10 a.m. to 2 p.m., Monday through Friday, for company employees. If you cannot schedule a flu shot during these times, they will also be available during the week of October 10. During that week, shots will be administered on an appointment basis only.

¶ If you would like to schedule flu shots for any of your dependents, the charge will be $10 per person. Flu shots for your dependents will be scheduled only during the October 10 session. Could you please have any of your dependents schedule their flu shots no later than October 5.

. polite request

cg

Keyboarding Connection

Capturing an Image from the Internet

Would you like to copy an image or graphic from the Internet? It's easy!

Point the mouse pointer to the image or graphic and press the right mouse button. When the shortcut menu appears, choose Save Picture As (or Save Image As). The Save Picture dialog box appears. Select the appropriate drive and name the file if necessary. Click Save. The image is usually saved with a .gif, .jpg, or .bmp file extension. To insert the image into a Word document, select the Insert tab, choose Picture, locate the file, and click Insert. You also could right-click the image, choose Copy, and then click the Paste button in Word.

Remember that images on the Internet are copyrighted and cannot be used without permission and possibly payment. This is especially important for business communication. Be sure to check the Web site for information about copyright and usage before you copy images or graphics.

Your Turn: Conduct a Web search, and locate an image or graphic to save. Right-click the image, choose Save Picture As, name the file, and save the image. Insert the image into a word processing document.

Medical Office Documents—B

Goals

- Type at least 46wpm/5'/5e.
- Correctly use Word's tab set feature to set and use tabs within a table.
- Correctly format a business report and a predesigned table.

A. WARMUP

alphabet	1	Jay visited back home and gazed upon a brown fox and quail.
one hand	2	exceed kimono ads mop geared opinion cast onion weave plump
easy	3	Jan and her son may make a bowl of fish and a cup of cocoa.

Skillbuilding

B. SUSTAINED PRACTICE: ALTERNATE-HAND WORDS

Take a 1-minute timed writing on the boxed paragraph to establish your base speed. Then take a 1-minute timed writing on the following paragraph. As soon as you equal or exceed your base speed on this paragraph, move to the next, more difficult paragraph.

4	A downturn in world fuel prices signals a lower profit	11
5	for giant oil firms. In fact, most downtown firms might	22
6	see the usual sign of tight credit and other problems. The	34
7	city must get down to business and make plans in the fall.	46
8	The hungry turkeys ate eight bushels of corn that were	11
9	given to them by our next-door neighbors. They also drank	23
10	the eight bowls of water that were left in the yard. All in	35
11	all, the birds caused quite a bit of chaos early that day.	46
12	A debate on what to do about that extra acreage in the	10
13	desert dragged on for four hours. One problem is what the	22
14	effect may be of moving the ancient ruins to a much safer	34
15	place. City officials must always protect our environment.	45
16	Molly was dressed in a plain pink dress at the annual	11
17	meeting that was taking place at the hotel in Tempe later	23
18	that last week in September. The agenda included four very	34
19	controversial topics that have often generated much debate.	46

1 | 2 | 3 | 4 | 5 | 6 | 7 | 8 | 9 | 10 | 11 | 12

Take two 5-minute timed writings.

Goal: At least 46wpm/5'/5e

C. 5-MINUTE TIMED WRITING

```
20      The first impression you make on a job interview will    11
21 be a lasting one, and you will want it to be favorable. A     23
22 safe choice is to dress conservatively. If you have time,     34
23 find out what people who are currently employed at this       45
24 company wear to work. You can acquire this information by     57
25 simply calling the human resources office. Or, you could      68
26 observe what the current employees are wearing when you       80
27 pick up a job application from a company.                     88
28      As you plan the details of your appearance before your   99
29 job interview, be cognizant of all the details. You will     110
30 want to present a neat and clean appearance. Your clothing   122
31 should be clean and very neatly pressed. Your hair and your  134
32 nails should be neatly groomed, and your shoes should be     146
33 clean and polished. You should use only a small amount of    157
34 perfume or cologne and wear only basic jewelry.              167
35      Next, plan to arrive for the appointment in time to     177
36 make a check of your appearance before the interview.        188
37      Your appearance may not be the sole factor that will    199
38 secure the job, but it will help you make a positive first   211
39 impression. Remember to dress for the position you would     222
40 like rather than the position you have.                      230
   1 | 2 | 3 | 4 | 5 | 6 | 7 | 8 | 9 | 10 | 11 | 12
```

Formatting

D. WORD PROCESSING: TABLE—TAB

GO TO Word Manual

Study Lesson 92 in your Word Manual. Complete all of the shaded steps while at your computer. Then format the documents that follow.

Document Processing

Situation: Today is September 2, the second day of your assignment at Bayfield Hospital. Today you are assigned to the Billing Office, where you will complete documents related to the activities in that office. Your first assignment is to prepare a report describing the billing procedure at Bayfield Hospital.

Report 92-67
Business Report

BAYFIELD BILLING PROCESS

September 2, 20--

¶ The billing process at Bayfield hospital will be under going a review during October. *the month of* Our last billing review was conducted 3 years ago. This report ~~will explain~~ *explains* how fees are determined, how transactions are ~~being~~ recorded, how payments are made, and how overdue accounts are collected.

(continued on next page)

Determining Fees

¶ Fees that a physician charges for service should be fair both to the patients that are under his or her care and to the Medical Profession. A doctors fees should be based on the following criteria:

- The amount of time involved in providing the service
- The level of skill required in providing the service
- The degree of expertise required to interpret the results of the service provided

¶ Fees should be identified in a schedule fee that lists doctor's and patient's names, procedures performed, and the charges assessed for those procedures. The patient's fee schedule should be made available us if it is requested. If patients inquire about the amount of the fee, an estimate should be given to the patient. In all instances, this estimate should not be made available to the patient before treatment has begun. An example of a fee schedule currently used by bayfield is shown in Table 1.

Apply a 25 percent shading to Row 2.

Bayfield Heart Clinic 1061 N. 3rd Place Eugene, OR 97477				
Date	**Doctor**	**Patient**	**Procedure**	**Fee**
02/02/--	Crispman	Diane Crowley	Place stent	1,875
02/04/--	Sanchez	Diane Crowley	Ultrasound intracoronary	2,911
02/04/--	Crispman	Diane Crowley	Catheterize left heart	540
06/02/--	Crispman	Diane Crowley	Imaging, pulmonary angio	105
02/07/--	Sanchez	Diane Crowley	Electrocardiogram	165
Total Fees				$5,596

RECORDING TRANSACTIONS

¶ A record of all patient visits must be maintained. A charge slip should be used to record procedures. The charge slip includes information such as a check list of all procedures; a checklist of all diagnosis; space for additional information; and an area for all charges, payments, and balances. As the doctor performs procedures annotations and changes are made to the charge slip so that it is kept current. The

(continued on next page)

charge slip should be attached to the patients' chart. When all procedures have been completed, a copy of the charge slip is sent to the patient to indicate the charges incurred during the patient's visit.

MAKING PAYMENT ARRANGEMENTS

¶ A patient's bill can be paid by one of the following methods:

- a patient can pay the bill by cash or check at the conclusion of the visit.
- A patient can pay amounts of the bill at designated times, weekly or monthly.
- A bill (statement) can be sent to the patient at the conclusion of the visit.
- A bill can be sent to the Health Insurance Carrier.

Regardless of which method of payment is used, the patient will not be assessed any overdue charges prior to 30 days after service has been rendered.

COLLECTING OVERDUE Accounts

¶ There are a number of reasons why a patient might not pay a bill. Whatever the reason, however steps must be taken to collect accounts delinquent. If you find that an account is overdue, here are some steps you can take to resolve the issue:

1. Attach a reminder when the bill is sent if payment is thirty days or more over due.
2. Call the patient if payment is received after the reminder is sent.
3. Attach a personal note to a statement that is over due, possibly as long as sixty days.
4. Make one further attempt to telephone the patient for payment.
5. Send a collection letter for payment. the letter should be firm but friendly.
6. Establish a payment plan to assist the patient in making payments on a schedule.
7. Go to court for legal action, or turn the account over to a collection agency.

We certainly do not wish to take legal action to collect any of our overdue accounts. Please make every attempt to collect overdue accounts so that we can avoid this step.

Table 92-48
Predesigned Table

Create a boxed table using a predesigned style. Use the following guidelines to create the table:

1. Apply a table style of your choice.
2. After the style has been applied, verify that the bolding shown in the illustration is used.
3. Remove any automatic hyperlink that might appear for the e-mail address in Row 1.

<table>
<tr><td colspan="5">18 pt BILLING STATEMENT

14 pt Allison Price, M.D.
12 pt ↓ Bayfield Hospital
254 Carmel Avenue
Eugene, OR 97440 ↓2X

Telephone: 541-555-3434 →tab E-Mail: billing@bayfield.org ↓1X</td></tr>
<tr><td colspan="5">↓1X
Patient: →tab Karen S. Fairchild
Address: 701 Maple Street
City, State, and ZIP: Eugene, OR 97438 ↓1X</td></tr>
<tr><td>Date</td><td>Description</td><td>Charge</td><td>Payment</td><td>Balance</td></tr>
<tr><td>7/18/--</td><td>EKG</td><td>$235.00</td><td>$125.00</td><td>$110.00</td></tr>
<tr><td>7/21/--</td><td>Laboratory work</td><td>175.00</td><td>50.00</td><td>125.00</td></tr>
<tr><td>7/28/--</td><td>X-ray</td><td>110.00</td><td>0.00</td><td>110.00</td></tr>
<tr><td>8/04/--</td><td>Laboratory work</td><td>80.00</td><td>50.00</td><td>30.00</td></tr>
<tr><td>8/18/--</td><td>Office medical</td><td>135.00</td><td>100.00</td><td>35.00</td></tr>
<tr><td colspan="5">Total Due →right tab $410.00</td></tr>
</table>

Strategies for Career Success

Enhancing Your Presentation With Visual Aids

Visual aids capture people's attention while increasing their retention. Use visual aids to present an outline of your presentation, explain detailed technical or numerical information, and summarize your key points.

Be selective. Don't bombard your audience with visuals. Your visual aids should support and clarify your verbal presentation. Consider the size of your audience and the size of the room before selecting your visuals. Audiences have little patience for visuals that are too small to read or too busy. Types of visual aids are slides, photographs, flip charts, maps, flowcharts, handouts, and computer graphics including tables, graphs, and charts. You can have printed visual aids if the room is small, or you can use a multimedia projector that attaches to a laptop computer to project your presentation. This is also useful for Web conferencing, so that people in different locations also can see your visual aids.

Limit the amount of information on a visual. Use simple graphics. Continue displaying the current visual until you are ready to discuss the next one. Always keep the projector on during your presentation.

Your Turn: In what ways would your visual aids differ if your audience had 10 people or 110?

Medical Office Documents—C

93

Goals

- Demonstrate improved speed and accuracy while typing.
- Demonstrate acceptable proofreading skills by editing copy.
- Correctly format a business letter and a business report.

A. WARMUP

alphabet
1 The quixotic knights' wives were found on jumpy old zebras.

practice: *s* and *d*
2 sad Sid deeds desks dosed dudes dusts sheds sides soda suds

easy
3 The ivory tusk may be a key to their ancient rogue rituals.

Skillbuilding

B. MAP+: NUMBERS

Follow the GDP software directions for this exercise to improve keystroking accuracy.

PPP PRETEST » PRACTICE » POSTTEST

C. PRETEST: Discrimination Practice

PRETEST
Take a 1-minute timed writing.

4 Did the new clerk join the golf team? James indicated 11
5 to me that Beverly invited her prior to last Wednesday. He 23
6 believes she must give you a verbal commitment at once. We 35
7 should convince her to join because she is a gifted golfer. 46
1 | 2 | 3 | 4 | 5 | 6 | 7 | 8 | 9 | 10 | 11 | 12

D. PRACTICE: Left Hand

PRACTICE
Speed Emphasis:
If you made no more than 1 error on the Pretest, type each *individual* line 2 times.
Accuracy Emphasis:
If you made 2 or more errors, type each *group* of lines (as though it were a paragraph) 2 times.

8 vbv bevy verb bevel vibes breve viable braves verbal beaver
9 wew went week weans weigh weave wedges thawed weaker beware
10 ded dent need deals moved ceded heeded debate edging define
11 fgf guff gift flags foggy gaffe forget gifted guffaw fights

E. PRACTICE: Right Hand

12 klk kale look kilts lakes knoll likely kettle kernel lacked
13 uyu buys your gummy dusty young unduly tryout uneasy jaunty
14 oio oils roil toils onion point oriole soiled ration joined
15 jhj jell heed eject wheat joked halved jalopy heckle jigsaw

POSTTEST

Repeat the Pretest timed writing and compare performance.

F. POSTTEST: Discrimination Practice

Language Arts

Edit the paragraph to correct any errors.

G. PROOFREADING

```
16      Suprising as it may seem, their has been a good deal
17 of interest in comunicating with a computer thrugh the
18 human voice for about fourty years. Researchers haev spent
19 millions ofdollars in hteir efforts to improve voice input
20 tecknology. It is likly that in the next decade we will
21 see many use ful applications in busness and in education.
```

Document Processing

Situation: Today is September 3, the third day of your assignment. You will work in a specialty area—the Dermatology Unit. Dermatology is a branch of science dealing with the skin and its structure, functions, and diseases.

Correspondence 93-87

Business Letter in Modified-Block Style

September 3, 20-- | Dr. Avery R. Childress | Professor of Medical Science | Kingswood General Hospital | 2832 Lincoln Street | Eugene, OR 97403-2512 | Dear Dr. Childress:

¶ We would like to invite you as one of six dermatology specialists to address the students in our medical science class on the topic of dermatology. We have the following dates open for your presentation: November 5, November 12, and December 10. The time frame we have scheduled is from 10 a.m. to noon or 2:30 p.m. to 4:30 p.m. on these three dates.

¶ Would it be possible for you to speak on the topic of skin rashes and their causes and treatments? Naturally, we would appreciate any comments based on the release of your latest article in the August 15 edition of the *Journal of Marketing Research.*

¶ We would be honored to include you in our program. If you agree to one of the above dates for your presentation, I will send you further information on how to reach the auditorium where your presentation will be held. I am enclosing a speaker's form that you can fill out to designate any presentation needs you have (Internet connection, computer, handouts, etc.).

Sincerely yours, | Stephanie Hill, M.D. | cg | Enclosure | PS: Please let me know no later than September 15 if you will be able to participate in our professional seminar.

Report
93-68
Business Report

COMMON SKIN RASHES

Their Causes and Cures

Dr. Stephanie Hill

¶ Skin rashes are caused by many different things. They are frequently recognized by symptoms of blistering, dryness, itching, reddening, or scabbing of the skin. Some of the more common ailments that fall into the category of skin rashes are eczema, dermatitis, and psoriasis. This paper discusses these three common types of skin rashes.

ECZEMA

¶ Eczema, also known as atopic dermatitis, causes the skin to appear red and blotchy. The disease can occur at any age, from infants to adults, but it typically occurs from infancy to childhood. It affects about 3 percent of the United States population. There are two types of eczema—atopic eczema and hand eczema.

¶ **Atopic Eczema.** Atopic eczema is caused by contact with woolen clothing, by heat, by detergents, by the house dust mite, and by stress.

¶ **Hand Eczema.** Hand eczema is caused by detergents, grease, oils, sensitive skin, and too much exposure to wet work.

DERMATITIS

¶ Dermatitis is often referred to as contact dermatitis. Some of the more common substances that cause dermatitis are cosmetics, jewelry, household and industrial chemicals, perfumes, plants, rubber, and soaps. Contact dermatitis is further classified as either allergic contact dermatitis or irritant contact dermatitis.

¶ **Allergic Contact Dermatitis.** This skin rash occurs after contact is made with certain substances, called allergens. The rash occurs as a reaction of the body's immune system to expel the allergen from the skin. Common allergens are often found in jewelry and cosmetics metals.

¶ *Irritant Contact Dermatitis.* This skin rash does not require exposure to an allergen but can develop when you come in contact with substances such as detergents, oils, skin cleansers, and solvents.

PSORIASIS

¶ Psoriasis is a chronic skin disease characterized by skin scaling and inflammation. This disease affects about 5.5 million people in the United States. It occurs in all age groups and affects both men and women. When psoriasis develops, patches of skin redden and become covered with scales. The skin then cracks and may cause severe irritation in places like the face, scalp, elbows, knees, and lower back.

¶ It is believed that psoriasis is a disorder of the immune system in which there are not enough white blood cells to help protect the body against infection and diseases of this type.

Medical Office Documents—D

Goals

- Type at least 46wpm/5'/5e.
- Correctly format a ruled table, a business letter, and a predesigned table.

A. WARMUP

alphabet	1	Jeb quickly drove a few extra miles on the glazed pavement.
frequent digraphs	2	on bon con none noon don ion one son ton won onto moon font
easy	3	When did the busy men fix the two fishbowls for the busman?

Skillbuilding

B. PROGRESSIVE PRACTICE: NUMBERS

Follow the GDP software directions for this exercise to improve keystroking speed.

C. TECHNIQUE PRACTICE: BACKSPACE KEY

Type each line 2 times, using your Sem finger to strike the BACKSPACE key.

The ← symbol means to backspace. For example, type *mar*, backspace, and type *p*, thus changing *mar* to *map*.

4 mar←p hex←y woe←k wow←n cot←p wag←n fro←y tea←n tar←p
5 has←y mad←n rid←p tot←p egg←o dug←n his←p gag←y box←y
6 cow←y tie←n nub←n via←m par←n has←y dab←y hot←p pie←n
7 ton←e why←o pot←p gee←l the←y job←y pub←n she←y bat←y

Take two 5-minute timed writings.

Goal: At least 46wpm/5'/5e

D. 5-MINUTE TIMED WRITING

```
 8      Innovative technology may bring new problems for our      11
 9 homes and businesses. A rising shift to use a cell phone is    23
10 causing many people to look at the etiquette of cell phone     35
11 usage. Are there times and places where a cell phone should    47
12 not be used?                                                   49
13      People want to be able to stay in touch, no matter        60
14 where they are or what they are doing. However, in some        71
15 places, cell phone usage is inappropriate or not allowed.      82
16      For example, you would not want a ringing cell call to    94
17 disrupt the entire production if you are enjoying a concert   106
18 or play. As a consideration to everyone in the audience,      117
19 the management may make an announcement asking audience       128
20 members to turn off their cell phones or pagers before the    140
21 production begins. Making this request gives everyone the     152
22 chance to enjoy the show.                                     157
23      Often you see someone driving a car while talking on     168
24 cell phone. Talking on the phone while you are driving is     179
25 not a good idea. When you are talking on the phone and not    191
26 concentrating on driving, you may cause an accident. If you   203
27 are driving a vehicle in traffic, your full focus should be   215
28 on the road. Be cognizant of this. Do not use your cell       226
29 phone when driving.                                           230
     1 | 2 | 3 | 4 | 5 | 6 | 7 | 8 | 9 | 10 | 11 | 12
```

Keyboarding Connection

Coping With Spam

Have you received those heaps of unsolicited e-mail, commonly known as spam? Everyone wants to get rid of those irritating online sales pitches. Unfortunately, there is not much you can do about them. You can make use of various filters, but they aren't foolproof.

If you end up on a spammer's list and receive a courteous e-mail asking you to reply if you wish to be removed from the list, *do not reply*. The spammer may interpret your reply to mean that you read e-mail, and you may be put on the hot list. The best action is to try to avoid divulging your e-mail address to spammers. Most importantly, use an alternate account if posting in any kind of online forum.

Your Turn: Other than relying on spam filters, are there any other actions you have taken to reduce the number of unsolicited e-mails you receive?

Document Processing

Situation: Today is September 4, the fourth day of your assignment. Today you are working in the Oncology Unit. Oncology is a branch of science dealing with the study of tumors. You will begin by typing this ruled table.

Table
94-49
Ruled Table

Proofread the medical terms very carefully.

DESCRIPTIONS AND TREATMENTS
OF ADULT BRAIN TUMORS ↓1X

Types of Tumors	Description and Treatment
Astrocytomas	Tumors that start in brain cells. Treatment includes surgery, chemotherapy, and radiation. ↓1X
Brain stem gliomas	Tumors located in the bottom part of the brain, which connects to the spinal cord. Treatment includes radiation and biological therapy.
Cerebellar astrocytomas	Tumors that occur in the area of the brain called the cerebellum. Treatment is similar to that for astrocytomas.
Craniopharyngiomas	Tumors that occur near the pituitary gland. Treatment includes surgery and radiation.
Oligodendrogliomas	Tumors that begin in brain cells that provide support and nourishment for the cells that transmit nerve impulses. Treatment includes surgery, chemotherapy, and radiation.

Correspondence
94-88
Business Letter in Block Style

September 4, 20-- | Dr. Victor D. Samuels | Oregon Medical Center | 782 Olive Street | Eugene, OR 97404-1410 | Dear Vic: | Subject: George M. Collins

¶ On August 21 I examined Mr. Collins and discovered a Stage 1A, Cleaved B cell follicular lymphoma in the right inguinal region. I conducted a surgical excision and recommended radiation therapy. Mr. Collins completed his radiation therapy three weeks ago and feels well at this time. He has no complaints, his appetite and energy are normal, and he looks good. His weight is down seven pounds upon my recommendation three weeks ago that he lose some excess weight.

¶ There are no abdominal or inguinal lymph nodes to his scrotal sac exam. There are, however, three- to four-millimeter nodes in the left inguinal region that appear totally unchanged from his original exam on August 21. His lungs are clear, his heartbeat is regular, the liver and spleen are not enlarged, and there are no palpable masses.

¶ It appears to me that Mr. Collins has recovered satisfactorily from his radiation therapy. He has requested a second opinion, and I am therefore recommending that he make an appointment with you at his earliest convenience. We will prepare a referral for Mr. Collins and forward it to your office by Friday of this week.

Sincerely, | Joan T. Rashid, M.D. | cg

Table
94-50
Predesigned Table

Open the file for Table 94-49 and make the following changes:

1. Add the following two entries to the table so that they appear in alphabetical order:
   - Gliomas
     The general name for tumors that come from the supportive tissue of the brain; for example, astrocytomas or oligodendrogliomas. They may be benign or malignant. Treatment includes surgery and radiation.
   - Plasmacytoma
     Under a microscope these tumors are round in shape; thus, they are called round cell tumors. They can appear as one single tumor or as multiple tumors and are usually located on the thoracic or lumbar areas of the spine. Treatment includes radiotherapy.
2. Apply a table style of your choice.
3. After the style has been applied, verify that the text in Rows 1 and 2 is bolded.

Strategies for Career Success

Letter of Resignation

When you plan to leave a job, you should write a resignation letter, memo, or e-mail to your supervisor and send a copy to Human Resources. Follow these guidelines to write an effective resignation.

Start a resignation letter positively, regardless of why you are leaving. Include how you benefited from working for the company, or compliment your coworkers.

In the middle section, state why you are leaving. Provide an objective, factual explanation and avoid accusations. Your resignation becomes part of your permanent company record. If it is hostile, it could backfire on you when you need references. Stipulate the date your resignation becomes effective (providing at least a two-week notice).

End the letter of resignation with a closing of goodwill (for example, "I wish all of you the best in the future").

Your Turn: List the benefits of *not* burning your bridges (showing anger or bitterness) in your letter of resignation.

Medical Office Documents—E

Goals

- Demonstrate improved speed and accuracy while typing.
- Demonstrate acceptable language arts skills by composing an e-mail message.
- Correctly format an open table, a business report, and an e-mail message.
- Successfully complete a Progress and Proofreading Check with zero errors on the first scored attempt.

A. WARMUP

alphabet 1 Four European jackdaws loved my big sphinx of quartz glass.
number/symbol 2 edow@msn.com 38% Ely & May (6/9) Wow! $4.12 *ibid. #573-012
easy 3 He may go with us to the giant dock down by the handy lake.

Skillbuilding

B. 12-SECOND SPEED SPRINTS

Take three 12-second timed writings on each line.

4 Glen may take apart the old robots when he comes into town.
5 Blanch may go with me to town to visit my son and his pals.
6 Due to the big quake, the city may start to move all autos.
7 Bob owns a pair of old bikes and a new car he got from dad.
' ' ' ' 5 ' ' ' ' 10 ' ' ' ' 15 ' ' ' ' 20 ' ' ' ' 25 ' ' ' ' 30 ' ' ' ' 35 ' ' ' ' 40 ' ' ' ' 45 ' ' ' ' 50 ' ' ' ' 55 ' ' ' ' 60

C. PACED PRACTICE

Follow the GDP software directions for this exercise to improve keystroking speed and accuracy.

Language Arts

D. COMPOSING AN E-MAIL MESSAGE

Compose an e-mail message to Dr. Natalie Benson, whose e-mail address is nbenson@bayfield.org, informing Dr. Benson of the appointments you have scheduled for Tuesday, September 29. The first appointment is with James Mitchell, who is coming for his annual physical—make this appointment at 9 a.m.

The second appointment is with Karen McDaniels, who is going to have her blood pressure and cholesterol checked. She will see Dr. Benson at 10 a.m. The final appointment is with Mary Ann Bradley, who will see the doctor about flu symptoms. Make her appointment at 2:30 p.m. Be sure you use an appropriate greeting, closing, and signature.

Save but do not send this e-mail message.

Document Processing

Situation: Today is September 5, the final day of your assignment, and you are working in the Surgery Unit. The specialty within this unit is knee surgery. Your first assignment is to create a table listing various medical terms and their definitions. Insert 1 blank line after each entry in Column B of the table.

Table
95-51
OpenTable

MEDICAL TERM & THEIR DEFINITIONS	
September 5, 20--	
Adenopathy	Swelling or enlargement of the lymph nodes
Auscultation	The act of listening to sounds made by the various structures as a diagnostic procedure
Cholcystectomy	Surgical removal of the gall bladder
Fibroperitonal	Related to the tissue that borders the abdominal cavity which covers most of the viscera
Enterstomy	An incision into the intestines that produces a hole in the abdoman through which the intestines are emptied
Femur	The extremely long bone of the thigh
Laparoscopy	A minimally evasive surgical technique that uses a fiber-optic instrument
Hemostasis	The arrest of bleeding
Laparotomy	Incision in to the abdominal wall
Trocar	An instrument for withdrawing fluid from a cavity

Correspondence
95-89
E-Mail Message

Hi, Dr. Sanchez:

¶ Mr. Shipman came in today with a lesion crusted in his back. Lesion was removed using 1% xylocaine with epinephrin loc. Wound was closed with 4.0 nylon suteres. stitches should be removed in aproximately 10 days. Suture should remain dry for 3 days. Mr. Walden is to call if he has questions or if problems arise.

Carrie

Carrie n. Garrison

E-mail: cgarrison@bayfield.org

phone: 541-555-3829

Report
95-69
Business Report

Progress and Proofreading Check

Documents designated as Proofreading Checks serve as a check of your proofreading skill. Your goal is to have zero typographical errors when the GDP software first scores the document.

RECOVERING FROM KNEE SURGERY

Dr. Paige Freidman

September 5, 20--

¶ Specific procedures should be followed by patients who are recovering from knee surgery. Depending on the particular surgery that was performed, postoperative needs of patients with knee replacements vary greatly. Healthy, young individuals may require only a few therapy sessions to recover from their surgery completely. Older individuals with no family or friends to help them at home may need special assistance or equipment to aid their mobility. Some patients may benefit from a short stay in a rehabilitation facility. To enhance the rate of recovery, patients should identify and address any special needs that may require attention before their operation.

¶ To promote full recovery, Bayfield Hospital has developed a coordinated pathway of physical and occupational therapy for patients' use. Patient Rehabilitation and Therapy Service (PRTS) and Bayfield Hospital have collaborated on recommending a specific sequence of procedures to follow.

¶ Prior to surgery, we recommend that patients determine any special equipment that will be required to promote recovery. Also, correct techniques should be learned for performing day-to-day activities such as getting in and out of bed, driving an automobile, taking showers, getting up from a seat, and going up and down stairs. Finally, patients need to be aware of what exercises will help facilitate their recovery.

¶ After surgery, patients must participate in physical therapy to ensure that they can:

1. Extend the knee straight or bend it past 90 degrees.
2. Place weight on the knee to test for strength and stability.
3. Use the knee without discomfort.

¶ If you have any questions regarding these procedures, do not hesitate to contact my administrative assistant, Carrie Garrison, at Extension 4400.

UNIT 20

Legal Office Documents

LESSON 96
Legal Office Documents—A

LESSON 97
Legal Office Documents—B

LESSON 98
Legal Office Documents—C

LESSON 99
Legal Office Documents—D

LESSON 100
Legal Office Documents—E

Legal Office Documents—A 96

Goals

- Type at least 47wpm/5'/5e.
- Correctly format a warranty deed, a boxed table, and an e-mail message.

A. WARMUP

alphabet	1	Ban all foul toxic smog which can quickly jeopardize lives.
concentration	2	counterinsurgencies individualistically interchangeableness
easy	3	Bob can use eight hand signals if he is proficient in them.

Skillbuilding

B. SUSTAINED PRACTICE: ROUGH-DRAFT

Take a 1-minute timed writing on the boxed paragraph to establish your base speed. Then take a 1-minute timed writing on the following paragraph. As soon as you equal or exceed your base speed on this paragraph, move to the next, more difficult paragraph.

4	Are you eating wisely? If you're like most Americans,	11
5	you have never been hungrier for information about food and	23
6	health. As medical research transforms yesterday's beliefs	35
7	into today's fallacies, many folks are changing their ways.	47
8	For example, many currant discussions have focussed on	11
9	the value of fiber in our deits, but did you know there are	23
10	two types of fiber? Oatmeal is high in soluble fiber, and	35
11	bran is known for it's high amount of insoluble fiber.	46
12	What are their diferences? Insoluble fiber adds bulk to	11
13	the content of the intestines, which might ward off colon	23
14	cancer. Soluble fiber adds bulk to the stomachs' contents,	35
15	making diets feel stuffed and help reduce cholstrol.	46
16	Americans typicaly eat half the amount daily of fiber	11
17	recomended by the national cancer institute. A serving of	23
18	some sereals can supply up to one third of the daily quoty.	35
19	Other first rate sources *are certain fruits and vegetables.*	47

1 | 2 | 3 | 4 | 5 | 6 | 7 | 8 | 9 | 10 | 11 | 12

Take two 5-minute timed writings.

Goal: At least 47wpm/5'/5e

C. 5-MINUTE TIMED WRITING

```
20      Many businesses across the country are adopting a new  11
21 dress code called business casual. Depending on the type of  23
22 place for which you work, business casual can have various  35
23 meanings. Most places allow their workers to dress down a  46
24 notch from what was expected in the past.  55
25      If people wore suits and ties in the past, then the  65
26 business casual code would allow them to stop wearing ties  77
27 and suit jackets. It is quite necessary for a company to  89
28 formulate dress code guidelines for workers to follow when  100
29 business casual goes into effect at the firm.  110
30      Surveys from a range of firms show mixed results when  121
31 employees were given a choice of dressing more casually.  132
32 Some firms feel business casual is a perk that works for  143
33 employees. But other firms report that job productivity  155
34 rates zoom down when workers are allowed to dress down.  166
35 More research is needed.  171
36      When you feel good about the way you look, you will  181
37 show this attitude in your performance. If your company has  193
38 adopted a business casual dress code, you must keep in mind  205
39 that business casual does not mean that you can dress in a  217
40 sloppy manner. A neat appearance and good grooming always  229
41 enhance a business casual look.  235
   1 | 2 | 3 | 4 | 5 | 6 | 7 | 8 | 9 | 10 | 11 | 12
```

Formatting

D. LEGAL DOCUMENTS

Legal documents can be classified as either noncourt documents or court documents. Examples of noncourt documents are a warranty deed and a last will and testament. Examples of court documents are an affidavit, a summons, a complaint, and a judgment. Line numbers are added to all court documents so that any part of a document can be easily referenced.

State statutes, court rules (federal, state, appellate, and so on), and law office preferences determine the format of legal documents, including margins, line numbering, line spacing, line lengths, page numbering, indents, alignment, and bolding. Therefore, the legal documents and formatting guidelines in this unit have been designed to serve as simplified examples of acceptable legal formats.

Follow these guidelines to format the legal documents in this unit:

- Type a legal document on 8.5- by 11-inch paper.
- Use default margins on all sides.
- Use single spacing and no bold.
- Indent paragraphs 1 inch; press ENTER 2 times between paragraphs.
- For multipage legal documents, insert a centered page number at the bottom of each page, including page 1.
- For all signature lines, set a 3.25-inch left tab. Then type a continuous underscore from the 3.25-inch tab to the right margin.

Document Processing

Report
96-70
Warranty Deed

A seller who provides a warranty deed warrants (or guarantees) that he or she has full ownership of a property and has the right to sell it. The seller also guarantees all rights of the property to the buyer.

Insert a space before and after the underscore representing the date.

WARRANTY DEED ↓2X

5 underscores

→tab 1" THIS INDENTURE, made this _____ day of February, 20--, between Alicia R. Carpenter, Grantor, and Karen T. Draper, Grantee, whose post office address is 3214 Benton Blvd., Kansas City, KS 66105-2843. ↓2X

WITNESS, for and in consideration of the sum of EIGHTY-SEVEN THOUSAND and 00/100 DOLLARS ($87,000), Grantor does hereby GRANT to Grantee, all of the following real property lying in the County of Wyandotte, State of Kansas, and described as follows, to wit:

Lots Fifteen (15) and Sixteen (16), Block Sixty-three (63), Original Townsite of Kansas City, Kansas, SUBJECT TO mineral conveyances, easements, special or improvement taxes and assessment, rights-of-way, and reservations of record.

(THIS DEED IS IN FULFILLMENT OF THAT CERTAIN CONTRACT FOR DEED ENTERED INTO BY AND BETWEEN THE SAME PARTIES ON THE DATE HEREOF.)

And the said Grantor for herself, her heirs, executors and administrators, does covenant with the Grantee that she is well seized in fee of the land and premises aforesaid and has the right to sell and convey the same in manner and form aforesaid: that the same are free from all encumbrances, except assessments for special improvements which have not been certified to the County Treasurer for collection or installments of special assessments, and the above lands and premises in the possession of said Grantee, against all persons lawfully claiming or to claim the whole or any part thereof, the said Grantor will warrant and defend.

WITNESS, the hand of the Grantor. ↓2X

underscores to the right margin

→ tab 3.25" ____________________________________

Alicia R. Carpenter ↓2X

STATE OF KANSAS ↓2X

County of Wyandotte ↓2X

On this _____ day of October, 20--, before me, a notary public for said County and State, personally appeared Alicia R. Carpenter, to me known to be the person described in and who executed the foregoing instrument and acknowledged to me that she executed the same as her free act and deed.

____

Boyd H. Fraser → 6.5" right tab Notary Public
Wyandotte County, Kansas
My Commission Expires August 21, 2015

Table 96-52
Boxed Table

Apply 25 percent shading to Row 2.

Press ENTER 1 time after each entry in Column B.

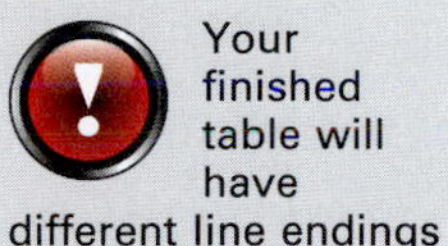
Your finished table will have different line endings for Column B when you resize the column widths to fit the contents.

WARRANTY DEED TERMINOLOGY State of Kansas	
Term	**Definition**
Appurtenance	Something attached to the land
Consideration	The value of the property
Escrow	A system of document transfer in which the document is given to a third party to hold until the conditions of the agreement have been met
Grantee	The person who is buying the property
Grantor	The person who owns the property
Mortgage	The pledge of property as security for a loan
Quitclaim	A document that transfers a property title to another
Warranty deed	A deed in which the seller forever guarantees clear title to the land

Keyboarding Connection

Transferring Text From a Web Page

Have you ever wished you could copy the text from a Web page? You can!

To select the desired text to copy, click at the beginning of the text and drag your cursor to the end of it, so all the text you want to copy is highlighted. On the Edit menu in your browser, click Copy. (Or you can right-click the selected text and click Copy.) Open your word processing document and position the cursor where you want to paste the text. In the Clipboard section of the Home tab, select Paste. The text will appear in your word processing document.

When you copy text information from the Web, you must cite the source in your document by giving information such as the URL (Web page address), Web page name, and author, if given.

Your Turn: Open a Web page. Copy some text, and paste it in a word processing document.

Correspondence
96-90
E-Mail Message

Type the e-mail below in correct format. Type Chao as the sender's name, and use the following as the writer's identification: Chao Chang | E-mail: cchang@webmail.net | Phone: 913-555-9962.

Hi, Daniel:

¶ You might recall last week that I indicated there might be a foreclosure property available and that it would be auctioned at the Wyandotte Courthouse. On January 19, 3 properties in Southern Wyandotte county will be auctioned as fore closures. These properties are located adjacent to the lots you purchased last year; I know that you would be interested in expanding your lot size with this purchase. Specifically they are located in 4 counties surrounding Wyandotte County, as follows:

1. Douglas County, Lot 9.
2. Jefferson County, Lot 15.
3. Johnson County, Lot 17.
4. Lot 23, Leavenworth County.

¶ I expect these properties will sell for $52,000 each; their excellent location may force the bidding into the $60,000 or $70,000 range. If you cannot be present for the auction but would like to place your bid on the properties, please let me know so that I can act as your agent. If you elect to do this, send me the bidding you wish to present for each of the properties. I need confirmation from you no later than January 8 so that I can register as your agent to present your bid.

Legal Office Documents—B

97

Goals

- Demonstrate improved speed and accuracy while typing.
- Demonstrate acceptable language arts skills in using semicolons.
- Correctly format a last will and testament and a business letter in block style.

A. WARMUP

alphabet	1	I quizzed five wine experts jokingly on samples of Chablis.
one hand	2	garage homily sea oil seated Honolulu ever jump eager plunk
easy	3	Do not blame their firms for the low quantity of auto fuel.

Skillbuilding

B. MAP+: ALPHABET

Follow the GDP software directions for this exercise to improve keystroking accuracy.

C. PROGRESSIVE PRACTICE: ALPHABET

Follow the GDP software directions for this exercise to improve keystroking speed.

Language Arts

Study the rules at the right.

D. SEMICOLONS

RULE
; no conjunction

Use a semicolon to separate two closely related independent clauses that are not connected by a conjunction (such as *and, but,* or *nor*).

Management favored the vote; stockholders did not.

But: Management favored the vote, but stockholders did not.

RULE
; series

Use a semicolon to separate three or more items in a series if any of the items already contain commas.

Staff meetings were held on Thursday, May 7; Monday, June 7; and Friday, June 12.

Note: Be sure to insert the semicolon between (not within) the items in a series.

Edit each sentence to correct any errors.

```
4  Paul will travel to Madrid, Spain; Lisbon, Portugal, and
5  Nice, France.

6  Mary's gift arrived yesterday, Margie's did not.

7  Bring your textbook to class: I'll return it tomorrow.

8  The best days for the visit are Monday, May 10, Tuesday,
9  May 18, and Wednesday, May 26.

10 Jan is the president; and Peter is the vice president.
```

Document Processing

Report
97-71
Last Will and Testament

A last will and testament is a legal document stating how a person wants his or her property distributed after death.

LAST WILL AND TESTAMENT
OF
EDUARDO D. HERNANDEZ ↓2X

I, EDUARDO D. HERNANDEZ, residing in Portales, New Mexico, do hereby make and declare this to be my Last Will and Testament, hereby revoking any and all former Wills and Codicils by me at any time heretofore made. ↓2X

ARTICLE I ↓2X

This will is made in New Mexico and shall be governed and administered according to New Mexico law, even though subject to probate or administered elsewhere. The New Mexico laws applied shall not include any principles or laws relating to conflicts of laws.

ARTICLE II

Whenever used herein, words using the singular shall include the plural, and words using the masculine shall include the feminine and neuter, and vice versa, unless the context requires otherwise.

ARTICLE III

; no conjunction

I am married, and my wife's name is Maria R. Hernandez. All references hereinafter made to "wife" or "spouse" shall refer to her and no other; if she is not my legal wife at the time of my death, then she shall be deemed for the purpose of this, my last Will and Testament, to have predeceased me. I was formerly married to Angela Sanchez, who is now deceased. There were three (3) children born of my marriage to Angela Sanchez. The names of those children are as follows: Rita Calderon, Timothy Sanchez, and Brian Sanchez.

1

(continued on next page)

ARTICLE IV

If My Spouse Survives. Except as may be provided hereunder in this Article IV, if my spouse survives me, I give to my spouse all my interest in household furniture and furnishings, books, apparel, and similar personal effects; art objects, gun collections, and jewelry; sporting and recreational equipment; all other tangible property for personal use; all other like contents of my home and any vacation property that I may own or reside in on the date of my death; all animals; any motor vehicles that I may own on the date of my death; and any unexpired insurance on all such property.

; series

ARTICLE V

If My Spouse Does Not Survive. Except as may be otherwise provided in this Article IV, if my spouse does not survive me, I give the property described above in this Article (except motor vehicles) to my children who survive me, to be divided among them as they shall agree, or in the absence of such agreement, as my Personal Representative shall determine, which determination shall be conclusive.

ARTICLE VI

If any beneficiary named or described in this Will fails to survive me for 120 hours, all the provisions in this Will shall lapse, and this Will shall be construed as though the fact were that he or she predeceased me.

ARTICLE VII

All estate, inheritance, transfer, succession, and any other taxes plus interest and penalties thereon that become payable by reason of my death upon property passing under this instrument shall be paid out of the residue of my estate without reimbursement from the recipient and without apportionment. All death taxes upon property not passing under this instrument shall be apportioned in the manner provided by law.

IN WITNESS WHEREOF, I have hereunto affixed my hand and seal this _____ day of ____________________, 20--. ↓2X

20 underscores

↑ 5 underscores

Insert a space before and after the underscores representing the day and the month.

→ tab 3.25″ ______________________________ underscores to the right margin

EDUARDO D. HERNANDEZ Testator

↑ 6.5″ right tab

The foregoing instrument, consisting of TWO (2) pages (this page included), was on this _____ day of ____________________, 20--, subscribed on each page and at the end thereof by Eduardo D. Hernandez, the above-named Testator and by him signed, sealed, published, and declared to be his Last Will, in the presence of us, and each of us, who thereupon, at his request, in his presence, and in the presence of each other, have hereunto subscribed our names as attesting witnesses thereto. ↓2X

34 underscores

__________________________________ residing at __________________________________ ↓2X

__________________________________ residing at __________________________________

2

Correspondence
97-91
Business Letter in Block Style

; no conjunction

April 10, 20-- | Mr. Eduardo Hernandez | 248 Oklahoma Dr. | Portales, NM 88123-3342 | Dear Mr. Hernandez: | Subject: Will provisions

¶ Your last will and testament has been drafted; it is enclosed for your review. Please review it carefully for any omissions or deletions.

¶ Although your will has been drafted as you indicated, there are still a couple of alternative inclusions that I would suggest:

- Do you wish to include a fiduciary summary power in the will?
- What division of estate do you wish to include for your family?

¶ These inclusions could be rather comprehensive. Therefore could we schedule a meeting for next Monday to accomodate these changes? Please call my Administrative Assistant so she can put you on my calendar.

Sincerly, | Paula T. Tisdale | Attorney at Law | urs | Enclosure | c: T. Bailey, Roland, B. Wells

Strategies for Career Success

Designing a Page for Readability

A well-designed document is appealing to the eye, is easy to read, and shows you are professional and competent. Follow these simple guidelines to increase the readability of your documents.

Use white space (that is, empty space) to make material easier to read by separating it from other text. Side margins should be equal. Create white space by varying paragraph length. The first and last paragraphs should be short—three to five typed lines.

Use bulleted or numbered lists to emphasize material. Make sure all items in the list are grammatically parallel in structure. Use headings to introduce new material. Use full caps sparingly. Consider desktop publishing software to visually enhance your document. Remember to balance graphics, lists, and text.

Your Turn: Review a document you have recently written. What page design and format techniques did you use to make the document more readable?

Legal Office Documents—C 98

Goals

- Type at least 47wpm/5′/5e.
- Correctly use Word's line numbering feature.
- Correctly format an affidavit and a business letter in block style.

A. WARMUP

```
alphabet           1 My woven silk pajamas can be exchanged for the blue quartz.
practice: f and d  2 fad fold fed Fido doffs defy find fled deaf fund deft faded
easy               3 Sue and I may fish for cod and smelt when I am at the lake.
```

Skillbuilding

B. PACED PRACTICE

Follow the GDP software directions for this exercise to improve keystroking speed and accuracy.

C. 5-MINUTE TIMED WRITING

Take two 5-minute timed writings.

Goal: At least 47wpm/5′/5e

```
 4      From the time you start attending school, you begin to   11
 5 develop new skills in making friends and getting along with   23
 6 people. These skills are used throughout your life journey.   35
 7 If you want to be successful in any business or career, you   47
 8 can't be a loner. You must learn skills for working with      59
 9 people from all cultures.                                     64
10      In a corporation, people use their unique skills to      74
11 work as a team in order to accomplish their goals. Like a     86
12 finely tuned orchestra or a football team, all members must   98
13 work together to achieve a desired objective. If a person    110
14 does not work efficiently within the group, then other team  122
15 members may have to work harder to compensate so that the    133
16 effort of the team will not fall short.                      141
17      Working with others allows you the chance to learn      152
18 from other people. You may also learn some things about      163
19 yourself. To get along with your coworkers, you may have to  175
20 overlook the personal faults of others. Everyone has some    186
21 faults, and your faults may be just as disconcerting to      198
22 other people as their faults are to you.                     206
23      The ability to work with people will also enhance       216
24 your quest for career advancement. You can expect amazing    228
25 results when you work with your team.                        235
     1 | 2 | 3 | 4 | 5 | 6 | 7 | 8 | 9 | 10 | 11 | 12
```

Formatting

D. WORD PROCESSING: LINE NUMBERING

Study Lesson 98 in your Word Manual. Complete all of the shaded steps while at your computer. Then format the documents that follow.

Document Processing

Report
98-72
Affidavit of Possession

Add line numbers to all lines in this court document. When your document is typed, the line that appears next to the line number will vary from some of those shown here.

An affidavit is a sworn written statement made under oath. It is a court document.

1 ←Line numbers for a court document AFFIDAVIT OF POSSESSION ↓2X
2
3 STATE OF SOUTH CAROLINA ↓2X
4
5 COUNTY OF CHARLESTON ↓2X
6
7 Travis Bradley, being first duly sworn, deposes and says: ↓2X
8
9 That he is an adult person and is a resident of Charleston County,
10 South Carolina, and that his mailing address is 105 Livingston Lane, Rockville, SC
11 29487.
12
13 That he knows the ownership, occupancy, and history of the
14 following property located in Charleston County, South Carolina, to wit:
15
16 All that part of the Southwest Quarter of the Northwest Quarter of
17 Section Ten (10), Township Sixty-two (62), further described as follows:
18 Beginning at the Northeast corner of said Southwest Quarter of the Northwest
19 Quarter; thence South along the East line of said quarter 2000.00 feet; thence
20 West 425.00 feet; thence North 150.00 feet; thence West 315.00 feet; thence
21 North 600.00 feet; thence East 882.00 feet.
22
23 That the record title holder in fee simple of the above property is
24 Travis Bradley, a single person; that he is presently in possession of the
25 above-described premises;
26
27 That ownership of the aforesaid property is based upon an unbroken
28 chain of title through immediate and remote grantors by deed of conveyance
29 which has been recorded for a period of more than twenty-five (25) years, to
30 wit: Since August 21, 1985; at 4 a.m.;
31

(continued on next page)

32 That the purpose of this Affidavit of Possession is to show proof of
33 ownership by providing and recording evidence of possession for marketable
34 title as required by the Marketable Record Title Act of the State of South
35 Carolina.
36
37 DATED this _____ day of May, 20--, at Rockville, South Carolina.
38
39 ______________________________
40 James Cates Attorney at Law
41
42 Subscribed and sworn to before me this _____ day of May, 20--.
43
44 ______________________________
45 Denise Crocker Notary Public
46 Charleston County, South Carolina
47 My Commission Expires April 18, 2015

Correspondence 98-92
Business Letter in Block Style

June 15, 20-- | Mr. Douglas Stengel | 1338 Phobe Street | Mt. Pleasant, SC 29464 | Dear Mr. Stengel:
¶ Enclosed is a copy of an Affidavit of Possession that was filed on your behalf with the Charleston County Courthouse. After checking with the County Recorder's Office, we have determined that your affidavit was filed on November 17, 1985. To your knowledge, have there been any legal transactions that have not been recorded that would reveal a change of ownership since your affidavit was filed?
¶ If you are aware of any unrecorded transactions that might change the ownership status of your property, please contact our office immediately to update your property records.
¶ If you have any questions, you can contact my office at 843-555-3838.
Sincerely yours, | Brandon Whitfield | Attorney at Law | urs | Enclosure | c: Sharon Steeley, Cameron Estrada

Keyboarding Connection

Searching the Yellow Pages

Do you find the Yellow Pages of your phone directory handy? Try the Internet as an alternate source. Many of the Web's search engines allow you to search for phone numbers, addresses, and e-mail addresses.

You can use the Yellow Pages feature to search for mailing addresses and phone numbers of businesses and organizations. Access your search engine and type "yellow pages." You'll see a list of links for a variety of sites where you can search for location and contact information of businesses. The site http://www.yellowpages.com is the online equivalent of the Yellow Pages books. Search engines also might provide you with a map of the location of the business or organization.

Using the Yellow Pages online is like having all of the phone directories in the United States at your fingertips.

Your Turn: Access the Yellow Pages online via your favorite search engine. Search for a business in your city by name and then by category. Did you retrieve the address and phone number of the business using both search methods?

Legal Office Documents—D

Goals

- Demonstrate improved speed and accuracy while typing.
- Demonstrate acceptable language arts skills in spelling.
- Correctly format a summons, a memo, and a predesigned table.

A. WARMUP

alphabet	1	The wolves exited quickly as the fanged zoo chimp jabbered.
frequent digraphs	2	en end den deny gene hen men lend menu pen ten oven yen Ben
easy	3	Vivian may risk a penalty if she is privy to the right bid.

Skillbuilding

B. MAP+: SYMBOL

Follow the GDP software directions for this exercise to improve keystroking accuracy.

PPP PRETEST » PRACTICE » POSTTEST

PRETEST

Take a 1-minute timed writing.

C. PRETEST: Horizontal Reaches

```
4      Art enjoyed his royal blue race car. He bragged about  11
5  how he learned to push for those spurts of speed which made 23
6  him win races. The car had a lot of get-up-and-go. He had   35
7  daily meetings with his mechanics when a race date was set. 46
     1 | 2 | 3 | 4 | 5 | 6 | 7 | 8 | 9 | 10 | 11 | 12
```

PRACTICE

Speed Emphasis:
If you made no more than 1 error on the Pretest, type each *individual* line 2 times.

Accuracy Emphasis:
If you made 2 or more errors, type each *group* of lines (as though it were a paragraph) 2 times.

D. PRACTICE: In Reaches

```
8  oy ahoy ploy toys loyal coyly royal enjoy decoy Lloyd annoy
9  ar fare arch mart march farms scars spear barns learn radar
10 pu pull push puts pulse spurt purge spuds pushy spurs pupil
11 lu luck blue lure lucid glued lumps value lulls bluff lunge
```

E. PRACTICE: Out Reaches

```
12 ge gear gets ages getup raged geese lunge pages cagey forge
13 da dare date data dance adage dazed sedan daubs cedar daily
14 hi high hick hill hinge chief hires ethic hiked chili hitch
15 ra rate rare brag ranch brace ratio bravo rayon prawn races
```

F. POSTTEST: Horizontal Reaches

POSTTEST

Repeat the Pretest timed writing and compare performance.

Language Arts

G. SPELLING

Type these frequently misspelled words, paying special attention to any spelling problems in each word.

16 distribution executive extension requested specific carried
17 recommended alternative programs access budget issued seize
18 objectives indicated calendar family could these until your
19 administrative accommodate possibility students fiscal past
20 transportation employee's categories summary offered estate

Edit the sentences to correct any misspellings.

21 The execitive requested an extention on spicific programs.

22 I have recomended alternitive programs for early next week.

23 These objectives were indacated for the new calender year.

24 These passed administrative goals will accomodate the team.

25 These categories could be included in the employee summery.

26 I offerred early access to the estate's budjet distributions.

Document Processing

Report 99-73
Summons

A summons is a court document that notifies a defendant that a lawsuit has been filed and that an appearance must be made before the court, at a specified time, to answer the charges.

Type the title (SUMMONS) on the same line as *vs.*

Add line numbers to all lines in this court document. When your document is typed, the line that appears next to the line number will vary from some of those shown here.

```
 1  STATE OF TEXAS                          → 6.5" right tab IN DISTRICT COURT
 2                                                                        ↓2X
 3  COUNTY OF HUNT                               NORTHEAST JUDICIAL DISTRICT
 4                                                                        ↓2X
 5  FIRST NATIONAL BANK     → tab 3.25" ) → 6.5" right tab NO. ____20 underscores____
 6  105 Royal Lane                      )
 7  Commerce, TX 75428-2230             )
 8                                      )
 9  → tab 1"        Plaintiff,          )
10                                      )
11                  vs.                 )            → 6.5" right tab SUMMONS
12                                      )
13  JAMES MCFEELEY                      )
14                                      )
15                  Defendant.          )
16
17  THE STATE OF TEXAS TO THE ABOVE-NAMED DEFENDANT:
18
19  → tab 1"        You are hereby summoned and required to appear and defend
20  against the Complaint in this action, which is hereby served upon you by serving
21  upon the undersigned an Answer or other proper response within twenty (20)
22  days after the service of the Summons and Complaint upon you, exclusive of the
23  day of service.
24
25                  If you fail to do so, judgment by default will be taken against you
26  for the relief demanded in the Complaint.
27
28                  SIGNED this _____ day of July, 20--.
29
30                                  → tab 3.25" ______________________________
31                                      Rachel Simmons        Attorney at Law
32                                      334 Alamo Street    ↑ 6.5" right tab
33                                      Commerce, TX 75428-3110
34                                      Telephone: 903-555-1130
35                                      Attorney for Plaintiff
```

Correspondence
99-93
Memo

MEMO TO: Christopher Redding

FROM: Darlene Ruzi

DATE: October 13, 20--

SUBJECT: Client listing

¶ As you requested, I am enclosing an up-to-date new client summary for our Dallas area clients. This list is current as of this week and it shows the distribution of clients in the counties of Dallas, Ellis, hunt, Kaufman, and Rockwall. Please note that the billing hours total are also indicated in this list. Dallas and Kaufman counties represents the greatest number of clients per county. Just in the past quarter, these 2 counties represented nearly 70% of our client base. Rockwall County clients do not represent a sizable percentage of our client base but the opening of two new family law offices in that county will certainly generate considerable new business in the next calendar year.

¶ We will send you an updated list bi weekly. The next list could show the possibility of client gains in Rockwall county, and we expect business in Ellis and Hunt counties to continue growing to accommodate the population growth in those specific areas.

urs | Enclosure | c: Blake Zachry

Table
99-53
Predesigned Table

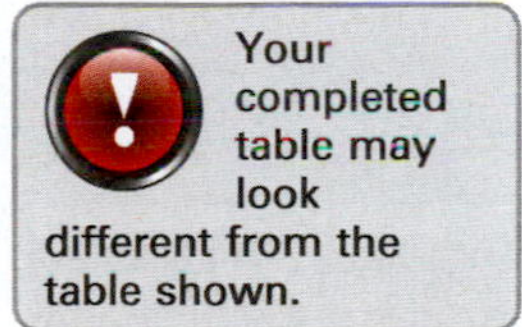
Your completed table may look different from the table shown.

1. Apply a table style of your choice.
2. In Rows 1 and 2, verify that all text is bolded.
3. In Row 2, align the column headings at the bottom center.

CLIENT LIST **October 15, 20--**			
Name	**Address**	**County**	**Billing Hours**
Carroll Azteca	423 North Avenue	Hunt	25
Thomas Bryan	302 Bradley Lane	Rockwall	30
Maria Calhoun	1204 Park Street	Kaufman	23
Raymond Cooper	144 Cypress Circle	Rockwall	14
Denise Johnson	3076 Burns Avenue	Hunt	18
Vickie Nichols	483 Laurel Trace	Ellis	7
Margie Rambert	291 Shelby Drive	Kaufman	9
Pearl Sibley	402 Waverly Way	Dallas	32
Heather Wong	2421 Hope Road	Ellis	12
Ray Zhen	2232 Alvin Lane	Dallas	28

UNIT 20 LESSON 100

Legal Office Documents—E

Goals

- Type at least 47wpm/5'/5e.
- Correctly format a complaint, a warranty deed, and a judgment.
- Successfully complete a Progress and Proofreading Check with zero errors on the first scored attempt.

A. WARMUP

alphabet 1 Brown jars prevented the mixture from freezing too quickly.
number/symbol 2 coy20@cox.net 70% Hsu & Van 5/7 Win! ($4.93) *op. cit #16-8
easy 3 Jay may ask if my own neighbor is proficient in such a job.

Skillbuilding

B. 12-SECOND SPEED SPRINTS

Take three 12-second timed writings on each line.

4 Keith must work with a tutor when he has need of more help.
5 Chris may clap his hands when they chant the songs at camp.
6 Do not blame my firm for the low level of fuel in the tank.
7 The new city law may allow us to fish for cod on the docks.
' ' ' ' 5 ' ' ' ' 10 ' ' ' ' 15 ' ' ' ' 20 ' ' ' ' 25 ' ' ' ' 30 ' ' ' ' 35 ' ' ' ' 40 ' ' ' ' 45 ' ' ' ' 50 ' ' ' ' 55 ' ' ' ' 60

C. TECHNIQUE PRACTICE: SPACE BAR

Type each line 2 times, using your right thumb to strike the SPACE BAR in the center.

8 A toy dog in the pen is apt to be a big hit at the new gym.
9 We may go to the zoo for the day if the sun is not too hot.
10 Eli and Max may use a map to see how to get to the new pub.
11 If it is to be, it is up to you and Ben to do it for a fee.

Take two 5-minute timed writings.

Goal: At least 47wpm/5'/5e

D. 5-MINUTE TIMED WRITING

12	Company loyalty may be a thing of the past. A worker	11
13	who stayed and worked in one place for thirty or more years	23
14	is rare these days. People are moving to different jobs at	35
15	a faster pace than in the past. Changing jobs many times	46
16	over a career no longer carries the stigma of the past.	57
17	Some workers are just looking for new challenges.	67
18	Those who change jobs are able to market their skills	78
19	and to get a salary increase. Hopping from job to job can	90
20	pay amazing returns for some careers. Firms may be quite	101
21	willing to offer higher pay and more perks to attract the	113
22	best and most skilled people. People who change jobs a lot	125
23	have the experience and knowledge that other firms may be	136
24	eager to get.	139
25	The chance to change jobs is there not only for the	150
26	younger worker but also for older workers who are well into	162
27	their careers. For example, computer technology has been	173
28	experiencing a boom. The Internet industry has a big demand	185
29	for computer programmers. People with knowledge in this	196
30	field can request higher salaries.	203
31	A firm may even offer additional benefits in order to	214
32	attract experienced workers with great credentials. It is	226
33	really up to each person to decide what to do.	235
	1 | 2 | 3 | 4 | 5 | 6 | 7 | 8 | 9 | 10 | 11 | 12	

Document Processing

Report 100-74
Complaint

Add line numbers for all lines in this court document, and restart line numbers on each page. When your document is typed, the line that appears next to the line number will vary.

A complaint is the initial document filed with a court by a plaintiff to initiate a lawsuit by establishing the facts or legal claims. A complaint is a court document.

1	STATE OF IOWA		IN DISTRICT COURT
2			
3	COUNTY OF DES MOINES		CENTRAL JUDICIAL DISTRICT
4			
5	PEOPLE'S COUNTY BANK	)	NO. ____________
6	215 Grand Avenue	)	
7	Des Moines, IA 50304	)	
8		)	
9	Plaintiff,	)	
10		)	
11	vs.	)	COMPLAINT
12		)	
13	COLEMAN FARMS, INC.	)	
14	STEVEN R. COLEMAN	)	
15		)	
16	Defendant.	)	
17			

(continued on next page)

Press ENTER 2 times before each roman numeral. Center all roman numerals between the margins.

1 PLAINTIFF FOR ITS CAUSE OF ACTION AND COMPLAINT AGAINST THE
2 DEFENDANT, COMPLAINS, ALLEGES, AND SHOWS TO THE COURT:
3
4 I.
5 That defendant owes plaintiff $10,885.00, plus interest and charges,
6 under the terms of a promissory note executed April 18, 20--, a copy of which is
7 attached hereto and incorporated by reference as "Exhibit A."
8
9 II.
10 That defendant has not, upon due demand, satisfied his obligation
11 under the terms of the promissory note.
12
13 III.
14 That Coleman Farms is an Iowa for-profit corporation duly organized
15 under the corporate laws of the State of Iowa.
16
17 IV.
18 That the registered agent of Coleman Farms is Steven R. Coleman.
19
20 V.
21 That Steven R. Coleman executed a Commercial Guaranty for the
22 note dated April 18, 20--, a copy of which is attached hereto and incorporated
23 herein as "Exhibit B."
24
25 VI.
26 That Steven R. Coleman executed a Commercial Guaranty on the
27 prior promissory note No. 7249, and the Commercial Guaranty provides that the
28 guaranty extends to ". . . all renewals of, extensions of, modifications of,
29 refinancings of, consolidations of, and substitutions for the promissory note or
30 agreement." A copy of that Commercial Guaranty is attached hereto and
31 incorporated hereby by reference as "Exhibit C."
32
33 VII.
34 That the indebtedness was the renewal of a prior promissory note
35 executed by Coleman Farms to People's County Bank on June 28, 20--, which
36 was in the original principal amount of $10,480, a copy of which is attached
37 hereto and incorporated by reference as "Exhibit D."
38
39 VIII.
40 That Steven R. Coleman is personally liable for the amount of the
41 debt, as is the corporation, Coleman Farms.
42
43 WHEREOF, PLAINTIFF DEMANDS JUDGMENT AGAINST THE
44 DEFENDANT, AS FOLLOWS:
45

For the numbered list, press TAB 1 time, then create the numbered list.

46 1. For the amount of $5,780.00, plus interest on that amount from
47 and after April 18, 20--, at the rate of 12.75% per annum; and for
48 its costs, late charges, and disbursements in this action;
49

(continued on next page)

1 2. For such other and further relief as the Court may deem
2 appropriate.
3
4 SIGNED this _____ day of December, 20--.
5
6 ______________________________
7 Barry R. Jacobs Attorney at Law
8 484 Grand Avenue
9 Des Moines, IA 50305
10 Telephone: 515-555-3399
11 Attorney for Plaintiff

Report
100-75
Warranty Deed

WARRANTY DEED

¶ THIS DEED, is made this _____ day of August, 20--, between Edward J. Garcia, hereby called the Grantor, whose address is 937 Ludlow Street, Hamilton, OH 45012, and Samuel Ramsey, hereby called the Grantee, whose address is 1104 Buckeye Street, Hamilton, OH 45014.

¶ *THE GRANTOR, in consideration of the sum of TWO HUNDRED TWENTY-FIVE THOUSAND and 00/100 DOLLARS ($225,000), does hereby grant, bargain, sell, and convey unto the Grantee, in fee simple, all of the property described in Exhibit "A" attached hereto and made a part thereof;*

¶ *And the remainders, rents, issues, and profits thereof and all of the estate, right, title, and interest of the Grantor, therein and thereto;*

¶ *TO HAVE AND TO HOLD the same, together with all structures, improvements, rights, easements, privileges, and appurtenances thereon and thereunto belonging or held and enjoyed therewith, unto the Grantee according to the tenancy hereinafter set forth.*

¶ *WITNESS, the hand of the Grantor.*

____
Edward J. Garcia

STATE OF OHIO

County of Butler

(continued on next page)

¶ On this ______ day of August, 20--, before me, a notary public within and for said County and State, personally appeared Edward J. Garcia, to me known to be the person described in and who executed the within and foregoing instrument and acknowledged to me that he executed the same as his free act and deed.

____

Marcia H. Gates Notary Public
Butler County, Ohio
My Commission Expires May 15, 2015

Report 100-76
Judgment

Add line numbers to all lines in this court document. When your document is typed, the line that appears next to the line number will vary from some of those shown here.

Progress and Proofreading Check

Documents designated as Proofreading Checks serve as a check of your proofreading skill. Your goal is to have zero typographical errors when the GDP software first scores the document.

A judgment is a decision by a court to resolve a controversy. A judgment is a court document; it determines the rights and obligations of the parties.

1 STATE OF GEORGIA IN DISTRICT COURT
2
3 COUNTY OF DOUGLAS NORTH-CENTRAL JUDICIAL DISTRICT
4
5 James S. Crenshaw)
6 d/b/a Crenshaw Computers) CIVIL NO. 45-98-C-00127
7 6823 Creekwood Drive)
8 Douglasville, GA 30135)
9)
10 Plaintiff,)
11)
12 vs.) JUDGMENT
13)
14 Peachtree Hospital Association)
15 d/b/a Peachtree Nursing Care)
16)
17 Defendant.)
18
19 The defendant, Peachtree Hospital Association, d/b/a Peachtree
20 Nursing Care, having been regularly served with process, and having failed to
21 appear and answer the plaintiff's Complaint filed herein, and the default of said
22 defendant having been duly entered, and it appearing by the affidavits of
23 plaintiff that plaintiff is entitled to judgment herein.
24
25 IT IS THEREFORE ORDERED AND ADJUDGED, that the plaintiff have
26 and recover from the defendant, Peachtree Hospital Association, d/b/a
27 Peachtree Nursing Care, the sum of $12,000.00 plus interest thereon from and
28 after October 10, 20--, until paid, together with costs in the sum of $343.75.
29
30 SIGNED this _____ day of ____________________, 20--.
31
32 ______________________________
33 Clerk of the District Court

Outcomes Assessment on Part 5

Test 5

5-Minute Timed Writing

```
 1      When you submit your resume to apply for a job, you      11
 2  want your resume to be noticed. Here are some things you     22
 3  might do to make certain your resume receives the time and   34
 4  focus it deserves.                                           38
 5      First, be neat. Review each page to make sure that it    49
 6  is free of typos and spelling errors. Check each page for    60
 7  correct grammar. Remember that this document will make the   72
 8  first impression with a potential employer. You want the     83
 9  document to represent you in the best way. Use white paper   95
10  of good quality to print your resume.                       103
11      Second, try to be creative. Make your resume unique. A  114
12  future employer may be looking for specific things when he  126
13  or she scans the pages of your resume. Be sure to provide   137
14  facts that explain exactly what skills you have acquired in 149
15  positions you have held in the past. Avoid using the same   161
16  buzzwords that everyone else uses.                          168
17      Finally, state a career objective on your resume. Some  179
18  experts suggest that by stating a career objective, you are 191
19  showing a career path. Others think that stating a career   203
20  objective may limit many job possibilities. If you state a  215
21  career objective, make sure the objective is in line with   226
22  the specific job for which you are applying.                235
      1 | 2 | 3 | 4 | 5 | 6 | 7 | 8 | 9 | 10 | 11 | 12
```

Correspondence Test 5-94

Business Letter in Block Style

17 March 20-- | Mr. Antoine Devereux | Plant Manager | Technik Group | 3148, Rue Richer | 75214 | Paris | France | Dear Mr. Devereux:

¶ We have astounding news to share with you regarding our Lyon plant in Genesis. Sales at the Lyon plant during its first 3 months of operation have surpassed our Bremen and Leipzig sales over the same period. Much of this sucess is due to your unique marketing effort to promote the ~~Jefy~~ Genesis throughout France.

¶ We are going to promote the same marketing approach at our Bremen and Leipzig plants because of the success you experienced at the Lyon plant. I would like you to lead the effort in that campaign. Therefore would you please put together ~~for me~~ a proposal and send it to me by the end of the month.

¶ We look forward to receiving your proposal.

Sincerely, | Alex Defforey | V.P., Marketing | urs | c: Mary Kay Summers, Richard Laforgue

Table Test
5-54
Boxed Table

Add 25 percent shading to Row 2.

PATIENT MEDICAL REPORT		
Patient Name:		
Chest X-Ray (Code 410)	Normal	Abnormal
Cholesterol—HDL (Code 466)	Normal	Abnormal
Cholesterol—LDL (Code 724)	Normal	Abnormal
Cholesterol—Total (Code 682)	Normal	Abnormal
EKG (Code 562)	Normal	Abnormal
Kidney Function (Code 401)	Normal	Abnormal
Liver Function (Code 382)	Normal	Abnormal
Sugar (Code 790)	Normal	Abnormal
Thyroid Level (Code 242)	Normal	Abnormal
Triglycerides (Code 491)	Normal	Abnormal

Report Test
5-77
Summons

Add line numbers to all lines in this court document. When your document is typed, the line that appears next to the line number will vary from some of those shown here.

1 STATE OF MINNESOTA IN DISTRICT COURT
2
3 COUNTY OF PENNINGTON NORTHERN JUDICIAL DISTRICT
4
5 DALE E. MATTHEWS) NO. ____________
6 248 Hughes Street)
7 Thief River Falls, MN 56701)
8)
9 Plaintiff,)
10)
11 vs.) SUMMONS
12)
13 MELANIE D. HILL)
14)
15 Defendant.)
16
17 THE STATE OF MINNESOTA TO THE DEFENDANT:
18
19 YOU ARE HEREBY SUMMONED and required to appear and defend,
20 within the time designated in this action and in this Court. You shall appear
21 and defend within 20 days after the service of the Complaint against you,
22 exclusive of the day of service. Service by publication is complete 30 days
23 after the date of first publication.
24
25 YOU ARE HEREBY NOTIFIED that in case of your failure to appear
26 and defend within the time designated, judgment by default shall be rendered
27 against you for the relief demanded in the Complaint.
28
29 SIGNED this _____ day of March, 20--.
30
31 ______________________________
32 Donna Farrington Attorney at Law
33 879 James Street
34 Thief River Falls, MN 56702
35 Telephone: 218-555-8844
36 Attorney for Plaintiff

Using and Designing Business Documents

6 PART

Keyboarding in Legal Services Careers

A career in legal services can take many forms. Lawyers, of course, are responsible for legal work, but a number of other positions in the legal services field are available. Often, lawyers assign tasks to paralegals. Paralegals—also referred to as legal assistants—have taken on a larger percentage of responsibilities in recent years. Another profession in the law field, that of court reporter, requires excellent communication skills. Court reporters must take exact notes of proceedings. Keyboarding skills are important for many job functions in legal services careers, and they can prove to give a job candidate an advantage.

Paralegals can work in many different business settings, but they are found most commonly in law firms and government offices. Court reporters are responsible for providing an accurate and detailed legal record of any proceeding. For individuals working in the legal services field, strong communication skills, written and spoken, are very important, but being able to convey ideas in a typed report in a timely manner is even more important.

Goals

Keyboarding

- Demonstrate improved speed and accuracy when operating the keyboard by touch.
- Type at least 50 words per minute on a 5-minute timed writing with no more than 5 errors.

Language Arts

- Demonstrate acceptable proofreading skills, including using proofreaders' marks correctly.
- Demonstrate acceptable language arts skills in punctuation, grammar, and mechanics.
- Demonstrate acceptable language arts skills in composing and spelling.

Word Processing

- Use appropriate word processing commands necessary to complete document processing activities successfully.

Document Processing

- Correctly format office forms, office publications, online resumes, and form letters.

Objective Test

- Answer questions with acceptable accuracy on an objective test.

UNIT 21

Using and Designing Office Forms

LESSON 101
Using Correspondence Templates

LESSON 102
Using Report Templates

LESSON 103
Designing Letterheads

LESSON 104
Designing Notepads

LESSON 105
Designing Miscellaneous Office Forms

Using Correspondence Templates

Goals

- Demonstrate improved speed and accuracy while typing.
- Demonstrate acceptable language arts skills in adjective and adverb agreement.
- Correctly use Word's correspondence templates.
- Correctly format a memo using a template.

A. WARMUP

alphabet	1	Jimmy quit and packed the seventy extra bags for Liz Owens.
concentration	2	paleoanthropologist extraterritoriality oversimplifications
easy	3	Cory works with a tutor when he works with theory problems.

Skillbuilding

B. MAP+: ALPHABET

Follow the GDP software directions for this exercise to improve keystroking accuracy.

C. PROGRESSIVE PRACTICE: ALPHABET

Follow the GDP software directions for this exercise to improve keystroking speed.

Language Arts

D. ADJECTIVES AND ADVERBS AND AGREEMENT

Study the rules at the right.

RULE
adjective/adverb

Use comparative adjectives and adverbs (*-er*, *more*, and *less*) when referring to two nouns or pronouns; use superlative adjectives and adverbs (*-est*, *most*, and *least*) when referring to more than two.

The shorter of the two training sessions is the more helpful one.
The longest of the three training sessions is the least helpful one.

RULE
agreement nearer noun

If two subjects are joined by *or*, *either/or*, *neither/nor*, or *not only/but also*, make the verb agree with the subject nearer to the verb.

Neither the coach nor the players are at home.
Not only the coach but also the referee is at home.
But: Both the coach and the referee are at home.

Edit each sentence to correct any errors.

```
4  Of the three printers, the faster one was the most
5  expensive.

6  Of the two phones purchased, the first one is the better
7  model.

8  The quietest of the five printers is also the less
9  expensive.

10 Not only the manager but also the employees wants to attend.

11 Neither the printer nor the monitors is in working order.

12 Either Mr. Cortez or his assistants have to sign the order.

13 Coffee or soft drinks is available for the afternoon
14 session.

15 Not only the manual but also the software were mailed.
```

Formatting

E. FILLING IN FORMS

Business forms can be created by using templates that are provided within word processing software. When a template is opened, a generic form is displayed on the screen. Specific information that is appropriate for that form may then be added.

Template forms contain data fields that correspond to blank sections on printed forms. For example, a memo template may include the guide words *To:*, *CC:*, *From:*, *Date:*, and *Re:* for the subject. Templates are usually designed so that you can replace data in fields easily by clicking in the field or by selecting the information you want to replace and typing the needed data. You can also delete fields that you do not wish to have included in your template. Built-in styles are also readily available.

You can customize a generic template by filling in repetitive information (such as the company name and telephone number) and saving it as a new template. Then each time you open that newly created template, the customized information appears automatically.

F. WORD PROCESSING: TEMPLATES—CORRESPONDENCE

Study Lesson 101 in your Word Manual. Complete all of the shaded steps while at your computer. Then format the documents that follow.

Document Processing

Form
101-1
Memo Template

Note: You may want to print the information in the template before deleting it.

1. Type this memo using the preselected blank memo template that has opened automatically.
2. Type the information for the memo from the copy shown next.

To: Philip Acoosta, Senior web designer

CC: Delores Easterwood, Manager

From: Bradley Pollard, General Manager

Date: April 14, 20--

Re: Web Site Update

agreement nearer noun

¶ Neither the Arbor Station Web site nor the Chapel Hills Web site have been updated in the last 2 years. The older of the two Web sites is the one that needs the greatest number of revisions. It is essential that our web sites reflect all the choices and amenities that are available to only not our current residents but also to those interested in joining our neighborhood.

adjective/adverb

¶ Philip, could you please draft a proposal that focuses on changes you make to our Web site. Most certainly, you will want to include the new villages that have been added the last 2 years: Creekwood village and Springwood village. These 2 add a total of 42 units to our sub division, and we want to make certain all home owners are aware of these new additions when they visit our Web site. | urs

Form
101-2
Memo Template

To: Bradley Pollard, General Manager | **CC:** Delores Easterwood, Design Manager | **From:** Philip Acosta, Senior Web Designer | **Date:** April 30, 20-- | **Re:** Revising the Web Sites

agreement nearer noun

¶ Brad, I am in the process of revising subdivision Web sites. Neither the Arbor Station Web site nor the Chapel Hills Web site has updated links. As you might recall, we updated the other subdivision Web pages last February so that we could add the real estate, local resources, and classified ads links to their sites. Of these three links, the real estate link will involve the greatest amount of revision because of all the graphic images that will be displayed.

adjective/adverb

¶ I plan to complete the first draft of the Web site revisions on May 5, but this draft will not include an update for the real estate link. Because of the complexity of this link, I am planning to send you my first draft of that link on May 10.

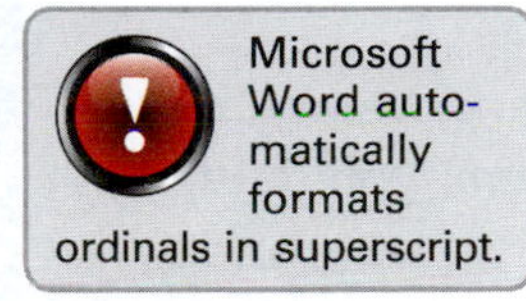

Microsoft Word automatically formats ordinals in superscript.

¶ If you have any questions regarding the status of the Web sites, feel free to call me at Extension 224 or stop by my office on the 4th floor. | urs

Form
101-3
Memo Template

To: Delores Easterwood, Design Manager | **CC:** Bradley Pollard, General Manager | **From:** Philip Acosta, Senior Web Designer | **Date:** May 11, 20-- | **Re:** Web Site Presentation

¶ Delores, I have finished my update of the Web sites and would like to schedule Meeting Room 120 to present my finished product. Brad indicated that this update was a top priority for the Design Department; therefore, I would like all department heads to attend the presentation and provide any feedback they wish to share.

¶ Would you please make reservations for Room 120 for May 15, preferably at 1 or 2 p.m. I expect the presentation and follow-up questions will take the better part of an hour.

¶ I'm excited about the changes we have made to the Web sites, and I believe through my revisions our subdivision sites will see a tremendous surge in hits in the coming months. | urs

Using Report Templates

Goals

- Type at least 48wpm/5'/5e.
- Correctly use Word's report templates.
- Correctly format a report using a template.

A. WARMUP

alphabet 1 That crazy man waved a quart jug of bad milk at the sphinx.
one hand 2 rebate minion red mom desert lumpily draw imply erase jolly
easy 3 Ken had a dish of lamb and cut up a mango and ripe apricot.

Skillbuilding

B. SUSTAINED PRACTICE: SYLLABIC INTENSITY

Take a 1-minute timed writing on the boxed paragraph to establish your base speed. Then take a 1-minute timed writing on the following paragraph. As soon as you equal or exceed your base speed on this paragraph, move to the next, more difficult paragraph.

4 People continue to rent autos for personal use or for 11
5 their work, and the car-rental business continues to grow. 23
6 When you rent a car, look carefully at the insurance cost. 35
7 You might also have to pay a mileage charge for the car. 46

8 It is likely that a good deal of insurance coverage is 11
9 part of the standard rental cost. But you might be urged 23
10 to procure extra medical, property, and collision coverage. 35
11 If you accept, be ready to see your rental charge increase. 46

12 Perhaps this is not necessary, as you may already have 11
13 the kind of protection you want in a policy that you have 23
14 at the present time. By reviewing your own auto insurance 34
15 policy, you may easily save a significant amount of money. 46

16 Paying mileage charges could result in a really large 11
17 bill. This is especially evident when the trips planned 22
18 involve destinations that are many miles apart. Complete a 34
19 total review of traveling plans before making a decision. 45

1 | 2 | 3 | 4 | 5 | 6 | 7 | 8 | 9 | 10 | 11 | 12

Take two 5-minute timed writings.

C. 5-MINUTE TIMED WRITING

```
20      Job stress is not so uncommon in today's workplace.       11
21 There may be many causes of job stress; but the most likely  23
22 reasons it occurs are overwork, possible layoffs, conflicts  35
23 with people at work, or just simply working in a job that    46
24 is no longer to your liking.                                 52
25      Symptoms of job stress are common to many people, and   53
26 they include changes in sleeping patterns, short temper,     74
27 upset stomach, headache, and low morale. Although many of    86
28 us suffer from one or more of the above symptoms, we should  98
29 take them seriously if the symptoms continue or if we tend  110
30 to experience three or four of the symptoms at the same     121
31 time continuously.                                          125
32      Sometimes it is possible to reduce the stress in your  136
33 work by taking a commonsense approach to the situation. If  148
34 you think that you are being overworked, take a vacation or 160
35 avoid taking work home with you. If you are concerned about 172
36 layoffs, then be certain that you are prepared to make a    183
37 career change if it is required.                            190
38      If you have conflicts with your boss or with others at 201
39 the office, try to work them out by discussing the issues   213
40 with the people involved to be certain they understand all  224
41 aspects of the conflict. Then, work together to minimize    236
42 any future conflicts.                                       240
     1 | 2 | 3 | 4 | 5 | 6 | 7 | 8 | 9 | 10 | 11 | 12
```

Formatting

D. WORD PROCESSING: TEMPLATES—REPORT

Study Lesson 102 in your Word Manual. Complete all of the shaded steps while at your computer. Then format the documents that follow.

Document Processing

Form
102-4
Report Template

1. Type this report using the preselected blank report template that has opened automatically.
2. Type `TopDesign` as the company name.
3. Type the following as the address:

   ```
   3724 Woodbine Avenue
   Knoxville, Tennessee 37903
   ```

4. Type `Web Page Mistakes` as the title.
5. Type `Designing a Web Page` as the subtitle.
6. Move to the second page and type the same title as you did in step 4; then type the subtitle again on the second page.
7. Type the rest of the information into the template, as indicated in the copy shown next.

¶ Look closely and you'll find that almost all Web pages have design mistakes embedded with in. There are millions of Web pages on the WWW, and most of them were created by users who have never studied the finer points of web page design. Here are a few of the more common mistakes made in Webpage design.

Top 3 Mistakes

¶ Don't use fancy fonts or multiple fonts on your Web Page. There are literally 1,000s of fonts from which to choose. If you don't have them on your computer, you can search for any font you want on the WWW. Don't use many fonts that are too small or fonts that are difficult to read, such as script fonts.

¶ Don't use music on your Site! When Web pages were in there infancy, Web designers attempted to use music to attract visitors. Guess what—it miserably failed! If you must use an audio link, let the visitor choose as to whether or not he or she wishes to use it. People are attracted to your site on a quest for information. Unless that quest involves a search for songs, music is not the key to keeping them there!

¶ Don't use blinking text or animated GIFs. Such techniques detract the visitor from the content of your Web page. In today's world of Web page design, blinking text and animated GIFs make your site look unprofessional.

Other Common Mistakes

¶ Although we're discussing Web page design mistakes, spelling and grammar play still a critical role in designing a sucessful Web page. A page that contains these errors leads the visitor to believe that, if you have not taken the time to check for spelling and grammar mistakes, then the content may also be compromised.

¶ You should attempt to con struct your page with an easy-to-understand navigation structure. If a visitor clicks on one of the links on your page, it should lead him or her to the information that is being sought. If you take someone to a page that is totally irrelevant to the topic being searched there's a pretty good chance that you will loose that visitor forever.

Form 102-5
Report Template

1. Type this report using the preselected blank report template that has opened automatically.
2. Type `Home Planning Inc.` as the company name.
3. Type the following as the address:

```
580 Market Street
Lexington, Kentucky 40505
```

4. Type `Creating a Budget` as the title.
5. Type `Solutions for the Home` as the subtitle.
6. Use the same title on the second page of the report; then repeat the subtitle on the second page.
7. Type the rest of the information into the template, as indicated in the copy shown next.

¶ To begin your budget analysis, write down every time you spend money; list what your expenses are during the month. Think also about different categories that you can list under which your expenses will fall. Keep your expenses in a columnar arrangement so they can be added up easily at the end of the month.

¶ You also need to list all your sources of income. As you did with your list of expenses, arrange all your income sources in a columnar format.

Reviewing Your Budget

¶ During the month, review both your income and your expenses. Do you notice any large or unusual amounts that don't typically appear every month? If there are, you might want to exclude them or place them in a different section of your budget. Leaving them categorized as typical monthly expenses may distort your budget. Look also to see if you have expenses that don't occur on a monthly basis. Maybe you have auto insurance that renews every six months. If that is the case, set aside the monthly equivalent of that six-month expense so that you know how much will be assigned each month.

¶ After listing all your expenses and all your income, look at the grand totals for both categories. Does the expense column total exceed the income column total? If so, you are spending more than you are earning, and some adjustments need to be made. You could possibly reduce the amount you spend on items such as entertainment or cut back on the number of times you eat out in a restaurant rather than preparing your meals at home.

¶ During the month, be sure that you record every time you spend money. If it looks like you are spending too much money and that you might run out of money before the month is over, you will have to cut back on some of your expenses. You cannot spend money you do not have!

Looking Back

¶ At the end of the month, see how well you have done with your expenses. Did you record every expense? Did you have to cut back because you were spending too much? What expenses did you cut back to make certain that you did not exceed your monthly income? After analyzing your month's budget, make adjustments and start with a new budget the next month. After a few months of preparing and analyzing your budget, you will be a better caretaker of your money.

Designing Letterheads

Goals

- Demonstrate improved speed and accuracy while typing.
- Demonstrate acceptable proofreading skills by comparing lines.
- Correctly use Word's features for small caps and text boxes.
- Correctly format a letterhead form.

A. WARMUP

alphabet
1 Jackson believed that we quizzed the old sphinx from Egypt.

practice: *v* and *b*
2 verb bevel bevy above Bev livable vibe bovine brave visible

easy
3 Rodney may risk half of his profits for the old oak mantel.

Skillbuilding

B. MAP+: NUMBERS

Follow the GDP software directions for this exercise to improve keystroking accuracy.

PPP PRETEST » PRACTICE » POSTTEST

PRETEST
Take a 1-minute timed writing.

C. PRETEST: Vertical Reaches

4 The senior lawyer was able to tackle the case in June. 11
5 He knew he would be making himself available to the court 23
6 for a fourth time in a month. He said he needed to revamp 34
7 his vacation plans to guard against whatever might go awry. 45
1 | 2 | 3 | 4 | 5 | 6 | 7 | 8 | 9 | 10 | 11 | 12

PRACTICE
Speed Emphasis:
If you made no more than 1 error on the Pretest, type each *individual* line 2 times.
Accuracy Emphasis:
If you made 2 or more errors, type each *group* of lines (as though it were a paragraph) 2 times.

D. PRACTICE: Up Reaches

8 aw awry away paws drawer awakes spawns brawny awards aweigh
9 se self seen sewn bosses paused senior seller seizes itself
10 ki kiln kilt kite skirts joking kinder bikini making unkind
11 rd hard lard cord hurdle overdo lizard inward boards upward

E. PRACTICE: Down Reaches

12 ac acid ache aces jacked facial actors tacked jackal places
13 kn knot knee knob knives kneels knight knotty knocks knaves
14 ab able blab ably tables fabric babies rabbit cabana cables
15 va vase vain Vail evades revamp valley avails ravage canvas

POSTTEST

Repeat the Pretest timed writing and compare performance.

F. POSTTEST: Vertical Reaches

Language Arts

G. PROOFREADING

Compare these lines with lines 38–42 on page 419. Edit the lines to correct any errors.

```
16      If you have conflicts with your boss or with others at
17  your office, try to work them out by discusing the issue
18  with the people involved to be curtain they understand all
19  all aspects of the conflict. Work together to minimize any
20  any future conflict.
```

Formatting

H. DESIGNING A FORM

Use the following guidelines to design an attractive, effective form:

1. Keep all elements of your design simple and balanced.
2. Limit the number of fonts, attributes (bold, italics, and so on), and sizes. Using no more than two fonts is a good rule of thumb.
3. Use white space liberally to separate and open up text and graphics.
4. Use different alignments (left, center, right, and full) to add interest and emphasis and to improve readability.
5. Experiment and change—Word makes both easy to do.

I. WORD PROCESSING: FONT—SMALL CAPS AND TEXT BOXES

Study Lesson 103 in your Word Manual. Complete all of the shaded steps while at your computer. Then format the documents that follow.

Document Processing

Form
103-6
Letterhead Form

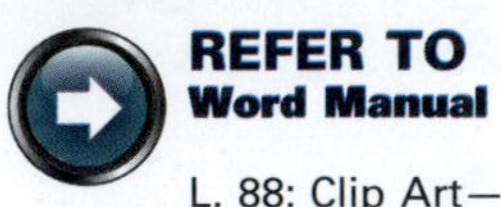

REFER TO
Word Manual

L. 88: Clip Art—Insert

1. Change the top, left, and right margins to 0.3 inch.
2. Insert a text box at the top of the page that is 1.4 inches high and 7.8 inches wide.
3. Center the text box horizontally and position it relative to the top margin.
4. Click inside the text box, and change the text alignment to right.
5. Change to Calibri 24 pt. Bold, Small Caps, and type this:

   ROCKWALL REAL ESTATE

6. Press ENTER 1 time, change the font to Calibri 11 pt., and type this:

   893 Shoreview Drive
   Rockwall, TX 75032
   972-555-8900

7. Change the font to Calibri 11 pt. Italic, and type this:

   www.rockwallhomes.com

8. Click outside the text box, and then insert clip art related to real estate.
9. Set the clip art wrap style so the clip art is on top of the text box; and then size and move it so that it fits inside the text box as shown in the illustration below.
10. Change the text box and clip art shapes to appear as rounded rectangles.
11. Select a text box border and shading that complement the colors in the clip art.
12. Select all text, and change the font color to one that complements the colors in the clip art.
13. Compare your finished letterhead to the illustration that follows. Make any necessary changes, including removing any automatic hyperlink.

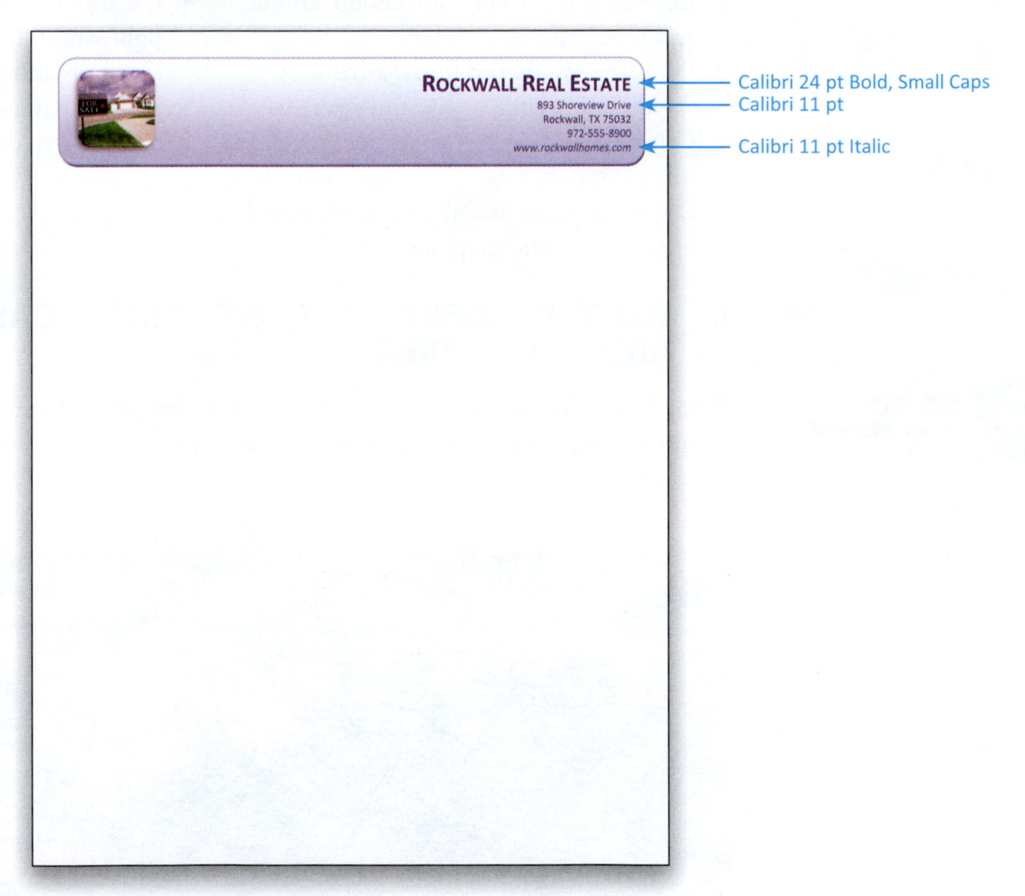

Form
103-7
Letterhead Form

1. Change the top, left, and right margins to 0.3 inch.
2. Insert a text box at the top of the page that is 1.1 inches high and 7.8 inches wide.
3. Click inside the text box, and change the text alignment to center.
4. Change to Cambria 24 pt. Bold Italic, Small Caps, and type this:

   Jack's Matting and Framing

5. Press Enter 1 time, and change the font to Calibri 12 pt. Bold, and type this:

   123 Pearl Street

6. Press the Space Bar 2 times, and then insert a square bullet symbol from the Wingdings font group.
7. Press the Space Bar 2 times and type this:

   Boulder, CO 80306

8. Press the Space Bar 2 times, insert a square bullet symbol, press the Space Bar 2 times, and type this:

   303-555-9022

9. Press Enter 1 time, then change the font to Calibri 12 pt. Bold Italic, and type this:

   www.weframe.com

10. Click outside the text box, and then insert clip art related to picture framing.
11. Set the clip art wrap style so the clip art is on top of the text box; and then size and move it so that it fits inside the left side of the text box as shown in the illustration below.
12. Copy the clip art; then paste it to the right side of the text box, in a position similar to the clip art on the left side of the text box as shown in the illustration below.
13. Change the text box and clip art shapes to appear as rounded rectangles.
14. Select a text box border and shading that complement the colors in the clip art.
15. Select all text, and change the font color to one that complements the colors in the clip art.
16. Compare your finished letterhead to the illustration that follows. Make any necessary changes, including removing any automatic hyperlink.

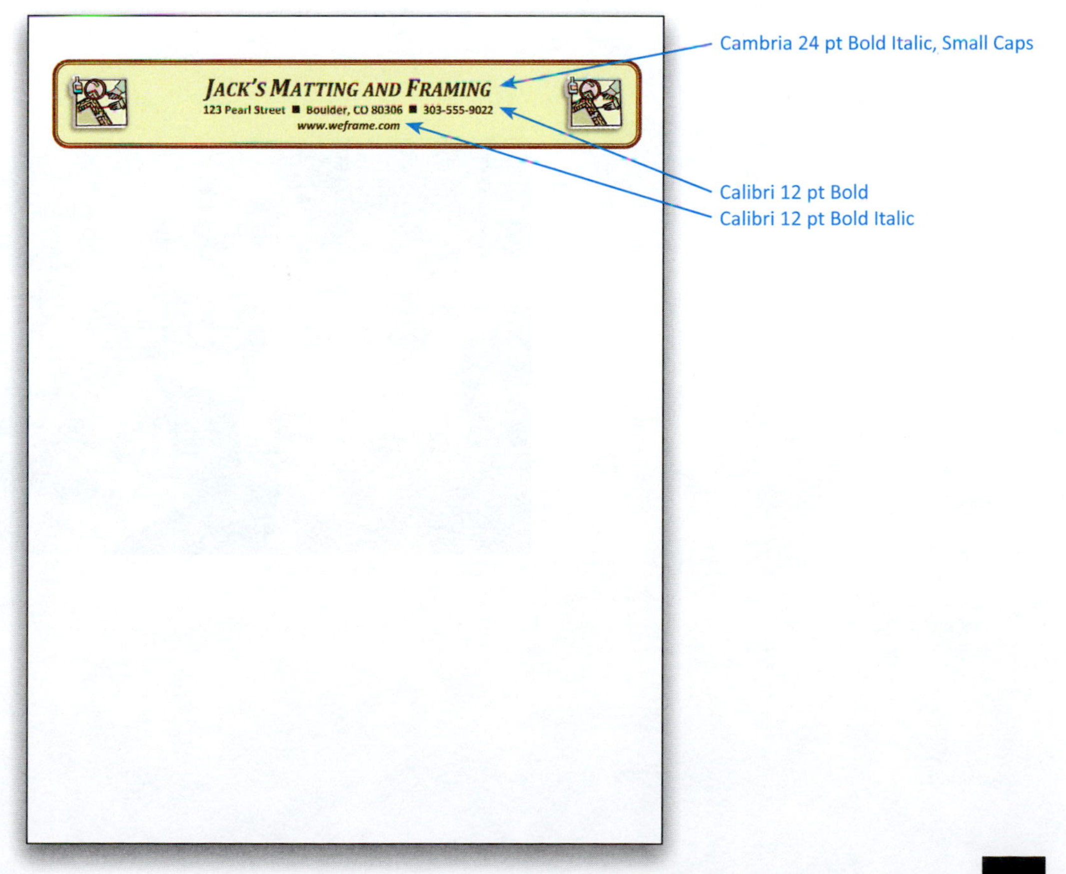

Form 103-8
Letterhead Form

1. Create a letterhead design of your own—for you personally, for your institution, or for a business.
2. Insert at least one picture that enhances the theme of the letterhead.
3. Remember to include complete information in the address block.
4. Try using fonts that you have not yet applied—experiment with point sizes and attributes.

Strategies for Career Success

Managing Business Phone Time

The average American spends an hour a day on the phone. Phone calls can be extremely distracting. Time is spent taking care of the call and following up after the call. You can take steps to reduce wasted time on the phone.

Before you make an outgoing call, organize the topics you want to discuss. Have all the materials you need: pens, paper, order forms, and so on. Consider sending an e-mail when appropriate, rather than making a phone call. E-mail is less intrusive and can be answered when the recipient has time instead of when it's sent. If you do decide to use e-mail, be prepared to follow up later if you don't get a response.

When you take an incoming call, answer it promptly. Identify yourself. It is common to answer the phone with your first and last name (for example, "Mary Smith speaking" or "Mary Smith"). Limit social conversation; it wastes time. Give concise answers to questions. At the end of the call, summarize the points made. End the conversation politely.

Your Turn: Keep a log of your time on the phone for one day. What is your average conversation time? What can you do to reduce your average phone conversation time?

UNIT 21 LESSON

Designing Notepads 104

Goals

- Type at least 48wpm/5'/5e.
- Correctly use Word's print options.
- Correctly format a notepad form.

A. WARMUP

alphabet	1	Save his quiz by fax; I jammed it in a plain brown package.
frequent digraphs	2	es ewes yes espy eves less desires west exes eyes fees mess
easy	3	The giant world map is the handiwork of the man in Langley.

Skillbuilding

B. PROGRESSIVE PRACTICE: NUMBERS

Follow the GDP software directions for this exercise to improve keystroking speed.

C. TECHNIQUE PRACTICE: TAB KEY

Press TAB 1 time between words. Type each line 2 times.

4	Kim→	apt→	Mac→	art→	Nat→	Meg→	ads→	arm→	all→	ado→	Joy
5	Orr→	awl→	Jan→	Ida→	Moe→	Lin→	zap→	Joe→	zed→	ark→	awe
6	Kai→	Lev→	add→	ask→	Mom→	Uri→	Jeb→	Nan→	aid→	Lot→	amp
7	Jay→	Hal→	Ima→	Ira→	ail→	aim→	Ian→	Max→	Pat→	Liv→	Jim

Keyboarding Connection

Effective E-Mail Management

Are you bombarded with e-mail? Take a few simple steps to manage e-mail more efficiently and reduce wasted time.

Create separate accounts, or perhaps different folders with filters for routing incoming messages, for receiving messages that require your direct attention. Keep your mailbox clean by deleting or archiving messages you no longer need. Create folders to organize messages you need to keep (for example, set up folders for separate projects).

Keep backups of important files. Be cautious of e-mail from people you do not know. Check your e-mail on a regular basis to avoid buildup of messages. Set up an automatic responder message for when you are out of the office, so people know not to expect an immediate response, and tell whom they should contact in your absence.

Your Turn: Review the current organization of your e-mail. List ways you can improve your e-mail management.

Take two 5-minute timed writings.

Goal: At least 48wpm/5'/5e

D. 5-MINUTE TIMED WRITING

```
 8      Employers are always searching for people who have       10
 9 salable skills. Having salable skills makes you unique and    22
10 desirable as an employee. Developing skills and qualities     34
11 such as a pleasing personality, a good sense of humor, a      45
12 positive attitude, an ability to get along with people, and   57
13 the ability to manage your time and prioritize your work      69
14 may help you find a job.                                      74
15      A tenacious person is persistent and maintains strong    85
16 work habits. He or she does not give up on a task easily      96
17 and always expects to finish the assigned task.              106
18      A good sense of humor and a positive attitude are two   117
19 traits that can help a person advance on the job. Although   128
20 there are times to be serious at work, sometimes you have    140
21 to look at things humorously. If you maintain a positive     151
22 attitude, other workers will like to work with you.          162
23      When you acquire the skills to manage your time and     172
24 prioritize your work, you will be successful in anything     184
25 you try to do. When you are given an assignment, ask for     195
26 guidelines so that you will know what needs to be done and   207
27 in what order. Then try to complete the assignment in a      218
28 timely fashion. The skills may be difficult to learn, but    230
29 you will be glad you can manage your time and work.          240
     1 | 2 | 3 | 4 | 5 | 6 | 7 | 8 | 9 | 10 | 11 | 12
```

Formatting

GO TO Word Manual

E. WORD PROCESSING: PRINT OPTIONS

Study Lesson 104 in your Word Manual. Complete all of the shaded steps while at your computer. Then format the documents that follow.

Document Processing

Form
104-9
Notepad Form

Many ink-jet printers do not print beyond the bottom half inch on a sheet of paper. Keep this in mind when positioning objects at the bottom of a page.

1. Insert a picture of an appointment book or a picture related to a day planner.
2. Drag and size the picture so that it looks similar to the one in the illustration that follows.
3. Create a text box, about the same size and in the same position as the one in the illustration, to hold the words "A Note From Sheila McDaniel."
4. Remove the border around the text box.
5. Change to Calibri 36 pt. Bold, and center and type this:

   `A Note From Sheila McDaniel`

6. Create a text box at the bottom of the page, about the same size and in the same position as the one in the illustration, to hold the company name, address, and telephone number.
7. Remove the border around the text box.
8. Change to Calibri 20 pt. Bold Italic; then type this:

   `Computer Solutions Made Simple`

9. Press ENTER, change to Calibri 14 pt. Bold; then type this:

   `4829 Kramer Street, Boise, Idaho 83702`

10. Press ENTER; then type this:

    `208-555-1344`

11. Display formatting marks; then anchor all objects to the first blank line at the top of the page.
12. Change to a whole-page view, click outside any objects, and select and copy the entire document.
13. Move to the end of the document, and insert three manual page breaks to create three additional blank pages.
14. Paste the copied document, into each of the three newly created pages: click in the fourth page, and paste; click just *before* the Page Break formatting code on the third page, and paste; click just *before* the Page Break formatting code on the second page, and paste.
15. Use the print option to print four pages per sheet on 8.5- by 11-inch paper.

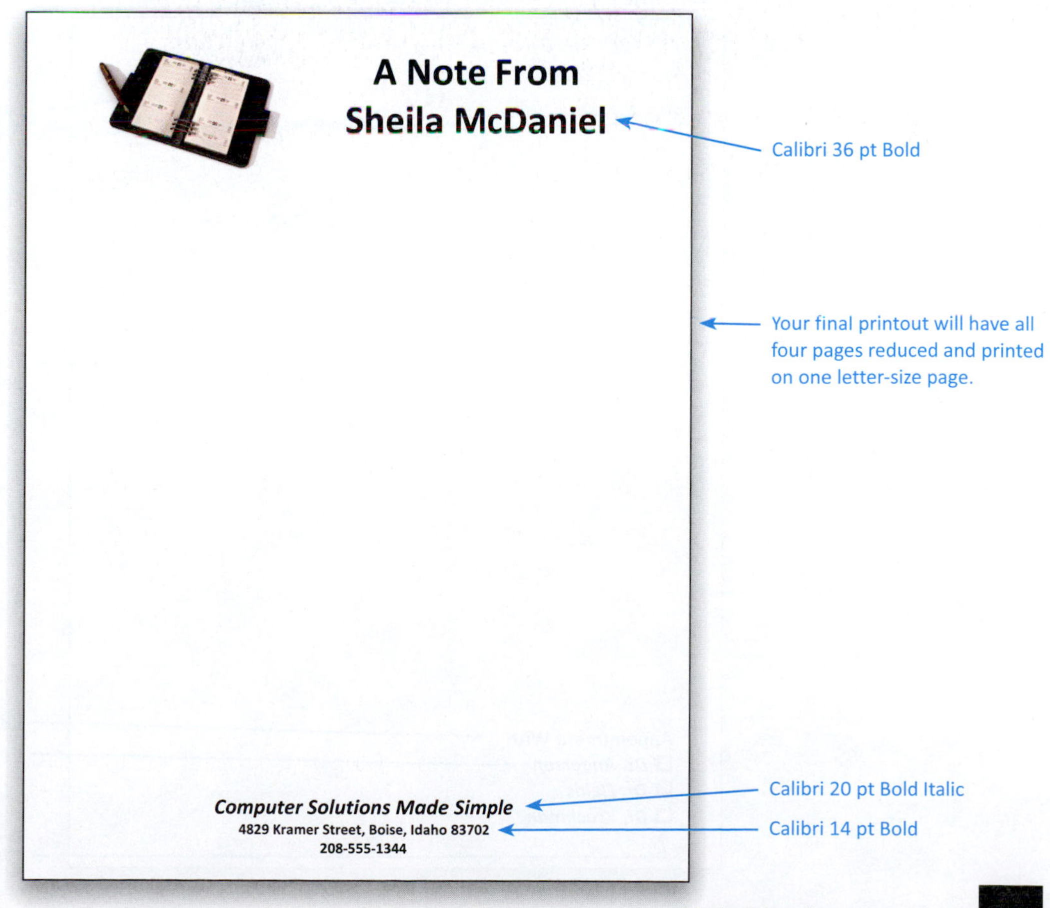

Form
104-10
Notepad Form

1. Insert a picture of a heart or a hospital.
2. Drag and size the picture so that it looks similar to the one in the illustration that follows.
3. Create a text box, about the same size and in the same position as the one in the illustration, to hold the words "The Heart Clinic."
4. Remove the border around the text box.
5. Change to Calibri 36 pt. Bold, Small Caps, and center and type this:

   `The Heart Clinic`
6. Apply a color to the text that complements the picture you inserted in step 1.
7. Press Enter, change to Calibri 16 pt. Bold Italic, and type this:

   `www.heartclinic.org`
8. If necessary, remove the hyperlink from www.heartclinic.org.
9. Create a text box, about the same size and in the same position as the one in the illustration, to hold the doctors' names displayed at the bottom of the page.
10. Remove the border around the text box.
11. Change to Calibri 20 pt. Bold, and type this:

    `Appointment With`
12. Insert a check box from the Wingdings font group, using 20 pt.
13. Change to Calibri 20 pt. Bold Italic, then type `Dr. Anderson` and press Enter.
14. Repeat steps 12 and 13 for the remaining names in the list: `Dr. Fields` and `Dr. Krachman`.
15. Display formatting marks; then anchor all objects to the first blank line at the top of the page.
16. Change to a whole-page view, click outside any objects, and select and copy the entire document.
17. Move to the end of the document and insert three manual page breaks to create three additional blank pages.
18. Paste the copied document into each of the three newly created pages: click in the fourth page, and paste; click just *before* the Page Break formatting code on the third page, and paste; click just *before* the Page Break formatting code on the second page, and paste.
19. Use the print option to print four pages per sheet on 8.5- by 11-inch paper.

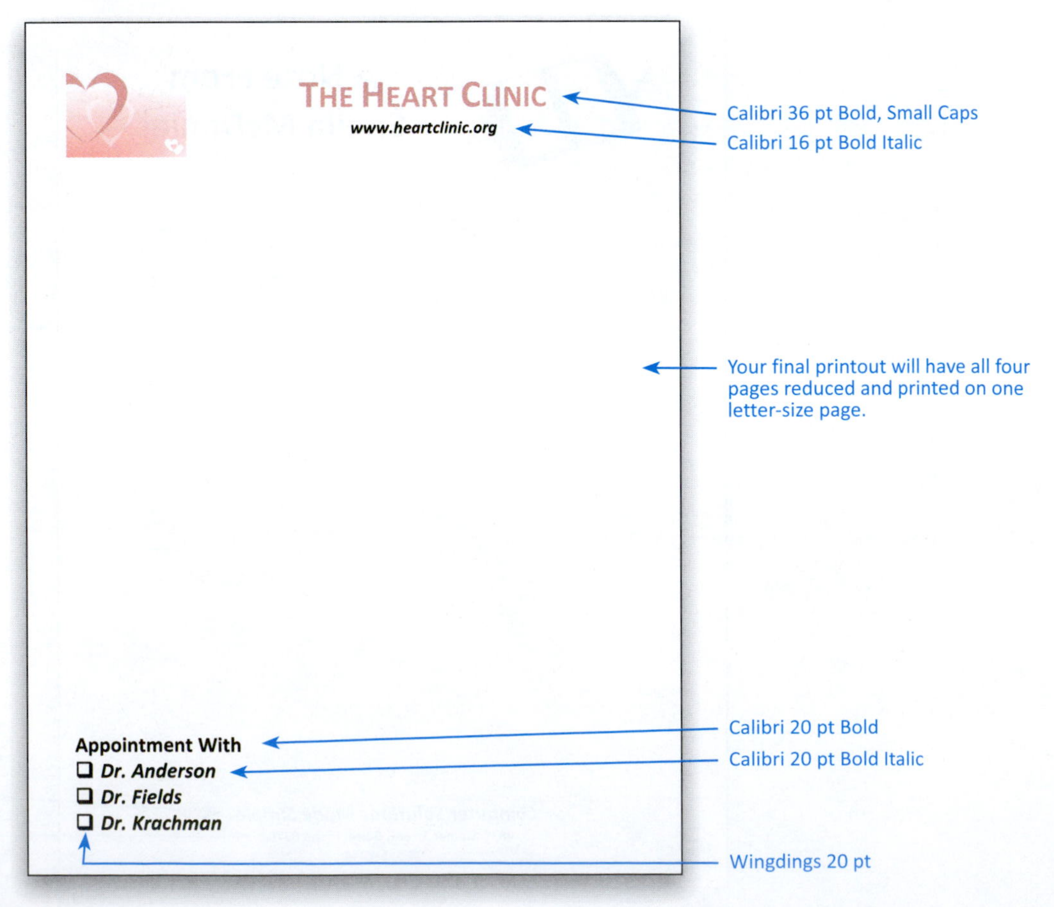

Form
104-11
Notepad Form

1. Create a notepad design of your own—for you personally, for your institution, or for a business.
2. Insert at least one picture that enhances the theme of the notepad.
3. Insert at least one text box with a fill.
4. Try using fonts that you have not yet applied. Experiment with point sizes and attributes.

Keyboarding Connection

Using Hyperlinks

Do you know how to surf the Web? It's easy! The Web contains pages, which are blocks of text, visuals, sound, or animation. Hyperlinks are certain words in the text of the Web page that are highlighted, underlined, or colored differently from the other words. These words link to other pages on the Web.

When you point your cursor at a hyperlink and click, the page connected to that word is displayed. Therefore, one page on the Web can connect to many other pages. Hyperlinked pages do not have to be read in any specific order.

Hyperlinks enable you to connect and retrieve Web pages from computer networks worldwide. With hyperlinks, you can point and click or surf your way all over the Web. You also can bookmark pages that you find, so you can find them again later.

Your Turn: Open a page on the Web. Surf the Web using the hyperlinks displayed on the page.

UNIT 21

LESSON

Designing Miscellaneous Office Forms

105

Goals

- Demonstrate improved speed and accuracy while typing.
- Demonstrate acceptable language arts skills in composing an e-mail message.
- Correctly format a directory form, a sign-in form, and a memo template.
- Successfully complete a Progress and Proofreading Check with zero errors on the first scored attempt.

A. WARMUP

```
alphabet        1 Xylophone wizards quickly begat a lively form of jive beat.
number/symbol   2 pnoe@att.net 270% Ivy & Day 3/8 Go! $17.59 *sic (#6423-145)
easy            3 The turkeys and hogs may spend the day in the mango fields.
```

Skillbuilding

B. 12-SECOND SPEED SPRINTS

Take three 12-second timed writings on each line.

```
4 The man with the rifle may signal us to take the sign down.
5 Hale saw a bible of the gospel in the chapel near the lake.
6 Half of the maps may be for the land and half for the lake.
7 The firm did not sign a form that may name me to the panel.
  ''''5''''10''''15''''20''''25''''30''''35''''40''''45''''50''''55''''60
```

C. PACED PRACTICE

Follow the GDP software directions for this exercise to improve keystroking speed and accuracy.

Language Arts

D. COMPOSING AN E-MAIL MESSAGE

Compose the body of an e-mail message to explain basic design guidelines. Refer to page 423—Section H, Designing a Form. Using your own wording, include the following ideas:

Paragraph 1. Explain that a simple, balanced design is essential and that typefaces (fonts), attributes, and sizes should be limited.

Paragraph 2. Explain that white space should be used to make text easier to read and graphics easier to see.

Paragraph 3. Explain that word processing software is a powerful tool that makes experimenting easy.

Document Processing

Form
105-12
Directory Form

1. Change the page orientation to landscape.
2. Change the top margin to 2 inches, the bottom margin to 0.75 inch, and the side margins to 0.5 inch.
3. Insert clip art associated with a home about the same size in the same position as the one in the illustration. **Note:** Change text wrap to In Front of Text before moving the clip art.
4. Click outside the clip art; then insert a text box, about the same size in the same position as the one in the illustration, to hold the headings.
5. Press ENTER 1 time, then change to Calibri 48 pt. Bold, Small Caps.
6. Center and type this:

   ARBOR STATION SUBDIVISION

7. Change the font color to complement the clip art inserted in step 3.
8. Press ENTER 1 time; then change to Calibri 24 pt. Bold, Small Caps.
9. Center and type DIRECTORY OF RESIDENTS as the subtitle.
10. Remove the border around the text box.
11. Click outside the text box; then insert a boxed table with 4 columns and 17 rows.
12. Move the table below the clip art and text box, as shown in the illustration.
13. Select the entire table, and change the font to Calibri 18 pt. Bold.
14. Type these column headings in Row 1: Name | Address | Telephone | E-Mail
15. Change the alignment in Row 1 to center.
16. Add shading to Row 1, using a color that complements the picture.
17. Change the font color to white.

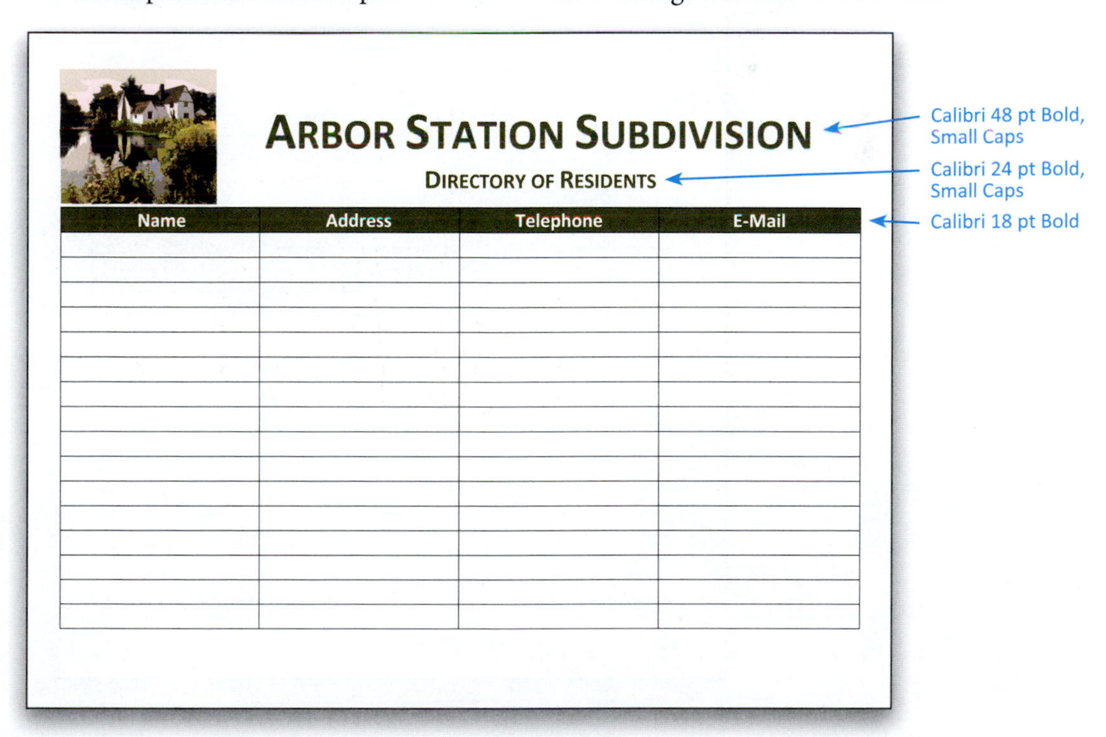

Form
105-13
Sign-In Form

1. Change the top margin to 2 inches, the bottom margin to 0.75 inch, and the side margins to 0.5 inch.
2. Insert a boxed table with 4 columns and 28 rows.
3. Select the entire table, and change the font to Calibri 16 pt. Bold.
4. Type these column headings in Row 1: `Name | Time In | Time Out | Date`, and then change the alignment in Row 1 to center.
5. Add shading of 25 percent to Row 1.
6. Move to the top of the document, and insert clip art, associated with a check mark, in the same position and about the same size as the one in the illustration that follows. **Note:** Before moving the clip art, set text wrapping so that the image appears on top of the text without rearranging the text.
7. Click outside the clip art, then insert a text box, about the same size and in the same position as the one in the illustration, to hold the heading and the doctors' names.
8. Remove the border around the text box.
9. Change to Calibri 36 pt. Bold, Small Caps; then center and type this:

   `Physician Sign-In Sheet`
10. Press Enter 1 time, and change the alignment to left.
11. Press Tab 2 times; turn off Small Caps; then insert a round bullet using Wingdings 20 pt. Bold.
12. Press Tab 1 time, then type `Dr. Eleanor Clemmons` and press Enter 1 time.
13. Repeat steps 11 and 12 for the remaining names in the list: `Dr. Paul Davis` and `Dr. Jeanine Sordhoff`.

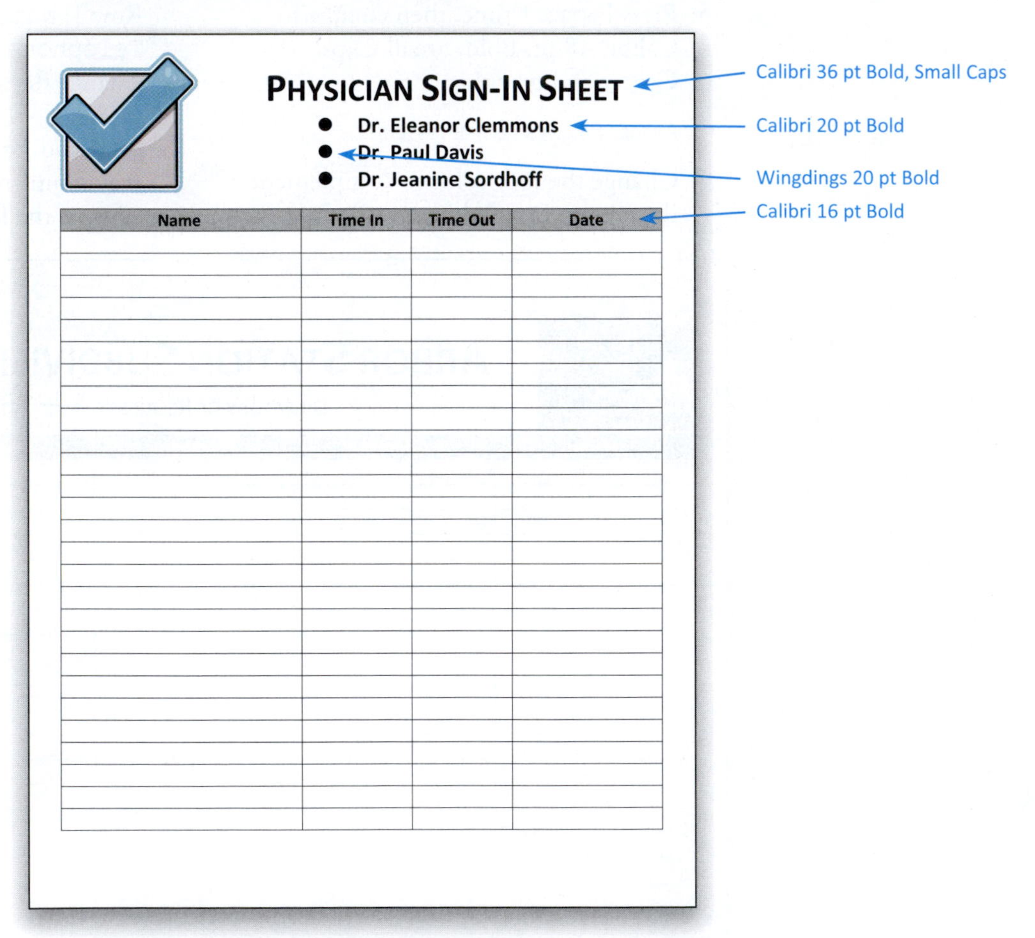

Form
105-14
Memo Template

Progress and Proofreading Check

Documents designated as Proofreading Checks serve as a check of your proofreading skill. Your goal is to have zero typographical errors when the GDP software first scores the document.

Type this memo using the preselected blank memo template that has opened automatically.

To: All Employees

CC: Shelley Castle, Benefits Department

From: Brett R. Cecoli, Human Resources Dept.

Date: November 10, 20--

Re: Company Well ness Program

¶ With the flue season just around the corner we are again planning to administer free flu shots to all company employees. Last year we administered a similar program, and employee absence due to illness was considerably reduced. A signup schedule will be distributed to all Departments on December 5th. The schedule will list all dates, times, and locations for flu shots to be given administered. Please put December 5 on your calender and be sure to sign up for your flu shot. | urs

Keyboarding Connection

Choosing a Different Home Page

You don't have to start at the same home page every time you start your browser. You can change the browser's home page to start at one of your favorite Web pages or even a blank page. Refer to your browser's help feature for details.

Some companies require all browser windows to open with the company's home or internal use page. Check your company's Internet usage policy before making any changes to your computer or browser settings.

Your Turn: Using your browser, access a favorite Web page. Make it your browser's home page.

UNIT

22

Designing Office Publications

LESSON 106
Designing Cover Pages

LESSON 107
Designing Announcements and Flyers

LESSON 108
Designing Newsletters—A

LESSON 109
Designing Newsletters—B

LESSON 110
Designing Newsletters—C

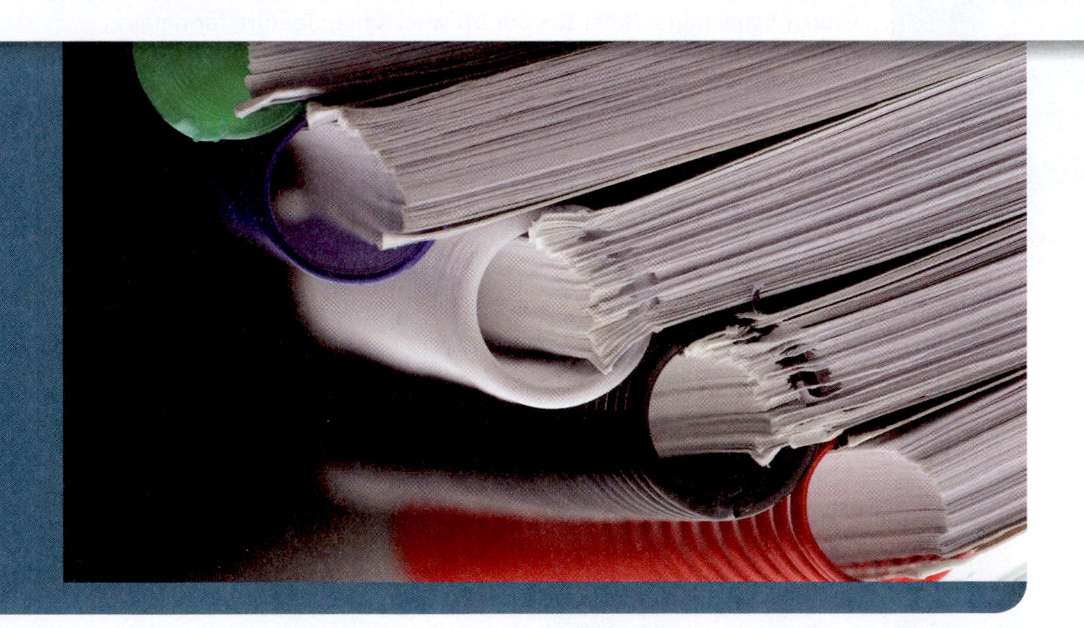

Designing Cover Pages 106

Goals

- Type at least 49wpm/5'/5e.
- Correctly use the WordArt feature.
- Correctly format a cover page.

A. WARMUP

alphabet 1 Few black taxis drove up major roads on a quiet hazy night.
concentration 2 nonrepresentational professionalization straightforwardness
easy 3 Glen may dismantle the authentic robot when he is downtown.

Skillbuilding

B. SUSTAINED PRACTICE: NUMBERS AND SYMBOLS

Take a 1-minute timed writing on the boxed paragraph to establish your base speed. Then take a 1-minute timed writing on the following paragraph. As soon as you equal or exceed your base speed on this paragraph, move to the next, more difficult paragraph.

4 Shopping in the comfort and convenience of your own 11
5 living room has never been more popular than it is right 22
6 now. Shopping clubs abound on cable channels. You could 33
7 buy anything from exotic pets to computers by mail order. 45

8 Sometimes you can find discounts as high as 20% off 11
9 the retail price; for example, a printer that sells for 22
10 $565 might be discounted 20% and be sold for $452. You 33
11 should always investigate quality before buying anything. 44

12 Sometimes hidden charges are involved; for example, 11
13 a printer costing $475.50 that promises a discount of 12% 22
14 ($57.06) has a net price of $418.44. However, if charges 34
15 for shipping range from 12% to 15%, you did not save money. 45

16 You must also check for errors. Several errors have 11
17 been noted so far: Invoice #223, #789, #273, and #904 had 22
18 errors totaling $21.35, $43.44, $79.23, and $91.23 for a 34
19 grand total of $235.25. As always, let the buyer beware. 45

1 | 2 | 3 | 4 | 5 | 6 | 7 | 8 | 9 | 10 | 11 | 12

Take two 5-minute timed writings.

Goal: At least 49wpm/5'/5e

C. 5-MINUTE TIMED WRITING

```
20      Why do people choose a particular career? Your first    11
21 instinct might likely be to say that people work to make     22
22 money. That may be true, but extensive research has shown    34
23 that many other factors are considered just as important     45
24 and that these factors should be carefully considered when   57
25 you are about to accept a new position.                      65
26      There are many rewards that a job can provide, such     76
27 as a chance to be creative, the chance to spend time with    87
28 people whose company you enjoy, or the feeling that you are  99
29 doing something useful for yourself or for your employer.   111
30 The quality of the work environment is also an important    122
31 consideration in choosing a career, as is the chance to     134
32 work closely with people on a daily basis.                  142
33      Obviously, your career should allow you to advance in  153
34 your field and to be competitive for promotions. You should 165
35 be able to see a clear line for advancement in your job and 177
36 be given a chance to demonstrate your abilities so that     188
37 your coworkers and supervisors recognize your strengths.    200
38      Parallel to these factors is the need for your job to  211
39 give you adequate challenges on a daily, continuing basis.  223
40 If your work is not challenging, boredom will set in, and   234
41 you might soon be looking for a change in your career.      245
      1 | 2 | 3 | 4 | 5 | 6 | 7 | 8 | 9 | 10 | 11 | 12
```

Formatting

D. WORD PROCESSING: WORDART

Study Lesson 106 in your Word Manual. Complete all of the shaded steps while at your computer. Then format the documents that follow.

Document Processing

Report
106-78
Cover Page

1. Insert clip art related to health or the medical profession.
2. Drag and size the clip art so that it looks similar to the one shown in the illustration that follows.
3. Apply an attractive visual style of your choice for the clip art.
4. Insert WordArt, about the same size and in the same position as the one shown in the illustration. Type these words for the WordArt:

   `Health Care Basics`

5. Use Calibri 36 pt. Bold for the Word-Art text; choose a style and color for the WordArt to coordinate with the clip art.
6. Create a text box, about the same size and in the same position as the one below the clip art.
7. Type "Making the Right Choice" inside the text box using Cambria 36 pt. Bold Italic. Choose a font color for the text to coordinate with the clip art.
8. Remove the border around the text box.
9. Create a text box, about the same size and in the same position as the one at the bottom of the page shown in the illustration that follows.
10. Type A SEMINAR SPONSORED BY BOYD MEDICAL CENTER inside the text box using Calibri 24 pt. Bold, Small Caps.
11. Press ENTER 2 times, change to Calibri 20 pt. Bold, and then type this:

    `Tanner Auditorium`

12. Press ENTER 1 time; then type this:

    `1:00 to 2:30 p.m.`

13. Press ENTER 2 times; then type this:

    `July 10, 20--`

14. Remove the border around the text box.

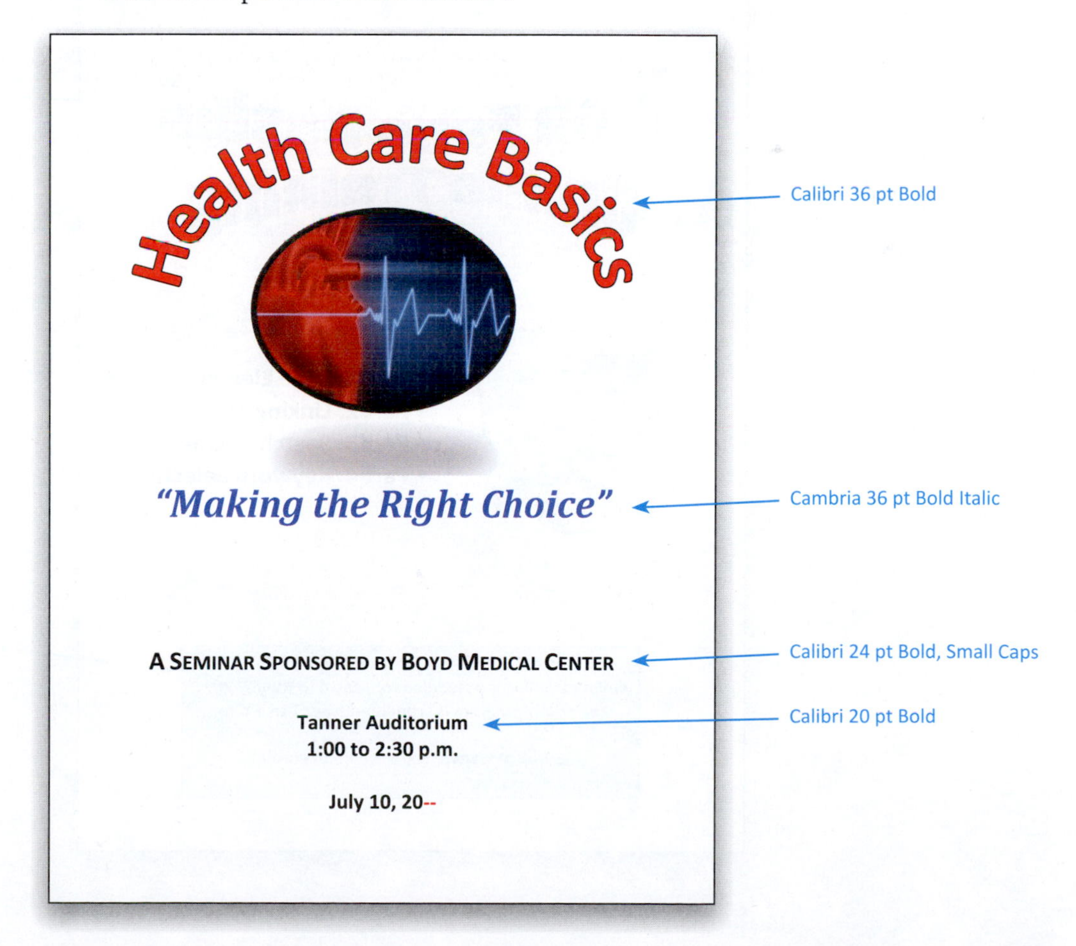

Report 106-79
Cover Page

1. Insert clip art related to the Internet or education.
2. Drag and size the clip art so that it looks similar to the one in the illustration that follows.
3. Apply an attractive visual style of your choice to the clip art.
4. Insert WordArt, about the same size and in the same position as the one at the top of the illustration, and then type `Web Page Design` on the first line and `Online Training` on the second line.
5. Use Impact 36 pt. Bold font for the WordArt text; choose a style and color for the WordArt to coordinate with the clip art.
6. Create a text box, about the same size and in the same position as the one shown in the illustration that follows.
7. Use Calibri 24 pt. Bold to type the following inside the text box:
   - `Part 1: Page Elements`
   - `Part 2: Linking Tools`
   - `Part 3: Search Engines`
   - `Part 4: Keyword Selection`
8. Remove the border around the text box.
9. Create a text box, about the same size and in the same position as the one shown at the bottom of the page in the illustration that follows.
10. Use Calibri 18 pt. Bold to center and type the following inside the text box:

    `Cost of 16 hours of instruction is $300. Online training is scheduled for May 4 to May 7, 20--. Each daily program is scheduled from 1 to 5 p.m.`
11. Press ENTER 2 times, and then center and type this:

    `Enroll at www.webdesign.com/enroll.`
12. Add a text box fill color that coordinates with the picture.

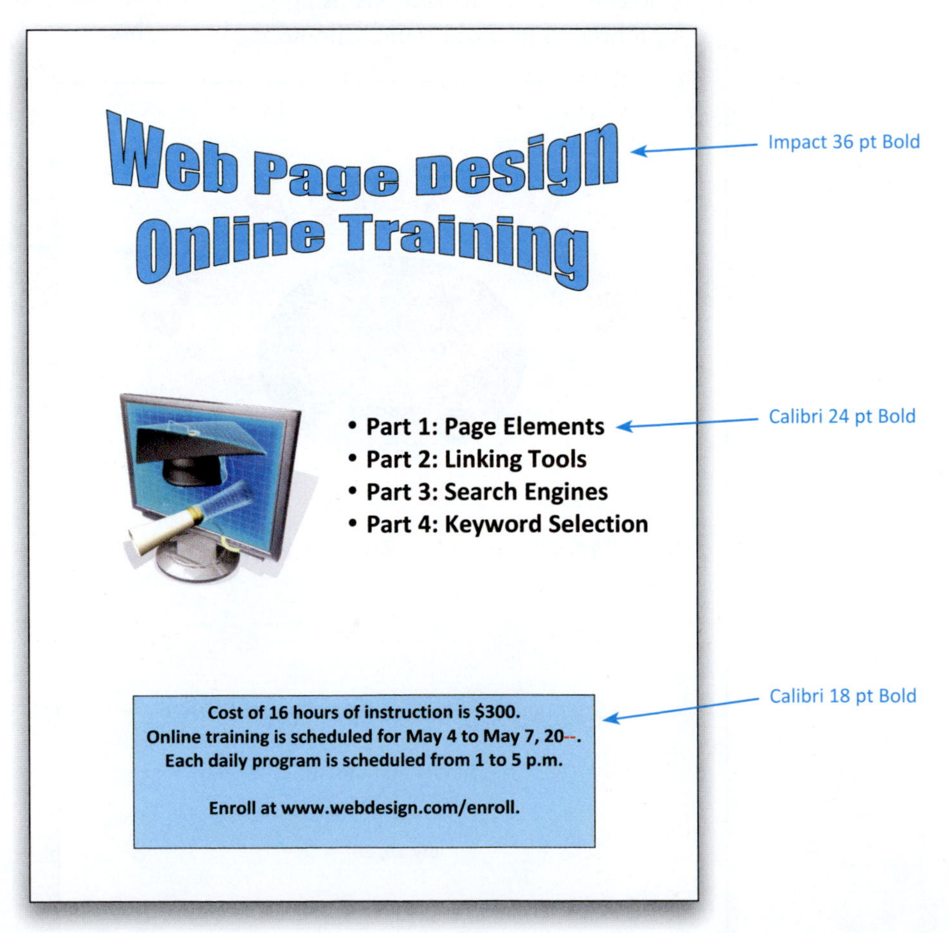

Report
106-80
Cover Page

1. Create a cover page design of your own to be used as the insert for a view binder that holds information for one of your courses.
2. Insert at least one picture related to the subject of the course.
3. Insert at least one text box with a fill.
4. Insert some WordArt.
5. Change any of the font colors to coordinate with the picture or WordArt as desired.

Designing Announcements and Flyers

Goals

- Demonstrate improved speed and accuracy while typing.
- Demonstrate acceptable language arts skills in pronoun usage.
- Correctly use Word's features to move a table and add a background page color.
- Correctly format an announcement and a flyer.

A. WARMUP

alphabet	1	Six big devils from Japan then quickly forgot how to waltz.
one hand	2	revert unhook act him access pumpkin gave lymph fever union
easy	3	Rob's work as the auditor in Lakeland may help us in a way.

Skillbuilding

B. MAP+: ALPHABET

Follow the GDP software directions for this exercise to improve keystroking accuracy.

C. PROGRESSIVE PRACTICE: ALPHABET

Follow the GDP software directions for this exercise to improve keystroking speed.

Language Arts

Study the rules at the right.

D. PRONOUNS

RULE
nominative pronoun

Use nominative pronouns (such as *I, he, she, we, they,* and *who*) as subjects of a sentence or clause.

The programmer and he are reviewing the code.
Barb is a person who can do the job.

RULE
objective pronoun

Use objective pronouns (such as *me, him, her, us, them,* and *whom*) as objects of a verb, preposition, or infinitive.

The code was reviewed by the programmer and him.
Barb is the type of person whom we can trust.

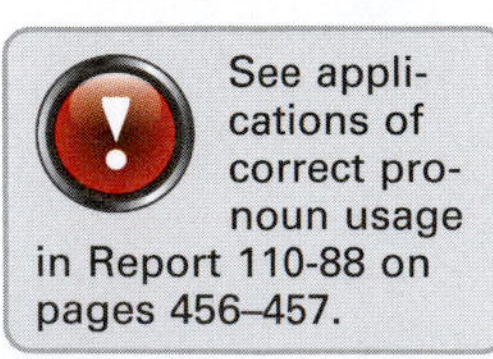
See applications of correct pronoun usage in Report 110-88 on pages 456–457.

Edit each sentence to correct any errors.

4 We hope they will take all of them to the concert tomorrow.

5 John gave the gift to she on Monday; her was very pleased.

6 If them do not hurry, Mary will not finish her work on time.

7 The book was proofread by her; the changes were made by he.

8 It is up to them to give us all the pages they read today.

9 Me cannot assure they that it will not rain for the picnic.

Formatting

E. WORD PROCESSING: TABLE—MOVE AND PAGE COLOR

Study Lesson 107 in your Word Manual. Complete all of the shaded steps while at your computer. Then format the documents that follow.

Document Processing

Report 107-81
Announcement

1. Insert WordArt, about the same size and in the same position as the one at the top of the illustration that follows.
2. Use a shape similar to the one shown in the illustration, with the words Dade County; choose the desired font and font size for the text.

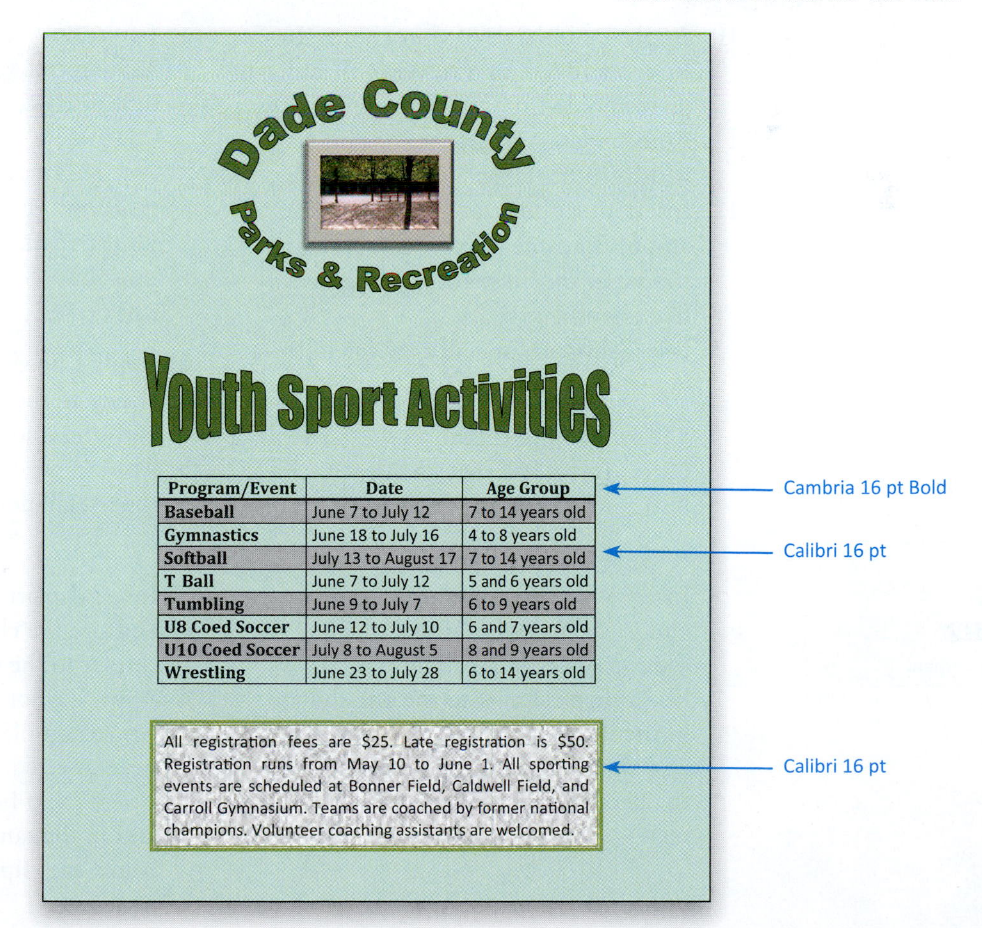

Dade County
Parks & Recreation

Youth Sport Activities

Program/Event	Date	Age Group
Baseball	June 7 to July 12	7 to 14 years old
Gymnastics	June 18 to July 16	4 to 8 years old
Softball	July 13 to August 17	7 to 14 years old
T Ball	June 7 to July 12	5 and 6 years old
Tumbling	June 9 to July 7	6 to 9 years old
U8 Coed Soccer	June 12 to July 10	6 and 7 years old
U10 Coed Soccer	July 8 to August 5	8 and 9 years old
Wrestling	June 23 to July 28	6 to 14 years old

All registration fees are $25. Late registration is $50. Registration runs from May 10 to June 1. All sporting events are scheduled at Bonner Field, Caldwell Field, and Carroll Gymnasium. Teams are coached by former national champions. Volunteer coaching assistants are welcomed.

3. Insert WordArt, similar in size and shape and in a position beneath the first WordArt you inserted in step 1. Use a shape similar to the one shown in the illustration, with the words `Parks & Recreation`; choose the desired font and font size for the text.
4. Insert clip art related to parks; drag and size the clip art so that it looks similar to the one in the illustration.
5. Select a picture style of your choice for the clip art.
6. Apply a color to the text in the WordArt to complement the clip art you have inserted.
7. Insert WordArt, about the same size and in the same position as the one below the WordArt you inserted in step 3. Type the words `Youth Sport Activities` and apply a font color that complements the overall design.
8. Insert a 3-column, 9-row boxed table. Drag the table to a position immediately below the WordArt inserted in step 7 as shown in the illustration that follows.
9. Use Calibri 16 pt. for all entries in the table. Type the following table entries:

Program/Event	**Date**	**Age Group**
Baseball	June 7 to July 12	7 to 14 years old
Gymnastics	June 18 to July 16	4 to 8 years old
Softball	July 13 to August 17	7 to 14 years old
T-Ball	June 7 to July 12	5 and 6 years old
Tumbling	June 9 to July 7	6 to 9 years old
U8 Coed Soccer	June 12 to July 10	6 and 7 years old
U10 Coed Soccer	July 8 to August 5	8 and 9 years old
Wrestling	June 23 to July 28	6 to 14 years old

10. Apply a table style of your choice. In Row 1 and Column A, verify that all text is bolded.
11. Automatically adjust the column widths in the table.
12. Insert a text box, about the same size and in the same position as the one shown in the illustration, using justified alignment.
13. Use Calibri 16 pt, and type the following words in the text box:

    All registration fees are $25. Late registration is $50. Registration runs from May 10 to June 1. All sporting events are scheduled at Bonner Field, Caldwell Field, and Carroll Gymnasium. Teams are coached by former national champions. Volunteer coaching assistants are welcomed.

14. Apply a border and a texture of your choice to the text box that coordinate with the color used in the WordArt.
15. Apply a page color that complements the overall design.

Report 107-82
Announcement

1. Insert WordArt, about the same size and in the same position as the one at the top of the illustration that follows.
2. Use a shape similar to the one shown in the illustration, with the words `Breckenridge Rentals`; choose the desired font and font size for the text.
3. Insert clip art related to skiing; drag and size the clip art so that it looks similar to the one in the illustration.
4. Apply a color to the text in the WordArt to complement the clip art you have inserted.
5. Insert a text box, about the same size and in the same position as the one below the clip art.

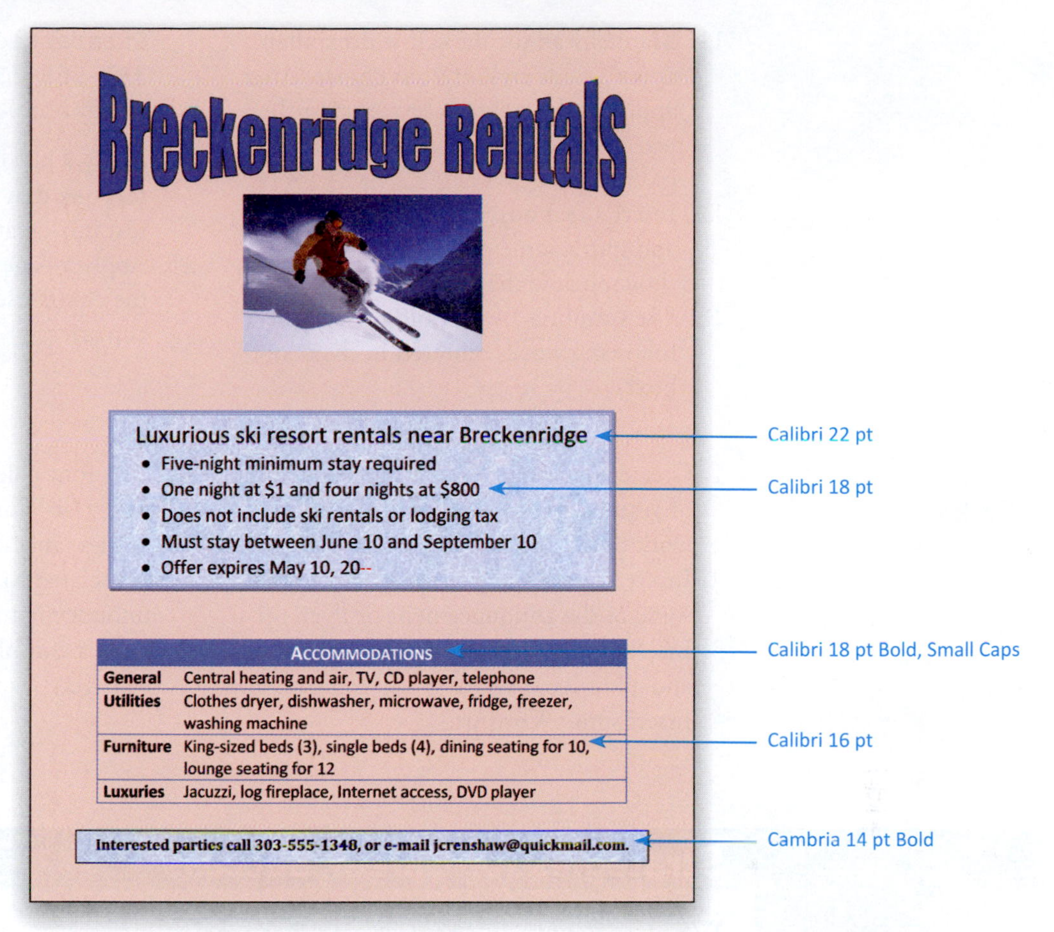

6. Type the following information in the text box. Use Calibri 22 pt. for the centered heading; then change to Calibri 18 pt. to format the remaining lines as a bulleted list:

   Luxurious ski resort rentals near Breckenridge
   - Five-night minimum stay required
   - One night at $1 and four nights at $800
   - Does not include ski rentals or lodging tax
   - Must stay between June 10 and September 10
   - Offer expires May 10, 20--

7. Apply a border and texture of your choice to the text box that coordinates with the colors used in the WordArt and clip art.
8. Insert a table with 2 columns and 5 rows. Drag the table to a position immediately below the text box created in step 5.
9. Merge the cells in Row 1.
10. Use Calibri 18 pt. Bold, Small Caps for Row 1; use Calibri 16 pt. for Rows 2 through 5. Type the following table entries:

Accommodations	
General	Central heating and air, TV, CD player, telephone
Utilities	Clothes dryer, dishwasher, microwave, fridge, freezer, washing machine
Furniture	King-sized beds (3), single beds (4), dining seating for 10, lounge seating for 12
Luxuries	Jacuzzi, log fireplace, Internet access, DVD player

11. Manually adjust the cell widths; then apply a table style of your choice. After applying the style, make sure that the text in Row 1 and Column A appears in bold.
12. Insert a text box, about the same size and in the same position as the one shown below the table.
13. Use Cambria 14 pt. Bold to type the following words centered in the text box:

```
Interested parties call
303-555-1348, or e-mail
jcrenshaw@quickmail.com.
```

14. Apply a border and a texture fill to the text box that match those used in the text box created in step 5.
15. Apply a page color that complements the colors used in the WordArt and clip art.

Report
107-83
Announcement or Flyer

1. Create an announcement or flyer design of your own for an upcoming event at work or on campus.
2. Insert at least one picture related to the topic of the announcement or flyer.
3. Insert at least one text box with a fill and a border.
4. Insert some WordArt.
5. Use a font color to coordinate with the clip art or WordArt.
6. Insert a table that contains information related to the topic of the flyer or announcement.
7. Apply a complementary page color to the page.

Strategies for Career Success

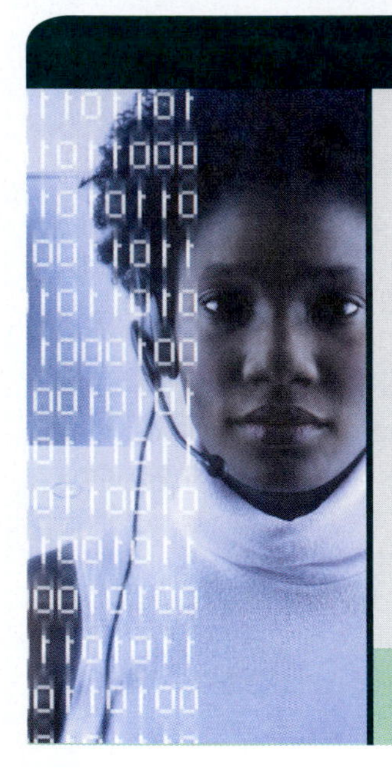

What to Exclude From Your Resume

What items should you omit from your resume? Don't list salary demands. If the job posting requires a salary history, create a separate page listing the salaries for each position you've held. If the job posting wants your salary requirements, in the application letter state, "Salary expectation is in the range . . . ," and provide a range (usually a $5,000 range).

Exclude personal information such as race, gender, health status, age, marital status, religious preference, political preference, national origin, and physical characteristics (for example, height and weight). Do not provide your Social Security number or your photograph.

Exceptions to listing personal information do exist. For example, if you are applying for a job at a political party's headquarters and you are a member of that party, listing your party affiliation might be important to your potential employer.

Your Turn: Review your resume. Have you included any personal information? If your answer is yes, does it serve a purpose for being in your resume?

Designing Newsletters—A

Goals

- Type at least 49wpm/5′/5e.
- Correctly format a newsletter masthead.

A. WARMUP

alphabet 1 In the North, quick waxy bugs jumped over the frozen veldt.
practice: *w* and *e* 2 wet were where we elbow wed dew wide ewe wee wade web endow
easy 3 Jane can buy fuel for the antique auto at the downtown lot.

Skillbuilding

B. PACED PRACTICE

Follow the GDP software directions for this exercise to improve keystroking speed and accuracy.

C. 5-MINUTE TIMED WRITING

Take two 5-minute timed writings.

Goal: At least 49wpm/5′/5e

```
 4      Purchasing a home is probably one of the most major        11
 5 financial decisions you will make in your lifetime. Dozens      22
 6 of questions need to be answered when buying a home. For        34
 7 example, how much of a down payment will you make and how       45
 8 much of a monthly payment on your mortgage will you be able     57
 9 to afford?                                                      60
10      In addition to your mortgage payment, there are other      71
11 costs associated with buying a new home. The mortgage will      82
12 cover the principal and interest for your loan, but you         94
13 will also have homeowner's insurance and utilities to pay,     105
14 such as water, sewer, electricity, or gas.                     114
15      You may want to purchase a home through a real estate     125
16 agent, and it is important that you find out how much of a     137
17 commission will be charged for that service.                   146
18      When working with a real estate agent, you need to let    157
19 that person know about the kind of community in which you      169
20 would prefer to live. Do you want to be close to schools,      180
21 shopping centers, and restaurants, or would you rather         191
22 purchase a home in a secluded neighborhood away from the       203
23 noise and congestion of a metropolitan city?                   212
24      When you find the home that you like, look at it very     223
25 carefully to see if it is structurally well built, if you      234
26 like the floor plan, and if it is big enough for you.          245
     1 | 2 | 3 | 4 | 5 | 6 | 7 | 8 | 9 | 10 | 11 | 12
```

Formatting

D. NEWSLETTER DESIGN

Newsletters are an excellent forum for communicating information on a wide range of subjects. A well-planned newsletter will employ all the basic principles of good design. However, because newsletters usually include information on a wide variety of topics, they are generally complex in their layouts.

Most newsletters have the following elements in common: mastheads, main headings and subheadings, text arranged in flowing newspaper-column format using various column widths to add interest, text boxes to emphasize and summarize, pictures to draw readers' attention and interest to a topic, and a variety of borders and fills.

The design of a multipage newsletter must look consistent from one page to the next. This consistency provides unity to the newsletter design and is often achieved through the use of headers and footers.

Document Processing

Report 108-84
Newsletter

Follow these steps to create the masthead and footer for the first page of the newsletter shown on the next page.

1. Set all margins to 0.75 inch.
2. Create an open table with 2 columns and 2 rows. Drag the middle column border to the left so that Column A is about 2.0 inches wide.
3. Right-align Column B, Row 1.
4. In Column B, Row 1, change to Calibri 36 pt. Bold and type `Planning Today for a Fire Emergency` on two lines.
5. Press ENTER 1 time, change to Calibri 14 pt. Bold, and type `A Newsletter From HLS Security Systems`; then press ENTER 1 time.
6. Move to Column A, Row 2, change to Calibri 12 pt. Bold Italic, and type `Volume 5, Issue No. 2`
7. Move to Column B, Row 2, and change to right alignment; then change to Calibri 12 pt. Bold Italic and type this:
   `February 20--`
8. Apply a left, right, and bottom border to Row 2.
9. In Column A, Row 1, insert clip art associated with security. Drag and size the clip art so that it looks similar to the one shown in the illustration that follows.
10. Select the newsletter title, and change the font color to coordinate with the picture in Column A.
11. Apply a double-line border to Row 1 using a color that complements the color in the newsletter title.
12. Insert a blank footer, and center and type `Page` followed by 1 space.
13. Insert a page number and close the footer.
14. Apply a page color to coordinate with the picture and newsletter title.

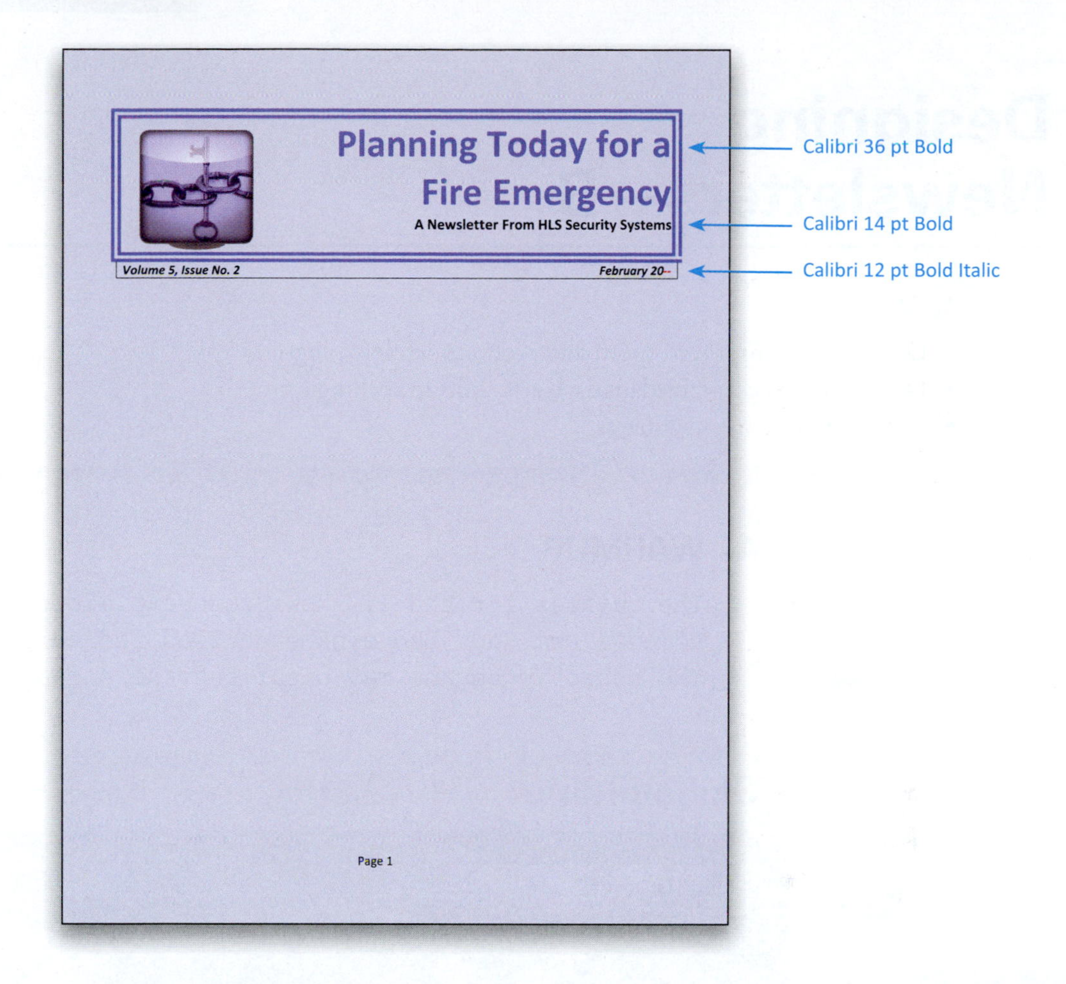

Report
108-85
Newsletter

1. Create a newsletter masthead of your own related to home safety.
2. Use any picture that enhances the purpose of your newsletter.

UNIT 22 LESSON

Designing Newsletters—B

109

Goals

- Demonstrate improved speed and accuracy while typing.
- Demonstrate acceptable language arts skills in spelling.
- Correctly format a newsletter.

A. WARMUP

alphabet	1	The quizzes for the TV shows were explained by Mick Jagger.
frequent digraphs	2	ed edge wed Eddy bed eyed cede lied fed edited led axed red
easy	3	The neurotic iguana may disorient the neighbor and her dog.

Skillbuilding

B. MAP+: SYMBOL

Follow the GDP software directions for this exercise to improve keystroking accuracy.

PPP PRETEST » PRACTICE » POSTTEST

PRETEST

Take a 1-minute timed writing.

C. PRETEST: Alternate- and One-Hand Words

```
4      In their opinion, the ornamental bicycle from Honolulu 11
5  may be regarded as an authentic antique. It deserves to be 23
6  treated well because it may attract many new visitors from 35
7  Texas and Ohio to most downtown streets in July and August. 47
     1 | 2 | 3 | 4 | 5 | 6 | 7 | 8 | 9 | 10 | 11 | 12
```

PRACTICE

Speed Emphasis:
If you made no more than 1 error on the Pretest, type each *individual* line 2 times.

Accuracy Emphasis:
If you made 2 or more errors, type each *group* of lines (as though it were a paragraph) 2 times.

D. PRACTICE: Alternate-Hand Words

```
8  maps visual suspend amendment turndown visible height signs
9  form profit penalty shamrocks blandish problem thrown chair
10 snap emblem dormant authentic clemency figment island usual
11 half signal auditor endowment ornament element handle amend
```

E. PRACTICE: One-Hand Words

```
12 serve uphill exceeds killjoy carefree homonym terrace onion
13 trade poplin greater pumpkin eastward plumply barrage holly
14 defer unhook reserve minimum attracts million scatter plump
15 exact kimono created phonily cassette opinion seaweed union
```

POSTTEST

Repeat the Pretest timed writing and compare performance.

F. POSTTEST: Alternate- and One-Hand Words

Language Arts

Type these frequently misspelled words, paying special attention to any spelling problems in each word.

G. SPELLING

```
16 operations health individual considered expenditures vendor
17 beginning internal pursuant president union written develop
18 hours enclosing situation function including standard shown
19 engineering payable suggested participants providing orders
20 toward nays total without paragraph meetings different vice
```

Edit the sentences to correct any misspellings.

```
21 The participents in the different meetings voted for hours.
22 The presdent of the union is working toward a resolution.
23 The health of each individal must be seriously considered.
24 Engineering has suggested providing orders for the vendor.
25 One expanditure has been written off as part of oparations.
26 He is inclosing the accounts payible record as shown today.
```

Document Processing

Report
109-86
Newsletter (Continued)

Open the file for Report 108-84. Follow these steps to continue the newsletter as shown below:

1. Move your insertion point to the end of the document; then press ENTER 1 time.
2. Insert File 109, and turn on automatic hyphenation.
3. Carefully place your insertion point in front of the first character of the text you inserted from File 109.
4. Select all the newly inserted text, including 1 blank line below the last line of text.
5. With the text still selected, create a 3-column page layout.
6. Select the following side headings in the newsletter, and change the font to Calibri 20 pt. Bold:

   ```
   Plan Ahead
   Make a Diagram
   Plan Your Escape
   Avoid Smoke
   ```

7. Insert clip art in the space below the first two side headings. The clip art should be related to the topic of each of the paragraphs (*plan* and *drawing*).
8. Set text wrapping to place text above and below the image, but not beside the image.
9. Set the clip art height to 1.8 inches; let the width adjust proportionally to the height.
10. Drag the clip art into a position similar to the clip art shown in the illustration.
11. Compare the placement of the columnar text to see if it's similar to that shown in the illustration. Check to see if the side heading "Plan Your Escape" appears at the top of Column C. If not, adjust the size and placement of the clip art.

Adjust the size and placement of the pictures on this page so that the heading **Plan Your Escape** displays at the top of Column C.

Highlighted words are spelling words from the language arts activities.

Planning Today for a Fire Emergency

A Newsletter From HLS Security Systems

Volume 5, Issue No. 2 *February 20--*

All family members must know what to do in case of a fire emergency in the home. Fighting a fire should be left to professional firefighters; family members should exit a burning home without delay.

There are several individual steps that must be taken to initiate a fire-evacuation plan.

Plan Ahead

One of the first steps at the beginning of your plan is to install smoke detectors and be sure they are operating. Also, close bedroom doors while sleeping. It takes 10 to 15 minutes for a fire to burn through a wooden door. Those few minutes could mean the difference between escaping or being trapped by the fire.

Make a Diagram

Develop a drawing of the floor plan in your home. Mark all exits, windows, doors, stairs, halls, and the locations of all fire alarms. Be sure that the children know how to identify an alarm sound when it is activated.

Plan Your Escape

Each family member must know how to exit the home by at least two different routes. The first route will most likely be the door normally used to exit; the second route might be through a window. Make sure that all windows open freely without restriction.

If a door is going to be used as an emergency exit, be sure that it is checked carefully before it is opened. If the door is hot, it means that the fire is immediately outside the door and that another exit should be chosen.

Avoid Smoke

If you are caught in a room filling with smoke, be sure to stay as low as

Page 1

possible to the floor and crawl toward the nearest exit. Smoke and heat rise, so the cleanest air will always be at the floor level.

If the door is closed between you and the fire and it is not possible for you to exit, stuff the cracks and cover vents to keep the smoke out.

Page 2

Report 109-87
Newsletter (Continued)

1. Open the file for Report 108-85 with the newsletter masthead you created.
2. Follow the steps for Report 109-86, and then delete the "Avoid Smoke" section at the bottom of Column C.
3. Insert a picture after the side heading "Plan Your Escape."
4. Drag and size the picture so that it is similar to the ones previously inserted on the page. Make certain that all of the text remains on that page and does not wrap to a second page.

Keyboarding Connection

E-Mail Privacy

How private are your e-mail messages? Although there has been a lot of discussion about hacking and Internet security, e-mail may be more secure than your phone or postal mail. In fact, most new-generation e-mail programs have some kind of encryption built in.

It is not hackers who are most likely to read your e-mail. It is anyone with access to your incoming mail server or your computer. If your computer and incoming server are at work, then you can assume your supervisor can read your e-mail. In some companies, it is normal practice to monitor employees' e-mail. Therefore, you should not send e-mail from work that you don't want anyone there to read.

If you are serious about e-mail privacy, you may want to examine other encryption methods. Different products are available to ensure that your e-mail is read only by the intended recipient(s). However, some companies don't allow employees to add software to their computers for legal reasons, so check your company's computer policies. It may be wiser to send personal e-mail from your own computer outside of work.

Your Turn: Perform a keyword search using a search engine for information on different products that are available to protect your e-mail privacy.

Designing Newsletters—C

Goals

- Type at least 49wpm/5'/5e.
- Correctly format a newsletter.
- Successfully complete a Progress and Proofreading Check with zero errors on the first scored attempt.

A. WARMUP

alphabet
1 The glum, wavy-haired ex-cons bequeathed fake topaz jewels.

number/symbol
2 gilp@comcast.net (11%) Ng & Ma 4/5 No! $13.86 *Est. #20-972

easy
3 Nancy and Blanche cut six bushels of corn in the cornfield.

Skillbuilding

B. 12-SECOND SPEED SPRINTS

Take three 12-second timed writings on each line.

4 He may go with us to the giant dock down by the handy lake.
5 The old chapel at the end of the big lake has an odd shape.
6 His body of work may charm the guests who visit the chapel.
7 His civic goal for the city is for them to endow the chair.

' ' ' ' 5 ' ' ' ' 10 ' ' ' ' 15 ' ' ' ' 20 ' ' ' ' 25 ' ' ' ' 30 ' ' ' ' 35 ' ' ' ' 40 ' ' ' ' 45 ' ' ' ' 50 ' ' ' ' 55 ' ' ' ' 60

C. TECHNIQUE PRACTICE: ENTER KEY

Type each line 2 times. Type each sentence on a separate line by pressing ENTER after each sentence.

8 Don't! We are. Give. Speak. Type it. Beg. Be there. We did?
9 Step on it. See to it. Wait. Find it? Says who? We do. Sit.
10 Who knows? See me. Get up. Eat! Where? Who is he? Finished?
11 When? Today. Do it now. We are up. Al saw her. Do not. All?

Take two 5-minute timed writings.

Goal: At least 49wpm/5'/5e

D. 5-MINUTE TIMED WRITING

```
12     When the rate of unemployment is very low, jobs are        11
13 easier to find. Although you may find a job easily, what       22
14 can you do to make sure your job is one you will enjoy?        33
15 Here are some suggestions to assist you.                       41
16     First, be certain you receive a job description when       52
17 you are hired. The job description should list all of the      64
18 requirements of the job and the details of what you will be    78
19 expected to do.                                                79
20     Second, you should receive some type of orientation to     90
21 your job and the company. During orientation, you will fill   102
22 out various tax forms, benefit forms, and insurance papers.   114
23 You may view a video that will help you learn more about      126
24 the company and available benefits.                           133
25     Third, when you start your training, you should take      144
26 notes, pay attention, and ask questions. You should also      155
27 have your trainer check your work for a period of time to     167
28 be sure you are performing your duties correctly. If your     178
29 tasks are complex, you can break them down into smaller      189
30 parts so you can remember all aspects of your job.            200
31     Finally, when you know your job requirements, chart       210
32 your work each day. Concentrate on being part of the team.    222
33 Be zealous in striving to work beyond the expectations of     234
34 your supervisor. Then, you will achieve job satisfaction.     245
     1 | 2 | 3 | 4 | 5 | 6 | 7 | 8 | 9 | 10 | 11 | 12
```

Document Processing

Report 110-88
Newsletter (Continued)

Open the file for Report 109-86. Follow these steps to finish creating the newsletter shown below.

1. Verify that automatic hyphenation is on.
2. Place your insertion point directly after the final period at the end of the sentence in Column A. Then press ENTER 2 times.
3. Change to Calibri 20 pt. Bold, and type `Practice the Plan` as a side heading. Then press ENTER 1 time.
4. Change to Calibri 14 pt., press ENTER 1 time, and then type the following paragraph:

   Effective fire evacuation is only as good as family members are aware of how it is supposed to function. Have them practice the plan, and be certain all family members are aware of all escape routes. Practice the escape plan at different hours.

5. With your insertion point after the final period you typed in step 3, press ENTER 2 times; then insert File 110.
6. Select the following side headings in the text that was inserted, and change the font to Calibri 20 pt. Bold:

```
Exit Safely
Plan to Meet
Assist Others
```

7. Insert clip art in the space below the side heading "Exit Safely." The clip art should be associated with the topic of the paragraph (*exit*).
8. Set the clip art with a height of 1.55 inches; let the width adjust proportionally to the height.
9. Apply the same picture style to the clip art that was used for the clip art on page 1 of the newsletter.
10. Drag the clip art into a position similar to the clip art shown in the illustration below. Set text wrapping to place text above and below the image, but not beside the image.
11. Move your insertion point to the end of the newsletter.
12. Insert a text box at the bottom of Column C, about the same size and shape and in the same position as the one shown in the illustration.
13. Change to Calibri 16 pt. Bold; then center and type this in the text box:

```
Future Issues
```

14. Press ENTER 1 time, change to Calibri 11 pt. Bold, and then center and type this:

```
March: Homeland Security
April: Updating Your System
May: Emergency Supplies
June: Safety Seminars
```

15. Apply a textured fill to the text box that complements the page color of the newsletter.
16. Change the shape of the text box to complement the shape used for the clip art in the newsletter.
17. Make whatever adjustments are needed to make your newsletter look attractive.
18. The newsletter should look similar to the illustrations that follow.

Planning Today for a Fire Emergency

A Newsletter From HLS Security Systems

Volume 5, Issue No. 2 ***February 20--***

All family members must know what to do in case of a fire emergency in the home. Fighting a fire should be left to professional firefighters; family members should exit a burning home without delay.

There are several individual steps that must be taken to initiate a fire-evacuation plan.

Plan Ahead

One of the first steps at the beginning of your plan is to install smoke detectors and be sure they are operating. Also, close bedroom doors while sleeping. It takes 10 to 15 minutes for a fire to burn through a wooden door. Those few minutes could mean the difference between escaping or being trapped by the fire.

Make a Diagram

Develop a drawing of the floor plan in your home. Mark all exits, windows, doors, stairs, halls, and the locations of all fire alarms. Be sure that the children know how to identify an alarm sound when it is activated.

Plan Your Escape

Each family member must know how to exit the home by at least two different routes. The first route will most likely be the door normally used to exit; the second route might be through a window. Make sure that all windows open freely without restriction.

If a door is going to be used as an emergency exit, be sure that it is checked carefully before it is opened. If the door is hot, it means that the fire is immediately outside the door and that another exit should be chosen.

Avoid Smoke

If you are caught in a room filling with smoke, be sure to stay as low as

Page 1

nominative pronoun
Column A (*"they"*)

possible to the floor and crawl toward the nearest exit. Smoke and heat rise, so the cleanest air will always be at the floor level.

If the door is closed between you and the fire and it is not possible for you to exit, stuff the cracks and cover vents to keep the smoke out.

Practice the Plan

Effective fire evacuation is only as good as family members are aware of how it is supposed to function. Have them practice the plan, and be certain all family members are aware of all escape routes. Practice the escape plan at different hours.

Exit Safely

Exiting safely through a ground-floor window or door is usually uneventful. However, if you are on the second floor or higher, exiting will require you to take some precautions. If you attempt to jump from an upper floor, you might injure an ankle or leg. One suggested solution would be to purchase a ladder for the upstairs bedrooms to use for emergency exits. Make sure to inspect the ladders annually to be sure they operate properly.

If living in an apartment, never use an elevator in case of fire. An elevator may cease operating during a fire and stop between floors or at a floor where the fire is located. As an alternative, use a fire escape or stairwell to escape.

Teach your family that, once they are outside a burning building, they should never go back into the building.

Plan to Meet

A special meeting place should be considered that is always located a safe distance from the house. Knowing where this meeting place is will assist all family members in determining where to meet to see if everyone is safe and has exited the home.

Assist Others

You may have to provide some special assistance to young children.

If children are afraid, they may choose to hide under a bed or in the closet. Encourage them to exit outside the home, a safe distance away from the fire. Make certain that your children can operate all windows, open all doors, descend a ladder, or lower themselves to the ground.

You may also need to consider assistance for the elderly, who may have difficulty in exiting the premises.

Future Issues

March: Homeland Security
April: Updating Your System
May: Emergency Supplies
June: Safety Seminars

Page 2

nominative pronoun Column B (*"they"*)
objective pronoun Column C (*"them"*)
objective pronoun Column A (*"them"*)

objective pronoun Column C (*"themselves"*)
nominative pronoun Column C (*"who"*)

Report 110-89
Flyer

Progress and Proofreading Check

Documents designated as Proofreading Checks serve as a check of your proofreading skill. Your goal is to have zero typographical errors when the GDP software first scores the document.

1. Insert WordArt about the same size as the one in the illustration that follows. Center the WordArt horizontally, and apply a color of your choice for the text. Use the following text for the WordArt:

   `Premier Real Estate`

2. Insert clip art related to homes; drag and size the clip art so that it looks similar to the one in the illustration.
3. Select an attractive visual style of your choice for the clip art.
4. Apply a font color to the text in the WordArt to complement the clip art you have inserted.
5. Create a text box, about the same size and in the same position as the one in the illustration. Use Calibri 20 pt. Bold Italic to type and center the words `"Serving the Canton area for 55 years"` in the text box. Use a shape fill that complements the color of the WordArt.
6. Create a boxed table with 3 columns and 9 rows. Drag the table to a position immediately below the text box created in step 5.
7. Use Calibri 16 pt. for Row 1; use Calibri 14 pt. for Rows 2 through 9. Type the table entries as follows:

Weekly Specials: April 10 Through April 16		
Address	**Price**	**Agent**
224 Birchfield Run, Green Bay	$242,000	Angie Summers
4134 Diamond Court, DePere	$257,000	Doug McClure
812 Eagles Nest Circle, Allouez	$263,000	Angie Summers
427 Matthews Avenue, Green Bay	$269,000	Connie McCormack
1280 Timbermill Circle, Allouez	$283,000	Doug McClure
628 Clifton Terrace, DePere	$297,000	Chad Burnett
829 Cypress Court, Green Bay	$323,000	Angie Summers

8. Apply a style of your choice to the table. After applying the style, make sure that the text in Row 1, Row 2, and Column A appear in bold.

9. Apply a page color that complements the colors used in the WordArt and clip art.

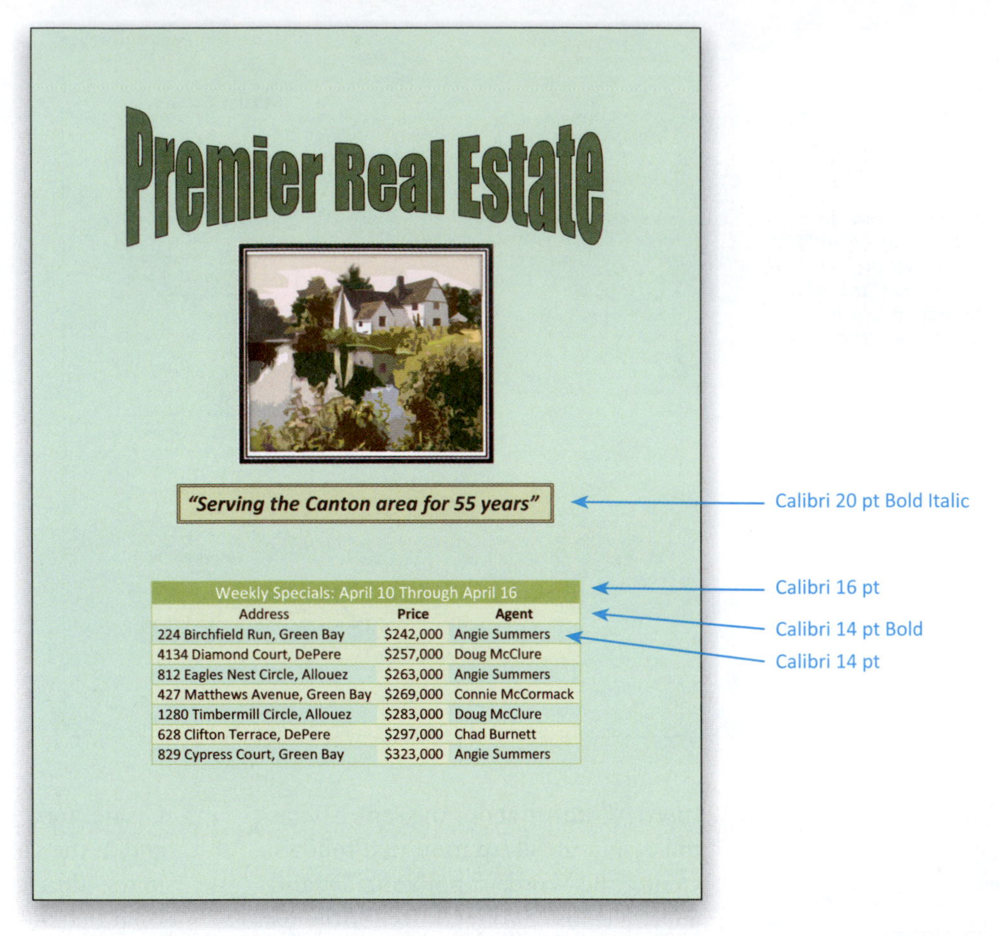

Premier Real Estate

"Serving the Canton area for 55 years"

Weekly Specials: April 10 Through April 16		
Address	**Price**	**Agent**
224 Birchfield Run, Green Bay	$242,000	Angie Summers
4134 Diamond Court, DePere	$257,000	Doug McClure
812 Eagles Nest Circle, Allouez	$263,000	Angie Summers
427 Matthews Avenue, Green Bay	$269,000	Connie McCormack
1280 Timbermill Circle, Allouez	$283,000	Doug McClure
628 Clifton Terrace, DePere	$297,000	Chad Burnett
829 Cypress Court, Green Bay	$323,000	Angie Summers

UNIT 23

Online Resumes and Merged Documents

LESSON 111
Designing an Online Resume

LESSON 112
Mail Merge—A

LESSON 113
Mail Merge—B

LESSON 114
Mail Merge—C

LESSON 115
Mail Merge—D

Designing an Online Resume

Goals

- Demonstrate improved speed and accuracy while typing.
- Demonstrate acceptable language arts skills in capitalization.
- Correctly use Word's custom borders and shading feature.
- Correctly format an online resume.

A. WARMUP

alphabet	1	Big July earthquakes confounded the zany experimental vows.
concentration	2	uncommunicativeness departmentalization electrocardiography
easy	3	It is the duty of the busy ensigns to dismantle the panels.

Skillbuilding

B. MAP+: ALPHABET

Follow the GDP software directions for this exercise to improve keystroking accuracy.

C. PROGRESSIVE PRACTICE: ALPHABET

Follow the GDP software directions for this exercise to improve keystroking speed.

Language Arts

Study the rules at the right.

D. CAPITALIZATION

RULE
= organization

Capitalize common organizational terms (such as *advertising department* and *finance committee*) only when they are the actual names of the units in the writer's own organization and when they are preceded by the word *the*.

The report from the Advertising Department is due today.

But: Our advertising department will submit its report today.

RULE
= course

Capitalize the names of specific course titles but not the names of subjects or areas of study.

I have enrolled in Accounting 201 and will also take the marketing course.

Edit each sentence to correct any errors.

```
4  The advertising department at their firm is excellent.

5  The Finance Committee here at Irwin will meet today.

6  I think I am going to pass keyboarding 1 with flying colors.

7  Their marketing department must approve the proposal first.

8  A class in Business Communications would be very helpful.

9  To take Math 102, you must have taken a beginning math
10 course.
```

Formatting

E. ONLINE RESUME

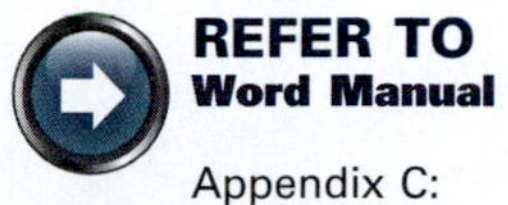

Appendix C: Saving a Word File in PDF Format.

An online resume is an opportunity to showcase your technical expertise and creativity in Word as you use customized borders and shading. Also, because an online resume is electronically available and could be posted online in PDF format, your resume is accessible to a wider range of prospective employers.

If desired, you can include hyperlinks to actual documents if those documents are available with your resume or posted on the Internet. Text shown in square brackets on an electronic resume, such as [Transcript], would be converted to a hyperlink to jump to the related item.

F. WORD PROCESSING: TABLE—BORDERS AND SHADING, CUSTOM

Study Lesson 111 in your Word Manual. Complete all of the shaded steps while at your computer. Then format the documents that follow.

Document Processing

Report
111-90
Online Resume

1. Create a table structure, and type in the information as shown in the completed resume. Use the default Calibri 12-pt. font unless directed otherwise.
2. Select Row 1, set a right tab at the right margin, and apply italic.
3. Type the information in Row 1, aligning the phone number and e-mail address at the right margin.
4. Select "Ted C. Campos," and change the font to Calibri 24 pt. Bold.
5. Type the headings in the appropriate rows using Calibri 14 pt. Bold.
6. Type the information under each heading in the corresponding rows.
7. Type the bulleted lists in Calibri 11 pt.
8. Italicize the job titles in the "Experience" section.
9. Increase the indent on the line under the "References" section to align with the text following the bullets in the bulleted lists.
10. Type the last line of text in the resume, center it, and change the font to Calibri 9 pt. Italic.
11. Apply custom borders and shading as desired.
12. Apply a theme color palette and theme font of your choice.

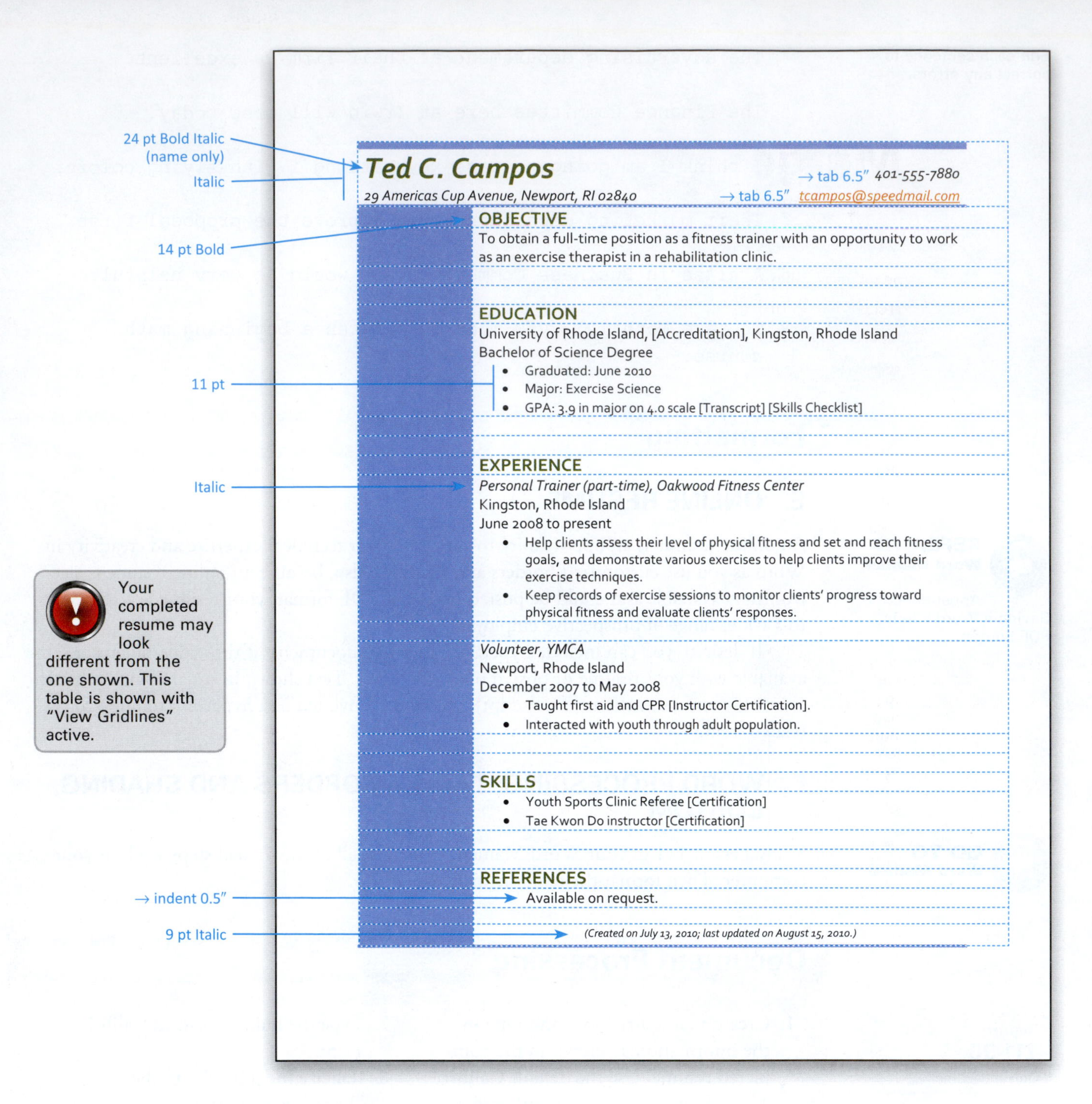

Ted C. Campos 401-555-7880
29 Americas Cup Avenue, Newport, RI 02840 tcampos@speedmail.com

OBJECTIVE
To obtain a full-time position as a fitness trainer with an opportunity to work as an exercise therapist in a rehabilitation clinic.

EDUCATION
University of Rhode Island, [Accreditation], Kingston, Rhode Island
Bachelor of Science Degree
- Graduated: June 2010
- Major: Exercise Science
- GPA: 3.9 in major on 4.0 scale [Transcript] [Skills Checklist]

EXPERIENCE
Personal Trainer (part-time), Oakwood Fitness Center
Kingston, Rhode Island
June 2008 to present
- Help clients assess their level of physical fitness and set and reach fitness goals, and demonstrate various exercises to help clients improve their exercise techniques.
- Keep records of exercise sessions to monitor clients' progress toward physical fitness and evaluate clients' responses.

Volunteer, YMCA
Newport, Rhode Island
December 2007 to May 2008
- Taught first aid and CPR [Instructor Certification].
- Interacted with youth through adult population.

SKILLS
- Youth Sports Clinic Referee [Certification]
- Tae Kwon Do instructor [Certification]

REFERENCES
Available on request.

(Created on July 13, 2010; last updated on August 15, 2010.)

Your completed resume may look different from the one shown. This table is shown with "View Gridlines" active.

Report 111-91
Online Resume

1. Open Report 111-90.
2. Apply borders and shading with customized widths and colors of your choice different from the ones used in Report 111-90.
3. Apply a theme color palette and theme font of your choice different from the ones used in Report 111-90.
4. Change the content of the first bulleted item in the first portion of the EXPERIENCE section to this:

```
Help clients set and reach
fitness goals and improve
their exercise techniques.
```

5. Change the content of the second portion of the EXPERIENCE section to this:

```
Strength Coach (part-time),
Fitness Emporium
Jamestown, Rhode Island
January 2007 to April 2008
• Selected fitness equipment;
  coordinated personal
  training programs.
• Demonstrated several
  methods of strength
  training.
```

Mail Merge—A

Goals

- Type at least 50wpm/5′/5e.
- Correctly use Word's mail merge feature to create merged letters.
- Correctly format a form letter in block style.

A. WARMUP

alphabet	1	Dr. Jekyll vowed to finish zapping the quixotic bumblebees.
one hand	2	secret hominy dew hip beasts nonunion edge monk staff nylon
easy	3	Susie's sorority is proficient in their work with the city.

Skillbuilding

B. SUSTAINED PRACTICE: CAPITALS

Take a 1-minute timed writing on the boxed paragraph to establish your base speed. Then take a 1-minute timed writing on the following paragraph. As soon as you equal or exceed your base speed on this paragraph, move to the next, more difficult paragraph.

```
 4      Even though he was only about thirty years old, Jason   11
 5  knew that it was not too soon to begin thinking about his    23
 6  retirement. He soon found out that there were many things    34
 7  involved in his plans for an early and long retirement.      45

 8      Even without considering the uncertainty of social      10
 9  security, Jason knew that he should plan his career moves    22
10  so that he would have a strong company retirement plan. He   33
11  realized that he should have an Individual Retirement Plan.  45

12      When he became aware that The Longman Company, the      10
13  firm that employed him, would match his contributions to a   22
14  supplemental retirement account, he began saving even more.  34
15  He used the Payroll Department funds from the Goplin Group.  46

16      He also learned that The Longman Company retirement     11
17  plan, his Individual Retirement Plan, and his supplemental   22
18  retirement account are all deferred savings. With those      34
19  tax-dollar savings, Jason bought New Venture Group funds.    45
      1 | 2 | 3 | 4 | 5 | 6 | 7 | 8 | 9 | 10 | 11 | 12
```

Take two 5-minute timed writings.

Goal: At least 50wpm/5'/5e

C. 5-MINUTE TIMED WRITING

```
20      Employers want the people who work for them to have      11
21 many qualities of good character. Character is defined as a 23
22 distinctive feature of a person or thing. Character may be   34
23 what you are known for and may be why you remember someone   46
24 else. What are some of the traits you think of that are      57
25 linked with good character? A few traits might be respect,   69
26 honesty, trust, caring, leadership, attitude, tolerance,     81
27 fairness, and patience.                                      85
28      All people should have respect for themselves and for   96
29 others. If you respect people, you have a high regard for   108
30 the way they conduct themselves in all aspects of life.     119
31 However, before you can respect others, you need to have    131
32 respect for yourself.                                       135
33      Honesty and trustworthiness are similar traits. In     145
34 business dealings, people expect honesty and will admire    157
35 people who have this quality. They like to build business   168
36 relationships with companies whose employees are honest,    180
37 just, and trustworthy.                                      184
38      Your attitude is reflected in the way you act toward   195
39 other people or in the way you speak to them. You can make  207
40 great strides in advancing your career by taking a look at  219
41 the way you interact with people. You may want to take a    230
42 closer look at some character traits you want to improve.   242
43 Such improvements in life will amaze you.                   250
     1 | 2 | 3 | 4 | 5 | 6 | 7 | 8 | 9 | 10 | 11 | 12
```

Formatting

D. FORM LETTERS

A form letter is a letter that combines standard and variable information for a number of different recipients to create a set of merged documents. Mail merge is also very useful when creating corresponding envelopes and labels for a form letter. The same variable information used to create the address block in the form letter may be used to create the address block in envelopes or labels.

Two files must be created before a merge can occur. The main document (in this example, a form letter) contains generic content that doesn't change. The data source file contains variable information specific to the recipient (the person receiving the finalized merged document), such as the inside address block and the first and last name in the salutation.

After these two files are created, placeholder fields (codes that will be replaced with actual text after the files are merged) are inserted into the main document. These fields link the variable content from the data source file to the generic text in the main document. Finally, the main document file is merged with the data source file to create a number of finished documents that combine generic text from the main document with variable text from the data source file into a single file.

When the main document or data source is updated, all changes will be reflected in each new merged document. The following illustration shows a letter created as a main document with corresponding placeholder fields inserted.

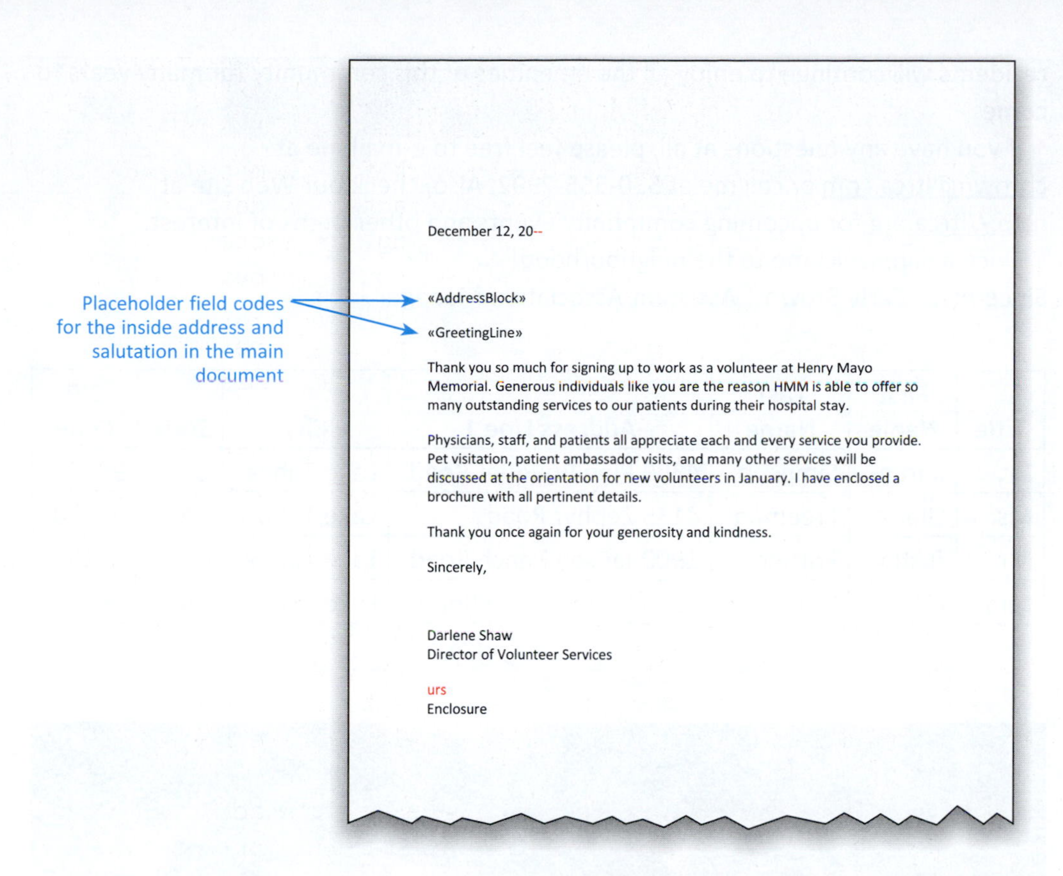

December 12, 20--

«AddressBlock»

«GreetingLine»

Thank you so much for signing up to work as a volunteer at Henry Mayo Memorial. Generous individuals like you are the reason HMM is able to offer so many outstanding services to our patients during their hospital stay.

Physicians, staff, and patients all appreciate each and every service you provide. Pet visitation, patient ambassador visits, and many other services will be discussed at the orientation for new volunteers in January. I have enclosed a brochure with all pertinent details.

Thank you once again for your generosity and kindness.

Sincerely,

Darlene Shaw
Director of Volunteer Services

urs
Enclosure

E. WORD PROCESSING: MAIL MERGE—LETTERS

Study Lesson 112 in your Word Manual. Complete all of the shaded steps while at your computer. Then format the documents that follow.

Document Processing

Correspondence 112-95
Business Letter in Block Style

1. Create the main document without any placeholder fields, and save the main document file as *Correspondence 112-95-main.*
2. Create a data source file for each recipient listed, and save the data source file as *Correspondence 112-95-data.*
3. Insert the appropriate placeholder fields in the form letter; select a colon as the punctuation mark for the salutation.
4. Adjust the blank lines above or below the placeholder fields as needed to format the inside address and salutation correctly.
5. Preview your results and make any adjustments as needed.
6. Merge the main document and the data source file to create one file with the four merged letters, and save the file as *Correspondence 112-95.*

Main Document

February 14, 20--
«AddressBlock»
«GreetingLine»
¶ Welcome to Lakeshore Terrace! I hope you are enjoying the stunning vistas of nearby Lake Tahoe, the golf course, and the recreation center that are all part of the amenities available to every homeowner in our planned community.
¶ Be assured that the Lakeshore Terrace Residential Community Association is committed to maintaining the guidelines set forth by our association so that our

(continued on next page)

residents will continue to enjoy all the amenities of this community for many years to come.
¶ If you have any questions at all, please feel free to e-mail me at cbrown@ltrca.com or call me at 530-555-2992. Also, check our Web site at http://ltrca.org for upcoming community events and other items of interest.
¶ Once again, welcome to the neighborhood!
Sincerely, | Carly Brown | Assistant Association Manager | urs

Data Source

Type the data shown in the table in the appropriate fields in the dialog box.

Title	First Name	Last Name	Address Line 1	City	State	ZIP Code
Dr.	Karen	Simpson	4309 Pine Bouquet Road	Lake Tahoe	CA	96150
Ms.	Gloria	Freeman	4135 Zephyr Road	Lake Tahoe	CA	96150
Mr.	Justin	Frazier	1900 Jansen Beach Road	Lake Tahoe	CA	96150
Mrs.	Lillian	Hunt	1135 Pioneer Trail Road	Lake Tahoe	CA	96150

Mail Merge—B

Goals

- Demonstrate improved speed and accuracy while typing.
- Demonstrate acceptable proofreading skills by editing lines.
- Correctly format a form letter in modified-block style.

A. WARMUP

alphabet
1 Prized waxy jonquils choked the weeds in the big farm vats.

practice: *f* and *g*
2 fig finger flag frogs gift golf gulf goofs gruff fogs flags

easy
3 The new formal audit may be paid for by the downtown firms.

Skillbuilding

B. MAP+: NUMBERS

Follow the GDP software directions for this exercise to improve keystroking accuracy.

PRETEST » PRACTICE » POSTTEST

PRETEST

Take a 1-minute timed writing.

C. PRETEST: Common Letter Combinations

4 The condo committee was hoping the motion would not be 11
5 forced upon it, realizing that viable solutions ought to be 23
6 developed. It was forceful in seeking a period of time for 35
7 tensions to cool. All concerned wanted the problem solved. 47

1 | 2 | 3 | 4 | 5 | 6 | 7 | 8 | 9 | 10 | 11 | 12

PRACTICE

Speed Emphasis:
If you made no more than 1 error on the Pretest, type each *individual* line 2 times.

Accuracy Emphasis:
If you made 2 or more errors, type each *group* of lines (as though it were a paragraph) 2 times.

D. PRACTICE: Word Beginnings

8 for forum forge forced forgot formal forest foreign forerun
9 con conks conic consul confer convey convex contact concern
10 per perks peril person period perish permit percale percent
11 com combs comet combat comedy comics common compete complex

E. PRACTICE: Word Endings

12 ing tying hiking liking edging bowing hoping having nursing
13 ble fable pebble treble tumble viable dabble fumble fusible
14 ion union legion nation region motion potion option bastion
15 ful awful cupful fitful joyful lawful earful artful tearful

POSTTEST

Repeat the Pretest timed writing and compare performance.

F. POSTTEST: Common Letter Combinations

Language Arts

Edit this paragraph to correct any errors.

G. PROOFREADING

```
16 The idea and practise of sharing risk originated in
17 antiquetry. Many years ago, Chinesemerchants deviced an
18 injenious way of protecting themselves against the chance
19 of a financialy ruinous accadent in the dangerous river
20 along the trade routes when they were delivring goods.
```

Document Processing

Correspondence 113-96

Business Letter in Modified-Block Style

1. Create the main document without any placeholder fields, and save the main document file as *Correspondence 113-96-main.*
2. Create a data source file for each recipient listed, and save the data source file as *Correspondence 113-96-data.*
3. Insert the appropriate placeholder fields in the form letter; select a colon as the punctuation mark for the salutation.
4. Adjust the blank lines above or below the placeholder fields as needed to format the inside address and salutation correctly.
5. Preview your results and make any adjustments as needed.
6. Merge the main document and the data source file to create one file with the four merged letters, and save the file as *Correspondence 113-96.*

Main Document

July 21, 20--

«AddressBlock»

«GreetingLine»

¶ Thank you for registering for the American Association of Retired Teachers annual convention to be held in Las Vegas, Nevada, on October 10-12.

¶ You can look forward to three days of noted speakers, engaging educational presentations, interactive exhibitors, prizes, and events. Your evenings will be filled with concerts, dinners, and Las Vegas entertainment! If you wish to take some excursions to nearby attractions, such as Hoover Dam and Red Rock Canyon, visit the concierge booth upon arrival to make all the necessary arrangements.

(continued on next page)

¶ AART has contracted with several Las Vegas hotels to provide you with luxury accommodations at a price you can afford. Reserve your hotel room soon to secure your accommodations. Visit our Web site at http://www.aart.org for details and online reservations.

¶ Please feel free to e-mail me at rholt@aart.org if you have any further questions.

Sincerely, / Ms. Robbie Holt / Event Coordinator / urs

Data Source

First Entry

Mr. / Richard / Lampman / 1237 Winterson Road / Baltimore / MD / 21201

Second Entry

Ms. / Penny / Cutler / 915 Fairmont Boulevard / Rapid City / SD / 57701

Third Entry

Dr. / Todd / Dabney / 1531 Paseo de Peralta / Santa Fe / NM / 87501

Fourth Entry

Mrs. / Tanya / Benjamin / 931 Talbot Street / Taylor / TX / 76574

Mail Merge—C

Goals

- Type at least 50wpm/5′/5e.
- Correctly format a form letter in block style.

A. WARMUP

alphabet
frequent digraphs
easy

```
1 Why did Max become eloquent over a zany gift like jodhpurs?
2 te tee ate byte tell tea termite ten Ute tent teed teen Ted
3 The auditor's panel had the right to risk a firm's profits.
```

Skillbuilding

B. PROGRESSIVE PRACTICE: NUMBERS

Follow the GDP software directions for this exercise to improve keystroking speed.

C. TECHNIQUE PRACTICE: SHIFT KEY

Type each line 2 times. After striking the capitalized letter, return the Shift Key finger immediately to home-row position.

```
4 Alex Bly and Clara Dye wed. Ella Fochs and Gil Hall talked.
5 Ida Jackson met Kay Lang for a fast lunch at Mamma Nancy's.
6 Otis Pike should call Quint Richards about Sophia Townsend.
7 Urich Volte will take Winona Xie to visit Yadkin in Zurich.
```

Take two 5-minute timed writings.

Goal: At least 50wpm/5'/5e

D. 5-MINUTE TIMED WRITING

```
 8      Before you apply for a job, you will want to do some     11
 9 detective work. First, choose a company where you want to     23
10 work, and then use the Internet to find out about the firm.   34
11 If you find a site for the business, then you can learn all   46
12 about the company, its hiring policies, the job listings,     58
13 or ways to apply for a job there.                             65
14      When you are researching a business, you want to         75
15 learn about the history of the company. You may be able       86
16 to find out how stock analysts expect the company stock       97
17 to perform in the coming months if the firm is publicly      108
18 traded. When you find a job opening for which you know that  120
19 you want to apply, read carefully to see what type of work   132
20 experience and education the business requires for the job.  144
21      When you prepare your resume, emphasize your major      155
22 qualifications based on the requirements listed for the      166
23 job. If the person who will receive the job inquiries is     177
24 not listed, contact the company by phone or e-mail to learn  189
25 his or her name. You should personalize the cover letter     201
26 and resume to stress what the firm needs.                    209
27      The information you find in your research will be       219
28 very helpful during the interview with a manager at the      230
29 company. Ask good questions and speak confidently about      242
30 the job. Emphasize how your skills fit in.                   250
    1 | 2 | 3 | 4 | 5 | 6 | 7 | 8 | 9 | 10 | 11 | 12
```

Document Processing

Correspondence
114-97
Business Letter in Block Style

1. Create the main document without any placeholder fields, and save the main document file as *Correspondence 114-97-main.*
2. Create a data source file for each recipient listed, and save the data source file as *Correspondence 114-97-data.*
3. Insert the appropriate placeholder fields in the form letter; select a colon as the punctuation mark for the salutation.
4. Adjust the blank lines above or below the placeholder fields as needed to format the inside address and salutation correctly.
5. Preview your results and make any adjustments as needed.
6. Merge the main document and the data source file to create one file with the four merged letters, and save the file as *Correspondence 114-97.*

Main Document

Nov. 1, 20--

<<GreetingLine>>

<<AddressBlock>>

¶ Welcome to Movie Flix! As a new member youre entitled to 6 months of free dvds by mail. Because we have over 150 shipping points across the Nation you can count on receiving your DVD in about one business day. Due dates and late fees are a thing of the past. For every new member yuo refer, you will receive anadditional 2 months of free premium membership. You have a wide array of DVDs to choose from. Many new-release movies and and current-season TV episodes are available. If you prefer, we can stream all your entertainment to you via a Movieflix device or directly online to your personal computer at extra charge. Please visit our site at www.mflix.com for complete listings.

¶ If you have any questions or concerns whatsoever, don't hesitate to contact me at 800-555-7662 or e-mail me at rphillips@mflix.com. I'm at your service.

Sincerely, | Roy Phillips | Subscriber RelationsSpecialist | urs

Data Source

Mr. | Estrada | Andres | 123 N. Thomas Road | Phoenix | AZ | 85400

Joyce | Evans | 1172 Yellowstone High way | Cody | WY | 82414

Mr. | Ken | Newwton | 459 South Meridian | Oklahoma City | OK | 73108

Mr. | Brandy | Burgess | 29 Riverside Dr. | Corning | NY | 14830

Mail Merge—D

Goals

- Demonstrate improved speed and accuracy while typing.
- Demonstrate acceptable language arts skills in composing a personal business letter.
- Correctly use Word's mail merge feature to create merged envelopes and labels.
- Correctly format merged envelopes and labels.
- Correctly format a form letter in block style.
- Successfully complete a Progress and Proofreading check with zero errors on the first scored attempt.

A. WARMUP

```
alphabet        1 I have just quoted for nine dozen boxes of gray lamp wicks.
number/symbol   2 wroe@gmail.com 82% Dye & Cox (5/7) Oh! ($6.90) *8:45 #12-63
easy            3 My mangy dog then ran to his bowl in the den to take a sip.
```

Skillbuilding

B. 12-SECOND SPEED SPRINTS

Take three 12-second timed writings on each line.

```
4 I am at my best when I am on a boat on an icy lake at home.
5 Ray may work in the field of coal when he is not busy here.
6 If they work in town, they may make a visit to the old gym.
7 Jake may try to fix the leaks in the pipes in the city gym.
  ''''5'''10'''15'''20'''25'''30'''35'''40'''45'''50'''55'''60
```

C. PACED PRACTICE

Follow the GDP software directions for this exercise to improve keystroking speed and accuracy.

Language Arts

D. COMPOSING A PERSONAL BUSINESS LETTER

Compose the body of a letter to a former instructor of yours. You want him or her to agree to serve as a reference for you when you apply for jobs after college. In the letter, discuss the following:

Paragraph 1: Start with a pleasant introduction, and remind the instructor of which class(es) you had with him or her and perhaps something specific about yourself to help the instructor remember you.

Paragraph 2: Describe the kind of position for which you're applying so that the instructor will know what to include in the letter of reference.

Paragraph 3: Close on a positive, appreciative note.

Formatting

E. MERGED ENVELOPES AND LABELS

Creating a set of merged envelopes and labels is very similar to creating a set of merged letters. The basic difference is that the main document is a blank envelope, an envelope with a return address, or a blank label rather than a letter with generic content. A new data source can also be created and used, or an existing data source can be reused.

F. WORD PROCESSING: MAIL MERGE—ENVELOPES AND LABELS

Study Lesson 115 in your Word Manual. Complete all of the shaded steps while at your computer. Then format the documents that follow.

Document Processing

Correspondence
115-98
Envelopes

Main Document

1. Create the main document without any placeholder fields, and save the main document file as *Correspondence 115-98-main.*
2. Delete any return address that might appear.
3. Create a data source file for each recipient listed, and save the data source file as *Correspondence 115-98-data.*
4. Insert the appropriate placeholder fields in the inside address area of the envelope.
5. Preview your results and make any adjustments as needed.
6. Merge the main document and the data source file to create one file with the four merged envelopes, and save the file as *Correspondence 115-98.*

Data Source

First Entry

Mrs. | Esther | Page | Alpha Sound Systems | 720 East Adams Street | Springfield | IL | 62701

Second Entry

Ms. | Jennie | Guthrie | Advanced Solar Heating Systems | 3421 West Markham Street | Little Rock | AR | 72201

Third Entry

Dr. | Ruth | Mendoza | Henry Mayo Hospital | 6439 Vista Way | Carlsbad | CA | 92008

Fourth Entry

Mr. | Benjamin | Ong | World Appliance Service | 2394 Graves Road | Tallahassee | FL | 32303

Correspondence
115-99
Mailing Labels

1. Create the main document without any placeholder fields, and save the main document file as *Correspondence 115-99-main.*
2. Choose Avery US Letter as the label vendor and 5160 as the product number.
3. Create a data source file for each recipient listed, and save the data source file as *Correspondence 115-99-data.*
4. Insert the appropriate placeholder fields in the label.
5. Preview your results and make any adjustments as needed.
6. Merge the main document and the data source file to create one file with the four merged labels, and save the file as *Correspondence 115-99.*

Main Document

Data Source

First Entry

Mr. | Carlos | Bedolla | 500 Stoneridge Drive | Columbia | SC | 29210

Second Entry

Dr. | Julie | Bergman | 5331 Grand Canyon Drive | Madison | WI | 53713

Third Entry

Ms. | Shannon | Beckam | 111 North Grand Avenue | Lansing | MI | 48917

Fourth Entry

Mrs. | Debra | Mack | 1444 Fairview Avenue | Boise | ID | 83702

Correspondence
115-100
Business Letter in Block Style

1. Create the main document without any placeholder fields, and save the main document file as *Correspondence 115-100-main.*
2. Create a data source file for each recipient listed, and save the data source file as *Correspondence 115-100-data.*
3. Insert the appropriate placeholder fields in the form letter; select a colon as the punctuation mark for the salutation.
4. Adjust the blank lines above or below the placeholder fields as needed to format the inside address and salutation correctly.
5. Preview your results and make any adjustments as needed.
6. Merge the main document and the data source file to create one file with the four merged letters, and save the file as *Correspondence 115-100.*

Main Document

March 28, 20--
«AddressBlock»
«GreetingLine»
¶ Summer is rapidly approaching, and Southern California Electrical has a great idea to help save you money on your electric bill. SCE is offering a special Summer Discount Plan to help conserve energy and prevent power emergencies.
¶ If you agree to enroll in our plan, we will install a remote-controlled device on your air-conditioning unit. During hours of peak demand, this remote device will cycle your air conditioning on and off based on an interval of your choosing. You will be interested to know that a temperature shift of only a few degrees is typical—you probably won't even notice it. But you will notice the savings in your energy bill.
¶ There are two convenient options to choose from—one plan will maximize your savings and the other plan will maximize your comfort. Log on to www.scelectrical.com/sdp to enroll online and to review all details of each plan. The earlier you sign up, the faster you'll begin saving money.
Sincerely, | George Morimoto | Customer Programs Representative | urs

Data Source

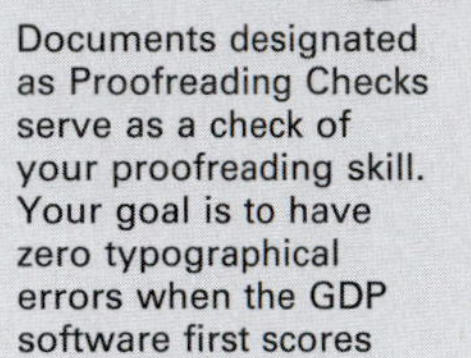

Progress and Proofreading Check

Documents designated as Proofreading Checks serve as a check of your proofreading skill. Your goal is to have zero typographical errors when the GDP software first scores the document.

First Entry
Mr. | Martin | Galindo | 1599 South Raymond Avenue | Fullerton | CA | 92831

Second Entry
Ms. | Colleen | Westridge | 1029 West Ball Road | Anaheim | CA | 92802

Third Entry
Dr. | Michelle | Hardey | 431 North Doheny Drive | Beverly Hills | CA | 90210

Fourth Entry
Mrs. | Carolyn | Wong | 325 North Pass Avenue | Burbank | CA | 91505

UNIT 24

Skillbuilding and In-Basket Review

LESSON 116
Skillbuilding and In-Basket Review—Banking

LESSON 117
Skillbuilding and In-Basket Review—Education

LESSON 118
Skillbuilding and In-Basket Review—Nursing Facility

LESSON 119
Skillbuilding and In-Basket Review—Government

LESSON 120
Skillbuilding and In-Basket Review—Software Development

UNIT 24 LESSON

Skillbuilding and In-Basket Review—Banking

116

Goals

- Type at least 50wpm/5'/5e.
- Correctly format a memo template, boxed table, and letterhead form.

A. WARMUP

alphabet	1	We promptly judge antique ivory buckles for the next prize.
concentration	2	gastroenterologists interdenominational individualistically
easy	3	Dirk may visit the island by the oaks with his tan bicycle.

Skillbuilding

B. SUSTAINED PRACTICE: PUNCTUATION

Take a 1-minute timed writing on the boxed paragraph to establish your base speed. Then take a 1-minute timed writing on the following paragraph. As soon as you equal or exceed your base speed on this paragraph, move to the next, more difficult paragraph.

4	Have you ever noticed that a good laugh every now and	11
5	then really makes you feel better? Research has shown that	22
6	laughter can have a very healing effect on our bodies. It	33
7	is an excellent way to relieve tension and stress all over.	46
8	When you laugh, your heart beats faster, you breathe	11
9	deeper, and you exercise your lungs. When you laugh, your	22
10	body produces endorphins--a natural painkiller that gives	34
11	you a sense of euphoria that is very powerful and pleasant.	46
12	Someone said, "Laugh in the face of adversity." As it	11
13	happens, this is first-rate advice. It's a great way to	22
14	cope with life's trials and tribulations; it's also a good	34
15	way to raise other people's spirits and relieve tension.	45
16	Finding "humor" in any situation takes practice--try	11
17	to make it a full-time habit. We're all looking for ways	22
18	to relieve stress. Any exercise--jogging, tennis, biking,	34
19	swimming, or golfing--is a proven remedy for "the blues."	45

1 | 2 | 3 | 4 | 5 | 6 | 7 | 8 | 9 | 10 | 11 | 12

Take two 5-minute timed writings.

Goal: At least 50wpm/5'/5e

C. 5-MINUTE TIMED WRITING

```
20      A few factors should be considered before you buy a       11
21 new printer for your computer. First, decide how you will      22
22 use your new printer. If you plan to use the printer for       34
23 typing letters and reports, you may decide you want a laser    45
24 printer at a reasonable price and that is capable of doing     57
25 general tasks you will need.                                   63
26      If you are buying the printer for office use, you may     74
27 decide to shop for a printer that prints documents more        85
28 quickly and is of exceptional value. Then, if you plan to      97
29 use a digital camera with the printer, you will want to get   109
30 a printer that is made to print documents of photo quality.   121
31      Resolution, speed, and paper handling are some other     132
32 factors you should consider when you buy a new printer.       143
33 Resolution refers to how sharp the image appears on the       154
34 paper. With printers that have a higher resolution, the       165
35 image gives you output of higher quality. You will see an     177
36 amazing difference when you compare some samples of print     188
37 from the other kinds of printers.                             195
38      If you expect to print long documents, then you will     206
39 want to search for a reliable printer with a feed tray that   218
40 holds a large amount of paper. The more expensive printers    230
41 are usually faster printers. After assessing your printer     241
42 needs, you are ready to make your purchase.                   250
      1 | 2 | 3 | 4 | 5 | 6 | 7 | 8 | 9 | 10 | 11 | 12
```

Document Processing

Situation: Today is October 10. You are employed in the office of First National Savings in Del Mar, California. Ms. Sabrina Talavaro, vice president, has written the memo shown next. Type it using a memo template; send it to all bank employees with a copy to T. J. Hurley, president. Ms. Talavaro prefers to use her name and title in the From field. The subject of the memo is "Revision to Online Access Agreement."

Form 116-15
Memo Template

¶ *The revised OAA (Online-Access Agreement) becomes effective on October 20. Our customers have been notified of the new agreement via e-mail and letters. However, we do anticipate customer inquiries for specific details and individual account questions. Below is a recap of significant changes made to the OAA.*

(continued on next page)

¶ The agreement was simplified and includes two important changes. First, the rights and responsibilities of account owners and delegates have been amended to add an option for an account owner to delegate account-management authority to another person. Second, online banking terms and conditions have been incorporated into the OAA for the convenience of our customers.

¶ The revised OAA also specifically clarifies details regarding the "Payment-Send-on Date" for Automatic Bill Pay that has historically been a source of confusion. Also, the sections related to online banking were revised to better describe the enrollment process.

¶ Please visit www.fns.com/oaa/about to review all changes in depth. I have also attached a table that can be used as a quick reference to relevant sections in the OAA. Contact me at stalavaro@fns.com if you have any questions.

When the memo is distributed, the table below should be attached. Ms. Talavaro asks you to use attractive borders and shading to give this table a desktop-published appearance.

Table
116-55
Boxed Table

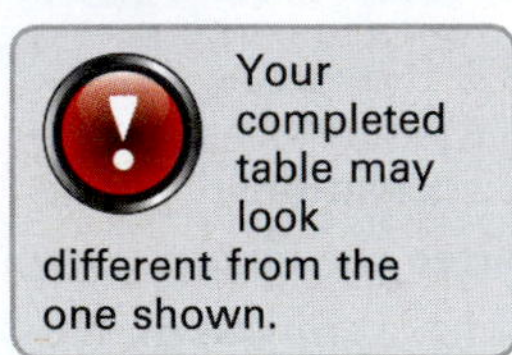
Your completed table may look different from the one shown.

ONLINE ACCESS AGREEMENT* First National Savings	
Topic	**Section**
Online banking terms and conditions	1, 3, 4, and 29
Guest users and authorized users defined	2A, 2B, and 5D
Bill Pay Account name change	7A
Bill Pay Account number changes	10A
Online billing provider definition	6A
Enrollment process for eligible accounts	10
Legal disclosures	20A and 20B
*Update effective October 20, 20--.	

Ms. Talavaro has sketched out a letterhead form and wants you to design the finished letterhead for First National Savings. The top of the letterhead should include the company name, address, phone number, and Web site address with each element separated by a diamond-shaped symbol. The main office address is 1701 Coast Boulevard, Del Mar, CA 92014; the phone number is 800-555-2447, and the Web site address is www.fns.com. Type the company slogan `First National Savings: the key to your financial future` at the bottom of the letterhead form.

Form
116-16
Letterhead Form

To begin the form, change all margins to 0.6 inch.

Insert clip art that relates to the company slogan.

Company Name

Street Address • City, State ZIP • Phone • Web site

Company slogan with a border above it.

Skillbuilding and In-Basket Review—Education

117

Goals

- Demonstrate improved speed and accuracy while typing.
- Demonstrate acceptable language arts skills in word usage.
- Correctly format an academic report, a flyer, and a left-bound business report.

A. WARMUP

```
alphabet  1 Jackie quietly gave the dog owner most of his prize boxers.
one hand  2 stages phylum wet pop affect jumpily tact junky beard pinky
easy      3 Duane's handy bicycle is to be thrown in the dormant field.
```

Skillbuilding

B. MAP+: ALPHABET

Follow the GDP software directions for this exercise to improve keystroking accuracy.

C. PROGRESSIVE PRACTICE: ALPHABET

Follow the GDP software directions for this exercise to improve keystroking speed.

Language Arts

D. WORD USAGE

Study the rules at the right.

RULE accept/except

RULE affect/effect

RULE farther/further

RULE personal/personnel

RULE principal/principle

***Accept* means "to agree to"; *except* means "to leave out."**

All employees except the maintenance staff should accept the agreement.

***Affect* is most often used as a verb meaning "to influence"; *effect* is most often used as a noun meaning "result."**

The ruling will affect our domestic operations but will have no effect on Asian operations.

***Farther* refers to distance; *further* refers to extent or degree.**

The farther we drove, the further agitated he became.

***Personal* means "private"; *personnel* means "employees."**

All personnel agreed not to use personal e-mail for business.

***Principal* means "primary"; *principle* means "rule."**

The principle of fairness is our principal means of dealing with customers.

Edit each sentence to correct any errors.

4 The company cannot accept any collect calls, except for his.

5 The affect of the speech was dramatic; everyone was affected.

6 Further discussion by office personal was not appropriate.

7 Comments made during any meeting should never be personal.

8 If the meeting is held any further away, no one will attend.

9 The principle reason for the decision was to save money.

10 Office ethics are basic principles that should be practiced.

11 He cannot except the fact that the job was delegated to Jack.

12 Any further effects on office personnel will be evaluated.

Document Processing

Situation: Today is September 25. You are employed in the office of Dr. Daniel Lopez, dean of online education, at Arizona Technical College in Phoenix. Dr. Lopez has written the report shown next and left it in your in-basket for you to type and format. The title of the report is "PREPARING TO TEACH ONLINE." In his reports, he uses "Dr. Daniel V. Lopez, Dean" as the byline followed by the complete date.

Report 117-92
Academic Report

affect/effect
principal/principle

There are many strategies for becoming a successful online instructor. Adapting class management strategies and developing related course management systems will affect the outcome and success of any online course. A few basic principles are discussed here.

CLASS MANAGEMENT STRATEGIES

affect/effect

To make a successful transition from a traditional class setting to an online class setting, you must be very cognizant that class management strategies must be adapted. In particular, course policies related to due dates and timelines as well as the effects of late work on student success must be spelled out and strictly enforced.

principal/principle
affect/effect

Dr. Bill Maedke, a principal expert in online teaching, says that if students are not held accountable for delivering assignments on time, student success is greatly affected.

(continued on next page)

farther/further

accept/except

Attrition increases as they procrastinate beyond the point of no return. When they finally realize they are getting further and further behind, many will drop out rather than accept a failing grade.[1]

COURSE MANAGEMENT SYSTEMS

A course management system that supports the course requirements and facilitates the exchange of work between instructor and student is critical. Take time to research the various courseware management systems and compare their features. For a comprehensive list of accepted course management systems at ATC, visit www.atc.edu/online/courseware. The article "The Fine Art of Teaching at a Distance" by Dana Evans is another excellent resource.[2]

accept/except

STAFF-DEVELOPMENT TRAINING SESSIONS

The best way to prepare to teach online at Arizona Tech is to attend a series of upcoming staff-development training sessions entitled "Teaching Online @ ATC" that will be available to all interested instructional personnel. Look for a flyer in your mailbox and in your school e-mail soon that will provide further details on these training sessions.

personal/personnel

farther/further

[1]Bill Maedke, "Class Management Strategies for Teaching at a Distance," The Collegian Journal, February 1, 2010, p. 29.
[2]Dana Evans, "The Fine Art of Teaching Online," Education Today, April 17, 2010, pp. 85-91.

Italicize publication titles.

Dr. Lopez has left a sketch of a flyer for the staff-development workshop entitled "Teaching Online @ ATC" that he would like you to design. He has asked you to use WordArt for the title, a rounded text box for the announcement, a predesigned table format for the workshop schedule, and landscape orientation for the page layout.

Report 117-93
Flyer

personal/personnel

farther/further

Teaching Online @ ATC

Insert a picture that relates to the @ symbol.

Dr. Daniel V. Lopez, dean of online education, would like to extend a personal invitation to all instructional personnel to attend a series of staff-development workshops that will focus on strategies for teaching at a distance.

- *The workshops will be held at the Faculty Conference Center at Arizona Technical College beginning November 2.*
- *The schedule and topics are listed below.*

Date, Time, and Location	Topic
Monday, November 2, Room 1A	Online Pedagogy
Tuesday, November 10, Room 1B	Course Design
Wednesday, November 18, Room 2A	Learning Objects
Monday, November 30, Room 2C	Online Resources
For further details, visit www.atc.edu/online/workshops.	

Report 117-94
Left-Bound Business Report

Open the file for Report 117-92, and make the following changes:

1. Change the format from an academic report to a left-bound business report.
2. Change the report title to this: ONLINE TEACHING AND LEARNING RESOURCES.
3. Change the date to September 30, 20--.
4. Delete the second sentence in the first paragraph.
5. Insert this side heading and the paragraph that follows it into the report just above the "COURSE MANAGEMENT SYSTEMS" heading:

   INSTRUCTIONAL TECHNOLOGY
   A learning object is an online instructional resource that supports learning via the use and reuse of digital instructional components designed to deliver small amounts of information in different contexts. For example, a set of digital flash cards might include a course concept on one side of the card and the corresponding definition on the other side. The flash card content could be written by an instructor or purchased as part of a digital instructional package.

Skillbuilding and In-Basket Review—Nursing Facility

Goals

- Type at least 50wpm/5′/5e.
- Correctly format a business letter in block style, an itinerary, and a newsletter.

A. WARMUP

alphabet	1	Jacqueline was vexed by the folks who got the money prizes.
practice: *o* and *i*	2	oil boil folio polio Rio coin icon into Ohio olio silo void
easy	3	Her ruby handiwork is fine, and she is so proficient at it.

Skillbuilding

B. PACED PRACTICE

Follow the GDP software directions for this exercise to improve keystroking speed and accuracy.

C. 5-MINUTE TIMED WRITING

Take two 5-minute timed writings.

Goal: At least 50wpm/5′/5e

4	Job sharing is a current concept that many places are	11
5	using to keep valued workers. People are finding a wide	22
6	range of reasons for not wanting to work full time. Here	34
7	are some tips on how to approach your boss if you would	45
8	like to attempt job sharing.	51
9	First, check your company handbook for an authorized	61
10	policy regarding this concept. If there is no rule that	73
11	prohibits the concept, then try to enlist a coworker who	84
12	would like to job-share and help you in writing a proposal	96
13	for job sharing where you work.	102
14	Next, define your needs and your goals. Develop a work	113
15	schedule that will meet all of your personal and monetary	125
16	needs. Be sure that you include enough time to get the work	137
17	done. If you want to work at your home on occasion, be sure	149
18	to state your desires.	154
19	You might find it is often quite helpful to maintain a	165
20	journal of your job duties, noting how much time is devoted	177
21	to each task. Your plan must also include details about the	189
22	logistics of the proposal. Decide how to handle unexpected	201
23	crisis situations.	205
24	Finally, time your presentation so there will be no	215
25	unnecessary interruptions. Be organized, persistent, and	227
26	professional in your presentation. Prepare to be successful	239
27	by compiling clearly defined ideas to support your plans.	250
	1 | 2 | 3 | 4 | 5 | 6 | 7 | 8 | 9 | 10 | 11 | 12	

Document Processing

Situation: Today is February 10. You work at The Meadows at Ivy Glen, an assisted-living residence in Connecticut, for Ms. Angelica Casillas, director. Ms. Casillas has written the letter shown next. It should be sent to Mrs. Sandra Elliott, 1122 King Street, Greenwich, CT 06831. Ms. Casillas uses "Sincerely yours" as her standard complimentary closing, uses "Ms. Angelica Casillas" as her writer's identification, and prefers her business title typed under her name in the closing lines.

Correspondence 118-101
Business Letter in Block Style

¶ Thank you for your inquiry regarding the assisted-living facilities here at The Meadows at Ivy Glen. We know that you, like so many of our residents, wish to live as independently as possible for as long as possible. We're here to help bridge the gap between independent living and living with assistance.

¶ I've spoken with Molly Fitzgerald, your dear friend who has been a resident for the past six months. She speaks fondly of you and believes that you would be very happy living here. I would like to meet with you in person to evaluate which level of assistance would best meet your needs. Based on the information in your application, I believe that you would benefit from basic assistance with laundry, housekeeping, and medications.

¶ Please call me at your earliest convenience at 203-555-2435 to set up an appointment. I will be happy to give you a personal tour of our lovely grounds and review our range of services and facilities at that time. I will also arrange for Molly to join us for a leisurely lunch.

¶ Thank you again for your interest in The Meadows at Ivy Glen, and I look forward to meeting you very soon.

Report 118-95
Itinerary

Ms. Casillas will be attending the Assisted-Living Federation of America Conference in Philadelphia in June and has asked you to prepare an itinerary with the title `ASSISTED-LIVING FEDERATION OF AMERICA CONFERENCE`. Type `Itinerary for Angelica Casillas` as the subtitle. The inclusive trip dates are June 12–14.

THURSDAY, JUNE 12	
7:09 a.m. - 8:28 a.m.	Flight from New York city, La Guardia Airport, to Philadelphia; Continental 1282 (800-555-3668); eticket; Seat 24C; nonstop.
	¶ Roz Jorgensen (Cell: 215-555-7635; Office: 215-555-2121) will meet your flight on Thrusday, provide transportation during your visit, and arrange for transportation back to the airport on Saturday morning.
	¶ Philadelphia Courtyard Suites (215-555-1200)
	King-sized bed, non smoking room; late arrival guaranteed; Reservation No. 35762-M1.
Friday, MARCH 13	ALFA Conference and Expo
	Philadelphia Royale Hotel
	1239 Market St.
	Philadelphia, PA 19107
	(215-555-1876)
8 p. m.	Dinner at the Amalfi Eatery next door to the Philadelphia Hotel Royale
SAT., MARCH 14	
6:30 a.m.	Meet ~~Tom Clinton~~ Roz Jorgensen in the ~~hotel restaurant~~ lobby of the Philadelphia Courtyard Suites for transportation to the airport.
9:30 a.m.-10:40 ~~p~~a.m.	Flight from New York City to Philadelphia, LaGuardia Airport; Continental 1541; e-ticket; Seat 11A; nonstop.

Report
118-96
Newsletter

Ms. Casillas has written the spring newsletter and has sketched out a masthead. She would like you to design the newsletter using these guidelines:

1. Set all margins at 0.75 inch.
2. For the masthead table, use clip art that is inspired by the spring season, and set the height to 2 inches.
3. Press ENTER 2 times outside the masthead table to begin typing the body.
4. Select a page color and font colors for titles and headings that complement the clip art.
5. Add or remove borders to enhance the design.
6. For the 2-column body, use automatic hyphenation, full justification, and Calibri 16 pt. so the residents will be able to read the newsletter more easily.
7. After you type the body, format the headings in bold and change the font to Cambria 24 pt.

Insert clip art that relates to spring. Set the height to 2 inches.

The Meadows at Ivy Glen

Spring 20--

With summer just around the corner, it's time to pull out your social calendars and reserve time for the great activities we have planned. Read on, and let Joyce Fontana know if you plan to participate.

Healthy Sleep

Are you getting enough sleep? Sleep debt might be keeping you from having the energy you need to participate in our fitness fun. Try this to improve your sleep time:

- Exercise early in the day to help you relax at night.
- Avoid coffee and nicotine as they can both disturb the quality of your sleep.
- Take a warm bath or shower just before bed.
- Establish a sleep pattern by going to bed and getting up at the same time each day.

Spring Fitness Fun

With the warmer months approaching, many folks are thinking about stepping up their exercise regimen. Join Ray Kirk in the rose garden for an energizing fitness walk beginning March 20 at 9 a.m.

Tee Time

Beginning April 1, join Alex Taylor on the putting green each day at 10-11 a.m. for two weeks for some golf instruction. At that time, you can sign up for excursions to our fabulous local golf courses.

Fat Burners

We've added new items to our menu that are low in calories but high in taste and are nutritious! Give them a try.

Skillbuilding and In-Basket Review—Government

Goals

- Demonstrate improved speed and accuracy while typing.
- Demonstrate acceptable language arts skills in spelling.
- Correctly format a business letter in block style, a ruled table, and an e-mail message.

A. WARMUP

alphabet
1 My grandfathers picked up quartz and a valuable onyx jewel.

frequent digraphs
2 at ate bat cat eat tat fat hat mat oat pat rat sat vat beat

easy
3 The girls may fish for cod in the lake or buy them in town.

Skillbuilding

B. MAP+: SYMBOL

Follow the GDP software directions for this exercise to improve keystroking accuracy.

PPP PRETEST » PRACTICE » POSTTEST

C. PRETEST: Close Reaches

PRETEST
Take a 1-minute timed writing.

4 Casey hoped that we were not wasting good grub. After 11
5 the sun went down, he swiftly put the oleo and plums in the 23
6 cart. Bart opened a copy of an old book, Grant had a swim, 35
7 and Curt unearthed a sword in a hole in that grassy dune. 46
1 | 2 | 3 | 4 | 5 | 6 | 7 | 8 | 9 | 10 | 11 | 12

D. PRACTICE: Adjacent Keys

PRACTICE
Speed Emphasis:
If you made no more than 1 error on the Pretest, type each *individual* line 2 times.
Accuracy Emphasis:
If you made 2 or more errors, type each *group* of lines (as though it were a paragraph) 2 times.

8 as mask last past easy vase beast waste toast reason castle
9 op hope flop open mops rope opera droop scope copier trophy
10 we west owed went weld weep weigh weary wedge wealth plowed
11 rt hurt port cart dirt fort court party start hearty parted

E. PRACTICE: Consecutive Fingers

12 sw swat swim swan swig swap swift sweet sword switch swirly
13 un tune spun unit dune punt under prune sunny hunter uneasy
14 gr grow grim grab grub grew great graze gripe greasy grassy
15 ol role oleo pool sold hole troll folly polka stolen oldest

POSTTEST

Repeat the Pretest timed writing and compare performance.

F. POSTTEST: Close Reaches

Language Arts

Type these frequently misspelled words, paying special attention to any spelling problems in each word.

G. SPELLING

16 practice continue regular entitled course resolution assist
17 weeks preparation purposes referred communication potential
18 environmental specifications original contractor associated
19 principal systems client excellent estimated administration
20 responsibility mentioned utilized materials criteria campus

Edit the sentences to correct any misspellings.

21 It is the responsability of the administration to assist.

22 The principle client prepared the excellent specifications.

23 He mentioned that the critiria for the decision were clear.

24 The contractor associated with the project referred them.

25 He estamated that the potential for resolution was great.

26 I was told that weeks of reguler practice were required.

Document Processing

Situation: Today is April 25. You work as an administrative assistant at the Centers for Disease Control and Prevention for Ms. Tina Min, traveler health specialist. Ms. Min has written the letter shown next. The letter should be sent to Mr. Carlos De Leon, 539 Locust Street, Des Moines, IA 50309. Ms. Min uses "Sincerely" as her standard complimentary closing, uses "Ms. Tina Min" as her writer's identification, and prefers her title typed under her name in the closing lines.

Correspondence 119-102
Business Letter in Block Style

¶ Your inquiry regarding vaccinations required for international travel was referred to me, and I am happy to answer your excellent questions. Preparation for a trip abroad does require a few weeks of planning to avoid potential problems associated with the timing of vaccinations.

¶ You mentioned that you are leaving in three months. Have you scheduled a visit to your doctor? Ideally, you should

(continued on next page)

set up a visit at least four to six weeks before your trip. Because so many environmental factors are at play when international travel is involved, you would be wise to go to a travel medicine provider specialist who can assist you with all details related to vaccinations. A principal responsibility of a provider of this type is to inform patients about the latest specifications for all health-related aspects of international travel.

¶ Please visit http://www.cdc.gov/travel.aspx for more helpful details and informative travel podcasts, or call CDC at 1-800-CDC-INFO. Enjoy your vacation, and I wish you continued good health.

Table
119-56
Ruled Table

HEALTH INFORMATION FOR TRAVELERS TO AUSTRALIA

Vaccination or Disease	Recommendations or Requirements for Vaccine-Preventable Disease
Routine	Recommended if you are not up to date with routine shots, such as measles/mumps/rubella (MMR) vaccine and the diphtheria/pertussis/tetanus (DPT) vaccine.
Hepatitis B	Recommended for all unvaccinated persons who might be exposed to blood or body fluids, have sexual contact with the local population, or be exposed through medical treatment, such as for an accident, even in developed countries, and for all adults for the purpose of protection from HBV infection.
Japanese encephalitis	Recommended if you visit Torres Strait and any zones associated with far Northern Australia.

This e-mail message should be sent to Regina Crawford, a close associate of Ms. Min. They address each other on a first-name basis. Ms. Min's e-mail address is tmin@cdc.gov. Her office phone number is 323-555-1876.

Correspondence
119-103
E-Mail Message

Hi, Regina:

¶ I mentioned to you yesterday that I am researching an inquiry related to health information for travelers to Australia. Please review the attached table, and let me know if it is complete or requires further information. I utilized the CDC Web site as my principal resource.

¶ Thank you, Regina, for your excellent assistance.

Skillbuilding and In-Basket Review—Software Development 120

Goals

- Type at least 50wpm/5′/5e.
- Correctly format a business report and a business letter in modified-block style.
- Successfully complete a Progress and Proofreading check with zero errors on the first scored attempt.

A. WARMUP

alphabet	1	Brown jars prevented the mixture from freezing too quickly.
number/symbol	2	coy20@cox.net 70% Hsu & Van 5/7 Win! ($4.93) *op. cit #16-8
easy	3	Jay may ask if my own neighbor is proficient in such a job.

Skillbuilding

B. 12-SECOND SPEED SPRINTS

Take three 12-second timed writings on each line.

```
4 Leo may visit the island by the giant oaks on his tan bike.
5 Nan may sign over the title to her car when she is in town.
6 She is so good at her work and likes what she does as well.
7 The old men may have a duel down by the lake at noon today.
  ''''5''''10''''15''''20''''25''''30''''35''''40''''45''''50''''55''''60
```

C. TECHNIQUE PRACTICE: BACKSPACE KEY

Type each line 2 times, using your Sem finger to strike the BACKSPACE key when you see the ← symbol. For example, type *kid*, backspace, and type *n*, thus changing *kid* to *kin*.

```
8  kid←n jag←m law←y oaf←k pat←y tag←m hid←m ice←y inn←k
9  fro←y mud←m rat←p sue←m flu←y bog←o gym←p big←n hug←m
10 dug←n and←y zag←p hex←y mow←p art←m tow←y age←o her←n
11 dad←m fur←n sin←p elf←k bar←n bud←m spa←y log←o fad←n
```

Take two 5-minute timed writings.

Goal: At least 50wpm/5'/5e

D. 5-MINUTE TIMED WRITING

```
12      With modern technology, it is possible to work at a       11
13 job full time and never leave your house. You can set up a     22
14 home office with a phone line, a facsimile, and a computer     34
15 system. Before choosing to work at home, however, you will     46
16 want to examine carefully your reasons for working at home.    58
17      Some people think about working at home so they can       69
18 have more time to spend with their families. Other people      80
19 like to have more flexibility in their work schedule. They     92
20 are looking for the opportunity to enjoy a better quality     104
21 of life or to participate in other activities.                113
22      There are some factors to consider before you make       123
23 the decision to work at home. You will want to consider the   135
24 ultimate cost of benefits that you could give up if you       147
25 change your place of work. You will want to check with your   159
26 employer to see if you are entitled to paid vacation days     170
27 and health insurance or if you can make contributions to      182
28 your retirement plan. Another factor to consider is the       193
29 limited contact with peers.                                   198
30      Before making the ultimate decision to work at home,     209
31 develop some realistic expectations of how you will spend     221
32 each day. Although you can organize your work to fit your     232
33 schedule, you will find the real challenge is to determine    244
34 a routine that works for you.                                 250
      1 | 2 | 3 | 4 | 5 | 6 | 7 | 8 | 9 | 10 | 11 | 12
```

Document Processing

Situation: Today is September 1. You work for Software Solutions, a software development company in Washington. Your boss is Mr. Jeffrey Hill, software development manager. Mr. Hill has written the business report shown next and left it in your in-basket for you to type and format. The title of the report is "NEW PROJECT-DEVELOPMENT STRATEGIES." He prefers to use "Jeffrey Hill, Software Development Manager" as the report byline followed by the above date and the current year.

Report
120-97
Business Report

¶ In january, our company was given the Bantam and Jones Project. As you know, this project was critical from a monetary stand point. We also knew that ~~Bantam and Jones~~ our customer was carefully scrutinizing the quality of this project. Because this was a fixed-price project, ~~and~~ we had to deliverthe work by the end of July in order to avoid huge customer fees. The problem was that the project was out sourced to a different project team in a different location, and the quality of the end product that was turned over to us for final review was questionable. ¶ As we later found out, the

(continued on next page)

project remote team had slowly disintegrated, and our home-based Seattle team had to come in at the last moment to rescue this project. In order to avoid this type of in the future, we will be implementing some new development project strategies.

TEAM COMMUNICATION

¶ The design phase of any project is always exciting and energizing. Our analysts are talking to our clients, softwarearchitects are meeting with developers and managers are coordinating the flow of communication. As the pofject progresses, communication breaks down. The analysts has moved on to the next project, the architects have finished their design, and the manager is reviewing status reports only occasionally. The developers are working at a feverish pace to get the project out on time, and the team is no longer working in unison. The following changes are going to be implemented to avoid this type of communication breakdown:

¶ Pair Programming. Studies show that 2 programmers work harder on a given task than they would if they were working independently and produce 15 % fewer bugs. On all future projects programmers will work to keep each other in check. One person will type in code while the other reviews each line of code as it is being typed at the same keyboard. We will provide programmers with “people-skills training, since issues related to personal interaction are the biggest drawback to successful pair programming.

¶ **Customer Status Reports.** Our customer is going to be an integral part of this team approach. A weekly status report will keep our customer in the loop and hold our teams account able for both content and deadlines. The project manager will oversee and coordinate communication between all parties.

CONCLUSION

¶ Our company has earned a reputation for exceptional control quality in this industry. We are makinga renewed commitment to maintain that reputation and hopefully surpass our own impressive standards. Another Status Report will be issued in 2 weeks regarding how these meas ures will be implemented on what the effects will be for specific projects currently underway.

Correspondence 120-104
Business Letter in Modified-Block Style

Mr. Hill has written the letter shown next. The letter should be sent to Ms. Patty Chang, Project Director, Silicon Valley Consulting Services, 15125 South Market Street, San Jose, CA 95113. Mr. Hill uses “Sincerely” as his standard complimentary closing and prefers his title typed under his name in the writer’s identification. Add this postscript to the letter: `Our president is very impressed with all your recommendations to date.` Send a blind copy to Hong Chan Cho.

Progress and Proofreading Check

Documents designated as Proofreading Checks serve as a check of your proofreading skill. Your goal is to have zero typographical errors when the GDP software first scores the document.

¶ Thank you for your prompt input as we have worked through ideas on the Bantam and Jones project. Your recommendations are sure to have a very powerful and positive impact on future projects.

¶ I have enclosed a copy of the report that was distributed to all Software Solutions employees involved in project development. Please review it and let me have your reactions. I feel confident that once our teams are comfortable with the new strategies and see the positive outcomes, they will embrace the recommendations.

¶ Please let me have your recommendations regarding training for our programmers as we implement our new pair-programming strategy. Here is a table with the proposed training schedule:

PROPOSED TRAINING SCHEDULE Pair Programming, Phase I	
Date	**Workshop Topic**
September 30	Communication Techniques
October 10	Tools for Pair Programming
October 20	Refactoring to Patterns
October 30	Design Patterns

¶ I need your final recommendations no later than September 15. I would assume that it makes more sense to begin with a workshop on communications techniques since the typical reaction to change by most employees is resistance. Perhaps if our programmers realize that the transition to pair programming will take place in phases, they will be more likely to accept the new approach and react positively.

(continued on next page)

¶ We need to arrange a face-to-face meeting for in-depth discussions on this very important transition. The following individuals will be invited to attend as they will play key roles during this transitional period:

- Hong Chan Cho
- Alicia King
- Barry Kidd
- Steven Cozell
- Colleen Cunningham

¶ Please call me when you receive this letter so that we can make the proper arrangements and coordinate schedules.

Outcomes Assessment on Part 6

Test 6

5-Minute Timed Writing

```
 1      The potential to reach your career goals has never    10
 2  been better. The person who will move forward in a career 22
 3  is the one who will make the bold moves to follow his or  33
 4  her dreams. He or she will have the required attributes of 45
 5  initiative and motivation to put forth maximum efforts in 57
 6  order to realize a fulfilling position.                   65
 7      If you want to get ahead in the highly competitive    75
 8  business world today, you need a personal coach or mentor 87
 9  who is experienced in motivating people who want to reach 98
10  their potential. You may be afraid to go after your dream 110
11  career because you are afraid of failure. Your personal   121
12  mentor will help you to minimize any problems you incur. He 132
13  or she will encourage you to strive for more.             142
14      When you decide to work with a qualified coach, you   153
15  are investing in yourself. You can trust your coach to help 165
16  you through this joyful process of expanding your horizons 177
17  until you reach your goals.                               182
18      When you think you have reached your limit, your coach 194
19  will make suggestions for additional improvement. He or she 206
20  will present the strategies you can use to be successful. 217
21  Your coach will guide you in making the critical decisions 229
22  for advancing your career. The final decision to improve  240
23  your skills and be successful is yours, however.          250
      1 | 2 | 3 | 4 | 5 | 6 | 7 | 8 | 9 | 10 | 11 | 12
```

Form Test 6-17
Memo Template

Type this memo using the preselected blank memo template that opens automatically.

To: Brian Collins, Director of human resources

CC: Vincent Alvarez, President

From: April Mendoza, Chair Committee

Date: May 15, 20--

Re: Sierra Madre Health Run

The Sierra Madre Health Run is being scheduled again this year on June 17, 20--. As you may recall, last year we were able to raise $ 12,000 for the Sierra Madre home for youth. Since its inception 5 years ago, we have raised over $75,00 0 that has gone directly to the building fund at the home.

(continued on next page)

Thank you for participating in this annual event and a special thanks goes to all those who donated there time and effort to make this event such a tremendous success over the years.

As Human Resources Director, we hope you'll again encourage all your employes to participate in the Health Run. We hope to exceed last year's donations by 10%. With Crosby international's participation, we know that will be a reasonable goal to reach.

urs

Report Test
6-98
Online Resume

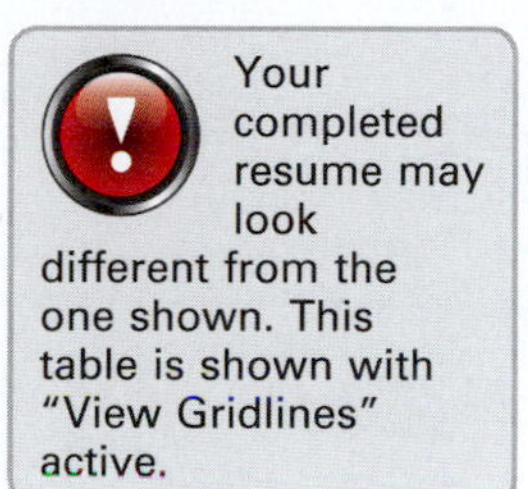

Marilyn Alexander — *607-555-6475*

8142 Lawton Avenue, Binghamton, NY 13901 — *malexander@quickmail.com*

OBJECTIVE

To obtain a full-time position as an event or meeting planner.

EDUCATION

Ithaca College, Ithaca, New York
Bachelor of Science Degree

- Graduated: August 2010
- Major: Event Planning
- GPA: 3.85 in major; 3.75 overall [Transcript] [Skills Checklist]

EXPERIENCE

Event Planner, Empire Facilities Inc.
Binghamton, New York
June 2006 to present

- Inspect and evaluate meeting space, lodging, and related venues and services to ensure a high standard of quality for scheduled events.
- Select key suppliers, prepare budgets, and negotiate contracts.
- Develop and maintain strong business relationships with hotels, conference centers, restaurants, gift suppliers, and audiovisual companies.

Administrative Assistant to Event Planner, Kramer Conferences Inc.
Flushing, New York
June 2005 to May 2006

- Scheduled conference calls and conference rooms for events.
- Ordered computer equipment and software used to plan events.
- Arranged for Web site and brochure updates; scheduled monthly meetings.

SKILLS

- Computing skills in Microsoft Word, Excel, and PowerPoint.
- Strong Interpersonal and organizational skills.

REFERENCES

Available on request.

(Created on July 13, 2010; last updated on August 15, 2010.)

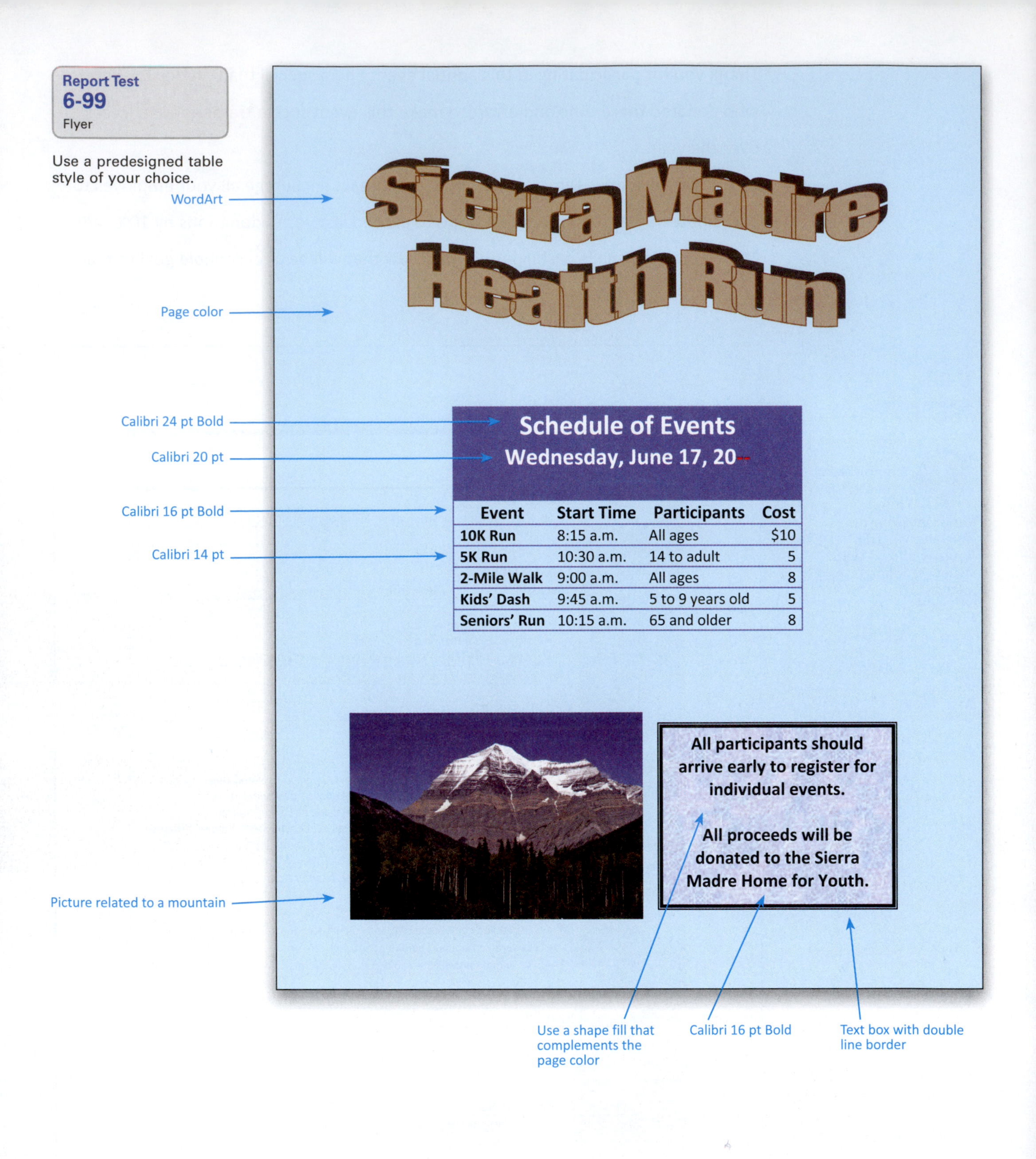

Report Test
6-99
Flyer

Use a predesigned table style of your choice.

Sierra Madre Health Run

Schedule of Events Wednesday, June 17, 20--			
Event	**Start Time**	**Participants**	**Cost**
10K Run	8:15 a.m.	All ages	$10
5K Run	10:30 a.m.	14 to adult	5
2-Mile Walk	9:00 a.m.	All ages	8
Kids' Dash	9:45 a.m.	5 to 9 years old	5
Seniors' Run	10:15 a.m.	65 and older	8

All participants should arrive early to register for individual events.

All proceeds will be donated to the Sierra Madre Home for Youth.

Skillbuilding

Progressive Practice: Alphabet SB-2

Progressive Practice: Numbers SB-7

Paced Practice SB-10

Supplementary Timed Writings SB-26

Progressive Practice: Alphabet

This skillbuilding routine contains a series of 30-second timed writings that range from 16 wpm to 104 wpm. The first time you use these timed writings, take a 1-minute timed writing with 3 or fewer errors on the Entry Timed Writing paragraph. Push moderately for speed.

Select a passage that is 1 to 2 wpm *higher* than your Entry Timed Writing speed. Then take up to six 30-second timed writings on the passage.

Your goal each time is to complete the passage within 30 seconds with no errors. When you have achieved your goal, move on to the next passage and repeat the procedure.

Entry Timed Writing

```
     Bev was very lucky when she found extra quality in the  11
home she was buying. She quietly told the builder that she   23
was extremely satisfied with the work done on her new home.  35
The builder said she can move into her new house next month. 47
  1  |  2  |  3  |  4  |  5  |  6  |  7  |  8  |  9  |  10  |  11  |  12
```

16 wpm The author is the creator of a document.

18 wpm Open means to access a previously saved file.

20 wpm A byte represents one character to every computer.

22 wpm Hard copy is usually text that is printed out on paper.

24 wpm Soft copy is text that is displayed on your computer screen.

26 wpm Memory is that part of your word processor that stores your data.

28 wpm The menu is a list of choices used to guide a user through a function.

30 wpm A sheet feeder is a device that will insert sheets of paper into a printer.

32 wpm An icon is a small picture that illustrates a function or an object in software.

34 wpm Active icons on your desktop represent the programs that can be run on your computer.

Skillbuilding

36 wpm To execute means to perform an action specified by the user or also by a computer program.

38 wpm Output is the result of a word processing operation. It can be either printed or magnetic form.

40 wpm Format refers to the physical features which affect the appearance and arrangement of your document.

42 wpm A font is a type style of a particular size or kind that includes letters, numbers, or punctuation marks.

44 wpm Ergonomics is the science of adapting working conditions or equipment to meet the physical needs of employees.

46 wpm Home position is the starting position of a document; it is typically the upper left corner of the display monitor.

48 wpm The purpose of a virus checker is to find those programs that may cause your computer to stop working as you want it to.

50 wpm An optical scanner is a device that can read text and enter it into a word processor without the need to type the data again.

52 wpm Hardware refers to all the physical equipment you use while computing, such as the display screen, keyboard, printer, and scanner.

54 wpm A peripheral device is any piece of equipment that will extend the capabilities of a computer system but is not required for operation.

56 wpm A split screen displays two or more different images at the same time; it can, for example, display two different pages of a legal document.

58 wpm To defrag the computer means that you are reorganizing the files so that related files will be located in the same general place on a hard drive.

60 wpm With the click of a mouse, one can use a button bar or a toolbar for fast access to features that are frequently applied when using a Windows program.

62 wpm

Gadgets are typically controls which are placed on your desktop to allow you to have immediate access to frequently used information such as time and date.

64 wpm

Turnaround time is the length of time needed for a document to be keyboarded, edited, proofread, corrected if required, printed, and returned to the originator.

66 wpm

A local area network is a system that uses cable or another means to allow high-speed communication among many kinds of electronic equipment within particular areas.

68 wpm

To search and replace means to direct the word processor to locate a character, word, or group of words wherever it occurs in the document and replace it with newer text.

70 wpm

Indexing is the ability of a word processor to accumulate a list of words that appear in a document, including page numbers, and then print a revised list in alphabetic order.

72 wpm

When a program needs information from you, a dialog box will appear on the desktop. Once the dialog box appears, you must identify the option you desire and then choose the option.

74 wpm

A facsimile is an exact copy of a document, and it is also a process by which images, such as typed letters, graphs, and signatures, are scanned, transmitted, and then printed on paper.

76 wpm

Compatibility refers to when a computer is able to share information with other computers or also to communicate with different hardware. It could be accomplished by other methods.

78 wpm

Some operators like to personalize their desktops when they use Windows by making various changes. For example, they can change their screen colors or the pointer so that they will have more fun.

80 wpm

Wraparound is the ability of a word processor to move words from one line to another line and from one page to the next page as a result of inserting and deleting text or changing the size of margins.

82 wpm

It is possible when using Windows to evaluate the contents of different directories on the screen at the very same time. You can then choose to copy or move a particular file from one directory to another.

84 wpm

List processing is a capability of a word processor to keep lists of data that can be updated and sorted in alphabetic or numeric order. A list can also be added to any document that is stored in your computer.

86 wpm

A computer is a device that accepts data that are input and then processes those data to produce the output. A computer performs its work by using various stored programs that provide all the necessary instructions.

88 wpm

A word processor is more than a program that can process words. Word processors have many other capabilities such as merging documents; executing some mathematical equations; and inserting clip art, shapes, and pictures.

90 wpm

Help and support in Windows are available to assist you in finding answers to questions you may have about just how the computer functions. You can find help on topics like security, files, folders, printing, and maintenance.

92 wpm

When you want to look at the contents of two windows when using Windows, you might want to reduce the window size. Do this by pointing to a border or a corner of a window and dragging it until the window is the size that you want.

94 wpm

Scrolling means to display a very large quantity of text by rolling it horizontally or vertically past your display screen. As text disappears from the top section of your screen, new text will appear in the bottom area of your screen.

96 wpm

You have several options available to you when you print a document. For example, you can determine which printer to use, the pages you desire to print, the number of copies to be printed, the print quality desired, and the paper size used.

98 wpm

An ink-jet printer and a laser printer are popular printers used in a home office. Many users prefer an ink-jet printer because it is not as expensive to buy. But a laser printer provides a higher-quality print and is often the preferred choice.

100 wpm

E-mail, text messaging, cell phones, and chat rooms have enabled us to communicate quickly with people all around the globe. We can transmit a call or a message on the spur of the moment and receive a response to our call or message almost instantly.

102 wpm

Many different graphics software programs have been brought on the market in past years. These programs can be very powerful in helping with a business presentation. If there is a requirement to share data, using programs like these could be very helpful.

104 wpm

Voice mail is an essential service used by many people in the business world. This technology enables anyone placing a call to your phone to leave you a message if you cannot answer it at that time. This unique feature can help many workers be more productive.

Progressive Practice: Numbers

This skillbuilding routine contains a series of 30-second timed writings that range from 16 wpm to 80 wpm. The first time you use these timed writings, take a 1-minute timed writing with 3 or fewer errors on the Entry Timed Writing paragraph. Push moderately for speed.

Select a passage that is 1 to 2 wpm *higher* than your Entry Timed Writing speed. Then take up to six 30-second timed writings on the passage.

Your goal each time is to complete the passage within 30 seconds with no errors. When you have achieved your goal, move on to the next passage and repeat the procedure.

Entry Timed Writing

```
     Their bags were filled with 10 sets of jars, 23 cookie  11
cutters, 4 baking pans, 6 coffee mugs, 25 plates, 9 dessert  23
plates, 7 soup bowls, 125 recipe cards, and 8 recipe boxes.  35
David delivered these 217 items to 20487 Mountain Boulevard. 47
  1 | 2 | 3 | 4 | 5 | 6 | 7 | 8 | 9 | 10 | 11 | 12
```

16 wpm There are 37 chairs in Rooms 24 and 156.

18 wpm About 10 of the 39 boxes were torn on June 8.

20 wpm Only 3 papers had errors on pages 28, 40, and 197.

22 wpm My 46 letters were sent on May 10, June 3, and June 27.

24 wpm The 79 freshmen, 86 juniors, and 54 seniors arrived at home.

26 wpm The school needs 150 pens, 38 reams of paper, and 42 new folders.

28 wpm Only 1 or 2 of the 305 new books had errors on pages 46, 178, and 192.

30 wpm They met 10 of the 23 tennis players who received 4 awards from 5 trainers.

32 wpm Those 8 vans carried 75 passengers on the first trip and 64 on the next 3 trips.

34 wpm I saw 2 eagles on Route 86 and then 4 eagles on Route 53 at 9 a.m. on Monday, May 10.

36 wpm

The 17 firms produced 50 of the 62 records that received awards for 3 of the 4 categories.

38 wpm

The 12 trucks hauled 87 cows, 65 horses, and 49 pigs to the farm, which was 30 miles northeast.

40 wpm

She moved from 87 Bayview Drive to 659 Bay Street and then 3 blocks south to 4012 Gulbranson Avenue.

42 wpm

My 2 or 3 buyers ordered 5 dozen in sizes 6, 7, 8, and 9 after the 10 to 14 percent discounts were added.

44 wpm

There were 134 men and 121 women waiting in line at Gate 206 for the 58 to 79 tickets to the Cape Cod concert.

46 wpm

Steve had listed 5, 6, or 7 items on Purchase Order 243 when he saw that Purchase Requisition 89 contained 10 more.

48 wpm

Your items numbered 278 will sell for about 90 percent of the value of the 16 items that have code numbers shown as 435.

50 wpm

The managers stated that 98 of those 750 randomly selected new valves had about 264 defects, far exceeding the usual 31 norm.

52 wpm

Half of the 625 volunteers received over 90 percent of the charity pledges. Approximately 38 of the 147 agencies might enjoy this.

54 wpm

Merico hired 94 part-time workers to help the 378 full-time employees during the 62-day period when sales go up by 150 percent or more.

56 wpm

Kaye only hit 1 for 4 in the first 29 games after an 8-game streak in which she batted 3 for 4. She then hit at a .570 average for 16 games.

58 wpm

The mail carrier delivered 98 letters during the week to 734 Oak Street and also took 52 letters to 610 Faulkner Road as he returned on Route 58.

60 wpm

Pat said that about 1 in 5 of the 379 swimmers had a chance of being among the top 20. The best 6 of these 48 divers will receive special recognition.

Skillbuilding

62 wpm

It rained from 3 to 6 inches, and 18 of those 20 farmers were fearful that 4 to 7 inches more would flood about 95 acres along 3 miles of the new Route 79.

64 wpm

Those 17 sacks weighed 48 pounds, more than the 30 pounds that I had thought. All 24 believe the 92-pound bag is at least 15 or 16 pounds above its true weight.

66 wpm

They bought 7 of the 8 options for 54 of the 63 vehicles last month. They now have over 120 dump trucks for use in 9 of the 15 new regions in the big 20-county area.

68 wpm

Andy was 8 or 9 years old when they moved to 612 Glendale Street and away from the 700 block of Henry Lane, which is about 45 miles directly west of Boca Raton, FL 33434.

70 wpm

Doug had read 575 pages in the 760-page book by August 30; Darlene had read only 468 pages. Darlene has read 29 of those optional books since October 19, and Doug has read 18.

72 wpm

The school district has 985 elementary students, 507 middle school students, and 463 high school students. This total represents the greatest increase in total enrollment for us.

74 wpm

Attendance at last year's meeting was 10,835. Your goal for this year is to have 11,764 people. This might enable us to plan for an increase of 929 participants, a rise of 8.57 percent.

76 wpm

David's firm has 158 stores, located in 109 cities in the South. The company employs 3,540 males and 2,624 females, a total of 6,164 employees. About 4,750 of those employees work part-time.

78 wpm

Memberships were as follows: 98 members in the Drama Guild, 90 members in Zeta Tau, 82 members in Theta Phi, 75 in the Bowling Club, and 136 in the Ski Club. This meant that 481 joined the group.

80 wpm

The association had 684 members from the South, 830 members from the North, 1,023 members from the East, and 751 from the West. This total membership was 3,288; these numbers increased by 9.8 percent.

Paced Practice

The Paced Practice skillbuilding routine builds speed and accuracy in short, easy steps by using individualized goals and immediate feedback. You may use this program at any time after completing Lesson 9.

This section contains a series of 2-minute timed writings for speeds ranging from 16 wpm to 96 wpm. The first time you use these timed writings, take the 1-minute Entry Timed Writing with 2 or fewer uncorrected errors to establish your base speed.

Select a passage that is 2 wpm higher than your Entry Timed Writing speed. Then use this two-stage practice pattern to achieve each speed goal: (1) concentrate on speed and (2) work on accuracy.

Speed Goal. To determine your speed goal, take three 2-minute timed writings in total. Your goal each time is to complete the passage in 2 minutes without regard to errors. When you have achieved your speed goal, work on accuracy.

Accuracy Goal. To type accurately, you need to slow down—just a bit. Therefore, to reach your accuracy goal, drop back 2 wpm from the previous passage. Take consecutive timed writings on this passage until you can complete the passage in 2 minutes with no more than 2 errors.

For example, if you achieved a speed goal of 54 wpm, you should then work on an accuracy goal of 52 wpm. When you have achieved 52 wpm for accuracy, move up 4 wpm (for example, to the 56-wpm passage) and work for speed again.

Entry Timed Writing

If you can dream it, you can live it. Just follow your heart. There are many careers, which range from the mundane to the exotic to the sublime.

Start your career planning now by quizzing yourself about your talents, skills, and personal interests.

1 | 2 | 3 | 4 | 5 | 6 | 7 | 8 | 9 | 10 | 11 | 12

16 wpm

Your future is now,[1] so you must seize [2]every day.

After [3]exploring your interests,[4] quickly check the[5] sixteen career clusters[6] for a wide range[7] of potential jobs.[8]

18 wpm

When exploring various[1] career options, think[2] about what a job means[3] for you.

Recognize[4] that it can mean what [5]you do just to earn money[6] or what you find quite[7] challenging overall.[8]

20 wpm

If you acquire a job[1] that you enjoy, then it[2] means even more than simply [3]earning an excellent wage.[4]

It also means making a[5] contribution, taking pride[6] in your work, and utilizing[7] all of your talents.[8]

Skillbuilding

22 wpm

What is the difference between[1] a job and a career? Think[2] carefully. A job is work[3] that you have to do for money[4].

A career is a sequence[5] of related jobs that optimize[6] your interests, experience[7], knowledge, and training[8].

24 wpm

Learn all about the world of work[1] by looking at the sixteen[2] career clusters. Most jobs are[3] included in one of the clusters[4] that have been organized by[5] the government.

When exploring[6] careers, list all the unique[7] clusters that interest you[8].

26 wpm

Once you identify the career clusters[1] that interest you, look at[2] the jobs that are within each cluster[3].

Analyze exactly what skills[4] and aptitudes are needed, what[5] training is required, what the[6] work setting is like, and what your[7] chances for advancement are[8].

28 wpm

Use your career center and your school[1] or a public library to research[2] your career choice. Go on the Internet[3], and ask experts for their unique[4] views of certain careers.

As you[5] gather data about your job options[6], you might learn about new career[7] options that are on the horizon[8].

30 wpm

You must gain insight into a career.[1] You can become a volunteer, sign up for[2] an internship, or even work in a part-time[3] job in the field.

You will become[4] more familiar with a specific job[5] while you develop your skills. You will[6] quickly gain prized experience,[7] whether you choose that career or not.[8]

32 wpm

No matter which path you choose, strive[1] for a high level of pride in yourself and[2] in your job. Your image is affected by[3] what other people think of you as well[4] as by what you think of yourself.

Next,[5] analyze your level of confidence. If you[6] have any self-doubts, strive to acquire[7] more self-confidence and self-esteem.[8]

34 wpm

Confidence is required for a positive attitude,[1] and a positive attitude is required[2] for success at work. While you may not control[3] all that happens at work, recognize that[4] you must control how you react to what[5] happens.

Become more confident and cultivate[6] positive thoughts, which will provide you[7] with extra power in life and on the job.[8]

36 wpm

Quite a few factors lead to success on the job.[1] People who have analyzed these factors say[2] that it is the personal traits one exhibits[3] that determine who is promoted and who is not.[4]

One of the best traits a person can have[5] is the trait of being likable. That means that[6] you are honest, loyal, courteous, thoughtful,[7] pleasant, kind, considerate, and positive.[8]

38 wpm

If you are likable, you will relate well with[1] most people. If you have excellent social contact[2] with others, it will humanize the workplace and[3] make your work there more enjoyable. Think of[4] all the hours you are required to spend with one[5] another each day.

If you show that you are willing[6] to collaborate with your coworkers, most[7] likely you will also receive their cooperation.[8]

40 wpm

Cooperation begins on the first day of your new [1] job. When you work for a firm, you quickly become [2] a part of that team. Meeting people and learning [3] new skills can be quite exciting.

For some people, [4] though, a new situation can trigger some anxiety. [5] The best advice is to remain calm, do your job [6] with zeal, learn the workplace policies, be flexible, [7] avoid being too critical, and always be positive. [8]

42 wpm

When you begin a new job, even if you have recently [1] received your college degree, chances are you will [2] start at the bottom of the organizational chart. Each [3] of us has to start somewhere. Do not despair or become [4] lazy.

With hard work, you should start your climb [5] up the corporate ladder. If you are smart, you will [6] quietly take on even the most tedious task, take [7] everything in stride, and exercise any chance to learn. [8]

44 wpm

If you think learning is restricted to an academic setting, [1] think again. You have much to learn on the job, [2] even if it is a position for which you have been trained. [3]

As a new employee, you will not be expected to know [4] everything. When necessary, do not hesitate to ask your [5] employer questions. Learn all you can about your job [6] and the company. Capitalize on the new information to [7] enhance your job performance and to build toward success. [8]

46 wpm

Begin every valuable workday by prioritizing all of your [1] tasks. Decide which tasks must be done immediately and [2] which can wait. List the most important items first; then [3] determine the order in which each item must be done.

After [4] you complete a task, then quickly cross it off your [5] priority list. Maximize your time; that is, do not put off [6] work you should do. If a job must be done, just do it. You [7] will stay on top of your list when you utilize time wisely. [8]

48 wpm

Do not let the phone control your time. Learn how to manage[1] all your phone calls. Phone calls can be extremely distracting[2] from other duties, so be jealous of your quiet time. When[3] making a phone call, organize the topics you want to discuss[4]. Gather needed supplies such as pencils, papers, and files[5].

Set a time limit and stick to the topic. Give concise answers[6], summarize the points discussed, and end your talk politely[7]. Efficient phone usage will help you manage your time[8].

50 wpm

As with everything, practice makes perfect, but along the way[1], we have all made some mistakes. Realize that the difference [2]between successful people and those who are less successful is[3] not that the successful people make fewer mistakes. It is just[4] that they will never quit.

Instead of letting mistakes bring[5] you down, use your mistakes as opportunities to grow. If you make[6] a mistake, be patient with yourself. You might be able to fix[7] your mistake. Look for success to be just around the corner.[8]

52 wpm

Be patient as you learn how to take care of problems and accept[1] criticism. Accepting criticism may be quite a test for you. Still[2], it is vital to many of us at work. Criticism that is given in a[3] way to help you learn, expand, or grow is called constructive criticism[4].

If you look at criticism as being helpful, it will be easier[5] to deal with. You might be amazed to learn that some people[6] welcome it since it teaches them the best way to succeed on the[7] job. Try to improve how you accept helpful criticism from others.[8]

54 wpm

People experience continuous growth during a career. Goal setting[1] is a key tool to acquire for any job. Some people believe that goals[2] provide the motivation we need to get to the place we want to be.[3] Setting goals encourages greater achievements. The higher that we set[4] our goals, the greater the effort we need to reach them.

Each time[5] we reach a target or come closer to a goal, we should realize an[6] increase in our confidence and in our performance, which leads to greater[7] accomplishments. And the cycle continues to spiral for years.[8]

56 wpm

One goal we must all strive for is punctuality. When employees are absent[1] or just tardy, it costs the company money. If you are frequently[2] tardy or absent, others have to do extra work to cover for you. If you[3] are absent often, your peers may begin to resent you, which causes everyone[4] stress in the department.

Being late and missing work might penalize[5] your own relationship with your manager and have a negative effect[6] on your career. To avoid such potential problems, develop a personal[7] plan to ensure that you arrive every day on time and ready to work.[8]

58 wpm

To hold a job is a chief part of being an adult. Some people start their[1] work careers as teens. From the start, a range of work habits are developed[2] that are as crucial to success as the actual job skills and knowledge[3] that someone brings to his or her job.

What traits are expected of workers?[4] What do employers look for when they rate their own workers? Vital[5] personal traits would include being confident, helpful, positive, and loyal.[6] If you are also kind, passionate, and organized, you may now have[7] many of these qualities that employers value most of all in their staffs.[8]

60 wpm

Being dependable is a required work trait. If a job must be done by a special time, the manager will be pleased to learn that his or her workers are going to meet that deadline. Those who are dependable learn to utilize their time to attain maximum results. Loyal workers can also be counted on, they have good attendance records, they are well prepared, and they get to work on time and ready to start.

If the firm wants to meet its goals, it must have a team of loyal and dependable workers. You, your peers, your supervisors, and your managers are all team members who work to reach their goals.

62 wpm

The ability to organize is an important quality for the worker who would like to display good work habits. The worker should have the ability to plan the work that needs to be done and then to be able to execute that plan in a timely manner.

An employer requires a competent worker to be well organized. If the office worker is efficient, he or she handles requests swiftly and deals with messages without delay. The organized worker does not allow his or her work to accumulate on the desk. Also, the organized worker will return all phone calls quickly and make lists of the jobs that still need to be done each day.

64 wpm

Efficiency is one work habit that is important. The efficient worker does each[1] task quickly and starts work on the next task eagerly. He or she thinks about ways[2] to save steps or time. For example, an efficient worker may plan just one trip[3] to the copier with a number of copying jobs rather than take many trips to do[4] each separate job.

Being efficient also means that you have all of the required[5] supplies to finish each job. An efficient worker zips along on each project, uses[6] his or her time wisely, and then stays focused on that one task. With careful[7] and detailed planning, a worker who is efficient can finish tasks in less time.[8]

66 wpm

Cooperation is another ideal work habit. It begins on the first day of the job and[1] means that you quietly think of all team members when you make a decision. A person[2] who cooperates is willing to do what is needed for the good of the whole group.[3] For you to be a team player, you must take the extra steps to cooperate.

Cooperation[4] may mean that you need to be a good sport if you are asked to do something you[5] would rather not do. It may mean that you have to correct some mistakes made by another[6] person in the office. When each employee has the interests of the company at[7] heart and works well with other workers, then everyone is a good corporate citizen.[8]

68 wpm

Enthusiasm is still another work trait that is eagerly sought after by employers. If[1] you are enthusiastic, then you have lots of positive energy. This is reflected in your[2] actions toward your work, coworkers, and employer. It has been noted that eagerness[3] can be catching. If you show you are excited to try any project, then you may quickly[4] not only achieve the highest praise but also will be considered for career advancement.[5]

How much enthusiasm do you show at the workplace? Do you encourage people or complain[6] to people? There should always be lots of good jobs for workers who are known[7] to have a wealth of zeal and a positive approach to the jobs that they are assigned.[8]

70 wpm

Acceptance is a work trait required of all of us. In the work world of today, each business[1] includes both men and women of different religions, races, cultures, skills, and beliefs.[2] You will interact with many types of people as customers, coworkers, and owners.[3] Treat each one fairly, openly, and honestly.

All types of prejudice are hurtful, hateful,[4] and, in short, unacceptable. Prejudice is not allowed at work. Each of us must learn[5] to accept and even prize the many kinds of differences that are exhibited by all of us.[6] Since so many diverse groups work side by side in the work world, it is vital that all[7] workers maintain a high degree of shared insights. Embrace each of us for who we are.[8]

72 wpm

It can be concluded that certain work habits or traits should play the major role in deciding[1] the success of all workers. Most managers would be quick to agree on the high importance[2] of these traits. It is most likely that these habits would be analyzed on performance[3] appraisal forms. Promotions, pay increases, new duties, and your future with the company may[4] be based on these yearly job assessments.

You should request regular job performance assessments[5] even if your company does not conduct them. This feedback might then expand your[6] job skills and career development by helping you grow. If you always look for ways to improve[7] your work habits and skills, you will enjoy success in the world of work and beyond.[8]

74 wpm

You can be sure that no matter where you work, you will use some form of technology. Almost[1] every business depends on computers. Firms use such devices as voice mail, fax machines, cell[2] phones, and personal digital assistants. These tools help us to do our work quickly and efficiently.[3] They also take some of the drudgery out of our lives.

One result of the use of these[4] tools is globalization, which means worldwide communication links between people. Our world[5] has turned into one global village. We should expand our thinking beyond the office walls.[6] We must become aware of what happens in other parts of the world. These events may directly[7] affect you and your job. The more you know, the more valuable you will become to a company.[8]

76 wpm

Each advance in technology has had an effect on all aspects of our lives. For example, the dawn[1] of the age of the Internet has changed how people get and send data. It is the largest data network[2] in the world. It is called the information superhighway since it is a vast network of big[3] computers that can link people and resources around the world. It is an exciting medium to help[4] you access current data and be more useful on the job and at home.

Without a doubt, we are [5] all globally linked, and data technology services can support those links. The industry offers [6] different job opportunities in dozens of fields. Keep in mind that keyboarding skills are required[7] in this field as well as in most others. Touch-typing skills are just assumed in most jobs.[8]

78 wpm

It is amazing to learn about the many jobs in which keyboarding skill is needed today. The use of[1] a computer keyboard by executive chefs is a prime example. The chefs in large restaurants must prepare[2] parts or all of the meals served while they direct the work of their staff of chefs, cooks[3], and others in and near the kitchens.

The computer has become a prime tool for a wide range of tasks[4], including tracking stocks of their food supplies. By seeing which items are favorites and which[5] items are not requested, the chef can work out the food requirements, order food, and supervise[6] the purchase of foods. Also, the computer has proved to be a very practical tool for such tasks[7] as helping to plan budgets, prepare purchase orders for vendors, write menus, and print reports.[8]

80 wpm

Advanced technology has opened the doors to a wide variety of amazing new products and services to [1] sell. It seems that the more complex the products get, the higher the price of the products is and [2] that the larger the sales commission is, the stiffer the competition is. To sell a technical product [3] requires detailed product knowledge, good verbal skills, smooth sales rapport, and also expert typing [4] skills.

Business favors those who have special training. For example, a pharmacy company may choose [5] a person who has a strong knowledge of chemistry to sell its products. Sales is for those who enjoy [6] using their command of persuasion to make the sales. The potential for good pay and commissions [7] is quite high for the salesperson who is trained well. You should perhaps think about a job in sales. [8]

82 wpm

As you travel about in your sales job or type a report at the office or create the Friday night pizza [1] special for your new diner, you should always plan to put safety first. Accidents happen, but they do [2] not have to happen regularly or to have such severe results. Accidents cost businesses billions of dollars [3] each year in medical expenses, lost wages, and insurance claims.

Part of your job is to make certain [4] that you are not one of the millions of people injured on the job each year. You may believe you [5] work in a safe place, but accidents occur in all types of businesses. A few careless people cause most [6] accidents, so ensure your safety on the job. Safety does not just happen. It is the result of the very [7] careful awareness of those people who plan and put into action a safety program that benefits everyone. [8]

84 wpm

In the world of today, you need more than the needed skills or the personal qualities to succeed on the [1] job. Managers also expect all workers to have ethics. Ethics are the codes of conduct that tell a person [2] or a group how to act. Workers who act ethically do not lie, cheat, or steal. They are honest and fair [3] in all their dealings with others. In short, they are good citizens.

Workers who act ethically gain a good [4] reputation for themselves and for their companies. They are known to be dependable. Unethical behavior [5] can have a spiraling effect. A single act can do a lot of damage. Even if you have not held a job yet, you [6] have had some experience with ethical problems. Life is full of a range of occasions to behave ethically. [7] Do the right thing when faced with decisions. The ethics you follow will carry over into the workplace. [8]

86 wpm

Now that you know what will be expected of you on the job, how do you make sure you will get the job in the [1] first place? Almost everyone has at least once gone through the interview process for a job. For some, the [2] interview is a traumatic event, but it does not have to be so stressful. Research is the key. Learn about [3] the firm with whom you are seeking a job. Form a list of questions to ask. Interviews also provide you the [4] chance to interview the organization.

Take a folder of items with you. Include copies of your data sheet with [5] a list of three or more professional references, your academic transcript, and your certificates and licenses. [6] Be sure to wear appropriate business attire. The outcome of the interview will be positive if you have [7] enthusiasm for the job, match your skills to the needs of the company, ask relevant questions, and listen. [8]

88 wpm

How can you be the strongest candidate for the job? Be sure that your skills in reading, writing, math, speaking,[1] and listening are strong. These skills should enable you to listen well and communicate clearly, not only[2] during the job interview but also at your place of work. This exchange of information between a sender and a[3] receiver is known as communication.

It does not matter which career you choose; you will still spend most of[4] your time using these basic skills to communicate with others. You should use the skills as tools to gain information,[5] solve problems, and share ideas. You can also use these skills to help you meet the needs of your customers.[6] Most of the new jobs in the next few years will be in industries that will require direct customer contact.[7] Do not jeopardize your chances for success; make sure that you are able to communicate well with others.[8]

90 wpm

Writing well can help you gain a competitive edge in your job search and throughout your career. Most of us have[1] had occasion to write business letters whether to apply for a job, to comment on a product or service, or to place[2] an order. Often it seems easy to sit back and let our thoughts flow freely. At other times, we seem to struggle[3] to find the best words to use to express our thoughts in precisely the correct way. We all sometimes have these[4] issues.

Writing skills can improve with practice. Use these principles to develop your writing skills. Try to[5] use words that you would be comfortable using in person. Use words that are simple, direct, kind, and confident.[6] When it is possible, use words that emphasize only the positive side. Remember to proofread your work. Well-organized[7] thoughts and proper grammar, spelling, and punctuation will show your reader that you care about quality.[8]

92 wpm

Listening is such a vital part of the communication process. It is the key for learning, getting along, and forming[1] rapport. Do you think that you are an active or a passive listener? Listening should not be just a passive process.[2] To listen actively means to analyze what is being said and to interpret what it means. Active listening makes you[3] a more effective worker because you react to what you have heard as well as to what you have not heard.

Study these[4] steps to expand your listening skills: Do not cut people off; let them finish their remarks before you speak.[5] If what they said is unclear, write down your questions, and wait for the discussion to be finished until you ask them.[6] Reduce personal and environmental noise so you can focus on the message. Keep an open mind. Remain attentive and[7] maintain eye contact when possible. By using these skills, you can become even more confident and more effective.[8]

94 wpm

Speaking is also a form of communication. In the world of work, speaking is an important way in which to share information.[1] Regardless of whether you are speaking to an audience of one or one hundred, you will want to be sure that your[2] listeners hear your message. Be clear about your purpose, your audience, and your subject. A purpose is the overall[3] goal or reason for speaking. An audience is anyone who receives information. The subject is the main topic or key idea[4] that you wish to analyze.

Research your subject. Use specific facts and examples to give you credibility. As you speak,[5] be brief and direct. Progress logically from point to point. Speak slowly and pronounce clearly all your words.[6] Is the quality of your voice friendly and pleasant or is it shrill and offensive? These factors influence how your message[7] is received. A good idea is worthless if you cannot present it well, so take all the time you need to get ready.[8]

96 wpm

Building a career is a process. You have looked at all your interests, values, skills, talents, and feelings. Your look[1] into the world of work has begun, but the journey does not stop here, for the present is the perfect place to start thinking[2] about the future. It is where you start to take steps toward your goals. It is where you can really make a difference[3].

As you set personal and career goals, remember the importance of small steps. Each step toward a personal goal or[4] a career goal is a small victory. The feeling of success encourages you to take other small steps. Each step builds onto[5] the next. Continue analyzing your personal world as well as the world you share with others. Expect the best as you go[6] forward. Expect a happy life, loving relationships, success in life, and fulfilling and satisfying work in a job that you[7] really love. Last but not least, expect that you have something unique and special to offer the world, because you do.[8]

Supplementary Timed Writings

Supplementary Timed Writing 1

All problem solving, whether or not it is personal or academic, involves decision making. You make decisions in order to solve problems. On occasion, a problem occurs as a result of a decision you have made. For example, you may decide to smoke, but later in life, you might then face the problem of nicotine addiction. You may decide not to study math and science because you think that they are difficult. 11 23 35 46 58 70 82

Because of this choice, some career options may be closed to you. There is a consequence for each action. Do you see that events in your life do not just happen, but that they are the result of your choices and decisions? 93 108 116 127

How can you best prepare your mind to help you solve problems? A positive attitude is a great start. Indeed, your attitude will determine the way in which you may solve a problem or make a decision. Approach your studies, such as science and math courses, with a positive attitude. Try to think of academic problems as puzzles to be solved and not just as work to be avoided. 138 149 161 173 185 195 203

Critical thinking is a type of problem solving that allows you to decode, analyze, reason, assess, and process data. Since it is basic for all successful problem solving, you should try to explore, probe, question, and search for all the right answers. 213 224 235 248 253

A problem may not always be solved on the first try, so do not give up. Try, try again. To find a solution may take a real effort. Use your critical thinking skills to achieve success in a world that is highly competitive and demanding. 263 275 286 298 300

1 | 2 | 3 | 4 | 5 | 6 | 7 | 8 | 9 | 10 | 11 | 12

Supplementary Timed Writing 2

For many of us, the Internet is an important resource 11
in our private and public lives. The Internet provides us 23
with quick access to countless Web sites that may contain 34
news, products, games, and other types of data. The Web 45
pages on these sites can be designed, authored, and posted 57
by anyone from anywhere around the world, so you must use 69
critical thinking skills when reviewing these Web sites. 80

Just because something is said on the radio, printed 91
in the newspaper, or shown on television does not mean that 103
it is true. This applies to data found on the Internet as 115
well. Do not fall into the trap of believing that if it is 126
on the Net, it must be true. A wise user of the Internet 138
thinks critically about data found on the Net and evaluates 150
this material before he or she decides to use it. 160

When you assess a new Web site, think about who, what, 171
how, when, and where. Who refers to the author of the Web 183
site. The author may be a business firm, an organization, 194
or a person. What refers to the validity of the data. Can 206
this data be verified by a reputable source? 215

How refers to the viewpoint of the author. Are your 225
data presented without prejudice? When refers to the time 237
frame of your data. Do you have recent data? Where refers 249
to your data source. Are the data from a trusted source? 260

By answering these critical questions, you will learn 271
more about the accuracy and dependability of a Web site. 283
When you surf the Net next time, be quite cautious. Anyone 294
can publish on the Internet. 300

1 | 2 | 3 | 4 | 5 | 6 | 7 | 8 | 9 | 10 | 11 | 12

Supplementary Timed Writing 3

Most office workers perform a wide range of tasks in	11
their workday. These tasks may require them to handle phone	23
calls or forward personal messages, to send short e-mail	34
notes or compile complex office reports, or to write simple	46
letters or assemble detailed letters with tables, graphics,	58
and imported data. Office workers are thus a basic part of	70
the structure of the firm.	75
The office worker must use critical thinking in order	86
to carry out a wide array of daily tasks. Some of the tasks	98
are more urgent than other tasks and should be done first.	110
Some tasks take only a short time, while others take a lot	122
more time. Some tasks demand a quick response, while others	134
may be taken up as time permits or even postponed until the	146
future. Some of these tasks might require input from other	158
people.	159
Whether a job is simple or complex or big or small,	170
the office worker must decide what is to be done first by	182
setting the priority for each task.	189
When setting priorities, critical thinking skills are	200
essential. The office worker must assess each aspect of the	212
task. It is a good idea to identify the size of the task,	223
learn about its complexity, estimate the effort needed,	235
judge its importance, and set its deadline.	243
Once the office worker assesses a task that is to be	254
done within a certain span of time, then the priority for	266
completing all those tasks can be set. Critical thinking	277
skills, if applied well, can save the employer money, but	289
if they are applied poorly, they might cost an employer.	300

1 | 2 | 3 | 4 | 5 | 6 | 7 | 8 | 9 | 10 | 11 | 12

Supplementary Timed Writing 4

```
     Each day business managers must make choices that keep  11
their firms running in a smooth, skillful, and gainful way.   23
Every decision needs to be quick and sure.                    32
     To make good decisions, all managers must use critical   43
thinking. They must gather all the needed facts so that       54
they can make sound, well-informed choices. Over time, they   66
can refine their skills. Then, when they face a similar       77
problem, they can use their knowledge to help them solve      89
new problems with ease and in less time.                      97
     What types of decisions do you think managers make      107
that involve critical thinking? Human resource managers      119
need to decide whom to hire, what to pay the new worker,     130
and where to place him or her. In addition, human resource   142
managers should be able to help resolve conflicts between    153
workers.                                                     155
     Office managers must purchase copy machines, software,  166
computers, and supplies. Top executives must make business   178
policies, appoint other managers, and assess the success of  190
the firm. Plant supervisors must set schedules, gauge work   202
quality, and assess workers. Sales managers must study all   214
of the new sales trends, as well as provide sales training.  226
     Most managers use critical thinking to make wise and    237
well-thought-out decisions. They carefully check all the     248
facts, analyze these facts, and then make a final judgment   259
based upon these facts. They should also be able to clearly  271
discern fact from fiction. Through trial and error, most     283
managers learn their own ways to solve problems and find a   294
solution for their firms.                                    300
  1 | 2 | 3 | 4 | 5 | 6 | 7 | 8 | 9 | 10 | 11 | 12
```

Supplementary Timed Writing 5

```
     In most classes, teachers just want the students to        11
analyze situations, draw conclusions, and solve problems.       22
Each of these tasks requires students to use good thinking      34
skills. How do students acquire these skills? What process      46
do students follow to develop these skills?                     55
     During early years of life, children learn words and       65
then combine these words into sentences. From there, they       77
learn to declare ideas, share thoughts, and express their       89
feelings. Students learn numbers and math concepts. They       100
may learn to read musical notes, to keep rhythm, to sing       111
songs, and to recognize popular and classical pieces of        123
music. Students learn colors and shapes and start to draw.     134
     During their early years, students learn the basic        145
models of problem solving. One way for students to solve       156
problems and apply thinking skills is to use the scientific    168
approach. This approach requires a student to state the        179
problem to be solved, collect the known facts about that       191
problem, analyze the problem, and pose viable solutions.       202
Throughout this process, teachers ask questions that force     214
students to expand their thinking skills.                      222
     Teachers may want to ask questions such as these: Did     233
you clearly state the problem? Did you get all the facts?      245
Did you get the facts from the right place? Did you assume     257
anything? Did you pose other possible answers? Did you keep    269
an open mind to all solutions? Did you let your bias come      280
into play? Did you take the time to listen to other people?    292
Finally, does the solution make sense?                         300
  1 | 2 | 3 | 4 | 5 | 6 | 7 | 8 | 9 | 10 | 11 | 12
```

Supplementary Timed Writing 6

```
     A major goal for all instructors in school is to teach  11
critical thinking skills to their class. This skill is the   23
process of deciding in a logical way what we should do or    35
believe, and it also involves an ability to compare and      46
contrast, solve problems, make decisions, analyze results,   58
and combine and use knowledge. Can you see that these are    69
important skills you can use all your life?                  78
     These skills help the student who later becomes a part  89
of the workforce. Whether someone is in a small business,   101
is in a corporate setting, or is self-employed, the world   112
of today is a competitive one, and skilled employees are    124
always in demand.                                           127
     One part of gaining success in the workforce is having 139
the skill to deal with the mixed demands of the fast-paced  150
business world. A few of the required skills are insightful 162
decision making, creative problem solving, and productive   174
contact among diverse groups.                               180
     In school, we learn the basics of critical thinking.   191
This skill extends far beyond the borders of the classroom  203
and lasts a lifetime. We use critical thinking in all of    214
our daily lives. We constantly analyze and assess pursuits  226
such as music, movies, speech, fashion, magazine articles,  238
and television shows.                                       242
     We all had experience using critical thinking skills   253
well before we even knew what they were. So you should keep 265
on learning and growing. The classroom can be the perfect   276
place for your exploration, so use that time to learn how   288
others solve problems. There are always new goals to reach. 300
  1  |  2  |  3  |  4  |  5  |  6  |  7  |  8  |  9  |  10  |  11  |  12
```

Supplementary Timed Writing 7

One of the first steps you should take to unlock your	11
creativity is to realize that you have control over your	22
mind; your mind does not control you. Creativity is just	34
using a new or different way to solve a problem.	44
Many of our inventions have involved breakthroughs in	55
traditional ways of thinking, and the result has often been	67
amazing. For example, Einstein broke with the old ways and	78
tried obscure formulas that have changed all scientific	90
thought. Your attitude can form a mental block that may	101
keep you from exercising creativity. When you free up your	113
mind, the rest will follow.	118
Do your best to unleash your mind's innate creativity	129
by turning problems into puzzles. When you think of the	140
task as a puzzle, a challenge, or a game instead of as a	152
difficult problem, you will open up your mind and free your	164
creative side to operate. Creative ideas come when you are	176
enjoying yourself and are involved in unrelated tasks.	187
Old habits often restrict you from trying new ways of	198
solving problems. There is often more than one solution, so	210
strive to see each situation in a fresh, new light. How	221
many times have you told yourself that you must follow the	233
rules and perform tasks only in a certain way?	242
If you want to be creative, then look at situations in	253
a new light, break the pattern, explore new opportunities,	265
and challenge old rules. If you are facing a hard problem	277
and cannot find an answer, take a quick walk or relax for a	289
few minutes; you can then go back to the problem renewed.	300
1 | 2 | 3 | 4 | 5 | 6 | 7 | 8 | 9 | 10 | 11 | 12	

Supplementary Timed Writing 8

Keyboarding is a very popular business course that	10
most students take. The major goals of a keyboarding course	22
are to develop touch control of the keyboard, to use proper	34
typing techniques, to build basic speed and accuracy, and	46
to receive considerable practice in applying those basic	57
skills to format letters, reports, tables, memos, and other	69
kinds of personal and business documents.	78
In the first part of a keyboarding course, you must	88
learn to stroke the keys by touch, using proven techniques.	100
You learn to strike the keys in a quick and accurate way.	112
After the keys are learned, you then focus your attention	123
on producing documents of many sizes and types.	133
When you first learn to keyboard, there may be certain	144
steps, guidelines, and exercises that should be followed.	156
There are rules to help you learn and in due time to master	168
the keyboard. To create each document requires that you	179
apply critical thinking. What format or layout should be	190
used? What font and font size would be best? Are all the	202
words spelled correctly? Does the document look neat on the	214
page? Are the figures accurate? Are the punctuation and	225
grammar correct?	228
Being creative also has a lot to do with risk taking	239
and courage. It takes courage to explore new ways to think	251
and to risk looking different and even to risk being wrong.	263
Your path to creativity is such a vital component of your	274
critical thinking skills. Allow your creative thoughts to	286
flow freely when you produce each keyboarding task. Enjoy	298
the journey.	300
1 | 2 | 3 | 4 | 5 | 6 | 7 | 8 | 9 | 10 | 11 | 12	

Supplementary Timed Writing 9

More employees are injured using the computer keyboard	11
in the United States than using any other equipment in the	23
workplace. Therefore, you should find the most comfortable	35
and ergonomic position when you are keyboarding.	45
Your chair should be on rollers, be adjustable to fit	56
your individual height, and have substantial support for	67
your lower back. You should sit with your hips pushed as	78
far back in the chair as possible, and your thighs should	90
not touch the underside of the workstation.	99
Your monitor should be aligned with your keyboard and	110
centered opposite you. The display should be just slightly	122
below eye level and tilted away from you slightly. When you	134
sit back in the chair and hold your arm out horizontally,	145
your middle finger should touch the middle of the monitor.	157
That way you won't need to make excessive head movements to	169
see the viewing area of your screen.	176
A document holder should be positioned at the same	187
height and distance as the screen in order to minimize any	199
head movements and at the same angle as the screen. Place	210
the document holder to the side of the screen opposite the	222
mouse. Position the mouse at the identical height as the	233
keyboard, and you should move the mouse with your whole arm	245
and not just with your wrist.	251
There's no research to show that an ergonomic keyboard	263
is any more beneficial than the standard keyboard layout.	274
If your keyboard has pop-up legs, these should not be used	286
because a negative slope to the keyboard is by far the most	298
healthful.	300

1 | 2 | 3 | 4 | 5 | 6 | 7 | 8 | 9 | 10 | 11 | 12

Supplementary Timed Writing 10

One of the most important decisions we all have to face is choosing a career. Your options can appear to be a bit overwhelming at first. But you should not worry because your critical thinking skills will help.

Start with a self-assessment. What are your interests? Would you prefer to work inside or outdoors? Would you like to work with numbers or with words? Are you an independent type or would you rather work within a group? What are your preferred courses? Think about each of these questions, and then make a list of your interests, skills, aptitudes, and values. What you learn about yourself might help you find the career that is just right for you.

After you have explored your own interests, look at the sixteen career clusters for a wide range of possible jobs. Most jobs are included in one of these clusters that have been organized by the government. During your search, make a note of the clusters that interest you and look into all the clusters.

Get as much information as you can by making use of all available resources. Scan the employment section in the major Sunday newspapers for job descriptions and salaries. Search the Internet, which provides access to job listings around the world. If you want to evaluate closely a certain company, access its home page and look around.

Sign up for interviews with companies that visit your campus. Talk with people in your field of interest to ask questions and get advice. Taking the initiative in your job search will pay off.

Line word counts: 10, 22, 34, 42, 54, 66, 77, 89, 101, 113, 125, 133, 143, 155, 166, 178, 190, 194, 204, 216, 228, 240, 252, 261, 272, 284, 296, 300

1 | 2 | 3 | 4 | 5 | 6 | 7 | 8 | 9 | 10 | 11 | 12

Index

NOTE: Page numbers preceded by R- indicate material in References Manual; page numbers preceded by SB- indicate material in Skillbuilding supplement.

INDIVIDUAL KEYS (alphabet)
A, 3–5, 34
B, 18–20, 34
C, 18–20, 34
D, 3–5, 34
E, 8–9, 34
F, 3–5, 34
G, 28–30, 34
H, 11–13, 34
I, 14–17, 34
J, 3–5, 34
K, 3–5, 34
L, 3–5, 34
M, 23–24, 34
N, 8–9, 34
O, 11–13, 34
P, 25–27, 34
Q, 28–30, 34
R, 11–13, 34
S, 3–5, 34
T, 8–9, 34
U, 18–20, 34
V, 31–34
W, 22–24, 34
X, 25–27, 34
Y, 31–34
Z, 31–34

INDIVIDUAL KEYS (numbers)
0, 55, 71
1, 57–58, 71
2, 38–40, 71
3, 47–49, 71
4, 44–46, 70
5, 41–43, 70
6, 47–49, 70
7, 44–46, 70
8, 41–43, 70
9, 38–40, 70

INDIVIDUAL KEYS (punctuation, functions, and symbols)
& (ampersand), 54–55
' (apostrophe), 41–43, 48, 134–135, R-17
* (asterisk), 64–65, 125
@ (at sign), 58
BACKSPACE key, 4–5, 29, 58, 161, R-2B
: (colon), 44–45, 48, 84, 152, R-18
, (comma), 28–30, 35, 75, 92–93, 151–153, 192, R-15–R-16
. (decimal), 71
/ (division), 72
$ (dollar sign), 54–55, 142
ENTER key, 3–4, 122, 225, R-2B
! (exclamation mark), 63–65
– (hyphen), 38–39, 90, 214, R-17
LEFT SHIFT key, 14–15, 48
- (minus), 72
* (multiplication), 72
# (number or pound), 61
¶ (paragraph), 86, 128–129, 205
( ) (parentheses), 60–61
% (percent), 60–61, 174, R-13B, R-13D
. (period), 15, 35, R-18
+ (plus), 72
? (question mark), 57–58
" (quotation mark), 63–65, 151–152
RIGHT SHIFT key, 22–24, 48
; (semicolon), 5, R-16
SHIFT key, 14–15, 22–24, 48, 55, 144, R-28
/ (slash), 47–48
SPACE BAR, 3–4, 32, 51, 61, 81, 185
TAB key, 25–27, 51, 65, 106, 166, 202, R-28

A
Abbreviations, 259
  lowercase, 359
  measures, 353, 356
  rules, 257, 353–354, R-22
  from U.S. Postal Service, R-14B
Academic report
  document processing, 200–201, 483–485
  multipage, 243, R-8C–D
    document processing, 124–125
    formatting, 123–124
    with lists, 124
    parts of, 123
    proofreading, 127–129
    skillbuilding, 122
Accent mark, 332–333
Accept/except, 482–484, R-20
Address
  commas in, 75, 192, R-15
  e-mail, 99
  inside address, 89, 152, R-3A
  international address, 327, R-3D, R-5A
  mailing/return address, 155, R-3D, R-12B
  multiple, 257–258
  return address, R-3D, R-12B
  See also International formatting of addresses and dates
Adjacent adjectives, comma and, 277, 279, R-16
Adjacent keys, skillbuilding, 100, 221, 360, 490
Adjectives
  adjacent, 277, 279, R-16
  and adverbs and agreement, 415–417, R-20
  compound, R-17
Administrative services career, 73
Advanced formatting, 236–237
Adverbs, 415–417, R-20
Affect/effect, 482–484, R-20

Affidavit, 391, 400–401
Agenda, meeting, R-11A
  document processing, 283–285, 298
  formatting, 281–282
Agreement, rules for
  adjectives and adverbs, 415–417
  intervening words, 325, 328, 333, R-19
  pronoun, 325–326, 328, 333, R-19
  singular and plural, 257, 260, R-19
Alignment, table, 138
Alphabet
  home-row keys, 3–5
  keyboarding, 3–35
  progressive practice, 39, 50, 369, 395, SB-2–SB-6
  skillbuilding, 5, 9, 12, 15, 19, 23, 26, 29, 32, 34–35, 39, 48, 55, 58, 75, 110, 134, 151, 173, 176, 192, 214, 235, 256, 276, 325, 353, 369, 395, 442, 460, 482, SB-2–SB-6
Alternate-hand words, 114, 180–181, 238, 373, 450–451
Alternate keys, R-2B
American Management Association, 247
American Psychological Association (APA) style. *See* APA style
Ampersand (&), 54–55
Announcement, 443–446
Annual report reference, R-9B
APA style, 18
  reference list pages in, 182, 184
  for reports, 173–176, R-10A–B
Apostrophe ('), 41–43, 48, 134–135, R-17
Application letter, 196–199, 228, 250, R-12B
Area, as unit of measurement, 40
Arrow keys, R-2B
Art, Audio, Video Technology, and Communication Services cluster, 1
Ask.com, 80
Asterisk (*), 64–65, 125
At sign (@), 58
Attachment feature, in e-mail program, 84, 103
Attachment notation, 102–104, R-4D, R-7C
Audience, 299, 367
Author/page citations, R-10C. *See also* Writer's identification
Author/year citations, 175, R-10A
Avery labels, 97

B

Backspace key, 4–5, 29, 58, 161, 271, 382, 493, R-2B
Banking documents, 479–481
Beginnings, word, 45, 79, 199
Bias, reducing, in communication, 202
Bibliography, R-9B
  for business report, 366–367
  document processing, 273
  formatting, 181–182
Blind copy notation (BCC), 84, 263–264, R-5B
Block style, R-3A. *See* Business letter, in block style; Personal-business letter, in block style; Personal-business letter, in modified-block style
Blog, 51
Bloomberg.com, 247
Body
  academic report, 123
  business letter, 89
  business report, 111, 115
  correspondence, R-3A
  e-mail message, 84–85
  memo, 102
  table, R-13A
Book
  author reference, R-9B
  italicized title of, 107, 172
Bookmarks, 361
Border, table, 135, 461
Boxed table, 131–133, 224, 246, 329, 338, 346, 362, 480, R-5A, R-8B, R-13A
  in medical office documents, 371
  in warranty deed, 393
Building, word, 5, 23, 26
Bulleted and numbered lists, 119–121, 249, 259–260, 283–284, R-12C
Business and administrative services careers, 73
Business document
  correspondence, 87–108
  e-mail message, 83–86
  word processing, 75–82
Business letter, 108
  in block style, 90–91, 93–94, 146, 153, 187, 211–212, 226–227, 237, 254–255, 259–260, 264, 341, 345, 384, 398, 401, 465–466, 468–469, 471–472, 491–492, 495–497, R-3A
  document processing, 90–91, 163
  with enclosure notation, 92–94
  on executive stationery, R-4A
  folding, R-6B
  formatted for window envelope, R-4C
  formatting, 89–90
  on half-page stationery, R-4B
  medical office documents, 379–381
  in modified-block style, 216, 265–266, 328, 379, R-3B
  multipage, R-5A, R-5B
  parts of, 89
  personal, R-12B
    in block style, 203–204, 206, 208, 237
    composing, 474
    document processing, 155–157
    formatting, 155–157
    in modified-block style, 197–198, 204, 206, 208, R-3D
  in simplified style, R-3C
Business reports, 341, R-9A
  bibliography, 366–367
  cover page, 365–367
  document processing, 112–113, 120–121, 216–217, 222–223, 242–243, 358–359, 362, 374–377, 494–495
  formatting, 111–112
  language arts, 110–111, 361
  left-bound, with indented displays and footnotes, 169–172, 190
  with lists, rough draft of, 118–121

medical office documents, 380, 388
multipage, 114–117, 349–352, 354, R-8A–B
document processing, 362–363
formatting, 358, 361
tables in, 355–356
one-page business, 110–113
with paragraph headings, 115
paragraphs blocked in, 128–129
parts of, 111–112
with side headings, 112
skillbuilding, 110
with table, 333
table of contents, 366
See also Reports
Byline, 111, 123, R-8A, R-10A

C

Canada
country code for telephone dialing, 336–337
formatting letter with address and date, 326–329
URLs, 331
Canadian provinces, U.S. Postal Service abbreviations, R-14B
Capitalization
column capitalization in tables, R-13D
of compass points, R-21
course titles, 460–461
for emphasis in e-mail, 125
of first word in sentence, 110, 112–113
Left Shift key, 14–15
mechanics, R-20
and netiquette, 290
organizational terms, 460–461, R-21
proper nouns, 110, 112
Right Shift key, 22–24
skillbuilding, 42, 77, 196
sustained practice, 42, 330
times (week day, months, holidays, religious days), 110–113, R-21
Capitals, skillbuilding, 463
Caps Lock key, R-2B
Career opportunities
in business and administrative services, 73
in education, 149
in health services, 233
in information technology (IT) services, 323
in legal services, 413
in media, 1
See also Strategies for Career Success (feature)
CD/DVD drive, R-2A
Cells, merge in table, 135
Chamber of Commerce, 247
Channel, in communication process, 367
China. *See* People's Republic of China
Citation
author/year, 175
report, 180–184, R-9D, R-10A–D
Clause, 9, 12, 92–93
Clip art, 358–359, 363
Close reaches, skillbuilding, 100–101, 221, 360–361, 490–491
Closing
of business letter, 89
comma after complimentary, 152–153
in e-mail message, 85
formatting, 153
in letters, 151–153, R-3A
Closing line, company names in, 262
Colon (:), R-18
in greeting of e-mail message, 84
to introduce explanatory material, 369–370, 372
with salutation, 152
skillbuilding, 45, 48
spacing, 44
Column entries, of table, 132
Column headings
open table with, 137–139
in tables, 132, R-4D, R-5A, R-8B, R-13A–D
Columns, report formatting in, 292–296
Comma (,), 29–30, R-16
in addresses, 192
and adjacent adjectives, 277, 279
with complimentary closing, 152–153
with coordinate conjunctions, R-15
in dates, 192
with direct quotation, 151
between independent clauses, 92–93
and introductory expression, 93
with name in direct address, 75
and nonessential expression, 276, 278–279
series, 235, 237
skillbuilding, 35
spacing around, 28
transitional expression, 235–236, R-16
Common letter combinations, 45, 79, 200, 335–336, 467–468
Communication, components of, 367. *See also* Feedback
Company name, 262, R-5B
Comparative adjectives, R-20
Compass points, capitalization of, R-21
Complaint document, 339, 391, 407–409
Complimentary closing
of business letter, 89
comma after, 152–153
formatting, 153
in letters, 151–153, R-3A
Compound adjective, hyphen and, 256, 259–60, R-17
Compound numbers, hyphen and, 214–215
Computer keyboard, R-2B
Computer system
keyboard, R-2B
major parts of, R-2A
Computer technology, use of, in educational setting, 149
Computer virus, 359
Conjunction, semicolon and, 395–396, 398, R-16
Consecutive fingers, skillbuilding, 100, 221, 360, 490
Control keys, R-2B
Cookies, Web site, 167
Coordinate conjunction, 92, R-15

Copy
image or graphic from Internet, 372
in word processing, 127
Copy notation
in correspondence, 162, R-3C, R-5B
e-mail with, 84, 162
Correspondence
business letters (*See* Business letter; Personal-business letter)
day/month/year format, 328
e-mail (*See* E-mail)
memos, R-4D, R-7C, R-9C
with attachments, 100–105
with lists, 158–160
transmittal, 236, R-16
See also E-mail; Employment documents; *entries for specific letter types*
Correspondence template
document processing, 416–417
formatting, 416
Course titles, capitalization of, R-21
Court documents, 391
Court reporter, 413
Cover letter, 186
Cover page
document processing, 365–367, 439–441
formatting, 365, 438
Cut, in word processing, 127

D

Dashes, for emphasis, 125
Data source file, in mail merge, 464, 466, 469, 472, 475–476
Date
of academic report, multipage, 123
of business letter, 89
commas in, 192, R-15
of memo, 102
of report, 111, R-8A
use figures for, 173, R-22
See also International formatting of addresses and dates
Date line, in correspondence, R-3A
Day/month/year format, in international correspondence, 328
Days of week, capitalization of, 110, R-21
Decimal (.), 71
Delivery notation, in correspondence, 263, R-3C, R-4A, R-5B
Diagonal (/). *See* Slash (/)
Dice.com, 51
Direct address
comma before and after name in, 75
commas and, R-15
Directory form, 433
Direct quotation, 153
comma before and after, 151
commas and, R-15
and quotation marks, 151, R-18
Discrimination practice, 118–119, 241–242, 378–379
Disk drive, R-2A
Display screen, R-2A
Distance, use figures to express, 174, R-22
Division (/), 72
Document processing
academic report, 145–146, 200–201, 243, 483–485
agendas, 283–285, 298
agreement nearer noun, 417
announcement, 443–446
application letter in block style, 250
bibliography, 183–184, 273
boxed table, 246, 338, 362, 371, 480
business letter in block style, 237, 254–255, 259–260, 264, 337, 341, 465–466, 468–469, 471–472, 487, 491–492, 495–497
business letter in modified-block style, 265–266
business report, 112–113, 120–121, 216–217, 222–223, 242–243, 341, 349–351, 358–359, 494–495
in APA style, 175–176
left-bound, 171–172, 190
in MLA style, 179
multipage, 116
report citations, 183–184
resume, 195, 206–207
table of contents, 189
tables in, 138–139, 215, 227
title page, 188–189
with View Gridlines, 135
works cited (MLA style), 184
China, 345–346
clip art, 363, 424
correspondence
business letter, 90–91, 108
in block style, 146, 163, 211–212, 226–227
with enclosure notation, 93–94
in modified-block style, 166–167, 216
e-mail message, 85–86, 105, 108, 163, 219, 227
envelopes, View Gridlines, and labels, 98–99
letters of application, 197–198
memo, 104–105, 107–108, 212, 219, 228
personal-business letter
in block style, 155–157, 203–204, 206, 208
in modified-block style, 197–198, 204, 206, 208
in personal letters, 153
references in APA style, 184
cover page, 365–367, 439–441
directory form, 433
e-mail message, 239–240, 265, 338, 341–343, 492
envelopes, 474–475
flyer, 446, 457–458, 485
follow-up letter in block style, 250
with international addresses and dates, 328–329
itinerary, 278–279, 487–488
judgment, 410
left-bound business report, 244, 485
legal documents, 392–394, 396–398, 404–405, 407–410
letterhead, designing, 424–426
letterhead form, 481
magazine article, 294–296, 299
mail merge, 465–466, 468–469

medical office documents, 370–372, 374–377, 379–381, 384–385, 387–388
memo, 239–240, 268–270, 405
memo report, 272–273
memo template, 416–417, 435, 479–480
minutes of meeting, 298
multipage business report, 254, 354–356
multipage letters, 254
newsletters, 448–449, 451–453, 455–456, 488–489
notepad form, 429–431
online resume, 461–462
open table, 247
personal-business letter in block style, 237
procedures manual, 288–290
and report templates, 419–421
resume, 249
ruled table, 247, 492
sign-in form, 434
tables
boxed, 133, 224
boxed tables, 133, 224
open, 138–139, 215, 227
open tables, 138–139, 215, 227
ruled, 146, 201, 220
ruled tables, 146, 201, 220
warranty deed, 409–410
Dollar sign ($), 54–55, 142, R-8B, R-13A–B, R-13D
Dot leaders, 188
Dot-style telephone numbers, 336
Down reaches, 158, 286, 422

E

Education careers, 149
Education documents, 483–485
Effect/affect, R-20
E-mail
attachments, 103
with blind copies, 264
with copies, 162–163
creating signature file for, 266
document processing, 85–86, 105, 108, 159–160, 163, 219, 227, 341–342, 492
effective management of, 427
flame wars, avoiding, 213
language arts, 83
management of, 427
in Microsoft Outlook, R-5C
in MSN Hotmail, R-5D
parts of address, 99
style guide for business, 125
E-mail message, 239–240, 338, 387
composing, 83, 344, 432–433
document processing, 265
formatting, 84–85, 159, 332
as legal correspondence, 394
parts of, 84–85
E-mail privacy, 453
E-mail reference, R-9B
Em dash (—), 90, 243
Employment documents
application letter, 196–199, 228, 250, R-12B
follow-up letter, 202–204, 250
integrated employment project, 205–208
interview communications, 199–201, 231
resume, 192–195, 206–207, 220, 249, 461–462, R-12A
Employment project, integrated, 205–208
Enclosure notation
in correspondence, R-3B, R-5B
formatting, 93
Endnotes, in report, R-8C–D, R-9C
Enter key, 3–4, 122, 225, 339, 454, R-2B
Envelopes, R-6A
formatting, 95–96
and mail merge, 474–475
metric size for, 326–327
word processing, 98
Escape key, R-2B
Except/accept, R-20
Exclamation mark (!), 63–65
Executive stationery, R-4A
Explanatory material, 369–370, 372, R-18

F

Facebook, 329
Farther/further, 482–485, R-20
Feedback, 287, 367
Figures. *See* Numbers (#)
Find and replace, 268
Flame wars. *See* E-mail, flame wars, avoiding
Flyer, 446, 457–458, 485
Follow-up letter, to interview, 202–204, 250
Font, 194, 423
Footers, 288
Footnotes, in report, 170–171, R-8A–B, R-9A
Form, R-14A
designing, 423
filling in, 416
Formatting
advanced, 236
agendas, 281–282
announcement, 443–446
author/year citations, 175
bibliographies, 181–182
blind copy notation, 263
bulleted and numbered lists, 119
column headings, 138
company names in closing lines, 262
cover page of business report, 365
day/month/year format, 328
delivery notation, 263
designing form, 423
dot-style telephone numbers, 336
e-mail with blind copies, 264
e-mail with copies, 162
e-mail messages, 84–85

Formatting *(continued)*
enclosure notations, in business letter, 93
envelopes, 95–96, R-6A
filling in forms, 416
footnote references, 170–171
headers, 175
indented displays, 162
international addresses in letter, 327
international telephone access codes, 336–337
itineraries, 277
labels, for business letter, 97
left-bound reports with footnotes, 170–171
legal office documents, 391
letter
of application, 197
business, 89–90
with copy notations, 162
folding, 96, R-6B
follow-up, 203
modified-block style, 165
personal-business, 155
personal titles in, 152
magazine article, 292–294
margins and footnotes, 171
memo, 102–103
metric envelope size, 326–327
metric paper size, 326
metric units of measurement, 340
minutes of meeting, 282–283
multipage business report, 115–116
multipage letters, 53
multiple addresses, 257–258
on-arrival notations, 258
online resume, 461
postscripts, 263
procedures manual, 287–288
reference list pages in APA style, 18
report, 111–112
academic, 123–124
in APA style, 174–175
with list for business, 119
in MLA style, 178
rough-draft business for business, 127
report headings in memos, 272
resume, 193–194, 220
review, 144–146
ruled tables with number columns, 141–142
subject lines, 258
table, parts of, 132–133
table heading block, 135
table of contents, 187–188
tables within documents, 262
tab set
dot leaders, 188
ruler tabs, 166
title page, 186–187
titles, 111, 123, 132, 151–153, 172
word processing, 76–78, 80, 82, 107, 163, 183, 188, 194
clip art, insert, 358
columns and hyphenation, 294
file, insert and bookmarks and hyperlinks, 361
find and replace, 268
font, small caps and text boxes, 423
footers, 288
line numbering, 400
mail merge envelopes and labels, 474
mail merge letters, 465
paper size, 328
print options, 428
sort, 259
styles, 349
table
move and page color, 443
shading and e-mail blind copies, 264
tab, 374
templates
correspondence, 416
report, 419
WordArt, 438
works-cited pages in MLA style, 183
Form letter, formatting, 464–465
Fractions, R-17
spell out, 214
using figures to express, R-22
Fragment, sentence, 75, R-19
France
address in letters, 327
telephone dialing code, 337
URLs, 331
Function keys, R-2B
Further/farther, R-20

G

GDP Reference Manual, 85, R-1–R-22
Germany
address in letters, 327
formatting letter with address and date, 340–343
telephone dialing code, 337
URLs, 331
Goodwill messages, 86
Google, 247
Government document reference, 491–492, R-9B
Grammar, R-19–R-20. *See also* Language arts
Greeting, in e-mail message, 84

H

Half-page stationery, R-4B
Hanging indent, in report, R-10D
Heading(s), 175, R-9A
braced column, R-13A
column, 132, 137–139
in memos, 102, 105
paragraph, 115, 123
in report, R-8A–C, R-8C, R-9A, R-9D, R-10A, R-10C
side, 111–112, 123
2-line, R-13B
Heading block, in tables, R-5, R-8B, R-13A–D
Health services, careers in, 233

Holidays, capitalization of, 110–111, 113, R-21
Home-row keys, 3–5
Horizontal reaches, 140–141, 267–268, 402–403
Hospitality documents, 214–217
Hyperlinks, 361, 431
Hyphen (-)
  automatic, 243
  columns and, 294
  in compound adjectives, 256, R-17
  in compound numbers, R-17
  and em dash (—), 90
  expressing fractions, 214
  skillbuilding, 39
  spacing, 38
  in U.S. telephone numbers, 336

I

IDD. *See* International Direct Dialing (IDD)
In-basket review
  banking documents, 479–481
  education documents, 483–485
  government documents, 491–492
  hospitality documents, 214–217
  insurance documents, 210–213
  manufacturing documents, 225–228
  nonprofit documents, 221–224
  nursing facility documents, 486–489
  retail documents, 218–220
  software development documents, 494–497
Indented display, 183
  in business reports, 356
  in correspondence, R-3A
  formatting, 162–163
  in report, R-8B, R-8C
Independent clause, 92–94, R-15
Information technology (IT) services, careers in, 323
In reaches, 140, 267, 402
Inside address
  of business letter, 89
  in correspondence, R-3A
  of personal letter, 152
Instructor assistant, 149
Insurance documents, 210–213
Integrated employment project, 205–208
International address, 327, R-3D, R-5A
International Direct Dialing (IDD), 336
International formatting of addresses and dates
  Canada, 326–329
  China, 345–346
  France, 336–338
  Germany, 340–343
  Mexico, 331–334, 336–338
  URLs, 331–334
International telephone access codes, 336–337
Internet
  business information on, 247
  cookies, 137
  copy image or graphic from, 372
  defined, 51
  e-mail (*See* E-mail)
  evaluating sources, 190
  hyperlinks, 431
  international URLs, 331
  transferring text from Web page, 393
  use of, in classrooms, 149
  Web searching and browsing, 80, 143
  Yellow Pages on, 401
Interview
  communications regarding, 199–201, 231
  ending, 201
  process of, 8
  See also Job application letter; Job interview portfolio, preparing
Interviewing techniques, 279
Introductory expression, 93
  colon and, R-18
  commas and, R-15
Italics
  in bibliography, 183–184
  text to be emphasized, 107
  titles of published works, 151, 172, 208, 243, 484, R-18
  See also Underline
Italy, telephone dialing code, 337
Itinerary
  document processing, 278–279
  formatting, 277–278
  in report, 487–488, R-11C

J

Japan, telephone dialing code, 337
Job application letter, writing, 228
Job interview portfolio, preparing, 82
Journal article reference, R-9B
Judgment, 391, 410

K

Keyboard, computer, R-2A–B
Keyboarding Connection (feature)
  antivirus programs, 359
  copy image or graphic from Internet, 372
  e-mail
    flame wars, 213
    management of, 427
    parts of address, 99
    privacy, 453
    signature file, 266
    style guide for business, 125
  evaluating Internet sources, 190
  home page, choosing different, 435
  hyperlinks, 431
  Internet, defined, 51
  netiquette, 290
  search
    for business information, 143, 247
    for people, 329
    Yellow Pages, 401
  search engine, 80
  spam, 383
  teleconferencing for meetings, 346

Keyboarding Connection (feature) *(continued)*
transferring text from Web page, 393
Web site cookies, 167
Yellow Pages, searching, 401
Keys. *See* INDIVIDUAL KEYS (alphabet) *and entries for specific keys*

L

Labels, formatting, 97–99, 474
Language arts
abbreviations, 257, 353–354, R-22
adjectives and adverbs, 415–416, R-20
agreement, 257, 325–326, 415–416, R-19
apostrophes ('), 134–135, R-17
capitalization, 110–111, 460–461, R-21
colons, 369–370, R-18
commas, 75–76, 92–93, 192–193, 235–236, 276–277, R-15–R-16
e-mail message, composing, 344, 386, 432–433
formatting, 80
grammar, R-19–R-20
hyphenation, 214–215, 256, R-17
italics, R-18
mechanics, R-21–R-22
number expression, 173–174, 214–215
paragraphs, composing, 205, 248, 297
periods, 369–370, R-18
personal business letter, composing, 474
pronouns, 134, 443
agreement, R-19
nominative, 442, 456–457, R-20
objective, 442
possessives and, R-17
proofreading, 80, 119, 200, 242, 287, 379, 468
punctuation, 369–370, R-18
quotation marks and italics (or underline), 151–152
semicolon, 395–396, 398, R-16
sentences, 83, 92–93, 126, 164, R-19
spelling, 101, 141, 181, 222, 268, 361, 403, 451, 491
underline, R-18
word usage, 482–483, R-20
Last will and testament, 391, 396–398
LED display, multifunction printer with, R-2
Left-bound report, 190, 244, 485, R-9A
Left hand, 118, 241, 378
LEFT SHIFT key, 14–15, 48
Legal assistant, 413
Legal documents, R-11D
affidavit, 391, 400–401
complaint, 391, 407–409
court documents, 391
document processing, 392–394, 396–398, 400–401, 404–405, 407–410
formatting, 391, 400
judgment, 391, 410
last will and testament, 391, 396–398
noncourt documents, 391
summons, 391, 404
types of, 391
warranty deed, 391–393, 409–410
Legal services, careers in, 413
Length, as unit of measurement, 340
Letterhead
for business letter, 89, R-3A
document processing, 424–426
formatting, 423
Letterhead form, 481
Letter of complaint, 339, 391, 407–409
Letter of resignation, 385
Letters
closing lines in, 151–153
with copy notations, 162
cover, 186
folding, 96, R-6B
international address in, 327
multipage, 253–255
personal titles and complimentary closings in, 151–153
See also Correspondence; Mail merge; INDIVIDUAL KEYS (alphabet); *entries for individual letter types*
Line numbers, 400, R-11D
Line spacing, 124
LinkedIn, 329
List(s)
academic reports with, 123–124
business reports with, 111, 118–121
in correspondence, R-3B–C, R-5B, R-12C–D
in e-mail message, 332
formatting, 332
numbered, 119
in report, R-8A, R-8C, R-9A, R-9C, R-11A, R-12A, R-12C–D
See also Bulleted and numbered lists; Numbers (#), in table
Listening skills, 65
Lowercase abbreviation, 359, R-22

M

Magazine article
document processing, 295–296, 299
formatting, 292–294
quotation marks around title of, 151
Mailing label, 97–99. *See also* Address
Mail merge
data source file in, 464, 466, 469, 472, 475–476
defined, 464
document processing, 465–466, 468–469, 471–472, 474–476
formatting envelopes and labels, 474
formatting form letters, 464–465
letters, 465
main document in, 464–465, 468–469, 472, 474–476
Main document, in mail merge, 464–465, 468–469, 472, 474–476
Manufacturing documents, 225–228
Margins, 171, R-9D
Mass, as unit of measurement, 340
Measurements
abbreviate, 356, R-22
metric units of, 340
use figures to express, 174, R-22
Medical office documents
composing e-mail message, 386

document processing, 370–372, 374–377, 379–81, 379–381, 384–385, 387–388
formatting, 374
Meeting
minutes of, 282–283, 298, R-11B
preparing to conduct, 101
teleconferencing for, 346
See also Interview
Memo, R-4D, R-9C
with attachment notation, 103–104
document processing, 104–105, 107–108, 159–160, 212, 219, 228, 239–240, 268–270, 372, 405, 479–480
formatting, 102–103, 159
language arts, 101
parts of, 102
report headings in, 272
template for, 416, 435
transmittal, R-7C
MEMO FROM heading, 105
Memo headings, 102
Memo report, 272–273, R-9C
MEMO TO heading, 102
Message, in communication process, 367
Metric units of measurement, 340
Mexico
document processing, 337–338
formatting letter with address and date, 327, 331–334
telephone dialing code, 337
URLs, 331
Microsoft Bing.com, 80
Microsoft Outlook, e-mail message in, R-5C
Microsoft Outlook/Internet Explorer, 84
Minus sign (–), 72
Minutes of meeting, 282–283, 298, R-11B
Mixed numbers, 174, R-22. *See also* Numbers (#)
MLA style
reports in, 177–179, R-10C–D, R-11B
works-cited pages in, 183–184
Modern Language Association (MLA). *See* MLA style
Modified-block style
in business letter, 216, R-3B
in correspondence, 165–167, 216, R-3B, R-3D
in personal-business letter, 197–198, 204, 206, 208, R-3D
Money, use figures to express, R-22
Monitor, computer, R-2A
Monster.com, 51
Months, capitalization of, 110, R-21
Mouse, R-2A
MSN Hotmail, 84, R-5D
Multifunction printer with LED display, R-2
Multiline list
in correspondence, R-3B, R-5B, R-12C–D
in reports, R-8A, R-8C, R-11A–R-12A, R-12C–D
Multipage academic report, 122–125, 127–129, 243, R-8C–D
Multipage business letter, R-5A, R-5B
Multipage business report
document processing, 116–117, 349–352, 354–356, 362–363, R-8A–B
formatting, 114–115, 258, 349, 361
lowercase, 353
tables in, 355–356
Multipage correspondence, R-5A–B, R-8A–D, R-13C
Multipage letter, 250, 253–255
Multiple addresses, 257–258
Multiplication sign (*), 72
MySpace, 329

N

National Business Employment Weekly, 244
Navigation keys, R-2B
Negative language, 136
Netiquette, observing, 290
NetMeeting, 346
Newsletter
design and elements of, 448
document processing, 448–449, 451–453, 455–457, 488–489
Newspaper article title, 151, R-9B
Nominative pronoun, 442, 456–457, R-20
Noncourt document, 391
Nonessential expression, 276, 278–279, R-16
Nonprofit document, 221–224
Nonverbal communication, 157
Notepad, designing
document processing, 429–431
formatting, 428
Notes, in tables, R-8B, R-13A
Nouns
and agreement, 415–416
apostrophes to form possessive plural, 134
capitalization of, R-21
possessives, 134, R-17
See also Proper nouns
Number columns, ruled tables with, 140–143
Numbering, 119–121, 283–284
Numbers (#), 437
and dates, R-22
expressing, 173–174, 214–215
hyphenate compound, 214–215
hyphens and, R-17
mixed, R-22
progressive practice, 339, 470, SB-7–SB-9
skillbuilding, 61, 64, 81, 118, 122, 140, 158, 161, 169, 175–176, 176, 199, 202, 241, 245, 286, 291, 335, 378, 382, 422, 427, 437, 442, 460, 467, 470, 482, SB-2–SB-9
in table, R-4D, R-8B, R-11A, R-12C, R-13A–C
when to spell out, R-21–R-22
See also INDIVIDUAL KEYS (numbers)
Nursing facility documents, 487–489

O

Objective pronoun, 442, 457, R-20
Occupational Outlook Handbook, 244
Office forms, miscellaneous, 433–435
On-arrival notation, 258, R-5A
One-hand words, 180–181, 450–451
Online database reference, R-9B
Online learning, 149
Online resumes, 461–462

Open punctuation, in correspondence, R-4C
Open tables, 247, 387, R-13B
with column headings, 137–139, 227
document processing, 135–136, 215
formatting, 135, 141
Ordinal numbers in superscripts, 417
Organizational terms, capitalization of common, 460–461, R-21
Orphan control, 116
Outline, R-7A
Out reaches, 140, 267, 402

P

Page break, 116
Page numbers
of academic report, 123
of business report, 115–116
in correspondence, R-5A–B, R-8A–D, R-10A–D, R-13C
in report, R-8B, R-8D, R-10A–B
Paper
for correspondence, 326
executive stationery, R-4A
folding, 96, R-6B
half-page stationery, R-4B
metric size, 326
word processing, 328
Paragraph (¶)
blocked in business report, 128–129
composing, 205, 249, 297
symbol as new blocked paragraph, 86
Paragraph heading
of academic report, multipage, 123
of business report, 111, 115
in report, R-8A, R-8D
Paralegal, 413
Parentheses (), 60
Paste, in word processing, 127
People's Republic of China
address in letters, 327
telephone dialing code, 337
URLs, 331
Percentage, using figures to express, R-22
Percent sign (%), 60–61, 174, R-13B, R-13D
Period (.), R-18
to end polite request sentence, 369–370, 372
skillbuilding, 15, 35
spacing rules, 15
See also Sentence(s)
Personal-business letter, R-12B
in block style, 203–204, 206, 208, 237
composing, 474
document processing, 155–157
formatting, 155–157
in modified-block style, 197–198, 204, 206, 208, R-3D
See also Business letter
Personal/personnel, 482–485, R-20
Pew Internet and American Life Project, 51
Phone time, managing business, 426
Placeholder fields, in mail merge, 464–465
Places (locations), commas in, 192, R-15
Plural nouns, 134, 136
Plus sign (+), 72
Polite request, period to end, 369–370, 372, R-17
Positive language, 136
Possessive plural nouns, 134
Possessives, 134, R-17
Postscript notation, 263, R-5B
Pound sign (#), 61
Predesigned table, 377, 385, 405
Preliminary report pages, 185–190
Prepositional phrase, 93, R-15
Presentation, and visual aids, 377
Principal/principle, 482–483, R-20
Printer, R-2A
Print options, in word processing, 428
Privacy, e-mail, 453
Procedures manual
document processing, 288–290
footers, 288
formatting, 287–288
Pronouns, 443
agreement, 325–326, 328, 333, R-19
nominative, 442, 456–457, R-20
objective, 442, 457
possessives and, 134, R-17
Proofreaders' marks, 120–121, 127, 200, 208, 212–213, 222, 237, R-14C
Proofreading, 119
academic report, 127–129
practice, 242, 287, 379, 468
techniques for, 80
Proper nouns, 110, 122, R-20
Publication titles, italicize, 260, 484
Punctuation, R-18
apostrophe ('), 41–43, 48, 134–135, R-17
colon (:), 44–45, 48, 84, 152, 369–370, 372, R-18
comma (,), 29–30, R-16
in addresses, 192
and adjacent adjectives, 277, 279
after complimentary closing, 152–153
with coordinate conjunctions, R-15
in dates, 192
with direct quotation, 151
between independent clauses, 92–93
and introductory expression, 93
with name in direct address, 75
and nonessential expression, 276, 278–279
series, 235, 237
skillbuilding, 35
spacing around, 28
transitional expression, 235–236, R-16
in correspondence, R-4C
hyphen (-), 243, 256
automatic, 243
columns and, 294
in compound adjectives, R-17

in compound numbers, R-17
and em dash (—), 90
expressing fractions, 214
skillbuilding, 39
spacing, 38
in U.S. telephone numbers, 336
italics
in bibliography, 183–184
text to be emphasized, 107
titles of published works, 151, 172, 208, 243, 484, R-18
period (.), R-18
to end polite request sentence, 369–370, 372
skillbuilding, 15, 35
spacing, 15
quotation mark ("), 63–65, 151–152
semicolon (;), 5, 395–396, R-16
to separate three or more items in series, 395
separating two related independent clauses, 395–396
skillbuilding, 88, 210, 348, 390, 478
standard, of business letter, 89, R-3A
underline, 92, 107, R-18
See also entries for specific punctuation marks

Q

Question mark (?), 57–58
Quick Reference for the Automated Office, 107
Quotation mark ("), 63–65, 151–152
Quotations
in correspondence, R-3A
in report, R-8B, R-8D

R

Reference initials
in business letter, 89, 91
in correspondence, R-3A, R-4D, R-5B
in memo, 102
References, in APA style, 182, 184
Religious days, capitalization of, 110, R-21
Report citations, 180–184
Report headings, in memos, 272
Report review, 298–299
Reports
academic (*See* Academic report)
agenda, meeting, R-11A
APA style, 173–176, R-10A–B
bibliography, R-9B
business (*See* Business reports)
byline, R-8A, R-10A
citations, R-9D, R-10A–D, R-10C
date, R-8A
endnotes, R-8C–D, R-9C
footnotes, R-8A–B, R-9A
hanging indent, R-10D
header, R-9A
headings, R-9D, R-10C
main, R-10A
paragraph, R-8A, R-8C, R-9A
side, R-8–R-9A, R-9C
indented display, R-8B, R-8C
itinerary, R-11C
language arts, 126
left-bound, R-9A
legal document, R-11D
line numbers, R-11D
lists, R-8A, R-8C, R-9A, R-9C, R-11A, R-12A, R-12C–D
margins, R-9D
memo report, R-9C
minutes of meeting, R-11B
MLA style, 177–179, R-10D, R-11B
multiline lists, R-8A, R-8C, R-11A–R-12A, R-12C–D
outline, R-7A
page number, R-8B, R-8D, R-10A–B
paragraph heading, R-8A, R-8D
preliminary pages, 185–190
quotation, long, R-8B, R-8D
rough-draft
document processing, 127–129
formatting, 127
skillbuilding, 126
single-line lists, R-9A, R-9C, R-11A, R-12A, R-12C–D
spacing, R-9D
special feature, R-9D
subheadings, R-10A
subject line, 2-line, R-9C
table of contents page, R-7D
tables in, R-8B
title, R-7A–B, R-8A–C, R-10A, R-10C
title page, R-7C
works-cited page, MLA style, R-10D
See also Report templates
Report templates
document processing, 419–421
formatting, 419
Resignation, letter of, 385
Resumes, 192
document processing, 195, 206–207, 249
formatting, 193–194, 220
online, 461–462
parts of, 193
Retail documents, 218–220
Return address
in correspondence, R-3D, R-12B
in personal-business letter, 155
Right hand, 118, 241, 378
RIGHT SHIFT key, 22–24, 48
Rough-draft business reports with lists
document processing, 120–121
formatting, 119–120
language arts, 119
skillbuilding, 118–119
Ruled table, 146, 201, R-4D, R-13C
document processing, 220, 247, 492
in medical office documents, 384
with number columns, 140–143
Ruler tabs, 166
Run-on sentence, 76, R-19

S

Salutation
- of business letter, 89
- in correspondence, R-3A
- of personal letter, 152

Search engine, 80
Seasons, and capitalization, 110
Selected Business Resources on the Web, 247
Sem (semicolon) finger, 3–4. *See also* INDIVIDUAL KEYS (punctuation, functions, and symbols)
Semicolon (;), 5, R-16
- to separate three or more items in series, 395
- separating two related independent clauses, 395–396

Sender, in communication process, 367
Sender's name, in e-mail message, 84
Sentence(s)
- capitalization in, 110–113
- commas and, 92–93
- composing, 83, 126, 164
- fragment, 75, R-19
- run-on, 76, R-19
- skillbuilding, 16, 19, 24, 27, 29, 32

Sentence fragment, 75, R-19
Series, use of comma/semicolon in, 235, 237, R-16
Shading, in tables, 461
Shift key, R-2B
- Left Shift, 14–15, 48
- Right Shift, 22–24, 48
- technique practice, 48, 55, 144, 245, 364, 470

Side heading
- of academic report, 123
- of business report, 111–112
- in report, R-8A–B, R-9C–D

Signature, of business letter, 89
Signature file, creating e-mail, 266
Sign-in form, 434
Simplified style, in correspondence, R-3C
Single-line lists
- in correspondence, R-3C, R-12C–D
- in report, R-9A, R-9C, R-11A, R-12A, R-12C–D

Singular noun, 134, 136
Skillbuilding
- alphabet, 176, 235, 256, 442, 460, 482, SB-2–SB-6
- alphabet practice, 39, 55, 58, 75, 110, 134, 151, 173, 192, 214, 276, 325, 353, 369, 395
- clauses, 9, 12
- close reaches, 100–101, 101, 221, 361, 490–491
- horizontal reaches, 140–141, 141, 267–268, 402–403
- hyphen practice, 39
- key review and new keys
  - 2, 48
  - 4, 7, colon (:), 45, 48
  - 6, 3, slash, 48
  - 8, 5, apostrophe ('), 42, 48
  - A–H, 34
  - B, U, C, 19
  - comma, 35
  - E, N, T, 9, 48
  - I–Z, 35
  - Left Shift, 15
  - O, R. H, 12
  - period, 35
  - Q, G, 29
  - Right Shift, W, M, 23
  - V, Y, Z, 32
  - X, P, Tab, 26
- minimum-change practice, 8, 12, 15, 19
- numbers, 61, 64, 81, 118, 122, 158, 161, 169, 199, 202, 240, 286, 467, 470, SB-7–SB-9
- paced practice, 64, 126, 137, 164, 177, 205, 218, 248, 261, 297, 432, 447, 473, 486, SB-10–SB-25
- pretest-practice-posttest
  - adjacent keys, 100, 221, 490
  - alternate-hand words, 114, 180, 180–181, 238, 373, 450, 450–451, 451
  - close reaches, 100–101, 221, 490
  - common letter combinations, 45, 79, 200, 467–468
  - consecutive fingers, 10, 221, 490
  - discrimination practice, 118, 241–242
  - down reaches, 158, 286
  - in reaches, 140, 267
  - horizontal reaches, 140–141, 267–268
  - left hand, 118, 241
  - one-hand words, 180, 450
  - out reaches, 140, 267
  - right hand, 118, 241
  - up reaches, 158, 286
  - vertical reaches, 158–159, 286–287
  - word beginnings, 45, 79, 199, 467
  - word endings, 45, 79, 199, 467
- progressive practice
  - alphabet, 235, 256, 276, 442, 460, 482, SB-2–SB-6
  - numbers, 245, 291, 470, SB-7–SB-9
- sentences, 16, 19, 24, 27, 29, 32
- slash (/), 48
- sustained practice
  - alternate- and one-hand words, 180–181, 238
  - capitals, 77, 196, 463
  - numbers and symbols, 140, 169, 437
  - punctuation, 88, 210, 478
  - rough draft, 131, 252
  - syllabic intensity, 154, 280
- symbol practice, 140, 267, 450, 490
- technique practice
  - Backspace key, 29, 58, 161, 271, 493
  - Enter key, 122, 225, 454
  - hyphen, 39
  - quotation marks, placement of, 64
  - Shift key, 48, 55, 144, 245, 364, 470
  - Space Bar, 32, 61, 81, 185, 291
  - Tab key, 65, 106, 202
- timed writing (*See* Timed writing)
- 12-second speed sprints, 39, 52, 106, 126, 144, 164, 185, 205, 225, 248, 271, 297, 432, 454, 473, 493

vertical reaches, 158–159
words
alternate-hand keys, 180
beginnings, 199
endings, 45, 79, 199
one-hand words, 180
right hand, 118
word beginnings, 45, 79
word building, 5, 23, 26
See also In-basket review
Skills in communications and media, 1
Slash (/), 47–48
Small caps, 423
Software development documents, 493–497
Source table, R-8B
Space Bar, 3–4, 32, 51, 61, 81, 185, 291, 406
Spacing
comma, 28
hyphen, 38
line, 124
periods, 15
in report, R-9D
semicolon, 5
See also Backspace key
Spam, coping with, 383
Special feature
in report, R-9D
in tables, R-13D
Speed sprints, 12-second, 39, 52, 106, 126, 144, 164, 185, 205, 225, 344, 364, 386, 406, 454
Spelling, 101, 181, 222, 268, 361, 403, 451, 491
Spell out numbers. *See* Numbers (#), expressing
Standard punctuation
of business letter, 89
in correspondence, R-3A
States, U.S. Postal Service abbreviations, R-14B
Strategies for Career Success (feature)
audience analysis, 299
business communication, 367
complaint letter, 339
corrective feedback, 287
cover letters, 186
designing page for readability, 398
goodwill message, 86
interviewing techniques, 279
interview thank-you letter, 231
job application letter, writing, 228
job interview portfolio, 82
job search, 244
listening, 65
managing business phone time, 426
meeting preparation, 101
nonverbal communication, 157
positive *vs.* negative language, 136
presentation with visual aids, 377
reducing bias in communication, 202
resignation letter, 385
resume
formatting, 220
what to exclude from, 446
Style guide, business e-mail, 125
Subheadings, in report, R-10A
Subject line or box, 258
in correspondence, R-3C, R-4D, R-5A, R-7C
in e-mail message, 84
in memo, 102
2-line, in report, R-9C
Subtitle
of academic report, multipage, 123
of business report, 111
of table, 132, R-8B, R-13A–B, R-13D
Summons, 391, 404
Superscripts, and Microsoft Word formatting, 417
Syllabic intensity, 56, 154, 280, 418
Symbols
insert, 332
skillbuilding, 140, 169, 267, 360, 382, 402, 437, 450, 490
in word processing, 332
See also INDIVIDUAL KEYS (punctuation, functions, and symbols)

T

Tab key, 25–27, 51, 65, 106, 166, 202, 427, R-2B
Table(s), 144–145, R-12A–C
autofit to contents, 133
body, R-13A
border, 135
borders and shading, custom, 461
bottom-aligned, R-13A–B
boxed, 131–133, 224, 329, 393, 480, R-5A, R-8B, R-13A
braced column headings, R-13A
capitalization, columns, R-13D
column entries of, 132
column headings, 132, 137–139, 214, R-4D, R-5A, R-8B, R-13A–D
column width, change, 194
in correspondence, R-4D, R-5A, R-13C–D
document processing, 133
within documents, 262
dollar signs, R-8B, R-13A–B, R-13D
format, 133
heading block, 135, R-5, R-8B, R-13A–D
insert, 133
merging cells in, 135
note, R-8B, R-13A
numbers in, R-4D, R-8B, R-13A–C, R-13C
open, 134–139, 141, 215, R-13B
open, with column headings, 137–139, 227
parts of, 132–133
percent signs, R-13B, R-13D
predesigned, 377, 385, 405
in reports, 355–356, R-8B
ruled, 146, 201, 220, 492, R-4D, R-13C
ruled, with number columns, 140–143
source, R-8B

Table(s) *(continued)*
special features, R-13D
subtitle of, 132, R-8B, R-13A–B, R-13D
table number, R-8B, R-13C
title, R-5A, R-8B, R-13A–D
total line, R-13A, R-13C–D
2-line column heading, R-13B
vertical placement, R-13D
Table heading block, 135
Table note, R-13D
Table number, R-8B, R-13C
Table of contents, 187–189, 366, R-7D
Tab set, dot leaders, 188
Taiwan, telephone dialing code, 337
Telecommunications design, 323
Teleconferencing, for meetings, 346
Telephone access codes, international, 336–337
Telephone numbers, dot-style, 336
Template forms. *See* Correspondence template; Report templates
Ten-key numeric keypad, R-2B, 70–72
Territories, U.S. Postal Service abbreviations, R-14B
Text boxes, 423
Thank-you letter, for interview, 231
Time
capitalization of, 110, 112–113
using figures to express, R-22
Timed writing
1-minute, 348
10 wpm, 5
11 wpm, 9
12 wpm, 12
13 wpm, 16
14 wpm, 19
15 wpm, 23
16 wpm, 26
17 wpm, 29
18 wpm, 32
19 wpm, 35
2-minute
19 wpm, 39
20 wpm, 42
21 wpm, 45
23 wpm, 51
24 wpm, 55
25 wpm, 58
26 wpm, 61
27 wpm, 65
28 wpm, 68
3-minute
28 wpm, 77, 115
29 wpm, 81
30 wpm, 89
31 wpm, 95
32 wpm, 107
34 wpm, 122
35 wpm, 132, 137
36 wpm, 145, 155
37 wpm, 161, 170
38 wpm, 177, 186
5-minute
39 wpm, 197, 203
40 wpm, 211, 218, 226, 239, 246
41 wpm, 253, 261, 272
42 wpm, 281, 292
44 wpm, 331, 340
45 wpm, 349, 357, 365
46 wpm, 374, 383
47 wpm, 391, 399, 407
48 wpm, 419, 428
49 wpm, 438, 447, 455
50 wpm, 464, 471, 479, 486, 494
supplementary, SB-26–SB-35
12-second speed sprints, 39, 52, 106, 126, 144, 164, 185, 205, 225, 248, 271, 297, 344, 386, 406, 432, 454, 473, 493
Time measurement, use figures to express, 174
Title(s)
of academic report, multipage, 123
in bibliography, 183–184
of business report, 111
and italics (or underline), R-18
of newspaper, magazine article, book chapter, report, 151, 208
personal, in letters, 151–153
of published works, 151, 172, 208, 243, 260, 484–485, R-18
and quotation marks, R-18
of report, R-7A–B, R-8A–C, R-10A, R-10C
of table, 132, R-5A, R-8B, R-13A–D
2-line, R-8C, R-9A, R-10A, R-10C
Title page, R-7B
document processing, 188–189
formatting, 186–187
of report, R-7C
TO box, in e-mail message, 84
Total line, in table, R-13A, R-13C–D, R-13D
Transitional expression, comma in, 236, R-16
Transmittal memo, R-7C
12-second speed sprints, 39, 52, 106, 126, 144, 164, 185, 205, 225, 248, 271, 297, 432, 454, 473, 493. *See also* Timed writing

U

Umlaut symbol, 332, 341–342
Underline, 92, 107, R-18. *See also* Italics
United Kingdom, telephone dialing code, 337
United States
hyphen in telephone numbers, 336
telephone dialing code, 337
Up reaches, 158, 286, 422
URLs, international, 331
U.S. Postal Service abbreviations, R-14B

V

Vertical reaches, 158–159, 286–287, 422–423
Vertical table placement, R-13D

View Gridlines, 98–99, 135, R-11B
Virus, computer, 359
Volume, as unit of measurement, 340

W

Warranty deed, 391–393, 409–410
Web
  searching, 143
  transferring text from page on, 393
  See also Internet
Web browser, 143
WebEx, 346
Web site cookies, 137
Weight
  as unit of measurement, 340
  use figures to express, 174, R-22
Widow/orphan control, 116
Window envelope
  business letter formatted for, R-4C
  correspondence formatted for, R-4C
  folding for, R-6B
Windows keys, R-2B
WordArt, 438, 443–444, 446
Word beginnings, 45, 79, 199, 335, 467
Word building, 5, 23, 26
Word endings, 45, 79, 199, 335, 467
Word processing
  alignment, 112, 138
  bullets and numbering, 120–121
  columns and hyphenation, 294
  cut and copy; paste, 127
  e-mail with attachment notations, 103
  file, insert and bookmarks and hyperlinks, 361
  find and replace, 268
  font, small caps and text boxes, 423
  font size, 112
  font and table, change column width, 194
  formatting, 76–78, 80, 82
  headers, 175
  indentation and e-mail copies, 163
  indentation (hanging and autocorrect) hyperlink, 183
  italic, 107
  language arts, 75–76, 80
  line numbering, 400
  line spacing, 124
  merge cells and table, 135
  page break, 116
  page number, 116
  paper size, 328
  print options, 428
  skillbuilding, 75, 77, 79, 81
  sort, 259
  symbol, insert, 332
  table
    borders and shading, custom, 461
    insert and autofit to contents, 133
    shading and e-mail, 264
    tab, 374
  tab set
    dot leaders, 188
    ruler tabs, 166
  templates
    correspondence, 416
    reports, 419
  underline, 107
  widow/orphan control, 116
  WordArt, 438
Word usage, 482–483, R-20
Works-cited page, in MLA style, 183–184, R-10D
Writer's identification, 84, 89, R-3A
WWW page reference, R-9B

Y

Yahoo!, 80, 247
Year in complete date, commas and, R-15
Yellow Pages, searching, 401

Z

0 (zero) key, 55

PHOTO CREDITS

Stockbyte/Getty xiii, 2, 324, 347; Medioimages/Photodisc/Getty Images xiv, 130, 139; C Squared Studios/Getty xvi, 209; it Stock/Punchstock xviii, 234; Brooklyn Production/Corbis xx, 368; Flying Colurs/Getty xxii, 414; Eric Audras/PhotoAlto/PictureQuest xxvi, 105; Mark Dierker, McGraw-Hill Companies R-2; Veer 16, 382; Medio Images/Alamy 21; Dynamic Graphics/Jupiter Images 37, 53; Ryan McVay/Getty 65, 82, 86, 101, 136, 157, 186, 202, 217, 220, 228, 231, 244, 279, 287, 299, 309, 319, 339, 367, 377, 385, 398, 426, 446; Getty 74; DigitalVision/Getty 78, 146, 282; Jason Reed/Getty 80, 99, 125, 143, 167, 190, 213, 247, 266, 290, 304, 329, 346, 359, 372, 383, 393, 401, 427, 435, 453; PhotoDisc/Getty 87, 431; DigitalVision/Punchstock 109; PhotoAlto 117; Brand X Pictures/Punchstock 150; Creatas/PictureQuest 160; Steve Cole/Getty 168, 389, 469; C Sherburne/PhotoLink 191; 2008 Masterfile Corporation 198; RF/Corbis 224; Corbis 245, 477; Thinkstock 251; Artifacts Images 264, 366; Anderson Ross/Getty 275; Comstock/PictureQuest 300; Steve Ide 307; Joseph Sohm/Visions of America/Corbis 334; Ross Anania 343; DigitalVision 350; Stockbyte 361, 481; Comstock/Jupiter Images 381; Jack Star/Photolink/Getty 394; Comstock Images 403, 406; Getty Images/PhotoDisc 423; Tetra Images 428; Ingram Publishing/Superstock 436; AbleStock/Alamy 441; Moodboard/Corbis 449; AFP/GETTY 453; Banana Stock/Jupiter Images 458; Image Source/Jupiter Images 459; Stockbyte/Punchstock 466; InDeed 476; Ingram Publishing/AGE Photostock 489; Red Chopsticks 497; Barbara Penoyar/Getty SB-1.